T0234802

Communications
in Computer and Information Science 1785

Editorial Board Members

Rationale

The CCIS series is devoted to the publication of proceedings of computer science conferences. Its aim is to efficiently disseminate original research results in informatics in printed and electronic form. While the focus is on publication of peer-reviewed full papers presenting mature work, inclusion of reviewed short papers reporting on work in progress is welcome, too. Besides globally relevant meetings with internationally representative program committees guaranteeing a strict peer-reviewing and paper selection process, conferences run by societies or of high regional or national relevance are also considered for publication.

Topics

The topical scope of CCIS spans the entire spectrum of informatics ranging from foundational topics in the theory of computing to information and communications science and technology and a broad variety of interdisciplinary application fields.

Information for Volume Editors and Authors

Publication in CCIS is free of charge. No royalties are paid, however, we offer registered conference participants temporary free access to the online version of the conference proceedings on SpringerLink (http://link.springer.com) by means of an http referrer from the conference website and/or a number of complimentary printed copies, as specified in the official acceptance email of the event.

CCIS proceedings can be published in time for distribution at conferences or as post-proceedings, and delivered in the form of printed books and/or electronically as USBs and/or e-content licenses for accessing proceedings at SpringerLink. Furthermore, CCIS proceedings are included in the CCIS electronic book series hosted in the SpringerLink digital library at http://link.springer.com/bookseries/7899. Conferences publishing in CCIS are allowed to use Online Conference Service (OCS) for managing the whole proceedings lifecycle (from submission and reviewing to preparing for publication) free of charge.

Publication process

The language of publication is exclusively English. Authors publishing in CCIS have to sign the Springer CCIS copyright transfer form, however, they are free to use their material published in CCIS for substantially changed, more elaborate subsequent publications elsewhere. For the preparation of the camera-ready papers/files, authors have to strictly adhere to the Springer CCIS Authors' Instructions and are strongly encouraged to use the CCIS LaTeX style files or templates.

Abstracting/Indexing

CCIS is abstracted/indexed in DBLP, Google Scholar, EI-Compendex, Mathematical Reviews, SCImago, Scopus. CCIS volumes are also submitted for the inclusion in ISI Proceedings.

How to start

To start the evaluation of your proposal for inclusion in the CCIS series, please send an e-mail to ccis@springer.com.

Crina Damşa · Amanda Barany
Editors

Advances in Quantitative Ethnography

4th International Conference, ICQE 2022
Copenhagen, Denmark, October 15–19, 2022
Proceedings

Editors
Crina Damşa ⓘD
University of Oslo
Oslo, Norway

Amanda Barany ⓘD
Drexel University School of Education
Philadelphia, PA, USA

ISSN 1865-0929   ISSN 1865-0937 (electronic)
Communications in Computer and Information Science
ISBN 978-3-031-31725-5   ISBN 978-3-031-31726-2 (eBook)
https://doi.org/10.1007/978-3-031-31726-2

This Springer imprint is published by the registered company Springer Nature Switzerland AG
The registered company address is: Gewerbestrasse 11, 6330 Cham, Switzerland

Preface 2022

This volume contains the proceedings of the Fourth International Conference on Quantitative Ethnography (ICQE 2022). The success of this conference and its predecessors is due in large part to the resilience and cohesion of the ICQE community that has prevailed and flourished during and after the last few turbulent pandemic years. From October 15–19, 2022, our community gathered in person for the first time since our inaugural ICQE in 2019 for a rich and insightful onsite conference at the University of Copenhagen in Denmark. Founders, long-standing members, and newcomers all came together in the beautiful city of Copenhagen to share emergent research, collaborate in lively discussions, expand their networks, and enjoy the amazing Danish cuisine and culture.

The contributions in this volume illustrate the expanding diversity of the ICQE field. Authors hail from diverse fields and perspectives, contributing not only empirical studies that apply QE tools and techniques, but also methodological and theoretical advances. Collectively, these papers exemplify the multifaceted ways that a quantitative ethnographic approach can extend our understanding of complex processes such as human thought, behavior, and interaction in a number of different domains and contexts. Methodological advancements include innovations in the application of mathematical and statistical procedures, visualization and modeling techniques, and coding and analysis approaches.

With record numbers of conference submissions and acceptances, ICQE22 featured work exploring the nature of online collaboration, student learning and self-regulation, policy in practice, professional engagement, and ways to engage participants in research. Our goal for ICQE22 was to identify and implement thematic submission tracks to support connection-making and collaboration between scholars. This year's submission tracks featured applications of quantitative ethnographic approaches and techniques in the learning sciences, health sciences, policy, and a variety of inter- and multidisciplinary contexts, as well as methodological innovations and theoretical work on the relationship between QE and Epistemic Network Analysis (ENA) and practices in Quantitative Ethnography. Submissions featured at the conference were evaluated by two primary reviewers and one meta-reviewer from the ICQE international Program Committee using double-blind review. The fourth volume of Advances in Quantitative Ethnography features 29 full papers: twelve papers that extend and advance theory and methods, ten papers that present applications in education contexts, and seven that employ quantitative ethnographic approaches across a variety of multidisciplinary fields and topics including healthcare, politics, COVID-19, social security, and community growth. All poster submissions, symposia, doctoral consortium submissions, and keynote abstracts can be found in the ICQE22 Conference Proceedings Supplement (www.qesoc.org/proceedings).

A significant number of submissions to this year's conference were the direct result of the activities organized by the QE community. Since its establishment in 2019, the

International Society for Quantitative Ethnography (www.qesoc.org) has been active in connecting and supporting a vast community of international QE scholars. The 2022 Data Challenge, held in April, focused on fostering new QE collaborations and attracting new researchers and practitioners, resulting in projects that leveraged data sources such as news and current events, pop culture and media, and multimodal data sources from humanitarian and sociohistorical contexts. The QE Webinar Series hosted five webinars on topics ranging from issues in the exploration of political and ethical topics using QE methods, the application of QE in adaptive learning systems, the value of QE for examining dialogue, the development of QE tools, methodological discussions on how QE can enrich qualitative analyses, and QE teaching practices. This year also featured monthly virtual QE Sandbox Events hosted by the Open Science SIG with the goal of creating an open-ended space for QE scholars to ask questions, develop connections, and enhance their technique skills. The International Society for Quantitative Ethnography also continued the pre-conference workshop series aimed at providing an opportunity for researchers new to QE and ENA to develop introductory technical exposure to topics such as data formatting, segmentation, coding, validation, and modeling using the ENA software tool.

The program chairs would like to thank the National Science Foundation (NSF) for their support for the conference, which contributed to registration scholarships that reduced costs for returning attendees and fully covered registration for first-time attendees, students, and post-doctoral researchers. We also offer our heartfelt thanks to the reviewers and committee members, and for the tremendous efforts from the ICQE support team.

ICQE22 embodied the value of in-person community-building and sharing of knowledge, expertise and experiences within the QE field, and especially the value of collaboration across disciplinary areas and across continents. ISQE is a growing community making strides to expand interdisciplinary and international collaboration and prepare for new epistemological challenges ahead. We invite new and returning scholars and disciplines to join this adventure!

March 2023

Crina Damşa
Amanda Barany

Organization

Program Committee Chairs

Crina Damşa | University of Oslo, Norway
Amanda Barany | Drexel University, USA

Program Committee

Alexis Andres | University of Pennsylvania, USA
Gol Arastoopour Irgens | Clemson University, USA
Gideon Dishon | Ben-Gurion University of the Negev, Israel
Aroutis Foster | Drexel University, USA
Karin Frey | University of Washington, USA
Dragan Gašević | Monash University, Australia
Rogers Kaliisa | University of Oslo, Norway
Shamya Karumbaiah | Carnegie Mellon University, USA
Vitomir Kovanovic | University of South Australia, Australia
Adam Lefstein | Ben-Gurion University of the Negev, Israel
Florian Meier | Aalborg University, Denmark
Kamila Musiejuk | University of Bergen, Norway
Ha Nguyen | University of California Irvine, USA
Ayano Ohsaki | Musashino University, Japan
Michael Phillips | Monash University, Australia
Andrew Ruis | University of Wisconsin-Madison, USA
Mamta Shah | Elsevier, Inc., USA
Amanda Siebert-Evenstone | Nelson Institute for Environmental Studies, USA
Zachari Swiecki | Monash University, Australia
Vitaly Popov | University of Michigan, USA

Conference Committees

Daniel Spikol (Co-chair) | University of Copenhagen, Denmark
Morten Misfeldt (Co-chair) | University of Copenhagen, Denmark
Jun Oshima (Keynote) | Shizuoka University, Japan
Karin Frey (Keynote) | University of Washington, USA
Eric Hamilton | Pepperdine University, USA

Olga Viberg	KTH Royal Institute of Technology, Sweden
Ryan Baker	University of Pennsylvania, USA
Brendan Eagan	University of Wisconsin-Madison, USA
Szilvia Zörgő	Maastricht University, The Netherlands
David Williamson Shaffer	University of Wisconsin-Madison, USA

Contents

QE Theory and Methodology Research

The Foundations and Fundamentals of Quantitative Ethnography 3
  Golnaz Arastoopour Irgens and Brendan Eagan

LSTM Neural Network Assisted Regex Development for Qualitative
Coding 17
  *Zhiqiang Cai, Brendan Eagan, Cody Marquart,
  and David Williamson Shaffer*

Does Active Learning Reduce Human Coding?: A Systematic Comparison
of Neural Network with nCoder 30
  *Jaeyoon Choi, Andrew R. Ruis, Zhiqiang Cai, Brendan Eagan,
  and David Williamson Shaffer*

Reducing Networks of Ethnographic Codes Co-occurrence
in Anthropology 43
  *Alberto Cottica, Veronica Davidov, Magdalena Góralska, Jan Kubik,
  Guy Melançon, Richard Mole, Bruno Pinaud, and Wojciech Szymański*

Multiclass Rotations in Epistemic Network Analysis 58
  *Mariah A. Knowles, Amanda Barany, Zhiqiang Cai,
  and David Williamson Shaffer*

Is QE Just ENA? 71
  David Williamson Shaffer and Andrew R. Ruis

The Role of Data Simulation in Quantitative Ethnography 87
  Zachari Swiecki and Brendan Eagan

Ordered Network Analysis 101
  *Yuanru Tan, Andrew R. Ruis, Cody Marquart, Zhiqiang Cai,
  Mariah A. Knowles, and David Williamson Shaffer*

Creating and Discussing Discourse Networks with Research Participants:
What Can We Learn? 117
  Hazel Vega

Modeling Collaborative Discourse with ENA Using a Probabilistic
Function 132
  Yeyu Wang, Andrew R. Ruis, and David Williamson Shaffer

Segmentation and Code Co-occurrence Accumulation: Operationalizing
Relational Context with Stanza Windows 146
  Szilvia Zörgő

Parsing the Continuum: Manual Segmentation of Monologic Data 163
  Szilvia Zörgő and Jais Brohinsky

Applications in Education Contexts

An Examination of Student Loan Borrowers' Attitudes Toward Debt
Before and During COVID-19 185
  Dara Bright and Amanda Barany

Learning Through Feedback: Understanding Early-Career Teachers'
Learning Using Online Video Platforms 201
  *Lara Condon, Amanda Barany, Janine Remillard, Caroline Ebby,
  and Lindsay Goldsmith-Markey*

How Can We Co-design Learning Analytics for Game-Based Assessment:
ENA Analysis 214
  Yoon Jeon Kim, Jennifer Scianna, and Mariah A. Knowles

Automated Code Extraction from Discussion Board Text Dataset 227
  *Sina Mahdipour Saravani, Sadaf Ghaffari, Yanye Luther,
  James Folkestad, and Marcia Moraes*

Mathematics Teachers' Knowledge for Teaching Proportion: Using Two
Frameworks to Understand Knowledge in Action 239
  Chandra Hawley Orrill and Rachael Eriksen Brown

Self-regulation in Foreign Language Students' Collaborative Discourse
for Academic Writing: An Explorative Study on Epistemic Network
Analysis 254
  Ward Peeters, Olga Viberg, and Daniel Spikol

Community at a Distance: Understanding Student Interactions
in Course-Based Online Discussion Forums 270
  *Jennifer Scianna, Monique Woodard, Beatriz Galarza, Seiyon Lee,
  Rogers Kaliisa, and Hazel Vega Quesada*

Modeling Students' Performances in Physics Assessment Tasks Using
Epistemic Network Analysis 285
    Hamideh Talafian and Hosun Kang

Computational Thinking in Educational Policy –The Relationship
Between Goals and Practices 299
    Andreas Lindenskov Tamborg, Liv Nøhr, Emil Bøgh Løkkegaard,
    and Morten Misfeldt

Understanding Detectors for SMART Model Cognitive Operation
in Mathematical Problem-Solving Process: An Epistemic Network
Analysis 314
    Mengqian Wu, Jiayi Zhang, and Amanda Barany

Applications in Interdisciplinary Contexts

Change the Museum: Examining Social Media Posts on Museum
Workplace Experiences to Support Justice, Equity, Diversity and Inclusion
(JEDI) Efforts 331
    Danielle P. Espino, Bryan C. Keene, and Payten Werbowsky

Ukraine War Diaries: Examining Lived Experiences in Kyiv During
the 2022 Russian Invasion 347
    Danielle P. Espino, Kristina Lux, Heather Orrantia, Samuel Green,
    Haille Trimboli, and Seung B. Lee

Political Discourse Modeling with Epistemic Network Analysis
and Quantitative Ethnography: Rationale and Examples 359
    Eric Hamilton and Andrew Hurford

What Makes a Good Answer? Analyzing the Content Structure of Answers
to Stack Overflow's Most Popular Question 374
    Luis Morales-Navarro and Amanda Barany

Analyzing the Co-design Process by Engineers and Product Designers
from Perspectives of Knowledge Building 388
    Ayano Ohsaki and Jun Oshima

Leveraging Epistemic Network Analysis to Discern the Development
of Shared Understanding Between Physicians and Nurses 402
    Vitaliy Popov, Raeleen Sobetski, Taylor Jones, Luke Granberg,
    Kiara Turvey, and Milisa Manojlovich

Quantitative Ethnography of Policy Ecosystems: A Case Study on Climate
Change Adaptation Planning 414
  Andrew R. Ruis

Correction to: Reducing Networks of Ethnographic Codes Co-occurrence
in Anthropology C1
  Alberto Cottica, Veronica Davidov, Magdalena Góralska, Jan Kubik,
  Guy Melançon, Richard Mole, Bruno Pinaud, and Wojciech Szymański

Author Index 429

QE Theory and Methodology Research

The Foundations and Fundamentals of Quantitative Ethnography

Golnaz Arastoopour Irgens[1](✉) ⓘ and Brendan Eagan[2](✉)

[1] Clemson University, Clemson, USA
garasto@clemson.edu
[2] University of Wisconsin-Madison, Madison, USA
beagan@wisc.edu

Abstract. As the Quantitative Ethnography (QE) community becomes more inter-disciplinary, it will need multiple theoretical accounts to fit with the multiple epistemologies of researchers. Thus, in this paper, we provide one theoretical account. We argue that ethnography is foundational to QE, quantification augments ethnographic accounts, and that *critical reflexivity* is necessary in QE. Then, we outline ten iterative steps of QE analyses, explained through two examples, and articulate five main practices. Our goals for this paper are to 1) distill fundamental aspects of QE for new adopters, 2) offer a summarized account for established QE practitioners, 3) clarify underlying values and practices that drive the methodology, and 4) highlight which practices are essential to QE and which are flexible. This paper provides one accessible summarization of QE for an inter-disciplinary field.

Keywords: Modeling · Philosophy · Processes · Critical Reflexivity

1 Introduction

Quantitative Ethnography (QE) is a methodology that integrates qualitative and quantitative analysis methods. With roots in educational research, QE has been used by researchers in a variety of fields. The QE methodology became formalized with the release of Shaffer's *Quantitative Ethnography* book in 2017. However, as the community grows and become more interdisciplinary, it will need multiple accounts of the methodology from different perspectives. The purpose of this article is to provide an accessible, distilled description of QE for the broader developing community with new emphases on critical reflexivity practices. Blending our own ideas with Shaffer's, we begin by describing how ethnography is foundational to QE, meaning that ethnographic techniques provide the essential grounding. We continue by describing how quantification is fundamental, meaning that mathematical techniques are necessary to augment the power of ethnographic methods. Then, we outline ten steps in the iterative QE modeling process and provide two examples of studies that used these processes. Finally, we end by articulating five main practices for QE.

© The Author(s), under exclusive license to Springer Nature Switzerland AG 2023
C. Damşa and A. Barany (Eds.): ICQE 2022, CCIS 1785, pp. 3–16, 2023.
https://doi.org/10.1007/978-3-031-31726-2_1

2 Ethnography is Foundational

Although QE has two facets, ethnography is at the heart. The science of ethnography is about making sense of how and why people do the things that they do. More specifically, an ethnographer interprets a culture by going through formal and systematic procedures. For example, in Hutchins' [1] landmark study of officers in the U.S. navy, he observed sailors tracking the position of their ship. The sailors needed to work together to succeed in the complex task of safely navigating their ship through sea and to land. Hutchins argued that the key system to facilitate communication and correct each other's mistakes was through a radio system in which sailors could hear all communications, even if they were not directly involved. This form of widely overheard conversation and communication is what Hutchins referred to as a wide horizon of observation and led to useful error detection and correction that kept the sailors efficient and safe in their work.

The purpose of ethnographic studies, such as the one conducted by Hutchins, is to make claims about one specific culture or community of people and weave these claims into an interpretation of the culture for a broader audience. Such claims are not necessarily meant to be generalizable beyond the community that was studied. Rather, the stories and conceptualizations that emerge from such ethnographic studies can be used as effective tools in other contexts and inspire related scientific explorations. For example, although Hutchins' study made claims about one particular group of sailors at one point in time, his work advanced the concept of how what an individual sees or hears influences cognition and teamwork. Years later, this general idea of horizon of observation inspired Blandford and Furniss's (2005) development of a methodological framework to analyze collaboration in small teams. The researchers tested their framework with telephone dispatchers at emergency ambulance centers in London and were able to draw similar conclusions to Hutchins.

To draw conclusions in ethnography, researchers collect data that are rich enough to yield a "thick description" [2] of a particular culture. Such data are collected through observational recordings, participant-observational recordings, interviews, and other artifacts of cultural meaning. These data contain evidence of the culturally specific ways of how people talk, listen, interact, and use tools in the community that is being studied. These forms of big-D Discourse [3] are the "overt manifestations of culture: what it actually looks like when someone is expressing meaning within some community" [4]. One of the goals of ethnographers and quantitative ethnographers is to shift from observable actions to interpreted meanings to provide an evidence-based account of why and how people from a particular community do what they do. To cross this bridge, ethnographers categorize data by tagging it with big-C Codes, which are categories of meaning derived by the ethnographer to make sense of collected data. This process is often, unsurprisingly, referred to as coding.

Once the data are associated with the appropriate Codes, the ethnographer analyzes how the Codes relate to one another in order to communicate a thick description of a culture. The thick description is created by linking multiple emic observations and interpretations (perspectives of the people in the culture) to etic observations and interpretations (perspectives of the researcher). As Shaffer [4] notes, Hutchins' study is a strong example of developing the etic description of horizon of observation from the emic contexts of U.S. sailors but can be applied across multiple emic contexts, such as with dispatchers at emergency ambulance centers in London.

When ethnographers systematically develop etic interpretations of emic observations, they construct knowledge through their own lens. Thus, the researcher themself plays a key role in the methodological process and "is the primary 'instrument' of data collection and analysis" [5] and knowledge creation. This knowledge is inherently situated within the researcher's intersecting identities of race, gender, class, and their ethical, theoretical, and epistemic commitments. To maintain scientific rigor, the researcher's "view from somewhere" [6] must be addressed through *critical reflexivity* practices [7]. Critical reflexivity involves interrogating the ethical decisions ethnographers make during the research process and making the encountered tensions visible to the scientific community [8]. This form of reflexivity becomes especially important when working with vulnerable or marginalized populations who are at risk of being exploited or harmed when participating in research [9].

3 Quantification is Fundamental

For quantitative ethnographers, critical reflexivity extends beyond human interactions to computational tools. In addition to the researcher being a primary instrument of data analysis in quantitative ethnography, the computational tools play a significant role. All tools were developed by people with particular worldviews that influence decision-making during development. Those people's assumptions, opinions, and biases are embedded into the tool [10]. Thus, computational tools are not neutral or objective artifacts for meaning-making. When researchers exercise critical reflexivity, they commit to uncovering the tools' limitations and ethical obligations in order to better understand the ways in which power and privilege amplify a particular point of view and obscure marginalized voices [11]. To exercise critical reflexivity, quantitative ethnographers should ask questions such as: Who designed this tool and for what purposes? What are the assumptions made in this tool about discourses and cultures? Which social, cultural, and political values are amplified and which are minimized? How does the tool (re)enforce inequities and oppression when creating samples, making statistical calculations, and visualizing data?

Through a critical reflexivity lens, the computational tools in QE are quite powerful. The unique combination of human researcher and digital tools in QE allows for an exploration of data and reveal of stories that likely would not have been uncovered without this analytical process [12]. For large datasets that emerge from modern digital spaces, such as social media, computational QE tools allow for researchers to access a "thick description" of such growing and changing digital cultures [4]. Even for comparatively smaller datasets, such as interview transcriptions, computational QE tools augment traditional qualitative analyses by exposing the researcher to new visualizations and quantifications that reveal and inspire stories grounded in the data [13].

Moreover, statistics provide forms of validity for qualitative analyses beyond accounts of "trustworthiness" or "authenticity" criterion [14]. Statistical tools in QE are used to generalize within the sample of data collected and not necessarily to generalize beyond the sample of data to a larger population. As mentioned before, although the broader ideas uncovered in ethnography may be useful in other contexts, limited generalizability is a fundamental aspect of ethnography. Thus, sampling and statistical tools in QE are not used in the same way that they are used in traditional quantitative studies. The goal is not to generalize findings to a broader population but rather, to provide some level of confidence that the interpretations and stories told about one particular culture are persistent throughout the group of people that were studied. In other words, statistical analyses in QE provide additional warrants or evidence for reaching a point in which analyzing additional data does not provide new insights. This point is called reaching *theoretical saturation* in qualitative analysis and is an important amalgamation of qualitative and quantitative in QE. As Shaffer [4] aptly puts it, "By reframing the role of sampling and statistical significance... the distinct logic of quantitative inquiry and the distinct logic become compatible. We find a point of contact between these two very different epistemological stances toward research."

4   Ten Steps in the Iterative QE Modeling Pathway

The interpretation techniques that are typically associated with qualitative analyses occur throughout the QE process. Likewise, the quantitative mindset is consistently active, as ethnographic data is organized, sorted, and coded in preparation for quantitative models. Here, we offer ten steps that incorporate both mindsets for developing quantitative models from ethnographic data. The ten steps are split into five categories: collection, segmentation, codification, accumulation, and measurement (Fig. 1).

4.1   Collection

Because ethnography is the foundation of QE, data collection (Step 1) aligns with traditional qualitative procedures. Observations are central to ethnographic data collection and include researcher notes on how people talk and act in a particular setting [15]. Researcher-created data may be in the form of field notes in paper or digital forms containing observations and interpretations, photographs or videos and corresponding transcriptions, and researcher reflective diary entries. Data may also be in the form of participant-created documents or artifacts that have particular meaning to people within a culture. These include letters, multi-media art, emails, digital log data, articles, discussion boards, and social media postings. In some studies, data may be created by researchers and participants collaboratively.

4.2   Segmentation

After data are collected in a form that is likely to enable thick descriptions, the researcher prepares this data for statistical analyses. First, the researcher identifies and segments the data into *lines* (Step 2), which are defined as "the smallest unit of continuous action that is of interest in the data" [4]. In discourse data, lines can be defined in various ways including turns of talk, responses to a question, or moves made in a digital game. Lines are then grouped into *stanzas* (Step 3), which are "a set of lines that are within the same relevant context, and therefore related to one another" [4]. Stanzas are often compared to chapters in a book, verses in a song, or, quite literally, stanzas in a poem. Stanzas can be classified in various ways including as activities, interview sessions, or conversational topics on a discussion board. If a moving stanza window model is used, additional segmentation is completed to designate the start and end boundaries of the *conversation* as the moving stanza window slides through the discourse [16]. Researchers justify their segmentation choices theoretically by operationalizing existing conceptualization of theoretical discourse structures, if available. Alternatively, researchers justify their segmentation choices empirically by experimenting and choosing segmentation that is most aligned with a story grounded in the data. For example, Zörgő and colleagues [17] developed an approach for testing various segmentation choices in one dataset and discovered that segmentation choices change the interpretations of the findings in their particular dataset.

4.3 Codification

After segmentation, each line is codified numerically. Because of the ethnographic ideologies in QE, the coding process in QE is often grounded and derived from the data itself. In actual practice, steps three and four are interchangeable and iterative. Researchers may segment data into lines, code the data, and then segment the coded data into stanzas. To progress through the model-making process, codes must be represented as numbers. Many QE studies have used binary coding: displaying a 1 if the code appears in the line and 0 if the code does not appear in the line. Other studies have explored weighted code values. For example, Frey and colleagues [18] analyzed adolescents' emotions during peer victimization and used weighted coding in their analysis to model the strength of the emotions at the coding level. As of now, most QE researchers rely on "hand-coding" in which a human identified the codes in each line of data [19]. However, researchers also develop automated classifiers using regular expressions, topic modeling, and nCoder. Other tools, such as the Rho R Package, use statistics to validate that the automated classifiers are coding the data consistently in ways that align with human interpretations. The Reproducible Open Coding Kit (ROCK) also available on R, provides QE researchers with tools to segment and code data and transfer their codes to a model [20].

4.4 Accumulation

After codes are represented quantitatively, the data are accumulated in steps five through seven. A value is computed for each stanza based on the codes, represented as S1 in the figure. For example, when using ENA, S1 is represented as a vector that captures the number of co-occurrences among codes. Then, stanza values are accumulated for each unit of analysis. Units of analysis can be defined in many ways including each person in the community, teams of people, or documents. In practice, steps five and six may happen concurrently, in which a stanza value is determined for each unit of analysis. As of now, ENA is the most widely used tool for accumulating data [19]. In ENA, the observation of the unit is visualized in two forms: 1) as a weighted network representation of the accumulated, and often scaled, co-occurrences of codes, and 2) as a point in space that roughly corresponds to the centroid of the weighted network. Other tools that have been developed to accumulate and visualize coded data include Social Epistemic Network

Signature (SENS) [21], Socio-Semantic Network Analysis (SSNA) [22], and using R to merge sentiment analysis with domain-specific discourse [23]. Some QE analyses have stopped at step seven of computing and visualizing observations. In these studies, the main purpose is to provide a description of the data and tell a visual story but not to make claims about statistical differences within dataset.

4.5 Measurement

If researchers are interested in measuring differences between or within groups in the data, then they can continue to steps 8, 9, and 10 in which statistical analysis are conducted. A parameter is computed for each sample and a statistic is computed to determine whether there is a difference between samples that is statistically significant. Examples of parameters could be calculating a mean or a median. Examples of statistics could be a t statistic from a t-test or a u statistic from a non-parametric Mann-Whitney test. Although two-sample inferential statistics are commonly used, other forms of statistical tests could be conducted that align with study's goals. For example, one study used k-means clustering as an exploratory way to group and measure samples [24]. In a more recent study, one-sample inferential statistics were used to determine whether observed ENA models were statistically different from models created by chance and thus, making statistical claims for theoretical saturation within the dataset [25].

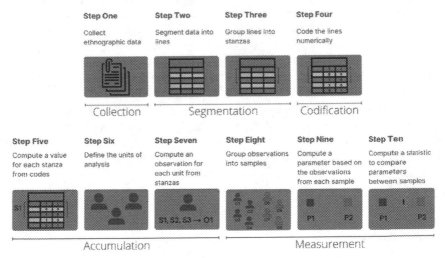

Fig. 1. Ten iterative steps for creating a QE model modified from Shaffer [10].

5   Examples of QE Processes

5.1   Augmenting Descriptive Analyses

In this first example, we describe a QE analysis by Vega and colleagues [26] in which they explored the identity process of four Costa Rican pre-service teachers in training to become English as a foreign language teachers. Given that pre-service education is a critical period for teacher identity formation, the purpose of the study was to illuminate the ways in which dominant discourses can contribute to tensions in identity development. One researcher conducted semi-structured, open ended interviews via video calls. Interviews, which ranged from 45–75 min, were recorded and transcribed. Researchers were interested in characterizing tensions that pre-service teachers felt in their training programs when negotiating and managing their identity development and wanted to provide a powerful descriptive analysis. Thus, the research team employed steps one through six of the iterative QE modeling pathway and did not engage with the measurement aspects.

The research team segmented the data into 143 lines by turns of talk (Step 2) and grouped the lines into stanzas that represented a sliding window of two turns of talk (Step 3) bounded by each interview session. To code the dataset, the team engaged in three iterative rounds of coding. In the first round, they created deductive codes derived from a theoretical framework, and then followed an inductive process to extend and add codes. In the third round, for reduction of the codes and reaching theoretical saturation, categories generated in the previous round were collapsed. Using the refined coding scheme, two of the researchers coded the data separately and met to discuss the inconsistencies until they reach mutual agreement. The coding was coded numerically through binary coding (Step 4).

To accumulate and visualize the dataset, Vega and colleagues relied on ENA. They chose pre-service teachers as the unit of analysis (Step 5). Then, they computed a value for each stanza and accumulated these stanzas for each unit to create an observation (Steps 6 and 7). The observations were represented as weighted networks for each teacher. Analysis of the networks and discourse revealed that all four participants positioned themselves as inferior non-native English speakers and negatively compared themselves to native English speakers from the U.S. or U.K. In the paper, the researchers tell the stories of the four pre-service teachers who made strong connections between the Native speaker as a standard and Tensions, indicating concerns around their linguistic practices as language learners.

At the conclusion of the paper, the researchers argue for the affordances of ENA and QE that strengthen qualitative analyses of language teacher identity. First, they were able to test the deductive and inductive coding categories and refine based on their persistence and connectivity on the visualizations. They claim that "the iterative process of interaction between the qualitative data and ENA network visualizations provided grounded evidence of salient codes in our data set and clarity for the story that the data were telling." Second, ENA allowed for descriptive storytelling at multiple levels. There were aspects of the teachers' developing identities that were prevalent between two teachers but even within a particular pair of teachers there were nuanced experiences that the networks could explain and visualize that were not visible in previous qualitative studies of this data. These distinctions between and within groups revealed undiscovered tensions at personal, group, and aggregated levels that participants experienced. The authors conclude that the use of ENA on previously analyzed qualitative data revealed new descriptive interactions in the data that were not seen before, thus augmenting the original qualitative analyses.

5.2 Employing Statistical Models to Make Claims

In this second example, we describe a QE analysis by Sweicki and colleagues [27] in which they examined a dataset of transcripts from 16 teams comprised of 94 naval officers during air defense warfare team training. The dataset was segmented into 12,027 lines of talk and split into an experimental condition, teams with access to a decision-support system, and a control condition, teams that did not have access to this system. The researchers were interested in determining if there was a statistical difference between the commanding officers in the experimental and control group in terms of collaborative problem-solving approaches. To make this comparison they segmented the transcripts of the Navy air defense warfare team training scenarios in lines determined by turns of talk and grouped the lines of data by team and condition (Steps 2 & 3). Then, the research team qualitatively analyzed the data starting with a grounded analysis and triangulation with related previous related studies to develop a coding scheme. They then applied this coding scheme using nCoder to develop and validate automated qualitative coding of the data (Step 4).

After segmentation and codification, Swiecki and colleagues used ENA to achieve accumulation and measurement. Through the ENA webtool, they identified units of analysis as the commanders in each condition (Step 6) and used a sliding stanza model with a window size of five to capture the recent temporal context of the conversation (Step 3). The ENA webtool then created a value for each stanza (Step 5) for each commander in each condition and accumulated these values to create one observation for each officer (Step 7). The observations were represented as weighted networks in which one network was created for each officer that revealed the connections they made between codes. To address their original research question, Swiecki and colleagues compared the patterns of connections made by commanders in the experimental and control conditions. They found that the discourse patterns of commanders in the control condition spent more time making connections related to Seeking Information while the commanders in the experimental condition we able to make more connections that Contributed Information and Linking Information about the tactical situation and tactical actions. Taking the analysis further, the research team used an alternative observational representation in ENA which represents each observation as a numeric value that roughly corresponds to the center of mass of the weighted network. Because each observation is a number, a distribution can be created for each group of interest and in turn, inferential statistics can be employed. In this study, the research team conducted a two-sample Mann-Whitney U test between distributions of the projected points in ENA space for commanders in the two conditions (Steps 8, 9, and 10). The results revealed that the discourse patterns in the control group ($Mdn = -0.21, N = 13$) were significantly different from the experimental group ($Mdn = 0.25$, $N = 16$; $U = 206$, $p < 0.01$, $d = 2.98$, power $= 1.00$). This quantitative result supported the claim that commanders in the control condition made stronger connections to Seeking Information, while commanders in the experimental condition made stronger connections to codes related to tactical decision-making.

Finally, prior to reporting their quantitative results, the research team identified qualitative examples of all of the aspects of their quantitative results and provided interpretive explanations of the qualitative data. Moreover, after providing their qualitative results they used both the qualitative examples and linked quantitative models in ENA to frame further examples of individual commander performance to reinforce the linkages between their qualitative understanding and the computational model they were using.

6 Five Main Practices in QE

In addition to a set of ten iterative steps, we offer five main practices in QE. These practices differ from the iterative steps in that they are ways of thinking and doing that the researcher engages in throughout QE.

6.1 Practice the 3 C'S of Data Hygiene: Clean, Complete, and Consistent

Because QE researchers integrate qualitative and quantitative ways of thinking, they must use data organization approaches that align with an integrated mindset. One way to frame such integrative practices is by referring to having proper "data hygiene." In everyday terms, hygiene is defined as the set of cleanliness practices conducive to maintaining health and preventing disease. Extending this metaphor to QE, having proper data hygiene means making qualitative and quantitative techniques compatible such that ethnographic data can be analyzed statistically without compromising validity and thick descriptions [4]. In actual practice, QE researchers practice proper data hygiene by organizing ethnographic data into a single qualitative data table that is clean, complete, and consistent. As stated above, the data table is comprised of lines, which are the smallest unit of action that is of interest in the data, and stanzas, which are groups of lines that are topically related. These lines and stanzas must be represented in the data table such that the data table is machine-readable but not necessarily human-readable. Bold borders, shading, and merged columns may help readers understand information presented in a data table [28]. However, these aesthetics are not usable for a computational program.

Researchers can ensure their data table is machine-readable by following the three C's of proper data hygiene. First, the same notation should be used throughout the table to indicate the same information. For example, if the location of the study is referred to as "Los Angeles" in some parts of the data table and "L.A." in other parts of the table, the quantitative analysis will assume these are two different locations although a human reader will assume they are the same location. The data table should be *clean* in terms of notation. Second, each row in the table should have all the information related to that unit of analysis. For example, if a row represents one line of discourse from a particular participant, then that row should also have all the data collected that is related to that participant, such as age, location, or dietary preferences. Again, completeness is not aesthetically pleasing to a human reader because the same information will be repeated in every row, but it is necessary for computation. Thus, each row in the data table should be *complete* and include all the data collected for that particular participant or unit of analysis. Last, not only should every row be complete but it should also only contain information related to that particular unit and line of discourse. The same idea applies to the columns in the data table–every column must contain one type of information. For example, if a column is labeled as "Location," then it should only have data about location. The "Location" column could have different data entries such as, "Los Angeles," "Lagos," or "Buenos Aires," but there is no other information except for location. Thus, each column and row in the data table should be *consistent* in terms of the information provided.

6.2   Get a Grip

After data collection and organization, ethnographers develop stories about a particular culture. The analysis process can be thought of as putting together pieces of a socio-cultural puzzle [29] but one with multiple possible solutions. Just like most research processes, quantitative ethnography, is a messy, ambiguous process. To navigate through making sense of the collected data, QE researchers must "get a grip" on the story that they would like to tell from the data. Shaffer [4] describes this process as getting a mechanical grip on a Discourse. He argues that the term emphasizes how the mechanical tools of research are used to "grab hold" of the complex phenomena in the world that we are trying to explain. In practice, QE researchers are consistently getting and refining a grip on the Discourse throughout the analytical process. The first move towards getting a grip is by familiarizing oneself with the data and developing initial Codes. As indicated by the example from Vega and colleagues in Sect. 5.1, researchers may refine their Codes during the coding process but also after modeling their data and interpreting their models. In QE, this iterative process of Codes informing models and models informing Codes continues until the grip has tightened sufficiently and a fair thick description has been developed. Getting a grip is a metaphor for how QE researchers consistently use the mechanisms of ethnography and statistics to reveal the underlying Discourse in a culture.

6.3   Have a Conversation with the Tools

One thing that makes QE a unique methodology is that researchers get a grip on their data by using ethnographic and statistical tools together. Even in the initial stages of data organization, a seasoned QE researcher will rely on digital and computational tools to ensure that data tables are clean, complete, and consistent. In later stages of QE analysis, the digital tools play a more significant role. As stated in Sect. 4.2, a researcher may rely on natural language processing tools to help identify phrases or lines that should be coded in the data. Such tools are skilled at finding additional Codes (or lines that should have been coded) that a researcher may have overlooked. However, such tools do not understand the discourse data in the way that human researchers understand and interpret discourse—at least, not yet anyway. Each party—computational tool and human researcher—have certain strengths and weaknesses. And what makes QE such a powerful approach is the way it leverages the strengths of the automation power of computational tools with the interpretative power of human researchers. But to ensure rigor and quality, the researcher must check the outputs of the tool to see if the results make sense, are fair, and grounded in the data. What often happens is that the researcher and the tools engage in iterative cycles of feedback in which the research inputs information into the tools, the tools process the information, the tools output new information, the researcher interprets this information and decides their next move. This is called *having a conversation* with the tool. Similar to a conversation between two people, the researcher may decide to "ask" the tool a clarifying question by exploring the output further or move the conversation along by "asking" a new question and running a new analysis. The computational tool essentially becomes a member of a well-functioning research team that has shared responsibilities and goals, utilizes the talents of its team members, and promotes the exchange of feedback.

6.4 Close the Interpretative Loop

While conversations with the tools happen throughout QE, there is one particular class of conversations that occurs during modeling that is of critical importance. In this conversation, the researcher inputs coded data into a modeling tool, the tool produces a model, the researcher interprets the model, and then goes back to the original data to see if the interpretation is supported by the data. If the interpretation does not align with the collected data, then the researcher must reevaluate the Codes and the assumptions made in the model. This unique conversation is called *closing the interpretative loop*. It is a central mindset in QE because it is the fundamental pathway of validating a model and provides the qualitative evidence that created the quantitative result. Although a central aspect of QE, closing the interpretative loop is susceptible to being forgotten by researchers. One reason this process is ignored is because the conversations between tools and researchers can be lengthy and intense. After many long hours and dead ends, a researcher may be excited to find a model that has a significant result and seems to make sense at face value. However, by not grounding the interpretation of the model in the data, the researcher violates a central tenet in the science of ethnography. Thus, closing the interpretative loop is an important way of establishing validity in QE and should be a consistent mindset.

6.5 Embrace Multiple Forms of Validity

In quantitative research, validity is defined as the accuracy of measurement and the extent to which the tools are measuring what is intended to be measured. However, in QE, validity is a much broader concept that takes up multiple forms. Closing the interpretive loop is the fundamental validity philosophy that supports QE, but there are other validity checks that occur throughout. As Winter [30] argues, "validity is not a single, fixed or universal concept, but rather a contingent construct, inescapably grounded in the processes and intentions of particular research methodologies and projects." For example, when coding data, QE researchers establish construct validity by building a codebook with definitions of Codes and examples of discourse that are categorized by a Code [31]. The definitions provide defined constructs that can be traced back to theory and examples of discourse provide evidence grounded in the data. A researcher may also establish validity by doing member-checking or other forms of participatory QE research in which researchers discuss the Codes with the participants from the study [32]. Researchers may strengthen emic-etic connections for building thick descriptions and co-construct meaning with participants. However, member-checking may also result in tensions between researcher and participants and highlight unequal power dynamics [33]. Thus, when engaging in participatory QE research, researchers should engage in their critical reflexivity practices by interrogating power dynamics, reflecting on how participants will be harmed or put at risk by member-checking, and the roles of the "researcher" and the "researched" [34].

In some studies, one researcher will code all the data alone. In other studies, two or more researchers will code the data and inter-rater reliability metrics will be used to determine if the interpretations are relatively the same across two or more people and therefore, offer some confidence in the conceptual validity of the interpretations. In some cases, researchers will engage in social moderation and code all the data and discuss until mutual consensus is reached. When the dataset is too large, two researchers select a sample of the data, code the sample individually, calculate inter-rater reliability using a statistic, determine if the statistic has met a pre-determined cut-off or threshold of performance, and if it has, then split the dataset and code the remaining data individually. These steps confirm reliability for the sample that was coded but it is unclear if the sample is representative of the remaining dataset and thus, it is unclear whether the remaining dataset will have the same level of validity. Eagan and colleagues [35] recommend using rho as a statistical technique to take representative samples of the dataset and to control for Type I error (false positives) when coding data with two or more raters. In addition to two human raters, QE researchers may also train and use an automated classifier to code large datasets. In these cases, inter-rater reliability is measured between two human raters to determine conceptual validity. It is also measured between each human rater and the automated classifier to determine computational validity and whether the automated classifier is capable of consistently coding the data in ways that align with human interpretations. Whether during coding or modeling, validity checks such as exercising critical reflexivity, closing the interpretive loop, and inter-rater reliability facilitate the rigor that establishes QE as a science.

7 Conclusion

In this paper, we argue that ethnography is foundational, and quantification is fundamental to the science of QE. We provided ten iterative steps for creating QE models and two examples of how these steps are visible. In parallel to the steps, we provided five main practices that we have observed and experienced as seasoned QE researchers. We drew from Shaffer's visionary book [4] but have reconceptualized and summarized key ideas. The goals of this article were to 1) provide a distilled version of the fundamental tenets of QE to provide an access point for new scholars, 2) provide a summarized reference guide for those who are established users of the methodology, 3) bring clarity to the potentially hidden values and practices that drive the methodology, and 4) bring clarity to processes that are essential in QE and processes that are flexible and context-dependent. Overall, this work provides one form of an accessible description of QE for the broader inter-disciplinary community.

References

1. Hutchins, E.: Cognition in the Wild. MIT press (1995)
2. Geertz, C.: The Interpretation of Cultures. Basic books (1973)

3. Gee, J.P.: An Introduction to Discourse Analysis: Theory and Method. Routledge, Milton Park, Abingdon, New York (2011)
4. Shaffer, D.W.: Quantitative Ethnography. Cathcart Press, Madison, WI (2017)
5. Watt, D.: On Becoming a qualitative researcher: the value of reflexivity. Qual, Report **12**, 82–101 (2007)
6. Haraway, D.: Situated knowledges: the science question in feminism and the privilege of partial perspective. Fem. Stud. **14**, 575–599 (1988). https://doi.org/10.2307/3178066
7. Corple, D.J., Linabary, J.R.: From data points to people: feminist situated ethics in online big data research. Int. J. Soc. Res. Methodol. **23**, 155–168 (2020). https://doi.org/10.1080/136 45579.2019.1649832
8. Arastoopour Irgens, G.: Using knowledgeable agents of the digital and data feminism to uncover social identities in the #blackgirlmagic Twitter community. Learn. Media Technol. **47**, 79–94 (2022). https://doi.org/10.1080/17439884.2021.2018608
9. Pacheco-Vega, R., Parizeau, K.: Doubly engaged ethnography: opportunities and challenges when working with vulnerable communities. Int. J. Qual. Methods **17**, 160940691879065 (2018). https://doi.org/10.1177/1609406918790653
10. Pea, R.: Practices of distributed intelligence and designs for education. In: Salomaon, G. (ed.) Distributed Cognitions: Psychological and Educational Considerations. Cambridge University Press, New York (1993)
11. D'Ignazio, C., Klein, L.F.: Data Feminism. The MIT Press, Cambridge, Massachusetts (2020)
12. Arastoopour Irgens, G.: Quantitative Ethnography Across Domains: Where We Are and Where We Are Going. Madison, WI (2019)
13. Hod, Y., Katz, S., Eagan, B.: Refining qualitative ethnographies using Epistemic Network Analysis: a study of socioemotional learning dimensions in a Humanistic Knowledge Building Community. Comput. Educ. **156**, 103943 (2020). https://doi.org/10.1016/j.compedu.2020.103943
14. Guba, E.G., Lincoln, Y.S.: Fourth Generation Evaluation. Sage (1989)
15. Glesne, C.: Becoming Qualitative Researchers: An Introduction. Pearson, Boston (2014)
16. Siebert-Evenstone, A.L., Arastoopour Irgens, G., Collier, W., Swiecki, Z., Ruis, A.R., Shaffer, D.W.: In search of conversational grain size: Modeling semantic structure using moving stanza windows. J. Learn. Anal. **4**, 123–139 (2017)
17. Zörgő, S., Swiecki, Z., Ruis, A.R.: Exploring the effects of segmentation on semi-structured interview data with epistemic network analysis. In: Ruis, A.R., Lee, S.B. (eds.) ICQE 2021. CCIS, vol. 1312, pp. 78–90. Springer, Cham (2021). https://doi.org/10.1007/978-3-030-677 88-6_6
18. Frey, K.S., McDonald, K.L., Onyewuenyi, A.C., Germinaro, K., Eagan, B.R.: "I Felt Like a Hero:" Adolescents' understanding of resolution-promoting and vengeful actions on behalf of their peers. J. Youth Adolesc. **50**(3), 521–535 (2020). https://doi.org/10.1007/s10964-020-01346-3
19. Kaliisa, R., Misiejuk, K., Irgens, G.A., Misfeldt, M.: Scoping the emerging field of quantitative ethnography: opportunities, challenges and future directions. In: Ruis, A.R., Lee, S.B. (eds.) ICQE 2021. CCIS, vol. 1312, pp. 3–17. Springer, Cham (2021). https://doi.org/10.1007/978-3-030-67788-6_1
20. Peters, G.-J., Zörgő, S.: Introduction to the Reproducible Open Coding Kit (ROCK) (2019). https://psyarxiv.com/stcx9/
21. Gašević, D., Joksimović, S., Eagan, B.R., Shaffer, D.W.: SENS: Network analytics to combine social and cognitive perspectives of collaborative learning. Comput. Hum. Behav. **92**, 562–577 (2019). https://doi.org/10.1016/j.chb.2018.07.003
22. Oshima, J., Oshima, R., Fujita, W.: A mixed-methods approach to analyze shared epistemic agency in jigsaw instruction at multiple scales of temporality. J. Learn. Anal. **5**, 10–24 (2018). https://doi.org/10.18608/jla.2018.51.2

23. Arastoopour Irgens, G.: Facilitating a sense of belonging for women of color in engineering. In: Roscoe, R.D., Chiou, E.K., Wooldrige, A.R. (eds.) Advancing Diversity, Inclusion, and Social Justice Through Human Systems Engineering, pp. 221–239. CRC Press, Boca Raton (2019)

24. Arastoopour Irgens, G., Chandra, S., Dabholkar, S., Horn, M., Wilensky, U.: Classifying emergent student learning in a high school computational chemistry unit. In: American Education Research Association (AERA) Conference. Toronto, CA (2019)

25. Swiecki, Zachari: The expected value test: A new statistical warrant for theoretical saturation. In: Wasson, Barbara, Zörgő, Szilvia (eds.) Advances in Quantitative Ethnography: Third International Conference, ICQE 2021, Virtual Event, November 6–11, 2021, Proceedings, pp. 49–65. Springer International Publishing, Cham (2022). https://doi.org/10.1007/978-3-030-93859-8_4

26. Vega, H., Irgens, G.A., Bailey, C.: Negotiating tensions: a study of pre-service English as foreign language teachers' sense of identity within their community of practice. In: Ruis, A.R., Lee, S.B. (eds.) ICQE 2021. CCIS, vol. 1312, pp. 277–291. Springer, Cham (2021). https://doi.org/10.1007/978-3-030-67788-6_19

27. Swiecki, Z., Ruis, A.R., Farrell, C., Shaffer, D.W.: Assessing individual contributions to Collaborative Problem Solving: A network analysis approach. Comput. Hum. Behav. **104**, 105876 (2020). https://doi.org/10.1016/j.chb.2019.01.009

28. Wong, D.M.: The Wall Street Journal Guide to Information Graphics: The Dos and Don'ts of Presenting Data, Facts, and Figures. W. W. Norton & Company, New York; London (2013)

29. Burns, A.: Analyzing ethnographic data. In: Tyner-Mullings, A., Gatta, M., and Coughlan, R. (eds.) Ethnography Made Easy. CUNY Open Educational Resource (2019)

30. Winter, G.: A Comparative Discussion of the Notion of "Validity" in Qualitative and Quantitative Research. TQR (2000). https://doi.org/10.46743/2160-3715/2000.2078

31. Shaffer, D.W., Ruis, A.R.: How we code. In: Ruis, A.R., Lee, S.B. (eds.) ICQE 2021. CCIS, vol. 1312, pp. 62–77. Springer, Cham (2021). https://doi.org/10.1007/978-3-030-67788-6_5

32. Vega, H., Arastoopour Irgens, G.A.: Constructing interpretations with participants through epistemic network analysis: towards participatory approaches in quantitative ethnography. In: Wasson, B., Zörgő, S. (eds.) Advances in Quantitative Ethnography, pp. 3–16. Springer International Publishing, Cham (2022)

33. Candela, A.: Exploring the Function of Member Checking. TQR (2019). https://doi.org/10.46743/2160-3715/2019.3726

34. Shum, S.B., et al.: Participatory Quantitative Ethnography. In: Advances in Quantitative Ethnography, pp. 126–138. Malibu, CA

35. Eagan, B., Rogers, B., Serlin, R., Ruis, A.R., Arastoopour Irgens, G., Shaffer, D.W.: Can we rely on irr? testing the assumptions of inter-rater reliability. In: International Conference on Computer Supported Collaborative Learning (2017)

LSTM Neural Network Assisted Regex Development for Qualitative Coding

Zhiqiang Cai(✉) ⓘ, Brendan Eagan ⓘ, Cody Marquart ⓘ,
and David Williamson Shaffer ⓘ

University of Wisconsin-Madison, Madison, USA
{zhiqiang.cai,beagan,cody.marquart}@wisc.edu,
dws@education.wisc.edu

Abstract. Regular expression (regex) based automated qualitative coding helps reduce researchers' effort in manually coding text data, without sacrificing transparency of the coding process. However, researchers using regex based approaches struggle with low recall or high false negative rate during classifier development. Advanced natural language processing techniques, such as topic modeling, latent semantic analysis and neural network classification models help solve this problem in various ways. The latest advance in this direction is the discovery of the so called "negative reversion set (NRS)", in which false negative items appear more frequently than in the negative set. This helps regex classifier developers more quickly identify missing items and thus improve classification recall. This paper simulates the use of NRS in real coding scenarios and compares the required manual coding items between NRS sampling and random sampling in the process of classifier refinement. The result using one data set with 50,818 items and six associated qualitative codes shows that, on average, using NRS sampling, the required manual coding size could be reduced by 50% to 63%, comparing with random sampling.

Keywords: Negative reversion · Qualitative coding · LSTM neural network

1 Introduction

Coding in qualitative research is traditionally a complex manual process of theory discovery [10]. Qualitative researchers go through the data item by item to extract information they find interesting or pertinent to their study. They discover patterns or themes to form big-C *Codes* [12]. Once a code is well defined, they go back to the data and systematically identify where each code occurs through out the entire dataset. As Shaffer and Ruis [13] pointed out, coding is basically a process of "defining concepts and identifying where they occur" [13]. While a researcher may be able to find the patterns for code definition using a relatively small part of a data set, "identifying where they occur" requires the researcher to go through every item in the data set. Such manual coding is often very

Supported by Natural Science Foundation

expensive and can be impossible for quantitative ethnographers, because they often deal with data that is too large to code by hand.

In contrast to manual coding, machine learning algorithms have been used to train classifiers for automatic coding. Such algorithms use part of the data that researchers manually coded to train a classification model, which is then used to classify the rest of the data [1, 9]. Researchers have identified challenges in using machine learning for automatic coding [2, 4]. The so called "black box" issue is a major challenge for ethnographers, qualitative researchers, or people working in the digital humanities interested in adopting automated qualitative coding methods. Namely, when an excerpt is coded as *positive* for a certain code, the *evidence* for the coding is often unclear from the output of the machine learning model, which makes it difficult for researchers to be successful in the *interpretation* stage in the analyses. Another challenge is that the amount of human coded data required for training machine learning algorithms is large, especially when the base rate (positive rate or frequency) of a code is small. For example, if a code occurs in about 1% of the items in the data set, to train a reliable neural network classifier often requires about 4,000 manually coded training items. In addition, machine learning algorithms tend to build classifiers based on high frequency expressions (words, phrases). Thus, the expressions used by minority groups or sub-populations could be under represented, resulting in biased and unfair coding.

Regex based coding has been proven to be a more efficient method for qualitative coding, which often requires manually coding only a few hundreds of excerpts in order to develop a reliable regex-based classifier. Once regexes are well developed, the coding is an automatic process and the matched text elements provide explicit coding evidence [12, 13]. However, regex based classifiers suffer from the *low recall* problem [2, 3]. That is, regex based classifiers can suffer from too many false negatives, where a researcher or domain expert would identify that a code is present, but the classifier does not. Various ways have been proposed to overcome the challenge of the low recall problem. For example, Latent Semantic Analysis [11] can be used to form a "snowball" method to help recursively expand keyword set for regex construction [3]. The latest discovery is the so called *"negative reversion set"* (NRS) in which false negative items are denser than in the negative set of regex classifiers [2]. This discovery makes it possible to greatly shorten the time in searching for missing patterns in regex development because researchers can use this set to focus on coding cases that are more likely to be false negatives and use the patterns shown in those examples to improve their classifiers.

Researchers developing new methodologies often conduct simulation studies to examine or compare the performance of different statistics or analytical approaches [6, 7]. This paper simulates the use of NRS in real world scenario and tackles the issue of required manual coding size. The main question we want to answer is, how much manual coding efforts can be reduced by using the NRS?

2   Negative Reversion Set and Research Questions

2.1   Negative Reversion Set

The usefulness of Negative Reversion Set (NRS) was discovered by the *triangulation* of three "raters": 1) a human; 2) a regex based classifier; and 3) a neural network model trained from the regex classifier. For a given data set D and a given code C, the human classification is denoted by $D = P + N$, where P is the set of human classified positive items and N the set of human classified negative items. The plus sign "+" denotes the union of the two sets. The classification by the regex classifier is denoted by $D = \tilde{P} + \tilde{N}$, where $\tilde{P}$ and $\tilde{N}$ are the regex classified positive and negative sets, respectively.

Taking human classification as ground truth, the four intersection sets of the two classifications by human and regex classifier are denoted by

- true positive set $P\tilde{P}$: both human and regex classify as positive;
- false positive set $N\tilde{P}$: human classifies as negative but regex classifies as positive;
- false negative set $P\tilde{N}$: human classifies as positive but regex classifies as negative; and
- true negative set $N\tilde{N}$: both human and regex classify as negative.

In the formulas above, "XY" denotes the intersection of two sets "X" and "Y".

The error and accuracy of the regex classification are determined by the size of the above four sets. The following metrics are used in this paper to measure the error and accuracy of the regex classifier:

- proportion of true positives:

$$tp = \frac{|P\tilde{P}|}{|D|};$$

- proportion of false positives:

$$fp = \frac{|N\tilde{P}|}{|D|};$$

- proportion of false negatives:

$$fn = \frac{|P\tilde{N}|}{|D|};$$

- proportion of true negatives:

$$tn = \frac{|N\tilde{N}|}{|D|};$$

- precision:

$$precision = \frac{tp}{|\tilde{P}|} = \frac{tp}{tp + fp};$$

- recall:

$$recall = \frac{tp}{|P|} = \frac{tp}{tp + fn}; \quad \text{and}$$

– Cohen's kappa:

$$k = \frac{p_o - p_c}{1 - p_c}$$

where $p_o = tp + tn$ is the observed agreement and $p_c = (tp + fp)(tp + fn) + (tn + fp)(tn + fn)$ is the chance agreement.

A regex classifier provides input to a neural network model to train another classifier, which classifies the data as $D = \tilde{P} + \tilde{N}$. Replacing $\tilde{P}$ and $\tilde{N}$ by $\bar{P}$ and $\bar{N}$ in the above formulas, the metrics about the performance of the neural network model are computed the same way as the regex classifier described above.

Table 1 shows the intersections of the three classifications. The so called "Negative Reversion Set" is the set of items that regex classifies as negative but the neural network model classifies as positive, i.e., the intersection of the regex negative set $\bar{N}$ and the neural network positive set $\tilde{P}$, which can be written as the union of two sets—a "correct" negative reversion set $PN\bar{P}$ and an "incorrect" negative reversion set $NN\bar{P}$:

$$NRS = \bar{N}\tilde{P}$$

$$= PN\bar{P}^{\tilde{}} + NN\bar{P}^{\tilde{}}$$

(1)

Table 1. Intersect sets of three classifications.

Human	Regex	Neural Network
P	$P\tilde{P}$	$PP^{\tilde{}}\tilde{P}$
	$P\tilde{N}$	$PP^{\tilde{}}\tilde{N}$
		$PN^{\tilde{}}\tilde{P}$
		$PN^{\tilde{}}\tilde{N}$
N	$N\tilde{P}$	$NP^{\tilde{}}\tilde{P}$
	$N\tilde{N}$	$NP^{\tilde{}}\tilde{N}$
		$NN^{\tilde{}}\tilde{P}$
		$NN^{\tilde{}}\tilde{N}$

In Eq. 1, the "correct" negative reversion set $PN\tilde{P}$ is the set of items that are falsely classified by regex as negative but correctly "reversed" back to positive by neural network. The "incorrect" negative reversion set $NN\tilde{P}$ is the set of items that regex correctly coded as negative but wrongly reversed by the neural network as positive. The proportion of correctly reversed items in the negative reversion set is used to measure the false negative density in the negative reversion set. For any two sets $X \subseteq Y$, we define the density of X in Y by

$$d(X, Y) = \frac{|X|}{|Y|}.$$

Thus the density of correctly reversed false negative items in the negative reversion set can be written as

$$d(P∩P, \tilde{}~ N∩P\tilde{}~) = \frac{|P\tilde{N}\tilde{\tilde{P}}|}{|\tilde{N}\tilde{\tilde{P}}|},$$

and the false negative density in the regex negative set is given by

$$d\left(P\tilde{N}, \tilde{N}\right) = \frac{|P\tilde{N}|}{|\tilde{N}|}.$$

Cai et al. [2] found that the density of false negative items in NRS could be much higher than in the regex negative set. That is,

$$d(P∩P, \tilde{}~ N∩P\tilde{}~) \gg d(PN, \tilde{}~ N∩).$$

As a side note, we point out that similar notations can be used to define "Positive Reversion Set (PRS)" which could be written as the union of "Correct Positive Reversion" and "Incorrect Positive Reversion":

$$PRS = P∩N\tilde{}~ = PP∩N\tilde{}~ + NP∩N.\tilde{}~$$

Positive reversion set could be useful for improving precision of regex classifiers, which is an interesting issue but out of the scope of this paper.

2.2 NRS Assisted Regex Development

Based on their discovery, Cai et al. [2] proposed a regex development procedure (see Fig. 1). In their procedure, the regex development starts from an initial list. This regex list is a set of "atomic regex", each of which cannot be decomposed as two regexes combined by the symbol "|". For example, "\bchair|\btable" is not an atomic regex because it can be decomposed as "\bchair" and "\btable". A researcher provides one or more keywords that can represent a part of the code. The keywords are then used to construct the atomic regexes.

Once the initial regex list is obtained, the data is coded by the regex list and a neural network model is then trained using a part of the data classified by the regex list. The reversion sets, including negative reversion set and positive reversion set, are then identified by intersecting the regex classification and neural network classification. Items from reversion sets are then selected and presented to the researcher to rate the occurrence of the code. A conflict occurs if the researcher's rating is different from the regex classification. The researcher may resolve the conflict by changing the rating or modifying the regex list. When the regex list is modified, a new neural network model is re-generated and new reversion sets are identified. New items are continuously selected and presented to the researcher, until the researcher's rating and the regex classification reach an acceptably high level of agreement. In this procedure, reversion sets serve as providers of most likely conflict items.

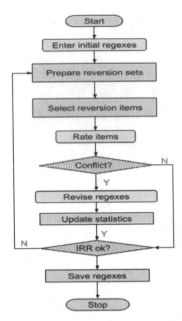

Fig. 1. Neural network assisted regex development for qualitative coding.

2.3 Research Questions

The regex development procedure suggested by Cai et al. [2] assumed that selecting items from a set with denser false negatives helps shorten the searching of new regexes. However, exactly how much such selection helps increase the efficiency of regex based classifier refinement remains an unanswered question. In this paper, we attempt to answer this question. Specifically, we ask:

RQ1 How does the false negative density change over multiple iterations? We know that the false negative density in the negative reversion set $N\tilde{}P\tilde{}$ could be much higher than in the regex negative set $N\tilde{}$. However, for each subsequent iterations, the number of false negative items reduces and thus the density could reduce quickly. This leads to the following questions, 1) How dense could it be at the beginning of the process? and 2) How quickly would it drop?

RQ2 Is using the negative reversion set more efficient than random sampling for the purpose of regex based classifier refinement, if so how much more? We hypothesize that sampling from a set with dense false negatives could help a researcher more quickly identify missing regexes. The question is, for a given level of required coding accuracy, how many fewer items would a researcher need to examine when using the negative reversion set compared to random sampling?

3 Method

3.1 Data

The data we used in this study were collected by previous researchers from an engineering virtual internship called *Nephrotex* [5, 8]. Participants worked as interns at a fictitious company that designs and manufactures ultrafiltration membranes for hemodialysis machinery used to treat end-stage renal failure. The work was divided into two phases. In the first phase, participants were grouped into teams of five. Each team worked on a specific task. In the second phase, participants were regrouped, or jigsawed, into new teams of five members from different teams in the first phase. The task in the second phase was to reflect the work each member did in the first phase to collaborate with their new team with varied expertise. The utterances in all online team chat conversations were collected, resulting in a data set with 50,888 utterances. After filtering out 70 longest utterances, 50,818 utterances were used in this study, each of which had a length not more than 100 words.

3.2 Codes

Previous researchers created six codes, including *Tech Constraints, Performance, Collaboration, Design, Data* and *Requests*. They developed and validated regexes for each code. Table 2 shows the name, description, example regex and IRR (Inter-Rater Reliability) of the six codes. The three numbers in the IRR column are the kappa values between three pairs of raters: human rater 1: human rater 2, regex : human rater 1, and regex : human rater 2. Since the regexes were well developed and validated, in this study we consider the regex lists "complete" and use the full regex classification as human classification.

3.3 Three Classifiers

This study involves three types of classification processes. The first type named "Full Regex", which uses the complete regex list developed and validated by previous researchers. This classification is used as "ground truth" and is considered equivalent to "human" classification. The second type is called "Partial Regex", which uses a subset of the a full regex list to classify the data. This type is used to simulate incomplete regex classifiers that are under development. The third type is the LSTM neural network (see Fig. 2), which uses a small part of the data classified by a partial regex classifier to train a predictive model. Details about this neural network model can be found in Cai et al. [2].

Table 2. Code definition, example regexes and IRR. (All codes were validated at a kappa threshold of 0.65 and a rho threshold of 0.05)

Code	Description	Example	IRR
TECH CONSTRAINTS	Referring to inputs: material, processing method, surfactant, and CNT	\bPESPVP, \bdry-jet, \bnegative charge, \bsurfactant,...	0.96|1.00|0.96
PERFORMANCE	Referring to attributes: flus, blood cell reactivity, marketability, cost, or reliability	\bafforda, \bBCR, \bflux, \bexpensive, \bmarketa,...	0.88|0.93|0.84
COLLABORATION	Facilitating a joint meeting or the production of team design products	\bmeeting, \bwe all, \bdiscussion, \bwhat should,...	0.76|0.87|0.76
DESIGN	Referring to design and development prioritization, tradeoffs, and design decisions	\bfinal decision, \bdecision, \bwent with, \bbased each design,...	0.89|0.86|0.84
DATA	Referring to or justifying decisions based on numerical values, results tables, graphs, research papers, or relative quantities	\bchart, \bequal value, \bresults,...	0.94|0.90|0.89
REQUESTS	Referring to or justifying decisions based on internal consultant's requests or patient's health or comfort	\buser, \bDuChamp, \bPadma, \bsafety, \bhospital,...	0.88|0.94|0.94

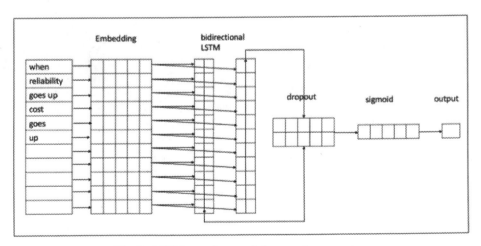

Fig. 2. LSTM neural network for negative reversion.

3.4 Simulation Procedure

To answer our research questions, we simulated coding process under two conditions, one was called "nn" condition and the other was called "random" condition. In "nn" condition, the neural network modeling was included in the loop to identify negative reversion sets. The "nn" condition procedure went as follows.

1 Select one of the six codes;
2 Select a single regex with base rate not less than 0.001 from the full regex list as lead regex (there are a total of 119 such regexes in the six classifiers);
3 Use the selected lead regex as partial regex list;
4 Code the data with the partial regex list;
5 Compute kappa between full regex coding and partial regex coding;
6 Sample 400 items containing at least 10 positive items and train a neural network model;
7 Code the data using the neural network model;
8 Find the negative reversion set;
9 Sample 30 items from the negative reversion set;
10 Compute the false negative density in the 30 items; 11 If there are no false negative items, go to step 14;
12 Find the regexes in the full regex list that match any of the false negative item in the 30 items and add the matched regexes into the partial regex list;
13 Go to step 4;
14 If there are more regexes that have not been selected as lead regex, go to 2; 15 If there are more codes, go to 1; 16 Stop.

The procedure for the random condition was the same as the "nn" condition, except that the 30 items in each iteration were randomly selected from the regex negative set, instead of NRS.

3.5 Data Aggregation

The false negative density and the achieved kappa in each iteration were averaged over the 119 leading regexes. The 95% confidence intervals were also computed for these means.

4 Results

4.1 False Negative Density

Figure 3 shows the average false negative density in each 30-item iteration under the two conditions (nn and random). In the first iteration, the 30 items from NRS (nn condition) had about 36% false negatives on average, while the random sampling from the regex negative set (random condition) had only around 11% on average. The density in both conditions dropped quickly in the earlier iterations and became about the same from the 6th iteration on. This indicates that the use of NRS is more effective at the beginning stages of regex list development.

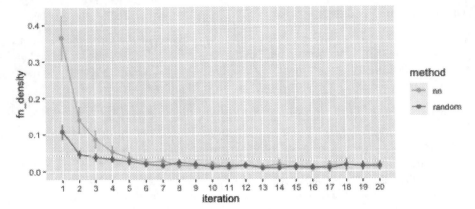

Fig. 3. False negative density in neural network identified negative reversion set (NRS) and in random sample from partial regex negative set

4.2 Required Manual Coding

Figure 4 shows the average kappas with 95% confidence intervals for each iteration, each condition. At iteration 1, for a given code and given lead regex, the partial regex list for both conditions were the same. And that is because both conditions started with the same lead regex. Therefore, the kappas between full regex list and partial list for both conditions were the same. From iteration 2 on, the items in the partial regex list for the nn condition were sampled from negative reversion set, while unsurprisingly, items were randomly sampled form the negative regex set for the random method condition, which is why we see the divergence in kappas from itteration 2. The kappa values for nn condition immediately became higher than the random condition, which implies that, the full regex list could be more quickly identified using the nn method. For example, to get a kappa $\kappa = 0.8$, the nn condition needed to iterate up to the 4th iteration, which

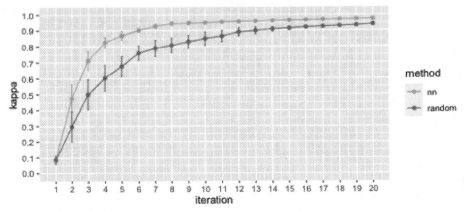

Fig. 4. Kappa between full regex coded data and partial regex coded data at each iteration for two methods

required 90 items; while the random condition needed to iterate up to 9th iteration, which required 240 items. Table 3 shows the estimated average number of required items for the two conditions. Overall, the nn to random ratio is less than 0.5. For higher kappa, the ratio is even smaller.

Table 3. Estimated number of manually coded items for developing regex with (nn)/without (random) NRS.

kappa	0.5	0.6	0.7	0.8	0.9
nn	45	60	70	90	180
random	90	120	150	240	420

5   Conclusions and Limitations

In this paper, we explored the use of the negative reversion technique in regex classifier development through a simulated coding procedure. We obtained two major results. One result is about the change of the density of the false negative items in the iterative procedure. We found that the false negative items were dense in early regex development but quickly dropped as the procedure iterated. This result has multiple implications. One is that the use of negative reversion set is more effective at the beginning of the iterations. When the regex list gets close to complete, the benefit from using negative reversion set is limited. Another implication is that, the dropping rate of the false negative density may be used as an indicator of the convergence of the iterative procedure. Namely, when the density and the dropping rate become small, further iteration may not be needed and the quality of the regex list under development may be high enough. However, if we consider the quality of the regex list as a function of density change, the code base rate needs to be taken into account, because for codes with smaller base rate, density is smaller and the change rate may be different. Further exploration on this issue is needed but is beyond the scope of this paper.

In addition, we found that sampling from the negative reversion set could be two or three times more efficient than random sampling from the regex negative set. In other words, using negative reversion set could largely reduce the number of items human needs to manually code when developing regex based classifiers.

Our results are averaged over 119 lead regexes from six classifiers with fairly tight confidence intervals providing evidence for the robust of our conclusions and the use of the NRS more broadly. However, when this technique is applied to other data sets, several factors may impact the results. The first factor is the code base rate. The six codes used in this paper have base rates ranging from 7% to 16%. When this technique is applied to codes with base rates far away from this range, the density drop rate, the kappa growth rate, and, more importantly, the number of required manual coding items could be different. The second factor is the number of items selected in each iteration. In this paper, we chose 30 items in each iteration just because it was easier for demonstrating performance. However, this number may affect the results. A smaller number may further reduce required manual coding. Meanwhile, a smaller number also implies more frequent updating of the neural network models, which takes computing time. The R code we ran on a mac laptop needs about 1 min to update an LSTM neural network model with 400 items in the training data. When the computing time is an issue, less frequent neural network updating could be considered. However, if the neural network updating can be further optimized and becomes fast enough, fewer items, or even single item per iteration could be considered.

Training size for neural network models is another factor that may impact the results. In this paper, we chose training size as 400 items and required that there are at least 10 positive items among these 400 items. How much the results rely on this choice is unclear. Future work in finding ways to optimize this choice is under consideration. One note on this is that, we don't believe using a very large training size will give us better results. The reason is that, larger the training size is, closer the neural network model will be to the regex classifier. That is, with a large training size, the training data could "force" the neural network to have a high level of agreement with the regex classifier and thus reduce the density of false negatives in the negative reversion set. We also point out that, any text classification models, not necessarily neural network models, could be used to construct the negative reversion set. It wouldn't be a surprise to us that there are models work better than the one we used in this paper.

As a final note, while this paper only considered false negatives, similar logic can be applied to construct "positive reversion set". In practical use, we believe both positive reversion set and negative reversion are useful. However, the negative reversion set could be more helpful when a code has a low base rate.

Acknowledgements. This work was funded in part by the National Science Foundation (DRL-1661036, DRL-1713110, DRL-2100320, LDI-1934745), the Wisconsin Alumni Research Foundation, and the Office of the Vice Chancellor for Research and Graduate Education at the University of Wisconsin-Madison. The opinions, findings, and conclusions do not reflect the views of the funding agencies, cooperating institutions, or other individuals.

References

1. Bai, X.: Text classification based on LSTM and attention. In: Thirteenth International Conference on Digital Information Management (ICDIM), pp. 29–32 (2018)
2. Cai, Z., Marquart, C., Shaffer, D.: Neural recall network: a neural network solution to low recall problem in regex-based qualitative coding. In: Mitrovic, A., Bosch, N. (eds.) Proceedings of the 15th International Conference on Educational Data Mining, pp. 228–238. International Educational Data Mining Society, Durham, United Kingdom (2022). https://doi.org/10.5281/zenodo.6853047
3. Cai, Z., Siebert-Evenstone, A., Eagan, B., Shaffer, D.W., Hu, X., Graesser, A.C.: ncoder+: a semantic tool for improving recall of ncoder coding. In: Advances in Quantitative Ethnography: ICQE Conference Proceedings. pp. 52–65 (2019)
4. Chen, N.C., Drouhard, M., Kocielnik, R., Suh, J., Aragon, C.R.: Using machine learning to support qualitative coding in social science: Shifting the focus to ambiguity. ACM Trans. Interact. Intell. Syst. **8**(2), 9:1–9:20 (2018). https://doi.org/10.1145/3185515, https://doi.org/10.1145/3185515

5. Chesler, N., Ruis, A., Collier, W., Swiecki, Z., Arastoopour, G., Shaffer, D.: A novel paradigm for engineering education: virtual internships with individualized mentoring and assessment of engineering thinking. J. Biomech. Eng. **137**(2), 1–8 (2015)

6. Eagan, B., Brohinsky, J., Wang, J., Shaffer, D.: Testing the reliability of interrater reliability. In: Proceedings of the Tenth International Conference on Learning Analytics and Knowledge, pp. 454–461 (2020)

7. Eagan, B., Swiecki, Z., Farrell, C., Shaffer, D.: The binary replicate test: Determining the sensitivity of CSCL models to coding error. In: Proceedings of the 13th International Conference on Computer Supported Collaborative Learning (CSCL), pp. 328–335 (2019)

8. Gautam, D., Swiecki, Z., Shaffer, D.W., Graesser, A.C., Rus, V.: Modeling classifiers for virtual internships without participant data. In: Proceedings of the 10th International Conference on Educational Data Mining, pp. 278–283 (2017)

9. Georgieva-Trifonova, T., Duraku, M.: Research on n-grams feature selection methods for text classification. In: IOP Conference Series: Materials Science and Engineering, vol. 1031, p. 012048. IOP Publishing (2021)

10. Glaser, B., Strauss, A.: The Discovery of Grounded Theory: Strategies For Qualitative Research. Aldine, Chicago (1967)

11. Landauer, T.K., Foltz, P.W., Laham, D.: An introduction to latent semantic analysis. Discourse Process. **25**(2–3), 259–284 (1998)

12. Shaffer, D.: Quantitative Ethnography. Cathcart Press, Madison, WI (2017)

13. Shaffer, D.W., Ruis, A.R.: How we code. In: Advances in Quantitative Ethnography: ICQE Conference Proceedings, pp. 62–77 (2021)

Does Active Learning Reduce Human Coding?: A Systematic Comparison of Neural Network with nCoder

Jaeyoon Choi[✉] , Andrew R. Ruis , Zhiqiang Cai , Brendan Eagan ,
and David Williamson Shaffer

University of Wisconsin-Madison, Madison, WI 53706, USA
jaeyoon.choi@wisc.edu

Abstract. In quantitative ethnography (QE) studies which often involve large datasets that cannot be entirely hand-coded by human raters, researchers have used supervised machine learning approaches to develop automated classifiers. However, QE researchers are rightly concerned with the amount of human coding that may be required to develop classifiers that achieve the high levels of accuracy that QE studies typically require. In this study, we compare a neural network, a powerful traditional supervised learning approach, with nCoder, an active learning technique commonly used in QE studies, to determine which technique requires the least human coding to produce a sufficiently accurate classifier. To do this, we constructed multiple training sets from a large dataset used in prior QE studies and designed a Monte Carlo simulation to test the performance of the two techniques systematically. Our results show that nCoder can achieve high predictive accuracy with significantly less human-coded data than a neural network.

Keywords: Coding · Automated Classifiers · Machine Learning · Active Learning · nCoder

1 Introduction

Coding is a process of defining concepts of interest (Codes) and identifying where they occur in qualitative data [23]. Broadly speaking, coding can be accomplished in two ways: (a) a human can read each segment of data and decide whether or not a given Code is present (or to what extent it is present); or (b) a computer can apply a classification algorithm that takes each segment of data as input and returns a coding decision as output. Because many quantitative ethnography (QE) studies involve more data than a human could reasonably read—let alone code—researchers often use automated classifiers to code their data. In order to do that, however, QE researchers need to develop classification algorithms that reliably predict the coding decisions of a human rater. Of course, developing an automated classifier typically requires some amount of human-coded data, which raises a key question: How much data does a human need to code in order to produce an accurate classification algorithm?

QE researchers typically use machine learning (ML) techniques to develop classification systems [6, 18]. Most commonly, they use either (a) traditional supervised learning techniques—such as support vector machines or neural networks—which induce a classifier from a set of human-rated excerpts (linear process), or (b) active learning techniques, in which the machine can repeatedly query a human rater to induce a classifier (iterative process).

However, it is impossible to determine *a priori* the size of the sample needed to train a classifier using any supervised learning technique, so comparison of machine learning techniques can only be done empirically [8]. To do this, researchers typically train classifiers on the same training data using traditional supervised learning techniques—and in some cases, active learning approaches (see, e.g., [4, 11]). While this makes it possible to compare the performance of classifiers on a given sample, it does not control for sampling bias, and thus generalizability is limited. Furthermore, and most importantly, these studies typically do not reflect the non-deterministic nature of the human-in-the-loop active learning process. Because the outcomes of active learning processes are contingent on the specific interactions between the machine and the human, conducting an experiment to examine this requires a significant investment of human labor. Hence, to the best of our knowledge, there have been no systematic comparisons between traditional supervised learning and active learning techniques, and thus no basis for determining the amount of human coding required to train a classifier with sufficient predictive accuracy.

In this paper, we systematically compare the performance of a traditional supervised learning approach and an active learning approach on a given dataset. Specifically, we compare an artificial neural network, a powerful traditional supervised learning technique, with nCoder, an active learning technique commonly used in QE studies. In a pilot study using one large dataset to develop automated classifiers for two Codes, we found that nCoder can achieve high predictive accuracy with significantly less human-coded data than a neural network.

2 Theory

2.1 Coding

At the most basic level, a Code is a label that is applied to some segment of data. But each time we apply a label to a piece of data, we are making an assertion about *meaning*. In the context of QE research, coding decisions create a linkage between some record of *events* (data) and *interpretation* of those events, reflecting the linkage asserted by Codes between the cultural meanings that people in some community construct and researchers' theoretically grounded interpretations of that culture [23].

Because coding is the lowest level at which assertions about the meaning of data are made, it is particularly important that coding decisions are accurate interpretations—that is, interpretations that both members of the community being studied and informed researchers would agree are fair representations of the community, of theory, and of the data itself. If we lack sufficient certainty that the codes in data mean what we think they mean, then any analysis conducted on those codes will be at best useless and at worst epistemically violent.

To achieve the high level of coding accuracy that this requires, researchers traditionally code data by hand. While there are many approaches to manual coding [15, 17, 21], all of them involve reading segments of data and deciding whether or not a code is present (or to what extent it is present). That is, the researcher makes each assertion about the interpretation of a segment of data based on close reading and expertise. But this approach is also slow, laborious, and prone to random error [19], and many communities now produce records of events that are far too large to code in this way.

As a result, researchers often use *automated classifiers* to code data at scale. Automated classifiers are algorithms, or sets of rules, that take features of data as input and return coding decisions as output. In the case of text data, the rules could be simple—for example, if the word "warbler" is present, the Code BIRD is applied—or they could involve complex interactions of words, grammar, syntax, capitalization, punctuation, sentence length or other features of written language. But whatever their rules are, automated classifiers are evaluated based on how well they *predict* the coding decisions of a human expert—that is, they are evaluated based on some measure of *inter-rater reliability* (IRR) between the classifier and a human expert [9]. Because codes are assertions of meaning, automated classifiers need to make the coding decisions that a human *would have* made if the human had read and coded the data.

To develop or *train* automated classifiers that achieve high predictive accuracy relative to human experts—that is, that meet or exceed some standard for IRR—researchers typically use one or more techniques broadly classed as *machine learning*.

2.2 Machine Learning

To develop automated classifiers for text data, machine learning techniques analyze corpora and combine features of text into classification rules [10]. These techniques can be broadly divided into (a) unsupervised learning and (b) supervised learning. *Unsupervised learning* techniques, such as those broadly classed as *topic modeling* (e.g., latent Dirichlet allocation [16]), consist of generative models that take a set of raw, uncoded text data and extract groups of keywords that are related to one another. These groups can be taken as codes, and human researchers can inspect the keywords (i.e., the classification rules) to try to discern the Codes to which they refer. Unsupervised models are often used in exploratory analyses, as they work quickly and require no initial coding—that is, they produce candidate automated classifiers with virtually no human effort. However, the resulting codes may not map to Codes grounded in theory, nor to meaningful elements of a community's culture. Moreover, codes generated by unsupervised learning techniques often achieve poor predictive accuracy [2, 6, 23].

To induce automated classifiers that better align with theory and the culture of the community being studied, researchers more commonly use *supervised learning* techniques, which operate not on raw text data but on coded text data. That is, supervised learning techniques are given information about which segments of text are associated with some Code and which are not. There are many supervised learning techniques, but they are broadly classed into *traditional supervised learning* and *active learning*. Traditional supervised learning techniques—including support vector machines, naïve Bayes, logistic regression, and neural networks—use a single set of human-coded data as an input to induce a model that predicts coding decisions on an unseen dataset. Active learning techniques—including Prodigy and nCoder—facilitate multiple cycles involving interactions between the machine and the human rater to guide incremental classifier refinement [22, 24, 25]. That is, where traditional supervised learning is linear, active learning is iterative.

However, all supervised learning techniques present several challenges for researchers. While such techniques generally perform better when the amount of human-coded data used to train the classifier is larger [20], it is not possible to compute *a priori* the size of the sample needed to train a classifier that achieves sufficient predictive accuracy. This is because the size of the sample needed to train a classifier is dependent in part on properties of that classifier (or its corresponding Code), which are difficult if not impossible to determine in advance. For example, a Code that appears infrequently in data may require more training data than one that appears frequently, and the frequency, or *base rate*, of a code in data can only be estimated once a human rater has coded some data. Thus, it is difficult to determine whether different techniques for developing automated classifiers differ significantly in the amount of human coding they require.

2.3 Assessing the Performance of Machine Learning Approaches

Research on the comparative advantages of different machine learning techniques has thus far been limited to (a) multi-case comparisons of traditional supervised learning approaches or (b) single-case studies of active learning approaches. In these studies, researchers compare traditional supervised learning techniques to one another using the same set of human-coded training data, and they compare traditional supervised learning with active learning by giving the active learning algorithm the same training data but uncoded. In such studies, the predictive accuracy of each machine learning technique is based on some IRR metric between the classifier and a human expert, and IRR scores can be compared directly because each technique received the exact same training data. For instance, Hartmann and colleagues [12] compared ten automated text classification algorithms—including support vector machines, random forest, and naïve Bayes—across 41 social media datasets, concluding that either random forest or naïve Bayes shows the highest accuracy values across the tasks. Goudjil and colleagues [11] compared support vector machines against a novel active learning method that supplemented the SVM algorithm, concluding that the active learning method can significantly reduce the amount of human inputs while enhancing predictive accuracy.

However, existing approaches for comparing machine learning techniques do not enable *systematic* comparison due to two critical limitations. (1) For a given dataset, techniques are only compared using a single training set—that is, a single sample of the dataset. While this enables performance measurement and ranking *based on that sample*, there is no control for sampling bias, and thus there is no control for error in the measurement of predictive accuracy *based on that dataset or the population from which it was drawn*. (2) This approach does not enable comparison of active learning techniques systematically, both because the need for a human in the loop is time- and labor-intensive and because the outcomes of active learning processes are dependent on the specific interactions between the machine and the human, which are non-deterministic. As a result, there are no studies that have systematically compared the performance of traditional supervised learning and active learning.

Researchers typically assess the performance of computational or statistical techniques systematically using Monte Carlo studies [13]. Monte Carlo studies use a large number of simulated datasets (or a large number of samples from a real dataset) and calculate a test statistic for each one, resulting in an empirical sampling distribution. To do this in the case of machine learning, however, requires (a) the ability to *construct large numbers of human-coded training sets* from a given dataset, and (b) the ability to *simulate a human-in-the-loop active learning process*.

In this paper, we present a systematic comparison between an artificial neural network, one of the most powerful techniques in traditional supervised learning, with nCoder, the most commonly used active learning technique in QE research. For a given Code, we use an automated classifier previously determined to have very high predictive accuracy (Cohen's $\kappa > 0.90$, Shaffer's $\rho < 0.05$) to code the entire dataset, which enables us to sample large numbers of different *coded* training sets. To simulate the nCoder active learning process, we designed an algorithm that approximates the human's input in the process, namely seeding the classifier with initial regular expressions and deciding what action(s) to take based on disagreements between the human and the classifier during training. This enables us to address the following research question: *Which machine learning technique requires the least human-coded data to train a classifier that achieves high predictive accuracy?*

3 Methods

3.1 Monte Carlo Simulation Study Design

In this pilot study, we compare two supervised learning approaches—a neural network (traditional supervised learning) and nCoder (active learning)—to determine how much human-coded data is necessary to achieve classifiers with high predictive accuracy. To do this, we used a single large dataset for which there is a set of existing automated classifiers (regular expression-based codes) that were validated by an expert human rater previously. These classifiers enable us to simulate human coding decisions at scale and also to simulate the active learning process. In what follows, we describe the general simulation design—which could be used with other datasets and other machine learning techniques—and in the subsequent sections, we describe in more detail how the Monte Carlo simulation was implemented in our study.

To test the performance of the two machine learning processes, we randomly split the dataset into two subsets: (a) a *development* set and (b) a *prediction* set. Each set was coded with the validated classifier to simulate human ratings. We used the development set to train automated classifiers, while the prediction set was used to evaluate the predictive accuracy of the classifiers.

After partitioning the data, we selected random samples of length n from the development set, where n was multiples of 100 up to 3,000 (i.e., 100, 200, 300, $\cdots$, 2,900, 3,000). We set 3,000 as the upper bound because it is well above the reasonable amount of data that human would typically code in order to train a classifier in QE context.

A classifier was constructed and developed for each sample. For the implementation of the neural network approach, each sample was given to the neural network algorithm. For nCoder, we designed a human-in-the-loop simulation algorithm where a classifier was developed iteratively using 100 items at a time, until a total of 3,000 lines was reached. (Detailed descriptions on the implementation of each algorithm are given below).

For each classifier, the classifier training process was repeated 100 times for each of two Codes used in this study. We used those developed classifiers to code the *prediction set* and computed Cohen's kappa against the simulated human coding decisions produced by the previously validated classifier. This allowed us to compute a confidence interval for the mean kappa values for each sample of length n for each approach and each Code.

3.2 Implementation of the Neural Network

Neural networks are a class of supervised learning techniques that loosely model the neurons in a biological brain. A neural network consists of (a) an input layer, a set of nodes that takes features from human-coded data; (b) an output layer, a set of nodes that produces an outcome of 0 or 1 in the case of binary classification; and (c) some number of hidden layers, sets of nodes that are in between the input and output layer that process features from the previous layer(s) and pass them to the next layer of nodes [3, 14].

There are multiple ways to implement a neural network, but for this pilot study, we used it as a traditional supervised learning technique. We implemented the neural network model that Cai et al. designed in [5]—the model uses an embedding layer that represents each unique word by a vector at the beginning, followed by one bidirectional Long Short Term Memory (LSTM) layer, and a sigmoid layer as the probability of the output, with a cutoff threshold of 0.50. That is, a probability output for a given excerpt that is greater than 0.50 is classified as 1, and otherwise 0.

For each sample, we preprocessed its text data with tokenization and lemmatization. Then, this preprocessed set, which was also coded with the pre-validated classifier to simulate a human-coded training set, was given to the neural network to develop an automated classifier. The algorithm randomly selected 20% of the given training set and used it as a validation set to tune the hyperparameters of a classifier.

3.3 Simulation of the nCoder Active Learning Process

nCoder is an active learning technique commonly used in QE research. nCoder facilitates construction and validation of a set of regular expressions, such that any excerpt in which one or more expressions occurs is classified as 1, and otherwise 0. To develop a classifier in nCoder:

1. A human rater seeds an automated classifier with one or more regular expressions.
2. nCoder randomly selects segments of previously unseen data and presents them to the human rater to evaluate for the presence or absence of the Code.
3. nCoder computes Cohen's kappa between the human coder and the classifier for the Code.

   a. If the agreement is above the threshold (typically $\kappa > 0.90$), the classifier development process terminates, and the current set of regular expressions is used as a classifier.

b. If the agreement is below the threshold, the machine shows the human rater the excerpts on which there is disagreement, the rater uses those disagreements to guide refinement of the classifier, and then the process is repeated beginning with Step 2 until the threshold for agreement is met (3a).

In order to model the human-in-the-loop process of nCoder, we designed the *Robocoder*, an algorithm that simulates this process. This algorithm compares the classifier being trained (which we term the *User Regex List* or URL) with a simulated human's coding decisions. Because the users who develop automated classifiers using nCoder possess expertise and deep knowledge of the data and the Code for which the classifier is being developed, we assume that the simulated human rater does not make errors in coding segments for this study. Therefore, we simulate the human's coding decisions as the classification results from a pre-validated set of regular expressions (the *Ideal Regular expression List* or IRL). To simulate the nCoder classifier development process for a given Code on a given dataset, the Robocoder uses the following process:

1. The Robocoder randomly selects five of the ten most frequent regular expressions from the IRL to seed the URL. We chose five because nCoder suggests starting with at least five regular expressions in the beginning, and we select them from the ten most frequent because human experts are likely to seed a classifier with common expressions first.
2. Each sample (length of 100) is coded with both the URL (classifier being developed) and the IRL (simulated human).
3. The *prediction set* is coded with both the URL and the IRL, and Cohen's kappa is computed between them.
4. The Robocoder identifies whether there are one or more excerpts from the sample drawn in Step 2 for which the coding decisions of the URL and IRL are different.

    a. If there are any discrepancies in the ratings, the Robocoder will resolve differences between the ratings of the URL and IRL as follows:

        i.   For each item where the coding decisions of the URL and IRL are different, the Robocoder finds all the regular expressions from the IRL that are not in the URL but that would have been satisfied by the excerpt.
        ii. Among those expressions, the Robocoder selects the one that has the highest base rate and adds it to the URL, simulating how a human would expand the regular expression list in response to a false negative by the URL.
        iii. After all differences are resolved, the Robocoder returns to step 2.

    b. If there are no discrepancies between the ratings of the URL and IRL, the Robocoder checks whether the length of the accumulated sample sets is 3,000.

        i.   If Yes, the Robocoder stops.
        ii. If No, the Robocoder returns to Step 2.

We repeated this process 100 times for each of the two Codes used in this study.

3.4 Data

The dataset used in this study consists of 50,888 chat utterances from an engineering virtual internship, *Nephrotex*, in which students work in teams to design a new filtration system for kidney dialysis machines [7]. We used the coding scheme developed by Arastoopour Irgens et al. [1], which includes a set of regular expression classifiers for each Code. For this study, we used two Codes: CLIENT/CONSULTANT REQUESTS and TECHNICAL CONSTRAINTS, as each has the lowest (0.07) and highest (0.16) base rate. The regular expressions validated by Arastoopour Irgens et al. [1] showed high κ values with a human expert, and thus can be used to simulate human coding decisions (See Table 1). Table 2 shows the frequency of each regular expression for each of the two codes.

Table 1. Base rate, the number of regular expressions, and the Cohen's kappa for each Code.

Code	Base Rate	Number of Regular Expressions	Agreement between Human Expert and Classifier
CLIENT/CONSULTANT REQUESTS	0.07	24	$\kappa = 0.94$
TECHNICAL CONSTRAINTS	0.16	21	$\kappa = 1$

Table 2. Regular expressions for CLIENT/CONSULTANT REQUESTS and TECHNICAL CONSTRAINTS (Base rates are sorted by the descending order and displayed up to three or four decimal point).

CLIENT/CONSULTANT REQUESTS		TECHNICAL CONSTRAINTS	
Regular Expression	Base Rate	Regular Expression	Base Rate
^(?:(?!\bexternal).)*\bconsultant(?!.*\bexternal)	0.034	\bmanufacturing process	0.034
\binternal consultant	0.012	\bprocesses	0.012
\bpatient	0.011	\bnano	0.011
\brequirement	0.010	\bhydro	0.010
\brequest	0.009	\bsteric	0.009
\bstandard	0.004	\bvapor deposition polymerization	0.004
\bminimum	0.004	\bphase inversion	0.004
\bPadma	0.002	\bnegative charge	0.002
\bAlan	0.002	\bPRNLT	0.002

(continued)

Table 2. (*continued*)

CLIENT/CONSULTANT REQUESTS		TECHNICAL CONSTRAINTS	
Regular Expression	Base Rate	Regular Expression	Base Rate
\bRudy	0.002	\bvapor	0.002
\bWayne	0.002	\bPolyamide	0.002
\bsatisfy	0.002	\bmaterials	0.002
\bMichelle	0.002	\bchemical	0.002
\bhospital	0.002	\bdry-jet	0.001
\bDuChamp	0.001	\bjet	0.001
\bcomfort	0.001	\bbiological	0.001
\bProctor	0.001	\bcarbon nanotube	0.001
\bAnderson	0.001	\bpolysulfone	0.001
\bRao	0.001	\bPESPVP	0.001
\bHernandez	0.001	\bsurfactant	0.0008
\buser	0.001	\bPMMA	0.0005
\bclient	0.0009	\bCNT	
\bsafety	0.0008		
\brecommendations	0.0005		

4   Results

Figures 2 and 3 show the mean Cohen's kappa values with 95% confidence intervals between the developed classifiers (URLs) and the pre-validated classifier used to simulate human coding (IRL) on the prediction set for samples of length n (See Fig. 1 for the Code CLIENT/CONSULTANT REQUESTS and Fig. 2 for the Code TECHNICAL CONSTRAINTS). These plots demonstrate that nCoder requires considerably smaller sample size to train an accurate classifier than a neural network. Even with 3,000 coded excerpts as a training set, the neural network's mean kappa remained below 0.90, a common threshold used in QE research. On both of the Codes, while nCoder required 700 segments to be coded in order for the lower bounds of the confidence intervals to be above 0.9, there is no case in our plots that the lower bounds of the confidence intervals are above 0.9 for the neural network, meaning that the neural network requires coding more than 3,000 segments to obtain an accurate classifier.

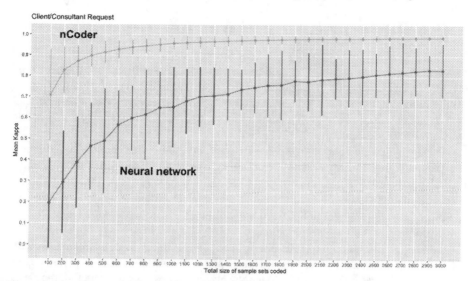

Fig. 1. Mean Cohen's kappa metrics with 95% confidence intervals between the developed classifiers (URLs) and the pre-validated classifier simulating human coding (IRL) on the prediction set for the Code CLIENT/CONSULTANT REQUESTS

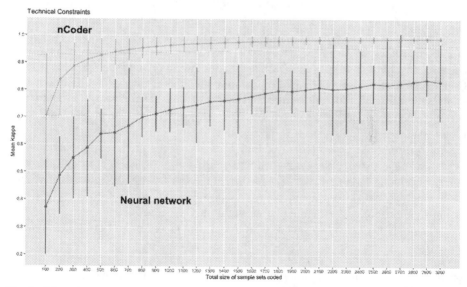

Fig. 2. Mean Cohen's kappa metrics with 95% confidence intervals between the developed classifiers (URLs) and the pre-validated classifier simulating human coding (IRL) on the prediction set for the Code TECHNICAL CONSTRAINTS

5 Discussion

In this paper, we present a comparative study that evaluates the amount of human-coded data needed by a neural network model (traditional supervised learning) and nCoder (active learning) to develop an automated classifier that achieves high accuracy. Our pilot results show that for the two Codes we tested, nCoder requires significantly less human-coded data to train a classifier that achieves sufficient predictive accuracy compared to the neural network technique.

This study enabled a systematic comparison between traditional supervised learning and active learning approaches by conducting a Monte Carlo Simulation. Using a pre-validated automated classifier to code the entire data that has very high predictive accuracy, large numbers of different coded training sets were sampled to control for sampling bias. Most importantly, we designed an algorithm that simulates nCoder, a human-in-the-loop active learning approach.

However, it is important to note that these results are largely dependent on the architectural design of machine learning approaches and the human-in-the-loop simulation. In our study, the design of the Robocoder closely resembles how the actual human user would update the classifier when resolving differences between the classifier and the human. Therefore, we can model the behaviors of the users without conducting cost and resource-intensive experiments with humans. However, we hypothesized that human raters do not make any mistakes or errors in coding process or when refining the classifier. For instance, if the human-coded inputs have a substantial amount of error in the beginning, while nCoder can correct the errors through iterations between the human and the machine, the neural network model would have low predictive performance, because it is a linear process that cannot rule out any errors once the process begins. On the other hand, if a human rater keeps adding incorrect regular expressions that they think are important, it will require more iterations, so the number of samples that human needed to code will increase in nCoder. Hence, we expect to address these issues in the future studies.

Yet one important contribution of this study is that the presented method can be expanded to any other Codes, datasets, and/or machine learning algorithms. By randomly generating large numbers of coded training sets from a given dataset, we can systematically control for the sampling bias that the previous studies using a single training set did not address. In addition, the ability to simulate a human-in-the-loop active learning process enables more thorough measurement by reflecting the iterative and complex nature of the human involvement process.

Acknowledgements. This work was funded in part by the National Science Foundation (DRL-1661036, DRL-1713110, DRL-2100320), the Wisconsin Alumni Research Foundation, and the Office of the Vice Chancellor for Research and Graduate Education at the University of Wisconsin-Madison. The opinions, findings, and conclusions do not reflect the views of the funding agencies, cooperating institutions, or other individuals.

References

1. Arastoopour, G., et al.: Teaching and assessing engineering design thinking with virtual internships and epistemic network analysis. Int. J. Eng. Educ. **32**(3), 1492–1501 (2016)
2. Bakharia, A.: On the equivalence of inductive content analysis and topic modeling. In: Eagan, B., Misfeldt, M., Siebert-Evenstone, A. (eds.) ICQE 2019. CCIS, vol. 1112, pp. 291–298. Springer, Cham (2019). https://doi.org/10.1007/978-3-030-33232-7_25
3. Baradwaj, B.K., Pal, S.: Mining educational data to analyze students' performance. ArXiv Prepr. ArXiv12013417 (2012)
4. Bull, L., et al.: Active learning for semi-supervised structural health monitoring. J. Sound Vib. **437**, 373–388 (2018)
5. Cai, Z., et al.: Neural recall network: A neural network solution to low recall problem in regex-based qualitative coding. In: Proceedings of the 15th International Conference on Educational Data Mining (2022)
6. Cai, Z., Siebert-Evenstone, A., Eagan, B., Shaffer, D.W.: Using topic modeling for code discovery in large scale text data. In: Ruis, A.R., Lee, S.B. (eds.) ICQE 2021. CCIS, vol. 1312, pp. 18–31. Springer, Cham (2021). https://doi.org/10.1007/978-3-030-67788-6_2
7. Chesler, N.C., et al.: A novel paradigm for engineering education: virtual internships with individualized mentoring and assessment of engineering thinking. J. Biomech. Eng. **137**, 2, 024701 (2015). https://doi.org/10.1115/1.4029235
8. Cho, J., et al.: How much data is needed to train a medical image deep learning system to achieve necessary high accuracy? ArXiv Prepr. ArXiv151106348 (2015)
9. Eagan, B.R., et al.: Can We Rely on IRR? Testing the Assumptions of Inter-Rater Reliability, vol. 4 (2017)
10. González-Carvajal, S., Garrido-Merchán, E.C.: Comparing BERT against traditional machine learning text classification (2021). http://arxiv.org/abs/2005.13012
11. Goudjil, M., Koudil, M., Bedda, M., Ghoggali, N.: a novel active learning method using SVM for text classification. Int. J. Autom. Comput. **15**(3), 290–298 (2016). https://doi.org/10.1007/s11633-015-0912-z
12. Hartmann, J., et al.: Comparing automated text classification methods. Int. J. Res. Mark. **36**(1), 20–38 (2019)
13. Harwell, M.R.: Summarizing Monte Carlo results in methodological research. J. Educ. Stat. **17**(4), 297–313 (1992)
14. Hernández-Blanco, A., et al.: A systematic review of deep learning approaches to educational data mining. Complexity **2019** (2019)
15. Holton, J.A.: The coding process and its challenges. Sage Handb. Grounded Theory. **3**, 265–289 (2007)
16. Jelodar, H., et al.: Latent Dirichlet allocation (LDA) and topic modeling: models, applications, a survey. Multimedia Tools Appl. **78**(11), 15169–15211 (2018). https://doi.org/10.1007/s11042-018-6894-4
17. Khandkar, S.H.: Open coding. Univ. Calg. **23**, 2009 (2009)
18. Larson, S., Popov, V., Ali, A.M., Ramanathan, P., Jung, S.: Healthcare professionals' perceptions of telehealth: analysis of tweets from pre- and during the COVID-19 pandemic. In: Ruis, A.R., Lee, S.B. (eds.) ICQE 2021. CCIS, vol. 1312, pp. 390–405. Springer, Cham (2021). https://doi.org/10.1007/978-3-030-67788-6_27
19. Miles, M.B., Huberman, A.M.: Qualitative data analysis: an expanded sourcebook. Sage (1994)
20. Ramezan, C.A., et al.: Effects of training set size on supervised machine-learning land-cover classification of large-area high-resolution remotely sensed data. Remote Sens. **13**, 3, 368 (2021)

21. Scott, C., Medaugh, M.: Axial coding. Int. Encycl. Commun. Res. Methods. **10**, 9781118901731 (2017)
22. Settles, B.: Active Learning Literature Survey **47**
23. Shaffer, D.W., Ruis, A.R.: How we code. In: Ruis, A.R., Lee, S.B. (eds.) ICQE 2021. CCIS, vol. 1312, pp. 62–77. Springer, Cham (2021). https://doi.org/10.1007/978-3-030-67788-6_5
24. Yu, D., et al.: Active learning and semi-supervised learning for speech recognition: a unified framework using the global entropy reduction maximization criterion. Comput. Speech Lang. **24**(3), 433–444 (2010). https://doi.org/10.1016/j.csl.2009.03.004
25. Prodigy · An annotation tool for AI, Machine Learning & NLP. https://prodi.gy. Accessed 23 May 2022

Reducing Networks of Ethnographic Codes Co-occurrence in Anthropology

Alberto Cottica(✉), Veronica Davidov, Magdalena Góralska, Jan Kubik,
Guy Melançon, Richard Mole, Bruno Pinaud, and Wojciech Szymański

Edgeryders, Tallinn, Estonia
alberto@edgeryders.eu

Abstract. The use of data and algorithms in the social sciences allows for exciting progress, but also poses epistemological challenges. Operations that appear innocent and purely technical may profoundly influence final results. Researchers working with data can make their process less arbitrary and more accountable by making theoretically grounded methodological choices.

We apply this approach to the problem of reducing networks representing ethnographic corpora. Their nodes represent ethnographic codes, and their edges the co-occurrence of codes in a corpus. We introduce and discuss four techniques to reduce such networks and facilitate visual analysis. We show how the mathematical characteristics of each one are aligned with a specific approach in sociology or anthropology: structuralism and post-structuralism; identifying the central concepts in a discourse; and discovering hegemonic and counter-hegemonic clusters of meaning.

1 Introduction

Since their inception, the social sciences have been split between qualitative and quantitative approaches. One of their most challenging undertakings has been to develop multi-method approaches that combine the strengths of both and minimize their weaknesses. We are working on a method that relies on both qualitative and quantitative techniques to increase the benefits of their complementarity. The former are employed at the stage of data collection – via in-depth interviews – and at the stage of analysis, when the ethnographically established contextual knowledge is employed in an iterative interpretation of the collected material in order to reveal repeatable, and thus in some sense "deeper", patterns of thought. Ethnographic coders – who are immersed in the studied societies and cultures – generate rich sets of codes. We analyze them not just to calculate frequencies of themes and motifs, but also to reveal their pattern of connectivity, that we then render in compelling visualizations. In these visualizations, an ethnographic corpus is represented as a network (Cottica et al. 2020), whose nodes correspond to ethnographic codes; the edges connecting them represent the co-occurrence

Supported by the European Commission's Horizon 2020 programme, grant agreement 822682.
The original version of this chapter was revised: The names of the two last co-authors have been corrected. The correction to this chapter is available at
https://doi.org/10.1007/978-3-031-31726-2_30

C. Damşa and A. Barany (Eds.): ICQE 2022, CCIS 1785, pp. 43–57, 2023.
https://doi.org/10.1007/978-3-031-31726-2_4

of codes in the same part of the corpus. We call this network a *codes co-occurrence network* (CCN).

A problem that commonly arises is that CCNs are too large and dense for human analysts to process visually. Network science has come up with several algorithms to reduce networks, based on identifying and discarding the least important edges in a network. It is relatively easy to apply them to this type of graph. What is harder is to justify the choice of one or the other of these techniques, and of the values assigned to the tuning parameters that they usually require. In previous work, we have proposed criteria for choosing a technique to reduce a CCN (Cottica et al. 2021), and evaluated four candidate techniques against those criteria. In this paper, we highlight the affinity of each of the four techniques with a prominent method of analysis, associated in turn with a specific school of thought in sociology or anthropology. Next, we use data from a study on Eastern European populism to demonstrate how they work. Our objective is to contribute to the rigor and transparency of the methodological choices of researchers when dealing with large ethnographic corpora.

We proceed as follows. After discussing work related to our own, we introduce the codes co-occurrence network, which is the network to be reduced. Next, we lay out criteria for choosing a technique to reduce a CCN for qualitative analysis, and introduce four such techniques. We then propose a mapping of reduction techniques onto methods of analysis widely used in sociology or anthropology. Finally, we proceed to apply them to our data, to show how the choice of a reduction technique sheds light on a specific facet of the studied phenomena.

2   Related Work

The turn towards big data, fueled by improvements in computing power, has led to renewed faith in the ability of quantitative work to provide knowledge that is more generalized than, yet as valid (that is, knowledge that preserves some of the richness of case-derived insights) as that obtainable by qualitative studies or quantitative projects relying on smaller numbers of cases (Beaulieu et al. 2021).

This has led to exciting progress. At the same time, however, it has highlighted a pressing need for methodological robustness. As scientific work based on large datasets addresses increasingly precise questions, more steps are needed to move from raw data to final result. As a consequence, the methods themselves may be hard to check against the insights derived from intimate familiarity with specific cases. In combination with "publish or perish" and with the premium placed by journals on counterintuitive, glamorous results, this has led to various epistemological crises. The replication crisis in social psychology is the most famous of them (Maxwell, Lau and Howard 2015), but not the only one. For example, it is claimed that half of the total expenditure on preclinical research in the US goes towards non-replicable studies (Freedman, Cockburn and Simcoe 2015); and that ostensibly innocent choices about data cleanup prior to analysis might lead to divergent results (Decuyper et al. 2016). Even controlled experiments with different researchers working with the same datasets on the same research questions have led to spectacularly divergent results, for reasons that are not yet entirely clear (Silberzahn et al. 2018; Breznau et al. 2021).

Qualitative sociological and anthropological research is not expected to be replicable. Rather, its claim to generating reliable knowledge comes from the rigor and account- ability of the methods applied systematically and self-consciously to a specific case or a small range of cases in well-defined spatial and temporal contexts. Therefore, careful, transparent choices about one's method are necessary every step of the way, even more so when research applies mixed methods (Beaulieu et al. 2021). This paper is offered as a contribution to the literature on the significance of such choices in a particular case: that of reducing semantic networks that express qualitative data. The literature on semantic networks originates in computer science (Sowa 1983; Sowa and others 2000; Woods 1975; Shapiro 1977); its main idea is to use mathematical objects – graphs – to support human reasoning. Building on this tradition, we focus on the idea of network reduction. In doing so, we factor in previous work on the cognitive limits of humans to correctly infer the topological characteristics of a network from visual inspection (Ghoniem, Fekete and Castagliola 2005; Melançon 2006; Munzner 2014; Soni et al. 2018). Such work confirms that large and dense networks are hard to process visually, and supports the case for network reduction.

It is important to maintain full awareness of the ways network reduction influences visual interpretation, and to account for them in the analysis. To enhance accountability, we require our mathematical techniques to directly support the specific requirements of knowledge creation in ethnography, and to be intuitive enough to ethnographers. In this sense, this work is inscribed in the tradition of scholars who aim to apply systematic visualization techniques, while still retaining sensitivity to informants' contextual, inter- actional, and socioculturally specific understandings of concepts (Dressler et al. 2005; Hannerz 1992; Strathern 1996; Burrell 2009).

3 The Codes Co-occurrence Network and Its Interpretation

Consider an annotated ethnographic corpus. We call any text data encoding the point of view of one informant (interview transcript, field notes, post on an online forum and so on) a *contribution*. Contributions are then coded by one or more ethnographers. Coding consists of associating snippets of the contribution's text to keywords, called *codes*. The set of all codes in a study constitutes an ontology of the key concepts emerging from the community being observed and pertinent to that study's research questions.[1]

We can think of such an annotated corpus as a two-mode network. Nodes are of two types, contributions and codes. By associating a code to a contribution, the ethnographer creates an edge between the respective nodes.

From the two-mode network described above, we induce, by projection, the one- mode CCN. Recall that this is a network where each node represents an ethnographic code. An edge is induced between any two codes for every contribution that is annotated with both those codes (Fig. 1). The CCN is undirected ($A \rightarrow B \equiv B \rightarrow A$). There can be more than one edge between each pair of nodes.

We interpret co-occurrence as association. If two codes co-occur, it means that one informant has made references to the concepts or entities described by the codes in

---

[1] For a complete description of the data generation process, see Sect. 3 of (Cottica et al. 2020).

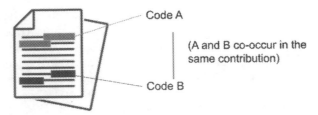

Fig. 1. Inducing a co-occurrence edge between ethnographic codes

the same contribution, seen as a unit. Hence, we assume, both concepts belong to this person's culture-generated mental map. The corpus-wide pattern of co-occurrences is taken to encode the *collective* mental map of informants.

CCNs tend to be large and dense, hence resistant to visual analysis. They are large because a large study is likely to use thousands of codes. They are dense as a result of the interaction of two processes. The first one is ethnographic coding. A rich contribution might be annotated 10 or 20 times, with as many codes associated to it. The second one is the projection from the 2-mode codes-to-contribution network to the 1-mode co-occurrence network. By construction, each contribution gives rise to a complete network of all the codes associated to it, each connected to all the others. Large, dense networks are known to be difficult to interpret by the human eye (Ghoniem, Fekete and Castagliola 2005; Melançon 2006).

4   Techniques for Network Reduction

Any network reduction entails a loss of information, and has to be regarded as a necessary evil. Reduction methods should always be theoretically founded, and applied as needed, and with caution. We propose four reductions techniques, each one related to a distinct theoretical tradition in the social sciences, particularly anthropology.

Following (King, Keohane and Verba 1994), we propose that a good reduction technique should:

1. Usefully support inference, understood as a simplifying interpretation of the emerging intersubjective picture of the world. The main contribution of network reduction to ethnographic inference is that it makes the CCN small and sparse enough to be processed visually (Melançon 2006; Ghoniem, Fekete and Castagliola 2005). A well-established literature – and techniques such as layout algorithms – help us define what a "good" network visualization is (Herman, Melancon and Marshall 2000).
2. Reinforce reproducibility and transparency. Reproducibility means that applying the same technique to the same dataset will always produce the same interpretive result (even if the technique has a stochastic component). Transparency means that how the researcher understands how the technique operates, and can explain to her peers how that particular technique contributes to addressing her research question.
3. Not foreclose the possibility of updating via abductive reasoning. Algorithms alone do not decide how parameters should be set to get optimal readability. Rather, the

values of the parameters are co-determined by the ethnographers, who possess rich empirical and theoretical knowledge of relevant contexts.

4. Combine harmoniously with other steps of the data processing cycle, such as coding and network construction. This means making sure that the interpretations of the data and their network representation are consistent across the whole cycle.

With that in mind, we turn to the discussion of four candidate techniques. Each of them can be tuned by choosing the value of a reduction parameter (different for each technique) that determines how many edges to discard. The value of this parameter is determined by the researcher, in function of the patterns she explores and of the network topology.

4.1 Association Depth

A first way to reduce the CCN is the following. For each pair of nodes in the network connected by at least one edge, remove all d edges connecting them, and replace them with one single edge of weight d. This yields a weighted, undirected network with no parallel edges.

d has an intuitive interpretation in the context of ethnographic research. Consider an edge $e = code1 \leftrightarrow code2$. $d(e)$ is the count of the number of times in which $code1$ and $code2$ co-occur. Since we interpret co-occurrence as association, it makes sense to interpret $d(e)$ as the depth of the association encoded in e. This gives us a basis for ranking edges according to the value of d. The higher the value of d of an edge, the more important that edge.

To reduce the network, we choose an integer d and drop all edges for which $d(e) \leq d$. As the value of d increases, so does the degree to which the reduced network encodes high-depth associations between codes.

4.2 Association Breadth

A second way of reducing the CCN is the following. For all pairs of nodes $code1$, $code2$ in the network, remove all edges $e : code1 \leftrightarrow code2$ connecting them, and replace them with one single edge of weight b, where b is the number of informants who have authored the contributions underpinning those edges. Like in the previous section, this yields a weighted network of codes with no parallel edges, but now edge weight has a different interpretation: it is a count of the related informants. This has a straightforward interpretation for ethnographic analysis. The greater the value of $b(e : code1 \leftrightarrow code2)$, the more widespread the association between $code1$ and $code$ is in the community that we are studying. We interpret it as association breadth. Notice that $b(e) \leq d(e)$.

As we did for depth, we reduce by choosing an integer b and dropping all edges for which $b(e) \leq b$. As the value of b* increases, so does the degree to which the reduced network encodes broadly shared associations between codes.

4.3 Highest Core Values

A third way of reducing the CCN is to consider a co-occurrence edge important if it connects two nodes that are both connected to a large number of other nodes. A community of such nodes can be identified by computing the CCN's k-cores. k-cores are subgraphs that include nodes of degree at least k, where k is an integer. They are used to identify cohesive structures in graphs (Giatsidis, Thilikos and Vazirgiannis 2011).

After computing all the k-cores of a network, its nodes can be assigned a core value. A node's core value is the highest value of k for which that node is part of a k-core.

To find the most important edges in the CCN, we again replace all edges between any pair of connected codes $code1$ and $code2$ with one single edge $e(code1, code2)$. Next, we choose an integer k and remove all the codes c whose core values $k(c) \leq k$.

4.4 Simmelian Backbone

A fourth approach to identify a network's most important edges is to extract its Simmelian backbone. A network's Simmelian backbone is the subset of its edges which display the highest values of a property called redundancy (Nick et al. 2013). An edge is redundant if it is part of multiple triangles. The idea is that, if two nodes have many common neighbors, the connection between the two is structural. This method applies best to weighted graphs; in this paper, we use association depth as edge weight.

This technique uses a granularity parameter, k. We set k to be equal to the average degree of the CCN, rounded to the nearest integer. At this point, for each pair of nodes n_1, n_2, we can compute the redundancy of the incident edge $e(n_1, n_2)$ as the overlap between the k strongest-tied neighbors of n_1 and those of n_2. To reduce the network, we choose an integer r and drop edges for which the redundancy $r(e) \leq r$.

5 Mapping Network Reduction Techniques onto Four Major Approaches in Sociology and Anthropology

Deciding which network reduction technique is best suited to a particular research project depends on the researcher's ontological and epistemological beliefs, as well as on the nature of the project itself and of its research questions. Each reduction technique reveals a different set of attributes semantic networks have. It also turns out that each technique fits the objectives of a prominent method of analysis, associated in turn with an identifiable approach in sociology or anthropology. Based on this fit, we propose that the researcher's approach suggests the choice of a reduction technique.

5.1 Association Depth

Determining association depth is in its essence a method of uncovering the structure of a society or culture. Key works in anthropology – *Anthropologie structurale* (Lévi-Strauss and Lévi-Strauss 1958) and *La Pensée sauvage* (Lévi-Strauss and others 1962) – and in social theory (Althusser 1965; Poulantzas 1973) initiated a whole host of structuralist and post-structuralist approaches.

For post-structuralist sociologists and anthropologists, social relations can only be understood by analysing how they are constituted and organized through discourse. In other words, social hierarchies, norms and practices are legitimized (or delegitimized) by granting the meaning attached to specific concepts a dominant position, enabling certain ideas to become hegemonic, i.e. widely accepted as then "Truth". For example, the idea that ethnic nations are natural entities growing out of shared kinship ties (all academic evidence to the contrary) is used to legitimize political control by the core nation and the marginalisation of minority ethnicities. Moreover, discourse scholars work from the assumption that the meaning respondents attach to floating signifiers is relational within a discourse. Within a patriarchal discourse, the meaning attached to 'woman' is directly determined by the meaning attached to 'man', for instance. To understand the meaning of concepts, it is thus essential to understand their interrelationships; discerning which meanings are hegemonic further requires us to understand which interrelationships between concepts are dominant. Focusing on association depth is thus a useful way of bringing into sharper focus the interrelationships between concepts that are most commonly used by informants, thereby providing a picture of the basic structure of discourse in a given community, within which informants create meaning and make sense of the world around them.

5.2 Association Breadth

We see association breadth as an alternative point of view on the structure of discourse. Whereas association depth encodes the raw number of co-occurrences between codes, association breadth emphasizes how widespread across different informants those co-occurrences are. In the analysis of Sect. 6 below, we used association depth to check that high-depth edges were not the artefact of just one (or very few) informant who happened to be obsessively associating those particular codes.

5.3 Highest Core Values

The technique based on core values of codes is designed to determine the centrality of certain concepts in a discourse. While it does not allow for the reduction of edges, it shows which concepts have most edges associated with them. It facilitates, therefore, a more systematic determination of which discursive elements constitute what is known in cultural anthropology as root paradigms, key metaphors, dominant schemata or central symbols of a given culture (Turner 1974; Aronoff and Kubik 2013).

5.4 Simmelian Backbone

Finally, the Simmelian backbone extraction can contribute to the discovery of hegemonic and counter-hegemonic clusters (subcultures) of meaning in an analyzed body of discourse (Gramsci 1975; Laitin 1986). No society or culture is fully integrated and each is subjected to centripetal and centrifugal forces simultaneously. As a result, even in the most "homogenous" societies and cultures one can identify at least embryonic subcultures or – in another formulation – for every hegemony there is a budding or fully articulated counter-hegemony. The point is that a hegemony or counter-hegemony is usually built not on a single symbol or concept but on their interconnected cluster. This reduction technique helps to identify such clusters and assess with greater precision their shape and internal coherence.

6 An Application

We used the corpus of a project we are working on to show how each of the four aforementioned reduction techniques can be seen as broadly corresponding to a paradigm in
anthropology – a convergence that attests to the utility of such a synthesis. This application is not meant as a full methodological primer. Rather, it means to be a "proof of concept", and show the possibilities of synthesizing quantitative and qualitative techniques
in the service of ethnographic insight.

The data were gathered in the spring and summer of 2021, as a part of a larger research
project on populism in Central and Eastern Europe, to be completed by the end of 2022.
They consist of 17 semi-structured interviews with Polish-speaking Internet users, who
used social media to seek and share information about health against the backdrop of
the COVID-19 pandemic. Research participants were asked about their opinion on the
current state of affairs in their respective countries, and their political choices over the
years and at present. The interviews' transcriptions (about 78,000 words) were then
split into contributions, in the sense of Sect. 3: each question of the interviewer, and
answer of the interviewee was considered as a contribution. In what follows, two codes
are considered to co-occur if, and only if, they were both used in annotating the same
contribution (as opposed to the same interview). Computed this way, the CCN from this
corpus includes 1,116 contributions, and 2,152 annotations. The latter use 600 unique
codes, connected by 16,370 co-occurrence edges.

We apply reduction techniques to the CCN in sequence, trying for different levels of
the respective reduction parameters (d, b, k, r) in order to achieve a good combination
of legibility (more edges discarded) and completeness (fewer edges discarded). In each
reduced network, we focus on the ego network of one code in particular, Catholic Church.
Ego network analysis is widely used in anthropology, for example in the conventions
of kinship charts. We selected this particular code in the expectation that the Catholic
Church would be fairly central in any ethnographic study of populism in Poland, and
that, therefore, it would appear in most reduced networks.

6.1 Highest Core Values

Anthropology as a discipline has a long history of trying to identify "core" dimensions
of culture, both to better theorize how a given culture is constituted, and as a useful
heuristic for ethnographic fieldwork (cf Boas's outer and inner forces (Boas 1932),
Kroeber's reality and value culture (Kroeber 1950), Steward's cultural core (Steward
1972)). In our approach we are particularly inspired by Victor Turner, a founding figure
in symbolic anthropology – a theoretical approach in British anthropology arising in
the 1960s – that viewed culture as an independent system of meaning deciphered by
interpreting key symbols and rituals (Spencer 1996) and theorized that "beliefs, however
unintelligible, become comprehensible when understood as part of a cultural system of
meaning" (Des Chene 1996). Turner subscribed to a definition of symbol as "a thing
regarded by general consent as naturally typifying or representing or recalling something
by possession of analogous qualities or by association in fact or thought" (Turner 1975).
As we are invested in holistically understanding and visualizing how cultural beliefs
and discourses are assembled, it is the recollection and association aspects that are of

particular interest to us. Turner did not seek to define a fixed core of concepts within a culture the way Steward, for example, did. Nevertheless, he did write about symbols "variously known as 'dominant,' 'core,' 'key,' 'master,' 'focal,' 'pivotal,' or 'central' [that] constitute semantic systems in their own right [with a] complex and ramifying series of associations as modes of signification."

We envision network reduction based on the highest core values as revealing something akin to such a semantic system. We approach it in the spirit of Turner's notion of "positional meaning" articulated in his methodology for studying rituals – a level of symbolic meaning derived from analyzing a symbol's association to other symbols and cultural concepts, in other words, contextual meaning: "The positional meaning of a symbol derives from its relationship to other symbols in totality, a *Gestalt* whose elements acquire their significance from the system as a whole. This level of meaning is directly related to the important property of ritual symbols... their polysemy. Such symbols possess many senses, but contextually it may be to stress one or a few of them only." (Turner 1975).

In our data, we see the highest core values reduction yielding an innermost nucleus of nodes (ethnographic codes) that recur most often in relation with each other. Catholic Church is close to the center of the symbols expressing this culture. Mathematically, it belongs to one of the innermost k-cores, ($k = 28$, containing 82 codes, shown in Fig. 2), though not the absolute innermost. Two k-cores exist in the graph where k is higher than 28 ($k = 29$, $k = 42$). The analysis supports the conclusion that the Catholic Church is one of the core symbols in this culture.

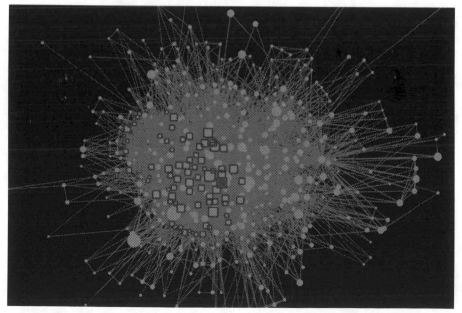

Fig. 2. The full CCN. The 28-core is shown highlighted in blue. It contains Catholic Church (in red). (Color figure online)

6.2 Simmelian Backbone

Next, we explore the neighborhood of Catholic Church through the lens of the Simmelian backbone reduction technique. Recall that this technique detects community of nodes connected by redundant links, and was developed to identify homophily and strong ties in a social network of actors (Nick et al. 2013). Here, we use it to identify communities of ethnographic codes. In a way, when applied to concepts rather than human actors, this approach literalizes the notion of certain ideas being "in conversation" with each other. The visualization reveals several such "conversations". The community structure itself maps onto the anthropological notion of culture as a field of competing forces, with different clusters of codes encoding different strands of culture. In the words of Jean and John Comaroff, "culture [is] the semantic space, the field of signs and practices, in which human beings construct and represent themselves and others, and hence their societies and histories… culture always contains within it polyvalent, potentially contestable messages, images, and actions." (Comaroff and Comaroff 2019) This approach stresses that culture is neither monolithic nor fixed, but rather always contingent and in flux, and allows us to see, from a bird's eye perspective, how various "signifiers-in-action" coalesce into identifiable semantic subspaces.

Catholic Church belongs to a community of codes that are political rather than spiritual– such as abuse of power, political marketing, and right wing (Fig. 3. In fact, the highest-redundancy edge incident to Catholic Church is to politicisation ($r = 55$). Our ethnographic interpretation is that people have concerns pertaining to the Catholic

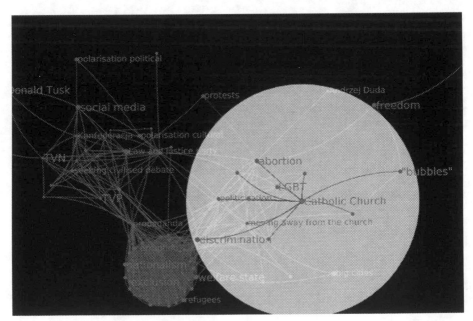

Fig. 3. The ego network of Catholic Church, with only edges with edge redundancy r > 30 shown.

Church, both in the context of what they conceive as this institution's excessive politicization and more personal concerns, anxieties, and anomic tendencies. This can be used as a foundation to build on iteratively in future research on a range of subjects, including but not limited to political cultures, epistemologies, various dimensions of trust and belief, and the position of the Catholic Church in the public space and the country's culture.

6.3 Association Depth and Association Breadth

We now turn to the association depth and association breadth reduction techniques, which work in tandem to deepen our understanding of the underlying structures of discursive associations. The association depth visualization shows us which associative links between concepts are the strongest – in other words, which codes emerge as being mentioned together most often. Association breadth helps evaluate the diffusion of these "deep" edges among informants. When the results produced through the depth and breadth reductions align, it confirms that deep associations are not generated by a small number of interviews with people who frame a topic by linking it repetitively with a constant, limited set of other topics, but rather a broad agreement that emerges from the analysis of many interviews or conversations. We can see how this plays out with Catholic Church code (Fig. 4): the three deepest associations are formed between it and the abuse of power, politicisation, and Polish catholicism codes. If we choose lower (but still significant, in the sense that the number of edges in the CCN is reduced by over 95%) levels of the reduction parameter d, codes like LGBT, discrimination and Law and Justice party appear.

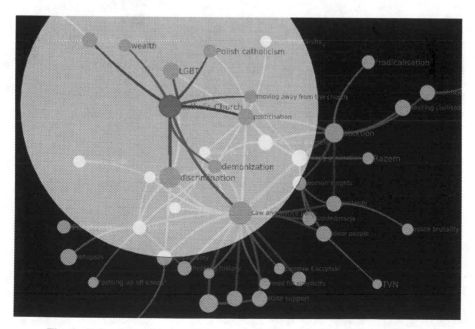

Fig. 4. Only edges with association depth d > 4, and incident codes are shown.

The association breadth-reduced CCN shows that the broadest links to Catholic Church are very similar to the deepest ones. The very broadest three connect it to politicization, Polish catholicism, and discrimination, and tolerance. Edges to "political" codes like LGBT, inequality, abuse of power and abortion resist to reductions by over 50% in the number of edges in the CCN (Fig. 5). In our case, these two reduction methods yield closely aligned results. Both attest to the Catholic Church figuring as an institution associated with politics more so than with faith or spirituality among the informants. Even though there are some codes visible in the graph that may correlate to spirituality, the broadest associations still link the Catholic Church with political codes and the issue of abuse of power.

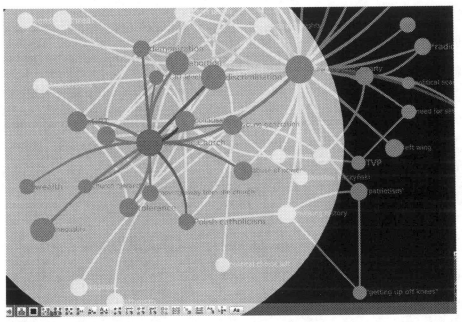

Fig. 5. Only edges with association breadth b > 3, and incident codes are shown. [fig_two_approaches]

7 Discussion and Conclusions

As ethnographers working with this form of data analysis, we look for patterns that are of interest to us either for their novelty (unexpected connections) or confirmation of either previous research, or initial impressions formed during data collection. In this particular example, this finding aligns with existing survey studies on Polish Catholicism today, which show that most Poles disapprove of the Church's direct involvement in politics (CBOS Foundation 2022).

More broadly, this approach is synergetic with anthropology's long-standing interest in structures. While we don't aspire to resurrect the classic structuralist goal of uncovering deep underlying structures or cross-cultural universals à la Claude Lévi-Strauss, *the figurehead of structural anthropology* there is methodological value in understanding cultural structures in a way aligned with schema theory developed by cognitive anthropologists rather than old-school structuralists. We are aware that such structures are historically contingent and subject to change. Nevertheless, these visualizations offer us a synchronic snapshot of how people mentally organize their experiences and understanding. From a methodological standpoint this can be valuable not only as new insight or confirmation, but also as a part of an iterative research process. Once we have a sense of what ideas the people under study believe link together most strongly, that knowledge can inform subsequent questionnaires, interviews, and selection of sites for participant observation. For example, perhaps the most salient participant observation in an ethnographic project on the Catholic Church in Poland today would have to take place, counterintuitively, outside the churches, in the domain of politics.

Lévi-Strauss believed that universal deep cognitive structures underpin all human cultural experience; in that, he exemplified the cross-cultural universalism position in anthropology. We do not subscribe to such a position; nevertheless, his approach to myth analysis resonates with our reduction techniques. According to him, all existing versions of the myth had to be aggregated, so that one could isolate what he called "gross constituent units" – clusters of specific types of relations that are present in all versions of the myths (e.g. characters overrating kinship relations, characters underrating kinship relations) (Lévi-Strauss 1955). These units, Lévi-Strauss posited, revealed deep structures expressed through the language of myth. In a similar way, we also look at the highest-redundancy edges in order to glean what they reveal about deep associations structuring cultural discourses in a corpus.

In conclusion, through this demonstration we aim to make a contribution to the ongoing and worthwhile conversations in the social sciences geared at synthesizing qualitative and quantitative methods. The reduction techniques discussed in this paper can be instrumental in supporting ethnographic insights, and the accountability of methodological choices in ethnographic research. The ethnographer's goal and research question inform the choice of a reduction technique; the appropriateness of such choice can be transparently argued by the researcher. Moreover, since the steps to build and reduce the CCN are reproducible (given the value of the reduction parameter), other researchers can validate, dispute, or improve upon her interpretation, thereby contributing to the accountability of qualitative research. The highest core values reduction identifies concepts of central significance, and can help map a starting point of entry into the data; the Simmelian backbone reduction maps heterogeneous communities of meaning, and may be especially helpful in identifying hegemonic and counter-hegemonic discourses at work within a community. Finally, the association depth and association breadth reductions, working in tandem, can help illuminate and validate the most significant associative structures of meaning in specific domains within a community under study.

References

Althusser, L.: For Marx. Verso Books (1965)

Aronoff, M.J., Kubik, J.: Anthropology and Political Science: A Convergent Approach, vol. 3. Berghahn Books (2013)

Beaulieu, A., Leonelli, S.: Data and Society: A Critical Introduction. Sage (2021)

Boas, F.: The aims of anthropological research. Science **76**(1983), 605–613 (1932)

Breznau, N., et al.: Observing Many Researchers Using the Same Data and Hypothesis Reveals a Hidden Universe of Data Analysis. MetaArXiv (2021). https://doi.org/10.31222/osf.io/cd5j9

Burrell, J.: The field site as a network: a strategy for locating ethnographic research. Field Meth. **2**(21), 181–199 (2009)

CBOS Foundation: Postawy Wobec Obecności Religii I Kościoła W Przestrzeni Publicznej (2022). https://www.cbos.pl/SPISKOM.POL/2022/K_003_22.PDF

Comaroff, J., Comaroff, J.: Ethnography and the Historical Imagination. Routledge (2019)

Cottica, A., et al.: Comparing techniques to reduce networks of ethnographic codes co-occurrence. Zenodo (2021). https://doi.org/10.5281/zenodo.5801464

Cottica, A., Hassoun, A., Manca, M., Vallet, J., Melançon, G.: Semantic social networks: a mixed methods approach to digital ethnography. Field Meth. **32**(3), 274–290 (2020)

Decuyper, A., Browet, A., Traag, V., Blondel, V.D., Delvenne, J.-C.: Clean up or Mess up: The Effect of Sampling Biases on Measurements of Degree Distributions in Mobile Phone Datasets. arXiv Preprint arXiv:1609.09413 (2016)

Mary, D.C.: Symbolic anthropology. In: Encyclopedia of Cultural Anthropology. Henry Holt (1996)

Dressler, W.W., Borges, C.D., Balierio, M.C., dos Santos, J.E.: Measuring cultural consonance: examples with special reference to measurement theory in anthropology. Field Meth. **17**(4), 331–355 (2005)

Freedman, L.P., Cockburn, I.M., Simcoe, T.S.: The economics of reproducibility in preclinical research. PLoS Biol. **13**(6), e1002165 (2015)

Ghoniem, M., Fekete, J.-D., Castagliola, P.: On the readability of graphs using node-link and matrix-based representations: a controlled experiment and statistical analysis. Inf. Vis. **4**(2), 114–135 (2005)

Giatsidis, C., Thilikos, D.M., Vazirgiannis, M.: Evaluating cooperation in communities with the K-Core structure. In: 2011 International Conference on Advances in Social Networks Analysis and Mining, pp. 87–93. IEEE (2011)

Gramsci, A.: I Quaderni Del Carcere. Einaudi (1975)

Ulf, H.: The global ecumene as a network of networks. In: Kuper, A. (ed.) Conceptualizing Society, pp. 34–56. Routledge (1992)

Herman, I., Melancon, G., Marshall, M.S.: Graph visualization and navigation in information visualization: a survey. IEEE Trans. Visual Comput. Graphics **6**(1), 24–43 (2000). https://doi.org/10.1109/2945.841119

King, G., Keohane, R.O., Verba, S.: Designing Social Inquiry: Scientific Inference in Qualitative Research. Princeton University Press (1994)

Kroeber, A.L.: Reality culture and value culture. Science **111**, 456–57 (2005). (Amer Assoc Advancement Science 1200 New York Ave, NW, Washington, DC)

Laitin, D.D.: Hegemony and Culture: Politics and Change Among the Yoruba. University of Chicago Press (1986)

Lévi-Strauss, C.: the structural study of myth. J. Am. Folklore **68**(270), 428–444 (1955)

Lévi-Strauss, C., Lévi-Strauss, C.: Anthropologie Structurale, vol. 171. Plon Paris (1958)

CLévi-Strauss, C., et al.: La Pensée Sauvage, vol. 289. Plon Paris (1962)

Maxwell, S.E., Lau, M.Y., Howard, G.S.: Is psychology suffering from a replication crisis? What does 'failure to replicate' really mean? Am. Psychol. **70**(6), 487 (2015)

Guy, M.: Just how dense are dense graphs in the real world? A methodological note. In: Proceedings of the 2006 Avi Workshop on Beyond Time and Errors: Novel Evaluation Methods for Information Visualization, pp. 1–7 (2006)

Munzner, T.: Visualization Analysis and Design. CRC Press (2014)

Nick, B., Lee, C., Cunningham, P., Brandes, U.: Simmelian Backbones: Amplifying Hidden Homophily in Facebook Networks. In: 2013 Ieee/Acm International Conference on Advances in Social Networks Analysis and Mining (Asonam), pp. 525–32 (2013)

Nicos, P.: On Social Classes. New Left Review (1973)

Shapiro, S.C.: Representing and locating deduction rules in a semantic network. ACM SIGART Bull. **10**(1145/1045343), 1045350 (1977)

Silberzahn, R., et al.: Many analysts, one data set: making transparent how variations in analytic choices affect results. Adv. Meth. Pract. Psychol. Sci. **1**(3), 337–356 (2018)

Soni, U., Yafeng, L., Hansen, B., Purchase, H.C., Kobourov, S., Maciejewski, R.: The perception of graph properties in graph layouts. Comput. Graph. Forum **37**(3), 169–181 (2018). https://doi.org/10.1111/cgf.13410

Sowa, J.F.: Conceptual Structures: Information Processing in Mind and Machine. Addison-Wesley Publication, Reading, MA (1983)

Sowa, J.F, et al.: Knowledge Representation: Logical, Philosophical, and Computational Foundations, vol. 13. Brooks/Cole Pacific Grove, CA (2000)

Jonathan, S.: Symbolic anthropology. In: Encyclopedia of Social and Cultural Anthropology. Henry Holt (1996)

Steward, J.H.: Theory of Culture Change: The Methodology of Multilinear Evolution. University of Illinois Press (1972)

Strathern, M.: Cutting the network. J. R. Anthropol. Inst. **2**(3), 517–535 (1996)

Victor, T.: Liminal to liminoid, in play, flow, and ritual: an essay in comparative symbology. Rice Inst. Pamphlet-Rice Univ. Stud. **60**(3) (1974)

Turner, V.:Symbolic studies. Ann. Rev. Anthropol. **4**(1), 145–61 (1975)

Woods, W.A.: What's in a link: foundations for semantic networks. In: Representation and Understanding: Studies in Cognitive Science, pp. 35–82. Elsevier (1975)

Multiclass Rotations in Epistemic Network Analysis

Mariah A. Knowles[1]([✉]) [iD], Amanda Barany[2] [iD], Zhiqiang Cai[1] [iD],
and David Williamson Shaffer[1] [iD]

[1] University of Wisconsin–Madison, Madison, WI 53711, USA
{mariah.knowles,zhiqiang.cai}@wisc.edu, dws@education.wisc.edu
[2] Drexel University, Philadelphia, PA 19104, USA
amb595@drexel.edu

Abstract. The task of succinctly and insightfully discussing themes in the differences between several (three or more) groups in naturalistic, ethnographic research faces a number of constraints. The number of all possible pairs is a quadratic function of the number of groups, and prior order and stand-out subsets may not exist to narrow that number down. We define and compare methods for guiding this task during Epistemic Network Analysis.

Keywords: Epistemic Network Analysis · Means Rotation · Linear Discriminant Analysis · Multiclass Rotations · Singular Value Decomposition

1 Introduction

It is a common task in naturalistic, ethnographic research to model and discuss the differences between multiple groups. Our focus in this paper is on the case where one has three or more (ie, $g \geq 3$) groups, as this presents a number of challenges when (i) the number of groups continues to increase, (ii) there is no meaningful prior order in which to guide one's comparison, and (iii) there is no clear subset of the data one can justify giving narrowed attention to. Generally, this task amounts to identifying themes of difference: imagine considering what it is that makes any two groups different from one another, then succinctly summing up what you find. Actually approaching the task exhaustively like this quickly becomes too burdensome without some way to guide one's analytic focus. For example, to compare 15 groups this way one would need to consider 105 distinct pairs.

To get at this task, we first summarize existing approaches to structuring themes of difference throughout the past three years of ICQE. Second, we define and compare a number of dimensionality reduction techniques usable in Epistemic Network Analysis (ENA), namely Singular Value Decomposition (SVD), Linear Discriminant Analysis (LDA), and a method we define here, Multi-Class Means Rotation (MCMR). And finally we illustrate our approach using a wellknown dataset in our community, Nephrotex, showing how one might choose among these methods and arrive at a story structured around a succinct number of themes of difference.

C. Damşa and A. Barany (Eds.): ICQE 2022, CCIS 1785, pp. 58–70, 2023.
https://doi.org/10.1007/978-3-031-31726-2_5

One of the strengths of multiclass methods is that they provide a reduced number of axes around which one can discuss the differences of their groups: to compare 15 groups, one would only need 4 (at least) to 14 (at most) axes. Axes provide themes of difference in terms of spectra, and structuring one's telling of the story around these spectra may help alleviate the complexity inherent in telling stories that move over multiple group difference. However, as we show, the existing approach (SVD) fails to identify trends that actually discriminate between multiple groups; LDA and MCMR both overcome this, balancing between discrimination and ENA goodness of fit scores differently.

2 Theory and Prior Literature

2.1 Multiclass Comparisons at ICQE

In the past three years of ICQE, data structured into multiple groups (that is, $g \geq 3$) has been approached in numerous ways. Generally, these boil down to comparing each group to the collective rest, comparing all possible pairs, justifying some focus, or discussing general trends instead. In each case, these strategies impose limitations when the number of groups continues to grow, and these limitations differ when one's groups have vs. don't have a pre-existing sense of order.

In some cases, groups in the data have pre-existing ordinality that often aligns with the passage of time, such as weeks in a course or stages in an intervention, and so there may be better reason to talk about them in one order or another [1–14]. In other cases, the groups in the data have no sense of ordinality, such as schools or countries, and so the order in which one ought to discuss and compare them depends on one's storytelling substance, constraints, goals, and commitments [10–22].

Researchers approached these cases in one of six ways (Fig. 1):

1. *Punt the Ball*—One can forego discussing group differences and instead describe each group in its own right without direct or inferred comparisons [15].
2. *One Against the Rest*—One can describe how each individual group in turn compared to all other groups together, perhaps after interpreting the grand mean of all groups [10, 11, 16–19].
3. *All Pairs*—One can describe each possible difference in each possible pairing of two groups [20]. In the ordinal case, one can also describe the differences of each adjacent pair of groups [6, 14].
4. *General Trend*—One can interpret possible meanings of the four plotted quadrants and use those to discuss overall trends in differences [14]. In the ordinal case, one can also fit or justify an overall temporal trend, then describe features of that trend [5, 7, 8, 12, 13].
5. *Justified Focus*—One can describe only a subset of possible pairings and provide a rationale for one's focus on that subset [11–13, 21, 22].
6. *Play the Tape*—One can, in the ordinal case only, describe the empirical qualities of individual groups in early-to-late order, perhaps running through this order multiple times to focus on the changes in particular qualities [1–5, 10]

With the exception of a few that used sequential pairwise means rotations (which only considered two groups at a time), most used an SVD projection to guide and/or illustrate these descriptions.

Each of these approaches impose limitations when g grows and one lacks a sense of ordinality. *All Pairs* approaches are prohibitively dense, as there are up to $(g^2 - g)/2$ possible pairs, which is too great a burden on one's page length and reader's attention to fully describe. *One Against the Rest* approaches are less dense as they require only g steps, and in some cases this may be appropriate, but in others this may lead to redundant descriptions of similar groups or not lead to clear insights about common patterns of difference among groups. *Justified Focus* approaches solve these issues, but only when one is fortunate enough to have data with immediately clear stand-out patterns. And while *General Trend* approaches exist in the ordinal case, authors have relied on SVD rotations to infer these trends in the non-ordinal case: as we show in our results below, SVD is ill-suited for this task, as it aims to maximize *overall* variance, not *between group* variance, and thus can fail to show differences that otherwise exist in the data. In theory, a *General Trend* approach could describe the themes of differences between all possible pairs of non-ordinal groups in as few as $\lceil \log_2 g \rceil$ axes, each axis dividing the groups in two in roughly orthogonal ways. At most, one would need $g - 1$ axes, which would amount to a *One Against the Rest* approach but dropping one axis, as it would be redundant with the rest. The method we propose achieves this lower bound in our worked example below, while capturing differences failed to be seen by SVD.

2.2 Singular Value Decomposition, Linear Discriminant Analysis, & Means Rotation

Let us consider two dimensionality reduction techniques commonly used in quantitative ethnography, Singular Value Decomposition (SVD) and Means Rotation (MR), as well as a related technique, Linear Discriminant Analysis (LDA). All three seek to find an axis of a high dimensional space that maximizes some aspect of variance: SVD maximizes overall variance, MR maximizes between-group variance of two groups, and LDA maximizes between-group variance while minimizing within-group variance (put another way, LDA maximizes effect size) [23, 24].

The calculations for SVD and LDA are closely related. Where X is one's high dimensional data, S_{cov} is the covariance matrix of X, $\bar{x}$ is the mean vector of X, S_b is the between-group scatter matrix of X given g groups, $\bar{x}^{(i)}$ is the mean vector of group i within X, and n_i is the sample size of the ith group, we first compute.

$$S_{cov} = \frac{1}{n-1}\left((X - \bar{x})^T (X - \bar{x})\right)$$

$$S_b = \sum_{i=1}^{g} n\left(\bar{x}^{(i)} - \bar{x}\right)\left(\bar{x}^{(i)} - \bar{x}\right)^T$$

then, in SVD, one finds the eigenvalues and eigenvectors of S_{cov} and uses those vectors with the highest eigenvalues to determine the axes of one's lower dimensional embedding; in LDA one does the same, instead finding the eigenvalues and eigenvectors of

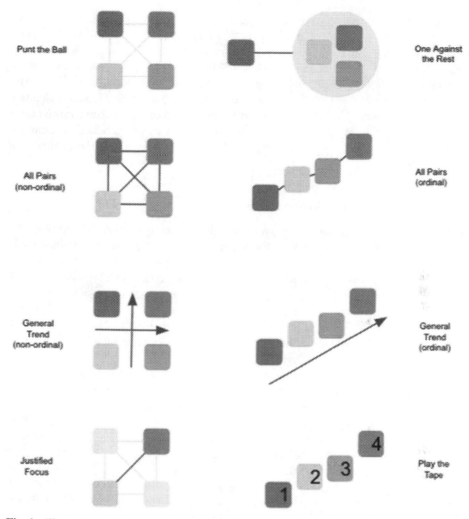

Fig. 1. Illustrations of the approaches taken in the past three years of ICQE for exploring themes of differences among three or more groups

$S_{cov}^{-1}S_b$. Note, SVD is guaranteed to find orthogonal axes in all cases, while LDA only guarantees this when S_{cov} is symmetric. A number of approaches have been proposed to address this and related limitations of LDA [24–35]. For the sake of demonstration, we consider a simple approach, discussed in the section below.

For MR, given two groups j and k, one instead takes $\bar{x}^{(k)} - \bar{x}^{(j)}$ as the x-axis and the first dimension of an SVD of the remaining dimensions as the y-axis.

In essence, each technique highlights different features of the data. SVD finds the dimensions that highlight the greatest overall differences between units in one's higher dimensional embedding, a useful task when one seeks to understand the major turns of one's global structure quickly. LDA maximizes the discrimination (effect size) between groups in one's data, a useful task when one seeks to design automated classifiers. And MR gives an easily interpretable x-axis for non-technical readers: the x-axis (in most cases) runs through the two group means. Moreover, MR can be generalized through a regression framework, which allows one to moderate this projection for possible conflations or hierarchical effects often seen in nested data (*eg.*, students within classes within schools within districts) [36]. However, MR is limited to the $g = 2$ case, and so unlike SVD and LDA, MR (as it currently stands) is not appropriate for modeling $g \geq 3$ groups simultaneously. As we show in the proposed method below, MR can be reformulated using the same framework as SVD and LDA, allowing it to be generalized to the multiclass case.

2.3 Epistemic Network Analysis Rotations

In this paper, we assume familiarity with Epistemic Network Analysis (ENA) [23, 37–40]. Still, some ground clearing is worthwhile about how ENA rotates high dimensional data.

The general process of ENA involves three steps: we construct a high dimensional model of the connections between qualitative codes; we reduce the dimensionality of that space while highlighting features of interest; and we project a network into that space as a way to illustrate its dynamics [11, 23, 38, 40]. Let X represent this high dimensional space, where X_{ij} corresponds to the ith unit's connection strength between the jth pair of qualitative codes.

In whatever rotation method one chooses in the ENA tool (rENA or WebENA [38–40]), the rotation amounts to reducing the dimensionality of X by finding a pair of vectors, v_x and v_y, such that Xv_x and Xv_y are the dimensions that most highlight one's features of interest. Because these dimensions are taken as the x- and y-axis of the ENA plot and the distances between plotted points must be uniformly interpretable (as in a rigid body rotation), we have the further requirements that v_x and v_y be orthogonal to one another and have equal length. In a case where one's underlying dimensionality reduction technique does not produce orthogonal axes (as with LDA), we can instead take as our y-axis an approximation found by rejecting v_y from v_x and re-normalizing [36]. Put another way, when v_x and v_y are not exactly orthogonal, we identify the *plane* they exist in, rotate that plane such that v_x aligns with our x-axis, and plot the result.

For the sake of demonstration, this is the technique we use for ensuring our proposed methods conform to ENA's rigid body requirements.

3   Methods

3.1   Proposed Method: Multiclass Rotations

To date, the only linear projection used (that we are aware of) for simultaneously comparing $g \geq 3$ groups in an ENA context is SVD. And by default, this is the behavior of WebENA except when $g = 2$ exactly, where MR is used instead [39].

We consider two alternatives to those methods, LDA and a multiclass generalization of MR (MCMR), which together we think of as members of a more general class of possible multiclass rotations: rotations of an ENA space designed to highlight differences among $g \geq 3$ groups when ordinality is not guaranteed. Moreover, the process of these two approaches is identical to SVD rotations, except LDA considers the eigenvalues and eigenvectors of $S_{cov}^{-1} S_b$ and MCMR considers that of just S_b. That is, SVD maximizes overall variance, LDA maximizes between-group variance while minimizing within-group variance, MCMR only maximizes between-group variance, and none of the these approaches is more or less conceptually complex than the other.

We claim that MCMR generalizes MR: the two are identical along the x-axis when $g = 2$. Let us sketch a proof: Let j and k be our two groups and $S_{cov}^{(j)}$ and $S_{cov}^{(k)}$ be their covariance matrices such that $S_{cov}^{(j)} + S_{cov}^{(k)} = S_{cov}$. MCMR's generalized eigenvalue problem is $S_b v = \lambda v$, where λ is an eigenvalue and v is an eigenvector. This is equivalent to an LDA eigenvector problem $S_b v = \lambda S_{cov} v$ when the covariance matrix is proportional to the identity matrix, $ie.$ when the columns of X are exactly independent. In such a case, it is known that the solution of LDA is proportional to the vector $\left(S_{cov}^{(j)} + S_{cov}^{(k)} \right)^{-1} \left(\overline{x}^{(k)} - \overline{x}^{(j)} \right) \propto x^{-(k)} - x^{-(j)}$. That is, MCMR is a special case of LDA which, when $g = 2$, reduces exactly to the definition of MR.

Whereas a generalization of MR based on a regression framework adds the ability to control one's projection in any way one can a regression [36], this generalization of MR based on an eigenvector framework adds the ability to explore differences between $g \geq 3$ groups even when ordinality is not guaranteed.

The question is, which of these two multiclass rotations is better (and when), what are the features of that difference, and what can these features tell us about telling stories around themes of difference between non-ordinal groups?

3.2 Data

To illustrate the task of telling a story of multiclass difference, we turn to Nephrotex [41]. We choose this dataset because (i) the ICQE community is familiar with it and (ii) it has a manageable number of multiple groups. Nephrotex was implemented across $g = 5$ schools (Iowa, KSU, Pitt, Rowan, and UW) during 2014 and 2015, and Nephrotex outcomes have been reported related to professional thinking [41], entrepreneurial mindsets [42], and complex collaborative thinking [43].

Nephrotex is a virtual internship designed to synchronously guide student groups through authentic biomedical engineering experiences. This provides students an educational task in which they can come to practice and understand the roles as engineers. This task has been designed with deliberate difficulties— problems to be overcome—to help guide students' learning and help them develop the skills necessary to achieve their goals. Nephrotex is also a collaborative environment where students are expected and encouraged to work together, and participants often ask each other for help in response to the data they encounter. As we show in the results below, on average, the discourse between the five sites differed in how students talked about these facets of the internship experience.

3.3 Evaluation

For our task of using one or more ENA plots to illustrate themes of difference, such plots need to be useful in a number of senses: they need to illustrate discrimination between one's groups (where there are differences), and the network embedding needs to aid interpretation of the space in trustworthy ways. So, to compare the usefulness of SVD, LDA, and MCMR, we will consider the discrimination between sites (Kruskal-Wallis H), the variance explained along the relevant axes (R^2), and the co-registration Pearson correlation of the network embedding along the relevant axes (r). Finally, we will use the best of these approaches to demonstrate how one might use it when closing the interpretive loop.

4 Results

4.1 Comparing Approaches

Table 1 summarizes the evaluation results for each method. SVD is designed to maximize variance explained, so naturally it outperforms the others along this metric. Moreover, it is worth noting that LDA explains only a small amount of variance. This suggests to us that LDA is too eager to minimize the variance within groups, and we see the results of this in the coregistration metrics: LDA is the only one that does not have a near-perfect score, scoring 10 percentage points lower than SVD and MCMR. Finally, SVD underperforms on discrimination between groups; LDA and MCMR have an H score more than 8 times that of SVD.

Because our goal is to tell a story about group differences, and because this task demands the ability to discriminate between groups, it is clear that LDA and MCMR are more appropriate models than SVD. However, the choice between LDA and MCMR depends on one's commitments: if one values fit of the network embedding higher, then MCMR wins out; if one values discrimination higher, then it's LDA; and if one values discrimination so long as network fit does not fall below some threshold, then it depends on where that threshold is set. Because, on inspection, MCMR and LDA were both able to discriminate between any pair of groups within their first three axes, and because we value network fit highly, we chose to explore and compare patterns in the Nephrotex dataset using MCMR.

Table 1. Statistical Evaluations

Model	R^2	r	H
SVD	.2830	.9964	8.201
LDA	.0685	.8921	74.22
MCMR	.1178	.9946	69.76

4.2 Quantitative Results

With $g = 5$ groups, the MCMR algorithm may produce up to $g - 1 = 4$ axes.

However, we focus on just the first three axes of the rotation (Fig. 3), *ie.* those that highlight the most between group variance. We do this because, altogether, these suffice to show how any one school was different from any other school. Along all three axes, there were significant differences between at least one pair of groups ($p_1 < .0001, H_1 > 69, p_2 < .0001, H_2 > 26, p_3 < .0001, H_3 > 24, g = 5$) and each had a high co-registration Pearson correlation which suggests strong goodnesses of fit between the visualizations and original models ($r_1 > .99, r_2 > .96, r_3 > .96$).

Figure 3 illustrates these axes. At a glance, the first MCMR axis discriminates between Pitt vs. Rowan vs. the rest in terms of client requests vs. technical constraints. The second discriminates between UW vs. Pitt and Iowa in terms of talk demonstrating the work of engineers vs. collaboration with one another within the virtual internship. And the third discriminates between KSU vs. the rest in terms of data-driven design vs. the affordances of the virtual platform. This suffices to show the differences between any pair of groups, and it achieves the theoretical lower bound of $\lceil \log_2 g \rceil = 3$ axes. These features of the data amount to a minimum number of themes of difference along which we might organize our qualitative account.

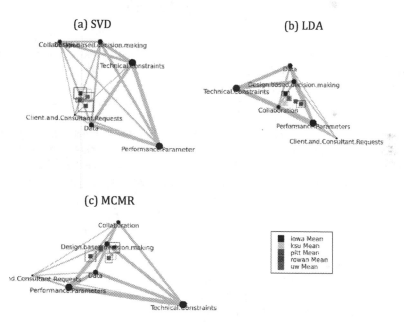

Fig. 2. ENA plots for all three models, showing the grand mean of connection strengths and confidence intervals for each school

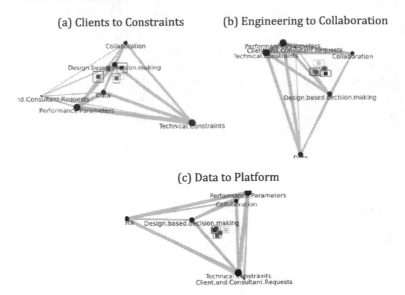

Fig. 3. First three axes of the MCMR rotation

4.3 Qualitative Description

One of the goals of Nephrotex as a virtual internship is for students to practice meeting stakeholder needs *as an engineer* (Fig. 3b). Throughout the internship's activities, students work together and with mentors, and as they do, they verbalize their understanding of the relationships between stakeholder needs and various engineering decisions. Along these lines, groups at UW, more often than Iowa or Pitt, discussed (1) hitting the design requirements of the virtual internship (*eg.*, "I have submitted my surfactant data to Alex twice and both times he has told me that some of my data is incorrect") and (2) using performance data to inform their design choices (*eg.*, "I agree with [student] in saying that steric hindering was the best option. It provided the most categories scoring in the higher ranges.").

Notably, the internship purposefully presented the students with tensions between stakeholder needs and constraints on the design space, and teams engaged with this *balancing act* in different ways (Fig. 3a). At Rowan, more so than other sites, this discourse centered around the requests of the internship's stakeholders as presented to students, as well as how students imagined future stakeholders' needs (*eg.*, "I found our reliability at least meets the required and preferred standard of both consultants"). On the other hand, at Iowa, KSU, or UW, groups talked more about the burdens of technical constraints themselves (*eg.*, "Cost was also a factor in my previous decision, otherwise the steric hindering surfactant would have been my top choice [goes on to list specific prices for choices in Nephrotex]"). Pitt, having much more variance in its implementation than the other schools, spanned this spectrum.

Finally, while setting parameter thresholds for their design in order to achieve their design goals, *in response to data*, and within the hard boundaries set by the internship tool, students often asked one another for help (Fig. 3c). This occurred least at KSU, where conversations favored more general discussions of the affordances of the Nephrotex platform (*eg.*, "The biological surfactant could be a good option if we could lower its cost or improve its reliability").

5 Discussion

In this work, we explore the use of three rotations for simultaneously comparing $g \geq$ 3 groups, SVD, LDA, and MCMR, seeking to understand the contexts in which each approach might best serve a research project based on data structure and goals. Using data from Nephrotex, which consists of a number of comparable groups, we applied all three approaches, choosing MCMR as the best fit for the further exploration. We then shared the visualizations of the dataset with the MCMR rotation applied across three axes, and illustrated how these visualizations can be used to tell stories of non-ordinal themes of differences among multiple groups simultaneously.

We see two main takeaways for this discussion: MCMR and LDA's improvement over SVD, and the role of multiclass rotations in illustrating themes of difference.

First, this work illustrated how MCMR and LDA approaches improved upon SVD in terms of discrimination between groups in the data. Yes, all three can be used to produce a set of axes that could guide an approach to storytelling organized around general trends in the data, but SVD may fail to identify trends that actually discriminate between groups. MCMR and LDA overcome this. The choice between these two depends on one's commitments. When one prioritizes network embedding, they should choose MCMR. And when one prioritizes discrimination between groups, and lower coregistration Pearson correlations are acceptable, LDA may be more appropriate.

And second, this work showcased how models generated using a multiclass rotation can help to tell an ethnographic story of differences between several schools' use of Nephrotex. We considered the first three axes of the MCMR rotation: this allowed us to illustrate the differences between any pair of schools in the fewest number of axes. Moreover, these axes illustrate the structure of one's themes of difference by providing a set of spectra identifying different aspects of the data. This modeling process helps to alleviate the complexity inherent in telling stories that move over multiple groups. Exhaustively exploring all possible pairs of groups, exploring all possible ways to compare one group against the rest, and being fortunate enough to see readily clear stand-out patterns—these are unreasonable asks of researchers as the number of groups grows. Instead, a well-chosen ENA rotation can more directly illustrate a minimum number of spectra around which one can structure their qualitative account.

In future work, the authors hope to explore the pros and cons of MCMR and LDA approaches across more diverse datasets and context, with the goal of offering a roadmap for future QE scholars for well-reasoned choice between available rotations.

References

1. Shah, M., Foster, A., Talafian, H., Barany, A.: Examining the impact of virtual city planning on high school students' identity exploration. In: Eagan, B., Misfeldt, M., Siebert-Evenstone, A. (eds.) Advances in Quantitative Ethnography. ICQE 2019. CCIS, vol. 1112. Springer, Cham (2019). https://doi.org/10.1007/978-3-030-33232-7_17

2. Espino, D.P., et al.: Reflections of health care workers on their in-hospital experiences during the onset of COVID-19. In: Wasson, B., Zörgő, S. (eds.) Advances in Quantitative Ethnography. ICQE 2021. CCIS, vol. 1522. Springer, Cham (2021). https://doi.org/10.1007/978-3-030-93859-8_17

3. Bressler, D.M.: Understanding off-topic utterances: do off-topic comments serve a purpose in collaborative learning? In First International Conference on Quantitative Ethnography: Conference Proceedings Supplement (2019)

4. Ha, S.Y., Lin, T.-J.L.: Development of epistemic cognition aboutsocial knowledge through collaborative small-group discussions. In: First International Conference on Quantitative Ethnography: Conference Proceedings Supplement (2019)

5. Brohinsky, J., Marquart, C., Wang, J., Ruis, A.R., Shaffer, D.W.: Trajectories in epistemic network analysis. In: Ruis, A.R., Lee, S.B. (eds.) ICQE 2021. CCIS, vol. 1312, pp. 106–121. Springer, Cham (2021). https://doi.org/10.1007/978-3-030-67788-6_8

6. Wakimoto, T., et al.: Student teachers' discourse during puppetry-based microteaching. In: Eagan, B., Misfeldt, M., Siebert-Evenstone, A. (eds.) Advances in Quantitative Ethnography. ICQE 2019. CCIS, vol. 1112. Springer, Cham (2019). https://doi.org/10.1007/978-3-030-33232-7_20

7. Wright, T., Oliveira, L., Espino, D.P., Lee, S.B., Hamilton, E.: Getting there together: examining patterns of a long-term collaboration in a virtual STEM makerspace. In: Wasson, B., Zörgő, S. (eds.) Advances in Quantitative Ethnography. ICQE 2021. CCIS, vol. 1522. Springer, Cham (2021). https://doi.org/10.1007/978-3-030-93859-8_22

8. Barany, A., Philips, M., Kawakubo, A.J.T., Oshima, J.: Choosing units of analysis in temporal discourse. In: Wasson, B., Zörgő, S. (eds.) Advances in Quantitative Ethnography. ICQE 2021. CCIS, vol. 1522. Springer, Cham (2021). https://doi.org/10.1007/978-3-030-93859-8_6

9. Mochizuki, T., et al.: Effects of perspective-taking through tangible puppetry in microteaching and reflection on the role-play with 3d animation. In: Eagan, B., Misfeldt, M., Siebert-Evenstone, A. (eds.) ICQE 2019. CCIS, vol. 1112, pp. 315–325. Springer, Cham (2019). https://doi.org/10.1007/978-3-030-33232-7_28

10. Espino, D.P., et al.: News media communication of risk and mitigation factors during early stages of the covid-19 pandemic. In: Second International Conference on Quantitative Ethnography: Conference Proceedings Supplement, p. 23 (2021)

11. Carmona, G., Galarza-Tohen, B., Martinez-Medina, G.: Exploring interactions between computational and critical thinking in model-eliciting activities through epistemic network analysis. In: Wasson, B., Zörgő, S. (eds.) Advances in Quantitative Ethnography. ICQE 2021. CCIS, vol. 1522. Springer, Cham (2021). https://doi.org/10.1007/978-3-030-93859-8_23

12. Knowles, M.A.: Telling stories of transitions: a demonstration of nonlinear epistemic network analysis. In: Wasson, B., Zörgő, S. (eds.) Advances in Quantitative Ethnography. ICQE 2021. CCIS, vol. 1522. Springer, Cham (2021). https://doi.org/10.1007/978-3-030-93859-8_8

13. Mohammadhassan, N., Mitrovic, A.: Discovering differences in learning behaviours during active video watching using epistemic network analysis. In: Wasson, B., Zörgő, S. (eds.) Advances in Quantitative Ethnography. ICQE 2021. CCIS, vol. 1522. Springer, Cham (2021). https://doi.org/10.1007/978-3-030-93859-8_24

14. Benna, A.M., Reynolds, K.: Teachers' beliefs shift across year-long professional development: ENA graphs transformation of privately held beliefs over time. In: Wasson, B., Zörgő, S. (eds.) Advances in Quantitative Ethnography. ICQE 2021. CCIS, vol. 1522. Springer, Cham (2021). https://doi.org/10.1007/978-3-030-93859-8_13

15. Bressler, D.M.: Differences in group communication between game and nongame collaborations. In: First International Conference on Quantitative Ethnography: Conference Proceedings Supplement (2019)

16. Barany, A., Shah, M., Foster, A.: Connecting curricular design and student identity change: an epistemic network analysis. In: Ruis, A.R., Lee, S.B. (eds.) Advances in Quantitative Ethnography. ICQE 2021. CCIS, vol. 1312. Springer, Cham (2021). https://doi.org/10.1007/978-3-030-67788-6_11

17. Phillips, M., Siebert-Evenstone, A., Kessler, A., Gasevic, D., Shaffer, D.W.: Professional decision making: reframing teachers' work using epistemic frame theory. In: Ruis, A.R., Lee, S.B. (eds.) Advances in Quantitative Ethnography. ICQE 2021. CCIS, vol. 1312. Springer, Cham (2021). https://doi.org/10.1007/978-3-030-67788-6_18

18. Ma, L.: Using epistemic network analysis to explore emergent discourse dynamics of a grade 2 knowledge building community. In: First International Conference on Quantitative Ethnography: Conference Proceedings Supplement (2019)

19. Vachuska, K.: Using epistemic network analysis to measure and identify racialidentity development stages. In: First International Conference on Quantitative Ethnography: Conference Proceedings Supplement (2019)

20. Schnaider, K., Schiavetto, S., Meier, F., Wasson, B., Allsopp, B.B., Spikol, D.: Governmental response to the COVID-19 pandemic - a quantitative ethnographic comparison of public health authorities' communication in Denmark, Norway, and Sweden. In: Ruis, A.R., Lee, S.B. (eds.) Advances in Quantitative Ethnography. ICQE 2021. CCIS, vol. 1312. Springer, Cham (2021). https://doi.org/10.1007/978-3-030-67788-6_28

21. Scianna, J., Kaliisa, R., Boisvenue, J.J., Zörgő, S.: Approaching structured debate with quantitative ethnography in mind. In: Wasson, B., Zörgő, S. (eds.) Advances in Quantitative Ethnography. ICQE 2021. CCIS, vol. 1522. Springer, Cham (2021). https://doi.org/10.1007/978-3-030-93859-8_3

22. Hamilton, E.R., Lee, S.B., Charles, R., Molloy, J.: Peering a generation into the future: assessing workforce outcomes in the 2020s from an intervention in the 1990s. In: Wasson, B., Zörgő, S. (eds.) Advances in Quantitative Ethnography. ICQE 2021. CCIS, vol. 1522. Springer, Cham (2021). https://doi.org/10.1007/978-3-030-93859-8_11

23. Bowman, D., et al.: The mathematical foundations of epistemic network analysis. In: Ruis, A.R., Lee, S.B. (eds.) Advances in Quantitative Ethnography. ICQE 2021. CCIS, vol. 1312. Springer, Cham (2021). https://doi.org/10.1007/978-3-030-67788-6_7

24. Van Loan, C.F., Golub, G.: Matrix computations (johns hopkins studies inmathematical sciences). Matrix Computations (1996)

25. Chu, D., Goh, S.R.: A new and fast orthogonal linear discriminant analysis on undersampled problems. SIAM J. Sci. Comput. 32(4), 2274–2297 (2010)

26. Dai, D.-Q., Yuen, P.C.: Regularized discriminant analysis and its application to face recognition. Pattern Recogn. 36(3), 845–847 (2003)

27. Friedman, J.H.: Regularized discriminant analysis. J. Am. Statist. Assoc. 84(405), 165–175 (1989)

28. Chen, L.-F., Mark Liao, H.-Y., Ko, M.-T., Lin, J.-C., Yu, G.-J.: A new lda-based face recognition system which can solve the small sample size problem. Pattern Recogn. 33(10), 1713–1726 (2000)

29. Howland, P., Jeon, M., Park, H.: Structure preserving dimensionreduction for clustered text data based on the generalized singular value decomposition. SIAM J. Matrix Anal. Appl. 25(1), 165–179 (2003)

30. Howland, P., Park, H.: Generalizing discriminant analysis using the generalized singular value decomposition. IEEE Trans. Pattern Anal. Mach. Intell. 26(8), 995–1006 (2004)

31. Huang, R., Liu, Q., Lu, H., Ma, S.: Solving the small samplesize problem of lda. In 2002 International Conference on Pattern Recognition, vol. 3, pp. 29–32. IEEE (2002)

32. Park, H., Drake, B.L., Lee, S., Park, C.H.: Fast linear discriminant analysis using QR decomposition and regularization. Technical report, Georgia Institute of Technology (2007)

33. Ye, J., Yu, B.: Characterization of a family of algorithms for generalized discriminant analysis on under sampled problems. J. Mach. Learn. Res. **6**(4) (2005)

34. Ye, J., Janardan, R., Park, C.H., Park, H.: An optimization criterion for generalized discriminant analysis on undersampled problems. IEEE Trans. Pattern Anal. Mach. Intell. **26**(8), 982–994 (2004)

35. Ye, J., Xiong, T., Madigan, D.: Computational and theoretical analysis of null space and orthogonal linear discriminant analysis. J. Mach. Learn. Res. **7**(7) (2006)

36. Knowles, M., Shaffer, D.W.: Hierarchical epistemic network analysis. In: Second International Conference on Quantitative Ethnography: Conference Proceedings Supplement. ICQE (2021)

37. Shaffer, D.W.: Quantitative ethnography. Lulu. com (2017)

38. Shaffer, D.W., Collier, W., Ruis, A.R.: A tutorial on epistemic network analysis: analyzing the structure of connections in cognitive, social, and interaction data. J. Learn. Anal. **3**(3):9–45 (2016)

39. Marquart, C.L., Hinojosa, C., Swiecki, Z., Eagan, B., Shaffer, D.W.: Epistemic network analysis (version 1.5. 2)[software] (2018)

40. Shaffer, D., Ruis, A.: Epistemic network analysis: a worked example of theory based learning analytics. Handbook of learning analytics (2017)

41. Arastoopour, G., et al.: Measuring first-year students' ways of professional thinking in a virtual internship. In: 2012 ASEE Annual Conference & Exposition, pp. 25–971 (2012)

42. Rogy, K.M., Bodnar, C.A., Clark, R.M.: Examining the entrepreneurial mindset of senior chemical engineering students as a result of exposure to the epistemic game "nephrotex". In: 2014 ASEE Annual Conference & Exposition, pp. 24–559 (2014)

43. Ruis, A.R., Siebert-Evenstone, A.L., Pozen, R., Eagan, B., Shaffer, D.W.: A method for determining the extent of recent temporal context in analyses of complex, collaborative thinking. In: 13th International Conference of the Learning Sciences (ICLS) 2018, vol. 3 (2018)

Is QE Just ENA?

David Williamson Shaffer$^{(\boxtimes)}$ and Andrew R. Ruis

University of Wisconsin–Madison, Madison, WI 53711, USA
`dws@education.wisc.edu`

Abstract. In the emerging field of quantitative ethnography (QE), epistemic network analysis (ENA) has featured prominently, to the point where multiple scholars in the QE community have asked some variation on the question: *Is QE just ENA?* This paper is an attempt to address this question systematically. We review arguments that QE should be considered a background and justification for using ENA as well as arguments that ENA should be considered merely one approach to implementing QE ideas. We conclude that ENA is used in QE, but not exclusively; and that QE uses ENA, but not exclusively; but that the answer to this question is less important than the reflexive thinking about methodology that has been a key focus of the QE community. Our hope is that, rather than a definitive answer to this question, this paper provides some ways to think about the relationships between theory, methods, and analytic techniques as the QE community continues to grow.

Keywords: Epistemic Network Analysis · ENA · Quantitative Ethnography · QE · Data Philosophy

1 Introduction

For the *Second International Conference on Quantitative Ethnography* (ICQE20), Porter et al. [39] conducted a systematic review of the literature from the field of *quantitative ethnography* (QE) and reported that "QE was often only discussed as a methodological framework from which ENA emerged." Indeed, walking into the poster session at ICQE19 looked like a veritable sea of *epistemic network analysis* (ENA) diagrams: 14 out of 25 (56%) of posters at ICQE19 used ENA.

By that metric, the predominance of ENA in the QE community has continued and even increased. ENA was used in 9 of 15 posters (60%) at ICQE20 and 17 of 19 posters (89%) at ICQE21. Thus, while QE studies have used other statistical and machine learning techniques—including process mining, quantitative multimodal interaction analysis, and non-negative matrix factorization [39]—it is easy to see why an undercurrent of discussions within the QE community asks about the relationship between QE and ENA.

This paper is an attempt to address this issue systematically. We review possible arguments that QE should be considered a background and justification for using ENA as well as arguments that ENA should be considered merely one approach to implementing QE ideas. (We also discuss reasons why the answers to these questions might not actually matter.)

So as not to be coy, let us state from the outset that based on these arguments, we think that neither view is correct: ENA is used in QE, but not exclusively; and QE uses ENA, but not exclusively. Of course, we do not anticipate that this overview will provide a definitive answer to the question—nor do we believe it should, as reflexive thinking on research methods is one of the hallmarks of a healthy community. Rather, our hope is to provide a framework that might make such discussions more productive as the community grows.

2   QE Is Just ENA

2.1   Argument from History

> The past is never dead.
> —William Faulkner, *Requiem for a Nun*

The application of statistics in qualitative research has a long history. It has been particularly prominent in the domain of interrater reliability measures [13], which are used to warrant the validity and reliability of coding schemes.

The earliest references to "quantitative ethnography" in Google Scholar are from the 1980 s, primarily in the work of Kleinman [26]. Building on a longer tradition of quantitative methods in ethnographic research (e.g., [12]), Kleinman argued that quantitative ethnography was a collection of "scaling techniques, ethnoscientific eliciting frames, sociolinguistic instruments, and measurement of time, space, change, and other coordinates of behavior and communication" which, when combined with qualitative data, "can be a standardized research method for assessing validity." Studies using this approach typically either counted the frequency with which themes appeared in interviews (see, e.g., [25]) or computed linguistic features of talk, such as measures of cohesion or linguistic complexity (see, e.g., [33]) that described the structure of talk but not its content.

In 1996, Bernard [6] described in general terms the process of using quantitative techniques on "qualitative data," including an argument that sounds strikingly similar to one of the core tenets of QE as it is used at ICQE:[1]

> It's tempting to think that qualitative analysis of text ... keeps you somehow "close to the data." When you do qualitative analysis of a text, you interpret it. You focus on and name themes and tell the story, as you see it, of how the themes got into the text in the first place.... In any event,

---

[1] Bernard also argued for the qualitative examination of quantitative data, again sounding strikingly similar to more recent arguments. He claims that qualitative analysis of quantitative data is "the search for, and the presentation of, meaning in the results of quantitative data processing." He argues that without such work, quantitative studies are "puerile."

you have to talk about the text, which means you have to produce labels for themes and labels for articulations between themes. All this gets you away from the data, surely as numerical coding does. Quantitative analysis involves reducing people (as observed directly or through their texts) to numbers, while qualitative analysis involves reducing people to words.

However, while this description of the quantitative analysis of qualitative data is consistent with QE research, neither Bernard nor his predecessors or contemporaries problematized the nature of the warrants that result from such work.

In 2004, Shaffer and Serlin [46] proposed *intrasample statistical analysis* as an approach to unifying qualitative and quantitative methods. Shaffer and Serlin argued that if individual students (or units of analysis more generally) were included as *fixed effects* in a statistical model, then a statistical analysis of events in thick data of the kind qualitative researchers use would generalize *within* the data.[2] That is, statistical measures could warrant *theoretical saturation* of qualitative analyses. As described in Shaffer [42], this statistical claim became the foundation of QE as a research method. However, Shaffer and Serlin (as well as Bernard and others) did not address a second fundamental question in QE research: namely, how to organize thick data of the kind that qualitative researchers typically use to make such statistical analyses possible.

Building on nearly a decade of research in the Learning Sciences, the question of organizing and quantifying thick data was addressed in detail by Chi [11], and it is on this framework that ENA was developed. More specifically, ENA combined Chi's organizational framework with *epistemic frame theory* [40], which was itself influenced by and extended theories of *situated* and *information-processing* views of cognition (see, e.g., [14,28]).

According to epistemic frame theory, complex thinking skills are developed (and deployed) in the context of specific *communities of practice*. These communities, in turn, have cultures of practice that consist of the skills, knowledge, values, identities, and epistemologies that members of the community use to ask and answer questions and solve problems. Critically, however, epistemic frame theory argues that becoming encultured into a community of practice meant understanding how these cultural elements were systematically *connected* to one another. Originally—and up to 2011 (see [4])—epistemic frames were analyzed qualitatively to document these connections.

The first reference to ENA itself is a paper from 2009 by Shaffer et al. [44]. The paper describes ENA by suggesting that a network is an appropriate way to model the connections among skills, knowledge, values, identities and epistemologies in a culture. Specifically, Shaffer et al. proposed (a) coding turns of talk (or chat messages) in data and (b) constructing a network model based on

---

[2] Technically, Shaffer and Serlin argued that such a statistical analysis would generalize to a *hypothetical sample* taken from "all the things that we might have recorded about these students in the given context from a particular perspective." Thus, statistical significance meant that the analysis was *saturated* in the sense that the results generalize to other possible data that might have been collected or examined under the original circumstances.

the co-occurrence of codes within a *strip* of activity—borrowing the notion of strips of activity from Goffman [21].

At this stage, there was no concept of a window (moving or otherwise), and the network representations and analyses drew on the existing tools of social network analysis, including non-deterministic Kamada-Kawai spring mass models analyzed using weighted density and relative centrality (see Fig. 1).

Between 2009 and 2018, new mathematical and graphical representations were proposed for analyzing epistemic frames, all of which were described as forms of ENA. For example, Hatfield and Shaffer proposed an *integration-cohesion index* for codes . Both *dimensional reduction* of network adjacency matrices [3] and *co-registration of network graphs and plotted points* [35] were proposed in 2012, as well as an impossible-to-read three-dimensional version of such a projection [36] (see Fig. 2). In 2014, Borden et al. released the first ENA Webkit [7], which introduced the scheme for displaying line weights that is used in the current ENA tools (see [48]). *Moving stanza windows* were proposed in 2016 [47], and were incorporated into a second version of the ENA Webkit [31] and rENA package [30] in 2018—the same year in which nCoder, first proposed in 2015 [43], was released as a web tool [32].

It was during this mathematical and conceptual development of ENA in 2015–2017 that *Quantitative Ethnography* [42] was written. *Quantitative Ethnography* was the first description of QE and first use of the term (as this community uses it) in print, although it had been used at conferences and in presentations earlier (see, e.g., [41]). Notably, the book is organized so as to lead up to ENA as the final expression of QE, and it is the topic of the penultimate chapter.

The development of QE and ENA were thus deeply intertwined. This history of co-development and co-presentation suggests that QE and ENA are on a very deep level inseparably connected.

2.2   Argument from Authorship

> *Every invention was once just a thought inside someone's head.*
> —William Federer, *Change to Chains*

As is more or less clear in this historical account of the development of QE and ENA, both of these contributions were developed by a single, relatively small group of researchers at the University of Wisconsin–Madison. Indeed, one criticism of QE is that the community is still dominated by work located in one research group [16]. The first QE conference (ICQE19) was in Madison, Wisconsin, and at the most recent conference (ICQE21), 13 out of 27 (48%) full papers had at least one person affiliated (concurrently or previously) with the University of Wisconsin–Madison. While it is true that the Epistemic Analytics Lab (the developers of QE and ENA) have developed tools other than ENA—nCoder [32] being only the most notable—in the years since the publication of *Quantitative Ethnography*, 39 out of 48 (81%) publications about QE from the lab have been related to ENA.

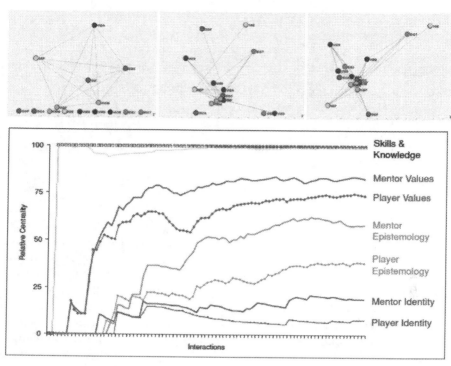

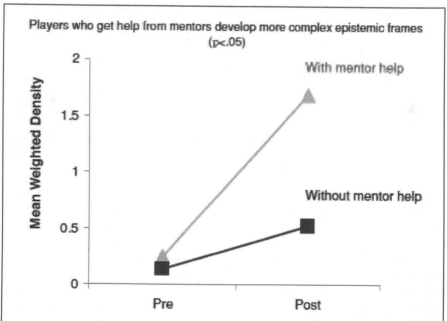

Fig. 1. Traditional network visualizations and summary statistics from the first paper on ENA.

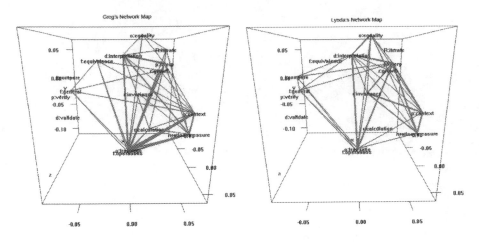

Fig. 2. A misguided attempt to construct three-dimensional ENA models (2013).

In other words, QE and ENA were both created at the University of Wisconsin–Madison. Researchers from the Univeristy of Wisconsin–Madison are involved in a large portion of papers published in and by the QE community. And an overwhelming proportion of QE papers from the University of Wisconsin–Madison involve ENA. Thus, the shared authorship of QE and ENA and the continuing presence of those authors in the QE community suggest that the distinction between QE and ENA may be small.

2.3   Argument from Usage

> *If you want to understand what a science is, you should look in the first instance not at its theories or its findings, and certainly not at what its apologists say about it; you should look at what the practitioners of it do.*
> —Clifford Geertz, *Thick Description*

> *Stupid is as stupid does.*
> —Mrs. Gump, *Forrest Gump*

As the statistics above show, what the practitioners of QE primarily do is ... ENA. But in addition to the historical and personal (or personnel) reasons above, ENA is a useful tool for QE researchers due to its alignment with QE practices.

In general, QE suggests that models should be *fair samples* in the sense that Goodman [22] describes. For Goodman, a fair sample is "one that may be rightly projected to the pattern or mixture or other relevant feature of the whole or of further samples" (p. 135). As an example, Goodman describes swatches from a bolt of cloth, arguing that some swatches would give a more accurate picture than others of the pattern that could be seen in the cloth as a whole. The most fair swatch is the one that gives us the most information about what we might expect to see in future swatches.

Shaffer and Ruis [45] (building on Shaffer [42]) describe four key forms of *QE fairness*:[3]

1. **Fairness to theory**: The methods used are a good reflection of the constructs used in the theories to which they relate—that is, a proponent of a theory would agree that the methods are aligned with it.
2. **Fairness to community**: The methods used are a good representation of the *emic perspective* of the community being studied—that is, a member of the community would agree that the methods are consistent with the cultural norms and meanings of the community.
3. **Fairness to data**: The methods used are a good model of the data and its structure—that is, relevant features or parts of the data are not omitted.
4. **Fairness to subgroups**: The methods used are equally fair to any relevant subgroups within the theory, community, or data—that is, there are not certain ideas, groups of people, or subsets of the data that are treated differently in some inappropriate way.

Shaffer and Ruis discuss these questions of QE fairness in the context of coding data: for example, the role of a clear code definition or inter-rater reliability measures in developing fair classifiers. However, these principles of QE fairness clearly apply to all aspects of QE work, including the models that are constructed using fair codes.

In this regard, ENA has specific affordances for creating fair QE models.

ENA Models Are Perceptual. Li [29] argues that effective data visualizations use *preattentive processing*: that is, they take advantage of low-level visual processing that takes place before conscious awareness to help viewers rapidly and accurately interpret an image.

The graphic design features of ENA network graphs are described elsewhere [48], but briefly, these graphs use a combination of color, saturation, size, and position that help viewers rapidly interpret the graphs. Specifically, ENA represents [C]odes as *nodes* with size proportional to their overall connection strength in the model, and connections between [C]odes as *edges* with thickness and saturation proportional to the strength of the connection. The result is to create a gestalt shape that has weight distributed across the connections.

Although reading any visualization requires a degree of *recognizability*, or the ability to identify features based on previous encounters [29]—ENA graphs make it relatively easy to identify influential codes (they are larger and have more connections coming into them) and influential connections (they are thicker and darker) in a model (see Fig. 3a).

---

[3] Shaffer and Ruis present three forms of fairness (theory, community, and data) together and then discusses subgroup fairness separately. However, we believe it is conceptually clearer to think of four co-equal criteria for fairness. We also note that these criteria do not explicitly reference ethical issues in theory (such as plagiarism), interactions with a community (such as informed consent), data (such as p-hacking), and subgroups (such as unconscious bias). However, we take these as shared assumptions about acceptable research practices.

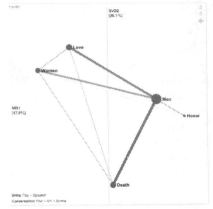

(a) Network graph for characters in *Romeo and Juliet*

(b) Network graph for characters in *Hamlet*

(c) Subtraction plot comparing characters in *Romeo and Juliet* and *Hamlet*

(d) Plotted points comparing characters in *Romeo and Juliet* and *Hamlet*

Fig. 3. ENA visualizations and data representations

ENA Models Are Consistent. The general problem of determining whether two network graphs are equivalent cannot be solved algorithmically [37]. However, it is possible to visually compare network graphs with high accuracy if their nodes are positioned isomorphically [23].

ENA uses a mathematical algorithm, specifically a dimensional reduction technique followed by an optimization, to position the nodes of its network graphs (see [8] for details). As a result, the positions of the nodes are *graph invariate*, which facilitates visual comparison of networks. For example, because the nodes in Figs. 3a (*Romeo and Juliet*) and 3b (*Hamlet*) are isomorphic, we can easily see that the connection between MEN and HONOR is stronger in *Hamlet* than in *Romeo and Juliet*, while the connection between LOVE and DEATH is stronger in *Romeo and Juliet* than in *Hamlet*—neither of which will surprise readers familiar with the plays.

ENA Models Are Interpretable. As a result, the differences between ENA models can be interpreted not just in terms of the differences in the *structure* of the networks (for example, which network is more densely connected, or which network has more central nodes) but based on their *content*—that is, which specific nodes are more or less strongly connected.

Thus, while both *Hamlet* and *Romeo and Juliet* are about LOVE and DEATH, by subtracting their networks (see Fig. 3c), we can see that these themes are more strongly connected to MEN in *Hamlet* and more strongly to WOMEN in *Romeo and Juliet*—again, not a surprise to those who know the plays.

Because the positions of the nodes are graph invariate, the *centroids* of the graphs can also be compared. The centroid is the weighted average of the connection strength of each node—which corresponds to the point where the connections in the graph balance left-to-right and top-to-bottom. Thus, the centroid of *Romeo and Juliet* (shown by the red square in Fig. 3c) is to the left of the centroid for *Hamlet* (the blue square) because the connections in *Romeo and Juliet* are stronger between the codes on the left side of the network graph and the connections in *Hamlet* are stronger on the right.

ENA Models Are Scalable. ENA's dimensional reduction technique represents each network with a *plotted point* (often referred to as an *ENA score*). The algorithm positions the nodes in space such that the centroid of each network *approximates* the location of the network's plotted point. Each network is thus represented by a point that is *co-registered* with its associated network graph.

This co-registration means that the networks are embedded in a space whose *dimensions* can be interpreted. Networks whose points have higher x coordinates make more connections to nodes on the right side of the space. Networks whose points have lower y coordinates make more connections to nodes in the lower part of the space. And so on.

As a result it is possible to compare very large numbers of networks statistically based on the locations of their points in the space, and to interpret those statistical differences using their co-registered network graphs. For example, Fig. 3d shows a comparison of characters in *Romeo and Juliet* and *Hamlet*. The points represent a network for each character. The mean networks are compared using a *t-test* and the difference can be interpreted using the subtracted network graphs of the means.

ENA Models Are Transparent. Critically, however, although ENA models are mathematically complex, they are not black boxes. It is possible to look at the edge of any network in the model and see the parts of the underlying data that generated the connections being modeled. Thus, it is possible to *close the interpretive loop* [42] and ground the results of the complex model in the original data.

As a result of these affordances, ENA models provide a continuous chain of co-registered representations: interpretations of a model can be linked to the dimensions of the ENA space, which are determined by specific plotted points in the model, which can be interpreted in terms of their associated network graphs, which are determined by—and can be linked back to—the original data. This chain of representations, in turn, makes ENA models open to inspection in terms of their fairness to theory, community, data, and subgroups. As a result, ENA exemplifies QE principles of fairness in modeling connections in [d]iscourse, which is the basis for inferences about the [D]iscourse of a community.[4]

In other words, the structure of ENA emerges from and exemplifies key concepts in QE. It is thus no surprise that *Quantitative Ethnography* describes steps in manipulating data that lead to ENA—and no surprise that ENA is the most prominent technique in QE research. The two are inextricably linked.

3 QE Is Not Just ENA

Having examined some of the strongest arguments that QE and ENA are linked in such a way that it is impossible to do QE without doing ENA (and vice versa), we now turn to arguments that QE and ENA should be though of as distinct, albeit related, approaches to data analysis.

3.1 Argument from Symbolic Logic

[T]he proposition "All X is Y" is interpreted to mean that there is no such class of things in existence as "X that is not-Y."
—John Venn, *On the Diagrammatic and Mechanical Representation of Propositions and Reasonings*

The most obvious problem with asserting that all QE is ENA is that it is logically inconsistent. If 14 out of 25 (56%) posters at ICQE19 used ENA, then it is equally true that 11 out of 25 posters (44%) did *not* use ENA. Similarly, if in the years since the publication of *Quantitative Ethnography*, 39 out of 48 (81%) of the publications about QE from the Epistemic Analytics Lab in Madison have been related to ENA, then 9 out of 48 (19%) have not been about ENA.

On one hand, tools exist (or are being developed) that have been used or can be used in QE studies that do not involve ENA: for example, ROCK [38], nCoder [32], ordered network analysis (Tan et al., this volume), network trajectory analysis [9], transmodal analysis [27], Quick Red Fox [24], process mining [34], quantitative multimodal interaction analysis [1], multimodal matrices [10], and non-negative matrix factorization [5]. Moreover, many of these tools were not developed at the University of Wisconsin–Madison or even with QE originally in mind.

---

[4] The use of capitalization denotes the difference between events in the world ([l]ower case) and claims about a culture ([U]pper case). This terminology comes from Gee [18] and Shaffer [45].

On the other hand, studies have used ENA without applying any of the theoretical machinery of QE. For example, Andrist et al. [2] used ENA to model the extent to which two people were looking at the same things during interactions documented in eye-tracking data.

The issue is that ENA is a method for producing perceptual, consistent, interpretable, scalable, and transparent network models. But as a mathematical modeling technique, it is agnostic as to the type of data, its source, or the chain of evidence that preceded the ENA model. Ultimately, ENA requires nothing more than a matrix of codes and associated metadata as parameters to the model.

QE, on the other hand, requires attention to the types and sources of data and the chain of evidence that precedes any model. QE studies thus highlight:

1. **Reflexive data collection.** QE researchers follow principles of good qualitative research, particularly with regards to ethical collection of data that provides a fair representation of the individuals and/or community being studied—recognizing, of course, that any study is an interaction between researcher and participants, and thus the researcher's own perspective and its impact needs to be taken into account [20].

2. **Grounded analysis.** QE researchers follow principles of good qualitative research to develop thick descriptions of the contexts from which their data comes, focusing on questions of why and how some specific people in some specific setting acted as they did. Critically, this includes developing familiarity with the data to the point where a claim is based on a theoretically-saturated interpretation of the context—recognizing, of course, that there are always multiple possible interpretations of a context being studied [19].

3. **Meaningful segmentation.** QE researchers construct qualitative data tables that operationalize the structure of their data based on a theory or theories of discourse rather than using arbitrary boundaries between segments of data [49]. Moreover, such segmentation has to provide lines of data that can be considered exchangeable for the purpose of quantification—that is, lines of data that can be meaningfully counted [42].

4. **Fair and valid coding.** QE researchers classify data based on a grounded understanding of the context, choosing [C]odes that are meaningful in the [D]iscourse in that setting and that can be used to explain that [D]iscourse in terms of the relationships among those [C]odes in the setting [42]. In operationalizing these [C]odes, they attempt to fairly represent the theoretical constructs, data, and community from whom the data was collected using methods whose reliability and validity can be systematically assessed. Because any classification method will produce some error in the resulting [c]odes, QE researchers strive to ensure fairness by using classifiers with very high levels of reliabililty [45].

5. **Interpretable and transparent models.** QE researchers construct models based on fair codes whose results can be interpreted meaningfully because they align a quantitative model with a grounded analysis. They construct models that make it possible to inspect all of the components of the model, and identify segments of data (and combinations of segments) that produce

specific model outcomes—and while recognizing that all models are inexact, they strive to ensure fairness through a process of *closing the interpretive loop*, or testing the validity of a model by qualitatively inspecting the data in light of the model that was produced.

In other words, QE is an approach to data analysis designed to warrant theoretical saturation of qualitative analyses using quantitative techniques. Because of its affordances, ENA is a particularly useful tool for conducting QE research. But the principles and practices of QE in no way constrain researchers to use ENA. Similarly, although ENA is a particularly useful tool for QE research, ENA can be used without reference to the principles and practices of QE.

3.2   Argument from the Nomenclature

> *Rose is a rose is a rose is a rose.*
> —Gertrude Stein, *Geography and Plays*

Adding to the conflation of QE and ENA has been an unfortunate tendency for people in the QE community to describe any network modeling tool used in QE as some form of ENA—for example, Threaded ENA, Directed ENA, or Trajectory ENA—including, in many cases, the developers of such tools.

One way to think about ENA is as a tool that accumulates co-occurrences of codes in data, performs a mathematical manipulation of the resulting matrices, and then displays the results using a network graph. The problem with viewing ENA at this level of generality is that by this definition, almost any network analysis tool could be considered a version of ENA.

Alternatively, one could think of ENA as a tool that accumulates co-occurrences of codes in data *using a particular algorithm*, performs a *specific mathematical manipulation*, and displays the results using *one form of network graph*.

By this more restricted definition, many of the tools that the community refers to as some flavor of ENA bear no more resemblance to the original ENA than the original ship of Theseus did to the ship after it was preserved by the Athenians.[5] For example, ordered network analysis (Tan et al., this volume)—a tool that uses different methods for accumulation, dimensional reduction, and visualization than ENA—should be considered a different tool, and to the extent that it is used in QE work, would provide another example of the separability of QE and ENA.

A more tenable view is perhaps somewhere in between, taking a core component of ENA as the concept of co-registration of network graphs and dimensional reduction. But even under this intermediate definition it is not clear whether QE appears to be equivalent to ENA based on their conceptual integration or because of a poor choice of naming convention.

---

[5] The Ship of Theseus is a paradox raised by Heraclitus of Ephesus (and others, including Thomas Hobbes) asking whether an object that had all of its parts replaced was still the same object.

4   Does It Matter?

In the preceding sections, we have attempted to articulate what seem to be the key arguments regarding the ontological status of QE and ENA. We argue that although QE and ENA share a common history and original authorship—and despite the large number of QE studies that use ENA—they should be considered as related but separable approaches to data analysis. There are QE studies that do not use ENA, and ENA studies that do not use QE. Rather, ENA is a particularly useful tool for enacting QE principles, but the principles of QE and the processes of ENA are distinct.

It is eminently possible to do (1) reflexive data collection, (2) grounded analysis, (3) meaningful segmentation, (4) fair and valid coding, and (5) construction of interpretable and transparent models to (6) close the interpretive loop and (7) warrant theoretical saturation using quantitative techniques—all without using ENA. Similarly, researchers have used models that rely on affordances that are (a) perceptual, (b) consistent, (c) interpretable, (d) scalable, and (e) transparent—without any reference to QE principles or practices.

In making these arguments, however, we recognize that the primary concern of scholars asking about the relationship may not be whether or not the two techniques are separable or not. Rather, we suspect, the concern is about the dominance and influence of this one tool (and by extension those who developed it) on the QE community and its work.

But we argue that the development of new fields often unfolds this way. For example, the field of *minimally invasive surgery* largely developed around a specific set of technologies, namely the *endoscope* and surgical tools that could be inserted through very small perforations in the skin, such as catheters and laparoscopic scissors. But minimally invasive surgery, though in many contexts used interchangeably with endoscopic procedures, is a theoretical perspective that surgical interventions should minimize tissue damage to accelerate postoperative recovery, lessen pain, and reduce the risk of complications and infection. Although most minimally invasive procedures, beginning in the 1980 s, consisted of some form of real-time moving imaging combined with keyhole or percutaneous tools operated manually, the field has since evolved to include a range of computer- and robot-assisted procedures, among other technical advances [17].

More generally, as Darden [15] argues, new fields of study emerge when a new scientific technique makes it possible to observe or construct something that, in turn, makes it possible to provide new solutions to old problems. This approach is generalized into a new theory, giving rise to new lines of research. In the case of QE, we suggest that the technique of ENA facilitated the construction of statistical models of grounded claims. This, in turn, made it possible to describe a more general approach to warranting theoretical saturation of qualitative analyses using quantitative techniques, which has led to the growth of the QE community.

But as with the example of endoscopy, despite the importance of some initial technique, a field expands on its origins rather than remains beholden to them—although it may be too soon to expect this process to have fully matured in a community that is only holding its fourth annual conference.

We conclude, therefore, that the question of the relationship between QE and ENA is important to keep in mind as we move forward. However, there are sound theoretical and practical advantages to recognizing that QE and ENA are two different, though related, ways of analyzing data.

Acknowledgements. This work was funded in part by the National Science Foundation (DRL-1713110, DRL-2100320, DRL-2201723), the Wisconsin Alumni Research Foundation, and the Office of the Vice Chancellor for Research and Graduate Education at the University of Wisconsin-Madison. The opinions, findings, and conclusions do not reflect the views of the funding agencies, cooperating institutions, or other individuals.

References

1. Andrade, A., Maddox, B., Edwards, D., Chopade, P., Khan, S.: Quantitative multimodal interaction analysis for the assessment of problem-solving skills in a collaborative online game. In: Eagan, B., Misfeldt, M., Siebert-Evenstone, A. (eds.) ICQE 2019. CCIS, vol. 1112, pp. 281–290. Springer, Cham (2019). https://doi.org/10.1007/978-3-030-33232-7_24

2. Andrist, S., Collier, W., Gleicher, M., Mutlu, B., Shaffer, D.W.: Look together: Analyzing gaze coordination with epistemic network analysis. Front. Psychol. **6** (2015)

3. Bagley, E.: Epistemic Mentoring in Virtual and Face-to-Face Environments. Ph.D. thesis, University of Wisconsin-Madison (2012)

4. Bagley, E.A., Shaffer, D.W.: Promoting civic thinking through epistemic game play. In: Ferdig, R. (ed.) Discoveries in Gaming and Computer-Mediated Simulations: New Interdisciplinary Applications, pp. 111–127. IGI Global (2011)

5. Bakharia, A.: On the equivalence of inductive content analysis and topic modeling. In: Eagan, B., Misfeldt, M., Siebert-Evenstone, A. (eds.) ICQE 2019. CCIS, vol. 1112, pp. 291–298. Springer, Cham (2019). https://doi.org/10.1007/978-3-030-33232-7_25

6. Bernard, H.R.: Qualitative data, quantitative analysis. CAM February, pp. 9–11 (1996)

7. Borden, F., Collier, W., Marquart, C., Arastoopour, G., Srinivasan, A., Shaffer, D.W.: Epistemic Network Analysis Webkit (2014)

8. Bowman, D., et al.: The mathematical foundations of epistemic network analysis. In: Ruis, A.R., Lee, S.B. (eds.) ICQE 2021. CCIS, vol. 1312, pp. 91–105. Springer, Cham (2021). https://doi.org/10.1007/978-3-030-67788-6_7

9. Brohinsky, J., Marquart, C., Wang, J., Ruis, A.R., Shaffer, D.W.: Trajectories in epistemic network analysis. In: Ruis, A.R., Lee, S.B. (eds.) ICQE 2021. CCIS, vol. 1312, pp. 106–121. Springer, Cham (2021). https://doi.org/10.1007/978-3-030-67788-6_8

10. Buckingham Shum, S., Echeverria, V., Martinez-Maldonado, R.: The multimodal matrix as a quantitative ethnography methodology. In: Eagan, B., Misfeldt, M., Siebert-Evenstone, A. (eds.) ICQE 2019. CCIS, vol. 1112, pp. 26–40. Springer, Cham (2019). https://doi.org/10.1007/978-3-030-33232-7_3

11. Chi, M.T.H.: Quantifying qualitative analyses of verbal data: A practical guide **6**(3), 271–315 (1997)
12. Clements, F.E.: Quantitative method in ethnography
13. Cohen, J.: Kappa: Coefficient of concordance. Educ. Psychol. Measur. **20**(37), 37–46 (1960)
14. Crowley, K., Jacobs, M.: Building islands of expertise in everyday family activity. In: Leinhardt, G., Crowley, K., Knutson, K. (eds.) Learning Conversations in Museums, pp. 333–356. Lawrence Erlbaum Associates (2002)
15. Darden, L.: Discoveries and the emergence of new fields in science. In: PSA: Proceedings of the Biennial Meeting of the Philosophy of Science Association, vol. 1978(1), pp. 149–160 (1978)
16. Elmoazen, R., Saqr, M., Tedre, M., Hirsto, L.: A systematic literature review of empirical research on epistemic network analysis in education. IEEE Access **10**, 17330–17348 (2022)
17. Fuchs, K.H.: Minimally invasive surgery. Endoscopy **34**, 154–159 (2002)
18. Gee, J.P.: An Introduction to Discourse Analysis: Theory and Method, 4th ed. Routledge (2014)
19. Geertz, C.: Thick description: Toward an interpretive theory of culture. In: The Interpretation of Cultures: Selected Essays, pp. 3–30. Basic Books (1973)
20. Glesne, C.: Becoming Qualitative Researchers: An Introduction. Pearson (2015)
21. Goffman, E.: Frame Analysis: An Essay on the Organization of Experience. Harvard University Press (1974)
22. Goodman, N.: Ways of Worldmaking. Hackett (1978)
23. Hascoët, M., Dragicevic, P.: Visual Comparison of Document Collections Using Multi-Layered Graphs (2011)
24. Hutt, S., et al.: Quick Red Fox: An App Supporting a New Paradigm in Qualitative Research on AIED for STEM (2021)
25. Keir, S.S.: Middle Class Black Families in Austin, Texas: An Exploratory Analysis of Husbands and Wives. Ph.D. thesis, University of Texas at Austin (1987)
26. Kleinman, A.: The cultural meanings and social uses of illness: A role for medical anthropology and clinically oriented social science in the development of primary care theory and research **16**(3), 539–545 (1983)
27. Knowles, M., Shaffer, D.W.: Hierarchical epistemic network analysis. In: Ruis, A.R., Lee, S.B. (eds.) Second International Conference on Quantitative Ethnography: Conference Proceedings Supplement, pp. 31–34. ISQE (2021)
28. Lave, J., Wenger, E.: Situated learning: Legitimate peripheral participation. Cambridge University Press (1991)
29. Li, Qi.: Embodying Data: Chinese Aesthetics, Interactive Visualization and Gaming Technologies. Springer, Singapore (2020). https://doi.org/10.1007/978-981-15-5069-0
30. Marquart, C., Swiecki, Z., Collier, W., Eagan, B., Woodward, R., Shaffer, D.W.: rENA: R statistical package for Epistemic Network Analysis (2018)
31. Marquart, C., Swiecki, Z., Hinojosa, C., Collier, W., Shaffer, D.W.: Epistemic Network Analysis Webkit (2018)
32. Marquart, C.L., Swiecki, Z., Eagan, B.R., Williamson Shaffer, D.: ncodeR: Techniques for automated classifiers (2018)
33. Mehl, M.R.: The Sounds of Social Life: Exploring Students' Daily Social Environments and Natural Conversations. Ph.D. thesis, University of Texas at Austin (2004)

34. Melzner, N., Greisel, M., Dresel, M., Kollar, I.: Using process mining (PM) and epistemic network analysis (ENA) for comparing processes of collaborative problem Regulation. In: Eagan, B., Misfeldt, M., Siebert-Evenstone, A. (eds.) ICQE 2019. CCIS, vol. 1112, pp. 154–164. Springer, Cham (2019). https://doi.org/10.1007/978-3-030-33232-7_13

35. Orrill, C., Shaffer, D.W.: Exploring connectedness: Applying ENA to teacher knowledge. In: Van Aalst, J., Thompson, K., Jacobson, M.J., Reimann, P. (eds.) The Future of Learning: Proceedings of the 10th International Conference of the Learning Sciences (ICLS 2012), vol. 1, pp. 175–179 (2012)

36. Orrill, C., Shaffer, D.W., Burke, J.: Exploring coherence in teacher knowledge using epistemic network analysis. In: Paper presented at the Annual Meeting of the American Educational Research Association (2013)

37. Pelillo, M.: Replicator equations, maximal cliques, and graph isomorphism. In: Kearns, M., Solla, S., Cohn, D. (eds.) Advances in Neural Information Processing Systems. MIT Press (1998)

38. Peters, G.J., Zörgő, S.: Introduction to the reproducible open coding kit (ROCK). PsyArXiv Preprints (2019)

39. Porter, C., et al.: A systematic review of quantitative ethnography methods. In: Ruis, A., Lee, S. (eds.) Second International Conference on Quantitative Ethnography: Conference Proceedings Supplement, pp. 35–38. International Society for Quantitative Ethnography (2021)

40. Shaffer, D.W.: Epistemic frames for epistemic games. Comput. Educ. **46**(3), 223–234 (2006)

41. Shaffer, D.W.: Quantitative ethnography: Measuring complex thinking using grounded data mining. Paper presented at Colorado State University (2016)

42. Shaffer, D.W.: Quantitative Ethnography. Cathcart Press (2017)

43. Shaffer, D.W., et al.: The nCoder: A technique for improving the utility of inter-rater reliability statistics (2015)

44. Shaffer, D.W., et al.: Epistemic network analysis: A prototype for 21st century assessment of learning, vol. 1, pp. 33–53 (2009)

45. Shaffer, D.W., Ruis, A.R.: How we code. In: Ruis, A.R., Lee, S.B. (eds.) ICQE 2021. CCIS, vol. 1312, pp. 62–77. Springer, Cham (2021). https://doi.org/10.1007/978-3-030-67788-6_5

46. Shaffer, D.W., Serlin, R.: What good are statistics that don't generalize?. vol. 33, pp. 14–25 (2004)

47. Siebert-Evenstone, A.L., Arastoopour, G., Collier, W., Swiecki, Z., Ruis, A.R., Shaffer, D.W.: In search of conversational grain size: Modeling semantic structure using moving stanza windows. In: Looi, C.K., Polman, J., Cress, U., Reimann, P. (eds.) Transforming Learning, Empowering Learners: The International Conference of the Learning Sciences (ICLS) 2016, vol. I, pp. 631–638 (2016)

48. Tan, S.C., Wang, X., Li, L.: The development trajectory of shared epistemic agency in online collaborative learning: A study combing network analysis and sequential analysis. J. Educ. Comput. Res. (2021) (in press)

49. Zörgő, S., Swiecki, Z., Ruis, A.R.: Exploring the effects of segmentation on semi-structured interview data with epistemic network analysis. In: Ruis, A.R., Lee, S.B. (eds.) ICQE 2021. CCIS, vol. 1312, pp. 78–90. Springer, Cham (2021). https://doi.org/10.1007/978-3-030-67788-6_6

The Role of Data Simulation in Quantitative Ethnography

Zachari Swiecki[1]([✉]) [iD] and Brendan Eagan[2] [iD]

[1] Monash University, Clayton, VIC 3800, Australia
zach.swiecki@monash.edu
[2] University of Wisconsin-Madison, Madison, WI 53711, USA

Abstract. Data simulations are powerful analytic tools that give researchers a great degree of control over data collection and experimental design. Despite these advantages, data simulations have not yet received the same amount of use as other techniques within the context of quantitative ethnography. In this paper, we explore the reasons for this and use examples of recent work to argue that data simulations can—and already do—play an important role in quantitative ethnography.

Keywords: data simulation · quantitative ethnographic methods · epistemic network analysis

1 Introduction

Data simulations are powerful analytical tools. Like statistical models, they can quantitatively represent phenomena that we observe in the world. Unlike statistical models, they are used to generate hypothetical data rather than predictions or inferences from real data. In turn, they afford researchers a high degree of control over parts of a study that are typically arduous, complex, and time consuming—things like data collection and experimental design.

Despite these advantages, data simulation has not been widely adopted as a quantitative ethnographic technique. Understanding why is not particularly difficult. Setting aside the training and experience required to develop data simulations, quantitative ethnography (QE) depends on the alignment between observed phenomena, qualitative claims, and quantitative warrants. More specifically, it depends on the alignment between *real* data about *real* events and qualitative and quantitative interpretations. Because data simulations by definition do not produce real data, they seem to have no place in QE.

In this paper, we argue that even though data simulations generate and operate on hypothetical data, they can—and already do—play a useful role in quantitative ethnographic analyses and the development of QE tools and methods.

2 Background

Before we describe the role of data simulation in QE, it will be useful to review some of the finer points of the QE process [14, 16] (Fig. 1). While these points are crucial to

C. Damşa and A. Barany (Eds.): ICQE 2022, CCIS 1785, pp. 87–100, 2023.
https://doi.org/10.1007/978-3-031-31726-2_7

QE, they may nonetheless be obfuscated in a typical analysis given the complexity of many QE techniques.

QE is fundamentally a process for providing quantitative warrants for qualitative claims. These claims are made in terms of the [D]iscourse of some culture—that is, the ways in which members of that particular culture act, talk, think, believe, value, solve problems, and so on. To make these claims, researchers observe the actual things members of the culture say and do and record them in some way—they observe the [d]iscourse of the culture and record their observations as some form of data (field notes, audio/video recordings, interaction logs, and so on).

The translation of [d]iscourse to data is the first of many simplifications of the [D]iscourse of a culture that are necessary to conduct any QE analysis. Of all the possible things researchers could observe members of a culture doing, they observe and record some subset of those things as data. And as happens in any human endeavour, they may make errors.

Prior to analyzing their data, researchers often make another simplification—they translate their data to some other—usually machine-readable—format. For example, field notes may be typed up or audio may be transcribed. Here again, errors may occur; notes may be mistyped, audio mistranscribed.

Using their recorded data, researchers attempt to understand the relationships between particular themes, ideas, or actions that members of a particular culture use to understand and operate on the world. In other words, they look for evidence of [C]odes in their data. Their evidence comes in the form of [c]odes, identifiable pieces of data that indicate the presence of [C]odes.

The act of coding is an act of pointing; it is a way of saying that some identifiable piece of data is representative of a higher-level concept [16]. To warrant these acts of pointing, QE researchers marshal a collection of qualitative and quantitative evidence. After qualitatively examining the data, they develop a *codebook* that describes examples of the links between the higher level concepts they are investigating ([C]odes) and how those concepts are instanced in the actual data they have ([c]odes).

Using a codebook, two or more raters apply it to the data—otherwise known as *coding*—annotating segments of the data for the presence or absence of the [C]ode. They then compare their ratings using inter-rater reliability (IRR) metrics such as Cohen's kappa and Shaffer's rho to demonstrate that these decisions can be reliably applied to the data. Of course, researchers may also develop automated classifiers to identify [C]odes using techniques such as regular expressions and evaluate them in a similar way.

The process of coding data is, of course, another simplification with the potential to introduce error. Quantitative metrics like kappa and rho are a way of controlling for these kinds of errors, a way of measuring the error and setting thresholds for how much of it they are willing to tolerate in the analysis.

Once codes have been identified and their relationship to [C]odes warranted, the next step is typically to identify relationships among the [c]odes that are salient to the purpose of the analysis. To warrant that these relationships, or connections, constitute systematic patterns in the data and not simply one-off or random occurrences—that is, to warrant theoretical saturation—researchers represent the relationships among [c]odes using statistical models such as epistemic network analysis (ENA) [15]. They then test whether a value derived from the sample of data is representative of what that value would be if calculated from the larger population of data that they might have collected about the same participants under similar conditions [17]. Here we denote the value from the sample as a [p]arameter and the value from the population as a [P]arameter.

Having found this quantitative warrant, researchers now have evidence that the relationships among [c]odes that they observed in their data are representative of the relationships among the corresponding [C]odes that shape the [D]iscourse of the culture they are studying. In other words, their qualitative claims are a systematic property of that culture's [D]iscourse. Crucially, however, the QE researcher's task is not complete until they re-examine these claims in terms of the actual data they have collected. That is, after the sometimes long, complicated, and reductive task of operationalizing qualitative claims in quantitative terms, researchers should check that their quantitative representations are aligned with—or not contradicted by—the actual observations they have made. In other words, they need to *close the interpretive loop*.

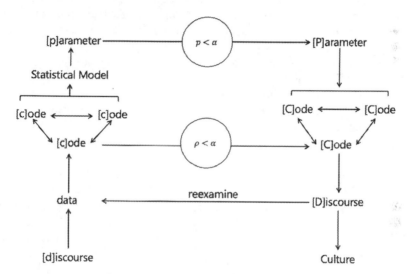

Fig. 1. The QE process. Adapted from [14]

The description above highlights two important features of the QE process. First—like any form of analysis—QE requires simplifications of the phenomena researchers wish to investigate. The things we observe members of a particular culture say and do we record as data; we categorise the kinds of things that members of that culture do by pointing to specific pieces of data; we look for connections among these categories by identifying relationships among these pieces of data. There is always the danger of oversimplification and error. Observations can be misrecorded; parties may not agree on whether some pieces of data actually correspond to categorizations of cultural activities; and identified connections may be meaningless. Second, the QE process hinges on the alignments between qualitative claims, quantitative representations, and real—that is, actually observed—data.

3 Data Simulation

As the term "data simulation" suggests, this technique does not traffic in real data. To highlight this feature, Gilbert and Troitzsch [9] argue that data simulation differs importantly from traditional statistical modeling (Fig. 2). In the latter, researchers have some real-world target that they want to understand. Their aim is to create a model of the target that is easier to study than the target itself. To do so, they collect data and develop a model (e.g., a set of regression equations) that abstracts salient features of the target. This model includes some parameters (e.g., beta coefficients) whose magnitudes are determined by fitting the model to the data on hand. Finally, they test whether the model generates predictions that are sufficiently similar to the collected data (e.g., using a coefficient of determination) and examine the significance and relative magnitude of the estimated parameters (e.g., using p values and measures effect size).

Simulation proceeds similarly except that the model may be in the form of an algorithm or computer program instead of a set of equations, and this model is used to generate simulated data rather than predictions from real data. If possible, the simulated data is compared to available real data to test how similar the two are and assess the validity of the simulation.

A representative example of data simulation in the social sciences is Jager and colleagues' [10] study of group conflict. They used data simulations to study conflict in crowds made up of groups with different allegiances, such as supporters of different football teams. By simulating groups of different sizes and different proportions of aggressive members, they found that conflict was most common when one group was larger than the other and the larger group had a relatively high proportion of aggressive members.

As this example suggests, data simulation has a number of affordances. First, it would be difficult—or at least unethical—to collect data about crowds of people fighting each other. Data simulation allows researchers to generate data that abstracts the situation in a relatively easy and safe way. Second, simulating data provides the researchers with a high degree of control over the design of the experiment. In the example above, Jager and colleagues were able to control the number of data points in each sample and the proportions of aggressive members; they did not have to rely on which participants happened to be available or consent to their study. Relatedly, data simulation allowed them to examine plausible cases that might have gone missed if they had relied on traditional data collection methods—for example, what would happen when the groups of supporters were exactly the same size? In this sense, the simulation allowed them to generalize their findings to a broader variety of situations.

Despite these advantages, at first glance data simulations do not seem to cohere with the QE process, which is so dependent on real data. The dashed links in Fig. 2 indicate steps that are technically unnecessary for data simulation to proceed. While it can be useful to collect real data and use it to assess the validity of the simulation, it is possible (and common) to operate solely on simulated data. However, such an approach is problematic in the context of QE. A QE researcher cannot arrive at qualitative claims when no real qualitative data exists; a researcher cannot close the interpretive loop if there is no real data to return to. In the next sections we overview four examples of applications

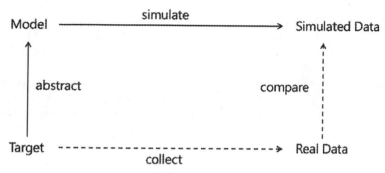

Fig. 2. The data simulation process. Adapted from [9]

of data simulation to QE to argue that despite these differences, data simulation can—and already does—have an important role in QE.

4   Data Simulation in Quantitative Ethnography

4.1   Transcription Error

QE researchers often rely on audio or video recordings of events as data. To analyze these data they typically transcribe it to some other machine-readable format—e.g., text—and then code the transcription [11, 24]. As a result, transcription provides a critical link in connecting events in the world to models and understandings of those events. Unfortunately, transcription processes are imperfect and transcription errors can lead to coding errors, each of which compound to negatively influence the integrity of the subsequent analysis.

To examine the impact of transcription error on coding performance, Eagan [6] used a data simulation. In terms of Fig. 2 above, his target was the relationship between transcription error and coding error—that is, the extent to which errors in a transcription impact the accuracy of labeling data for a [C]ode. To model this target, he investigated three main parameters that had previously been shown to influence coding performance:

- *base rate*: the frequency with which a code appears in a dataset [5, 14, 23].
- *token rate*: the number of unique tokens[1] used to code the dataset divided by the total number of unique tokens in the dataset [1, 4, 12].
- *redundancy rate*: for an individual dataset, the ratio of data segments with multiple independent examples of a code to the total number of positively coded data segments [8].

To examine how these parameters relate to the impact of transcription error on coding performance, Eagan developed the *sensitivity analysis for transcription error* (SATE) method. In statistics, sensitivity analyses measure the level of bias or error that

---

[1] In textual data, lines of text are composed of tokens: the individual, or unique combinations of, pieces of information that each line of data contains [22].

would need to be present in a dataset to invalidate a given inference, statistical result, or interpretation [7]—that is, the extent to which the data could be altered until an original result becomes invalid. This same approach can be used to examine the impact error has on the inferences or claims made in coding processes.

Eagan used the SATE method to study both real and simulated *data-classifier systems* (DCSs): the pairing of an individual dataset and a specific classifier or coding process. He did so by introducing transcription error to datasets and re-coding them to determine whether the resulting coding error was acceptable. Transcription errors were introduced using a 2-state Markov modulating failure process that goes through a dataset word by word with, in this case, a 5% chance of replacing each word with another word from the dataset.

First, Eagan used the SATE method on 18 DCSs from three different real world learning situations. For each DCS, 5% transcription error was introduced, then the dataset with error was re-coded with the automated classifier and kappa was calculated between the original coding and the coding of the data containing transcription errors. This process of transcription error introduction, re-coding, and kappa calculation was repeated 2,000 times creating a distribution of kappa for each DCS. If 95% of the distribution was greater than a coding performance threshold of kappa equal to 0.9, the DCS was considered robust to 5% transcription error; otherwise it was considered sensitive to 5% transcription error. He used this approach to demonstrated that SATE could discriminate between DCSs that were sensitive to 5% transcription error and those that were robust.

His analyses aligned with the previously specified mechanisms of transcription error influencing coding performance, however the analyses with actual data were too under-powered—that is he did not have enough data to find statistically significant relationships between these mechanisms or their interactions in real data. In addition, while the actual DCSs and prior work provided some guidance as to the ranges of the three parameters of interest, they did not offer examples or representations of all combinations of these parameters researchers could expect to encounter.

To investigate how transcription errors impact coding performance more thoroughly, Eagan created simulated data and associated classifiers to create *simulated DCSs* that are more representative of DCSs researchers could expect to see in the real world. As a result, he was able to assess the significant main effects and three-way interactions between base rate, token rate, and redundancy rate influencing the impact of transcription error on coding performance. In general, as base rate increases sensitivity to transcription error decreases; as token rate increases, sensitivity to transcription error increases; and as redundancy rate increases, some aspects of coding performance increase, but interactions make this relationship more complex (for more details see [6]).

4.2   Shaffer's Rho

The work by Eagan described above used data simulations to examine the relationships among data representations, classifier features, and classifier reliability. This work assumes that there is some defensible way to warrant classifier reliability—that the rate of agreement between two or more raters on some sample of data is suitably high and that the agreement would hold—allowing for some small level of disagreement—if they were to code the rest of the data. As many QE researchers know, this warrant comes in the form of Shaffer's rho [14]. However, it is likely less well known that the calculation of Shaffer's rho itself relies on data simulation.

To establish the reliability of coding approaches, researchers often use IRR metrics such as Cohen's kappa—especially when there is too much data or not enough time for one or more raters to code all of the data. The basic idea of using IRR metrics is to measure and control the amount of uncertainty—that is, disagreement between raters—involved in a coding process [16]. However, as Eagan and colleagues [4, 5] have argued, the way researchers commonly use IRR metrics is fundamentally flawed. Many researchers compute an IRR metric on a sub-sample of their data and simply assume that it generalizes to the rest of their dataset. That is, they do not control for cases where the IRR in a sample is over a reliability threshold (say Cohen's kappa > 0.65), but the IRR for the entire dataset is below that threshold—a Type I Error.

Shaffer's rho was developed to address this methodological gap. Here, the target of interest is the coding reliability of two raters. Given a real set of coded data, the algorithm that calculates Shaffer's rho simulates two coding processes over some hypothetical dataset where the agreement between the two raters is less than the IRR threshold of interest. In other words, a data simulation is used to generate a large number of coding pairs that are unreliable given some IRR threshold. Critically, this simulated data shares important characteristics with the real data on hand.

Next, a portion of this simulated data is sampled and the IRR measure is calculated. This process of simulating data and calculating IRR on a subsample of the simulated data is repeated hundreds of times and the IRR values from the samples generate a distribution of IRR measurements under a null hypothesis—namely that the observed IRR was sampled from a larger dataset for which the two raters would not have an acceptable level of agreement. If the observed IRR measurement—the measurement obtained by two raters on the real data for the code in question—is greater than 95% of the IRR values in the null hypothesis distribution, a researcher may conclude that their observed agreement generalizes to the rest of their dataset.

4.3 The Expected Value Test

In many QE analyses, the outputs of statistical models are used to as quantitative warrants for qualitative claims about the connections among [C]odes. One common type of model used in QE is ENA, which identifies the co-occurrence of [c]odes within data. [p]arameters derived from ENA can then be tested for statistical significance to warrant theoretical saturation.

As Swiecki [19] argues, these [p]arameters are often derived from the differences between two samples—say patterns of connections pre and post some intervention, or differences in connections between control and treatment groups. However, QE researchers may not always be able—or want—to compare samples. In some cases, they may be interested in the connections among [C]odes in the [D]iscourse of a single sample—say one classroom or one group of students. Swiecki (ibid.) developed a data simulation-based test—the *expected value test* (EVT)—to produce a [p]arameter appropriate for these kinds of single sample cases.

The method relies on comparing an ENA model developed from the real data to a distribution of ENA models developed from simulated data. In typical applications of

ENA, results are derived in terms of the dimensional reduced networks for each unit of analysis (ENA scores); however, for this test, the results are derived in terms of the full networks for each unit. These networks can be thought of as points in a high-dimensional space. Any collection of points has an average called a centroid and two points close together in this space are considered similar—that is the units of analysis corresponding to these points made similar kinds of connections (as identified by ENA). The method includes the following steps:

- Generate an ENA model from the real data on hand (observed model).
- Generate a distribution of ENA models from simulated data in which the codes and order of lines—e.g., turns of talk—have been repeatedly randomized—that is, a distribution of chance-based models.
- Calculate the similarity of the observed model to the average, or centroid, of the chance-based models. Calculate the distribution of similarities of the chance-based models to the centroid. Compare the observed similarity to the distribution.

Here, the data simulation takes the form of randomized data. The logic being that if the connections identified in the real data constituted a systematic pattern in the data, then they should statistically differ from connections identified in randomized sets of that data. Using this method, Swiecki (ibid.) was able to show that the EVT could distinguish between systematic and non-systematic connections in real data, suggesting that the method provided a plausible quantitative warrant for QE analyses of single samples.

4.4 Informational Interdependence

Collaborative problem-solving has been studied extensively by QE researchers (see, for example, [2, 13, 21]). As several researchers argue, collaborative problem-solving is characterized by different types of interdependence among group members. For example, DeChurch and Mesmer-Magnus [3] argue that *informational interdependence* arises when different individuals need to share different kinds of information to complete a task. Swiecki and colleagues [20] developed a data simulation to explore the nature of informational interdependence during collaborative problem-solving.

Prior to designing the simulation they examined data collected from a real world learning situation that made use of a jigsaw pedagogical design [18]. In a jigsaw design, each team is assigned a unique topic on which to become an "expert". After learning about their topic, new teams are formed in which each person has expertise in a different topic. In these new teams, individuals communicate their knowledge of their assigned topics with the others. Because informational interdependence involves the sharing of different information among individuals, the researchers hypothesized that the *interactivity* among teammates and the *dissimilarity* of the information they shared could be used to predict the amount of informational interdependence on the team, and thus, the impact of pedagogical designs like the jigsaw.

The data on hand consisted of digital records of conversations that teams had using an online chat messing tool. These teams were tasked with a mechanical engineering problem, namely, to design an exoskeleton for rescue workers that would perform well in terms of attributes like cost and user safety. Following a typical QE process, the researchers coded these data for the presence or absence of [C]odes related to engineering design in this context. In particular, they coded for concepts like design inputs and measurable design outcomes. To measure the effect of the jigsaw—and thus the extent of informational interdependence—they also included the jigsaw topics as [C]odes, which represented particular design inputs that individual team members were assigned to learn about before teams were re-formed.

Analyzing the data qualitatively, they found that chats from the pre-jigsaw sample were focused on the relationships between design inputs (other than the jigsaw topics) and design outputs. Chats from the post-jigsaw sample were focused on the relationships among the different jigsaw topics and the design outputs. They also noticed that the post-jigsaw sample was characterized by a higher level of interaction among teammates (individuals tended to exchange turns of talk rather than have monologue-like sequences of chats) and greater focus on sharing different kinds of information. In other words, interactivity and dissimilarity of information seemed to be related to informational interdependence.

To provide a quantitative warrant for these claims, the researchers developed an ENA model of the connections between [c]odes present in the data and compared the connections identified in the pre/post-jigsaw samples. This analysis yielded a statistically significant difference between the two samples that aligned with qualitative findings. A subsequent analysis regressed the ENA scores on the significant dimension on measures of interactivity and dissimilarity, controlling for team membership. The regression model showed that the mean dissimilarity metric of an individual's team was significantly associated with the ENA score, controlling for team effects—individuals on teams that shared different kinds of information tended to talk more like post-jigsaw teams. Put another way, sharing different kinds of information was positively related to informational interdependence.

While these results were useful, they were limited by the nature of the data on hand. Combinations of dissimilarity and interactivity were only present for limited ranges, raising the question of what the relationship among informational interdependence, dissimilarity, and interactivity would be if more complete data was available—that is, combinations throughout the range of both variables. To investigate this question, the researchers developed a data simulation.

The original data was the actual chat messages sent by the participants. These messages were coded for particular categories and then the relationships between these codes were modeled. Because it would be too difficult (and nonsensical) to attempt to simulate chat messages themselves, the researchers simulated the patterns of codes present in messages instead. Doing so required two generating mechanisms: one that determined the order in which the simulated participants "chatted" and the other to determine the codes present in their "chats".

To generate the sequence in which the simulated participants chatted, the researchers used a lag-1 transition matrix. To generate the codes present in the chats, they used a co-occurrence probability matrix for each simulated participant that was based on the their observed data. Given a pair of participants and a prior chat, the probabilities in these matrices determined which codes would be present or absent in the subsequent chat.

After validating the simulation by comparing its output to the actual data (see [20] for details), the researchers were able to simulate data under a larger variety of dissimilarity and interactivity combinations than were present in the real data and test the effect of these metrics on informational interdependence, which, as with the real data, was operationalized in terms of their location on the significant dimension of the original ENA space. The results suggested that dissimilarity and interactivity at the team *and* individual levels were significantly related to informational interdependence, expanding the results of the analysis of the real data.

5   Discussion

Thus far we have argued that QE analysis are characterized by two important features. First, QE analysis are simplifications of observed phenomena and are thus prone to error. Second, QE is an analytical process that fundamentally relies on the relationships among qualitative claims, quantitative representations, and real data. We have also given a brief overview of the application of data simulations in the context of QE. What remains is to explicitly link these examples of data simulation to the QE framework. These links are summarized in Fig. 3 and expanded upon below.

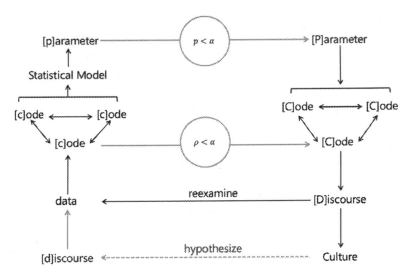

Fig. 3. The QE process with links to data simulation in green.

5.1   Link 1: [D]iscourse to Data

QE researchers record a subset of the [d]iscourse they observe as data. A common practice is to make audio or video recordings of [d]iscourse and then transcribe those recordings for analysis. Any transcription process, whether manual or automated, is prone to error. Words are mistaken, missed, or attributed to the wrong speaker. Because QE researchers code these data to make claims about the [D]iscourse of some culture, these errors, if left uncontrolled, can damage the coding, the analysis of connections, and consequently, the validity of the entire analysis. Put simply, if the data are bad to begin with, the analysis will be bad as well. Garbage in, garbage out.

The SATE method provides a means to investigate the tolerance of the coding process to transcription errors and guidance on how to control for transcription errors. By simulating a range of coding schemes and error prone data, the method can identify specific features that QE researchers can use to examine whether transcription errors in their data are likely to negatively impact the reliability of coding schemes applied to those data. In particular, [c]odes that are prevalent in a dataset and tend to appear multiple times within segments of data tend to be more robust to transcription error; [c]odes that are relatively unique compared to the data tend to be more sensitive to transcription error.

5.2 Link 2: [C]odes to [C]odes

QE researchers—as well as ethnographers more generally—come to understand the [D]iscourse of some culture by understanding the [C]odes of that culture—the kinds of things they say, do, feel, think, and believe that define them. To do so, they identify [c]odes in their data—actual pieces of data that they use to argue for the presence (or absence) of [C]odes. This act of pointing is reductive in the sense that it takes a high-level, sometimes vague and nuanced concept, and materializes it in the form of pieces of data. As a reductive act, it is prone to error and open for disagreement between parties—multiple researchers say, or the researcher and members of the culture.

To justify the link between [c]odes and [C]odes, QE researchers seek some measurable consensus or agreement. In many cases they code a subset of the data, measure the agreement, and determine if the agreement is good enough for the purposes of the analysis. Shaffer's rho—which is derived, in part, from a data simulation—provides evidence that the agreement reached on this sample of data would generalize to the rest of the data at hand, and thus supports and strengthens the link between [c]odes and [C]odes.

5.3 Link 3: Connections

[C]odes in isolation do not define the [D]iscourse of a culture; it is the relationships among [C]odes that allows us to understand the culture in some way. In turn, QE researchers often seek to identify the relationships among [c]odes in their data and warrant that these relationships are indicative of the patterns among [C]odes that help to define the culture. One way to warrant this link is to use ENA to identify co-occurrences between [c]odes in the data and then perform a statistical test, the result of which can suggest that the patterns observed in the data are systematic—signal, not noise.

While there are established ways of running these statistical tests for cases in which that are two samples of data that researchers wish to compare, the way forward is less clear when researchers can or want to only describe the nature of a single sample. Using a simulation to compare the connections observed in the data to the connections identified in a randomized version of that data, the EVT provides a statistical test of the connections between [c]odes for single samples. In turn, this method can support the link between the connections among [c]odes and the connections among [C]odes that characterize the [D]iscourse of some culture.

5.4 Link 4: Building Theory

Initiating a QE analysis requires observations of the [d]iscourse of a culture. These observations are recorded as data, and the analysis proceeds. When the analysis is finished, if we have done it well, we have evidence that the qualitative claims we are making are systematic properties of the [D]iscourse of the culture we are studying—we have evidence of theoretical saturation. These claims, however, are inherently limited by the [d]iscourse we have observed.

Although QE uses statistical tests, their function is not the same as in typical quantitative inquiry. Outside of QE, statistical tests are typically used to generalize claims made about some sample of observations—on people, say—to the larger population of observations we could have made about other people. In other words, typical statistical tests warrant generalizations *outside* the data we have. In QE, statistical tests are used to generalize claims made about some sample of observations on people to the larger population of observations we could have made about the same people. In QE, statistical tests warrant generalizations *within* the data we have.

Nonetheless, the data we have may be severely limited and thus our claims narrow. Data simulations can help to expand upon the data we have. As shown by the work of Swiecki and colleagues [20] as well as Eagan [6], data simulation can produce results that may have been missed if only real data had been examined. However, these results do not necessarily expand the kinds of claims we can make in the context of QE. The reason being that they are initially unverifiable.

A QE analysis is not finished when a significant statistical result is or is not obtained. The analysis is finished when the researchers re-examine the claims that they have supported or refuted in terms of the [d]iscourse they have recorded as data—that is, when they have closed the interpretive loop. When data in question is simulated, closing the loop is not possible—there is no qualitative account to check the results against. Of course, this does not mean that results from simulated data are useless. Instead, it reframes these results as the starting point for subsequent analysis; the results become hypotheses that can be tested by observing more [d]iscourse and conducting future QE analyses. In other words, they become mechanisms for testing and building theories about some culture.

6 Conclusion

In this paper, we provided an overview of the QE process and examples of the use of data simulation in QE. We argued that QE is reliant on real—that is, actually observed—data and that QE is error prone. In spite of the former and because of the later, we argued that data simulation has a role to play in QE. A look at Fig. 3 suggests that this role is more than just a cursory one. New links in the QE process can be created and existing links can be reinforced.

Our work here is limited in the sense that we have only provided evidence for the relationships between QE and data simulation. We have not discussed the major practical issues associated with using data simulations in QE nor have we provided guidelines for implementing simulations in the QE context. This paper is a prerequisite to that future work. For now, we hope that we have given insight to the usefulness of data simulation in QE and that this paper will spark debate and study about whether and how data simulation should be incorporated into future QE work.

Acknowledgements. This work was funded in part by Monash University, the National Science Foundation (DRL-1661036, DRL-1713110, DRL-2100320), the Wisconsin Alumni Research Foundation, and the Office of the Vice Chancellor for Research and Graduate Education at the University of Wisconsin-Madison. The opinions, findings, and conclusions do not reflect the views of the funding agencies, cooperating institutions, or other individuals.

References

1. Almuallim, H., Dietterich, T.G.: Learning with many irrelevant features. In: Proceedings of the Ninth National Conference on Artificial Intelligence AAAI, vol. 91, pp. 547–552 (July 1991)
2. Csanadi, A., Eagan, B., Kollar, I., Shaffer, D.W., Fischer, F.: When coding-and counting is not enough: using epistemic network analysis (ENA) to analyze verbal data in CSCL research. Int. J. Comput.-Support. Collab. Learn. **13**(4), 419–438 (2018)
3. DeChurch, L.A., Mesmer-Magnus, J.R.: The cognitive underpinnings of effective teamwork: a meta-analysis. J. Appl. Psychol. **95**(1), 32–53 (2010). http://doi.org/10.1037/a0017328, http://doi.apa.org/getdoi.cfm?doi=10.1037/a0017328
4. Eagan, B., Brohinsky, J., Wang, J., Shaffer, D.W.: Testing the reliability of inter-rater reliability. In: Proceedings of the 10th International Conference on Learning Analytics & Knowledge, pp. 454–461. Association for Computing Machinery (2020). http://www.epistemicanalytics.org/wpcontent/uploads/2020/06/LAK20_Eagan_IRR_Camera_Ready.pdf,https://doi.org/10.1145/3375462.3375508
5. Eagan, B., Rogers, B., Serlin, R., Ruis, A., Arastoopour, G., Shaffer, D.W.: Can we rely on reliability? Testing the assumptions of inter-rater reliability. In: Smith, B., Borge, M., Mercier, E., Yon Lim, K. (eds.) Making a Difference: Prioritizing Equity and Access in CSCL: 12th International Conference on Computer Supported Collaborative Learning (CSCL) 2017, vol. 2, pp. 529–532 (2017)
6. Eagan, B.R.: Measuring the Impact of Transcription Error. Doctoral Dissertation, University of Wisconsin - Madison (2020)
7. Frank, K., Min, K.S.: 10. Indices of robustness for sample representation. Sociol. Methodol. **37**(1), 349–392 (2007)
8. Gilad-Bachrach, R., Navot, A., Tishby, N.: Margin based feature selection-theory and algorithms. In: Proceedings of the Twenty-First International Conference on Machine learning, p. 43 (July 2004)
9. Gilber, N., Troitzsch, K.: Simulation for the Social Scientist. McGraw-Hill Education, UK (2005)
10. Jager, W., Popping, R., Van de Sande, H., Jager, W., Popping, R., Van de Sande, H.: Clustering and fighting in two-party crowds: simulating the approach avoidance conflict. J. Artif. Soc. Soc. Simul. **4**(3), 1–18 (2001)

11. Kaliisa, R., Misiejuk, K., Arastoopour, G., Misfeldt, M.: Scoping the emerging field of quantitative ethnography: opportunities, challenges and future directions. In: Ruis, A., Lee, S. (eds.) Advances in Quantitative Ethnography: Second International Conference, ICQE 2020, Malibu, CA, USA, February 1–3, 2021, Proceedings, pp. 3–17. Springer, Heidelberg (2021). https://doi.org/10.1007/9783-030-67788-6_1, https://link.springer.com/chapter/10.1007/978-3-030-67788-6_1

12. Liu, H., Setiono, R.: A probabilistic approach to feature selection-a filter solution. In: ICML, vol. 96, pp. 319–327 (July 1996)

13. Ruis, A.R., Siebert-Evenstone, A.L., Pozen, R., Eagan, B.R., Shaffer, D.W.: Finding common ground: a method for measuring recent temporal context in analyses of complex, collaborative thinking. In: A Wide Lens: Combining Embodied, Enactive, Extended, and Embedded Learning in Collaborative Settings: 13th International Conference on Computer Supported Collaborative Learning (CSCL), vol. 1, pp. 136–143 (2019)

14. Shaffer, D.W.: Quantitative Ethnography. Cathcart Press (2017). http://www.quantitativeethnography.org/

15. Shaffer, D.W., Collier, W., Ruis, A.R.: A tutorial on epistemic network analysis: analyzing the structure of connections in cognitive, social, and interaction data. J. Learn. Anal. 3(3), 9–45 (2016). http://learninganalytics.info/journals/index.php/JLA/article/view/4329

16. Shaffer, D.W., Ruis, A.R.: How we code. In: Ruis, A.R., Lee, S.B. (eds.) ICQE 2021. CCIS, vol. 1312, pp. 62–77. Springer, Cham (2021). https://doi.org/10.1007/978-3-030-67788-6_5

17. Shaffer, D.W., Serlin, R.: What good are statistics that don't generalize? Educ. Res. 33(9), 14–25 (2004)

18. Slavin, R.E.: Cooperative Learning. Learning and Cognition in Education, pp. 160–166. Elsevier Academic Press, Boston (2011)

19. Swiecki, Z.: The expected value test: a new statistical warrant for theoretical saturation. In: Wasson, B., Zörgő, S. (eds.) Advances in Quantitative Ethnography: Third International Conference, ICQE 2021 Virtual Event, November 6–11, 2021, Proceedings. Springer, Heidelberg (2022). https://doi.org/10.1007/978-3-030-93859-8_4

20. Swiecki, Z., Marquart, C., Eagan, B.: Simulating collaborative discourse. In: Paper Accepted to the ISLS Annual Meeting 2022 (2022)

21. Swiecki, Z., Ruis, A.R., Farrell, C., Shaffer, D.W.: Assessing individual contributions to collaborative problem solving: a network analysis approach. Comput. Hum. Behav. 104, 105876 (2020). https://doi.org/10.1016/j.chb.2019.01.009

22. Webster, J., Chunuy, K.: Tokenizaion as the initial phase in NLP. In: COLING 1992 Volume 4; the 14th International Conference on Computational Linguistics (1992)

23. Witten, I.H., Frank, E., Hall, M.A.: Data Mining: Practical Machine Learning Tools and Techniques. Morgan Kaufmann, USA (2011)

24. Zörgő, S., Peters, G.J.Y., Porter, C., Moraes, M., Donegan, S., Eagan, B.: Methodology in the mirror: a living, systematic review of works in quantitative ethnography. In: Wasson, B., Zörgő, S. (eds.) Advances in Quantitative Ethnography: Third International Conference, ICQE 2021 Virtual Event, November 6–11, 2021, Proceedings. Springer, Heidelberg (November 2021). https://doi.org/10.1007/978-3-030-93859-8_10

Ordered Network Analysis

Yuanru Tan[(✉)] [iD], Andrew R. Ruis[iD], Cody Marquart[iD], Zhiqiang Cai[iD],
Mariah A. Knowles[iD], and David Williamson Shaffer[iD]

Wisconsin Center for Education Research, University of Wisconsin, Madison, WI, USA
Yuanru.tan@wisc.edu

Abstract. Collaborative Problem Solving (CPS) is a socio-cognitive process that is interactive, interdependent, and temporal. As individuals interact with each other, information is added to the *common ground*, or the current state of a group's shared understanding, which in turn influences individuals' subsequent *responses to* the common ground. Therefore, to model CPS processes, especially in a context where the order of events is hypothesized to be meaningful, it is important to account for the ordered aspect. In this study, we present *Ordered Network Analysis* (ONA), a method that can not only model the ordered aspect of CPS, but also supports visual and statistical comparison of ONA networks. To demonstrate the analytical affordances and interpretable visualizations of ONA, we analyzed the collaborative discourse data of air defense warfare teams. We found that ONA was able to capture the qualitative differences between the control and experimental condition that cannot be captured using unordered models, and also tested that such differences were statistically different.

Keywords: Ordered Network Analysis · Collaborative Problem Solving · Directed Network · Network Visualization

1 Introduction

Collaborative Problem Solving (CPS) is often conceptualized as a process of constructing shared *cognitive* space through *social* interactions [8, 9]. Studies have found that successful CPS involves a large degree of mutual engagement, joint decision making, and discussions [12]. To model such socio-cognitive processes, the modeling approaches undertaken must not only account for the fact that events at any point in time are influenced by prior actions, but also that individuals make connections to the things their collaborators say and do [18]. However, current modeling approaches tend to either underrepresent or even neglect the *interactive* and t*emporal* nature of CPS by treating collaborations as a set of isolated events, or overrepresent the *interdependence* between CPS activities by assuming all events being equally related to each other.

In respond to such challenges, we introduce *Ordered Network Analysis* (ONA) in this study. ONA constructs directed network models of CPS by accounting for not only the interactive, interdependent, and temporal nature of collaborations, but also the *order of events* unfolding over time in CPS processes. We argue that ONA has three affordances for modeling CPS. First, ONA can model the order of events in CPS by tracking both

C. Damşa and A. Barany (Eds.): ICQE 2022, CCIS 1785, pp. 101–116, 2023.
https://doi.org/10.1007/978-3-031-31726-2_8

what units of analysis respond *with* and what they respond *to* as they interact with others in the group, and represent such connections in directed network models. Second, ONA supports comparison of network models at both the individual unit level and the aggregated group level. This enables the assessment of individual performance in group context and also statistical testing of differences between groups. Third, to facilitate the interpretation of analytical results, ONA visualizes models in network graphs that are intuitive to read and mathematically consistent with the model's summary statistics.

In what follows, we first discuss outstanding challenges in existing approaches for modeling CPS. Next, we describe ONA analytical procedures in detail and the rationale of ONA visualization design. Lastly, we demonstrate ONA using an example from a well-studied dataset documenting CPS in a context where the order of events is hypothesized to be meaningful. We conclude this paper with a discussion of contributions that ONA makes to Quantitative Ethnography (QE) research on CPS.

2   Background

2.1   Collaborative Problem Solving

Working in numerous domains involves groups of people collaboratively solve complex or ill-formed problems, CPS is increasingly emphasized in educational curricula and assessment frameworks [6]. In educational contexts, students' proficiency in CPS can be measured by the extent to which students respond to requests and initiate actions to advance the group goals [2]. In military contexts where tasks are often cognitively demanding and have high stakes, for example, intensive interactions are needed between team members to solve problems that might outpace the capabilities of any one individual [17]. Regardless of context, CPS is fundamentally *socio-cognitive* that both cognitive engagement and social interactions are needed to solve problems [8, 10, 18].

As a result, there are three key features that models of CPS need to account for: *interactivity*, *temporality*, and *interdependence* [18]. First, CPS is *interactive* because team members solve problems by interacting with each other rather than independently. Second, CPS has an important *temporal* dimension because events at any point in time are influenced by prior actions that are within some recent temporal context [11]. For example, when one team member asks a question, other team members are likely to respond soon after; and each response may address not only the original question but also any prior responses to it. Third, CPS is *interdependent* because the contributions of a given individual are related to and influenced by the contributions of others. For example, Clark [3] argues that information is added to the *common ground*, or the current state of a group's shared understanding, as individuals interact with each other, which in turn influences individuals' subsequent *responses* to the common ground. This directional relationship *from* the common ground *to* response indicates that the *order* in which events unfold in CPS may reveal important differences in individuals' contributions to the collaborative processes.

2.2   Existing Approaches to Modeling Collaborative Problem Solving

Currently, there exist different approaches that can be used to model CPS by accounting for interdependence, including the order of events. *Sequential* models and *temporal* models are two prevalent classes [19]. Figure 1 shows four common approaches that fall into these two classes. To illustrate the characteristics of the four approaches and how they differ from each other, considering the excerpt in Fig. 1 as an example, in which one commander and two coordinators who are on a navy ship are discussing whether a track's behavior is threatening. Each of them has a defined role to monitor ships and aircraft on radar, so that the team can collectively make an assessment as to whether its behavior is threatening.

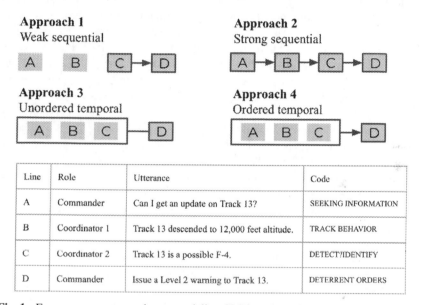

Fig. 1. Four common approaches to modeling CPS by accounting for the order of events.

In this excerpt, the Commander asks for an update on a track that is potentially threatening in line A and receives two relevant but different responses from two Coordinators in lines B and C. Coordinator 1 describes the track's behavior (a change in altitude that could signal preparation for an attack), and Coordinator 2 identifies that the track may be a fighter plane. Based on this information, the Commander decides to issue a warning in line D. That is, the commander's order in line D is a response to both Coordinators' contributions in lines B and C—and by extension, the commander's question in line A— which form the *common ground* for line D. Using this simplified example, we describe the affordances and limitations of the four main approaches to modeling collaborative interdependence.

Approach 1 represents sequential models that treat CPS processes as events that are weakly connected, such as Lag Sequential Analysis (LSA), where the sequential dependency is computed only between an event and its immediately preceding event. Such methods neglect the interdependent nature of collaboration and very limited temporal context is taken into account during modeling [4]. For example, the warning issued by Commander in line D is only considered as a response to its immediate precedent event line C in which Coordinator 2 identified what type of aircraft the track might be. In fact, the deterrent order issued in line D is because the track is likely a fighter plane (as indicated in line C) *and* its behavior is potentially threatening (as indicated in line B). Such conservative consideration of sequence undercounts the influence that Coordinator 1 has on the deterrent order.

Approach 2 is also a sequential method, but one that considers sequences of longer length. For example, Sequential Pattern Mining (SPM) is a common technique for the identification of frequent sequential patterns that emphasizes the specific local order of events. In SPM, every event is considered as a response to the immediately preceding event. This provides the most fine-grained information about the order of events. However, as Swiecki and colleagues [19] demonstrated, the micro-sequences that SPM produces are less effective predictors of collaborative performance than co-temporal models *even in contexts where order is hypothesized to matter*. In other words, SPM may overrepresent connections that are not meaningful. Although Approach 2 can count what is undercounted in Approach 1, i.e., the connection between A and B and between B and C, the example also shows that specific micro-sequences may introduce noise. For example, qualitative interpretation of the exchange in Fig. 1 would not change if the order of lines B and C were reversed, but SPM and other strong-sequential techniques will treat the sequences ABCD and ACBD as meaningfully different.

Approach 3 represents co-temporal methods, such as epistemic network analysis (ENA), that model the co-occurrence of Codes in common ground with Codes in the response [15]. ENA is sensitive to the order of events in the data, meaning changing the order of events changes which events are present in a given window, and thus changes the results of the model [19]. However, the order *from* common ground *to* response is not modeled in ENA. For example, an ENA model would not show that the warning the Commander issued in line D is a response to the common ground formed by lines A, B, and C; it would only show that there is a connection from D to each of A, B, and C. When the order of the connections is not modeled, the fact that the Commander issued a warning *after* gathering information from two Commanders can only be ascertained from qualitative triangulation. Consequently, it is difficult to compare how different Commanders might respond differently to similar situations.

In cases where the directionality of the connections from the common ground to response is hypothesized to be meaningful, techniques in Approach 4 can be applied. To our knowledge, the only extant technique that models CPS in this way is directed epistemic network analysis (dENA), a prototype technique presented at ICQE21 [5]. As Fig. 1 shows, the only difference between Approach 3 and Approach 4 is that the connection between common ground and response is unordered in Approach 3, and it is ordered in Approach 4. Adding such directionality makes it possible to model the influence of information *from* the common ground on individuals' response. For example, in line D where the Commander *responded with* DETERRENT ORDERS to the common ground formed by lines A, B, and C reveals important information about how the Commander's decision making is informed by his own question *and* the responses of the Coordinators. Compared to Approach 2 where ordered information is overcounted, and compared to Approaches 1 and 3 where ordered information is undercounted, Approach 4 is a relatively balanced approach to model CPS processes, especially in cases where the specific *local order* of collaborative discourse moves may be less important than their *local co-temporality*. For example, in ill-formed problem-solving scenarios where discussions do not strictly follow prescribed orders, such as in the example in Fig. 1, it may make little difference whether in a brief span of time the group talks about SEEKING INFORMATION, TRACK BEHAVIOR, and then DETECT/IDENTIFY, or any of the other possible ordering of those topics.

2.3 Remaining Challenges and Proposed Solution

As a proof of concept, dENA provided empirical evidence that besides modeling the *interactive, interdependent,* and *temporal* aspects of CPS, accounting for the *order of events co-temporally* can reveal additional insights about CPS that otherwise remain unknown in the model. Despite its thorough theoretical foundation, there are still two unsolved analytical challenges.

1. dENA does not support statistical comparison of networks. While visual comparison is supported by superimposing network graphs with isomorphic nodes to show graphical differences, there is no statistical method to test whether the differences between groups are significant. This severely limits the kinds of analyses that researchers can conduct.
2. dENA network spaces contain redundant information that negatively affects both the interpretability of the visualizations and model fit. Each unit of analysis is represented by a combination of two vectors: one representing what the unit responding *to*, the other representing responding *with*. These two vectors contain the same information because one is the transpose of the other. Including such redundant information in modeling leads to less-than-optimal models.

In the following section, we introduce ONA and explain how it addresses the challenges with existing unordered and ordered co-temporal models (ENA and dENA, respectively), and we demonstrate the technique by analyzing a well-studied dataset for which there are published findings on CPS for [5, 18, 19].

3 Methods: Ordered Network Analysis

3.1 Dataset

We analyzed discourse data collected from U.S. Navy air defense warfare teams engaging in training scenarios. Each team's goal was to detect and identify tracks with uncertain identities, then make an assessment as to the tracks' threatening level. Based on these assessments, teams decide to issue a warning or engage them in combat. Each team consisted of two commanders and four support roles. The teams were divided into two conditions with eight teams in each condition. The conditions differed regarding the technological support and training provided to the commanders on each team. Commanders in the experimental conditions had access to more advanced technologies and additional trainings compared to commanders in the control conditions.

The transcripts were segmented into lines corresponding to turns of talk, for a total of 12,027 lines. Our units of analysis were the individual team members across different training scenarios. In total, the analysis included 94 individuals. In light of the experimental design, we grouped individuals according to their experimental condition and their duties on the team: command or support. We focused the analysis on the 29 individuals who held command roles—16 in the experimental condition and 13 in the control—because the experiment was designed to affect their performance directly.

We analyzed the transcripts using the codes in Table 1, which were developed by [18] using a grounded approach. All codes were validated at a kappa threshold of 0.65 and a rho threshold of 0.05 using the nCoderR package [7].

Table 1. Qualitative codes, definitions, and examples

Code	Definition	Example
DETECT/IDENTIFY	Talk about radar detection of a track or the identification of a track, (e.g., vessel type)	NEW BEARING, BEARING 078 APQ120 CORRELATES TRACK 7036 POSSIBLE F-4
TRACK BEHAVIOR	Talk about kinematic data about a track or a track's location	TRACK NUMBER 7021 DROP IN ALTITUDE TO 18 THOUSAND FEET
SEEKING INFORMATION	Asking questions regarding track behavior, identification, or status	WE'VE UPGRADED THEM TO LEVEL 7 RIGHT?
DETERRENT ORDERS	Giving orders meant to warn or deter tracks	CONDUCT LEVEL 2 WARNING ON 7037
DEFENSIVE ORDERS	Giving orders to prepare defenses or engage hostile tracks	COVER 7016 WITH BIRDS

3.2 ONA Analytical Procedures

The ONA algorithm begins by accumulating connections for each unit of analysis using coded and segmented data. For each unit, the ONA algorithm uses a moving window to identify connections formed from a current line of data (e.g., turn of talk), or *response*, to the preceding lines within the window, or *common ground*. We chose a moving window length of five for this data based on prior analyses of the same dataset [16].

During connection accumulation, ONA accounts for the order in which the connections occur by constructing an *asymmetric adjacency matrix* for each unit: that is, the number of connections from code A to code B may be different than the number of connections from B to A.

This method was also implemented in dENA [5], however, in dENA, this single asymmetric adjacency matrix is copied and transposed, such that each unit of analysis is thus represented by two accumulated asymmetric adjacency matrices: one representing its ground connections, i.e., what the unit *responded to*; the other representing its response connections, i.e., what the unit *responded with*.

In ONA, each unit is represented by the original asymmetric adjacency matrix, which contains the same information as the two matrices used in dENA, but represents that information in a more parsimonious fashion. ONA transforms this single matrix into a single high dimensional *asymmetric adjacency vector*. Each unit is thus represented by a single high dimensional vector (as opposed to two high-dimensional vectors in dENA), which results in a more succinct network space and allows flexibility in dimensional reduction and statistical comparison, as described below.

The asymmetric adjacency vectors for all units are then normalized and centered and the algorithm performs a dimensional reduction. ONA currently implements *singular value decomposition* (SVD) and a *means rotation* (MR)[1] similar to the dimensional reductions in ENA.[2] In contrast, in dENA, some dimensional reductions (including SVD and MR) produce degenerate solutions when applied to the full set of high-dimensional vectors because each unit is represented by two vectors, one of which is the transpose of the other.[3] As a result, in dENA users had to choose to rotate by either the ground vectors or response vectors when applying SVD. To our knowledge, dENA has not yet provided users with recommendations on when to choose ground or response matrices to apply SVD or other dimensional reductions. Moreover, as a result of this mathematical limitation, dENA models suffer from low goodness-of-fit.

In contrast, by representing each unit's directed connections with a single vector, the dimensional reductions in ONA produce models with higher goodness-of-fit that are easier to interpret.

The dimensional reduction process results in an ONA score for each unit of analysis in the lower-dimensional space. The ONA scores are visualized by plotting them in the lower dimensional space resulting from the dimensional reduction. For each unit, its ONA score is represented as a point in the network space as shown in Fig. 2. Unlike the paired vectors (ground and response) used to represent units in dENA, the ONA scores are single points and thus can be used to conduct statistical tests or as predictors in regression models.

The ONA algorithm co-registers units' directed network graphs and projected points in the low-dimensional space.[4] As a result, the network graph visualizations meaningfully reflect the mathematical properties of the projected points that represent each network in the projected space. For each unit, its graph shows the strength and directionality

---

[1] MR is a dimensional reduction that can be applied when the units are divided into two discrete groups. The resulting space highlights the differences between groups (if any) by constructing a dimensional reduction that places the means of the groups as close as possible to the x-axis of the space. MR is frequently used in ENA analyses [1].

[2] Because each unit is represented by a single, high-dimensional adjacency vector, ONA can use any dimensional reduction technique that can be used with ENA.

[3] The mathematical proof that including vectors and their transpose cause degenerate solutions under SVD and other rotations is beyond the scope of this paper; however, we are happy to provide it upon request.

[4] The mathematical details of co-registration are beyond the scope of this paper and can be found in the work of Bowman et al. [1].

of the connections it made. Network nodes in ONA are positioned in the space using the same optimization routine used in ENA [1]: the algorithm minimizes the distance between the ONA scores and the centroids of the corresponding networks. As a result, the ONA metric space can be interpreted based on the locations of the nodes. Units with ONA points on the right side of the space have more frequent connections between the codes on the right side of the space. Similarly, units with points on the left have more frequent connections between the codes on the left side of the space.

3.3   ONA Visualization Design

Building on the graphic design principles used in ENA visualizations [20], in ONA, the node size is proportional to the number of occurrences of that code as a *response* to other codes in the data, with larger nodes indicating more responses. The color and saturation of the circle within each node is proportional to the number of *self-connections* for that code: that is, when a code appears in both the response and ground of a given window. Colored circles that are larger and more saturated reflect codes with more frequent self-connections. For example, Fig. 2 suggests that roughly 40% responses made with code A were responding to code A.

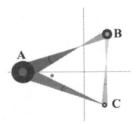

Fig. 2. Sample unit's ONA network. The overall size of the nodes represents the relative response strength with each code. The red dot in the middle of code A represents self-connections. Thicker and more saturated triangles represent stronger connections. The chevrons on the triangles indicate the order from common ground to response. The network is summarized by an ONA score, shown as a point. (Color figure online)

The directed connections in ONA are represented by edges between nodes, visualizing as a pair of triangles. Note that unlike most ordered network visualizations, which use arrows or spearheads to indicate directionality, ONA uses a "broadcast" model, where the source of a connection (ground) is placed at the apex of the triangle and the destination of a connection (response) is placed at its base. To facilitate interpretation, the dark chevrons place inside the triangles indicates the directionality of the connection from ground to response.

For example, in Fig. 2, between codes A and B, the thicker and more saturated triangle with a chevron on it represents the unit's *response with* code A to code B. In other words, code B is in the common ground that code A is a response to. Similarly, the thinner and less saturated triangle between A and B represents the unit's *response with* code A to code B. The dark chevron pointing towards A from B helps viewers identify that A is more often a response to B than the other way around. Between any pair of codes, if there is a bidirectional connection, the chevron only appears on the side with stronger connections. This helps viewers differentiate heavier edges in cases such as between codes B and C, where the connection strengths from both directions are similar. When the connection strengths are identical between two codes, the chevron will appear on both edges.

Taken together, ONA visualizations emphasize what the units of analysis *respond with*, rather than what they respond to. In other words, ONA visually emphasizes the units of analysis' active choice of reactions to what already happened in the common ground. To achieve such visual emphasis, we make sure that all the design elements (e.g., nodes, edges) and their attributes (e.g., size, saturation) in the visualizations consistently emphasize response strength. This is achieved by 1) using node size to represent the relative frequency of a code being present in a *response*, 2) using edge thickness and saturation to represent the relative frequency of a code being a *response* to the code it is connected to, and 3) using the chevron to represent the order of information flow from ground *to response*.

4 Results

In this section, we present the results of applying ONA to analyze the U.S. Navy air defense warfare teams discourse data that there are published findings for [5, 18, 19]. We compare ONA results against qualitative analysis results and ENA results, we found that ONA was able to capture qualitative differences between groups that were not shown in ENA model.

4.1 Qualitative Results

Qualitative analysis revealed both similarities and differences of the teams' CPS activities in the control and experimental conditions. In both conditions, teams were highly interactive, and individuals responded to and built upon the contributions of others as they pass information, make decisions, and take actions. However, commanders in the control and experimental conditions contributed to their teams in different ways. Specifically, in the experimental condition, since commanders in this condition had access to more advanced support system and were trained with additional curriculum materials, they did not need to acquire information verbally or hold it in their memory, so they were able to focus less on processing the tactical situation and more on contributing to and acting on that situation, such as issuing warnings in time. In contrast, commanders in the control condition, who only had access to standard technology support, often needed to clarify the tactical situation by asking questions. Consequently, they were often less able to take timely and appropriate actions toward tracks due to the increased burden of information management.

The following two excerpts illustrate such differences. The first excerpt is from a conversation between commanders and support roles from the control condition.

Line	Speaker	Utterance	Code
6241	CO	TAO CO, LET'S GO AHEAD AND ISSUE A THREAT LEVEL FOR THE PUMAS 13, 14, 15	DETECT IDENTIFY
6242	EWS	TAO, EW TRACK 012 IDENTIFIED AS F-4	DETECT IDENTIFY
6243	TAO	LEVEL 4, AYE	
6244	TAO	SAY AGAIN TRACK NUMBER F-4?	SEEKING INFORMATION
6245	EWS	14. CORRECTION 12, BEARING 094	TRACK BEHAVIOR
6246	TAO	TAO, AYE	

In line 6241, the CO asks the TAO to DETECT IDENTIFY the threat posed by the Puma helicopters. The TAO (line 6243) classifies the tracks as "level 4" threats, meaning that they are potentially hostile tracks that the team should monitor. Notice, however, between when the CO asks for a threat assessment and the TAO replies, the EWS (line 6242) reports another contact identified as an F-4 jet. The TAO then has to SEEKING INFORMATION by asking the EWS (line 6244) to repeat the information because they were busy making the threat assessment. The EWS repeats the track number of the F-4 and also adds additional information about TRACK BEHAVIOR (line 6245). The TAO acknowledges this message in line 6246.

As this excerpt shows, the members of this team were able to quickly distinguish similar sounding information (e.g., 14, level 4, F-4, 94). However, the commander (i.e., TAO) were often receiving new input while they were communicating decisions based on previous information. This means that they frequently had to request clarification by SEEKING INFORMATION from supporting members of the team to maintain an understanding of the tactical situation.

The next excerpt is from a conversation between commanders and support roles from the experimental condition. Typically, tracks are detected and reported by the supporting members of the team such as in the control condition, but the availability of the decision support system enabled the commander in the experimental condition to access this information directly, as the following excerpt illustrates.

Line	Speaker	Utterance	Code
9773	CO	OK 07 IS MOVING TOWARDS US SO WE'VE GOT TO COVER WITH GUNS OR BULLDOGS ON 07	TRACK BEHAVIOR DEFENSIVE ORDERS
9774	EWS	NEGATIVE	
9775	TAO	TIC GO OUT WITH LEVEL ONE QUERY ON 07 AND COVER WITH BULLDOGS	DEFENSIVE ORDERS DETERRENT ORDERS

The CO reports the detection of track 7, letting the team know its TRACK BEHAVIOR (line 9733). In the same turn of talk, the CO issues DEFENSIVE ORDERS to "cover with guns or bulldogs [anti-ship missiles] on 07". After adding an order to issue a level 1 warning to the track, the TAO passes the CO's orders to the TIC (line 9775). Thus, commanders on this team are reacting to the developing tactical situation by contributing new information about the TRACK BEHAVIOR (line 9733) and immediately responding to it with early actions from the detect-engage sequence: warning the track and covering it with weapons (lines 9733 and 97753).

As this excerpt shows, commanders in the experimental condition did not only contribute to their teams' understanding of the emerging tactical situation by passing information about tracks, also responded to these situations in a timely manner with appropriate decisions and actions. Although there were multiple simultaneous conversations that team members were participating it, but unlike the previous example, this did not lead to confusion because the commanders were not getting critical information only from the team.

4.2 ONA Results

Individual Unit Network. We first compared the individual network of one commander from the control condition (red, top) and another commander from the experimental condition (blue, bottom) as shown in Fig. 3.

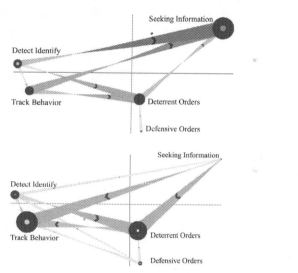

Fig. 3. Individual unit network for a commander from the control condition (red, top), and another commander from the experimental condition (blue, bottom). (Color figure online)

Both networks have strong connections between SEEKING INFORMATION and TRACK BEHAVIOR, as indicated by the relatively thicker and darker edges. However, ONA is able to show that the difference between how the two commanders made connections between TRACK BEHAVIOR and SEEKING INFORMATION was the *order* of the connections rather than their relative frequency. Such directional difference cannot be shown using ENA where the order of events is not accounted for. As the chevron indicates, in the network of the commander from the control condition, SEEKING INFORMATION is more commonly a response to TRACK BEHAVIOR. In the network of the commander in the experimental condition, TRACK BEHAVIOR is more commonly a response to SEEKING

INFORMATION. This difference in order is consistent with the qualitative findings. In the experimental condition, commanders were able to contribute to their teams' understanding of the emerging tactical situation by passing information about tracks supplied by the technological support system to which they had access to. Therefore, they were able to respond with TRACK BEHAVIOR when other team members SEEKING INFORMATION. In the control condition, due to the lack of support from the advanced technologies, SEEK-ING INFORMATION was the behavior commanders often initiated to ask for clarifications about TRACK BEHAVIOR.

Additionally, in the network for the commander in the experimental condition, there are two strong connections pointing towards DETERRENT ORDERS, one is from SEEKING INFORMATION, the other is from DETECT IDENTIFY. This means that orders to prepare defenses or engage hostile tracks are often issued *after* seeking information. In other words, the commander from the experimental condition was better able to use information to guide productive action, such as issuing orders, than the commander from the control condition.

Taken together, the SEEKING INFORMATION behavior in the experimental condition served as a common ground for commanders to respond to with productive actions such as issuing warnings through DEFENSIVE ORDERS and DETERRENT ORDERS. However, in the control condition, SEEKING INFORMATION was the behavior commanders initiated as a response to ask clarification questions about TRACK BEHAVIOR. In summary, compared to commanders in the control conditions, commanders in the experimental condition were thus better able to manage complex situations, ensuring that potentially hostile tracks were not lost from the tactical picture.

Group Comparison. Besides individual unit networks, we also compared the two conditions' aggregated mean ONA networks, as shown in Fig. 4 left. To illustrate the insights that ONA revealed about the group differences that otherwise remain unknown in unordered models such as ENA, we included an ENA network comparing the same groups, as shown in Fig. 4 right.

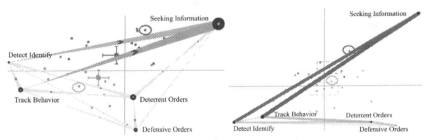

Fig. 4. Difference networks showing the most salient differences between the commanders in the control condition (red) and experimental condition (blue). Each edge is color-coded to indicate which of the two networks contains the stronger connection. Points represent ONA points (left) and ENA points (right), which summarize an individual unit network as a single point in the projection space. For example, the two individual networks shown in Fig. 3 are annotated in the network space in Fig. 4 using one red circle and one blue circle. (Color figure online)

Visual Comparison. By investigating ONA and ENA networks visually, we found that ONA contributed new insights to our interpretation of this dataset from two perspectives. First, for connections that have similar strength but differ in order, ONA preserved such directed connections while ENA counteracted it.

For example, in the ENA network, the connection between SEEKING INFORMATION and DETERRENT ORDERS is very weak, almost nonexistent. This means that there is very little or no difference in terms of how frequent those two codes co-occurred in the control and experimental conditions. However, recall that the qualitative results show that commanders in the control condition often had to request clarification by SEEKING INFORMATION from supporting members of the team to maintain an understanding of the tactical situation. In contrast, commanders in the experimental condition often responded to team members' SEEKING INFORMATION request in a timely manner with productive actions such as DETERRENT ORDERS. In other words, the differences in terms of how the two conditions made connections with SEEKING INFORMATION and DETERRENT ORDERS is not frequency, but *order*. ONA was able to capture such differences, representing by the chevron pointing from DETERRENT ORDERS to SEEKING INFORMATION.

Second, the *common ground* and *response* metaphor that ONA has helped differentiate the role of the same code in different connections. For example, ENA network shows that TRACK BEHAVIOR co-occurred frequently with SEEKING INFORMATION in the control group, as indicated by the corresponding red edge; and co-occurred frequently with DETERRENT ORDERS in the experimental group, as indicated by the corresponding blue edge. ONA makes it clear that the role TRACK BEHAVIOR acted in the two conditions is different. In the control condition, TRACK BEHAVIOR acted as the *common ground* for SEEKING INFORMATION, as indicated by the chevron pointing from TRACK BEHAVIOR to SEEKING INFORMATION. This means that *after* being shared with information about TRACK BEHAVIOR, commanders in this group often needed to SEEKING additional INFORMATION from other members. On the other hand, in the experimental condition, TRACK BEHAVIOR acted as a *response* to DETERRENT ORDERS. This means that *after* warnings being issued through DETERRENT ORDERS, TRACK BEHAVIOR information is presented to commanders to ensure that potentially hostile tracks were not lost from the tactical picture. The different role that TRACK BEHAVIOR has can be used as one of the aspects to characterize networks of different conditions.

Statistical Comparison. Since each unit's network is summarized as an ONA point in the projection space, we can compare the distribution of the projected ONA points for commanders in the control and experimental condition. Since most points in red locate on the upper right side, the points in blue locate on the left lower side of the space, we assume that the two groups are different with respect to their positions on both the first and second dimension. To test whether these differences were statistically significant, we conducted two sample t test between distributions of the projected points in ONA space for commanders in the two conditions. We found a significant difference between the experimental group (mean = -0.24, SD = 0.28) at the alpha = 0.05 level from the control (mean = 0.07, SD = 0.31) on the first dimension, as well as a significant difference between the control (mean = 0.24, SD = 0.08) and experimental (mean = -0.08, SD = 0.16) point distributions on the second dimension. However, in ENA, significant difference was only found on the second dimension between the control (mean = 0.32, SD = 0.17) and the experimental (mean = −0.05, SD = 0.20), with a smaller effective size compared to ONA (Cohen's d = 2.67 in ONA, Cohen's d = 1.69 in ENA).

Taken together, ONA was not only able to visually represent network differences between groups, but also allow researchers to make statistical claims about such differences. Similar comparison had also been conducted in the previous dENA study using the same dataset visually by investigating the difference network [5]. However, dENA was not able to further test if such differences observed visually are statistically different. Besides the test we demonstrated above, researchers can also conduct other statistical analysis such as using ONA points as predictors in regression analysis.

5   Discussion

In this study, we presented *Ordered Network Analysis* as a solution to model CPS by accounting for not only the interactive, interdependent, and temporal nature of collaborations, but also the order of events unfolding over time in CPS processes. We demonstrated the three major analytical and visual affordances of ONA. First, ONA can model both what units of analysis *respond with* and what they *respond to* as they interact with others in the group. Second, ONA supports the comparison of network models at both the individual unit level and the aggregated group level. This allows researchers to make statistical claims about how different individuals or groups respond to certain common ground differently. Third, through the co-registration process and the intentional visual design, ONA network visualizations are not only mathematically consistent with its summary statistics, but also intuitive to read.

5.1   Comparison of Methods

To extend the discussion in Sect. 2.2 where we reviewed extant CPS modeling approaches, in Table 2. We compare three QE approaches (i.e., ENA, dENA, ONA) by comparing their affordances. In summary, given its analytical and visual advancements, we suggest that ONA is preferable to dENA in all cases. When modeling weak sequential or temporally ordered data, we suggest that ONA should be used instead of ENA or other sequential methods such as SPM. For readers to make methodological choices for their CPS modeling, Table 2 serves as a brief summary rather than a meticulous description of the three approaches. We recommend that readers should refer to additional literature such as [1, 5, 14, 15] for more in-depth description.

Table 2. Different affordances of ENA, dENA, and ONA

Affordances	ENA	dENA	ONA
Connection matrix	Symmetrical	Asymmetrical	Asymmetrical
Summary statistics	ENA points	Vectors	ONA points
Rotations	Singular Value Decomposition, Means Rotation, hENA[5]	Singular Value Decomposition	Singular Value Decomposition, Means Rotation hENA
Node positions	Deterministic	Deterministic	Deterministic
Comparison of networks	Statistical, visual	Visual	Statistical, visual
Goodness of fit	High	Moderate	High
Best for	Temporal unordered data	ONA is preferrable to dENA in all cases	Weak sequential or temporal ordered data

5.2   Limitations and Conclusions

Although the ONA analysis in this study was only conducted using a single dataset, the data we used was only meant to provide an example of how ONA can model CPS by accounting for the order of events. Given its analytical and visual flexibility, we argue that ONA can not only be applied to model CPS processes, but also broadly in any research questions in situations where patterns of directed associations in data are hypothesized to be meaningful. In future work, we are interested in applying ONA in QE research in different domains.

Acknowledgement. This work was funded in part by the National Science Foundation (DRL-1661036, DRL-1713110), the Wisconsin Alumni Research Foundation, and the Office of the Vice Chancellor for Research and Graduate Education at the University of Wisconsin-Madison. The opinions, findings, and conclusions do not reflect the views of the funding agencies, cooperating institutions, or other individuals.

References

1. Bowman, D., et al.: The mathematical foundations of epistemic network analysis. In: Ruis, A.R., Lee, S.B. (eds.) ICQE 2021. CCIS, vol. 1312, pp. 91–105. Springer, Cham (2021). https://doi.org/10.1007/978-3-030-67788-6_7

---

[5] hENA, or Hierarchical Epistemic Network Analysis, is an extension to ENA that enables researchers to model nested effects of multiple grouping variables rather than one grouping variable using means rotation. Detailed description of hENA can be found in [13].

2. C. Graesser, A., Foltz, P.W., Rosen, Y., Shaffer, D.W., Forsyth, C., Germany, M.-L.: Challenges of assessing collaborative problem solving. In: Care, E., Griffin, P., Wilson, M. (eds.) Assessment and Teaching of 21st Century Skills. EAIA, pp. 75–91. Springer, Cham (2018). https://doi.org/10.1007/978-3-319-65368-6_5

3. Clark, H.H.: Using Language. Cambridge University Press, Cambridge (1996)

4. Csanadi, A., Eagan, B., Kollar, I., Shaffer, D.W., Fischer, F.: When coding-and-counting is not enough: using epistemic network analysis (ENA) to analyze verbal data in CSCL research. Int. J. Comput.-Support. Collab. Learn. 13(4), 419–438 (2018). https://doi.org/10.1007/s11412-018-9292-z

5. Fogel, A., et al.: Directed epistemic network analysis. In: Ruis, A.R., Lee, S.B. (eds.) ICQE 2021. CCIS, vol. 1312, pp. 122–136. Springer, Cham (2021). https://doi.org/10.1007/978-3-030-67788-6_9

6. Graesser, A.C., et al.: Advancing the science of collaborative problem solving. Psychol. Sci. Public Interest 19(2), 59–92 (2018)

7. Marquart, C.L., et al.: ncodeR: Techniques for Automated Classifiers (2018)

8. Miyake, N., Kirschner, P.A.: The social and interactive dimensions of collaborative learning. In: Sawyer, R.K. (ed.) The Cambridge Handbook of the Learning Sciences, pp. 418–438. Cambridge University Press, Cambridge (2014)

9. Roschelle, J., Teasley, S.D.: The construction of shared knowledge in collaborative problem solving. In: O'Malley, C. (ed.) Computer Supported Collaborative Learning, pp. 69–97. Springer, Heidelberg (1995). https://doi.org/10.1007/978-3-642-85098-1_5

10. Rosen, Y.: Computer-based assessment of collaborative problem solving: exploring the feasibility of human-to-agent approach. Int. J. Artif. Intell. Educ. 25(3), 380–406 (2015). https://doi.org/10.1007/s40593-015-0042-3

11. Ruis, A., et al.: Finding Common Ground: A Method for Measuring Recent Temporal Context in Analyses of Complex, Collaborative Thinking (2019)

12. San Martín-Rodríguez, L., et al.: The determinants of successful collaboration: a review of theoretical and empirical studies. J. Interprof. Care 19, 132–147 (2005)

13. Shaffer, D.: Hierarchical Epistemic Network Analysis (2021)

14. Shaffer, D.W., et al.: A tutorial on epistemic network analysis: analyzing the structure of connections in cognitive, social, and interaction data. J. Learn. Anal. 3(3), 9–45 (2016). https://doi.org/10.18608/jla.2016.33.3

15. Shaffer, D.W., et al.: Epistemic Network analysis: a worked example of theory-based learning analytics. In: Columbia University, USA et al. (eds.) Handbook of Learning Analytics, pp. 175–187. Society for Learning Analytics Research (SoLAR) (2017). https://doi.org/10.18608/hla17.015

16. Siebert-Evenstone, A.L., et al.: In search of conversational grain size: modeling semantic structure using moving stanza windows. J. Learn. Anal. 4(3), 123–139 (2017)

17. Smith, C.A.P., et al.: Decision support for air warfare: setection of deceptive threats. Group Decis. Negot. 13(2), 129–148 (2004)

18. Swiecki, Z., et al.: Assessing individual contributions to collaborative problem solving: a network analysis approach. Comput. Hum. Behav. 104, 105876 (2020)

19. Swiecki, Z., et al.: Does Order Matter? Investigating Sequential and Cotemporal Models of Collaboration, vol. 8 (2019)

20. Tan, Y., et al.: Epistemic network analysis visualization. In: Wasson, B., Zörgő, S. (eds.) Advances in Quantitative Ethnography, pp. 129–143 Springer International Publishing, Cham (2022). https://doi.org/10.1007/978-3-030-93859-8_9

Creating and Discussing Discourse Networks with Research Participants: What Can We Learn?

Hazel Vega(⊠)

Clemson University, Clemson, SC, USA
hvegaqu@clemson.edu

Abstract. In this paper, I argue that elements of Epistemic Network Analysis (ENA), a quantitative ethnography tool, can be adapted to facilitate co-construction of knowledge in an interview setting. ENA needs to be further explored in collaborative contexts with researchers and participants to generate nuanced examinations of its affordances and limitations. To respond to this challenge and continue the efforts of participatory QE, in this paper, I explain the outcomes of joint researcher-participant discussions of constructed discourse networks using ENA. For these discussions, I developed a simple tool using Google Slides, which I describe in detail. This tool allowed research participants and researcher to come together and delve into the themes and puzzles emerging from the creation and discussion of the networks. The outcomes of these network discussions shed light on the intricacies of joint cognition in discourse when data visualizations such as ENA are used to create a reflective and collaborative space for researchers and participants.

Keywords: Participatory QE · Constructionism · ENA networks · discussion · teacher identity

1 Introduction

As equitable researcher-participant relationships are sought and increasingly approached in participatory research [1], more attention is still needed to the development of the specific methods and tools required for such collaborative practices [2, 3]. Participatory research acknowledges the diversity of perspectives necessary for the co-construction of knowledge built on and for heterogeneity of epistemologies. Such an approach supports a view of research that works hand-in-hand with participants to create solutions to problems and issues in their communities, contexts, or professions [4–6]. In quantitative ethnography (QE), recent efforts have been steered in the direction of participatory research. Some community members have signaled their interest in extending QE through the formation of a SIG named participatory QE (PQE), publications [7–9], and scholarly discussions. This interest in PQE has raised questions about the affordances of already existing tools within QE, such as Epistemic Network Analysis (ENA) for collaborative sense-making.

C. Damşa and A. Barany (Eds.): ICQE 2022, CCIS 1785, pp. 117–131, 2023.
https://doi.org/10.1007/978-3-031-31726-2_9

In this paper, I argue that elements of ENA can be adapted to facilitate co-construction of knowledge in an interview setting. ENA creates visualizations of discourse through networks from qualitative data [10]. In QE, the ENA discourse networks have started to expand their functionality to include interactions between researchers and participants [8, 9]. However, as a rich tool, ENA still needs to be further explored in collaborative contexts with researchers and participants to generate nuanced examinations of its affordances and limitations. To respond to this challenge and continue the efforts of PQE, in this paper, I explain the reflections on outcomes of joint researcher-participant discussions of constructed discourse networks using ENA with teachers. These outcomes shed light on the intricacies of joint cognition in discourse when a data visualization such as ENA is used to create a reflective and collaborative space for researchers and participants in teaching contexts.

2 Theory

2.1 Discursive Constructionism

In this paper, I draw from the theory of discursive constructionism (DC) [11]. DC is grounded on the principles of constructionism [12], centering on the affordances for construction for knowledge building and reality-shaping. As part of knowledge construction, discourse is not fixed and depends on the multiple communicative resources individuals decide to use. As conceptualized by Tileagă and Stokoe [3, p. 10], discourse is "an action-oriented, world-building resource, rather than a tool of transmission and straightforward communication from one mind to another." Thus, DC focuses on how discourse and construction work together in interaction to achieve joint understandings of the world. According to Potter and Hepburn [11, p. 275], DC studies a world of descriptions, claims, reports, allegations, and assertions as parts of human practices, and it works to keep these as the central topic of research rather than trying to move beyond them to the objects or events that seem to be the topic of such discourse.

Furthermore, discourse can be constructed and constrictive [11]. It is constructed in the sense that it is made up of a set of communicative elements, from the smallest linguistic and literal units, such as words and grammar structures to broader and figurative resources, such as metaphors and interpretations. The constrictive dimension of discourse is constituted by its properties "stabilize versions of the world, of actions and events, of mental life and furniture" [11, p. 277]. Discourse makes action and phenomena recognizable in particular contexts and temporalities.

In the context of research interviews in which experiences and narrations are discussed, DC approaches the content and style of discourse as a construction of the experiences themselves through the invocation of the people, settings, time, and events [14]. As such, experiences and stories collected via interviews are discursive constructions in which interlocutors connect and uncover sociocultural and historical aspects of their world, identity, and roles [15]. This perspective recognizes "human interaction as collaboratively built, unfolding moment-by-moment and over time" [14, p. 3–4]. In this paper, DC helps to conceptualize researcher-participant interactions in interviews as spaces for co-construction of knowledge, keeping the centrality on human practices of interaction constituting joint understandings and explorations.

2.2 Teacher Learning and Data Visualizations

Teacher inquiry comprises research practices teachers employ to examine their instruction and ultimately improve their professional expertise [16, 17]. While more traditional alternatives to conduct teacher inquiry primarily relied on qualitative research, student artifacts, and observations, more recent developments in the field of learning analytics integrate student and teacher data visualizations [16]. A data-informed approach to teacher learning enables teachers to use datasets of classroom activity in technology-rich environments to gain retrospective insights of teaching and learning effectiveness [17]. However, these data-driven initiatives are scarce and need more robust support for teacher reflection [17]. Human-Centered Learning Analytics [18] is an emergent perspective with a participatory dimensions, aiming to involve stakeholders, like teachers, in the design of learning analytics tools. The attribute of human-centeredness ensures that designers and stakeholders collaboratively shape tools and systems that will influence learning and teaching [18]. Both, the potential of data-informed approaches and the human-centered attribute bring insights into how ENA data visualizations can be further developed fostering collaboration among designers, researchers, and participants. Nonetheless, the reach of these alternatives is not clear for pre-service teachers who are not yet in a classroom or for self-reported data, which embeds tacit beliefs and values. To this end, this paper argues that constructing data visualizations with teachers can be a critical tool for co-construction of knowledge helping with teacher reflection and the advancement of PQE.

3 Background: Information About the Research

To illustrate the outcomes of joint discussion of discourse networks, I use data from my dissertation, a narrative inquiry study [19] based predominantly on interview data. This research aims to examine the professional identity of English as a foreign language teachers in Costa Rica. Specifically, the study seeks to analyze the teacher identity tensions related to the English language and teaching. Tensions refer to teachers' reactions, feelings, and perspectives when who they are does not meet their own expectations or those of others. These tensions were explored through participants' narrative accounts in interviews. I used Seidman's [20] three-interview framework, in which interviews move from exploration to analysis of lived experiences. Interviews lasted from 60 to 120 min. They were audio recorded and transcribed manually and via an automated service. In this paper, I drew from interview 3 with one of the participants and researcher's analytical memos. Interview 3 was chosen because it was when experiences and perspectives discussed in previous interviews were revisited and analyzed. During this interview, I used a tool I developed to construct discourse networks with some ENA features. The purpose of developing and using this tool with participants was to create our own networks based on our understandings of previous discussion. Participants and researcher brought their individual network to the interview to support their reflection and interaction.

4 Description of the Tool to Construct Discourse Networks

In this section, I describe the tool and the procedures used with participants to create and discuss discourse networks.

4.1 Tool

To construct a network resembling the visualization of an ENA model, I opted for a practical tool participants could use with ease and minimal time investment. Through discussions with my dissertation advisor, we came up with the idea that a Google slide would provide an appropriate working space. We looked at the tool feasibility in terms of the elements of ENA we wanted to keep in our design. It was considered important to keep (1) the nodes and their size to identify possible key themes or codes and (2) the lines and their thickness to explore the connections among themes and their strength or importance for the network's creator. In the Google slide, I added lines of different thickness, dots of different sizes, and labels to name the themes. Under each of this, there are multiple copies so that they can be dragged and placed in the blank area (Fig. 1).

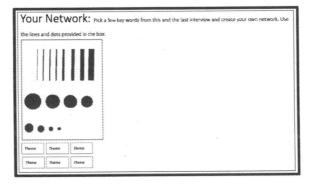

Fig. 1. Google slide to construct discourse networks

4.2 Procedure

I followed the steps and procedures below to use the Google slide tool with participants.

1. I introduced the tool to the participants at the end of interview two. This way, we would individually create our network and bring it to the third interview. I negotiated with the participants the time needed to complete this task and whether they wanted to take time from the following interview to work on their network. The purpose was to offer them sufficient time and adjust the procedure to their availability.
2. I chose a familiar topic for the participants and constructed a network to show them. I decided to create a network about their country, Costa Rica. To scaffold this procedure and reduce the cognitive load of the ENA elements complexity, I deconstructed the network, and showed it to the participants step-by-step in a series of slides. I designed the following steps, as shown in Figs. 2, 3, and 4.

   a. I told participants that we would see the results of a fictitious survey about Costa Rica in a different way to what they may have been accustomed. The survey was about what tourists thought about Costa Rica. First, using the slide on the left in Fig. 2, I asked them to say what they thought tourists said about each of the themes presented in the interview. Then, I said that we would create a visualization of the results, and the first element were dots (nodes). With the slide on the right, I asked them to look at the sizes, which meant that they were more or less important in the results.

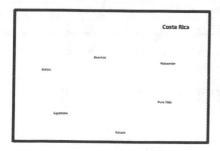 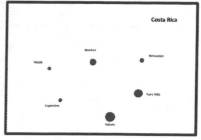

Fig. 2. Google Slides for representing themes and nodes in discourse networks.

b. In the next step, I introduced the element of the lines, considering their thickness and their connection to other nodes. Thus, I explained what a thicker or thinner line meant using the left slide in Fig. 3. Also, I asked participants what they thought about connections and showed them examples of fake responses associated with two of the nodes, one connection at a time (right slide).

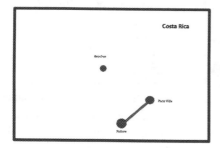 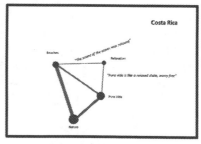

Fig. 3. Google Slides for representing lines and connections in discourse networks.

c. I continued showing the rest of the network and their connections until forming the whole network (left slide, Fig. 4). For the slide on the right, I eliminated the quotes used to illustrate the connections and highlighted a few words in a different color and asked participants to provide an idea of the story that the whole network told considering the elements reviewed. I also provided my interpretation. With this, I closed the network review and communicated to the participants that we were both going to construct networks using the Google Slides tool.

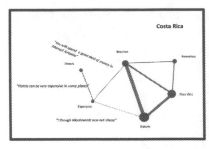 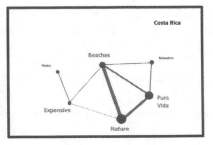

Fig. 4. Google Slides for illustrating the discourse networks and making interpretations.

5   Reflections on the Outcomes from the Joint Discussion of Discourse Networks

In this section, I provide reflections on the outcomes of the joint researcher-participant discussion of created discourse networks to co-construct understandings of the phenomenon under study. Namely, these outcomes are (1) constructing concept understandings, (2) giving meaning to the size of the nodes, and (3) making sense of connections. Before digging into the outcomes, I present a description of the participants that will help to contextualize this section.

5.1   A Note About the Participant

The research participant, Melissa, developed an interest in the English language early in her life, which later influenced her professional choice of becoming an English teacher. In her high school and pre-service years, Melissa kept a desire to approximate an ideal native English speaker. She developed a lack of confidence in her English proficiency (linguistic insecurity) when despite her efforts to improve, she perceived her level as inferior to that of a native speaker. As a novice teacher, Melissa kept a need to improve her English, but her interests and goals changed. She is beginning to understand that subjugating her identity to an ideology that privileges the native speaker was unrealistic. This shift has emerged as she focused on teaching and serving her students rather than attaining a perfect accent or being error-free. Her identity tensions have moved from giving center stage to native speakerism to focusing on ways to improve her language assessment methods.

5.2   Constructing Concept Understandings

When I shared my network with Melissa, she asked me about the word *tensions*; she wanted to know what I meant by that and why I had not connected to any dots, as shown in Fig. 5.

I explained that tensions in identity manifest in reactions, feelings, and thoughts when gaps between what teachers are or have and what they want or what is expected from them. This definition came from the literature on language teacher identity. To address her question about why I had placed the word tensions at the top and separate from the network, I said the following.

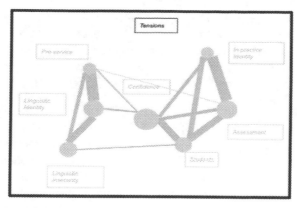

Fig. 5. Researcher's discourse network showing the word tensions at the top.

*[...] it's sort of embedded. So that's why I didn't want to put it in, like part of the network. Because I didn't know how to do it. But for me, that's like a very **general theme**, right? [...] **I haven't asked so much about the positive things** because my interest as a researcher is to see what are those tensions, what can do to solve those tensions for you, in the future for you and other teachers.*

When constructing the network, I made a conscious decision to include the word tension because it was central to the research. Since it was this *"general theme"*, I felt it connected to everything and did not know how to integrate it into the network. Despite this uncertainty, I included the word hoping that it would spark some discussion, and it did. Melissa's question brought to the front what we had been discussing throughout all the interviews, but this time, we had her personal experiences that we could refer to move past a theoretical concept. As a researcher, I debated whether to use this word with my participants because I thought that it would have a negative connotation. In my answer, I was still hesitant and said, *"I haven't asked about the positive things"*. This meant that I predominantly focused on experiences in which participants had struggled, and as a researcher, I knew there was so much more than hardship in their histories, but I was aware that my interest lied in the tensions. My uncertainty derived from avoiding that my research affected participants because of the constant revisitation of their challenges, so I did not know how to communicate this to them, and particularly, I did not know how to create a common understanding of such an overarching concept in my research. However, Melissa's question and my decision to include *tensions* in the network were an entry point for us to bring together our researcher and participant perspectives.

Following my answer, Melissa shared what she thought about *tensions*. Being this the third interview, she looked back at the experiences discussed that were tensions for her and provided the reflection below.

*[...] at the beginning, this thing of thing of tensions, [...], I saw it, like having maybe I don't want to say negative, but like, this sense, like **something bad is happening** [...]. But now that I'm thinking about it,**tensions don't have to be something negative. Maybe it's also something that relates to [...] situations***

*that [...] make you improve in life, because if you don't have tensions, you would not, like be a better teacher, be a better English speaker [...] So in a way I see tensions as something **necessary** maybe to be better in many different ways. Now it makes sense for me. So, as I told you, I saw it as something maybe a little bit negative, but now I see it as something **important** (interview 3).*

Melissa's phrase *"something bad is happening"* shows that we, as participant and researcher, shared a similar notion of tensions. Nonetheless, Melissa started to make a more nuanced sense of this concept, saying, *"tensions don't have to be something negative. Maybe it's also something that relates to [...] situations that [...] make you improve in life"*. Melissa was conceptualizing another side of tensions: how they can also help individuals to grow. For example, in our interviews, we had discussed how for many years, she had the goal of achieving native-like proficiency in English. More recently, she was starting to change that perspective because she thought she did not need to pursue a native speaker model to be an effective teacher and communicator. This was a perspective that focused on her strengths rather than on her perceived deficiencies. Thus, it helped her to appreciate her legitimacy and competence as a teacher of English. One of the reasons she came to that conclusion was because she had developed insecurities and frustration about her English. Reflection on these hard feelings made her consider changing her goal to achieve native-like English, a healthier alternative to pursuing a linguistic ideal. Also, Melissa claimed that tensions are *"necessary"* and *"important"*. Her statements stem from seeing how she had grown from her tensions. As explained above, her insecurities made her realize that there were better alternatives. Her tensions were necessary and important because they helped her focus on actions to validate her English and understand students struggling with insecurities like her.

Melissa's reflection on tensions helped me build on my own understanding of the term. After the interview with Melissa, I wrote an analytical memo examining my view of the term and how our conversation triggered a more profound sense of analysis for me.

*My conversation with Melissa made me realize **about my own conceptualization of tension as a negative word**, although I don't want to frame it like that, my research shows that way and unconsciously I think I was leaning towards this side thinking how I could discover tensions,**how bad they were**. [..] But I came to a more nuanced concept with her, she **made me see that based on data, yes, tensions are essential for LTI** [language teacher identity], but what attitude do we have towards them? How can we help teachers acknowledge those and use them? (researcher's analytical memo)*

Up to that point in the research, I had not confronted *"my own conceptualization of tension as a negative word"*. I was so involved in the study and worried about capturing those tensions that were the focus of my research, that I had not paused to see tensions from a different perspective. After Melissa's comment in the interview, I had to confront my bias and considered how it influenced my research and how I portrayed my participants. Thus, I was overly concentrating on *"how bad they were"*, just considering one angle of the concept. Although the literature on language teacher identity has conceptualized tensions as sites for reflection and growth, giving them a more "positive" characterization, my operationalization of the term in my research missed this piece. One of the reasons why this was happening was because I had not seen it directly in my research. However, Melissa "*made me see that based on data, yes, tensions are essential for LTI*". For me, that was a moment of realization of my own bias, and from there, I continued with the thought in mind that as a researcher, the data analysis procedures needed to embed this nuanced perspective.

5.3 Giving Meaning to the Size of the Nodes

During the interviews, a recurring theme was that Melissa's tensions in her pre-service years centered around her English proficiency; she wanted to develop her linguistic skills to the highest level possible. As soon as she started teaching, this tension shifted, and she became more concerned with her pedagogical skills. In the second interview, we discussed her challenges as a teacher, and she named them pedagogical insecurities, borrowing from her conceptualization of linguistic insecurities. She found a way to represent this shift in the network by using different sizes for the nodes corresponding to *pedagogical insecurities* and *linguistic insecurities*, as shown in Fig. 6.

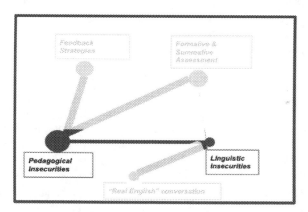

Fig. 6. Participant's network showing two different sizes of the nodes corresponding to pedagogical insecurities and linguistic insecurities.

Melissa further explained why she was very intentional about the sizes of the nodes and the meaning she was giving to this representation in the network. The following segment presents our discussion about these nodes in relation with the shift in her identity tensions.

*[1]-Melissa: [..] as I told you, I feel that [the shift in tensions] like a process, I do not know, like some of the insecurities, I see them as a process [...] let's say now I have changed, or my contexts have changed. Now **I'm here, but that doesn't mean that this [insecurities] disappeared, that my part of being an English learner***

disappeared,everything that comes with it, but now my life is more centered in this place [teaching], still , I have like, this background, all the situations here.

*[2]-Researcher: Yeah, I agree with you. And like my network, also, I think, and when out when I show it to you. I also made that connection that I wish like the network could have provided me with, like a timeline. Because I felt that just like you're saying, like, **those linguistic insecurities are not disappearing, but they're not taking center stage**. [...]*

*[3]-Melissa: I think there are a lot of things to think about, because maybe, right now, [...] it could be the case [...] that another person has pedagogical insecurities and had linguistic insecurities. When maybe in their present, they are living this, but maybe this is smaller.**They may think that it's pedagogical insecurities now, but it's smaller, compared to maybe a big linguistic insecurity in the past. [...] I think the dots and their size are really important to see, like, how much relevance that has had in your, [...], in your experience**. (Interview 3)*

Melissa's discussion of her discourse network examined the relevance of her tensions at different points in time. Her statement in turn of talk 1, *"Now I'm here, but that doesn't mean that this [insecurities] disappeared, that my part of being an English learner disappeared"* shows how she recognized a connection between her identity tensions across time. She said that she *"is here"* referring to being teaching, not studying English. But also, she meant that she has overcome some of those tensions associated with her English language learning, but they have not *"disappeared"* completely. I agreed with her in turn of talk 2, saying, *"those linguistic insecurities are not disappearing, but they're not taking center stage"*. We both saw them as part of her identity, only that in the present other more relevant areas capture her attention and give a secondary role to linguistic aspects.

The size of the nodes Melissa used for *pedagogical insecurities* and *linguistic insecurities* was deliberately chosen. She provided an example to explain how she interpreted size applied to her identity tensions. She stated in turn of talk 3, *"They [other teachers] may think that it's pedagogical insecurities now, but it's smaller, compared to maybe a big linguistic insecurity in the past."* In this example, Melissa described how for other teachers (or for herself), tensions may feel real now, but the intensity is weaker or "smaller" considering how strong it was in the past. Then, she added, *"I think the dots and their size are really important to see, like, how much relevance that has had in your, [...], in your experience."* Melissa associated the size of the dots with the perceived "relevance" of an identity tension in this case. She applied this ENA feature to her understanding of her identity, combining the intensity of the tensions and the temporality (past and present) to represent a shift. In my network, I struggled to represent this shift, and did not think about the size of the nodes to do it. Melissa's approach made much sense to me and confirmed that linguistic tensions had decreased in intensity, which was still a question I had.

Melissa's network and explanation illustrate a nuanced understanding of how her tensions evolved and shaped her identity. As a researcher, my bias may have been to assume that Melissa's linguistic tensions had disappeared entirely due to her experiences, new positioning, and identity exploration. Also, she could have lied to me and told me what I wanted to hear as a researcher, that she had risen above her struggles. Or we would not have had the opportunity to have this conversation at all. Nonetheless, our unfolding of the network components provided evidence of how her tensions were still part of her and are being integrated into her learning and professional trajectory. The network provided a visualization with different elements we could unpack through our discourse.

5.4 Making Sense of Connections

In our interview, Melissa and I agreed that there was a connection between her current pedagogical insecurities and linguistic insecurities. Our discourse networks linked these codes, as shown in Fig. 7. Melissa's visualization drew a direct link between the two types of insecurities, and my network connected linguistic insecurity with students, which indicated a link to her pedagogical area.

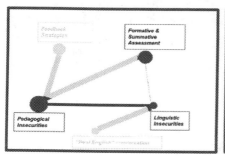 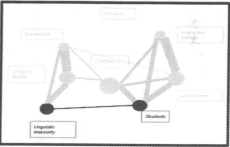

Fig. 7. Left: Participant's discourse network, showing a dotted line between *Formative & Summative Assessment* and *Linguistic Insecurities*. Right: Researcher's discourse networks representing a connection between *Linguistic Insecurity* and *Students*.

While we were both aware of the connection depicted in our networks, we were unsure of what it really meant in terms of Melissa's experiences. The next segment of our conversation unfolds how we discovered what lied at the heart of this connection.

[1]-Melissa: pedagogical insecurities have a connection to linguistic insecurities [...] both are part of my identity as a teacher, both of them as an English learner and speaker. [...] Maybe there is that connection, but I don't know what kind of connection. So I'm just gonna put this like, line forming a lot of dots, because maybe there's a connection but I don't know what connection.

[2]-Researcher: I feel exactly the same. And I don't have an answer to that. [...] I am exactly where you are right now.

[3]-Melissa: I think those things like those themes will stay with me because even those someday, I don't feel like I have that linguistic insecurity, I will still have like, the experience that I went through when I had that insecurity.

[4]-Researcher: [...] now that you're saying that; this is so interesting! How do you think this is maybe shaping or will continue to shape who you are as a

teacher ? [...] Like coming from that place of linguistic insecurity? What do you think?

*[5]-Melissa: [...] maybe **now it's a tool that I have to understand my students**, I guess [...], for example, [...] **going back to that example of some of my students say, and 'I'm sorry' when I give feedback, now, maybe that that's something that can help me to understand them**, and maybe they are feeling insecure. [...] I just remembered that example of them saying, 'I'm sorry'. And I guess that was because I have that knowledge of my linguistic insecurities.*

[6]-Researcher: I agree. Maybe if you hadn't had experience with these linguistic insecurities, you wouldn't even care [...]

[7]-Melissa: I think we just found the connection between that, that's the connection! [laughing]. I wasn't expecting [...]. So yeah, that that could be the connection. (Interview 3)

In this conversation segment, turn of talks 1 and 2 coincide with Melissa's words, "there is that connection, but I don't know what connection". She decided to represent this connection by adding a dotted line between Linguistic Insecurities and Formative and Summative Assessment. The latter code is linked to Pedagogical Insecurities because Melissa felt her assessment strategies could improve as she did not know how to respond to her students' oral performance. Thus, this dotted line indicated that Melissa knew that there was an underlying connection she still had not identified. She used this resource to show that she was unsure, but she had a strong intuition.

In turn of talk 3, Melissa acknowledged that *"those things like those themes [the tensions or insecurities] will stay with me"*. This statement made me think about the connection of her tensions to her teaching, so I asked the question, *"How do you think this is maybe shaping or will continue to shape who you are as a teacher?"* I wanted to know if, in her teaching, these past insecurities could play a role at all. At this point, I was unsure what the answer would be, but I thought it was worth asking it after she said that the insecurities *"will stay"* with her. I was struck by this phrase. In turn of talk 5, Melissa connects with one of the experiences we had analyzed in the previous interview. Briefly, this story was about a reaction she had noticed from one of her students when she provided error correction. This student would say *"I'm sorry"* every time after Melissa's correction. Melissa would tell the student that it was okay and that there was no need to apologize. However, the student continued to do it, and Melissa felt bad and uncomfortable about it. Melissa spontaneously brought this episode to our discussion as a puzzle that somehow was very meaningful to her. During the second interview, we just talked about it, but did not unfold the meaning behind it. In turn of talk 5, Melissa realized that her attention to her student's 'I'm sorry' was connected to her linguistic insecurities. She knew firsthand, as a learner, what it was to feel frustrated with her English, thinking that it was not proficient enough. In her student's response, she could see the same kind of shame, and that she was paying so much attention to that. That was when it clicked for her that her linguistic insecurities were a *"tool"* to understand her students. Her previous experience provided her with the empathy to put herself in the students' shoes. Now, she could use this tool to continue developing her assessment practices in more effectively. I was in total agreement with Melissa's realization. It made sense that her student emotionally struck her, and that she now felt more puzzles in that area of her teaching.

This moment provides evidence of how revisiting the networks and bringing the confusing or puzzling themes to the discussion could develop a collaborative space for the researcher and the participant. Melissa was creative with her network, adding a dotted line; she held to this line and used it to think through it in her discourse. I followed her cues as she made sense of the connection. This interaction demonstrates that joint thinking, listening, and conversing with our visualization unpacked discourse data.

In my analytical memo below, I reflected on how this experience, unraveling this connection meant for me as a researcher. I wrote,

> *One of my biggest realizations [from the interview] is that she [Melissa] knew all this, I did not come to give her the truth. She knew all this by herself, she can articulate it better now, but she had it in her. Teachers need more ways to express themselves. They have it in them. We just need to guide their reflection. (Researcher's analytical memo)*

My memo concludes this section by pointing to the collaborative nature of participant-researcher interactions. Creating and discussing an ENA network with Melissa proved that these interactions contribute to designing opportunities to examine participants' perspectives and come to joint understandings of the research phenomenon.

6 Discussion and Conclusion

The outcomes of the joint discussion of discourse networks presented in this paper suggest that researcher-participant interactions within a collaborative context set the stage for sense-making grounded in multiple perspectives. The reflection of the outcome of constructing concept understandings provided evidence for how themes or codes included in discourse networks, if chosen intentionally, can yield explorations not done in previous data collection. In the example provided, the participant and the researcher acknowledged a side of identity tensions that had been ignored. Additionally, such a deep dive into some well-established concepts may motivate the researcher to question bias, such as my focus on tensions only as negative. The outcome of giving meaning to the size of the nodes demonstrated the participant's appropriation of one of the ENA features. Understanding of the meaning of the node sizes helped the participant to apply it to a shift of intensity in different temporalities. Finally, the outcome of making sense of connections indicated that connections in networks can be brought up even if stakeholders are puzzled or do not know how to explain connections. There is a chance of co-constructing a possible explanation.

Overall, the examples illustrated show that the discussion of data visualizations between a researcher and a participant is a space for discursive constructionism [11]. This collaborative space enabled stakeholders to use the repertoires of discourse to construct meaningful moment-to-moment expansions of their ideas and realities to engage in joint sense-making. As acknowledged and requested by previous research [2, 3, 7, 9], QE tools have suitable features to continue expanding them to support the use and participation of multiple perspectives in addition to the one of the researcher. In this paper, some of the features of ENA provided a springboard for discursive constructions unfolding sociocultural and historical aspects of the researcher and participants, their context, and their positionings [15].

As a researcher, self-constructing the networks as a preliminary stage for coding prepared me to identify the big ideas within the data and specially to begin to understand how they were related from a more open perspective. The process kept me reflecting on my own biases, how they were helping, affecting, and hindering the data analysis. Retrospectively, I recognize that the network constructions in early stages of data analysis enabled me to incorporate participants' interpretations in the operationalization of codes. For example, "*linguistic insecurities*" became a major code that was broken down into subcodes to capture its complexity. I was able to laser-focus on this code because I was aware of the participants' concept interpretation and significance. For the participant, self-constructing the network first on her own and then discuss it with me opened the possibility for personal and multiple interpretations of her experience. She commented that this exercise was a much-needed summary of the puzzles and understandings she shared and developed in our interviews. This research and participant's experiences with the network construction denote the affordance of integrating discourse and construction in a collaborative space.

More broadly, the tool and procedures presented in this paper can be utilized in research contexts involving teacher or participant reflection. I recommend setting individual spaces for researchers and teachers to construct the networks first on their own and then come together to discuss. This model can be used when data are collected in different points in time to allow reflection. Limitations to the alternative proposed in this paper include the characteristics of participants, such as age or interest in this kind of activity as part of research. Also, it is important to consider the participants' and researchers' availability to invest time in the network construction prior to or during the interview. It should also be acknowledged that the procedures and tool discussed generate networks based on the perceptions and experiences of participants and researchers, not on statistical procedures. Further steps can be taken to continue designing tools that embed a fuller range of functionality.

References

1. Bang, M., Vossoughi, S.: Participatory design research and educational justice: studying learning and relations within social change making. Cogn. Instr. **34**, 173–193 (2016). https://doi.org/10.1080/07370008.2016.1181879
2. Arastoopour Irgens, G.: Quantitative ethnography across domains: where we are and where we are going. In: 1st International Conference of Quantitative Ethnography (ICQE). University of Wisconsin (2018)
3. Buckingham Shum, S.: Quantitative ethnography visualizations as tools for thinking. In: 2nd International Conference of Quantitative Ethnography (ICQE) (2021)
4. Brown, N.: Scope and continuum of participatory research. Int. J. Res. Method Educ. **45**, 200–211 (2021). https://doi.org/10.1080/1743727X.2021.1902980
5. Campbell, J.: A critical appraisal of participatory methods in development research. Int. J. Soc. Res. Methodol. **5**, 19–29 (2002). https://doi.org/10.1080/13645570110098046

6. Erickson, F.: Qualitative methods in research on teaching. In: Handbook of Research on Teaching. Collier Macmillan (1986)
7. Buckingham Shum, S., et al.: Participatory quantitative ethnography. In: Wasson, B., Zörgő, S. (eds.) Third International Conference on Quantitative Ethnography: Conference Proceedings Supplement (2021)
8. Phillips, M., Siebert-Evenstone, A., Kessler, A., Gasevic, D., Shaffer, D.W.: Professional decision making: reframing teachers' work using epistemic frame theory. In: Ruis, A.R., Lee, S.B. (eds.) ICQE 2021. CCIS, vol. 1312, pp. 265–276. Springer, Cham (2021). https://doi.org/10.1007/978-3-030-67788-6_18
9. Vega, H., Irgens, G.A.: Constructing interpretations with participants through epistemic network analysis: towards participatory approaches in quantitative ethnography. In: Wasson, B., Zörgő, S. (eds.) Advances in Quantitative Ethnography, ICQE 2021. Communications in Computer and Information Science, vol. 1522. Springer, Cham (2022). https://doi.org/10.1007/978-3-030-93859-8_1
10. Shaffer, D.W.: Quantitative Ethnography. Cathcart Press (2017)
11. Potter, J., Hepburn, A.: Discursive constructionism. In: Holstein, J.A., Gabrium, J.F. (eds.) Handbook of Constructionist Research, pp. 275–293. Guildford (2008)
12. Harel, I., Papert, S. (eds.): Ablex Publishing, Ney York (1991)
13. Tileagă, C., Stokoe, E. (eds.): Routledge, UK (2015)
14. Prior, M.T., Talmy, S.: A discursive constructionist approach to narrative in language teaching and learning research. System 102, 102595 (2021). https://doi.org/10.1016/j.system.2021.102595
15. Pavlenko, A.: Poststructuralist approaches to the study of social factors in second language learning and use. In: Cook, V. (ed.) Portraits of the L2 User, pp. 277–302. Multilingual Matters, Clevedon (2002)
16. Mor, Y., Ferguson, R., Wasson, B.: Editorial: learning design, teacher inquiry into student learning and learning analytics: a call for action: learning design, TISL and learning analytics. Br. J. Educ. Technol. 46, 221–229 (2015). https://doi.org/10.1111/bjet.12273
17. Sergis, S., Sampson, D.G.: Teaching and learning analytics to support teacher inquiry: a systematic literature review. In: Peña-Ayala, A. (ed.) Learning Analytics: Fundaments, Applications, and Trends. SSDC, vol. 94, pp. 25–63. Springer, Cham (2017). https://doi.org/10.1007/978-3-319-52977-6_2
18. Buckingham Shum, S., Ferguson, R., Martinez-Maldonado, R.: Human-centred learning analytics. J. Learn. Anal. 6, 1–9 (2019). https://doi.org/10.18608/jla.2019.62.1
19. Clandinin, D.J., Connelly, F.M.: Narrative Inquiry: Experience and Story in Qualitative Research. Jossey-Bass, San Francisco (2000)
20. Seidman, I.: Interviewing as Qualitative Research: A Guide for Researchers in Education and the Social Sciences. Teachers College Press, New York (2019)

Modeling Collaborative Discourse with ENA Using a Probabilistic Function

Yeyu Wang[(⊠)] ⓘ, Andrew R. Ruis ⓘ, and David Williamson Shaffer ⓘ

University of Wisconsin – Madison, Madison, WI, USA
ywang2466@wisc.edu

Abstract. Models of collaborative learning need to account for *interdependence*, the ways in which collaborating individuals construct shared understanding by making connections to one another's contributions to the collaborative discourse. To operationalize these connections, researchers have proposed two approaches: (1) counting connections based on the presence or absence of events within a temporal window of fixed length, and (2) weighting connections using the probability of one event referring to another. Although most QE researchers use fixed-length windows to model collaborative interdependence, this may result in miscounting connections due to the variability of the appropriate relational context for a given event. To address this issue, we compared epistemic network analysis (ENA) models using both a window function (ENA-W) and a probabilistic function (ENA-P) to model collaborative discourse in an educational simulation of engineering design practice. We conducted a pilot study to compare ENA-W and ENA-P based on (1) interpretive alignment, (2) goodness of fit, and (3) explanatory power, and found that while ENA-P performs slightly better than ENA-W, both ENA-W and ENA-P are feasible approaches for modeling collaborative learning.

Keywords: Collaborative Learning · Learning Analytics · Epistemic Network Analysis · Modeling Recent Temporal Context · Engineering Education

1 Introduction

A critical element of collaborative learning is that learners co-construct knowledge and make cognitive connections both intrapersonally and interpersonally [1]. That is, a learner forms links (a) between concepts that they themselves contribute to collaborative interactions and (b) between their own contributions and those of their collaborators. These links are operationalized in models of collaborative learning as connections between concepts. To accomplish this, Suthers et al. [2] suggest that in collaborative discourse, common ground can be represented in terms of the *recent temporal context* for an utterance: that is, the common ground for the current utterance in a conversation is composed of the utterances that precede it back to some prior point in time. Because both manual construction and natural language processing techniques face challenges in determining recent temporal context for each utterance at scale [3, 4], models of collaborative learning approximate the appropriate recent temporal context for utterances

C. Damşa and A. Barany (Eds.): ICQE 2022, CCIS 1785, pp. 132–145, 2023.
https://doi.org/10.1007/978-3-031-31726-2_10

using a *fixed-length moving window* or using a *probabilistic function*. Each of these approaches has advantages and disadvantages in approximating recent temporal context. Fixed windows are easy to compute but may over- or under-count connections in the model. Probabilistic models may, in some settings, be more accurate, but they can be more difficult to implement.

In this study, I examine one technique for modeling cognitive connections in collaborative contexts, Epistemic Network Analysis (ENA), which has been implemented primarily with a fixed-length moving window to operationalize recent temporal context. Using one dataset, I examine whether a novel approach, ENA with a probabilistic model, better models the process of collaborative learning.

2   Theory

2.1   Modeling Collaborative Learning

One important component of learning is the process by which individual learners work together to develop cognitive connections between concepts [5, 6]. For example, Suthers et al. [2] refer to a particular type of connection in collaborative learning, *uptake*, as the process of one student contributing to the conversation based contributions of another. Clark [7] in turn argues that critical to the notion of uptake is the concept of *common ground*: the shared knowledge and assumptions across individuals, groups, and communities that are relevant to a specific turn of talk. As Suthers and Desiato [8] suggest, in collaborative discourse, common ground can be operationalized as *recent temporal context*: that is, the common ground for some current utterance in a conversation is composed of the utterances that precede it back to some prior point in time.

Thus, Swiecki [1] argues that *interactivity* and *interdependence* are fundamental to collaborative learning. Interactivity refers to the process through which learners co-construct knowledge by responding to others' opinions or actions. This interactivity results in interdependence—that is, one learner's utterances or actions influence others. In other words, all learning can be characterized, at least in part, as a process of making connections between ideas. In collaborative learning, those connections are made from a learner's ideas to some collaborative recent temporal context.

2.2   Quantifying Interdependent Connections

In cognitive science, scholars make two claims about how humans understand information and make connections within the common ground. Each of these claims leads to a different approach to modeling connections.

Counting Cognitive Connections Based on Presence or Absence of Events Within the Window. The first claim is that people have limitations on their capacity for processing information. [9] argues that a speaker engages a listener's attention during a conversation by dividing big chunks of information into smaller, logically connected units, which is termed as *intonation units*. To construct appropriate intonation units, a speaker needs to make an assumption at each moment about how much understanding they share with others in a conversation. Thus, there is an underlying assumption about *what each person thinks the others can remember* in the process of conversational uptake. Based on this framework, researchers operationalize cognitive connections within the recent temporal context using a *fixed-length moving window*. The window is *fixed* on the assumption that all of the participants make a similar assumption about other participants' shared understanding. The window is *moving* in the sense that each line in the dataset has a window that represents its recent temporal context. Within each window, researchers develop *indicators* to described learning patterns, such as whether or not two events co-occur within the window.

Weighting Cognitive Connections Using the Probability of One Utterance Referring to Another. In addition to *how much* information a person can hold within their short-term memory, previous research has investigated *how likely* it is that a person can retain some piece of information in short-term memory as time passes. For example, Ebbinghaus [10] studied rates of retention and forgetting based on a test of vocabulary recall, resulting in an exponential decay function. Other research on information retention models forgetting based on power functions [11, 12]. Regardless of what function we use to model information retention, this perspective suggests that the *probability* of recalling information decays as time passes. Rather than claiming the connection strength between two codes is either 1 or 0, I propose to quantify the connection strength as a function of *distance* between the two lines where codes occur. To operationalize connection strength, I use a probabilistic function to model recent temporal context in collaborative discourse. The probabilistic function estimates *the probability of one utterance referring to another* based on the distance between two utterances.

2.3   Epistemic Network Analysis

Epistemic Network Analysis (ENA) is an approach to quantifying connections between concepts, behaviors and other elements to model collaborative learning [13]. ENA takes coded data generated by individuals during interactivity and represents connections among those codes as a network structure. Specifically, ENA computes connections based on the *presence* of the codes in each line of data and the codes in the previous lines of data that constitute its recent temporal context. That is, ENA currently is operationalized based on the first approach in Sect. 2.2. Using this approach to model a dataset, we need to construct a window for each utterance. However, the challenge is that not every line has the same window size. Ruis et al. [14] proposed to resolve this issue by choosing a *fixed* length for the window as a best *approximation*. They argue that the window size needs to be sufficient to capture the recent temporal context for 95% of utterances in a dataset and minimize improperly-included connections within the fixed size of the window. As Shaffer [13] argues, a fixed window is a good approximation because even though some responses are not direct responses to preceeding lines, they are part of the common ground. This kind of response is called a *dispreferred response* [15], a contribution that is "not an expected and direct reply to prior referents" ([13], p. 159). Therefore, even if covered by the fixed-length window, such dispreferred responses are still in the common ground and should be included in the recent temporal context.

In what follows, I refer to these two requirements for a fixed window model as the *maximum window postulate* and the *dispreferred response postulate*. The first says that we should choose a large fixed-length window to cover the recent temporal context for majority of utterances; and the second says that in choosing a large fixed window, we believe that dispreferred responses should be included in the recent temporal context.

Problems with Fixed-Length Window. The fixed-length window method thus depends on the dispreferred response postulate. That is, dispreferred responses should always be included in the recent temporal context for an utterance. However, it is not clear that this is always true. If we ignore the maximum window postulate and choose a shorter window, we will exclude lines which should be in the recent temporal context. That is, we produce a *Type II error* or a *false negative*, where we do not count connections which are relevant. If we follow the maximum window postulate, then we may include irrelevant responses within the window. That is, we produce a *Type I error* or a *false positive*, where we count connections which are actually irrelevant. This happens because, in this case, the dispreferred response postulate is not always valid: we cannot consider all dispreferred responses as relevant context for future utterances. Thus, situations where the dispreferred response postulate fails necessarily result in either Type I or Type II errors: either *overcounting* (Type I) or *undercounting* (Type II) connections.

Miscounting connections in an ENA model can lead to interpretive misalignment: the ENA model may include irrelevant connections or exclude relevant connections, which means the model is not aligned with a qualitative understanding of the data. Overcounting or undercounting connections also introduces error when constructing an ENA model, which may result in lower goodness of fit or lower the amount of variance explained.

2.4 Research Question

To address the issue of fixed window approach, I test whether ENA with a probabilistic approach provides a better model of collaborative discourse than a fixed-length window. In this study, I apply both ENA with a fixed-length *window* model (ENA-W) and ENA with a *probabilistic* model (ENA-P) to analyze the collaborative problem-solving processes in an engineering design training program, which consists of two primary learning activities: in the first half, student project teams explore a design space using a single material component, and in the second half, they attempt to create an optimal design using any available material. I compare these two models to answer the following research questions:

(1) Does ENA-P exhibit better interpretative alignment between qualitative and quantitative results than ENA-W?
(2) Does ENA-P have a better goodness of fit than ENA-W?
(3) Does ENA-P explain more variance between the two learning activities than ENA-W?

3   Methods

3.1   Dataset and Codebook

The dataset was collected from the virtual internship *Nephrotex* [16]. Nineteen engineering students participated in an online training simulation in which they designed a nanotechnology-based membrane for kidney dialysis machines at a fictitious company. The training program was divided into two activities. The goal for the first half was to help students explore the design space and learn the functional characteristics of a single material by analyzing graphs and data and conducting tests. The goal for the second half was to help students optimize the performance of a design across multiple parameters using a range of materials and other components. During these two activities, students communicated with their peers and a mentor through a persistent online chat tool that was a part of the simulation environment. To analyze the collaborative processes in this learning environment, researchers collected all 1443 chat posts across the 10 different groups in the simulation (5 in the first half, and 5 jigsawed groups in the second half). The chat posts were labeled by username and group number and arranged in a chronological order within each group.

To analyze the collaborative discourse, Siebert-Evenstone et al. [17] developed and validated a coding scheme with six codes: (1) PERFORMANCE PARAMETERS: criteria used to assess the design prototype including cost, marketability, reliability, flux, and blood cell reactivity; (2) DESIGN- BASED DECISION MAKING: processes of making design decisions, including prioritization and tradeoffs; (3) CLIENT AND CONSULTANT REQUESTS: concerns or needs of stakeholders in the simulation including suggestions and requirements for the final product; (4) DATA: specific technical or numeric information; (5) COLLABORATION: teamwork during decision making, including discussion of a team's collective action (e.g., "we need to…"); (6) TECHNICAL SPECIFICATIONS: characteristics of design prototypes, including selected materials, transformation processes, surfactant, and carbon nanotube percentage. All 6 codes were validated by two trained human raters (for each code, kappa > 0.83, $\rho(0.65) < 0.05$).

3.2   ENA

ENA takes binary-coded data as input and then constructs a fixed-length moving window to calculate connection counts between codes for each utterance. For each unit, ENA aggregates connection counts by summing across all windows for that unit's utterances. The aggregated connection counts are represented as an *adjacency vector*. ENA normalizes and centers the adjacency vectors, and the terms are used as *line weights* between nodes in the network representation. ENA performs a dimensional reduction technique to reduce the high-dimensional adjacency vectors to a low-dimensional space. In this study, the first dimension was constructed using a means rotation that maximizes the variance between the two primary activities in the simulation, and the second dimension was constructed using singular value decomposition, which maximizes variance among all units. ENA optimizes node positions in the resulting low-dimensional space to align the network centroids (based on line weights) with ENA scores (based on the dimensional reduction). To measure how aligned centroids and ENA scores are, ENA calculates the *goodness of fit* using Pearson's *r* correlation between these two values on all dimensions.

In the network representation, codes are represented as nodes, while connection strengths are represented by edge thickness and saturation. To compare patterns of connection-making in the first-half and second-half of activities, ENA creates a visualization called *difference plot*. That is, ENA calculates the mean line weights for units in each simulation activity separately and subtracts one group of mean line weights from the other, visualizing the differences with the color and thickness of the edges.

While network visualizations provide insights about different patterns of making connections between groups, ENA scores can be used to test whether these differences are *statistically* significant. In this analysis, I regressed the ENA scores from two different ENA models on a grouping variable of two activities. To test whether the variances explained by ENA-W and ENA-P are significantly different, I bootstrapped units and computed both regressions repeatedly, which created an empirical distribution of R^2 for both models. I applied Fischer's Z transformation and used a Monte Carlo rejection method to determine whether the difference in variance explained by the two ENA models was significant.

As a unified approach to data analysis, ENA integrates both qualitative interpretation and quantitative representation of data. Researchers establish *interpretive alignment* by showing that the conclusions derived from an ENA model is aligned with some qualitative interpretation of the original data. In my study, I checked the interpretive alignment in two ways:

- *Individual-Level*: I identified two segments of discussion and manually evaluated whether ENA-P addresses the potential over- and under-counting problems introduced by ENA-W.
- *Site-Level*: I evaluate whether the connection strengths in ENA-W or ENA-P provides a better representation of the expected outcomes based on the learning objectives for two activities.

3.3   Construction of ENA-W and ENA-P

Determining an Appropriate Window Size. To determine the window size for ENA-W, I adopted the method proposed by [14]. Two researchers randomly sampled 177 utterances from *Nephrotex* chat logs and determined the *furthest referent* for each utterance using social moderation. As proposed by [14], I identified the window size to be 7 utterances, accounted for recent temporal context in more than 95% of the sampled lines.

Determining an Appropriate Probabilistic Function. We derived the probabilistic function based on the same 177 samples. We define the sampled lines as an ordered set of lines $(l_1, l_2, \ldots, l_{177})$. Each line l_i has its furthest referent l_{x_i}. Based on our definition of the recent temporal context, each line is related to its referents and itself. Thus, we operationalized the window to represent the recent temporal context is an ordered set of lines, $W_i = (l_{x_i}, l_{x_i+1}, \ldots, l_i)$, where $|W_i| = i - x_i + 1$ (that is, the number of lines from l_{x_i} to l_i, , inclusive). For each line, l_i, we identified its furthest referent, l_{x_i}. We then constructed a histogram of window sizes, $|W_i|$, as shown in Fig. 1.

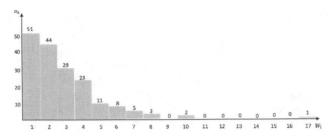

Fig. 1. Histogram for $|W_i|$ based on 177 Sampled Lines

The height of bars in the histogram indicates the total *counts* of a referring line l_r with the window length of W_i. We define the counts of referring lines given a window length k as $a_k = |\{ i|w_i = k\}|$. Let e be the maximum window length, $e = \max(W_i)$. The frequency distribution of window sizes lets us estimate the probability of a referring line (l_i) is related to any proceeding lines (l_λ), $\lambda < i$. We can also define the probability function $\pi(i - \lambda) = P(|W_i| > i - \lambda)$, which estimates the probability of the prior line l_λ is related to the referring line l_i. Thus, the frequency distribution of window sizes for all referring lines can be written as:

$$\pi(i - \lambda) = P(|W_i| > i - \lambda) = 1 - \frac{\sum_{j=0}^{i-\lambda} a_j}{\sum_{k=1}^{e} a_k}, \, a_0 \equiv 0.$$

4 Results

4.1 Research Question 1: Interpretive Alignment

Individual-Level Interpretive Alignment. In this section, I examined two examples from one student, Lily, who participated in the training program: one example illustrates that ENA-W may overcount connections, and the other illustrates that ENA-W may undercount connections. In both examples, I conducted a qualitative analysis on the recent temporal context of one utterance and manually derived the adjacency matrix of connection strengths using ENA-W and ENA-P.

Overcounting Problem. In the following example, a group of students is discussing different prototypes and evaluating their performance in preparation for choosing a final design:

Line	Team Member	Utterance
1	Abby	sounds good
2	Jina	Well the only other prototype i would consider is the one that was comprised of PMMA, vapor, using a hydrophilic surfactant, with a nanotube % of 4.0%

| 3 | Jina | this cost $100 dollars per unit, sold 500,000, had a reliability of 12 hours with a flux of 15 but a blood cell reactivity of 54.44 |

In line 1, Abby comments on a previous design, indicating that it "sounds good" as a candidate for the final prototype. Then Jina (line 2) proposes another candidate design "comprised of PMMA, vapor, using a hydrophilic surfactant, with a nanotube % of 4.0%." That is, she lists TECHNICAL SPECIFICATIONS as inputs for the design. In line 3, Jina continues by describing the PERFORMANCE PARAMETERS of the prototype, including cost, marketability, reliability, flux and blood cell reactivity. She further adds that the performance on the first four parameters is great, "but ... blood cell reactivity" is low at "54.44".

After summarizing the TECHNICAL SPECIFICATIONS and PERFORMANCE PARAMETERS of her prototype, Jina suggests that her teammates type the values of the PERFORMANCE PARAMETERS for their prototypes in the chat (line 4), which will be used to justify their design choices:

Line	Team Member	Utterance
4	Jina	If you guys could, can you type out the information from the prototypes on chat. We need it for the justifications
5	Bob	Flux: 29 BCR: 65.56 Reliability: 9 Marketability: 900,000
6	Abby	This resulted in a reliability of 8 h, marketability of 600,000 units, a flux rate of 13 m^3/m^2-day, and a low Bloodcell reactivity of 21.11. In total this prototype costs $130 dollars per unit
7	Lily	The BCR Type: Reliability-5, Market-800,000. Flux - 23. BCR- 10. Cost -$150

In response to Jina's proposal, Bob (line 5), Abby (line 6), and Lily (line 7) all enter the numerical values for the PERFORMANCE PARAMETERS of their prototypes. That is, they summarize how each of their prototypes performed on the metrics that the stakeholders care about.

Jina's response in line 4 is thus a dispreferred response. The previous discussion (lines 1–3) was focused on the TECHNICAL SPECIFICATIONS of the prototypes that each team member designed and tested. Jina (line 4) then abruptly shifted the discussion to the PERFORMANCE PARAMETERS of the prototypes, effectively beginning a new discussion.

How, then, should we model Lily's utterance in line 7? Based on the fixed window with 7 utterances, all lines in this segment, including any dispreferred responses, are relevant context because they are within the window, which in turn quantifies the connection between TECHNICAL SPECIFICATIONS and PERFORMANCE PARAMETERS as

1. In other words, the window models a connection between PERFORMANCE PARAME-TERS and TECHNICAL SPECIFICATIONS for line 7 even though qualitatively, Lily was not making that connection.

If we use a probabilistic function to quantify connection strength, line 7 comes 5 lines after line 2. Thus, the connection between Lily's reference to PERFORMANCE PARAMETERS in line 7 and Jina's reference to TECHNICAL SPECIFICATIONS is weighted by $\pi(7 - 2) = \pi(5) = \mathbf{0.107}$. Thus, the probabilistic model also shows a connection, but now with a weakened strength of only 0.107. This adjustment of connection strength suggests that the probabilistic model is a better representation—or perhaps in this case, a less imperfect representation—of Lily's response.

Undercounting Problem. In the following example, which comes at the beginning of the second half of the training program, students have switched groups. In their new group they introduce themselves, and then Abby describes (line 1) the conclusion by their team in the first half, suggesting that it was not particularly useful for designing a final prototype:

Line	Team Member	Utterance
1	Abby	basically the only thing i was able to conclude from my surfactant was that the BCR was constant in all of the prototypes. was 43.33%
2	Jina	The group i had previously worked with came up with a prototype that gave us an all around great dialyzer. It was comprised of PMMA for the material, Used the process of Vapor, and used a biological surfactant, and had a nanotube percentage of 1.5%
3	Jina	This resulted in a reliability of 8 h, marketability of 600,000 units, a flux rate of 13 m^3/m^2-day, and a low Bloodcell reactivity of 21.11. In total this prototype costs $130 dollars per unit
4	Abby	submit that prototype label in Team1 Batch1
5	Abby	do we want to stick to a specific material
6	Lily	I think we should include one prototype of each material
7	Abby	okay so each of us creates one from our material
8	Jina	Well what was the best one out of the previous prototypes for each material? It makes sense to do the best ones overall for each
9	Lily	well, change it up a bit. You can optimize your best result

Jina replies to Abby by reporting (line 2) the TECHNICAL SPECIFICATIONS for "an all around great dialyzer" that their group tested in the first half of the training program. Then, she provides (line 3) DATA about the PERFORMANCE PARAMETERS for her prototype.

Abby replies by suggesting (line 4) that the team use one of their prototypes from the first half of the training program in their next submission ("submit that prototype label in Team1 Batch1"). She asks (line 5) whether the whole team should use one material for the final submission. Lily replies (line 6) to Abby's question, saying that each person on the team should test a prototype for a different material. Abby confirms (line 7) that she understands what Lily had said: each student on the new team should design a prototype using the material studied by their old team. In response to Lily and Abby, Jina suggests (line 8) that they should use the "best ones overall" from their previous team. However, Lily disagrees and suggests (line 9) that they should consider changing the design from the previous team to achieve the best result possible.

This final comment about DATA (the "best result" of a design using one material) is thus a response to the previous 8 lines where students were deciding how to move to the next phase of their design process. More specifically, it relates to Jina's description (line 2) of the TECHNICAL SPECIFICATIONS for one specific device and its PERFORMANCE PARAMETERS (line 3).

But notice that with a window size of 7, DATA (line 9) is connected to PERFORMANCE PARAMETERS (line 3)—which is aligned with this qualitative analysis of the example. However, it is not connected to TECHNICAL SPECIFICATIONS (line 2), even though they are part of what would have been read as a single continuous comment by the same student (Jina). That is, the connection calculated by ENA-W is **0**. In other words, the window excludes a connection between DATA and TECHNICAL SPECIFICATIONS for line 9 even though qualitatively, Lily was making that connection.

If we use a probabilistic function to quantify connection strength (see 3.2.1), line 9 comes 7 lines after line 2. Thus, the connection between Lily's DATA in line 9 and Jina's TECHNICAL SPECIFICATIONS is weighted by $\pi(9 - 2) = \pi(7) = 0.034$. In other words, in this example, a qualitative analysis shows that Lily was making a non-zero connection between DATA and TECHNICAL SPECIFICATIONS.

In summary, the probabilistic model (1) reduces the type I error by decreasing the connection strength between PERFORMANCE PARAMETERS and TECHNICAL SPECIFICATIONS, which is overcounted by the fixed-length window model and (2) reduces the type II error by increasing the connection strength between DATA and TECHNICAL SPECIFICATIONS, which is undercounted by the fixed-length window model. These patterns persist throughout Lily's network throughout the training program: The connection strength between PERFORMANCE PARAMETERS and TECHNICAL SPECIFICATIONS is 0.70 in the ENA-W model, which decreases to 0.67 in the ENA-P model; the connection strength between DATA and TECHNICAL. SPECIFICATIONS is 0.42 in the ENA-W model, which increases to 0.51 in the ENA-P model.

Site-Level Interpretive Alignment. To assess interpretive alignment at the site level, I constructed an ENA-W and ENA-P model based on the chats from the whole class during the training program. Recall that the training program was designed to help students learn two abilities: the goal of the first half is to explore the performance of a single material based on different data sources (e.g., technical reports and graphs) and experimentation, while the goal of the second half is to optimize the performance (i.e., cost, safety, reliability, etc.) of a design prototype using any available material.

Thus, we would anticipate that students in the first half of the training program would make more connections between DATA and TECHNICAL SPECIFICATIONS because they are spending more time reading and discussing technical reports, collecting preliminary data, and constructing graphs to understand various design attributes for one single material. Students in the second half are more likely to make connections between DATA and PERFORMANCE PARAMETERS, as they are designing and testing prototypes to better understand the design space and maximize device performance across a range of parameters.

According to Fig. 2, the subtracted plot of ENA-P better aligns with expected difference between the first-half and the second-half of the training, based on the learning objectives of two halves. For example, students are expected to make more connections between DATA and TECHNICAL SPECIFICATIONS in the first-half of training. However, the edge between DATA and TECHNICAL SPECIFICATIONS in the subtracted plot for ENA-W is very weak, indicating little difference in the overall strength of that connection between the two halves: the edge weights differ by only 0.48. However, the ENA-P model shows that students made relatively more connections between DATA and TECHNICAL SPECIFICATIONS in the first half of training: the edge weights differ by 3.08. In other words, the ENA-W model does not reflect an expected difference in student discourse between the two halves of the simulation, while the ENA-P model does.

Similarly, students are expected to make more connections between DATA and PERFORMANCE PARAMETERS in their second-half, which is reflected in the subtracted plot of ENA-W: the edge weights differ by 1.60. However, the edge weight of this connection in ENA-P model shows even more salient difference, according to the thicker and darker blue edge. That is, the difference of this connections between two halves is larger in ENA-P: the edge weights differ by 4.01. In other words, the ENA-P model manifest and shows a more salient difference in network representation, compared to ENA-W.

Thus, in the individual-level, the individual network of Lily using ENA-P is more aligned with the qualitative evidence; in the site-level, the subtracted plot using ENA-P is more aligned with the expected difference based on the design and intervention of the. Thus, ENA-P models collaborative learning process and achieves a better interpretive alignment, compared to ENA-W.

4.2 Research Question 2: Evaluation of ENA Models Using Goodness of Fit

As described in Sect. 3.2., goodness of fit is a measure of discrepancy between dual representations for units. A higher goodness of fit provides a stronger warrant for the interpretation of the ENA scores based on the individual network. While goodness of fit for ENA-W is 0.93, goodness of fit for ENA-P is higher at 0.96. Thus, ENA-P has a better co-registration between dual representations than the ENA-W model.

4.3 Research Question 3: Evaluation for ENA Models Using Regression Analysis and Variance Explained

As described in Sect. 3.2. I applied a two bivariate regression models to predict ENA scores on the primary axis for the ENA-W and ENA-P and based on the condition of

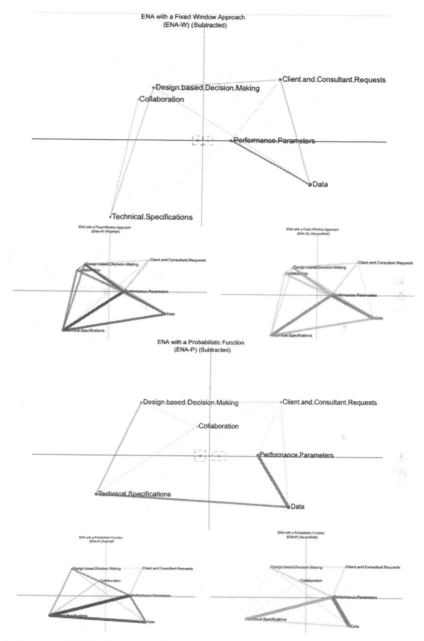

Fig. 2. Subtracted ENA Plots and Group ENA Plots Using Fixed Window Approach and Probabilistic Function

first-half and second-half of the game. Condition of first versus second half significantly predicts ENA scores for both models. However, the variance explained by ENA-W (R^2 = 0.22) is lower than the variance explained by ENA-P (R^2 = 0.38).

To explore whether the variance explained is significantly different between two models, as described in Sect. 3.2. I bootstrapped units from the whole set and ran the regression models repeatedly. With 1,000 iterations of bootstrapping, I calculated the 95% confidence interval (CI) for the R^2 of both models. The results show that the ENA-W model (95% CI $\in$ [0.20, 0.24]) has significantly lower variance explained than the ENA-P model (95% CI $\in$ [0.39, 0.43]). Thus, ENA-P has more explanatory power in accounting for differences between students in the first-half and second-half of the training program.

5 Discussion

This study explored two approaches to modeling collaborative learning in which the unit of analysis is individuals-in-a-group. Specifically, it compared ENA models constructed using two different methods for quantifying the strength of connections in collaborative discourse: (a) a fixed-length window approach (ENA-W), which quantifies connections as either present or absent within a set number of turns of talk; and (b) a novel probabilistic function approach (ENA-P), which estimates the likelihood that a connection is present. I hypothesized that ENA-P would better address the problem of over- or undercounting connections—that is, incorrectly quantifying connection strength—when a fixed-length window is used. To test this hypothesis, I conducted a pilot study to test the feasibility of ENA-P relative to ENA-W using data from 19 students who participated in a collaborative engineering design training program.

I compared ENA-P with ENA-W using three criteria: interpretive alignment, variance explained between groups, and model goodness of fit. Both models performed well, but ENA-P achieved slightly higher goodness of fit, explained significantly more variance, and was better aligned with both qualitative interpretation and expected learning processes based on the design of the training program. At the individual-level, given two discourse segments involving one particular student, ENA-P better quantified the connections overcounted or undercounted by ENA-W. Furthermore, this pattern persisted when all connections were aggregated for this student. At the site-level, the ENA-P model better reflected expected differences in student discourse between the first and second halves of the training.

This pilot study suggests that in at least some collaborative learning contexts, ENA-P may perform better than ENA-W; thus, ENA-P is a feasible method for quantifying connections in ENA models. While ENA-P models may perform better in some circumstances, they are also more difficult to construct. For example, in this study, we manually identified a probabilistic function based on an empirical distribution, which takes more time and effort. There are also other possible probabilistic models, such as exponential functions or power functions; thus, the findings of this study suggest that such approaches should be tested in future work.

In summary, while ENA-P performs slightly better than ENA-W based on the pilot test, both ENA-W and ENA-P are feasible approaches to model collaborative learning.

References

1. Swiecki, Z.: Measuring the impact of interdependence on individuals during collaborative problem-solving. JLA **8**, 75–94 (2021)
2. Suthers, D.D., Dwyer, N., Medina, R., Vatrapu, R.: A framework for conceptualizing, representing, and analyzing distributed interaction. Comput. Support. Learn. **5**, 5–42 (2010)
3. Rose, C., et al.: Analyzing collaborative learning processes automatically: exploiting the advances of computational linguistics in computer-supported collaborative learning. Int. Soc. Learn. Sci. **3**, 237–271 (2008)
4. Espinoza, C., Lämsä, J., Araya, R., Hämäläinen, R., Gormaz, R., Viiri, J.: Automatic content analysis in collaborative inquiry-based learning. In: European Science Education Research Association Conference. University of Bologna (2019)
5. DiSessa, A.A.: Knowledge in pieces. In: Forman, G., Pufall, P. (eds.) Constructivism in the Computer Age, pp. 47–70. Erlbaum, Hillsdale (1988)
6. Shaffer, D.W.: Models of situated action. In: Steinkuehler, C., Squire, K., Barab, S. (eds.) Games, Learning, and Society, pp. 403–432. Cambridge University Press, Cambridge (2012)
7. Clark, H.H. (ed.): Common ground. In: Using Language, pp. 92–122. Cambridge University Press, Cambridge (1996)
8. Suthers, D.D., Desiato, C.: Exposing chat features through analysis of uptake between contributions. In: 2012 45th Hawaii International Conference on System Sciences, pp. 3368–3377. IEEE, Maui (2012)
9. Chafe, W.: Discourse, Consciousness, and Time: The Flow and Displacement of Conscious Experience in Speaking and Writing. University of Chicago Press, Chicago (1994)
10. Ebbinghaus, H.: Memory: a contribution to experimental psychology. Ann. Neurosci. **20**, 155 (2013)
11. Rubin, D.C., Wenzel, A.E.: One hundred years of forgetting: a quantitative description of retention. Psychol. Rev. **103**(4), 734 (1996)
12. Wixted, J.T., Ebbesen, E.B.: Genuine power curves in forgetting: a quantitative analysis of individual subject forgetting functions. Mem. Cognit. **25**, 731–739 (1997)
13. Shaffer, D.W.: Quantitative Ethnography. Lulu.com (2017)
14. Ruis, A.R., Siebert-Evenstone, A.L., Pozen, R., Eagan, B.R., Shaffer, D.W.: Finding common ground: a method for measuring recent temporal context in analyses of complex, collaborative thinking. In: 13th International Conference on Computer Supported Collaborative Learning (CSCL), pp.136–143 (2019)
15. Pomerantz, A.: Agreeing and disagreeing with assessments: Some features of preferred/dispreferred turn shaped. Structures of Social Action: Studies in Conversation (1984)
16. Chesler, N.C., Ruis, A.R., Collier, W., Swiecki, Z., Arastoopour, G., Williamson Shaffer, D.: A novel paradigm for engineering education: virtual internships with individualized mentoring and assessment of engineering thinking. J. Biomech. Eng. **137**, 024701 (2015)
17. Siebert-Evenstone, A.L., Arastoopour Irgens, G., Collier, W., Swiecki, Z., Ruis, A.R., Williamson Shaffer, D.: In search of conversational grain size: modeling semantic structure using moving stanza windows. Learn. Anal. **4**, 123–139 (2017)

Segmentation and Code Co-occurrence Accumulation: Operationalizing Relational Context with Stanza Windows

Szilvia Zörgő[✉] [iD]

Care and Public Health Research Institute, Maastricht University, Maastricht, Netherlands
zorgoszilvia@gmail.com

Abstract. Depending on analytical goals and techniques, qualitative data may be coded and segmented to investigate code or code co-occurrence frequencies. As codes are relevant aspects of data vis-à-vis the topic of inquiry, segments are meaningful divisions of those data. To explore various modes of segmentation, their underlying assumptions, and effects on potential models, the framework and terminology of Epistemic Network Analysis was employed as an analytical tool where coding and segmentation both contribute to data visualization. Three operationalizations of segmentation are elaborated: moving, infinite, and whole conversation stanza windows and demonstrated through instances where each of these may be applicable to data.

Keywords: Data Segmentation · Methodology · Epistemic Network Analysis

1 Introduction

Working with qualitative data, such as audio recordings of focus group discussions and interviews, involves a series of decisions regarding how to transform data into a representation that enables analysis. If such techniques align with ontological and epistemological assumptions as well as research objectives, researchers may decide to transcribe, segment, and code qualitative data to identify patterns therein. Codes are sets of concepts, gestures, expressions that capture relevant aspects of data (as defined by the research questions) that help researchers systematically categorize phenomena in their data. Apart from coding, pattern identification may also equally depend on representing and analyzing the structure of data, which can be achieved through segmentation, that is, dividing data into "consistent and meaningful parts" [1].

As codes are relevant aspects of data vis-à-vis the topic of inquiry, segments are meaningful divisions of those data. What constitutes "meaningful division" depends crucially on the analytical goals and is in close interaction with similar decisions made regarding coding. Meaning can reside on many levels. For example, a researcher may be interested in character-level information to improve text prediction, but for effective text translation, information may need to be processed on a higher level, that of sentences or passages; yet, if a researcher is interested in identifying salient themes in, e.g., focus

C. Damşa and A. Barany (Eds.): ICQE 2022, CCIS 1785, pp. 146–162, 2023.
https://doi.org/10.1007/978-3-031-31726-2_11

group discussions or social media data, searching for meaning in character-level or even word-level information may be too "pixelized". Although, arguably, meaning resides on all levels simultaneously, a researcher's focus is guided by how they operationalize meaning and on which level(s) of the data they assume it is centered.

Coding is common in qualitative analyses of textual data, and several analytical approaches exist to aid code development, such as Interpretative Phenomenological Analysis, Grounded Theory, and Thematic Analysis. To the contrary, there is little guidance on systematic text segmentation. Many scholars differentiate between top-down and bottom-up approaches; the latter, also referred to as "word-based", involves utilizing lexical or linguistic features of a text to identify and describe its structure (including e.g., punctuation and syntax). Features of interest are established a priori, with assumptions like semantic dissimilarity and/or the introduction of novel words indicates shifts in meaning. A good example of this is KBDeX, a computational approach to segmentation based on word co-occurrences [2]. Top-down approaches, also referred to as "meaning-based" or "interpretive", involve utilizing content, context, and coherence to identify structure. In this approach, units of segmentation are first identified, and only then are their characteristics investigated to describe structure. While bottom-up techniques are easily automated, top-down techniques are usually performed manually, as hermeneutics is needed, and segmentation criteria are less precise than in word-based methods [3]. One could argue that any segmentation, which involves some scrutiny of the data is indeed "interpretive", thus a more accurate distinction may be differentiating between segmentation techniques that require no versus some level of qualitative engagement with the data.

Many researchers working with dialogue identify conversational turns or turns-of-talk as meaningful units. In cases of more continuous data or single data providers, segments may be constituted by e.g., phrases, sentences, or paragraphs. Text structure may often be hierarchically organized, that is, shorter segments may be nested in longer meaningful segments [4, 5]. Some types of analyses may only segment on a single level and consider these as a fragment of discourse that represent a single message, a distinguishing feature, or a change of subject [6]. Kleinheksel et al., suggest taking a fine-grained approach to ease the "cognitive burden of analysis", that is, identifying constructs of interest in longer segments. For example, dividing a paragraph into sentences or breaking a sentence up into phrases may be an option [7].

One could argue that the issue is not the "cognitive burden of analysis", as trained coders can label even relatively long sections, provided codes have a clear definition and method of application. Thus, even if a longer segment contains "multiple ideas of interest" [7], it is still possible to code reliably. Decisions on the granularity of segmentation more crucially depend on the mode of data analysis and modelling [8].

There are some comprehensive theoretical frameworks available in which segmentation assumes a central role, such as Goffman's Frame Analysis, which involves dividing activity continua into "strips", identifiable chunks of social behavior that are meaningful for a person or group. Participants of a particular strip make sense of behavior via "frames", that is, culturally determined descriptions of reality or schema of interpretation. [9] In another approach, Gee identifies five levels of structure in a narrative text, each building on the previous and contributing to interpretation. Namely, 1) Lines of data and groups of lines (stanzas); 2) Syntax and cohesion (deixis, syntactic devices); 3) Relation to narrative plot (main line or off line); 4) Psychological subjects (points of view from which the material in a stanza is viewed); and 5) Focusing system (where focus lies, e.g., new, vital, or salient information) [4].

In working with such theoretical frameworks, analysis need not necessarily involve quantification of qualitative data; for example, the notion of a strip (where a chunk of social behavior begins and ends) may not be operationalized and systematically applied to a dataset. The systematic application of such decisions becomes crucial when researchers aim to generate a quantitative model of qualitative data that relies on consistent coding and segmentation.

Epistemic Network Analysis (ENA), the flagship tool of Quantitative Ethnography (QE), can be utilized to quantify co-occurrences among elements in coded data and represent them in dynamic network models. A critical feature of ENA is that it enables researchers to compare networks by inspecting them visually and via summary statistics that reflect the weighted structure of connections. ENA provides a comprehensive framework and terminology for addressing questions in segmentation and code co-occurrence accumulation; hence the present paper employs it to ask: What are underlying assumptions behind systematic approaches to segmentation commonly used in ENA, and how do these affect data modelling?

2   The Epistemic Network Analysis Data Model

ENA is a tool that models and visualizes the relative frequency of co-occurrence between unique pairs of codes within designated segments of data. These frequencies are displayed as network graphs where nodes represent codes, and the thickness of edges represents the strength of co-occurrence. For a more detailed description of network construction, please see: [1, 10]. A dataset that can be processed by ENA, referred to as a qualitative data table, typically contains information in three major ontological domains: data, metadata, and codes.

Data: information analyzed in the study (e.g., transcribed audio-video, text)
Metadata: characteristics of the data itself (e.g., segmentation), the data providers (e.g., demographic data), or the data collection process (e.g., time of interview)
Codes: inductively or deductively developed, systematically applied constructs of interest.

Rows in a qualitative data table are constituted by the lowest level of segmentation called "utterances"[1]; apart from the data, columns in the table are the variables in the study (metadata and codes). Rows are characterized by "evidentiary completeness" in that each row contains values for all variables. Data is represented as one utterance per row (e.g., a turn-of-talk), metadata are commonly represented in numerical or categorical

---

[1] Some researchers use the term "utterance" to only describe the lowest level of segmentation in textual data, but here we refer to utterance as the smallest codable segment in any type of qualitative data.

form (e.g., male, female), and codes are usually represented in binary form[2] (0 if code is absent, 1 if code is present in utterance). Table 1 illustrates a schematic version of a qualitative data table with three data providers (two males, one female), two metadata variables (participant ID and sex), and four utterances coded with two codes.

Table 1. Schematic version of a qualitative data table

DATA PROVIDER ID	SEX	UTTERANCE	CODE 1	CODE 2
ID1	Female	Hello.	0	1
ID2	Male	Nice to meet you!	1	1
ID1	Female	Mind if I sit down?	0	0
ID3	Male	Please, join us!	1	0

Utterances, also referred to as "lines of data" in QE studies, are usually defined as a turn-of-talk, a sentence, a response, or a second in time [11]. Coding is performed on the level of utterances. All higher forms of segmentation can be described as groupings of one or more utterances; that is, utterances are nested within higher levels of segmentation that provide meaningful context to those utterances; this can be referred to as relational context. Relational context is provided by two variables: stanza and conversation. Conversations are groupings of lines that *can be* connected in a model, while stanzas are lines that *are* related and connote recent temporal context [1] or proximity of any kind (psychological, semiotic, etc.). In other words, conversations constitute a wider, stanzas a narrower context for specific utterances. For example, while all utterances in an interview can be considered related, as they were all uttered by the same data provider, not all lines in an interview are needed to understand a given utterance. The main ontological components[3] that contribute to segmentation in the ENA data model are as follows:

Utterance: smallest codable segment (e.g., a sentence in an interview)
Stanza: a set of one or more utterances (e.g., a topic within a response to an interview question)
Conversation: a set of one or more stanzas (e.g., a question-response segment in an interview)
Unit: the totality of utterances associated with a network within a model (e.g., all data from an interviewee); a model may consist of one or more networks in the same projection space

Note, that two or all of these components may be conflated in operationalization, such as considering e.g., individual social media posts lines of data and asserting that no other posts (for example, in a thread) provide relational context for them, thus code co-occurrences should not be able to take place across posts. In this case, a single post would be both utterance and conversation.

---

[2] Codes are always numerical; whether they are represented as binary, continuous, or scale is based on the analysis of the data and/or the output of the coding analysis.

[3] Note that any piece of metadata can potentially serve as segmentation.

Whereas there may be many types of stanzas applied to segment the same data (e.g., one based on temporality, another based on topic), any given utterance can only contribute to one stanza window within the same stanza type. This means that co-occurrences are computed for each line when they are the "referent line", the utterance that is determining co-occurrences[4]. Each line can only constitute the referent line once. Thus, with the exception of the last line in the conversation, utterances themselves do potentially "repeat" in windows (constitute multiple windows), but co-occurrences are only counted once for each line.

Utterances, thus, contribute to a single stanza, and stanzas are nested within conversations. A unit is the collection of referent lines assigned to a given unit designation, which is commonly operationalized as individuals or groups of data providers.

Each level of segmentation in the ENA data model is crucial to network construction: data is coded on the level of utterance, co-occurrences are computed on the level of stanza, and co-occurrence frequencies are aggregated in a given conversation and across conversations for each unit of analysis. These structures serve specific purposes in ENA modelling and are operationalized relative to each other.

In the book Quantitative Ethnography, Shaffer notes that segmentation should not be arbitrary, it should be based on rules, which should provide "ontological consistency" across the dataset. Ontological consistency in segmentation connotes having "the same kind of information" as lines of data and groupings of those lines (relational context) [1]. Similarity can be operationalized in many ways, such as based on length (e.g., how many words an utterance or stanza is), granularity (e.g., level of detail a segment should contain), or meaning (e.g., consistency in topics).

Stanza windows are ways of operationalizing stanza, that is, relational context in which all lines are related. Stanza windows define how co-occurrences are computed within conversations for a given unit of analysis. Thus, stanza windows serve as both segmentation and code co-occurrence accumulation. This paper investigates the three frequently employed windows in QE studies: moving stanza, infinite stanza, and whole conversation stanza window[5]. The following describes how these windows are conceptualized and some underlying assumptions about the data to which they are applied.

3   Establishing Relational Context

Moving Stanza Window
Quantitative ethnographers often operationalize stanza as a sliding window of fixed length (moving stanza window), where each utterance is associated with some prior segment within a conversation that forms its relational context. Moving stanza windows compute the co-occurrences of each line in a conversation relative to every line that comes before it *within the window*. Computations are made for the "referent line"; that is, the bottom-most line within the window, which is closest to the end of the conversation.

---

[4] For whole conversation stanza windows, there may not be a referent line, see Sect. 3.

[5] Stanza windows are examined in their "backward-facing" variations: co-occurrences are computed from a referent line to lines that precede it, as opposed to subsequent lines.

The default in the webtool is a moving stanza window of 4 lines; this means that each line within a conversation is considered to be related to the 3 lines that precede it, thus, relational context is determined as 4 lines of data. This window "slides down" from the top of the conversation (first lines) to the bottom (last lines). Code co-occurrences are aggregated along the way for each window to which a given unit had contributed the referent line. The co-occurrences in each window are then aggregated across all conversations to which a unit had contributed. The moving stanza "builds" up to the designated window size by beginning the conversation with a stanza of one line and adding a line to each subsequent stanza until the designated window size is reached.

Underlying assumptions: 1) The optimal size of the moving window can be determined based on theory and/or the data e.g. by qualitatively examining the distance between referent lines and references; 2) Relational context is uniform in length; stanza windows are the same size across a single conversation and across all conversations in the dataset; 3) Code co-occurrences beyond the given stanza window size are not possible; 4) Within the stanza window there is always a referent line; 5) In each moving stanza window, co-occurrences are only computed for the referent line; 6) Co-occurrences are only possible between the codes within the referent line or between the referent line versus the other lines included within the window; 7) Co-occurrences within a stanza window are only computed for a given unit if the unit contributed the referent line; 8) All successive stanzas partially overlap with each other within a conversation; 9) If the size of the moving window is equal to or larger than the number of lines in a given conversation, co-occurrence accumulation will be equivalent to an infinite stanza window (see below).

Infinite Stanza Window
Infinite stanza windows compute co-occurrences of each line in a conversation relative to every line that comes before it *within a conversation*. Thus, the infinite stanza works in the same way as a moving stanza, but there is no limit on the number of previous lines that are included in the window (except for the length of the conversation itself).

Underlying assumptions: 1) Stanza windows are not uniform length (size of window changes depending on referent line); 2) Code co-occurrences are possible in the entire conversation (e.g., codes at the beginning of a conversation have the potential to co-occur with codes in the middle or at the end of the conversation); 3) Within the stanza window there is always a referent line; 4) In each stanza window, co-occurrences are only computed for the referent line; 5) Co-occurrences are only possible between the codes within the referent line or between the referent line versus the other lines included within the window; 6) Co-occurrences within a stanza window are only aggregated for a given unit if the unit contributed the referent line; 7) With the exception of the very first stanza in a given conversation (1st line in a conversation), all stanzas completely overlap with each other within a conversation; 8) Codes located at the beginning of the conversation have more "weight" than those later on, as they are included in more stanza windows and thus have the potential to co-occur with more codes; 9) The location of the code within the conversation determines the size of their relational context: a code located on line eleven, for example, has a stanza window size of ten lines plus the referent line itself (eleven lines total); a code located on the thirty-seventh line in a conversation will have a stanza window size of thirty-seven lines, and so on.

Whole Conversation Stanza Window

Whole conversation stanza windows consider the entire conversation as the stanza window: this type of stanza window identifies whether a co-occurrence exists in the lines contributed by a given unit in a given conversation, then aggregates those across all conversations in the dataset. This approach equates conversation with stanza, thus, codes may co-occur anywhere in the conversation.

Underlying assumptions: 1) Stanza windows are conceptually the same length (i.e., the length of a given conversation), but operationally may differ in length if conversations vary in length; 2) From a theoretical perspective, there is no referent line within whole conversation windows, but co-occurrence computations may be operationalized with a referent line; 3) The location of any given code within a conversation/stanza window does not affect accumulation in any way; 4) The location of any given code compared to any other code within a conversation/stanza window does not affect accumulation in any way; 5) Co-occurrences within a stanza window are computed and aggregated for a given unit.

In the following, passages from two qualitative datasets are used to elaborate how moving, infinite, and whole conversation stanza windows function using binary summation and some implications of employing them.

4   Data in Use

Decisions regarding segmentation are highly dependent on research questions, objectives, modelling techniques, and most notably, the data itself. One crucial aspect of data is whether it is dialogic (two or more discussants) or monologic (single data provider). An example of the former may be multiple participants working together on a collaborative task, an example of the latter can be an interviewer and single interviewee having a discussion. Although a dialogue, interviews are usually conceptualized as data from a single data provider. Because these two types of data offer opportunities to highlight different aspects of segmentation and accumulation, both are used in the present paper.

Dialogic data were obtained from a discussion on gun violence between mass shooting survivors (MSS) and members of the National Rifle Association (NRA) conducted by Jubilee's Middle Ground[6]. To present a succinct example, 1) snippets were taken from the discussion and 2) utterances were represented as if they were contributed by four people, when in reality eight people participated in the conversation.

Monologic data were obtained from Soft White Underbelly[7], containing interviews and portraits of the human condition by photographer, Mark Laita. Specifically, a section of the 16-min-long interview with a teenaged runaway "Kristina" was chosen because its rhetorical characteristics provided an opportunity to demonstrate many forms of segmentation in a relatively succinct chunk of text.

---

[6] https://www.jubileemedia.com.
[7] https://www.softwhiteunderbelly.com; caution: contains language that may be upsetting.

Transcripts were obtained from the respective YouTube channels of Jubilee and Soft White Underbelly. In both dialogic and monologic data, utterance was operationalized as sentences. Sentences served as the smallest codable segments because the developed codes were most applicable to sentences (as opposed to e.g., smaller prosodic phrases or larger turns-of-talk). Furthermore, the intent was to present a concise chunk of text on a level of granularity that would enable a fair number of co-occurrences to take place through which the three window types can be sufficiently demonstrated. In illustrations with both dialogic and monologic data, conversation was specified as the entire chunk of text that is presented in the example.

5 Demonstrating Various Stanza Windows

In the following, three viable operationalizations of relational context are illustrated in a chunk of qualitative data: moving stanza window, infinite stanza window, and whole conversation stanza window. Utterances in dialogic and monologic data were coded with differing sets of codes. Co-occurrences were then aggregated per unit for each unique pair of codes. Lastly, network models were generated manually to illustrate the strength of co-occurrences and inspect the differences in models produced with the three stanza window types.

Dialogic Data

Dialogic data was coded for manifestations of the codes contained in Table 2. Figure 1 contains the lines of the narrative, segmented by sentence, and coded with the three codes (S, M, R) represented in binary form, as well as three modes of code co-occurrence accumulation.

Table 2. Codes applied to dialogic data and their brief descriptions.

CODE	DESCRIPTION
"Safety" (S)	holding a gun to feel safe, helping others feel safe with guns
"Mental health" (M)	naming mental health problems (depression, anxiety, isolation) as the underlying cause of mass shootings
"Regulation" (R)	State/national laws, advantages/disadvantages of regulating gun ownership, gun-free zones

Four individuals contributed to the conversation: Sally and Sue are members of the NRA, Joe and Fred are survivors of mass shootings. Their narratives are represented in brown and yellow, respectively. To compare network models, data providers were grouped according to whether they identified as members of the NRA or survivors of mass shootings; these comprised the units.

Figure 2 displays mean networks for NRA members and survivors of mass shootings. Code co-occurrences were accumulated with a moving stanza window of four, infinite stanza window, and a whole conversation stanza window. The conversation is the entire chunk of text (lines 1–14).

	Indiv.	Segmented data	S	M	R
1	Sally	So, you're in high school, do you feel safer or less safe being that your school is a gun-free zone?	1	0	1
2	Joe	I guess I feel safer.	1	0	0
3	Joe	But it doesn't matter if it's a gun or a knife or a bomb, I think he was going to do it no matter what.	0	1	0
4	Fred	I think mass shootings are a problem but we're focusing on the wrong thing.	0	0	0
5	Fred	We should focus on some sort of gun regulation, but at the same time acknowledge it is a mental health problem.	0	1	1
6	Sue	It's less about regulations, I think.	0	0	1
7	Sue	I'm a gun owner, and one of the proudest things I feel is when I teach, especially women.	0	0	0
8	Sue	I just feel like I've helped someone become safer in their life.	1	0	0
9	Joe	Yeah, it's almost like my equalizer.	0	0	0
10	Joe	So, like, it helps you and it gives you more peace of mind.	0	0	0
11	Joe	Like, I am not as vulnerable and unsafe as people think.	0	0	0
12	Sally	I believe we have a drug problem; I believe we have a racial problem.	0	0	0
13	Sally	The reason why I don't think mass shooting is a problem is because if we took all the guns it wouldn't stop the violence.	0	0	1
14	Sally	They could have used a car, they could have used a knife, that would not absolve these deaths.	0	0	0

Accumulation for NRA

	MSW			ISW			WCSW		
	S+R	S+M	M+R	S+R	S+M	M+R	S+R	S+M	M+R
Total	1	3	1	1	4	2	0	1	0

Accumulation for MSS

	MSW			ISW			WCSW		
	S+R	S+M	M+R	S+R	S+M	M+R	S+R	S+M	M+R
Total	2	2	2	3	3	2	1	1	1

Fig. 1. (Left) Qualitative data represented one utterance (sentence) per row, coded with three codes (Safety, Mental health, Regulation) line-by-line in binary form. Narratives from members of the National Rifle Association are in brown, narratives from survivors of mass shootings are in yellow. Code occurrences are highlighted in green. (Middle and right) Code co-occurrence accumulation for lines of data provided by members of the National Rifle Association (NRA) and mass shooting survivors (MSS) using a moving stanza (MSW), infinite stanza (ISW), and whole conversation stanza window (WCSW). (Color figure online)

UNIT	MOVING STANZA 4	INFINITE STANZA	WHOLE CONVERSATION
NRA			
MSS			

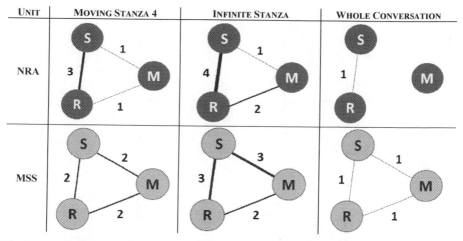

Fig. 2. Networks constructed with three different operationalizations of stanza: moving stanza window, infinite stanza window, and whole conversation stanza window. Network nodes represent codes, the thickness of the edges and numbers represent the strength of co-occurrence between codes.

Graphs depicting co-occurrence accumulation with a whole conversation window differ greatly from the other two window types. Only one edge was created in the NRA graph, three edges in the MSS graph; any number of co-occurrences in whole conversation models would be of equal strength if there are no other conversations to be summed across a unit, as in the discussed example. Networks generated with a moving stanza and infinite stanza window do not show marked differences compared to each other.

Monologic Data

Monologic data was coded for manifestations of the codes contained in Table 3. Figure 3 contains the lines of the narrative, segmented by sentence and coded with the three codes (A, S, D) represented in binary form, as well as three modes of code co-occurrence accumulation for lines contributed by the interviewee.

Table 3. Codes applied to monologic data and their brief descriptions.

CODE	DESCRIPTION
"Abandonment" (A)	Being left to one's own devices, loneliness
"Struggle" (S)	Life challenges, difficulties, hardship
"Desperation" (D)	Begging, pleading, last resorts

One individual contributed to the conversation: Kristina. Interviewer questions and comments are in grey. To compare network models produced with the varying operationalizations of stanza window, co-occurrences in the coded data were accumulated.

	SEGMENTED DATA	A	S	D	MSW A+S	MSW A+D	MSW A+S+D	ISW A+S	ISW A+D	ISW A+S+D	WCSW A+S	WCSW A+D	WCSW A+S+D
1	You know, everybody out here sees me and, people think I'm fine.	0	0	0	0	0	0	0	0	0			
2	You know?	0	0	0	0	0	0	0	0	0			
3	People don't know what people like me go through.	0	1	0	0	0	0	0	0	0			
4	Kind of sucks.	0	0	0	0	0	0	0	0	0			
	What do you think people don't understand?												
5	The struggle.	0	1	0	1	0	0	1	0	0			
6	It's hard to be out here by yourself with nobody to trust, nobody to go to.	1	1	0	1	0	0	1	0	0			
7	No family.	1	0	0	1	0	0	1	0	0			
8	I've called my parents a million times trying to beg 'em to go home.	1	0	1	1	1	1	1	1	1			
9	Nobody cares about nobody here.	1	0	0	1	0	1	1	1	1			
10	Out here it's all dog eat dog world.	0	1	0	1	1	1	1	1	1			
	Aha.												
11	People think that when they have a job and shit that they have it good, you know.	0	0	0	0	0	0	0	0	0			
12	They think that they are fucking struggling, that they're fucking going through it or whatever.	0	1	0	1	0	0	1	0	1			
13	They're not going through shit.	0	1	0	0	0	0	1	0	1			
14	They don't know what it's like to fucking eat out of the trash or to fucking not have, fucking clothes to wear or shoes that fit you.	0	1	1	0	1	1	1	1	1			
15	They don't know what it's like to be afraid for tomorrow.	0	1	0	0	0	1	1	0	1			
16	They don't know what it's like to do something that you don't want to do just to survive.	0	1	1	0	1	1	1	1	1			
17	This is the shit that I go through on a daily basis.	0	1	1	0	1	1	1	1	1			
					6	2	6	11	5	8	1	1	1

Fig. 3. (Left) Qualitative data represented one utterance (sentence) per row, coded with three codes (Abandonment, Struggle, Desperation) line-by-line in binary form. Code occurrences are highlighted in green. (Right) Code co-occurrence accumulation for lines of data provided by the interviewee using a moving stanza (MSW), infinite stanza (ISW), and whole conversation stanza window (WCSW). (Color figure online)

Figure 4 displays Kristina's networks. Code co-occurrences were accumulated with a moving stanza window of four, infinite stanza window, and whole conversation stanza window. The conversation is the entire chunk of text (lines 1–17).

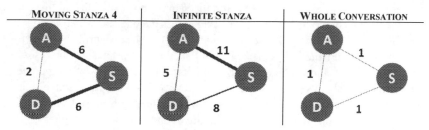

Fig. 4. Networks constructed with three different operationalizations of stanza: moving stanza window, infinite stanza window, and whole conversation stanza window. Network nodes represent codes, the thickness of the edges and numbers represent the strength of co-occurrence between codes.

The graph depicting co-occurrence accumulation with a whole conversation window again differs greatly from the other two window types; all connections are of equal strength. Yet, in monologic data, networks generated with a moving stanza and infinite stanza window also show marked differences compared to each other. The code pair Abandonment and Struggle exhibits substantially more co-occurrences in the infinite stanza model, even considering the increased proportions of the other two code pairs.

6   Circumstances and Implications of Using Various Windows

Moving Stanza Window

A moving stanza window of four was employed to accumulate code co-occurrences, which entailed taking each line and the three lines preceding it to determine which co-occurrences took place between the referent line and those within the window. Co-occurrences were aggregated for each unit, specified by which data provider contributed the referent line.

Typically, methodological papers have focused on challenges in determining the precise length of this sliding window, addressing the problem that a larger window may produce many false positive connections (overrepresenting connections that are not meaningful), while smaller windows may fail to capture valid connections. In most cases, appropriate window length is determined by manually coding a subset of data, identifying the furthest referents (e.g., utterances referring to each other are commonly max. 4 lines apart), and this is generalized to the entire sample [8, 12, 13]. Ruis and colleagues, for example, found that for one dataset documenting the interactions of engineering student project teams, statistical discrimination between two sub-populations was fairly robust to window length once a minimum length was reached (in their study, that minimum was four lines). However, they also found that model features and interpretation were more sensitive to window length, and did not stabilize until a window length of seven [8].

One of the numerous assumptions the researcher holds true when employing a moving stanza window to operationalize relational context is that referent lines and the utterances they refer to always reside within the same window length and that this uniform distance is adequate in capturing meaning across the dataset. Albeit fixed window lengths have successfully been applied to model e.g., collaborative problem-solving [14] and reasoning [15], it is not appropriate for all data types, datasets, and analyses.

Crucially, a fixed stanza window size implies that the window defining context for any given line will always be the same size. Whereas group conversations might have a faster pace and less references to previous topics or statements, narratives contributed by the same participant may be organic, iterative, and may have a higher chance of mixing proximal and distal self-referencing [16]. One consideration may be the general objectives of data collection, such as: is the researcher documenting a goal-oriented task (e.g., chatroom discussions on collaborative problem-solving) or a phenomenological description of an experience or opinion (e.g., semi-structured interview). The former may imply a more linear process of reaching a goal by working together where fixed window lengths are appropriate, the latter may imply a more iterative process of reflection where window sizes may need to vary. Another consideration may be whether underlying theory suggests that saying something more often indicates e.g., intensity of conviction or other psychological assumptions, in which case perhaps binary summed whole conversation windows would not suffice in modelling the data but moving or infinite stanza windows may as these operationalized stanza window and conversation separately.

In sum, justifications for employing a moving stanza window include assuming that the position of codes within the conversation (respective to its delimiters) is less important than the proximity of codes relative to each other (and relative to the employed window size). A further assumption is that a fixed window size can capture valid co-occurrences, which is justified if e.g., the pace of the conversation stays relatively constant in the entire dataset, such as, for example, with data that can be collected from a chat. An additional assumption in using fixed windows is that all discussants contribute a relatively similar number of utterances. If there is one discussant who generally utters more lines compared to other participants, this may complicate determining optimal window size. Using the other participants' narrative to determine a moving window size can cause the model to indicate that the discussant with more utterances responds less to those also in the conversation (as relatively distal connections cannot be made). Using a moving stanza window to operationalize relational context also connotes assuming there should be a referent line that determines which co-occurrences constitute meaningful connections within the window and that only preceding lines can form relational context with the referent line.

Infinite Stanza Window

Computing code co-occurrences with an infinite stanza window involved identifying a referent line and checking for co-occurrences in each line before it within the window. The first utterance constituted the first stanza, and all successive stanzas overlapped with the previous window until the last utterance in the conversation constituted the referent line and the entire conversation constituted the window. Co-occurrences were aggregated for each unit, based on the data provider contributing the referent line.

An infinite stanza window assumes that utterances in any part of the conversation can form relational context. Co-occurrences may form regardless of the location of codes within the conversation, and while the proximity of codes to each other is not presumed to be an important feature in the data, the position of codes within the conversation is crucial in their potential to interact with other codes. For example, in the case of an interview that was only segmented into utterances and the entire interview is the conversation, using an infinite stanza would imply that the researcher places more weight on what was said early in the interview rather than what was said later. This is because in an infinite window, codes in the beginning of the interview will constitute co-occurrences more often than those toward the end of the transcript. This operationalization of stanza window is analogous to the storytelling memory game where the first player begins with improvising a sentence, and every subsequent player must first repeat the sentences uttered by the players before them, only then can they add their own sentence to the story. Hence the beginning of the story will be uttered several times, while the last sentence only once. This also may mean that co-occurrence patterns, which were established earlier in the conversation, may repeat and that not all repetitions are necessarily meaningful but are a product of the mode of accumulation itself.

Another feature of employing a moving or infinite window is that the order of lines included in windows must be meaningful. Lines within a conversation should follow some kind of temporal (or other meaningful) order, but this requirement is not true for conversations themselves (as co-occurrences within windows are merely summed for each unit). Thus, using the windows discussed in this paper, a conversation in dialogic data should follow e.g., sequential order (as lines were uttered) and can only be reversed if the window itself is reversed (i.e., "forward-facing" rather than "backward-facing"). The extent of differences in the models due to order will depend on the differences in the location and frequency of codes within the dataset.

Another aspect of data to consider is how structured or focused the given data is perceived to be. For example, in the case of interviews, as data providers continue talking, they may digress farther and farther from their initial response to the question. Thus, if conversations are defined as question – response segments within a transcript, codes that are more central to the response could be located at the beginning of each conversation, hence it would be justified to assume responses are built on initial comments and those codes form meaningful connections to the latter part of the same response. Similarly, debates may exhibit a structure where the initial or central claims (arguments) are made at the beginning of a conversation and all statements following those are reactions to or extensions of the central ideas. Because arguments are usually logical successions to initial claims, it may be justified to consider codes interacting in this manner meaningful.

In sum, justifications for employing an infinite stanza window include assuming that the position of codes vis-à-vis conversation delimiters is more important than the position of codes relative to each other (i.e., co-occurrences may form regardless of codes' position in the conversation), and that codes appearing earlier in the conversation constitute the basis of later meaningful co-occurrences. Using an infinite stanza window to operationalize relational context also connotes assuming there should be a referent line that determines which co-occurrences form meaningful connections within the window and that only preceding lines can establish relational context with the referent line.

Whole Conversation Stanza Window

Accumulation with a whole conversation window entailed considering the entire conversation the stanza window and computing code co-occurrences accordingly. This technique does not enable multiple stanza windows within the same conversation, and binarizes code co-occurrences, which will generally lead to markedly different networks, compared to other modes of accumulation for the same dataset (provided all other model parameters are kept constant).

With regard to dialogic data, employing whole conversation windows can easily become problematic. There is no referent line in whole conversation windows, hence co-occurrences may form with both preceding and subsequent lines, provided they were contributed by the same unit. This means codes manifesting in lines contributed by a discussant will only co-occur with codes contributed by the same discussant within the conversation. In other words, despite multiple participants being in the same discussion, the model will, in essence, depict discussants conversing with themselves. Although this mode of accumulation may not be suited to model how discussants interact, it may be apt in depicting the individual mental model of each participant.

On the other hand, whole conversation stanza windows can be appropriate for monologic data, i.e., when there is only one data provider. In the case of diary entries, field notes, and unstructured, semi-structured or structured interviews, 1) the extent of relational context may vary across a dataset (thus, moving windows of fixed length are suboptimal), 2) both proximal and distal co-occurrences may be meaningful within a conversation (thus, stanza window and conversation can be operationalized as the same), and 3) the location of codes within the conversation do not necessarily matter (thus, moving windows are too constrictive and infinite windows attributing more weight to codes earlier in the conversation may be suboptimal). If the researcher is only interested in whether a co-occurrence took place within a conversation, then employing a whole conversation window with binary summation may be justified. If the frequency of these co-occurrences also matters, then a weighted summation may be applicable. When using the whole conversation method, to avoid overrepresenting connections that are not meaningful or underrepresenting those that are, often theory-based manual segmentation must be employed to delimit conversations of appropriate length. For more on manual segmentation and whole conversation windows, please see: [17].

7   Concluding Thoughts

The conceptual framework and terminology of ENA was utilized to address the effects of segmentation on quantitative analyses of qualitative data because both coding and segmentation contribute to the construction of ENA models. Employing a specific data model afforded delving into various operationalizations of stanza window (moving, infinite, whole conversation), illustrating how these affect network graphs, and elaborating some underlying assumptions.

Using the ENA data model itself entailed accepting a series of assumptions and implications, such as: segmentation can be hierarchical, meaning can reside on any or all levels of hierarchical segmentation, code co-occurrences are of interest, co-occurrences are influenced by segmentation decisions, code pairs constitute co-occurrences (rather than e.g., triads), relational context is operationalized as a mode of co-occurrence accumulation (stanza window) and aggregation (conversation), and both accumulation and aggregation are performed based on unit.

A significant feature of this data model is that stanza windows serve as both segmentation and co-occurrence accumulation. Many segmentation techniques involve a non-hierarchical conceptualization of data structure, in which case code accumulation may be less sensitive to temporality [12]. In the ENA data model, data can be hierarchically structured, utterances can be nested in larger contexts (e.g., stanza, conversation, unit), and although a subset or all of these can be conflated, this nested structure enables the grouping of lines of data based on temporality (e.g., order) or other metadata.

One could argue, the only "real" act of segmentation is defining what the smallest codable pieces of data should be, any other acts are mere groupings of those utterances. Yet, because utterances can indeed be grouped in various ways to establish relational context, this enables a myriad of operationalizations for co-occurrence accumulation (e.g., forward- and backward-facing stanza windows, binary or weighted summation, and so on).

In this paper, the ENA tool was not employed to generate networks, as the dataset was too small and manually created illustrations were more appropriate visualizations. Few publications have examined the effects of stanza windows on ENA models using complete datasets. One such study used a sensitivity analysis to compare different stanza window and conversation selections and found that these parameterizations may produce a marked difference between models on the level of individual data providers [18]. Precisely because coding and segmentation decisions influence each other greatly, more analyses are needed that investigate these questions. Observations in this paper should be taken with a grain of salt; general statements about utilizing various windows are challenging to formulate, as choices will always be dependent on the research question(s), analytical objectives, and the data itself.

Acknowledgements. This project received funding from the European Union's Horizon 2020 research and innovation program under the Marie Sklodowska-Curie grant agreement No. 101028644, as well as from University Fund Limburg/SWOL. The opinions, findings, and conclusions do not reflect the views of the funding agency, cooperating institutions, or other individuals. Thank you to Andrew Ruis for his insights on this paper.

References

1. Shaffer, D.: Quantitative Ethnography. Cathcart Press, Madison (2017)
2. Barany, A., Philips, M., Kawakubo, A.J.T., Oshima, J.: Choosing units of analysis in temporal discourse. In: Wasson, B., Zörgő, S. (eds.) ICQE 2021. CCIS, vol. 1522, pp. 80–94. Springer, Cham (2022). https://doi.org/10.1007/978-3-030-93859-8_6
3. Schnur, E., Csomay, E.: Triangulating text segmentation methods with diverse analytical approaches to analyzing text structure. In: Egbert, J., Baker, P. (eds.) Using Corpus Methods to Triangulate Linguistic Analysis. Taylor & Francis, New York (2020)

4. Gee, J.P.: A linguistic approach to narrative. J. Narrat. Life Hist. **1**, 15–39 (1991)
5. Collier, W., Ruis, A., Shaffer, D.W.: Local versus global connection making in discourse. In: Looi, C.-K., Polman, J., Cress, U., Reimann, P. (eds.) Transforming Learning, Empowering Learners Conference Proceedings, vol. I, pp. 426–433. International Society of the Learning Sciences (2016)
6. Kurasaki, K.: Intercoder reliability for validating conclusions drawn from open-ended interview data. Field Methods **12**, 179–194 (2000)
7. Kleinheksel, A.J., Rockich-Winston, N., Tawfik, H., Wyatt, T.R.: Demystifying content analysis. Am. J. Pharm. Educ. **84**, 7113 (2020). https://doi.org/10.5688/ajpe7113
8. Ruis, A.R., Siebert-Evenstone, A.L., Pozen, R., et al.: Finding common ground: a method for measuring recent temporal context in analyses of complex, collaborative thinking. In: Lund, K., Niccolai, G., Lavoué, E., et al. (eds.) A Wide Lens: Combining Embodied, Enactive, Extended, and Embedded Learning in Collaborative Settings, pp. 136–143. International Society of the Learning Sciences (2019)
9. Goffman, E.: Frame Analysis - An Essay on the Organization of Experience. Northeastern University Press, Boston (1974)
10. Williamson Shaffer, D., Collier, W., Ruis, A.: A tutorial on epistemic network analysis: analyzing the structure of connections in cognitive, social, and interaction data. J. Learn. Anal. **3**, 9–45 (2016). https://doi.org/10.18608/jla.2016.33.3
11. Zörgő, S., Peters, G.-J.Y., Porter, C., et al.: Methodology in the Mirror: Third International Conference on Quantitative Ethnography. Advances in Quantitative Ethnography, pp. 144–159 (2022). https://doi.org/10.1007/978-3-030-93859-8_10
12. Siebert-Evenstone, A.L., Arastoopour, G., Collier, W., et al.: In search of conversational grain size: modelling semantic structure using moving Stanza windows. J. Learn. Anal. **4**, 123–139 (2017)
13. Ruis, A.R., Siebert-Evenstone, A., Pozen, R., et al.: A method for determining the extent of recent temporal context in analyses of complex, collaborative thinking. In: Kay, J., Luckin, R. (eds.) Rethinking Learning in the Digital Age: Making the Learning Sciences Count. International Society of the Learning Sciences (2018)
14. Bressler, D., Bodzin, A., Eagan, B., Tabatabai, S.: Using epistemic network analysis to examine discourse and scientific practice during a collaborative game. J. Sci. Educ. Technol. **28**, 553–566 (2019)
15. Csanadi, A., Eagan, B., Shaffer, D.W., et al.: Collaborative and individual scientific reasoning of pre-service teachers: new insights through Epistemic Network Analysis (ENA). In: Smith, B., Borge, M., Mercier, E., Yon Lim, K. (eds.) Making a Difference: Prioritizing Equity and Access in CSCL: 12th International Conference on Computer Supported Collaborative Learning (CSCL) 2017, pp. 215–222. International Society of the Learning Sciences (2017)
16. Zörgő, S., Peters, G.-J.: Epistemic network analysis for semi-structured interviews and other continuous narratives: challenges and insights. In: Eagan, B., Misfeldt, M., Siebert-Evenstone, A. (eds.) ICQE 2019. CCIS, vol. 1112, pp. 267–277. Springer, Cham (2019). https://doi.org/10.1007/978-3-030-33232-7_23
17. Zörgő, S., Brohinsky, J.: Parsing the continuum: manual segmentation of monologic data. Preprint submitted to the Fourth International Conference on Quantitative Ethnography (2022). osf.io/79zxw
18. Zörgő, S., Swiecki, Z., Ruis, A.R.: Exploring the effects of segmentation on semi-structured interview data with epistemic network analysis. In: Ruis, A.R., Lee, S.B. (eds.) ICQE 2021. CCIS, vol. 1312, pp. 78–90. Springer, Cham (2021). https://doi.org/10.1007/978-3-030-677 88-6_6

Parsing the Continuum: Manual Segmentation of Monologic Data

Szilvia Zörgő[1]([⊠]) [iD] and Jais Brohinsky[2] [iD]

[1] Care and Public Health Research Institute, Maastricht University, Maastricht, Netherlands
zorgoszilvia@gmail.com
[2] University of Wisconsin-Madison, Madison, WI 53706, USA

Abstract. Segmentation is a crucial step in analyses of qualitative data where code or code co-occurrence frequencies are of interest. Decisions about how best to segment are inextricably connected to coding decisions, as well as wider analytical goals and research questions. These decisions directly affect resulting models and the interpretations derived from them. However, while there is a wealth of frameworks guiding code development and application, far fewer guidelines exist for segmentation. This paper reports on the development of an initial set of heuristics for the segmentation of monologic data. Using the framework of Epistemic Network Analysis, we demonstrate various approaches to segmentation and show how these segmentation decisions affect models and subsequent interpretations. We argue that segmentation should be aligned with research questions and developed in conjunction with coding, and we offer considerations and techniques for doing so.

Keywords: Data Segmentation · Methodology · Epistemic Network Analysis

1 Introduction

Qualitative data that are transcribed for analysis may be coded to identify relevant constructs and patterns. Often, these patterns are not only captured in codes, but in interactions among codes. A crucial factor contributing to code interactions is segmentation, that is, the "consistent and meaningful" division of data into codable pieces [1]. Segmentation decisions are critically linked with coding decisions, and both are highly dependent on research questions and analytical goals. When researchers aim to construct quantitative models of qualitative data, coding and segmentation are essential factors.

While several analytical frameworks, such as Interpretative Phenomenological Analysis and Grounded Theory, guide code development and application, few frameworks offer clear considerations of segmentation. Those that do (e.g., Goffman's Frame Analysis [2] or Gee's five-fold discourse structure [3]) rarely discuss the interaction between coding and segmentation decisions or the systematic and consistent application of segmentation to a dataset.

In the following, we offer considerations for manual segmentation of monologic data and develop heuristics for segmentation decision making. We then analyze publicly

C. Damşa and A. Barany (Eds.): ICQE 2022, CCIS 1785, pp. 163–181, 2023.
https://doi.org/10.1007/978-3-031-31726-2_12

available data in order to demonstrate these heuristics and, using the Epistemic Network Analysis data model, we show how segmentation decisions can affect models and the interpretations drawn from them. This worked example affords an empirically grounded examination of the interactions between segmentation, coding, and modelling as well as a discussion of manual segmentation applications and heuristics.

2 Theory

2.1 General Considerations in Segmentation

When code or code co-occurrence frequencies are of interest, segmentation should not be arbitrary, as it may influence these frequencies [4]. Ideally, the development of segmentation heuristics is informed by coding decisions, analytical goals, and the data themselves. According to Shaffer, segmentation should be based on heuristics, which should provide *ontological consistency* across a dataset. Ontological consistency in segmentation connotes similarity, or having "the same kind of information" as units of analysis [1]. Consistency can be operationalized in many ways, such as length (e.g., number of words), granularity (e.g., level of detail a segment should contain), or meaning (e.g., consistency in topics that segments represent). Some analyses may require data to be divided into equivalent chunks that are exchangeable for the purposes of quantification [5]. Depending on modelling technique, quantification may equally depend on coding and segmentation. Thus, these decisions ideally inform each other.

Meaningful segments are most often defined by analytical goals or utility. For example, text prediction development typically necessitates character-level segmentation, while text translation is processed on a higher level (e.g., sentences). Thus, meaning is markedly defined by the research objectives and resides on several levels simultaneously (e.g., character, word, sentence, document), any or all of which may be significant in achieving analytical goals. The specification of goals influences the operationalization of meaning and its localization on any given level(s) of segmentation.

Segmentation considerations are also influenced by coding decisions. In tokenization, for example, a text is broken down into words, numbers, and punctuation marks, which constitute the smallest units of analysis (lowest level of segmentation). These can then be used to develop codes through processes like stemming (truncating words to their assumed root) or lemmatization (specifying the base form of words using lexical knowledge). A code can be a specific word (e.g., leaf) or a set of words (e.g., leaf, leaves, foliage), in which case token-based segmentation would be appropriate. However, if a researcher uses codes to capture more abstract phenomena like jokes, for instance, then segmenting by words is suboptimal compared to sentences or sets of sentences. Thus, developed codes need to be applicable to designated segments.

In the case of textual data, scholars assert that text structures are often hierarchically organized, that is, shorter segments form the basis for longer ones [3, 6]. This hierarchical relationship among lines of data also establishes *relational context*, lines that are or can be related to each other, which is crucial for determining code interactions.

Some types of analyses may only segment on a single level and consider meaningful divisions to be a fragment of discourse that represents a single message, a distinguishing feature, or a change of subject [7]. Dialogic data are often segmented according to conversational turns or turns-of-talk. Without these structural indices, monologic data may be meaningfully segmented into e.g., phrases, sentences, or paragraphs. Kleinheksel et al. advocate for dividing segments that contain "multiple ideas of interest" (such as a paragraph) into sentences or breaking a sentence up into phrases to ease the "cognitive burden of analysis" [8].

Arguably, this "cognitive burden" may be eased substantially by developing a comprehensive codebook, clear coding instructions, and sufficiently training coders. However, the more crucial issues affecting the granularity of segmentation depend on the mode of data analysis and modelling [9]. To demonstrate the interdependence of segmentation, coding, and modelling, we employ the Epistemic Network Analysis (ENA) framework to elaborate ways in which segmentation heuristics can be developed and how these decisions affect models of code co-occurrences.

2.2 Components of Segmentation in Epistemic Network Analysis

ENA creates dynamic network models based on the relative frequency of code co-occurrence within designated segments of data. Both coding and segmentation decisions are crucial in determining code co-occurrences, which in turn form the basis for ENA models. ENA also offers an opportunity to examine how code co-occurrences are made meaningful by way of hierarchical segmentation, where codes are applied to the lowest level of segmentation and given context in relation to longer segments in which they are nested. Thus, ENA provides a suitable conceptual framework for examining the interactions between segmentation, coding, and modelling.

ENA displays code co-occurrences as network graphs where nodes represent codes, and the thickness of edges represents the strength of co-occurrence between unique pairs of codes. (For a more detailed description of network construction, please see: [1, 10].) ENA uses datasets that are curated in a specific manner, in accordance with its data model (see: [11]). Qualitative data are segmented according to their smallest codable pieces (lines or "utterances"), which constitute rows. Columns in the dataset are the data and variables of interest: metadata and codes (also referred to as discourse codes). Metadata are characteristics of the data itself (e.g., segmentation), the data providers (e.g., demographic data), or the data collection process (e.g., time of interview). Data are represented as one utterance per row, and codes are applied to each utterance. While most metadata are categorically represented (e.g., male, female), codes are usually represented in binary (0 if code is absent, 1 if code is present).

In ENA, lines are generally defined as a turn-of-talk, a sentence, a response, or a second in time [12]. All higher forms of segmentation can be described as groupings of one or more utterances. Utterances are nested within larger segments of qualitative data that provide relational context and make a given line meaningful.

Relational context in ENA is determined by two model parameters: stanza and conversation. A stanza is a set of one or more utterances; a conversation is a set of one or more stanzas. Code co-occurrences are computed on the level of stanza and are aggregated on the level of conversation. Stanza windows are specific ways of operationalizing stanza and, in this data model, function as both segmentation delimiters and modes of co-occurrence accumulation. The totality of utterances to be modelled in an ENA graph is referred to as a unit, which is commonly operationalized as individuals or groups of data providers. Co-occurrence computations in stanza windows are aggregated in each conversation for every unit of analysis.

One approach to operationalizing stanza with ENA is the whole conversation method, which equates conversation with stanza. Thus, codes may co-occur anywhere in the conversation. This type of stanza window identifies whether a co-occurrence exists in the lines contributed by a given unit in a given conversation, then aggregates those across all conversations in the dataset. Arguably, whole conversation stanza windows are not suited to model interactions among participants in dialogic datasets, as co-occurrences are only possible among lines to which a given unit has contributed. On the other hand, it offers affordances to models of monologic data, such as interviews, diary entries, or field notes. Employing a whole conversation is justified, provided codes are assumed to exhibit meaningful connections throughout the conversation, regardless of their position relative to each other or the conversation delimiters.

These circumstances often arise in monologic data, most notably in interviews. Yet, because the whole conversation method conflates stanza and conversation, manual segmentation must often be performed to delimit conversations of appropriate length, avoid overrepresenting connections that are not meaningful, and ensure the capture of meaningful ones. Given the lack of segmentation guidelines, we ask:

RQ1: How can segmentation heuristics be developed for monologic textual data?
RQ2: How can these heuristics be applied to establish meaningful relational context?
RQ3: What are the implications of these segmentation decisions for modelling?

3   Establishing Relational Context and Segmentation Heuristics

3.1   Spotlighting Critical Features

Segmentation heuristics are ideally based on meaningful, observed patterns and can be systematically applied across an entire dataset. Different forms of textual data, however, present varying challenges to segmentation, and so heuristics are best derived from the data themselves and in relation to analytical goals. *Spotlighting*, or collecting chunks of data that exhibit critical features, can aid in this process by providing evidence for the development of more general heuristics.

Zörgő and Peters emphasize the lack of "naturally occurring possibilities for segmentation [in] continuous narratives" like semi-structured interviews, not only in terms of designating ontologically consistent utterances, but also in defining stanzas as analytical units [13]. Furthermore, not all formal section breaks are necessarily meaningful. For example, a timestamp-based automatic transcription might be too fragmented or randomly parsed, and even brief responses to open-ended survey questions that are segmented based on individual responses may need to be split into smaller segments, like sentences, in order to be effectively coded.

These decisions can be facilitated by spotlighting. When examining what "closing the interpretive loop" can signify, Lefstein brings attention to the importance of theoretical assumptions: "To be able to say something meaningful about [our] data", we should search for instances that challenge (and confirm) our "favorite theory" [14]. This can be extended to spotlighting examples in data that are deemed typical or atypical by purposefully seeking out supporting and falsifying exemplars of a particular code constellation, theme, or assumption.

Conversely, there might be codes that the researcher assumes should not be connected in the model. For example, Nyirő et al. conducted interviews with bereaved parents and pediatric oncologists about the conversation in which parents are informed that their child's care has shifted from curation to palliation. An in-depth knowledge of the data suggested that parents and physicians had clear conversational preferences concerning positive sentiment (e.g., what "felt right") and negative sentiment (e.g., what "wasn't relevant"). This qualitative understanding guided the authors' segmentation choice to prevent connections between these sentiment codes in their models [15]. This is not to say contradiction or cognitive dissonance should not or cannot be modelled, but rather serves to illustrate that familiarity with one's data can aid segmentation based on critical code co-occurrences or their anticipated absence.

Spotlighting is thus an important step in the creation of segmentation heuristics, establishment of relational context, and employment of different types of segmentation based on the particularities of data and analytical goals.

3.2 Cycle or Repetition-Based Relational Context

Data features like *cycles* may help establish relational context. A cycle is a complete set of events or a series of states that often, but not necessarily, repeat in the same order. Researchers working with various data modalities have based their segmentation on such cycles. For example, Martin et al. used gameplay video to identify segments based on facial landmarks and emotional evidence: peaks and valleys of "joy values" designated their "learning windows" [16]. Andrist et al. analyzed coordinated referential gaze in collaborating dyads by segmenting interactions into a set of reference-action sequences, which were further divided using verbal reference or actions: pre-reference, reference, post-reference, action, and post-action [17].

In textual data, such as interview transcripts, cycles may be conceptualized as punctuation marks, paragraph markers, or question and response segments, which may or may not include follow-up questions and responses [18]. In think-aloud protocols or recursive interviewing, repeated (sets of) questions may serve as cycle-based segmentation. With multiple data providers in dialogue with each other, cycles may mean turns-of-talk. Andrade et al. defined "conversational turns" as an "attempt by a participant to create a meaningful exchange of information," a communication containing a text (verbalized ideas) and a subtext (nonverbal and paralinguistic elements) [19]. Barany et al. employed the absence of text as a segmentation heuristic when they defined meaningful segments: "any gap of more than a week between posts" [20].

3.3 Protracted Code-Based Relational Context

In studies involving ENA, metadata are most commonly attributes of the data provider or data provision [12] and make possible the attribution of units as individuals or groups (e.g., "novice vs. expert" or "ages 18–39 vs. 40 and above"). These metadata are usually specified with categorical values for each line in the dataset. This indicates that units are also a crucial parameter of segmentation insofar as accumulation (regardless of stanza window type) is performed for data contributed by any given unit.

It is possible to specify metadata that indicate content-related features of data and employ them as the basis for segmentation. Observing the fact that Twitter data "requires the creative use of multiple approaches to gain a richer understanding", Misiejuk et al. aimed to explore ways to integrate sentiment analysis with ENA. In their first approach, three sentiment codes were combined with codes about discourse content. In their second approach, sentiment was employed as "blocking variables" (metadata employed for segmentation). Thus, approach one placed sentiment within the ENA graphs as network nodes (exhibiting varying connections to the content codes), and approach two used sentiment as a way to segment data (utterances were grouped based on the sentiment that was expressed within them). Generated models were compared in terms of their "ability to differentiate between groups, increased accuracy, [and] enhanced interpretability to the model" [21]. This suggests that any piece of metadata may be employed as a foundation for segmentation, including metadata designated to indicate segmentation based on content-related features of the data.

Researchers may consider content-related codes as segmentation: for example, when a high relative frequency of certain codes within co-occurrences produces larger nodes in an ENA graph. This may occur due to 1) the critical role of these codes in analysis or 2) because, by virtue of their definition, they span several lines of data, while other codes in the coding scheme are only applicable to a single line. This can cause (qualitatively unjustified) exaggerated node sizes within epistemic networks. Two possible ways to address this issue are to change the operationalization of utterance or change the coding scheme. The operationalization of utterance interacts with the developed codes and merits a paper of its own. Changing the coding scheme entails inspecting whether codes differ in their applicability to a single utterance (henceforth: discrete codes) or a set of utterances (henceforth: protracted codes).

Provided there is a mix of discrete and protracted codes within the coding scheme, it may be justified to consider protracted codes as metadata describing characteristics of utterances, rather than employing them as discourse codes. The practical implication of this shift is that while values for discourse codes are usually represented in binary form within the dataset, protracted codes (functioning as metadata) are generally categorical. Note that no code is inherently discrete or protracted. It is by considering research questions, weighing segmentation decisions (most notably: operationalization of utterance), and testing implications for modelling that this decision can be made.

4   Exploring Examples of Relational Context

In the following, we demonstrate spotlighting critical features to develop segmentation heuristics for monologic data and use segmentation based on cycles and protracted codes to manually specify relational context. Data for our examples were obtained from the YouTube channel of Soft White Underbelly[1], containing interviews and portraits

---

[1] https://www.softwhiteunderbelly.com; this data contains language and imagery that may be upsetting for some readers.

of the human condition by photographer, Mark Laita. We chose a section of the 16-min interview of "Kristina", a teenaged runaway, because its rhetorical characteristics provided an opportunity to demonstrate our topics in a relatively succinct chunk of text.

In the narrative below, we have operationalized utterances as sentences. We coded these lines of data using codes contained in Table 1. Figure 1 contains our data, one sentence per row. Codes are represented per line in binary form on the right side of the table, and column U contains the ordinal numbering of utterances.

Table 1. Codes applied to monologic data and their brief descriptions.

CODE	DESCRIPTION
Physical abuse (P)	Explicit reference to or assumed instances of bodily violence, including rape.
Emotional abuse (E)	Explicit or assumed instances of verbal and affective mistreatment or trauma
Dissonance (D)	Discrepancies in how others perceive the speaker and how she feels, or between how the speaker behaves and feels
Loss (L)	Losing a loved one, an ideal, or a possession

Spotlighting Critical Features

Spotlighting involves pinpointing critical features of the narrative to derive segmentation heuristics. In the following example, we spotlight lines 5–7 as containing a meaningful pattern: Kristina equates the display of emotions with weakness, connects weakness to abuse, and notes a discrepancy between how she feels and what she allows others to see. This spotlighted piece of data may allow the formulation of heuristics based on lexical characteristics; for example, we may observe that she begins and ends this three-line segment with "fillers" ("yeah" on line 5 and "you know" on line 8), which may connote a meaningful delimiter. We may also note that lines 5–7 are self-contained as a topic (second topic in Fig. 1), although nested in a greater context of her describing life on the streets (lines 4–24). Our spotlighted example is also delimited by pauses in speech: the first pause was due to being asked a question, but the second pause was autonomous and lasted over three seconds. According to transcription timestamps, Kristina did not pause often, and so noting when she did may be significant. Lastly, we may note that our spotlighted section begins with a turn-of-talk delimiter, which can also be considered meaningful and occurs throughout the interview. Table 2 contains potential segmentation heuristics derived from the full chunk of data.

Segmentation heuristics derived from spotlighted data can be used to perform manual segmentation based on, for example, cycles or protracted codes. As a way of assessing a particular choice, it may be useful to triangulate segmentation heuristics, that is, to use other heuristics to qualitatively determine the viability of the decision. While not all heuristics will be meaningful in answering a given research question, some may serve to "cross-check" operationalizations of relational context. Below, we describe examples for segmentation based on cycles and protracted codes. We elaborate effects these choices have on the generated models, what changes they may prompt in interpretation, and how triangulation techniques may aid assessing segmentation viability.

T	P	TT	U		P	E	D	L
				Do you have any dreams or goals or anything you'd like to see happen in your future?				
1	1	1	1	I want to just be happy, bro.	0	0	0	0
1	1	1	2	The only dream I probably got is just to be happy.	0	0	0	0
1	1	1	3	'Cause just because I smile every day, just because I walk around like I'm cool, I'm not happy.	0	0	1	0
1	1	1	4	Sometimes I can't look at myself in the mirror without feeling like, "Damn, this is what life is."	0	0	1	0
				You get depressed a lot?				
2	2	2	5	Yeah, but I don't show it.	0	0	1	0
2	2	2	6	Because if you show it, then it's a sign of weakness and when you're weak is when the people prey on you most.	0	1	1	0
2	2	2	7	I just learned how to fake it and make sure that everyone thinks I'm cool.	0	0	1	0
				(pause)				
3	3	2	8	You know, these streets will take something beautiful and they'll just like crush it and just like make sure that that's nothingness.	0	1	0	1
3	3	2	9	Because out here there's just one thing.	0	0	0	0
3	3	2	10	Money talks, bullshit walks.	0	1	0	0
3	3	2	11	You could pay somebody to do anything out here, bro, and they'll do it.	0	0	0	0
3	3	2	12	If it's the price is right.	0	0	0	0
				(pause)				
3	4	2	13	So everything I ever thought was right, isn't really right out here, it's wrong.	0	0	0	1
3	4	2	14	Whatever I thought was wrong is right.	0	0	0	1
3	4	2	15	What is, isn't, what isn't is.	0	0	0	1
3	4	2	16	I seen children, old people, get killed just 'cause they don't want to comply with what the fuck these people want.	1	1	0	0
4	4	2	17	I've been raped so many times I can't even count on one hand.	1	1	0	0
4	4	2	18	My grandmother died I couldn't go to her funeral.	0	0	0	1
4	4	2	19	My father died I couldn't go to his funeral.	0	0	0	1
4	4	2	20	And yet I still find a reason to smile every day.	0	0	0	0
4	4	2	21	I've been kidnapped before at gunpoint.	1	1	0	0
4	4	2	22	I've been robbed.	1	0	0	1
4	4	2	23	I've been stabbed, all that shit.	1	0	0	0
5	4	2	24	Sucks, 'cause nobody will ever know what a person like me goes through on a daily basis or give a fuck really, honestly.	0	0	1	0
5	4	2	25	I go to the store I see people that have a life, they have somewhere to go, have somewhere to be.	0	0	0	0
5	4	2	26	They look at me with disgust and I just think to myself like, "Damn, I wonder how they would look at me if they knew what I've been through."	0	0	1	0
5	4	2	27	And the only reason I'm doing this because I hope that maybe somebody who gives a fuck will listen.	0	0	0	0
5	4	2	28	And somebody who gives a fuck would try and help.	0	0	0	0
5	4	2	29	That's what I'm hoping for.	0	0	0	0

Fig. 1. Narrative segmented according to change in topic (T), pause (P), and turn-of-talk (TT), coded with four codes (Physical abuse, Emotional abuse, Dissonance, and Loss) in binary form. Column U shows ordinal numbering of lines. Code occurrences are highlighted. (Color figure online)

Table 2. Segmentation heuristics developed from the data and evidence for each.

HEURISTICS	EVIDENCE
Use of fillers	"Yeah" (line 5) and "you know" (line 8)
Change in pronouns or narrative perspective	First person singular to indefinite pronoun (lines 4-23)
Code constellation	Listwise description of discrete events in personal history (lines 17-23); codes *Physical abuse*, *Emotional abuse*, and *Loss* should form a connection in the model
Absence of connection	Codes *Dissonance* in line 7 and *Loss* in line 8 should not be connected as it is not a meaningful co-occurrence
Repetition of words	"Happy" in lines 1 and 3; "I've" in lines 21-23
Change in tenses	Present (lines 13-15), past and present perfect (lines 16-23)
Change in topic	Personal experiences (lines 16-23), mentalization of others (lines 24-26)
Change in speaker	Speaker shifts after lines 4, 7, and 12
Pause in narrative	Pauses lasting over 3 seconds (e.g., after lines 4 and 7)

Employing Cycles or Repetition

In our examples below, we employ three segmentation heuristics that are conceptualized as meaningful cycles. Figure 1 contains these three operationalizations of relational context, from left to right: Topic (T) delimits segments by the topical focus of utterances; Pause (P) separates segments by a pause in interviewee speech lasting three or more seconds (including when they are being asked a question by the interviewer); and Turn-of-talk (TT) delimits segments by change of speaker (interviewer – interviewee).

Table 3 contains co-occurrence counts for unique pairs of our four codes for each type of relational context (topic, pause, turn-of-talk) computed with the whole conversation method. In accordance with this method, the stanza window is the conversation itself. Different relational contexts contain different numbers of conversations (this can be seen in Fig. 1 and is enumerated in Table 3 in column "Conv."). Code co-occurrences are highlighted in green. Co-occurrence summations are indicated in the dark grey rows for each type of relational context.

In the chunk of text presented in Fig. 1, each operationalization of relational context (T, P, TT) exhibited different numbers of conversations with varying code co-occurrences. These co-occurrence counts were summed for each unique pair of codes, which constitute the connections in our network models displayed in Fig. 2.

Topic-based segmentation was the only model without connections among all code pairs. Topics produced the greatest number of conversations (five), with no co-occurrences between the codes *Dissonance* and *Loss* or *Dissonance* and *Physical abuse*. The topic delimiter following line 23 separates Kristina's talk about herself and her history from her hypotheses about what others think of her. In a qualitative sense, this could indicate that Kristina works to conceal her experiences of loss and physical violence from others, which may be supported by her characterization of weakness in lines 5–7.

The model based on segmentation according to pauses longer than three or more seconds produced four conversations. All codes were still connected, but two code pairs (*Emotional abuse* and *Dissonance*, as well as *Emotional abuse* and *Loss*) exhibited connections that were twice as strong as other code pairs. Depending on the research

Table 3. Code co-occurrence accumulation for three operationalizations of relational context. Co-occurrences are highlighted in green. Summations for each are displayed in the grey rows.

Type	Conv.	P+E	P+D	P+L	E+D	D+L	E+L
Topic	1	0	0	0	0	0	0
	2	0	0	0	1	0	0
	3	1	0	1	0	0	1
	4	1	0	1	0	0	0
	5	0	0	0	0	0	0
Topic Sum		2	0	2	1	0	1
Pause	1	0	0	0	0	0	0
	2	0	0	0	1	0	0
	3	0	0	0	0	0	1
	4	1	1	1	1	1	1
Pause Sum		1	1	1	2	1	2
TT	1	0	0	0	0	0	0
	2	1	1	1	1	1	1
TT Sum		1	1	1	1	1	1

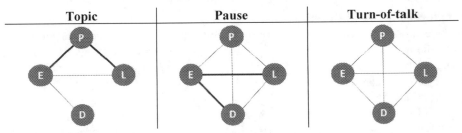

Fig. 2. Networks constructed with three different operationalizations of relational context: topic, pause, and turn-of-talk, computed with a whole conversation stanza window. Network nodes represent codes, the thickness of the edges represent the strength of co-occurrence between codes (Physical abuse, Emotional abuse, Dissonance, and Loss).

question, pauses may be of interest if it is hypothesized that they are linked to, e.g., underlying emotional or cognitive phenomena. In our example, there was no indication of this, and half of the exhibited pauses resulted from Kristina being asked a question, which may not be a meaningful pause in the same sense as pausing autonomously.

In the model built from turn-of-talk segmentation, there were uniform connections between all pairs of codes. This indicates that each code pair occurred with the same frequency in the two summed conversations. Since there were no co-occurrences in Kristina's response to the first interviewer question, all co-occurrences were localized in the second turn-of-talk. With this mode of accumulation, the only information that can be derived from the model is that each code pair occurred at least once within the second conversation, and no more or less than any other pair. Turn-of-talk-based segmentation included several changes in topic, tense, and pronouns in the second conversation, but this form of segmentation was not granular enough to reflect those changes.

All three operationalizations of relational context were executed based on meaningful segmentation heuristics involving cycles or repetition, and even within this relatively small chunk of text, the three types of segmentation exhibited considerable misalignment and produced markedly different models. Triangulation may be performed to assess the viability of chosen segmentations. For example, regarding sections delimited by pauses, we can observe that three conversations delimited by pauses were also delimited by fillers (lines 5, 8, 13), which may indicate Kristina placing more cognitive effort into phrasing a thought or processing an emotion. This would also signal a change in topic or verbal cues to support a change in cognition or emotion. This may be true for the first conversation (lines 5–7), which connects emotion display to vulnerability, but not necessarily for the next conversation (lines 8–12), which seems to interrupt the larger topic of describing life on the streets by excluding lines 13–15.

Thus, based on spotlighted pieces of data, we created segmentation heuristics with cycles (topics, pauses, turns-of-talk) that were then used to divide our data. Each type of segmentation yielded different models, where turn-of-talk showed uniform connections among all codes, while pause-based and topic-based segmentation exhibited markedly different code co-occurrences. Triangulating the latter two models showed that although pauses often aligned with fillers in Kristina's narrative, they did not always align with changes in topic. The results of triangulating various forms of segmentation can be interpreted by inspecting the rest of the data, correlating decisions with the research question(s), and/or by considering alternative ways of segmentation that are not based on cycles.

Employing Protracted Codes

To illustrate the use of protracted codes as segmentation, we employ two segmentation heuristics: change in narrative perspective (points of view) and change in topic. Changes in narrative perspective were considered meaningful based on established theory linking shifts in points of view (linguistic manifestations) with psychological distance (affective relation to narrated content). This theory states that first person point of view may be interpreted as emotionally proximal narration containing processed affect with which the speaker identifies, while second and third person perspectives may indicate distal narration of affect and events with which the speaker does not (yet) identify. [22] Our categorical values were: 1) first person point of view, 2) second person point of view, 3) third person or omniscient point of view. Figure 3 illustrates these narrative perspectives with colors purple, green, and blue, respectively. With this technique, all utterances labeled with a certain point of view can together constitute a meaningful segment. In our example, we could investigate how our codes *Physical abuse*, *Emotional abuse*, *Dissonance*, and *Loss* co-occurred against the "backdrop" of affective distance: for example, in emotionally proximal narration (network of all purple segments) and distal narration (network of all blue segments).

The second segmentation heuristic, change in topic, was employed as a cycle in the previous section. Now, we employ topics as protracted codes. This demonstrates that segmentation heuristics can be executed in various ways. To apply change in topic as a protracted code requires creating categorical values for each topic: Topic 1 was "desires" (lines 1–2 and 27–29), Topic 2 was "depression" (lines 5–7), Topic 3 was "street life" (lines 8–16), Topic 4 was "personal history" (lines 17–23), and Topic 5 was "mentalization of others" (lines 24–26). Figure 3 illustrates these topics with categorical values in the column labeled "Topic". These protracted codes allow the researcher to categorize segments based on their underlying content. Thus, co-occurrences can be interpreted against the "backdrop" of theme.

Topic	U		P	E	D	L
		Do you have any dreams or goals or anything you'd like to see happen in your future?				
Desires	1	I want to just be happy, bro.	0	0	0	0
Desires	2	The only dream I probably got is just to be happy.	0	0	0	0
Depression	3	'Cause just because I smile every day, just because I walk around like I'm cool, I'm not happy.	0	0	1	0
Depression	4	Sometimes I can't look at myself in the mirror without feeling like, "Damn, this is what life is."	0	0	1	0
		You get depressed a lot?				
Depression	5	Yeah, but I don't show it.	0	0	1	0
Depression	6	Because if you show it, then it's a sign of weakness and when you're weak is when the people prey on you most.	0	1	1	0
Depression	7	I just learned how to fake it and make sure that everyone thinks I'm cool.	0	0	1	0
		(pause)				
Street life	8	You know, these streets will take something beautiful and they'll just like crush it and just like make sure that that's nothingness.	0	1	0	1
Street life	9	Because out here there's just one thing.	0	0	0	0
Street life	10	Money talks, bullshit walks.	0	1	0	0
Street life	11	You could pay somebody to do anything out here, bro, and they'll do it.	0	0	0	0
Street life	12	If it's the price is right.	0	0	0	0
		(pause)				
Street life	13	So everything I ever thought was right, isn't really right out here, it's wrong.	0	0	0	1
Street life	14	Whatever I thought was wrong is right.	0	0	0	1
Street life	15	What is, isn't, what isn't is.	0	0	0	1
Street life	16	I seen children, old people, get killed just 'cause they don't want to comply with what the fuck these people want.	1	1	0	0
Pers. history	17	I've been raped so many times I can't even count on one hand.	1	1	0	0
Pers. history	18	My grandmother died I couldn't go to her funeral.	0	0	0	1
Pers. history	19	My father died I couldn't go to his funeral.	0	0	0	1
Pers. history	20	And yet I still find a reason to smile every day.	0	0	0	0
Pers. history	21	I've been kidnapped before at gunpoint.	1	1	0	0
Pers. history	22	I've been robbed.	1	0	0	1
Pers. history	23	I've been stabbed, all that shit.	1	0	0	0
Mentalization	24	Sucks, 'cause nobody will ever know what a person like me goes through on a daily basis or give a fuck really, honestly.	0	0	1	0
Mentalization	25	I go to the store I see people that have a life, they have somewhere to go, have somewhere to be.	0	0	0	0
Mentalization	26	They look at me with disgust and I just think to myself like, "Damn, I wonder how they would look at me if they knew what I've been through."	0	0	1	0
Desires	27	And the only reason I'm doing this because I hope that maybe somebody who gives a fuck will listen.	0	0	0	0
Desires	28	And somebody who gives a fuck would try and help.	0	0	0	0
Desires	29	That's what I'm hoping for.	0	0	0	0

Fig. 3. Data segmented according to narrative perspective (represented as colors: first person: purple; second person: green; third person/omniscient: blue) and change in topic (represented with categorical values in column "Topic"), coded with four codes (Physical abuse, Emotional abuse, Dissonance, and Loss) in binary form. Column U represents ordinal numbering of lines. Code occurrences are highlighted. (Color figure online)

Table 4 contains co-occurrence counts for unique pairs of codes for both types of relational context (narrative perspective and topic) computed with the whole conversation method. In accordance with this method, the stanza window is the conversation itself. Different relational contexts contain different numbers of conversations (listed with various labels in column "Conv."). Code co-occurrences are highlighted. Co-occurrence summations are indicated in the dark grey rows for each type of relational context.

Table 4. Code co-occurrence accumulation for two operationalizations of relational context. Co-occurrences are highlighted in green. Summations for both operationalizations are displayed in the grey rows.

Type	Conv.	P+E	P+D	P+L	E+D	D+L	E+L
	1st person (purple)	1	1	1	1	1	1
Perspective	2nd person (green)	0	0	0	1	1	1
	3rd person (blue)	0	0	0	1	1	1
Perspective Sum		1	1	1	3	3	3
	Desires	0	0	0	0	0	0
	Depression	0	0	0	1	1	1
Topic	Street life	1	0	1	0	0	1
	Personal history	1	0	1	0	0	0
	Mentalization of others	0	0	0	0	0	0
Topic Sum		2	0	2	1	1	2

In the text presented in Fig. 3, both operationalizations based on narrative perspective and topic exhibited different numbers of conversations with varying code co-occurrences. These co-occurrence counts were summed for each unique pair of codes, which constitute the connections in our network models displayed in Fig. 4.

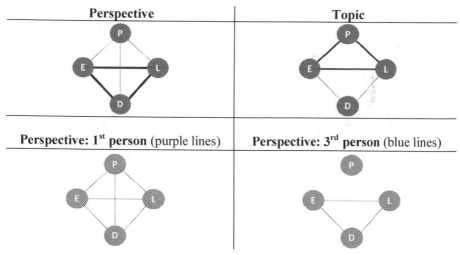

Fig. 4. (Top) Networks computed with a whole conversation stanza window and constructed with different relational context: narrative perspective and topic. (Bottom) Networks for 1st and 3rd person. Network nodes represent codes, and the thickness of the edges represent the strength of code co-occurrence (Physical abuse, Emotional abuse, Dissonance, and Loss). (Color figure online)

Employing three narrative perspectives to establish relational context created three conversations, and the generated model produced strong connections between *Emotional abuse* and *Dissonance*, *Emotional abuse* and *Loss*, as well as *Dissonance and Loss*. In other words, these co-occurrences were present in all three points of view within Kristina's narration. However, the interviewee connected all codes when speaking in first person, but left out *Physical abuse* when narrating with second and third person perspectives. We may conclude that emotionally proximal narration contains connections among all codes because she does not psychologically distance herself from the events and affects she reports. Furthermore, in cases where she exhibits connections in emotionally distal narration, for example narrating from a second person point of view, it is when she talks about being vulnerable or weak and taken advantage of by the social environment (lines 6 and 8). One conclusion may be that distal narration indicates unprocessed affect or emotions that were too intense to identify with during the interview.

Relational context determined by protracted codes on topic may be triangulated with observations and predictions on code connections or absences of our codes. For example, we could hypothesize that we would not see connections among any of our codes in the topic "Desires". If the data did, in fact, exhibit any co-occurrences between codes within the segments marked as belonging to the "Desires" conversation, a thorough qualitative inspection would be justified, as connections here would seem counterintuitive. On the other hand, the model representing connections in topic-based relational context did not exhibit connections between *Physical abuse* and *Dissonance*, which could have been an anticipated connection, especially since all our non-topic-based models exhibited a connection between these two codes. A qualitative examination is justified in this case as well, from which one could draw such conclusions as: 1) Kristina does not see any discrepancies in how others perceive her and how she feels, or between how she behaves and feels regarding physical abuse, but does with respect to emotional abuse and loss or 2) Kristina mostly mentions *Physical abuse* in relation to herself (lines 16–23) and *Dissonance* in relation to others (24–26).

Point of view as an operationalization of relational context may be triangulated with other segmentation heuristics, such as code constellations, change in topic, and change in pronouns. These support narrative perspective as a meaningful way to segment this particular chunk of text. On the other hand, change in topic did not always align with point of view. In fact, it produced a network exhibiting almost completely opposite connection strengths. In this instance, correlation between topics and perspectives may not be a justified requirement. In the former case, research questions may include inspecting connections among our four codes for each main topic, drawing conclusions such as *Physical abuse* and *Emotional abuse* were most strongly connected when Kristina was talking about life on the streets and her personal history. Narrative perspective, on the other hand, may be employed to ask questions about which connections or narrative perspectives are kept emotionally proximal versus distal.

These interpretations are not intended to be definitive but rather to illustrate how types of segmentation make possible different models and interpretations of data. Furthermore, they show that triangulating segmentation heuristics can effectively align interpretation with research questions and analytical goals.

5   Discussion

5.1   Summary

We employed the conceptual framework and terminology of Epistemic Network Analysis to explore different ways of manually establishing relational context in monologic data and to examine implications for modelling a quantified version of the data in network graphs. To illustrate our points, we chose a chunk of narrative from an interview with a teenaged runaway, Kristina. We began by using a spotlighting technique to pinpoint critical features of the narrative and derive more general segmentation heuristics. Some of these heuristics were used to establish two key forms of relational context: cycle-based and protracted code-based segmentation. Using the former, we employed change in speaker (turn-of-talk), pauses (lasting three or more seconds), and changes in topic to delimit the text. Protracted code-based segmentation was performed via categorical values indicating narrative perspective and change in topic. Code co-occurrences were computed with the whole conversation method, which equates stanza window with conversation, enabling co-occurrences within the entire conversation. Computed co-occurrences were aggregated for each operationalization of relational context.

We inspected differences in network graphs, noting distinctions between different forms of segmentation even within this succinct excerpt. The various relational contexts at times produced markedly different models. To evaluate types of segmentation, we employed different segmentation heuristics to qualitatively triangulate our results. We noted that depending on research questions, aligning or triangulating different forms of segmentation may not be meaningful. However, in many instances, it is an apt way to justify viable candidates for segmentation.

5.2   Plasticity in Operationalizing a Segmentation Heuristic

Through the use of topics as both cycle-based and protracted code-based segmentation, we demonstrated that any given segmentation heuristic may be used in many ways. For example, Yue et al., investigating student reflections on a piece of novel teaching support software, did not employ question-response segments within an interview to divide data, but rather based their segmentation on five pre-determined topics from the interview guide [23]. These topics were used to delimit meaningful segments within the data, but a pivotal question may be whether the segment delimiter was agnostic to these topics (e.g., ordinal numbering in each interview transcript) or not (e.g., categorical values repeating in each source of data, like "identity", "life events", etc.). In the former case, segments based on topic can only be aggregated across participants or data sources if the topics follow the same order (i.e., integers serve as categorical values). In the case of categorical identifiers, topics can be aggregated *regardless of their order* within sources. Thus, deciding on whether delimiters are agnostic to what they are delimiting implies utilizing them in a chronological order (ordinal, cycle-based) or anywhere in the dataset (categorical, protracted codes).

5.3 Differences in Segmentation Types

In general, metadata allows us to pinpoint a specific utterance or a group of utterances in a dataset. Agnostic delimiters enable us to locate a set of one or more utterances in a given dataset (e.g., a set of lines constituting a stanza in an interviewee's transcript), but they do not tell us anything about the content of the lines or the segmentation heuristic that underlies their grouping. Protracted codes allow the researcher to pinpoint sets of one or more utterances from one or more sources and disclose some information on the reason those utterances are grouped. They also enable various analyses to be performed on conversations aggregated based on the specific categorical value.

5.4 Using Protracted Codes

Research questions may invite analyses performed with protracted code-based segmentation. The most crucial prerequisite in employing protracted codes is to develop or adopt a coding scheme with at least two categorical values that can be applied to all utterances in a dataset. If none of the protracted codes used for segmentation can be applied to a given utterance, that line of data will be excluded from the dataset, as it will not contribute to a conversation. On the other hand, there may be instances where excluding such utterances is justified, in which case this prerequisite is moot.

If values used for segmentation repeat across an entire dataset, co-occurrences can be computed and aggregated according to these delimiters. For example, we may want to compare each participant's responses to specific questions within a structured interview or examine responses under specific conditions. Zörgő and Peters note that while investigating choice of therapy among patients using biomedicine versus those using alternative medicine, one collected piece of metadata was the primary illness and its comorbidities [13]. In their study, diagnosis was employed to form subsamples of data providers. However, a subsequent analysis could include segmenting patient narratives based on illness(es), since, as the authors describe, choices in therapy and lay etiology of illness may vary greatly within the same mental model depending on the specific illness to which the patient is referring. Similarly, Scheuer explored Reddit data sampling threads with posts referring to anti-depressants and sexual side-effects from r/depression to answer the question why patients discontinue the use of anti-depressants. Hypothesizing that side-effects and support type (how peers support each other captured in Social Support Behavior Codes) influence the discontinuation of a drug, Scheuer coded each post within her dataset with metadata on the specific class of anti-depressant that was being referenced (Selective Serotonin Reuptake Inhibitors or SSRIs versus non-SSRIs). This allowed the author to compare two network graphs (for data on SSRIs versus non-SSRIs) where side-effects and support types constituted the nodes against the "backdrop" of anti-depressant class [24].

5.5 Caveats, Limitations, and Strengths

There are several caveats and limitations to our study, most notably that whole conversation stanza windows, as a mode of code co-occurrence accumulation, may be employed with binary or weighted summation. The latter may be operationalized in a myriad of ways (e.g., with summing code occurrences, multiplying them, or using continuous code values). We employed binary summation, which enabled us to more easily elaborate topics that addressed our research questions, but this was done at the cost of oversimplifying the critical issue of co-occurrence accumulation.

Next, we utilized the conceptual framework and terminology of ENA, but we did not create epistemic networks. We saw choosing a specific framework as justified, as it was needed to address our questions and speak about segmentation in a coherent conceptual and terminological frame. However, the manner in which epistemic networks are constructed may have significant effects on the discussed segmentation decisions. For example, ENA performs spherical normalization on cumulative adjacency matrices produced for each unit of analysis that contain aggregated co-occurrence computations. This process accounts for the fact that different units may have various "lengths of talk" (i.e., stanzas) and results in a normalized vector quantifying the *relative frequencies* of co-occurrence among codes, independent of discourse length. This may greatly affect models, depending on the dataset and model parameterization.

Despite these limitations, this paper lends insight into how segmentation choices may affect models of coded data, as well as how codes and segmentation may inform and influence each other. Furthermore, although establishing relational context may seem more straightforward in some types of data than others, we highlight that segmentation based on formal section breaks in raw data (e.g., turn-of-talk or pauses) may not be meaningful depending on research questions, and that meaningful relational context can be operationalized in a myriad of ways. Finally, shedding light on the inherent interchangeability of codes and segmentation may deepen our understanding of what functions they serve and spur conversations about code and metadata construction, their use in segmentation, and how to justify these decisions. Congruently, the plastic use of segmentation heuristics also opens a vital dialogue on justifying the use of segmentation markers that are or are not agnostic to the segments of data they delimit.

6 Summary and Conclusions

In instances where code frequencies and/or co-occurrences are of analytical importance, segmentation should be considered as crucial as coding. Constructs of interest can potentially form the basis for either coding or segmentation, which should be considered vis-à-vis research questions. Segmentation should be developed in concert with coding decisions, and, much like coding, should be open to iterative development and social moderation. Spotlighting and triangulation are important steps in such a process. Various forms of segmentation can be applied to the same dataset to answer different research questions and/or validate the primary candidate for segmentation. Segmenting the data in different ways may lend a deeper understanding of the data and enable various ways of modelling. This paper serves as an initial investigation into segmentation heuristics and an invitation for further discussion.

Acknowledgements. This project received funding from the European Union's Horizon 2020 research and innovation program under the Marie Sklodowska-Curie grant agreement No. 101028644, as well as from University Fund Limburg/SWOL. The opinions, findings, and conclusions do not reflect the views of the funding agency, cooperating institutions, or other individuals.

References

1. Shaffer, D.: Quantitative Ethnography. Cathcart Press, Madison (2017)
2. Goffman, E.: Frame Analysis - An Essay on the Organization of Experience. Northeastern University Press, Boston (1974)
3. Gee, J.P.: A linguistic approach to narrative. J. Narrat. Life Hist. **1**, 15–39 (1991)
4. Zörgő, S., Swiecki, Z., Ruis, A.R.: Exploring the effects of segmentation on semi-structured interview data with epistemic network analysis. In: Ruis, A.R., Lee, S.B. (eds.) ICQE 2021. CCIS, vol. 1312, pp. 78–90. Springer, Cham (2021). https://doi.org/10.1007/978-3-030-677 88-6_6
5. Shaffer, D.W., Ruis, A.R.: How we code. In: Ruis, A.R., Lee, S.B. (eds.) ICQE 2021. CCIS, vol. 1312, pp. 62–77. Springer, Cham (2021). https://doi.org/10.1007/978-3-030-67788-6_5
6. Collier, W., Ruis, A., Shaffer, D.W.: Local versus global connection making in discourse. In: Looi, C.-K., Polman, J., Cress, U., Reimann, P. (eds.) Transforming Learning, Empowering Learners Conference Proceedings, vol. I, pp. 426–433. International Society of the Learning Sciences (2016)
7. Kurasaki, K.: Intercoder reliability for validating conclusions drawn from open-ended interview data. Field Methods **12**, 179–194 (2000)
8. Kleinheksel, A.J., Rockich-Winston, N., Tawfik, H., Wyatt, T.R.: Demystifying content analysis. Am. J. Pharm. Educ. **84**, 7113 (2020). https://doi.org/10.5688/ajpe7113
9. Ruis, A.R., Siebert-Evenstone, A.L., Pozen, R., et al.: Finding common ground: a method for measuring recent temporal context in analyses of complex, collaborative thinking. In: Lund, K., Niccolai, G., Lavoué, E., et al. (eds.) A Wide Lens: Combining Embodied, Enactive, Extended, and Embedded Learning in Collaborative Settings, pp. 136–143. International Society of the Learning Sciences (2019)
10. Williamson Shaffer, D., Collier, W., Ruis, A.: A tutorial on epistemic network analysis: analyzing the structure of connections in cognitive, social, and interaction data. J. Learn. Anal. **3**, 9–45 (2016). https://doi.org/10.18608/jla.2016.33.3
11. Zörgő, S.: Segmentation and code co-occurrence accumulation: operationalizing relational context with Stanza windows. In: Preprint submitted to the Fourth International Conference on Quantitative Ethnography (2022). https://psyarxiv.com/smkqr
12. Zörgő, S., Peters, G.-J.Y., Porter, C., et al.: Methodology in the Mirror: Third International Conference on Quantitative Ethnography. Advances in Quantitative Ethnography, pp. 144–159 (2022). https://doi.org/10.1007/978-3-030-93859-8_10
13. Zörgő, S., Peters, G.-J.: Epistemic network analysis for semi-structured interviews and other continuous narratives: challenges and insights. In: Eagan, B., Misfeldt, M., Siebert-Evenstone, A. (eds.) ICQE 2019. CCIS, vol. 1112, pp. 267–277. Springer, Cham (2019). https://doi.org/10.1007/978-3-030-33232-7_23
14. Lefstein, A.: Interpretation in linguistic ethnography: some comments for quantitative ethnographers. Work Pap Urban Lang Literacies Working Paper, vol. 297 (2022)
15. Nyirő, J., Zörgő, S., Enikő, F., et al.: The timing and circumstances of the implementation of pediatric palliative care in Hungarian pediatric oncology. Eur. J. Pediatr. **177**, 1173–1179 (2018)

16. Martin, K., Wang, E.Q., Bain, C., Worsley, M.: Computationally augmented ethnography: emotion tracking and learning in museum games. In: Eagan, B., Misfeldt, M., Siebert-Evenstone, A. (eds.) ICQE 2019. CCIS, vol. 1112, pp. 141–153. Springer, Cham (2019). https://doi.org/10.1007/978-3-030-33232-7_12
17. Andrist, S., Collier, W., Gleicher, M., et al.: Look together: analyzing gaze coordination with epistemic network analysis. Front. Psychol. **6**, 1016 (2015)
18. Wooldridge, A.R., Haefli, R.: Using epistemic network analysis to explore outcomes of care transitions. In: Eagan, B., Misfeldt, M., Siebert-Evenstone, A. (eds.) ICQE 2019. CCIS, vol. 1112, pp. 245–256. Springer, Cham (2019). https://doi.org/10.1007/978-3-030-33232-7_21
19. Andrade, A., Maddox, B., Edwards, D., Chopade, P., Khan, S.: Quantitative multimodal interaction analysis for the assessment of problem-solving skills in a collaborative online game. In: Eagan, B., Misfeldt, M., Siebert-Evenstone, A. (eds.) ICQE 2019. CCIS, vol. 1112, pp. 281–290. Springer, Cham (2019). https://doi.org/10.1007/978-3-030-33232-7_24
20. Barany, A., Foster, A.: Examining identity exploration in a video game participatory culture. In: Eagan, B., Misfeldt, M., Siebert-Evenstone, A. (eds.) Advances in Quantitative Ethnography: First International Conference, ICQE 2019, Madison, WI, USA, 20–22 October 2019, Proceedings, pp. 3–13. International Society for Quantitative Ethnography (2019)
21. Misiejuk, K., Scianna, J., Kaliisa, R., Vachuska, K., Shaffer, D.W.: Incorporating sentiment analysis with epistemic network analysis to enhance discourse analysis of Twitter data. In: Ruis, A.R., Lee, S.B. (eds.) ICQE 2021. CCIS, vol. 1312, pp. 375–389. Springer, Cham (2021). https://doi.org/10.1007/978-3-030-67788-6_26
22. Habermas, T.: Emotion and Narrative: Perspectives in Autobiographical Storytelling. Cambridge University Press, Cambridge (2019)
23. Yue, L., Hu, Y., Xiao, J.: Applying epistemic network analysis to explore the application of teaching assistant software in classroom learning. In: Eagan, B., Misfeldt, M., Siebert-Evenstone, A. (eds.) ICQE 2019. CCIS, vol. 1112, pp. 349–357. Springer, Cham (2019). https://doi.org/10.1007/978-3-030-33232-7_32
24. Scheuer, K.: Online support and antidepressant sexual side effects. In: Ruis, A., Lee, S. (eds.) Second International Conference on Quantitative Ethnography: Conference Proceedings Supplement, pp. 69–72. International Society for Quantitative Ethnography (2021)

Applications in Education Contexts

An Examination of Student Loan Borrowers' Attitudes Toward Debt Before and During COVID-19

Dara Bright(✉) and Amanda Barany

Drexel University, Philadelphia, PA 19143, USA
dnb66@drexel.edu

Abstract. Research has robustly documented the long-term life impacts of student loan debt on borrowers while in college and post-graduation. During the pandemic, repayment policies attempting to alleviate the debt burden were instituted to account for changes in income during government lockdowns. Since these reforms were implemented, what is needed is a more nuanced examination of the differences in post-graduation attitudes towards student loan debt in both pre-COVID and during the pandemic (after supportive government policy). This study utilizes Epistemic Network Analysis to identify and illustrate the connections in attitudes about debt between pre-COVID-19 and COVID-19 conversations. The results from this study illustrate statistically significant changes in attitudes towards debt, with pre-COVID-19 group members discussing how their negative feelings towards their debt drive their life choices while members of the COVID-19 conversations focused on repayment and hopeful feelings. Thus, this work positions itself to contribute to our understanding of the potential impact of debt-relief policies.

Keywords: Student Loan Debt · COVID-19 · Pandemic · Debt Relief Policies

1 Introduction

As the cost of education has increased in recent years, resulting in trillions of collective federal student loans, research aiming to understand long-term student impacts [1] and support changes in higher education have increasingly emerged. Pre-COVID-19, federal student loan balances increased more than sevenfold between 1995 and 2017 [2]. At the onset of the pandemic, the national student loan debt sat squarely at $1.56 trillion [3, 4] an increase from 1.12 trillion in 2014 [5], which translates to a 39% increase in only five years. The continually rising student loan debt comes despite several significant attempts at loan reform. In 2010, former President Obama reformed the Income Driven Repayment (IDR) program by decreasing the amount of discretionary income that must be paid monthly from 15% to 10% for borrowers on this repayment plan [6]. Despite this effort, scholars continued to note that student loan debt caused negative psychological, economic, and social effects on borrowers.

C. Damşa and A. Barany (Eds.): ICQE 2022, CCIS 1785, pp. 185–200, 2023.
https://doi.org/10.1007/978-3-031-31726-2_13

In 2020, the novel coronavirus (COVID-19) pandemic led to high unemployment rates and economic concern for many families and student loan borrowers. In an attempt to alleviate Americans from crippling financial disruptions, Congress authorized several flexibilities through the Higher Education Act (HEA) of 1965. These authorizations permitted additional loan deferment and forbearance opportunities. It also paused interest rate accruement on federal student loans from March 2020 to December 2022. Congress also suspended student loan debt collections such as wage garnishments and negative reporting to Credit Bureaus. While the expectation might be that debt-relief initiatives would help to alleviate financial stress felt by increased unemployment and financial instability, research on debt perception has lagged in examining this potential shift. There is a need to understand whether borrowers' attitudes changed after these COVID-19 policies were implemented in comparison to pre-COVID-19, and whether the implications of these policies possibly shifted borrowers' life outcomes.

This research contributes to the existing body of research on this topic by examining how policies may have influenced how borrowers feel about their student loan debt in a naturalistic setting. As student loan debt policies prior to COVID-19 were limited, many scholars have not had an opportunity to evaluate the relationship between debt relief and student loan debt attitudes. We explore differences in patterns of connection-making between debt-related themes and attitudes in Reddit users on a student debt forum before COVID-19 and after COVID-19, to understand how the recent robust efforts to reduce financial burden may have influenced debtholders' perceptions of student loan impacts. Thus, this research examines how online communities of borrowers discuss student loan debt over time using Epistemic Network Analysis to model connections between attitudes and debt.

2 Literature Review

There is growing consensus in scholarly literature that the rising costs of college are developing into an affordability crisis [7]. As a result of these tuition costs, students have increased the amount of student loan debt they have undertaken [8]. However, the exponential growth in tuition prices is unaligned with the rate of economic growth in the United States [9], which has led to higher default rates for recent generations and financial turmoil [10]. There are two primary causes of the college affordability crisis: (1) an overall decline in state funding and (2) higher education evolving into a privatized service, where institutions seek to make substantive profit. This literature review will evaluate how these COVID-19 student loan policies, compared to prior student debt relief policies, and student loan debt influences borrowers' behavioral patterns and life outcomes.

The exponentially growing student loan debt crisis remained largely unaddressed for decades until the Obama Administration (2008). As the United States experienced a substantive financial crisis in 2008, many of the Obama era Department of Education's higher education policy focused on alleviating the accumulating debt borrowers defaulting at higher rates than in previous cohorts (*see*: REPAYE Program, The American Opportunity Tax Credit Provision of the American Recovery and Reinvestment Act of 2009, and 2010 Fiscal Education Budget (FEB)). Most student loan-related policies and legislation before the Great Recession of 2008 (e.g., The Higher Education Reconciliation Act of 2005 and College Cost Reduction and Access Act of 2007 (CCRAA)) focused on increasing access to college through increased aid. The REPAYE Plan (2015) was an income-based student loan repayment plan that sought to alleviate some of the financial burdens that student loans were imposing on borrowers. Researchers have conducted policy analysis on the REPAYE Plan and noted that it had the potential to reduce long-term indebtedness [11]. However, little data follows up on the effects of this policy on lowering the default rates of various demographic groups and alleviating financial burden. In 2018, the Borrower Defense (BD) regulation was birthed out of guidance produced by the Department of Education in 2016. The BD regulation offered immediate forgiveness, or discharge, of student loans for borrowers who attended predatory universities. The DOE stated, the BD, aimed to protect borrowers from universities who "omi[tted] information and statements with a likelihood or tendency to mislead under the circumstances" [12]. Progress towards reducing the student loan debt crisis had otherwise been stagnant until the COVID-19 pandemic where millions of people lost their jobs and ability to repay their student loans. In response to this global crisis, the federal government has released some of the most progressive student loan debt relief policies.

This paper has established that the student loan debt crisis had mainly gone unchecked as evident by the limited policy presented, and as a result, the vast body of literature has focused its attention on the effects of student loan debt on borrowers' life outcomes. Research indicates that student loan debt affects graduates' life outcomes, including employment, further educational attainment, family decision-making, homeownership, and net worth [13]. Scholars have found that college students from low socioeconomic familial status tend to carry more debt-averse attitudes, which leads to less college matriculation due to this fear [14]. The authors found that affective attitudes toward student loan debt models debt aversion for students with low socioeconomic status (SES) [14]; however, more research is needed to explore *attitudes* toward the student debt loan *after graduation*.

The rise of student loan debt has profoundly affected borrowers' economic trajectory and socioeconomic mobility, specifically homeownership and increased net worth. Mezza and colleagues [15] evaluated whether having larger amounts of student loan debt influenced individuals' homeownership rates and found that for every $1,000 increase in loan debt, homeownership rates decreased by 1.8% for individuals in their mid-20s' who attended a public 4-year institution. These results remained consistent even when the authors controlled for local economic conditions. Other studies found even greater homeownership delays, such as a negative relationship between current homeownership rate and student loan debt for millennials, as more debt lowers the likelihood of owning a home [16]. Mountain and colleagues [16] argue that student loan debt pushes the homeownership timeline by several years for millennials with student loan debt compared to peers without debt.

Student loan debt also stems from several sources, including the federal government and private companies. Robb and colleagues [17] sought to understand the effects of federal student loans (versus private student loans) on homeownership decisions. This study adds nuance to prior studies as they found for every increase of $1,000 for a student's *private* loan balance, their likelihood of purchasing a home decreased by five percent. In contrast, there was no statistically significant impact on homeownership for students with federal loans. Although studies vary in how much impact student loan debt causes, it remains that this debt does influence homeownership. Moreover, for many students, homeownership is an opportunity at increasing their net worth and economic mobility.

As it relates to life choices, delayed marriage, child-birthing, and childrearing, are well-discussed, with people with student loan debt choosing to wait to engage in these behaviors [18–23]. Kuperbeg and Mzelis [24] found a link between student loans and delayed, or lowered, family formation rates, with college graduates who have substantial debt delaying childbirth and family formation. Min and Taylor [25] evaluated the relationship between child birthing delays and student loan debt by race and ethnicity. They found that Hispanic women with student loan debt "experience significant declines" in the likelihood of moving towards marital and nonmarital motherhood (p. 165). While indebted white women only experienced "a decrease in the probability of a marital first birth" (p. 165) [25]. It is critical to consider how marginalized populations, such as racially minoritized people, respond to incurring student loan debt because these secondary effects (e.g., birthing choices) have broader implications on future demographic patterns. In a study on marriage choice, Gineva [26] found a negative relationship between accumulated student loan debt and the probability of marriage by graduate students, specifically MBA students. Those students with more accumulated student debt and education expenditures had a lower probability of getting married; however, this effect decreased with age.

What can be synthesized from this existing literature on student loan debt is an emphasis on the effects of debt on life choices such as homeownership, marriage, and child-rearing. While these economic and social mobility effects and behavioral patterns are well-documented [18–20], fewer research examples exist that consider student loan borrowers' emotional well-being and cognitive attitudes towards student loan debt post-graduation because of these collective impacts.

Some nascent research examines how to relieve stress for student loan borrowers and suggests various debt reduction models such as student loan forgiveness and interest pauses [27]. As the pandemic has implemented interest pauses and other various measures of debt relief, it is important to contribute to the gap in the literature by evaluating how communities of borrowers discuss student loan debt in the repayment period before and during the COVID-19 pandemic to evaluate whether it influences attitudes and emotional responses.

3 Theoretical Framework

Cognitive appraisals (e.g., judgments, opinions, perceptions), mediate stressful events or experiences. This quantitative ethnographic study utilizes the Transactional Stress Model (TSM) [28] to evaluate how communities of borrowers perceive and discuss their student loan debt. The TSM argues that an individual's response to an event (stimulus) is informed by their beliefs about the stimulus and potential associated consequences. Lazarus [1, 29] (2000) argues that the presence of a stressful experience (i.e., student loan debt) does not inherently evoke negative emotions because the student loan debt can be appraised as a positive, negative, benign, or inconsequential experience (primary appraisals).

The TSM also emphasizes that different groups (with unique experiences, sociocultural contexts, etc.) may exhibit differential responses to stressful events. Lazarus and Folkman [7] argue that varying groups of individuals (e.g., demographic, geographic, historical) may experience different stressor intensities and have varying reactions based on group affiliation. Other studies examining debt that utilize the TSM have contextualized the notion of group differences in response to stressors as based on race or ethnicity [30]. As this is a comparative study between the pre-COVID-19 and COVID-19 groups, this study is drawing from the idea that there may be historical group differences in the degree to which respondents have a certain attitude towards debt. The COVID-19 pandemic was a collective experience, and individuals living through the pandemic are connected by shared pandemic-related experiences, including federally enacted debt relief policies. The strength and connections between pathways connecting attitudes and student loan debt may vary between these groups.

4 Methods

4.1 Data Collection

This study utilizes epistemic network analysis (ENA) as a quantitative ethnographic technique to model the connections between attitudes of student loan borrowers over time, which allows us to quantify qualitative discourse to visualize patterns of complexity that emerge in spaces such as public community forums. The data for this study was drawn from Reddit, which is an online platform that supports collective sharing, discussion, and rating of user-generated content. Engagement on Reddit is organized around topic-specific subreddits that users can create, seek out, join, view and contribute to as meets their specific needs or interests. Many online social platforms (e.g., Facebook, Quora, Twitter) could have been text-mined for this topic; however, Reddit was chosen because of its focus on protecting users' identities. In other forum-based platforms, such as Quora, there is an emphasis on creating an account with your real personal information. For example, Quora, Reddit's competitor, encourages its users to connect their Quora accounts to other social media platforms. As this research seeks to explore authentic responses and emotions toward student loan debt, Reddit was selected for its anonymity.

Users can create or engage with threads on a more specific question or topic within subreddits. For this study, several Reddit threads under the subreddit r/StudentLoans were used for data collection. Threads were selected based on five inclusion criteria. First, threads had to have robust responsiveness of at least 40 posts. Robust responsiveness indicates that the thread has comparatively active engagement. Second, threads had to be unarchived, or accessible to the research team. Third, included threads had to consist of posts made by at least 60% currently active users. This approach not only helped to ensure that posts were unarchived, but also suggested that the public-facing comments continued to represent users' perspectives and wishes. Fourth, the prompting post that began the thread had to include a question; researchers found that question-focused threads were more likely to garner responses that included respondents' opinions and experiences.

Included prompts often consisted of emotion-focused questions such as, *"I have all of this debt, am I screwed?"* or *"I have all of this debt, what do I do?."* It is important to note that different types of thread prompt may garner differential responses (e.g., more emotional versus technical), which the authors will explore in greater depth in subsequent work. This study emphasizes how borrowers on the Reddit forum are processing their own debt and potential attitudes before and during the pandemic. Fifth, only threads that emerged organically from the user base and not from posters who identified themselves as researchers (which were uncommon but featured high engagement), were included. This helped to ensure that the dataset consisted of a naturalistic data sample of reflections. After these inclusion criteria were applied, the final dataset included four prompts, forty-eight speakers, and 439 posts.

To collect the data from this subreddit thread (r/StudentLoans), the web pages were manually scraped into an Excel sheet for cleaning and coding. Since third and fourth-level posts were not included, some of the data cleaning co-occurred while collecting the data. Thereafter, these posts were broken into sentences for stanza prep, and inputted into a secondary Excel sheet, for analysis.

5 Data Analysis

5.1 Data Feature Choices

After setting the parameters of data inclusion, the data was collected from two tiers: the original poster (OP) of the topic and direct (second tier) respondents (DR). Data was not collected on responses to others' posts (third-tier posts and beyond). Typically, third-tier conversations tend to veer from the initial dialogue and topic of the original post. There was no demographic data collection as many users did not disclose their race, ethnicity, locality, gender, or disability status.

The standardized, interpretive, approach was employed to code this data, in which a reader reviewed data and marked line breaks by theme [31]. This segmentation approach allowed for a more detailed look at the range of sentiments expressed throughout the post. For example, a sample line of code may say, *"Now, I have made peace with my debt. I am not going to put life on hold."* While another line of code may be, *"The future sucks."* Noteworthy in this process, the TSM theory in tandem with the standardized interpretive approach informs the development of themes.

After inductively coding, the data yielded fifteen codes. Subsequently, a thematic analysis approach was employed in this data coding process. According to Fereday and Muir-Cochrane [32], thematic analysis is a "search for themes that emerge as being important to the description of the phenomenon" (p. 82). This process was engaged in by carefully "reading and re-reading [..] the data" [33] (p. 258). After several rounds of reading and re-reading by a single coder, the data was reorganized under five thematic topics (See Table 1).

Once the data was in the ENA webtool, it was critical to organize the data appropriately. This data's stanza, or conversation, segmentation refers to the collection of lines where connections between concepts were examined. This study sought to explore

Table 1. Data codebook.

Code	Definition	Example
Negative Feelings	This code was employed to describe occurrences where borrowers expressed negative feelings (e.g., fear, anger, regret) toward or about their student loan debt and repayment.	"My debt is a big contributor to my chronic depression and anxiety."
Acceptance	This code refers to occurrences in which borrowers express acceptance toward student loan debt and repayment.	"I'm still heavy in debt but it's manageable with budgeting still sometimes you just have to do what you have to do."
Positive Practical Response	This code encapsulates instances where the community of borrowers is offering the original poster (OP) advice, encouragement, or resources.	"Take 50–100 from each paycheck and invest in some stocks while they are down who knows in a year or 2 you could have a return that could cover your debt."
Negative Affective Response	This code captures the negative changes in behavior in response to student loan debt and repayment.	"It's crippling for sure. I've delayed buying a home, investing in my future and having kids."
Statement of Fact	The Statement of Fact (SoF) code refers to the borrower speaking about their debt with no emotional or affective responses.	"75k in student debt and made 51k last year."

the connection between time and feelings. Therefore, the conversation was during pre-COVID (2019 and before) and during COVID (after 2020). In the dataset, these conversations were labeled "0" for pre-COVID and "1" for during COVID. These conversations act as boundary confines that allow me to compare time periods and evaluate feelings over time. To further segment the data, a moving window of 4 was used because these posts were Reddit users who were storytelling. By the time the user was "mid-way" through their story, or roughly on their fourth sentence, the data reader found that the fourth sentence often would not be connected back to the first sentence. This sentence often marked a break from the Reddit user sharing their story to transitioning into offering advice or feedback to the initial post. Finally, the unit variable, time, had the "threads" (1–4) nested within them, and nested within the threads was the poster's set of lines or ID (Time -> Thread -> Poster ID).

nested in the conversation informed how I structured the data within the time periods. The primary unit variable (time) had conversations nested within it. Thread 1 and 2 were from the "during COVID" period, and Threads 3 and 4 were from pre-COVID (time). Under Thread 1, PosterIDs (A-P) were listed underneath, Thread 2 had PosterIDs, 2A-2J nested, Thread 3 had PosterIDs, 3A-3J, nested and Thread 4 had PosterIDs 4A-4G nested.

6 Results

Prior to utilizing ENA, two human raters coded 10% of random lines of data to ascertain rater agreement. Cohen's kappa and Shaffer's rho (p) were calculated for each of the six codes. Cohen's kappa was above .80 for each of the six codes, and Shaffer's rho (p) was below 0.04, indicating high agreement between human raters. Since codebook agreement was sufficient, one coder proceeded to code the remaining data. Table 2 below displays the epistemic network illustration of community of borrowers' student loan discussion before and during COVID-19. In the Pre-COVID dataset, there were 258 lines of codes in the two conversations. The distribution of themes across the pre-COVID data subset shows that 33% of responses were Negative Feelings, 10% expressed Acceptance, 23% displayed 23% showed practical positive response, 7% had negative affective response, 28% were statements of fact. In the subset COVID data, 12% of responses expressed negative feelings, 15% showed acceptance, 30% displayed negative affective response, 7% displayed negative affective response, 36% expressed a statement of fact. In the overall dataset, about 31% of the community showed negative feelings or negative affective responses (n = 141) and 26% shared positive practical responses.

Table 2. Distribution of codes' presence by time period.

Codes	Total Frequency (n)	Total Codes (%)	Pre-COVID codes frequency (n)	Pre-COVID Codes (%)	COVID-19 Codes (n) frequency	COVID-19 codes (%)
Negative Feelings	110	24%	85	33%	25	12%
Acceptance	58	12%	26	10%	32	15%
Practical Positive Response	121	26%	59	23%	62	30%
Negative Affective Response	31	7%	17	7%	14	7%
Statement of Fact	146	31%	71	28%	75	36%
Total	466	100%	258	100%	208	100%

Prior to evaluating the connections between codes, several features of the model were evaluated, including Goodness of Fit and Variance. Subsequently, the ENA webtool was employed to demonstrate the association between these codes and the time periods. The Goodness of Fit of the models was 0.96 for both Pearson and Spearman on the x-axis and 0.94 on the y-axis. This high Goodness of Fit indicates that "the network graphs provide a reliable interpretation of the dimensions of the projected metric space" [34] (p. 139).

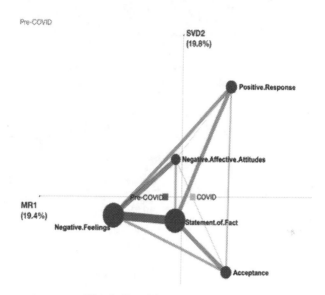

Fig. 1. Pre-COVID ENA Model.

Figure 1 shows the connections that appeared in the pre-COVID threads. In this figure, there is a moderate connection between negative feelings and statements of fact (0.35), negative affective attitudes and negative feelings (0.21), practical positive response and statement of fact (0.18), and practical positive response and negative feelings (0.16). Although, practical positive responses and negative feelings may seem contrary, it was relatively common. There is a connection between responders to the OP, who both lamented and offered advice. For example, one respondent said, "*I wish I finished my degree earlier. They can take your money but never your education.*" There is a connection between their personal regret and encouragement to OP to persist as education, to them, is invaluable.

Figure 2 depicts the COVID ENA model and illustrates there is a moderate association between statement of fact and acceptance (0.23), acceptance and statement of fact (0.22) and negative feelings and statement of fact (0.18). To a lesser degree, acceptance and practical positive response emerged (0.16). Similar to the other conversation, there was a small association between negative feelings and another, less dismal, emotion: acceptance (0.09). At first glance, this connection appears contrary; however, there is an association between respondents who felt regret and yet accepted that 'rigorous' repayment was the only way forward.

This ENA model illustrates the weighted associations between themes across borrowers' responses in the Pre-COVID and COVID time periods. Visual examination of

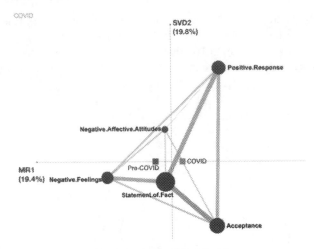

Fig. 2. COVID ENA Model.

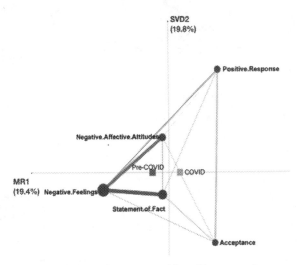

Fig. 3. ENA difference model displaying communities of borrowers' responses to student loan debt by time period.

the difference model illustrates a transition in overall sentiment pre-COVID and during COVID. Based on the ENA difference model (Fig. 3), communities of borrowers in the pre-COVID-19 period were more likely to express negative feelings and affective attitudes as they discussed their debt in contrast to their peers in the COVID-19 group.

Of noteworthiness is the increased prevalence of acceptance by borrowers from pre-COVID-19 to COVID-19 conversations. To evaluate the difference between the pre-COVID-19 community of borrowers and COVID-19 community of borrowers, a two-sample t-test (Mann-Whitney U test) assuming unequal variance was employed. Along the X-Axis, there was a statistically significant difference between in how the pre-COVID group (mdn $= -0.26$) and COVID group (mdn $= 0.27$) (U $= 4373$ p $= 0.02, r = -0.40$) discussed their student loan debt. In support of this data, the qualitative content analysis showed that these groups have considerable differences in the ways in which they discuss, and process, their student loan debt.

7 Discussion

The guiding theory of this study, Transactional Stress Model, suggests that potentially negative experiences such as having debt do not necessarily evoke negative emotions if the individual does not perceive the event in a negative manner. However, in both the pre-COVID-19 and COVID-19 sub-dataset, negative feelings permeated the discourse, which suggests the experience of having debt is negative for many borrowers. However, as theorized, there were group differences in the pre-COVID-19 attitudes and COVID-19 attitudes, with the pre-COVID-19 group having greater negative feelings than their peers in the other group. This statistically significant difference in attitude suggests that these COVID-19 student loan relief policies may have led to changes in how borrowers perceived them. These differences between groups may also suggest that living through a collective traumatic event, COVID-19, led individuals to re-prioritize what stressors they would focus on and how they felt about student loan debt.

This study is important because it illustrates that negative emotional experiences related to the debt burden extend post-graduation and are deeply interwoven into the core experience of student loan debt at every stage. Furthermore, this study expands on the existing findings in the literature, as it is heavily documented that college students experience negative health and social implications due to loan debt before and during college [35]. Moreover, the finding of negative feelings throughout both sub-groups shows that borrowers are not indifferent to student loan debt, although to a lesser degree in the post-COVID group. Although this finding – negative responses – is unsurprising as it aligns with the literature, it does indicate that many members in the communities of borrowers examined in this study have not normalized this debt as "rational" and commensurate with their job prospects. Reddit posters shared the following posts:

> When I graduated, I was honestly feeling pretty down in the dumps about having so much debt (~50k), especially when my higher paying jobs were not materializing after I went through a grueling MS program for teaching.

> Everyone I knew and spoke with was convinced that a college degree (of any sort) was a key into an amazing job. I am part of a generation where that was untrue, and it hits people hard when the reality of our choices exposes itself (usually with finances).

These borrowers' show a growing awareness that these student loans, which were once considered a necessary evil, do not offer the appropriate market return on the monetary investment that they have made. The above sentiments shared by the Reddit posters also highlight how normalized debt impacted their rational decision-making and college choices.

One of the most significant findings from this study is the change in prevalent attitudes from pre-COVID-19 to COVID-19 sub datasets. In the pre-COVID-19 sample, there was a substantial number of negative feelings expressed in relation to how they discussed their debt (statements of fact). Whereas, in the COVID sample, much of the data centers around practical positive responses in relation to how they discussed their debt (statements of fact). At first glance, this finding appears puzzling as the COVID pandemic caused financial devastation for many families, businesses, and individuals. Yet, this data illustrates a potentially illuminating phenomenon: student loan borrower relief policies. As shared in the introduction of this study, the federal government implemented debt relief policies to reduce the pandemic's negative effects, such as freezing the interest rates on loans. Therefore, in the COVID-19 discourse threads, there are far more borrowers discussing how to pay off debt. Interestingly, in the selected threads, no poster directly mentions COVID relief; however, they do hint at the role this relief plays in their ability to repay their debt. For example, one poster shared "I'm currently at 42k left and have money in my savings to pay it down to the 20ks by the time interest starts up in May."

Although the four threads mirror themselves with overarching themes of Ops looking for feedback and advice, the discourse in the COVID-19 threads focused less on the negative feelings associated with their debt. Instead, these borrowers discussed how to repay the debt as quickly as possible. In the pre-COVID-19 threads, the relationship between discussion about their debt (statements of fact) and acceptance has an association of 0.19; however, in the COVID-19 threads, this association increases to 0.23. This data suggests that the COVID-19 pandemic policies related to student loan debt relief may have mediated the connection between individuals' discussion of their debt and greater acceptance.

This emergent change between time periods also explains the rise in association between Practical Positive Responses as individual borrowers discussing their student loan debt (statements of fact). In the pre-COVID-19 sample, the association between Practical Positive Responses and statements of fact was 0.18; in the COVID-19 sample, this association rose to 0.22. In the pre-COVID-19 threads, one poster discussed their own relationship with student loan debt. They recommended to the OP to "forget those people who are telling you to figure things out faster" and in the COVID-19 sample threads, one poster speaks about the system in which the OP is operating and shares, "go easy on yourself about your loan debt. That's not some sign of you being a bad person, failing at life, or not being responsible. The system sucks. Especially if you're going for a nonprofit job where pay isn't great. So don't feel bad about your situation – it sounds like you're at a point to start figuring out what you need to do. You got this, OP. I'm rooting for you!" There is a tone change between the two cohorts of borrowers with the pre-COVID-19 being more about their own life lessons and regrets while the COVID-19 borrower offers contextual prospective about the job market and advice.

Although a less prevalent code across both groups, the presence of a negative affective response, is important because it has implications on borrowers' life choices and family making decisions. In both samples of data, the negative affective response, code appeared in 7% of the data. Assuming this data is representative of the 43.4 million student loan borrowers,' this negative affective response code could offer insight into how student loan debt affects life choices for over 3 million borrowers. Some of the sentiments highlight how financially devastating this debt is for individuals.

It's crippling for sure. I've delayed buying a home, investing in my future and having kids. Started working IT work at $38k/year.

I just feel like hopes of a happy life with kids and a house isn't really in the books for me because I'm not gonna have any savings for the next 10–15 years of my life.

I honestly think about killing myself like weekly because of student loans.

I do feel like the student loans have prevented me from buying a house or doing other things.

I haven't traveled as much as I wanted. I've put off buying a newer car and buying a house is definitely still years off in my mind.

These communities of borrowers show that many college graduates are delaying major life events which have substantial implications for the United States' economic and population growth. Research shows that the United States is likely to experience a slow-down of childbearing as adults in several cohort waves indicated that financial strain is the leading cause of delaying their choice to have children [4]. The literature also shows that the financial strain experienced by adults, in the 18–27 age group, is not felt equally, with lower-income women expressing greater desires to wait [4].

Overall, this study has salient implications for higher education. One notable contribution from this study is the highlighted need for improved financial aid counseling prior to matriculation. Several borrowers expressed regret at their major choice in college because of the disconnect between post-graduation salary, and future pay trajectories, to the amount of debt accrued. As this section illustrated, this study offers a comparative narrative of student borrowers' lived experiences and emotional responses to debt burden in a naturalistic setting. Thus, this study significantly augments the conversation about the importance of addressing the student loan debt crisis with meaningful policies.

Since this study was conducted, the Biden Administration has released the most substantive student loan forgiveness policy since this crisis began. In August of 2022, the Biden Administration announced a three-pronged plan to address the student loan debt crisis. In the first prong, the plan offers targeted debt forgiveness by cancelling up to $20,000 in federal student loans for Pell Grant recipients, who are students from low-income backgrounds, and up to $10,000 for non-Pell Grant recipients who hold federal student loans. The only criteria to be eligible for federal loan forgiveness, at the prescribed amounts, include making less than $125,000 a year. The second prong revises the income-driven repayment (IDR) plan which caps monthly payments at 5%, which is down from 10%, under prior rules. This modification to the IDR focuses solely on undergraduate loans. The third prong is tied to the second prong because this aspect of the plan seeks to ensure that borrowers' on IDR plans will not have loan balances that grow exponentially due to interest, by covering the growth of interest, as long as these students are making monthly payments. Relatedly, the Biden Administration fixed the Public Service Loan Forgiveness program (PSLF) to ensure that all who qualified were able to receive forgiveness by reducing the eligibility restrictions and challenges with implementation in the Department of Education (DOE) and documentation processes for borrowers. This debt relief plan seeks to ensure that individuals who are most impacted by student loan debt, low-income and middle-income individuals, are not negatively impacted by attending college.

Although this study did not consider the latest debt relief policy's effect on borrowers' attitudes, there are several boarder implications worth noting. The first implication suggests that women with a college education who are experiencing this debt relief may be more willing to engage in family planning. Secondly, this debt relief policy has the potential to contribute to economic growth, as individuals have more disposable income. Thirdly, education could potentially return to being a tool for economic mobility for low-income individuals; however, college affordability and costs remain an issue that must be addressed.

8 Conclusions

This study has offered the field of college borrower experiences with an in-depth, and raw, examination of their lived experiences. The ability to engage in this qualitative content analysis without the potential for social desirability biases in the responses, is afforded to me using a Quantitative Ethnography (QE) approach. The distinct affordances that Epistemic Network Analysis (ENA) allows me, as a researcher, to draw connections and evaluate unique patterns that appear in borrowers' emotional experiences before and after policy initiatives. Broadly speaking, both QE and ENA have aided in the understanding of borrowers' needs and corrective policies to address emotional distress and the economic implications of crippling debt.

One potential limitation to this work is how the Reddit threads were selected and organized. As the conversations were not selected on the premise of positively-worded and negatively worded threads, this mechanism may affect the types of responses that were garnered. For example, pre-COVID-19 and COVID-19 posts were not evaluated for whether they were positive or negatively framed, but rather the other inclusion criterion. However, by selecting on the premise of responsiveness, not framing, the authors avoided engaging in "cherry-picking" cases based on a biased perspective. By selecting emotion-focused questions, whether positive or negative, with high responsiveness, the Reddit respondents indicated to us what affective moods and questions were worthy of responding to. Thus, this inclusion criteria mitigates the negative effects of this potential limitation. Future studies should seek to explore differential responses based on thread prompts, and whether differences existed based on question type across cohorts.

References

1. Miller, B., Campbell, C., Cohen, B.J., Hancock, C.: Addressing the $1.5 trillion in federal student loan debt. Center for American Progress (2019). http://hdl.handle.net/10919/96079
2. Burk, D., Perry, J.: The Volume and Repayment of Federal Student Loans: 1995 to 2017. Congressional Budget Office (2020). https://eric.ed.gov/?id=ED610721
3. MacDonald, T.: Can Biden's plan for 'Education Beyond High School' solve the student loan crisis?. Advocate: J. Natl. Tert. Educ. Union 28(1), 30–31 (2021)
4. Brauner-Otto, S.R., Geist, C.: Uncertainty, doubts, and delays: economic circumstances and childbearing expectations among emerging adults. J. Fam. Econ. Issues 39(1), 88–102 (2018)

5. Di, W., Ryder Perlmeter, E.: Student loans part 1: get the numbers right (No. 10). Federal Reserve Bank of Dallas (2014). https://www.dallasfed.org/cd/FinAccess/ConsumerCredit/2014/1202.aspx
6. American Council on Education, Division of Government & Public Affairs: Summary of education provisions in the Health Care and Education Reconciliation Act of 2010. American Council on Education (2010). https://www.acenet.edu/Documents/Education-Provisions-in-the-Health-Care-and-Education-Reconciliation-Act-of-2010.pdf#search=Summary%20of%20Education%20Provisions%20in%20the%20Health%20Care%20and%20Education%20Reconciliation%20Act%20of%202010t-of-2010.aspx&usg=AOvVaw1Z7Mkpw3Fl5Ef0KeKhH-z0
7. Hillstrom, L.C.: The College Affordability Crisis. ABC-CLIO (2020). https://www.cbo.gov/publication/56754
8. Henager, R., Wilmarth, M.J.: The relationship between student loan debt and financial wellness. Fam. Consum. Sci. Res. J. **46**(4), 381–395 (2018)
9. De Koning, K.: US Government debts, a dangerous cocktail of borrowing, spending and inflation levels (2021). https://mpra.ub.uni-muenchen.de/id/eprint/109105
10. Mitchell, M., Palacios, V., Leachman, M.: States are still funding higher education below pre-recession levels. J. Collective Bargaining Acad. **0**(71), 1–27 (2015)
11. Bright, D., Pearson, W.: Race, social justice, and higher education financial aid in the United States: the case of African Americans. In: Pearson Jr., W., Reddy, V. (eds.) Social Justice and Education in the 21st Century. DIR, pp. 149–170. Springer, Cham (2021). https://doi.org/10.1007/978-3-030-65417-7_9
12. Student Assistance General Provisions, Federal Family Education Loan (2016). 81 FR 39329. https://www.federalregister.gov/d/2016-25448/p-27
13. Velez, E., Cominole, M., Bentz, A.: Debt burden after college: the effect of student loan debt on graduates' employment, additional schooling, family formation, and home ownership. Educ. Econ. **27**(2), 186–206 (2019)
14. Callender, C., Mason, G.: Does student loan debt deter higher education participation? New evidence from England. ANNALS Am. Acad. Polit. Soc. Sci. **671**(1), 20–48 (2017)
15. Mezza, A., Ringo, D., Sherlund, S., Sommer, K.: Student loans and homeownership. J. Labor Econ. **38**(1), 215–260 (2020)
16. Mountain, T.P., Cao, X., Kim, N., Gutter, M.S.: Millennials' future homeownership and the role of student loan debt. Fam. Consum. Sci. Res. J. **49**(1), 5–23 (2020)
17. Robb, C.A., Schreiber, S.L., Heckman, S.J.: The role of federal and private student loans in homeownership decisions. J. Consum. Aff. **54**(1), 43–69 (2020)
18. Catherine, S., Yannelis, C.: The distributional effects of student loan forgiveness (No. w28175). National Bureau of Economic Research (2020)
19. Cooper, D., Wang, J.C.: Student Loan Debt and Economic Outcomes. Current Policy Perspective No. 14-7. Federal Reserve Bank of Boston (2014). http://www.bostonfed.org/economic/ppdp/index.htm
20. Elliott, W., Lewis, M.: Student debt effects on financial well-being: research and policy implications. J. Econ. Surv. **29**(4), 614–636 (2015)
21. Addo, F.R., Houle, J.N., Sassler, S.: The changing nature of the association between student loan debt and marital behavior in young adulthood. J. Fam. Econ. Issues **40**(1), 86–101 (2019)
22. Haneman, V.J.: Marriage, millennials, and massive student loan debt. Concordia L. Rev. **2**, 103 (2017)
23. Nau, M., Dwyer, R.E., Hodson, R.: Can't afford a baby? Debt and young Americans. Res. Soc. Stratification Mob. **42**, 114–122 (2015)
24. Kuperberg, A., Mazelis, J.M.: Social norms and expectations about student loans and family formation. Sociol. Inquiry **21**(1), 90–126 (2021)

25. Min, S., Taylor, M.G.: Racial and ethnic variation in the relationship between student loan debt and the transition to first birth. Demography **55**(1), 165–188 (2018)
26. Gicheva, D.: Student loans or marriage? A look at the highly educated. Econ. Educ. Rev. **53**, 207–216 (2016)
27. Charron-Chénier, R., Seamster, L., Shapiro, T.M., Sullivan, L.: A pathway to racial equity: student debt cancellation policy designs. Soc. Curr. **9**, 4–24 (2021)
28. Lazarus, R.S., Folkman, S.: Stress, Appraisal, and Coping. Springer, New York (1984)
29. Lazarus, R.S.: Evolution of a model of stress, coping, and discrete emotions. In: Handbook of Stress, Coping, and Health: Implications for Nursing Research, Theory, and Practice, pp. 195–222 (2000)
30. Tran, A.G., Mintert, J.S., Llamas, J.D., Lam, C.K.: At what costs? Student loan debt, debt stress, and racially/ethnically diverse college students' perceived health. Cult. Diversity Ethnic Minor. Psychol. **24**(4), 459 (2018)
31. Barany, A., Philips, M., Kawakubo, A.J., Oshima, J.: Choosing units of analysis in temporal discourse. In: Wasson, B., Zörgő, S. (eds.) ICQE 2021. CCIS, vol. 1522, pp. 80–94. Springer, Cham (2021). https://doi.org/10.1007/978-3-030-93859-8_6
32. Fereday, J., Muir-Cochrane, E.: Demonstrating rigor using thematic analysis: a hybrid approach of inductive and deductive coding and theme development. Int. J. Qual. Methods **5**(1), 80–92 (2006)
33. Rice, P., Ezzy, D.: Qualitative Research Methods: A Health Focus. Oxford University Press, Melbourne (1999)
34. Wang, Y., Swiecki, Z., Ruis, A.R., Shaffer, D.W.: Simplification of epistemic networks using parsimonious removal with interpretive alignment. In: Ruis, A.R., Lee, S.B. (eds.) ICQE 2021. CCIS, vol. 1312, pp. 137–151. Springer, Cham (2021). https://doi.org/10.1007/978-3-030-67788-6_10
35. Baker, A.R., Montalto, C.P.: Student loan debt and financial stress: implications for academic performance. J. Coll. Student Dev. **60**(1), 115–120 (2019)

Learning Through Feedback: Understanding Early-Career Teachers' Learning Using Online Video Platforms

Lara Condon[1]([⊠]) [iD], Amanda Barany[2] [iD], Janine Remillard[1] [iD], Caroline Ebby[1] [iD],
and Lindsay Goldsmith-Markey[1] [iD]

[1] University of Pennsylvania, 3700 Walnut Street, Philadelphia, PA 19104, USA
condonl@upenn.edu
[2] Drexel University, 3141 Chestnut Street, Philadelphia, PA 19104, USA

Abstract. This study examines the patterns of feedback among early-career elementary mathematics teachers participating in an online inquiry group focused on the practice of number talk routines. Number Talk Routines are instructional practices designed to help facilitate students' computational fluency in ways that promote flexible number sense. Teachers facilitate these discussions using responsive teaching practices that elicit student thinking and highlight how students' strategies relate to each other and to key mathematical concepts. Data for this study come from time-stamped feedback comments posted by members of the inquiry group to correspond with specific moments during each participant's number talk routine. Epistemic network analysis was used to examine the patterns in the form and content of feedback over time. The results suggest that early-career teachers became more reflective in their feedback, connecting their own practices to the work of others and focusing more on teachers' decision making that supported enactment of responsive teaching practices.

Keywords: online professional learning communities · mathematics teaching and learning · feedback · epistemic network analysis

1 Introduction

Since the enactment of multiple mathematics reforms in the early 1990s, the focus mathematics teaching and learning is increasingly understood to be a social endeavor, where students learn through collective practices to develop conceptual understanding of mathematics [1]. Teachers are better equipped to foster deep mathematics understanding when they elicit, make sense of, and respond to students' ideas to help them make connections between themselves and the mathematical concepts they are learning, what is often referred to as *teaching responsively* [2]. Being able to make these in-the-moment decisions to teach responsively is complex and is therefore challenging for preservice teachers to learn during the span of teacher education programs. Further, despite reforms in mathematics education, more traditional, didactic forms of mathematics instruction persist [3], leaving early-career teachers lacking the necessary support to enact responsive teaching practices.

© The Author(s), under exclusive license to Springer Nature Switzerland AG 2023
C. Damşa and A. Barany (Eds.): ICQE 2022, CCIS 1785, pp. 201–213, 2023.
https://doi.org/10.1007/978-3-031-31726-2_14

In an effort to support early-career teachers in learning and employing responsive teaching practices, researchers designed an inquiry group format to help extend the learning of responsive mathematics teaching practices through video feedback of Number Talk Routines. In a number talk routine, the teacher poses a string of computational problems that build on one another, eliciting students' strategies for solving problems, helping students to understand one another's approaches, and highlighting connections between mathematical concepts. Participants in the inquiry groups learned to implement these routines in classrooms with students during a one-year masters-level preservice education program. The process included recording the number talk and posting it to a shared video platform that allowed for time-stamped comments from teacher educators and peers. Prior qualitative research using this data found that engaging in the process of feedback in the inquiry group helped teachers to recognize different elements in their own practice, helping them to develop skills of self-reflection. Grappling with instructional dilemmas and interrogating pedagogical reasoning help teachers to recognize and develop responsive teaching practices. This study aims to further interrogate the type and focus of time-stamped comments to understand the connections between feedback and teachers' ability to notice and offer guidance to one another towards responsive teaching practices using epistemic network analysis (ENA). ENA, a quantitative ethnographic technique, visualizes patterns of association between codes in discourse [4]. This form of analysis will help to surface deeper understanding of novices' ability to notice and provide feedback on responsive teaching practices throughout participation in an online community of inquiry, focusing on the following research question:

What patterns of feedback on number talk routines do early-career teachers enact through participation in an online inquiry group using a shared video platform?

Using ENA to understand the connections made through each participant's feedback over the course of their participation in the online video platform offers the potential to help improve our understanding of whether and how asynchronous feedback on number talks helps to support teachers' understanding and implementation of responsive teaching practices.

2   Background and Framing Concepts

2.1   Learning to Teach Responsively

The focal area of this study is on determining strategies for supporting novice teachers in developing responsive teaching practices through Number Talk Routines [5]. In a Number Talk Routine, teachers pose a string of related computation problems, usually ranging from 2–4 questions that build in complexity. Teachers facilitate a discussion of each problem through responsive teaching moves of eliciting and representing students' strategies and reasoning, helping students to see connections between the approaches, and making connections to key mathematical concepts. The nature and structure of number talks provide a prime opportunity for enacting responsive teaching practices [6]. *Responsive teaching* refers to the way that teachers elicit, interpret, and respond to student thinking in ways help to connect key disciplinary ideas to students' ideas and experiences [2]. Teaching responsively is complex and dependent upon the unique contexts of classroom learning environments [7]. Many teacher education programs have incorporated rehearsals or other simulations of practice to help preservice teachers learn to teach responsively by helping to foster pedagogical reasoning [8]. However, the limited duration of most teacher education programs and the lack of more contextual nuance makes it challenging for novices to be prepared to enact these practices when they first enter the classroom. This study provides a potential solution to extending the capabilities of teacher education programs to help novices continue honing their skills even after they graduate and begin teaching. The examination of how novice teachers engage with videos of one another in an online inquiry group provides insights into how novice teachers are thinking about responsive teaching practices once they enter the field as well as how their reflections and perceptions change over time.

2.2 The Role of Video Platforms and Feedback in Teacher Learning

Learning to teach is a complex practice, and as such, engaging in inquiry and conversations about in-the-moment teaching decisions through video of one's own practice and the practice of peers helps teachers to critically reflect on their pedagogical reasoning [9]. Prior research suggests that using video-sharing platforms allow teachers to have increased capacity to reflect on their practice and provide more focused feedback [10]. Borko and colleagues [11] suggest that "video can support collaborative learning focused on reflection, analysis, and consideration of alternative pedagogical strategies in the context of a shared common experience" (p. 419). Video of teaching episodes is necessary but not sufficient for providing teachers with opportunities to improve practice, as teachers need a clear framework or purpose through which to reflect on their practice or the practice of others [12]. Prior research on the use of video clubs as a form of professional development suggest that feedback and conversations about practice become more focused and in-depth over time [10]. Much of this research is situated within individual schools or districts, which can be logistically and financially challenging to implement. More recent studies explore the use of online platforms and video tagging to surface understandings of how video can improve teachers' ability to attend to and interpret student thinking and teaching responsively [13, 14].

Further, online platforms provide a unique opportunity for teachers and researchers to understand teachers' learning through the process of feedback itself. Prior quantitative ethnographic studies have examined how asynchronous posts in an online learning group can help to understand how learning develops through group communication based on the elements of teaching presence, social presence, and cognitive presence [15, 16]. The current study seeks to contribute to research on the use of asynchronous online learning communities by understanding how the nature of novice teacher thinking and understanding of responsive teaching practices shifts as they engage with one another and with teacher educators over the course of an academic year.

3 Methods

Participants in this project come from a larger study of video-feedback inquiry groups [14]. To explore the patterns of feedback over the course of the study, researchers used intensity sampling [17] to select the group that had the most consistent participation throughout the year. This group was comprised of five pre-kindergarten-1st grade early career teachers. The teacher educators were white female mathematics educators from the teacher education program the novice teachers had attended; two were faculty members and one was an advanced doctoral student/teaching assistant.

Data was collected via Vosaic, the video annotation platform used to conduct the inquiry groups. For each of four cycles, inquiry group participants uploaded a recording of a 10–20-min Number Talk, posted the video with a focusing question on the Vosaic platform, and posted comments on videos from other teachers in the inquiry group (Fig. 1). Teacher educators waited until at least one peer had provided feedback before commenting in order to avoid influencing the comments made by participants.

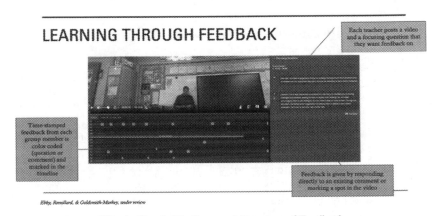

Fig. 1. Vosaic Platform and Structure of Feedback

Inquiry group interactions were downloaded from Vosaic into Excel for analysis. The spreadsheet contained information on the user, time stamps, moment duration, type, sequence, and the text of the comment. Posts were organized chronologically for each unique number talk video. To prepare the data for analysis, columns were added to group data based on time units, dividing the inquiry groups into First and Second half number talk groups (unit variable). Since feedback is focused on each individual's number talk and therefore connections should not be made across each individual in each round, an additional variable was created to indicate the unique number talk video, a combination of the Presenting Teacher and Number Talk Round.

Once the data were organized, two sets of codes were developed to help understand the form and responsive teaching content of the feedback, as underscored by the research on the framing concepts of this study, namely responsive teaching practices and the use of asynchronous feedback for teacher learning (Tables 1 and 2).

The full set of codes were applied to the data using 0 to 1 binary deductive coding, indicating 1 if the code was present and 0 if it was not. For example, the following line of data was coded with a 1 for three forms of feedback (compliment, question, and suggestion and two responsive teaching moves (selecting tasks and teacher decision making) and a 0 for all other codes:

Table 1. Codebook for Type of Feedback

Code	Definition	Example
Question	Asks for clarification or wonders about a decision	"Was Luca's strategy one you feel confident the other students know and use?"
Compliment	Highlights something that the teacher does well	"You do a really nice job of recording their ideas quickly so you can keep the number talk moving."
Suggestion	Points to something that the teacher could improve on or do differently	"You might ask, 'Who thinks they understand what ___ is saying?' Can you explain it in your own words? This will help more students engage."
Reflection	Connects to one's own teaching or to something they observe at another point during a number talk	"This has me thinking about how I can be more intentional about which students I am asking to share"

Table 2. Codebook for Responsive Teaching Content of Feedback

Code	Definition	Example
Elicit student thinking	How the teacher probes for student thinking, asks for different strategies, and refrains from filling in	"Love the question, 'why did you put 5 in your head?' VERY important to establish."
Represent student thinking	Highlights the use of visual models to support learning goals, uses board space effectively, and makes strategies visible	"What might happen if before you added 2 more on, you circled the 3 magnets that were there before…it might help some of them hold onto the idea."
Orient to others' ideas	How the teacher helps to make connections between strategies and/or engage students in understanding one another's strategies	"I think asking how two students' strategies are similar is a great way to keep students accountable for keeping track of and engaging with what their classmates said."
Establish norms	Facilitating the number talk in a way that communicates the value of making sense of different strategies and learning from mistakes	"This is a nice small discourse move. While you start with ___'s name, you phrase it, 'Let's pay attention to ___' which feels like a whole group reminder to remember to pay attention to the speaker."
Highlight the math	How the teacher advances key mathematical ideas or strategies by making connections, using conceptual press or representations, and deliberately sequencing the discussion	"By reiterating that these are two 10-frames, you are highlighting the idea that we can break up the numbers into multiples of 5s and 10s to see and subitize more effectively."

(continued)

Table 2. (*continued*)

Code	Definition	Example
Select tasks	The strategic selection and order of problems and tasks for the number talk	"These dots were nicely sequenced. Was there a specific strategy you had in mind? It might have helped them focus if they had a particular thing to think about through the number talk."
Teacher decision making	Instructional decisions not directly focused on responsive teaching practices but on the pedagogical choices made by the teacher during the number talk that help teachers to accomplish instructional goals	"It was a great decision to have them turn and talk here since this was the important mathematical idea you want everyone to engage with."

These dots were nicely sequenced. Was there a specific strategy or concept you had in mind when designing the sequence? It might have helped them focus if they had a particular thing to think about throughout the number talk.

To understand the form of feedback used by participants, comment type codes were developed inductively based on the form of feedback given by the commentor. Comment types included questions, suggestions, compliments, and reflections. Responsive teaching codes were deductive codes based on this number talk framework of responsive teaching moves.

Inter-rater reliability was calculated using Cohen's kappa for each of the 11 codes applied to the data based on 100 of the 360 lines in the data set. Good to excellent agreement with a minimum kappa of 0.75 was achieved on all codes except two. For the two code that did not reach moderate agreement, the two raters discussed areas of disagreement and coded another 10% data the data to recalculate IRR. Following recoding, moderate agreement with kappa of 0.67 was achieved for both codes.

3.1 Epistemic Network Analysis

In this study Epistemic Network Analysis [18, 19] was applied to the feedback data using the ENA1.7.0 [20]. Quantitative ethnographic techniques such as ENA were developed to help model associations that develop over time as participants engage with and learn from complex social and interactional systems [21]. Given the recursive and interconnected patterns of questions and comments enacted on the Vosaic platform, our online video inquiry groups serve as an ideal group for using ENA methods to understand how participants are reflecting on their own and others' teaching practices and thinking about responsive teaching moves within the context of number talk routines. Through their comments, teachers provide insights into their understanding of the teaching practices occurring in the videos as well as their own understanding of responsive teaching practices and what they believe can connect to their own work as teachers.

Units of analysis were defined as all lines of data associated with a single value of Time.Half subsetted by Number.Talk and Commentor. For example, one unit consisted of all the lines associated with Number.Talk NT1 and Commentor David (pseudonym). The ENA algorithm uses a moving stanza window to construct a network model for each line in the data, showing how codes in the current line are connected to codes that occur within the recent temporal context [22]. Based on the structure of the number talk videos, an initial analysis of the content in each of the lines of data build on references to a variety of prior moments in the number talk, and not just those in recent temporal context and are indicative of psychological proximity that spans the entire conversation [23]. As such, an infinite stanza window is used to capture the way that connections continue to progress throughout the conversation.

To understand how feedback changed over time both in terms of the form and content of the comments, two different epistemic network models were created. The first ENA model examined the type of feedback using comment codes, while the second ENA model examined the content of feedback using the responsive teaching codes. For both models, the variable "Person.NumberTalk" was set as the conversation variable for the model to ensure that associations were only drawn within each educators' unique video, as each video represented a unique set of data that would not necessarily relate to subsequent videos. For example, one conversation consisted of all the lines associated with Number Talk 1 and David 1.

Both ENA models normalized the networks for all units of analysis before they were subjected to a dimensional reduction, which accounts for the fact that different units of analysis may have different amounts of coded lines in the data. A means rotation maximized variance between each time half across the x-axis. These networks are visualized using graphs with nodes representing the codes and edges illustrating the co-occurrence, or connection, between the codes.

Excerpts from comments in the first half and second half of number talk feedback were reviewed to elucidate the meaning of these findings and complete the interpretive loop, helping to compare how the nature of feedback comments change as participants spent more time engaging in the online inquiry groups.

4 Results

4.1 Type of Feedback

The model examining associations between types of feedback had co-registration correlations of 0.96 (Pearson) and 0.95 (Spearman) for the first dimension and co-registration correlations of 0.97 (Pearson) and 0.98 (Spearman) for the second. These measures indicate that there is a strong goodness of fit between the visualization and the original model. Along the X axis (MR1), a Mann-Whitney test showed the type of feedback given in the First half of the number talks (Mdn $= -0.24$, N $= 14$) was statistically significantly different at the alpha $= 0.05$ level from Second half (Mdn $= 0.07$, N $= 13$ U $= 47.00$, p $= 0.03$, r $= 0.48$).

Overall, the model is driven by connections to the compliment code, with First half posts more likely to connect compliments and questions and compliments and suggestions. While relatively strong associations between compliments and both questions and suggestions manifested in both the First half and the Second half, these connections were somewhat stronger in the First half. This tendency to link questioning or suggestive

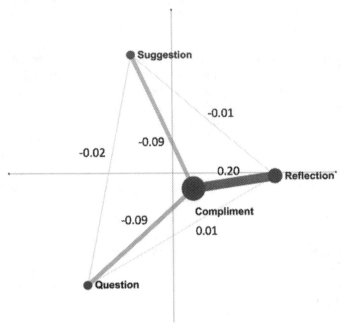

Fig. 2. Difference in the associations of type of comments from the first half to the second half of number talk inquiry groups.

feedback to a compliment may demonstrate the nature of teacher talk overall, as teachers often attempt to provide positive feedback alongside more suggestive feedback [24, 25]. Colloquially, teachers often refer to this pattern of feedback as "glows and grows", always coupling suggestions for improvement with commendations for areas of strength. In one such instance, Jennifer provides the following feedback: "you are doing a great job of keeping all of your students engaged and interested! I wonder if there is a way to communicate the difference between just seeing (subitizing) and counting." Jennifer's focus in this feedback comment is to provide a suggestion for how Nora, the presenting teacher, can highlight the mathematics. However, she begins by complimenting Nora's ability to keep students engaged in the discussion, thus creating a co-occurrence of the codes for compliment and suggestion. In other such instances, commentors would compliment a strategy or responsive teaching move, but also provide additional strategies or solutions that the presenting teacher could try in a subsequent number talk.

The models of the type of participants' feedback over time also suggest that the types of comments became more reflective throughout the course of the inquiry group study, specifically in reflective feedback that complimented the presenting teacher, as illustrated by Fig. 2. For example, in providing feedback to Becca in the third number talk, Katrina says:

Wow! I am so impressed by how Asher really took Melody's strategy and explained it so clearly and concretely. Did you intentionally choose him for that reason? This has me thinking about how I can be more intentional about which students I am asking to share and restate at different times in the number talk.

In this and similar complimentary and reflective comments, teachers engage in a form of dialogue with the presenting teacher [25] to highlight the responsive teaching move they would like to incorporate into their practice and to also understand the pedagogical reasoning that supported the presenting teacher's decision making.

4.2 Content of Feedback

The model examining associations in the content of participants' feedback had co-registration correlations of 0.95 (Pearson) and 0.96 (Spearman) for the first dimension and co-registration correlations of 0.98 (Pearson) and 0.95 (Spearman) for the second. These measures indicate that there is a strong goodness of fit between the visualization and the original model. Along the X axis (MR1), a Mann-Whitney test showed that the content of number talk feedback First half (Mdn $= -0.92$, N $= 14$) was statistically significantly different at the alpha $= 0.05$ level from Second half (Mdn $= 0.85$, N $= 13$ U $= 11.00$, p $= 0.0$, r $= 0.88$).

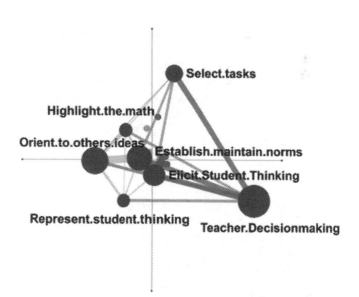

Fig. 3. Difference in the associations of the content of comments from the first half to the second half of number talk inquiry groups.

In the First half of the model, stronger connections can be seen from many of the responsive teaching practices to establishing and maintaining norms, as visualized in Fig. 3. The prevalence of establishing and maintaining norms as a focus during the First half is indicative of the emphasis during the beginning of the year of developing expectations for mathematics discourse communities during number talks. For example, David provides Katrina the following feedback on her first number talk: "this is a good discussion norm to establish. Getting students to pay attention to each other's comments and strategies is challenging but giving them a means to engage with each other's contributions helps with that." This type of feedback that focused on directing students to attend to one another's strategies was common throughout the First half of the number talks, as can be seen through the weight of the connection between establishing and maintaining norms and orienting to others' ideas.

The patterns of connection-making in the Second half of the number talks tended to be more balanced across all codes, with an increase in overall connections to teacher's decision making. Just as the type of feedback became more reflective over the course of the inquiry group, the content of teachers' feedback in the Second half focuses more on understanding why presenting teachers make certain decisions. These shifts in connections could suggest that participation in the inquiry groups helps to support teachers' reflection on pedagogical reasoning in number talks. An example of this can be seen in Emma's compliment on David's fourth number talk:

> This is a great conversation! I love "what would you do if you forgot a math fact" because it draws their attention to the fact that the strategies live together, and they don't lose access to the strategies they've used before just because they might have started using new, quicker ones.

Not only is Emma complimenting David's use of questioning to elicit student thinking, but it also highlights what this question does in terms of supporting other responsive teaching moves. Further, the increased balance of connections across codes in the Second half model suggests that the participants are thinking more flexibly in their analysis of teaching moments. The balanced distribution of connections along with the increased prevalence of focus on teacher decision-making also suggests that participants are demonstrating development of deeper pedagogical reasoning [26].

5   Discussion

The epistemic network analysis of novice teacher feedback in this study supports prior qualitative findings from the same data that suggest participants learned through the process of giving feedback to one another [14]. The shifts in both the nature and content of participants' feedback in this study suggest a growth in the novice teachers' pedagogical reasoning, as seen through increase in reflection in participants comments and through the diversification of connections and increased attention to teacher decision-making. The nature of sharing videos in an online platform and providing and receiving feedback allowed these early-career teachers to unpack the complexities of responsive teaching practices and reflect on the underlying pedagogical reasoning of their own work and that of their colleagues [26]. The process of giving and receiving asynchronous feedback allowed novice teachers to engage in discussions that helped develop their own professional knowledge and, in turn, provided them with opportunities for professional growth.

Prior research highlights the importance of pedagogical reasoning as core to teachers' practice [8, 26], as teachers consistently are faced with pedagogical dilemmas in the classroom that require rapid instructional decision making. The use of video platforms slows down the practice of teaching, allowing participants to unpack those complexities in their own practice and in one another's work. The results of this study support both the importance of growth of pedagogical reasoning as a mechanism for teacher learning as well as the use of video as a medium for helping novice teachers to develop their pedagogical reasoning.

This study also highlights the complimentary nature of teacher talk as novices engage in reflective feedback with one another. This finding could be demonstrative of peer colleagues as "empathic observers" [24] who situate themselves alongside the teacher for whom they are providing feedback. The nature of the inquiry group positioned participants as both teachers and researchers, and as such allowed them to engage in a constructive dialogue with one another [25], as with each comment, they were incorporating their own professional knowledge about teaching with reflections on how they would respond in-the-moment to different situations. This type of dialogic feedback positions novice teachers as capable, thus engaging them in a more agentic form of teacher learning than more traditional forms of professional development [25]. Further, the multiple roles participants played in both giving and receiving feedback helps to foster a reflective stance as empathetic observers based on the duality built into the structure of the inquiry group process. By noticing potential solutions to instructional dilemmas in the work of others, participants were better equipped to consider employing different strategies in their own classrooms in subsequent number talks based on their own reflections.

6 Conclusion

Together, the results of this study suggest that the nature and format of the online inquiry group provided teachers with windows into their own practice and into that of others in ways that helped to develop pedagogical reasoning and strengthen responsive teaching practices. Participation in the inquiry group strengthened novice teachers' identities as reflective practitioners, thinking about their own work while providing their professional knowledge and insights through feedback on others' teaching. Because learning is deeply embedded in teacher practice, novices were more able to make connections to their own work by learning through the work of others and make meaningful changes based on those reflections. Further studies should continue to explore opportunities for professional development that engage teachers as agentic and reflective in their own learning to help improve their pedagogical reasoning.

This study is limited in that it focuses on the networks of association of feedback in a single inquiry group and is thus not generalizable. However, it offers promise for the use of video feedback tools for pre-service and in-service professional learning. Further, the virtual nature of this inquiry group offers a potential way to support early-career teachers in continuing to enact responsive teaching practices that they learn in teacher education but may not be supported in their school culture. Further research in similar virtual professional learning communities across multiple cohorts of participant could help strengthen understanding of the efficacy of feedback in online video inquiry groups.

Acknowledgements. This research was funded by Spencer Grant Number [blinded for review]. This work was also supported by use of the Epistemic Analytics lab, funded in part by the National Science Foundation (DRL1661036, DRL-1713110), the Wisconsin Alumni Research Foundation, and the Office of the Vice Chancellor for Research and Graduate Education at the University of Wisconsin-Madison. The opinions, findings, and conclusions do not reflect the views of the funding agencies, cooperating institutions, or other individuals. All opinions are those of the authors and do not necessarily represent the views of the funder.

References

1. Boaler, J., Greeno, J.G.: Identity, agency, and knowing in mathematics worlds. In: Boaler, J. (ed.) Multiple Perspectives on Mathematics Teaching and Learning, pp. 171–200. Albex Publishing, Westport, CT (2000)
2. Robertson, A.D., Scherr, R., Hammer, D.: Responsive Teaching in Science and Mathematics. Teaching and Learning in Science Series. Routledge, Abingdon (2016)
3. Hill, H., McGinn, D., Dilbert, B.: Early findings report: Survey of U.S. middle school mathematics teachers and teaching. Center for Education Policy Research at Harvard University (2018). https://cepr.harvard.edu/files/cepr/files/mtts-early-findings.pdf
4. Wooldridge, A.R., Carayon, P., Shaffer, D.W., Eagen, B.: Quantifying the qualitative with epistemic network analysis: a human factors case study of task-allocation communication in a primary care team. IISE Trans. Healthc. Syst. Eng. **8**(1), 72–82 (2018)
5. Lampert, M., Graziani, F.: Instructional activities as a tool for teachers' and teacher educators' learning. Elementary Sch. J. **109**(5), 491–509 (2009)
6. Humphreys, C., Parker, R.: Making Number Talks Matter. Stenhouse, Portsmouth (2015)
7. Gay, G.:Culturally Responsive Teaching: Theory, Research, and Practice, 3rd edn. Multicultural Education Series, New York (2018)
8. Kavanagh, S.K., Conrad, J., Dagogo-Jack, S.: From rote to reasoned: examining the role of pedagogical reasoning in practice-based teacher education. Teach. Teacher Educ. **89**, 102991 (2020)
9. Van Es, E.A., Sherin, M.G.: Mathematics teachers "learning to notice" in the context of a video club. Teach. Teacher Educ. **24**, 244–276 (2008)
10. Lee, G.C., Wu, C.C.: Enhancing the teaching experience of pre-service teachers through the use of videos in web-based computer-mediated communication (CMC). Innov. Educ. Teach. Int. **43**(4), 369–380 (2006)
11. Borko, H., Jacobs, J., Eiteljorg, E., Pittman, M.E.: Video as a tool for fostering productive discussions in mathematics professional development. Teach. Teacher Educ. **24**, 417–436 (2008)
12. Brouwer, N., Besselink, E., Oosterheert, I.: The power of video feedback with structured viewing guides. Teach. Teacher Educ. **66**, 60–73 (2017)
13. Walkoe, J., Sherin, M., Elby, A.: Video tagging as a window into teacher noticing. J. Math. Teacher Educ. **23**, 385–405 (2020)
14. Blinded for review

15. Rolim, V., Ferreira, R., Lins, R.D., Găsević, D.: A network-based analytic approach to uncovering the relationship between social and cognitive presences in communities of inquiry. Internet High. Educ. **42**, 53–65 (2019)
16. Wright, T., Oliveira, L., Espino, D.P., Lee, S.B., Hamilton, E.: Getting there together: examining patterns of a long-term collaboration in a virtual STEM makerspace. In: Wasson, B., Zörgő, S. (eds.) Advances in Quantitative Ethnography: Third International Conference, ICQE 2021, Virtual Event, November 6–11, 2021, Proceedings, pp. 334–345. Springer, Cham (2022). https://doi.org/10.1007/978-3-030-93859-8_22
17. Patton, M.P.: Qualitative Research and Evaluation Methods, 2nd edn. Sage, Thousand Oaks (2002)
18. Shaffer, D.W.: Quantitative Ethnography. Cathcart Press, Madison, WI (2017)
19. Shaffer, D.W., Collier, W., Ruis, Λ.R.: A tutorial on epistemic network analysis: analyzing the structure of connections in cognitive, social, and interaction data. J. Learn. Anal. **3**(30), 9–45 (2016)
20. Marquart, C.L., Hinojosa, C., Swiecki, Z., Eagan, B., Shaffer, D.W.: Epistemic Network Analysis (Version 1.7.0) [Software] (2018). http://app.epistemicnetwork.org
21. Shaffer, D.W.: Epistemic frames for epistemic games. Comput. Educ. **46**(3), 223–234 (2006)
22. Siebert-Evenstone, A., Arastoopour Irgens, G., Collier, W., Swiecki, Z., Ruis, A.R., Williamson Shaffer, D.: In search of conversational grain size: modelling semantic structure using moving stanza windows. J. Learn. Anal. **4**(3), 123–139 (2017)
23. Zörgö, S., Peters, G.-J.Y.: Epistemic network analysis for semi-structured interviews and other continuous narratives: challenges and insights [Preprint] (2019). PsyArXiv https://doi.org/10.31234/osf.io/j6n97
24. Metz, M.L., Simmt, E.S.M.: Researching mathematical experience from the perspective of an empathic second-person observer. ZDM Math. Educ. **47**, 197–209 (2015)
25. Charteris, J.: Dialogic feedback as divergent assessment for learning: an ecological approach to teacher professional development. Crit. Stud. Educ. **57**(3), 277–295 (2016)
26. Loughran, J.: Pedagogical reasoning: the foundation of the professional knowledge of teaching. Teachers Teach. **25**(5), 523–535 (2019)

How Can We Co-design Learning Analytics for Game-Based Assessment: ENA Analysis

Yoon Jeon Kim(✉) ⓘ, Jennifer Scianna ⓘ, and Mariah A. Knowles ⓘ

University of Wisconsin – Madison, Madison, WI, USA
{yj.kim,jscianna,mariah.knowles}@wisc.edu

Abstract. The broader education research community has adopted co-design, or participatory design, as a method to increase adoption of innovations in classrooms and to support professional learning of teachers. However, it can be challenging, due to co-design's dynamic nature, to closely investigate how the co-process played out over time, and how it led to changes in teachers' perceptions, beliefs, and/or practices. Applying Quantitative Ethnography, we investigate how teachers and researchers collaboratively designed assessment metrics and data visualizations for an educational math game; we discuss the interactions among the co-design activities, teachers' learning, and qualities of the dashboard created as the output of the process.

Keywords: co-design · ENA · teacher professional learning · data visualization · human-centered learning analytics · game-based assessment

1 Introduction

By implementing educational games in classrooms, teachers can provide authentic and engaging opportunities to support learning of academic content as well as valuable cognitive and non-cognitive skills [1]. The advocates of game-based learning long recognized affordances of data generated from gameplay for improving teaching and learning in classrooms. For example, game data can be processed and presented to provide teachers with greater insights into students' learning, so they can provide timely feedback [2]. Making these data actionable and meaningful to teachers, however, poses several challenges. First, teachers must understand what kinds of data (or evidence) were collected and processed related to which learning outcomes. Second, teachers must be able to make sense of the presented data and trust its accuracy and validity. Third, data visualization tools coupled with games must be usable by teachers in real classroom contexts. In summary, making game-based assessment data useful to support teachers' pedagogical decision-making in classrooms is not trivial, and the disconnect between teachers' needs and learning analytics development has been consistently discussed as one of the main barriers to fully leveraging the data affordances of educational games, and educational technology more broadly [3].

C. Damşa and A. Barany (Eds.): ICQE 2022, CCIS 1785, pp. 214–226, 2023.
https://doi.org/10.1007/978-3-031-31726-2_15

In this paper, we aim to investigate the interactions among teachers' perceptions about assessment, data visualization and learning analytics, and the co-design process in the context of game-based assessment. We investigate these interactions in an iterative development process that engaged teachers as co-designers to develop teacher-facing, interactive dashboards for Shadowspect – a 3D puzzle game for assessing Common Core Geometry standards, student persistence, and spatial reasoning.

2 Theory and Relevant Work

2.1 Co-design

Co-design, participatory design, and co-creation all have the goal of involving stakeholders as collaborative designers [4]. In education research, co-design is increasingly adopted as a form of design-based research (DBR) that incorporates several types of stakeholders in the development and research processes. In this view of co-design, designers (or researchers) and stakeholders are on equal footing in the design process albeit with diverse roles. Teachers become designers seen as "experts of their experience," while designers become facilitators easing teachers' expression of creativity and as product experts under design.

As illustrated in Fig. 1 (adopted from [5]), a typical design process follows four phases: pre-design, generative, evaluative, and post-design. The first dot in the process indicates the determination of the design opportunity (or defining the problem), and the second dot indicates the finished product. While traditional design process brings the users in at the back end of the process, co-design aims to get end users involved in the front end. The key ingredient of successful co-design centers on an iterative and creative process of "making things" that illustrate future opportunities, concerns, values, and views on future ways of doing or living.

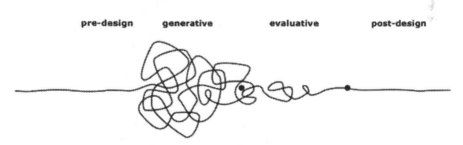

Fig. 1. Illustration of a design process

The co-design research community has been accumulating various co-design methods and tools to meaningfully engage end users who are not trained as professional designers in this creative process. Sanders and Stappers [5] describe three types of activities that occur during this creative, making process: probes, generative toolkits, and prototypes. The probes intend to get users to reflect on and express their experiences, feeling, and attitudes in forms and format that provide inspiration for designers. The generative toolkits intend to engage users to make expressive artifacts—artifacts that might not be directly related to the actual end product but demonstrate how they perceive and envision future opportunities and discuss them. These expressive artifacts can then be reviewed by the designers to identify underlying patterns and themes that can inform the prototype. Some better known toolkits include User Persona, User Journey Map, Role-Play, and Photo Studies (for the whole slew of toolkits see, for example, Kumar [6]). Prototypes are physical manifestations of ideas and concepts with varying degrees of fidelity and usually come later, closer to the evaluative phase, to get feedback from the end user. In summary, the key element of the co-design process is an iterative back and forth between divergent and convergent activities that are facilitated by the designers (in our case, design-based researchers) through "creative acts of making", in which both designers and users actively participate.

Beyond the immediate benefits of leading to products that better align with the end users' needs and values, many researchers have begun acknowledging the additional benefits of having teachers participating in this creative process as teachers' professional learning opportunities [7, 8]. For example, Voogt et al. [8] report that by engaging teachers as designers, teachers could learn how an innovation works rather than simply that it works.

2.2 Teachers' Assessment Literacy for Technology-Enhanced Learning Environments

Currently, one of the main challenges to developing meaningful learning analytics and complex assessment models for teachers is the limited understanding of what kinds of assessment (or data) literacy teachers need to have to fully leverage assessment in technology-enhanced learning environments [9]. The general tone is that teachers lack the requisite skills and expertise to make full use of the data available to them from interactive educational technologies [10].

One well-documented challenge for teachers' use of highly processed machine-learning driven assessment models is the non-transparent and inscrutable nature of these algorithms [11]. For example, if a teacher receives an alert message that a student is 90% likely to quit, the teacher might want to know both why the student is becoming disengaged and how the 90% estimation was reached. In most cases, however, no support is provided; teachers must interpret such estimations on their own. Additionally, as teachers may not necessarily be fluent with machine learning concepts, they may also struggle to critically examine these algorithms. In situations where teachers are asked to simply trust the outputs without understanding their intricacies, the "black-box" nature of the algorithms may lead to mistrust or uncertainty in the models and their results. Although recent work has begun to improve the interpretability of such algorithms, less attention has been paid to understanding what skills and knowledge teachers require and what features and qualities developers should consider to support teachers' use of such technologies.

In the current project, we define a teacher with assessment literacy in the context of educational games as follows [12]: (1) value non-academic, nontraditional, and process-oriented skills and attributes of learners that game environments can support; (2) understand what these constructs mean and can identify possible evidence for those constructs based on students' gameplay; (3) critically and curiously investigate how the data was processed, based on what rules, and understand the role of computing and artificial intelligence and its limitations even if it is not fully understand how the algorithms are being built; (4) use data and visualization tools to identify strengths, weaknesses, growth, and productive and unproductive struggles of learners beyond proficiency; and (5) strive to gain new, delightfully surprising insights about learners that they couldn't see with traditional forms of assessment; and finally (6) explore and dig into the data at various levels (i.e. individual, subgroup, classroom, grade) and with diverse goals (e.g. what's the puzzle that everybody is struggling with, so I can intervene?). This describes the secondary, professional development goals of the design team for the teacher fellows in addition to the creation of a meaningful, serviceable analytics platform.

3 Context

The research team selected 8 math teachers as *design fellows* from 16 secondary school teachers who applied in response to an open call for participation. The teachers were selected based on their interests in the educational value of games, data use in their classrooms, and interest and prior engagement in co-designing processes. The team and teachers met monthly during development iteration cycles for 12 months. A typical co-design session lasted 2 h. Due to COVID-19, all design sessions were conducted and recorded remotely via Zoom. The team collected several sources of data: design session discussions, teacher interviews, teachers' individual think-alouds, artifacts generated by the fellows, and the team's field notes.

The focus of individual co-design activities varied from generated activities using digital and nondigital toolkits to evaluative activities using prototypes. For example, the teachers used a digital toolkit called *Caterpillar* to come up with different instances for how persistence would be demonstrated in student's gameplay and how they would interpret them (Fig. 2a). The teachers also collaboratively created visualizations for possible prototypes (Fig. 2b), and later evaluated how these prototypes worked or didn't offering ideas to improve them.

For this paper, we analyzed all sessions, entry and exit interviews, and individual think-aloud activities to investigate the interplay between teachers' assessment literacy and the co-design process. To these ends, we address two questions:

RQ1: How did teacher discourse change throughout the co-design process to demonstrate changes in their thinking about the connection between assessment and student learning in game contexts?

RQ2: If change is demonstrated, how did the co-design activities support it?

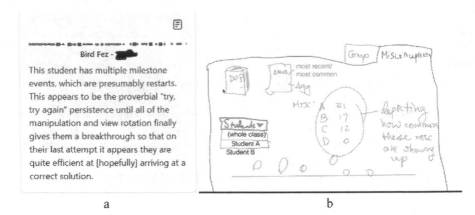

Fig. 2. Examples of co-design activities

4   Methods

4.1   Data and Pre-processing

Transcripts were generated based on audio recording and checked for accuracy. Transcripts were assigned metadata to compartmentalize the activities speakers were partaking in during each session; a single co-design session may have included several activities, some of which were based on group work. Activities were then labeled as the type of activity they were designed to be: probes, toolkits, and prototype reflections. Turns of talk were further segmented into individual sentences to isolate concepts the teacher fellows were bringing to the forefront of their discussions.

4.2   Coding

The research team approached the data by conducting a thematic analysis which yielded commonalities between the ways teacher fellows discussed their use of dashboards, desires for teaching, and thinking around artificial intelligence. These themes were iteratively defined into codes that incorporated elements of the role of technology (*AI*), teacher actions with the technology (*Manipulate*), teacher affect (*Trust*), teacher goals (*Teaching*), and teacher understanding of students' performance (*Comparison, Performance, Sequence, Thinking*) (See Table 1 for code definitions and examples). The researchers used the web-based nCoder [13] to reach agreement on the identified codes.

Table 1. Code Book - Kappa and Rho scores from nCoder are reported in order of Rater 1 vs. Classifier, Rater 1 vs. Rater 2, and Rater 2 vs. Classifier. *rho < 0.05, **rho < 0.01.

Label	Definition	Kappa
AI	algorithms, intelligent systems, automation, and artificial intelligence terminology, eg. "The computer program…instantly corrects the work for the students and gives them that feedback as soon as they submit it at the end"	.94* .96* 1.0**
Comparison	comparisons between student performance and other points of comparison, such as other students, class averages, explicit standards, and implied expectations, eg. "I can compare my students, how they're doing within school, which is like our district and school"	.97* .96* .96*
Manipulate	combining, filtering, sifting, selecting, or otherwise shifting one's perspective of data in general, such as sifting through student work, separating students, or identifying students, eg. "Or sorting by, like, the most missed question"	.96* .96* .93*
Teaching	things that teachers do, ie., pedagogical actions and strategies for instruction and intervention, such as checking in with students and planning concept review lessons, eg. "I would wanna sit down with that student and help them to develop strategies"	.96* .92* .92*
Performance	quantitative measures of student achievement, eg. "And again, I mean, just, I don't even know what growth looks like, but there's gotta be a way to measure it"	1.0* 1.0* 1.0*
Sequence	statistics, features, and descriptions of how students choose to link together, order, skip, or repeat complete educational tasks such as a problem, level, or assignment, eg. "So like, you know, a badge for, like, coming back to a level that you originally skipped"	.92* .91 .91
Thinking	what actions, thinking, or lack of those things, students performed within an educational task, eg. "And the other thing that I noticed, too, was that Player 1 was the only one who, like, changed the perspective so you weren't viewing it on an angle"	.93* .97* .97*
Trust	validity of metrics and trustworthiness of algorithms, eg. "Reliable's not the right word, but, it makes me question, like, how valid these scores are"	1.0** 1.0** 1.0**

4.3   Epistemic Network Analysis

Three models were generated using Epistemic Network Analysis to identify different elements of the teacher fellow discourse throughout the co-design experience in line with the research questions. Units were identified as Speakers in a given Session. As the focus of this study is on the teacher fellows' discourse, utterances by the design team were filtered out of the model.

Conversation size was defined as all lines belonging to a single group conversation during a particular activity in one session, e.g. three teachers in a breakout room using a toolkit activity to identify metrics of persistence would be one conversation. This segmentation allowed for comparison of the benefits of each activity type in the ENA plots. Furthermore, each model used the same moving window of 16 lines. This size was chosen to account for both longer teacher responses during think alouds and interviews (so the entire response would connect to itself) as well as rapid-fire communication during the brainstorming sessions where teachers were providing many, short responses to one another. The primary difference between the three models were the rotations used for visualization.

To address RQ1, we created a trajectory plot [14] (Model 1) to show the distribution of points "through time". In Model 1, the axes were rotated to maximize the variance between all sessions. This allows for better visualization of which codes and connections were dominant in the beginning, middle and end of the co-design process. To further address RQ1 about teacher fellows' growth, we created Model 2 using a Means Rotation to separate entry and exit interviews with the design fellows, which were the only two activities included in the model.

RQ2 considers how the co-design activities engaged teachers in discussion of student performance, metrics, and data literacy. Model 3 used hierarchical epistemic network analysis [15] to compare teacher discourse when they were interacting with prototypes, toolkits, and probes. We selected hierarchical epistemic network analysis because it allows us to see the independent effects of two binary variables simultaneously. The x axis in this rotation was defined by the presence of Probes while the y axis was defined by the presence of Toolkits. The third quadrant, where both probes and toolkits are absent, is where prototype activities are identified.

5 Results

5.1 Co-design Trajectory

RQ 1 focuses on the movement of design fellows through the co-design process. Model 1, the MCR trajectory plot, demonstrates that teacher fellows began the codesign experience focusing on *Performance* and *AI* before moving towards *Thinking* and *Teaching*, focusing on metrics of *Compare* and *Performance* while *Manipulating* data in the prototype before moving towards *Trust* and *AI* towards the end of the process (See Fig. 3). The x-axis can thus best be described as moving from a Tool orientation on the left side of the plot to a Trust orientation on the right. The y-axis is best described by the nature of the conversations. Conversations that are connected to *Performance* tend to focus on the scores and metrics that students are getting both in the game under study and in school more broadly. Thus, we define the lower end of the y-axis as being centered on quantitative discussions. The positive end of the y-axis centers most on *Sequence* and *Thinking* discussions which are both descriptors of what students are doing. Thus, we label this end of the axis as being focused on more qualitative ways of thinking and discussing performance.

Model 1 had coregistration values of .96 and .94 along the x and y axis respectively. This demonstrates that the plot is an accurate representation of the data. Each axis was responsible for explaining 15% of the variance within the data.

Early in Session 2 of the co-design workshops, teachers contemplated if *AI* could even be useful for the problem they were hoping to solve regarding assessment:

Teacher 1: But again like you talked about, the kind of technology that's out there with AI and your voice mail transcribing everything into texts, the possibilities, very soon, where all that stuff is going to be all set.

Teacher 2: I wonder if there is some technology that could see what they're doing and identify common mistakes. [...] I guess a systematized way to measure progress would be great. [...] Can a computer put our students into those categories related to their process?

While teachers were familiar with technology, they were unsure if computers and *AI* would be the right tools to be able to evaluate student *Performance*. By the end of the workshop, teachers were thinking more deeply about the implications of bringing *AI* into the classroom: "So we need to think about like, it's a for-profit company that makes this stuff. So like who makes it? And what kind of biases do they have? Because if it's all like white men who come up with the algorithms and, so anyway, it makes me think about that." Bringing ethical considerations into their discussion demonstrates a level of expertise with how algorithms and *AI* are made, not just that they exist within the dashboard program.

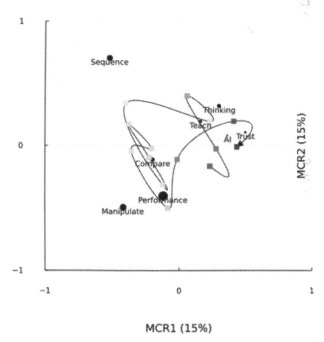

Fig. 3. The trajectory plot uses axes of MCR 1 and 2. Design fellows began and ended their experiences discussing *AI*; they began by focusing on *Performance* and *AI* and moved towards *Trust* and *AI* towards the end of the experience.

5.2   Teacher Discourse Shifts

Model 2 is visualized as an ENA plot (Fig. 4) that includes only entry and exit interviews that were conducted 1:1 with the design fellows. The entry interviews show strong
relationships among *Manipulate/Performance* and *Manipulate/Teach*. The strongest connection that emerged in the exit interview is the connection between *AI/Performance*.
Model 2 demonstrates the shift in teacher discourse from discussing their use of dashboards and analytics tools in the pre interview to their understanding of dashboards as a
computer-generated tool that they can control to show the nuances of student work and
learning.

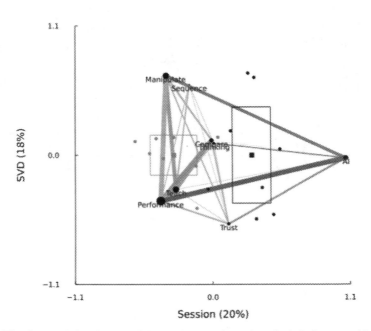

(f) #01 / pre vs. #11 / post

Fig. 4. A defining feature of the teacher post interviews is their focus on *AI*.

Interestingly, teachers were seemingly able to operationalize their *Trust* in *Thinking*
and *Manipulation* during the pre-interview to be offloaded onto *AI* by the post interview.
One teacher remark exemplifies this shift:

> "I had found something like we all did, when they put together teacher stuff, they
> try it, and students, and actually see how they feel about it, right? And so I think
> my trust issues go with like, like with the algorithm. Because I mean I don't fully
> understand the math or how it works, but I can trust that it's taking some important
> stuff that we teachers [inaudible] or that we value or weigh it as we think it is."

This teacher fellow is drawing the human sensemaking process into their interpretation of an algorithm's output. While they acknowledge that they do not feel capable

of the math behind the *AI,* if the output comes from being designed and operationalized with teachers, the output can be meaningful.

Additionally, while teachers make a greater connection between *AI/Trust/Thinking,* they also bring in more about *Manipulation* and *Performance* in connection with *AI.* One teacher compared the impact an *AI* could have on their *Teaching,* especially with students they perceived as under-performing,

> "You have like the really high-performing kids that you know, and the ones who are way behind that you know. And then the rest of them are kind of just like lost in the shuffle. And so having like the AI kind of make a suggestion or be like, hey, watch out for this kid because lately we haven't been doing this. [...]Like that AI to be able to, and I don't know if I'm using that correctly, but that AI to like be able to keep track of all that stuff."

It seems that the activities the teacher fellow participated in allowed them to improve their connections to *AI* to include ways that they could operationalize it in their classroom.

5.3 The Value of Co-design Activities

To tease apart the affordances of the different co-design activities, Model 3 used a hierarchical rotation to visualize the impact that probe and toolkit activities had on teacher discourse. When both probes and toolkits were present in the activities, there were strong connections between *Trust* and *Performance* as well as *Thinking* and *Sequence*. When probes were used without toolkits (noted with the blue down arrow), there were more likely to be connections between *Thinking* and *Teach*, and *Performance* and *Teach*.

Prototypes (shown as the red down arrow in Fig. 5 where both toolkits and probes were absent) largely focus on the connections between *Manipulate* and *Teach*. Teachers were active in reflecting on the value of the prototypes as they were interacting with them. They often played out scenarios of how they could use the tools with minor improvements to augment the *Teaching* they could do in the classroom: "That's why it's almost like, if we can come up with, like, filters that we know give important information, like: these are the students you should go help, or these are the students who you should reward."

Model 3 depicts some of the trends noted in the prior two models. While Model 1 shows the teacher fellows moving towards *Teach* and then *Performance, Manipulate,* and *Compare,* Model 3 correlates those motions to teacher fellow participation in probes early in the co-design process and toolkits towards the middle. One fellow clearly connects *Sequence* to *Performance* as they are trying to discern student behavior during a sense-making toolkit activity: "And I think, this is the only one that I would, like, like to see in a different way, the reattempts after failure. Cause I'm like, "Compared to the class, you only tried to rotate it eight times. Like, saying students that got better scores is because they tried to rotate it more times." The teacher fellow was able to articulate why the metric they were able to play with was not adequate for understanding why students were performing certain actions.

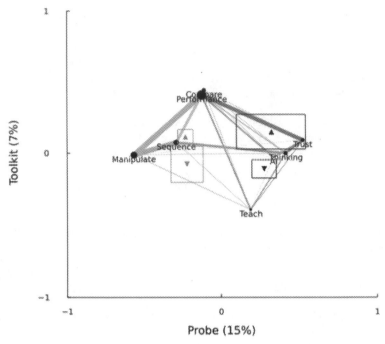

Fig. 5. Model 3 uses the x-axis to show the difference between discourse that occurred with a Probe, leading to more connections to *Trust* and *Thinking,* while the y axis depicts the impact of Toolkits leading to more connections to *Performance.* (Color figure online)

6   Discussion

This study leverages the theory of teacher learning through participating in co-design processes to develop educational innovations. Specifically, we investigate how a co-design process can facilitate teacher thinking about assessment metrics, the role of artificial intelligence and algorithms, and data visualizations in game-based learning environments. To investigate this interplay between teacher's assessment literacy and co-design process, we took a quantitative ethnographic approach to analyzing the discourse data collected from the co-design process.

Related to RQ1, our results indicate that by participating in this co-design process, teachers gained a more sophisticated understanding of the role that artificial intelligence plays in game-based learning and assessment. That is, while they started with rather naive beliefs about how AI is being used in assessment and how they trust it, at the end of this process, they were expressing more critical views about how these algorithms are being created and used in educational technology. In addition, they demonstrated how they now think about what makes for trustworthy algorithms in relation to their own teaching practices and beliefs.

Related to RQ2, our results indicate different affordances of probes, toolkits, and prototypes to support the co-design process. Our finding is also closely aligned with the existing literature of co-designing with teachers who do not hold technical or design expertise. That is, probes allowed teachers to envision innovative forms of assessment in game environments beyond their current practices, and toolkits were helpful for teachers to create tangible artifacts that better reflect their desires and needs to support their students.

Our findings provide a few implications for the field of game-based learning and assessment. First, in contrast to the common practice of developing learning analytics models and algorithms without involving teachers, co-design methods can be used to provide a creative process that engage teachers to generate metrics and algorithms that they can make sense with and trust, ultimately increasing validity of the analytics. Second, the use of data in game-based learning environments is a powerful link that helps teacher to think about learning beyond scores and contents, and the field needs to thoughtfully approach analytics and data dashboards with the goal of teachers' capacity building.

In relation to QE, this work demonstrates how QE methods can be used to address the challenges related to unpacking the dynamic and iterative nature of co-design processes, not just in relation to the product development, but how a co-design process influences the participants as well. This is significant, especially given the emerging efforts to engage practitioners meaningfully in development of learning analytics [16] as teachers and students in more educational research [17].

References

1. Clark, D.B., Tanner-Smith, E.E., Killingsworth, S.S.: Digital games, design, and learning: a systematic review and meta-analysis. Rev. Educ. Res. **86**, 79–122 (2016). https://doi.org/10.3102/0034654315582065
2. Shute, V.J., Masduki, I., Donmez, O.: Conceptual Framework for Modeling, Assessing and Supporting Competencies within Game Environments, pp. 1–25 (2011)
3. Lodge, J.M., Horvath, J.C., Corrin, L.: Learning Analytics in the Classroom: Translating Learning Analytics Research for Teachers. Routledge, Abingdon (2018)
4. Sanders, E.B.-N., Stappers, P.J.: Co-creation and the new landscapes of design. Co-design **4**, 5–18 (2008)
5. Sanders, E.B.-N., Stappers, P.J.: Probes, toolkits and prototypes: three approaches to making in codesigning. CoDesign **10**, 5–14 (2014)
6. Kumar, V.: 101 Design Methods: A Structured Approach for Driving Innovation in Your Organization. Wiley, Hoboken (2012)
7. Gravemeijer, K., van Eerde, D.: Design research as a means for building a knowledge base for teachers and teaching in mathematics education. Elementary Sch. J. **109**, 510–524 (2009)
8. Voogt, J., Laferrière, T., Breuleux, A., Itow, R., Hickey, D., McKenney, S.: Collaborative design as a form of professional development: in the context of curriculum reform. In: 2015 Annual Meeting of the American Educational Research Association: Toward Justice: Culture, Language, and Heritage in Education Research and Praxis (2015)
9. Tsai, Y.-S., Gasevic, D.: Learning analytics in higher education—Challenges and policies: a review of eight learning analytics policies. In: Proceedings of the Seventh International Learning Analytics & Knowledge Conference, pp. 233–242 (2017)
10. Luckin, R.: Machine Learning and Human Intelligence: The future of education for the 21st century. ERIC (2018)
11. Rudin, C.: Algorithms for interpretable machine learning. In: Proceedings of the 20th ACM SIGKDD International Conference on Knowledge Discovery and Data Mining, p. 1519 (2014)

12. Kim, Y.J., Lin, G., Ruipérez-Valiente, J.A.: Expanding teacher assessment literacy with the use of data visualizations in game-based assessment. In: Sahin, M., Ifenthaler, D. (eds.) Visualizations and Dashboards for Learning Analytics. AALT, pp. 399–419. Springer, Cham (2021). https://doi.org/10.1007/978-3-030-81222-5_18
13. Marquart, C., Swiecki, Z., Eagan, B., Shaffer, D.W.: ncodeR: techniques for automated classifiers [R package] (2019)
14. Brohinsky, J., Marquart, C., Wang, J., Ruis, A.R., Shaffer, D.W.: Trajectories in epistemic network analysis. In: Ruis, A.R., Lee, S.B. (eds.) ICQE 2021. CCIS, vol. 1312, pp. 106–121. Springer, Cham (2021). https://doi.org/10.1007/978-3-030-67788-6_8
15. Knowles, M., Shaffer, D.W.: Hierarchical epistemic network analysis. In: Second International Conference on Quantitative Ethnography: Conference Proceedings Supplement. ICQE (2021)
16. Buckingham Shum, S., Crick, R.D.: Learning analytics for 21st century competencies. J. Learn. Anal. **3**, 6–21 (2016)
17. Ahn, J., Campos, F., Hays, M., DiGiacombo, D.: Designing in context: reaching beyond usability in learning analytics dashboard design. JLA **6**, 70–85 (2019). https://doi.org/10.18608/jla.2019.62.5

Automated Code Extraction from Discussion Board Text Dataset

Sina Mahdipour Saravani⬥, Sadaf Ghaffari⬥, Yanye Luther⬥, James Folkestad⬥, and Marcia Moraes^(✉) ⬥

Colorado State University, Fort Collins, CO 80523, USA
{sinamps,sadaf.ghaffari,yanye.luther,james.folkestad,
marcia.moraes}@colostate.edu

Abstract. This study introduces and investigates the capabilities of three different text mining approaches, namely Latent Semantic Analysis, Latent Dirichlet Analysis, and Clustering Word Vectors, for automating code extraction from a relatively small discussion board dataset. We compare the outputs of each algorithm with a previous dataset that was manually coded by two human raters. The results show that even with a relatively small dataset, automated approaches can be an asset to course instructors by extracting some of the discussion codes, which can be used in Epistemic Network Analysis.

Keywords: Code extraction · Topic modeling · Unsupervised learning · Topic extraction

1 Introduction

Epistemic Network Analysis (ENA) has been used as an analysis technique in several different domains such as health care [1], educational games [2], and online discussion [3]. Recently, some researchers started to use ENA as a learning analytics visualization to support participatory Quantitative Ethnography (QE) [4] and instructor's assessment of student's participation in online discussions [5]. In that work, researchers presented the use of ENA as a tool to visualize connections among the codes that were discussed in the online discussion boards to assist instructors in assessing those discussions. Two human annotators manually coded the text data.

Based on the study presented in [5], we submitted a project proposal to our university's teaching innovation grant to examine the use of ENA as a visualization tool. One feedback provided by the reviewers was that instructors would not have time to be involved in the coding process, even if that process used nCoder [6]. The reviewers pointed out that they would like to have access to the visualization but not have the "burden" to build the codes. However, they would be willing to provide keywords that should be present in the codes. Considering that feedback, we decided to apply text mining and Natural Language Processing (NLP) algorithms to automate the extraction of codes from data and use the keywords that were provided by the instructors as guiding input to the algorithms. NLP has been applied to various applications [7–9] and

C. Damşa and A. Barany (Eds.): ICQE 2022, CCIS 1785, pp. 227–238, 2023.
https://doi.org/10.1007/978-3-031-31726-2_16

has improved drastically with deep learning [10, 11], motivating us to exploit it in this educational application.

We developed three text mining systems based on Latent Semantic Analysis, Latent Dirichlet Analysis, and Clustering Word Vectors to examine their capabilities for this task and determine the one that produced the best results. We compared the codes that were previously manually coded and validated by human coders in [5] with the outputs from the automated systems.

Previous work [12] on comparing coding from human raters and automatic algorithms found that the topic modeling algorithm was only compared with human coders for broad topics and that additional domain knowledge is necessary to identify more fine-grained topics. Similarly, another work [13] examined how keywords from codes manually extracted were presented in topics generated from topic modeling. It found that top keywords of a single topic often contain words from multiple manual codes. Contrarily, words from manual codes appear as high-probability keywords in multiple topics. It is important to notice that both studies used large datasets to run their topic modelling algorithms. Our study is different and more challenging in the sense that we have a relatively small dataset (Sect. 1.2). We will consider the findings from both previous works and will discuss how those are present in our work.

In this paper, we present a set of potential solutions to automatically extract codes from discussion data. We also propose detailed modifications to previously incorporated methods as a way to overcome the limitation of working with a small dataset. This is a challenging problem since there is no accurate mapping between this task and the well-defined tasks in Natural Language Processing (NLP) and Information Retrieval. This results in a lack of solid prior studies on the topic. We demonstrate that even with a small dataset, automated approaches can be an asset to course instructors by extracting some of the discussion codes. Further, instructors can provide input to the algorithms to guide them towards better results.

1.1 Research Questions

Considering the particularity of our study regarding the use of a small dataset, we aim to answer the following research questions.

- RQ1: Are Latent Semantic Analysis, Latent Dirichlet Analysis, and Clustering Word Vectors algorithms able to extract the codes previously coded by [5]?
- RQ2: What are the limitations of each algorithm?

1.2 Dataset

Our dataset consisted of online discussion data from seven semesters (Fall 2017, Fall 2018, Fall 2019, Spring 2020, Fall 2020, Spring 2021, Fall 2021) from an online class for organizational leaders as part of a Master of Education program at a Research 1 land-grant university. This dataset has 2648 postings and was provided to us by Moraes and colleagues [5]. The codebook established after meeting with Moraes and colleagues consists of the "a priori" codes presented in Table 1.

Table 1. Codebook.

Code Name	Definition	Kappa
Retrieval practice, Spacing out practice, Interleaving	Retrieval practice is the act of recalling facts or concepts or events from memory. The use of retrieval practice as a learning tool is known also as testing effect or retrieval-practice effect. Spacing out practice allows people to a little forgetting that helps their process of consolidation (in which memory traces are strengthened, given meaning, and connected to prior knowledge). Interleaving the practice of two or more concepts or skills help develop the ability to discriminate later between different kinds of problems and select the better solution	0.85
Elaboration	Elaboration is the process of giving new material meaning by expressing it in your own words and making connections with your prior knowledge. The more connections you create, the easy will be to remember it in the future	0.79
Illusion of mastery	Researches have pointed out that students usually have a misunderstanding about how learning occurs and engage with learning strategies that are not beneficial for their long-term retention, such as rereading the material several times and cramming before exams. When we got familiar with some content due to fluency in reading it, we create an illusion of mastering that content	0.89
Effortful learning	Learning is deeper and more durable when it is effortful, meaning that efforts, short-terms impediments (desirable difficulties), learning from mistakes, and trying to solve some problem before knowing the correct answer makes for stronger learning	0.85
Get beyond learning styles	There is no empirical evidence of the validity of learning styles theory in education. Researchers found that when instructional style matches the nature of the content, all learners learn better, regardless of their learning styles	0.86

2 Related Work

Previous works in the context of topic modelling mostly deal with using nCoder [6]. Although nCoder is a popular learning analytic platform used to develop a coding scheme, it is not fully automatic. In other words, it requires human in the loop to read through the text and validate if the coding is appropriate. nCoder+; [14] is another work in the same direction as of nCoder. This work specifically discusses an improvement to nCoder through semantic component addition to the nCoder process. This paper contributes to finding false negatives in the current nCoder version. Furthermore, as mentioned by authors of nCoder+, the idea is just a prototype and is not a public tool yet.

A very recent work by Cai, et al. [13] centers around nCoder as well. They investigate how close human created codewords are to topic models in large text documents. They also discuss whether the top keywords in topics match human codewords. There are distinct aspects between our work and others. First, we mainly take advantage of NLP approaches and compare three different unsupervised learning techniques to automate the topic extraction in our relatively small text documents. Second, we utilize coherence analysis as a way to determine the optimal number of topics in our text discussion data. Interestingly, in the context of our data, the established number of topics is the same as our acquired ground truth information from course instructors. In Sect. 3, we provide the details of our techniques for topic extraction.

3   Methods

For mining topics from our textual data, we begin our analysis with applying Latent Semantic Analysis (LSA) [15] to our discussion data. We then present two other methods for automatic code extraction from text data. The first method follows the efforts of previous researchers and is based on Latent Dirichlet Allocation (LDA) topic modeling [16]. The second method uses K-means [17] to cluster word embeddings. Both methods provide a way for the expert user to guide the automated learning process. Further details are provided in the following sub-sections.

3.1   Shared Preprocessing

Preprocessing is highly important in NLP tasks that are based on the bag of words modeling of the text, where the order of words in the sentences is ignored and a sentence is considered a bag of its words. Since our target task entails the retrieval of codes—in contrast with classification tasks like [9]—and the best outcome is to retrieve each of them in a uniform written form, such preprocessing steps are critical for better performance. Stop words, for example, do not carry any information that is useful for our task. Named-entity categories such as the name of authors and dates are also not relevant to the codes. We performed the following preprocessing steps that improved our experimental results. All these steps, except the last one, are also applied in the word embedding method. The term document refers to a post in our online discussion board dataset.

- *Tokenization.* We use the *simple_preprocess* from GENSIM [18] to tokenize the text using a regular expression from Python regex package.
- *Lowercasing.* We lowercase all words for uniformity and normalization of various writing styles and arbitrary capitalization.
- *Stop word removal.* Stop words do not contribute to codes and their removal would allow the algorithms to focus on useful words.
- *Applying minimum word length.* We assume that words with a length less than 3 characters in the English language do not contain useful information.
- *Irrelevant text removal.* We remove non-breaking space (NBSP), roman numerals, numbers, and URLs using regular expressions since these components do not contribute to the codes.

- *Named-entity removal.* Names of the students, authors, or books are not relevant to codes. After preliminary experiments, we concluded that they confuse the algorithms. We use SpaCy [19] to remove all tokens that are recognized as the name of a person or a work of art.
- *In-document frequency filtering.* Words that very rarely appear or are very frequent are not likely to be codes. We removed words that occur only in one single document. We also removed words that occur in more than 10% of the documents.
- *Generating bigrams and trigrams.* Since we are interested in code terms that contain more than one word—e.g. the code term "interleaved practice"—we extend the list of tokens in each document with its bigrams and trigrams: consecutive two and three words [20].

In our second proposed method, clustering word vectors: fastText + K-means, we do not consider bigrams and trigrams due to the lack of a natural operator to represent two or three single word vectors as a single vector of the same dimension. We leave further explorations of this path to future work.

3.2   Code Extraction Algorithms

One potential solution to the problem of code extraction, following the related work [13], involves using topic modeling algorithms. Another potential solution involves using word embedding vectors and clustering algorithms. We present a brief introduction to these algorithms and explain how we use them to discover the different topics of discussion in the class. Further, we provide qualitative comparisons between them for our objective.

Latent Semantic Analysis (LSA). LSA is a technique discovering statistical co-occurrences of words which appear together and provide further insights to the topic of words and documents. In this approach, a term-document matrix is formed from documents. The rows, in this matrix, are individual words and columns are documents. Specifically, the entries in a term-document matrix contain the frequency which a term occurs in a document. Singular Value Decomposition (SVD) is applied to the Term-Document matrix. As a result of applying SVD, we get the best k-dimensional approximation to the term-document matrix. The similarities among the entities in the lower dimension space are computed.

Latent Dirichlet Analysis (LDA). LDA is a generative probabilistic model in the context of NLP which represents documents over latent topics. These topics are each a distribution over words. The main assumption in topic modeling is that documents discuss the same topic if they use the same or similar set of words. Topics in LDA act as a hidden intermediate level between documents and words. This provides a path to dimensionality reduction, where a large matrix of association between all documents and words is broken into two matrices: one between documents and latent topics, and one between the latent topics and words [21, 22]. Being built upon the probabilistic latent semantic indexing (pLSI [23], LDA overcomes some of the shortcomings of pLSI. The pLSI has no natural way to assign a topic probability to an unseen document since it only learns a topic-document distribution for documents it has seen in its training. This is due to the use of a distribution that is indexed by training documents. Growth of pLSI's number of parameters with the number of documents also makes it prone to overfitting. Both of these limitations are resolved in LDA by using a parameterized hidden random variable as a topic-document distribution which is not explicitly linked to training documents.

LDA and the task of Topic Modeling for automated code extraction benefits from the separation of documents. The separation of documents is actually inherent in our target task. We intend to i) know what codes are covered in each discussion post, i.e. in each document, and ii) extract all codes that have appeared in all discussions. Hence, the separation of documents provides useful information for our objective.

After preprocessing, we create a LDA topic model over our aforementioned dataset (Sect. 1.2). We experiment with three variations: *without bigrams and trigrams, with bigrams and trigrams*, and *with bigrams and trigrams where prior topic-word distribution is modified*. The first two variations are self-explanatory. The third variation introduces the notion of a human user providing some codes or keywords in an input file to the program that are likely to be discussed in the course. We assume a constant topic for all keywords that are provided in a single line in the input file. For all keywords in a line, we assign a higher probability of belonging to that arbitrary constant topic compared to all other words in the dataset. We currently use a hyperparameter value (keywords_total_probability) to divide over the number of keywords and assign it to each of them. Thus, the probability for each keyword-topic pair is:

$$p(k_t, t) = \frac{keywords\_total\_probability}{n_{k_t}}. \tag{1}$$

For the rest of the words, the probability for that topic is the following uniform value,

$$p(w, t) = \frac{(1 - keywords\_total\_probability)}{(n_w - n_{k_t})}, \tag{2}$$

where n_w is the number of words in the whole dataset and n_{k_t} is the number keywords that user has provided for the arbitrary topic t. k_t is a provided keyword for topic t.

In case there are topics that the user has not provided any keywords for, the word-topic probability is

$$p(w, t) = \frac{1}{n_w}. \tag{3}$$

Since our experiments had a limited volume of data, this mechanism does not provide a significant improvement; however, it provides a natural way to optionally use human expert knowledge in the code extraction process using LDA. We implement this mechanism using the *eta* parameter of GENSIM's LDA implementation.

Clustering Word Vectors: fastText + K-means. This is another method which we present here as a potential solution to the code extraction problem. This approach is based on the idea of clustering algorithms. Although the code retrieval process is not evident, we propose a heuristic for that. The first requirement for clustering is representing the words in vectors. However, bag of words modelling is not sufficient here, as the clustering algorithm, being an unsupervised algorithm, only captures the already-present distinguishing characteristics of data rather than learning new features. Hence, the word vectors need to carry useful information for the latter use of the clustering algorithm. Exploiting the syntactic and semantic information contained in pre-trained word embedding vectors, which have successfully improved the accuracy on many NLP tasks [24–27], is a natural choice. To further handle out-of-vocabulary words that have not been observed in the pre-training process, we use fastText [25] word embeddings, which is a character-level word representation model. This ensures that even uncommon words that are discussed in a specific expert course would have appropriate vector embeddings. After preprocessing, we convert all of the words in the dataset to their embedding vectors. Unfortunately, in this step, we lose the information about which documents each word appeared in, which currently is a limitation of this approach. Next, we use the K-means clustering algorithm [17] to create groups of semantically and syntactically relevant words.

Word embedding models are pre-trained on huge amounts of digital text to learn the co-occurrence statistics of words. This pre-training objective results in a projection of syntactically and semantically relevant words to a close proximity in the resulting vector space. Furthermore, these word vectors have an interesting behavior against addition and subtraction operators where they prove capable of learning some relationships among words. For example, the arithmetic operation Paris − France + Italy equals Rome [24].

For the retrieval of words that represent each cluster, we utilize cluster centroids. We find the five closest word vectors to the center of each cluster and retrieve their words as the extracted codes. The closeness measure is the cosine similarity function. While this mechanism extracts interesting words, it has some limitations. The distance from cluster centroids does not necessarily imply irrelevance. Some code words may be closely related to two topics and far from the center of both associated cluster; hence, they would not be retrieved in either of the clusters. On the other hand, there is no reason to believe that the code words would appear in the center of the clusters.

For an analogous use of human expert input, the program accepts the same aforementioned keywords file. Here the input keywords, if present, are used to initialize the K-means cluster centroids. First, all words in a single line of the keywords file, which are assumed to represent one code, are converted to their respective fastText word embeddings. Then they are averaged and used as the initial center for one arbitrary cluster. During the training process of K-means, they are updated to fit the dataset. Generally, K-means algorithm without specific initialization is run multiple times with random initialization to find the best final convergence. However, since we specifically initialize all or some of the centroids using the keywords file, this variation of our implementation would execute K-means only once. In this case, it is reasonable to expect the code words to appear at the center of the clusters. This mitigates the aforementioned concern about the centers being ill-defined in terms of representing the actual codes, and further provides more computational efficiency by avoiding redundancy [10, 11].

The most important limitation of this approach is that the information about document boundaries and what words are contained is what documents are lost. While benefiting from the knowledge that is transferred from the pre-training of the word embedding model, this method treats the whole dataset merely as a dictionary of words.

4   Experimental Results

In order to answer the research questions we posed, we conducted experiments with the three aforementioned algorithms. To extract the topics from our discussion data, we were interested to find the optimal number of topics for our approach. Therefore, we conducted a topic coherence analysis [28] to achieve our aim. Given that text mining algorithms are in the category of unsupervised learning approaches, coherence analysis is considered an important measure as it gives structure to inherently unstructured textual data. Furthermore, it assesses the topics' quality and the coherence of words within each topic or cluster. The results in Table 2 indicate that the optimal number of clusters is five. For each of the five topics, we present the ten most representative words for the respective algorithms. The extracted topics from the Latent Semantic Analysis, Latent Dirichlet Allocation, and Clustering Word Vectors algorithms are demonstrated in Tables 3, 4, and 5 respectively.

To answer RQ1 and RQ2, we presented these results to Moraes and colleagues. Through qualitative analysis they determined that the outputs from LSA and LDA could extract some of the codes previously coded, but Clustering Word Vectors did not capture any code. They mentioned that the best code words are captured by the presented LDA algorithm where 4 of the 5 codes from the manual annotation have been extracted. In Table 4, **Topic 1** code words were related to *Effortful learning* code, **Topic 2** code words were related to *Get beyond learning styles*, **Topic 3** code words were related to *Illusion of mastery*, and **Topic 4** code words were related to *Retrieval practice*, *Spacing out practice*, and *Interleaving*. Only **Topic 0** did not represent any one of the codes. It is important to note that the *Elaboration* code, not present in any topic, had the lowest kappa between the two human coders (Table 1), meaning that even between human raters it wasn't an easy code to agree upon. Our results corroborate what was found in [12], as the topic modeling algorithm could only find broad topics. Assessing whether that is enough, in terms of accurately predicting codes in the remaining of our dataset, is something that still needs to be examined.

Table 2. Coherence Score for Various Number of Topics.

No. Clusters	Coherence Score
2	0.2851
3	0.2915
4	0.2944
5	0.5017
6	0.3776
7	0.4071
8	0.4067
9	0.3427
10	0.3773

Our LSA results present the same limitations found by [13]. As we can observe in Table 3, extracted code words of a single topic often contain words from multiple manual codes and words from manual codes appear as keywords in multiple topics.

Analyzing the extracted topics from the fastText + K-means algorithm, **Topic 2**, **Topic 3**, and **Topic 4** in Table 5 are not actual codes. **Topic 2** seems to contain only adverbs. As we expected and discussed this in Sect. 3.2, the pre-training process of the word embedding models (fastText) causes the vector space to have syntactically similar words positioned in a close proximity—the semantic closeness is not the only positioning objective of the pre-training process. As a result, the clustering algorithm (K-means) groups such words in a cluster. This is undesirable for the purpose of extracting codes. We discuss a potential solution to this problem in Sect. 5.

Table 3. Extracted Topics from Latent Semantic Analysis.

Topic 0	Topic 1	Topic 2	Topic 3	Topic 4
learn	practice	practice	memory	memory
practice	learn	forget	forget	difficulty
author	mass	mass	train	desire
think	author	lecture	difficulty	train
memory	time	inform	practice	example
time	memory	think	desire	story
wait	retrieve	learn	example	mindset
inform	forget	understand	mass	deliberation
knowledge	like	surgeon	learner	growth
skill	train	solution	help	plf*

* Stands for Parachute Landing Fall.

Table 4. Extracted Topics from Latent Dirichlet Allocation.

Topic 0	Topic 1	Topic 2	Topic 3	Topic 4
lecture	desire	dyslexia	confidence	mass
solution	desire_difficulty	learn_style	feedback	mass_practice
classroom	plf	individual	calibration	interleaving_practice
surgeon	resonate	learn_differ	confidence_memory	space_retrieval
acquire	parachute	disable	accuracy	tend
instruct	fall	intelligent	peer	day
learn_learn	land	prefer	answer	long_term
impact	jump	support	event	week
demand	parachute_land	dyslexia	state	myth
lecture_classroom	land_fall	focus	calibration_learn	practice_space

Table 5. Extracted Topics from fastText + K-means.

Topic 0	Topic 1	Topic 2	Topic 3	Topic 4
aspects	teacher	merely	pull	just
concepts	girl	simply	off	even
strategies	college	seemingly	down	know
perception	american	consequently	sticking-out	think
knowledge	school	ostensibly	underneath	going
understanding	junior	essentially	divits	get
implications	teacher	evidently	loose	thought
analysis	baylee	being	stick	really
approach	mom	therefore	rope	come
methodology	student	rather	sideways	but

5   Conclusion and Future Directions

The goal of this study is to investigate the capabilities of Latent Semantic Analysis, Latent Dirichlet Analysis, and Clustering Word Vectors to automatically extract codes from a relatively small discussion dataset. As previously stated, this is a challenging problem due to a lack of solid prior studies on the topic.

As observed in the experiments, LDA was the best approach and further examinations will be done in order to assess the prediction capabilities for the remaining dataset portions. The use of non-contextualized word embeddings, such as fastText (the third presented method—clustering word vectors) results in some clusters containing only syntactically relevant words—**Topic 2** in Table 5. However, syntactic similarity of words may not be necessarily useful in our target task of extracting codes because of the pre-training objective of the word embedding model. One possible solution is to use recent contextualized word embeddings such as BERT [27] as a substitute. Their word representation vectors are much richer in linguistic information and have been pre-trained to attend to important tokens in a text [29]. Such models also open up opportunities to keep the word-document information, as they are designed to use the context to generate the word vectors. However, due to their dynamic nature, the retrieval process is not trivial.

Another possible solution is exploiting the LDA2Vec [30] model for code extraction. As mentioned in Sect. 3.2, both the topic modeling and the clustering word embeddings have their advantages and disadvantages. To gain benefits from both, we intend to conduct experiments with LDA2Vec. Many advances in NLP focus on improving machines in processing text, while LDA2Vec aims to automatically extract information that is useful to from a large volume of text [30]. The LDA2Vec model is a modified version of the skip-gram word2vec model, where in addition to the pivot word vector a document vector is also exploited to predict the context, a modified architecture and pre-training objective. This makes LDA2Vec capable of capturing document-related information as well as word information. Since word vectors, document vectors, and topics are learned at the same time, they would be linked to each other and contain inherent information about the others.

Despite the limitations presented in this study which corroborates the findings of previous works [12, 13], we demonstrate that even with a relatively small dataset, automated approaches can be an asset to course instructors. Our intention is to incentivize further discussions on how text mining algorithms can be used to extract codes, even from relatively small datasets.

References

1. Zörgő, S., Jeney, A., Csajbók-Veres, K., Mkhitaryan, S., Susánszky, A.: Mapping the content structure of online diabetes support group activity on facebook. In: International Conference on Quantitative Ethnography (2021)
2. Bressler, D.M., Annetta, L.A., Dunekack, A., Lamb, R.L., Vallett, D.B.: How STEM game design participants discuss their project goals and their success differently In: International Conference on Quantitative Ethnography (2021)
3. Rolim, V., Ferreira, R., Lins, R.D., Găsević, D.: A network-based analytic approach to uncovering the relationship between social and cognitive presences in communities of inquiry. Internet Higher Educ. **42**, 53–65 (2019)
4. Vega, H., Irgens, G.A.: Constructing interpretations with participants through epistemic network analysis: towards participatory approaches in quantitative ethnography. In: International Conference on Quantitative Ethnography (2021)
5. Moraes, M., Folkestad, J., McKenna, K.: Using epistemic network analysis to help instructors evaluate asynchronous online discussions. In: Second International Conference on Quantitative Ethnography: Conference Proceedings Supplement (2021)
6. Marquart, C.L., Swiecki, Z., Eagan, B., Shaffer, D.W.: Package 'ncodeR', (2019). https://cran.r-project.org/web/packages/ncodeR/ncodeR.pdf. (Accessed 18 May 2022)
7. Esmaeilzadeh, A., Heidari, M., Abdolazimi, R., Hajibabaee, P., Malekzadeh, M.: Efficient large scale nlp feature engineering with apache spark. In: 2022 IEEE 12th Annual Computing and Commnication Workshop and Conference (CCWC) (2022)
8. Zuo, C., Banerjee, R., Shirazi, H., Chaleshtori, F.H., Zuo, C.: Seeing should probably not be believing: the role of deceptive support in COVID-19 misinformation on twitter. ACM J. Data Inf. Quality (JDIQ) (2022)
9. Saravani, S.M., Ray, I., Ray, I.: Automated identification of social media bots using deepfake text detection. In: International Conference on Information Systems Security (2021)
10. Saravani, S.M.: Redundant Complexity in Deep Learning: An Efficacy Analysis of NeXtVLAD in NLP, Colorado State University Theses and Dissertations (2022)
11. Saravani, S.M., Banerjee, R., Ray, I.: An investigation into the contribution of locally aggregated descriptors to figurative language identification. In: Proceedings of the Second Workshop on Insights from Negative Results in NLP (2021)
12. Bakharia, A.: On the equivalence of inductive content analysis and topic modeling. In: International Conference on Quantitative Ethnography (2019)
13. Cai, Z., Siebert-Evenstone, A., Eagan, B., Shaffer, D.W.: Using topic modeling for code discovery in large scale text data. In: International Conference on Quantitative Ethnography (2021)
14. Cai, Z., Siebert-Evenstone, A., Eagan, B., Shaffer, D.W., Hu, X., Graesser, A.C.: nCoder+: a semantic tool for improving recall of nCoder coding. In: International Conference on Quantitative Ethnography (2019)

15. Landauer, T.K., Foltz, P.W., Laham, D.: An introduction to latent semantic analysis. Discourse Process. **25**, 259–284 (1998)
16. Blei, D.M., Ng, A.Y., Jordan, M.I.: Latent dirichlet allocation. J. Mach. Learn. Res. **3**, 993–1022 (2003)
17. MacQueen, J., et al.: Some methods for classification and analysis of multivariate observations. In: Proceedings of the Fifth Berkeley Symposium On Mathematical Statistics And Probability (1967)
18. Řehůřek, R., Sojka, P.: Software Framework for Topic Modelling with Large Corpora. In: Proceedings of the LREC 2010 Workshop on New Challenges for NLP Frameworks, Valletta (2010)
19. Honnibal, M., et al.: Explosion/spaCy: v2.1.7: Improved evaluation, better language factories and bug fixes, Zenodo (2019)
20. Esmaeilzadeh, A., Cacho, J.R.F., Taghva, K., Kambar, M.E.Z.N., Hajiali, M.: Building wikipedia n-grams with apache spark. In Science and Information Conference (2022)
21. Ganegedara, T.: Intuitive Guide to Latent Dirichlet Allocation. https://towardsdatascience.com/light-on-math-machine-learning-intuitive-guide-to-latent-dirichlet-allocation-437c81220158. (Accessed 18 May 2022)
22. Seth, N.: Part 2: Topic Modeling and Latent Dirichlet Allocation (LDA) using Gensim and Sklearn. https://www.analyticsvidhya.com/blog/2021/06/part-2-topic-modeling-and-latent-dirichlet-allocation-lda-using-gensim-and-sklearn/. (Accessed 18 May 2022)
23. Hofmann, T.: Probabilistic latent semantic indexing. In: Proceedings of the 22nd Annual International ACM SIGIR Conference On Research And Development In Information Retrieval (1999)
24. Mikolov, T., Chen, K., Corrado, G., Dean, J.: Efficient estimation of word representations in vector space," arXiv preprint arXiv:1301.3781, (2013)
25. Bojanowski, P., Grave, E., Joulin, A., Mikolov, T.: Enriching Word Vectors with Subword Information, arXiv preprint arXiv:1607.04606, (2016)
26. Pennington, J., Socher, R., Manning, C.D.: Glove: Global vectors for word representation. In: Proceedings of the 2014 Conference On Empirical Methods In Natural Language Processing (EMNLP) (2014)
27. Devlin, J., Chang, M.-W., Lee, K., Toutanova, K.: BERT: Pre-training of deep bidirectional transformers for language understanding. In: Proceedings of the 2019 Conference of the North American Chapter of the Association for Computational Linguistics: Human Language Technologies, vol. 1 (Long and Short Papers) (2019)
28. Röder, M., Both, A., Hinneburg, A.: Exploring the space of topic coherence measures. In: Proceedings of the eighth ACM International Conference On Web Search And Data Mining (2015)
29. Vaswani, A., et al.: Attention is all you need. In: Advances in Neural Information Processing Systems, vol. 30 (2017)
30. Moody, C.E.: Mixing dirichlet topic models and word embeddings to make lda2vec, arXiv preprint arXiv:1605.02019, (2016)

Mathematics Teachers' Knowledge for Teaching Proportion: Using Two Frameworks to Understand Knowledge in Action

Chandra Hawley Orrill[1]([⊠]) [iD] and Rachael Eriksen Brown[2] [iD]

[1] University of Massachusetts Dartmouth, Dartmouth, MA 02747, USA
corrill@umassd.edu
[2] Pennsylvania State University Abington, Abington, PA 19001, USA
reb37@psu.edu

Abstract. In this paper, we consider how we could use two different frameworks, our own Robust Understandings of proportions plus the Knowledge Quartet, to better understand the relationship between mathematics teachers' knowledge and their teaching practices. We present both frameworks, then describe each of two teachers by describing their classroom, considering an ENA graph of their understanding of proportional reasoning and key patterns that emerged through use of the Knowledge Quartet. We end by discussing how we have been able to use these two frameworks together and why this research is important in ongoing efforts to make sense of the relationships between teachers' knowledge and practice.

Keywords: Epistemic Network Analysis · Knowledge Quartet · Teacher Knowledge · Proportional Reasoning

1 Introduction

Common sense and general consensus assert that the amount and kind of knowledge teachers have access to in their teaching impacts the experiences their students have. However, this has been a difficult assertion to test in practice. In mathematics teaching, many of the efforts to tie teacher understanding to practice to date have been large scale studies focused on assessments of teacher knowledge correlated to student outcomes (e.g., [1]). More modest efforts assess teachers' practices through particular lenses of practice that are tied to models of teacher knowledge (e.g., [2, 3]). And, other students try to connect teacher knowledge to teacher practice by asking teachers to respond to assessment items designed to engage the teachers in real-world scenarios about teaching specific content (e.g., [4, 5]).

In contrast to any of these approaches, we have paired in-depth clinical interviews [6] and think-alouds with teachers to understand their knowledge of proportions. Then, we followed those same teachers into their classrooms to watch them teach proportions to their students. However, we learned very quickly that the framework we created to analyze teachers' content knowledge outside the classroom did not fit the data inside the classroom. To address this, we adopted a framework known as the Knowledge Quartet (KQ; [7–10]) to analyze the use of knowledge in teaching. But, this left us with a unique challenge of trying to merge two different theories about teacher knowledge to create one vision of the ways in which knowledge mattered to classroom teaching. In this paper, we examine how we have worked to bring the two frameworks together and what we are learning about teacher knowledge by looking across the frameworks. In the sections below, we present brief discussion of teacher knowledge, the two frameworks we worked from, and an overview of the study.

2 Frameworks

2.1 Teacher Knowledge

In 1986, Shulman [11] proposed the model for teacher knowledge that is widely used today. His proposition was that teacher knowledge is multidimensional with three primary kinds of knowledge: content knowledge (CK), pedagogical knowledge (PK), and pedagogical content knowledge (PCK). CK, for our purposes, is the mathematics that teachers know and use. We are particularly interested in specialized knowledge of mathematics, which we define as the mathematics teachers know and are able to use to support learners in making sense of mathematics. This CK may or may not align with the mathematics knowledge of the 'person on the stress' as a non-teacher does not need to have deep understanding of the ways in which mathematics works or multiple models for making sense of such mathematics. PK is the knowledge of how to teach that is not content specific. It is not a focus of our study. PCK is the knowledge teachers have of how to teach mathematics. It tightly overlaps with specialized knowledge of mathematics in that it is the knowledge of representations and other tools that support students in making sense of mathematical ideas. For the purposes of our study, we focused on CK and PCK – with the interviews focusing on CK and the classroom observations focusing on PCK.

2.2 Knowledge in Pieces and ENA

The Knowledge in Pieces framework (KiP) [12, 13] guides our work around teachers' mathematical knowledge. This framework of conceptual change can also be used to create an image of a person's knowledge at a point in time, which is how we used it in this study. KiP posits that knowledge is comprised of fine-grained understandings, which we refer to as knowledge resources. These knowledge resources are connected in ways that allow people to draw on them as novel situations arise. Thus, "learning" could be a result of refining a knowledge resource, adding knowledge resources, or developing connections between knowledge resources. This is consistent with research on expertise that asserts that people who are more expert have both more understanding of a topic and a different organization of the topic than novices in that topic area [14, 15].

We have found Epistemic Network Analysis (ENA) [16–18] to be useful in making knowledge resources and the connections between them visible. ENA is a quantitative ethnography approach for showing the interactions between the codes in a dataset. In our analysis, ENA shows the co-occurrence of codes within an utterance. We view these co-occurrences as being connections between ideas for the participants. Thus, ENA allows us a mechanism through which we can see how teachers' ideas are connected together and drawn upon as they solve a variety of related mathematics tasks.

To use ENA for our KiP analysis, we developed a framework of Robust Understandings for Proportional Reasoning [19] that was used to code the data, with each code being a knowledge resource. Our codes captured knowledge resources such as implementing solution paths for proportional situations such as using unit rate or equivalent fractions; reasoning with proportional structures such as the multiplicative relationship or covariance; and other resources such as those relating ratios to proportions or applying rules to proportional situations. We used these codes to classify the thinking of 32 teachers, including the two teachers of interest in the current study. We then created ENA plots of the teachers' knowledge so we could make comparisons and develop richer understandings of patterns in the knowledge resources implemented by the teachers. The ENA plot informed our understanding of teachers' knowledge as well as the domain of proportional reasoning.

2.3 Knowledge Quartet

Because the Robust Understandings framework focused specifically on mathematics knowledge, it proved to be problematic for analyzing enacted knowledge in teachers' mathematics classrooms. We began our analysis with Matt and Tori (pseudonyms), who we discuss below, and found that we were unable to do much beyond making guesses about their knowledge as they worked with students. To address this problem, we adopted the Knowledge Quartet [7, 8, 9, 10] which was explicitly developed to operationalize aspects of content knowledge as they relate to mathematics teaching. Specifically, KQ is divided into four main categories. Foundational knowledge, the first category, is focused on content knowledge, background, and beliefs [9] that the teachers bring to the classroom. It is observable through particular teacher moved such as identifying student errors and using proper and precise terminology. The other three categories, Transformation, Connection, and Contingency are situated in PCK. They are the marriage of CK and PK in ways specific to mathematics teaching and learning.

3 Methods

3.1 Participants

In this paper, we focus on our efforts to make sense of teachers' knowledge in teaching proportions by focusing our attention on two middle school teachers, Matt and Tori. These two teachers were part of the larger group of 32 teachers with whom we did the interview study. They were two of the five teachers from that group for whom we have classroom video. The sample of 32 middle grades mathematics teachers was a convenience sample drawn from across four states that included six teachers identified by faculty/professional developers as being strong and the rest being volunteers who exhibited a range of strengths. Matt and Tori were in this latter group.

Matt was a white, male, 7th grade teacher in an urban district. He had been teaching mathematics for seven years at the time of data collection (all data were collected before COVID). Matt was certified as a grades 5–9 Math teacher, but had never taken any mathematics teaching methods courses or mathematics courses in college. The school he worked in was a K-8 school that felt more like an elementary school than a middle school. There were cutout paper fish on the windows and students' artwork throughout the halls. He had been allowed to "wrap" with his students, meaning that the class we observed was in their second consecutive year of mathematics with Matt as their teacher.

Tori was a white, female, 6th grade teacher in a suburban district. She had been teaching for two years at the time of data collection because she had changed career paths. Tori was certified as a Science teacher for grades 5–9, but had completed two mathematics teaching methods courses and more than six mathematics courses in college. Tori taught in a traditional middle school serving grades 6–8. The school was large with a hallway for each grade level and lockers lining all the walls.

3.2 Data Collected

As mentioned previously, Matt and Tori were part of a larger study. All 32 teachers in that study completed a task-based clinical interview plus a think-aloud interview. Five of those teachers, including Tori and Matt, also allowed us to videotape their classrooms as they taught proportional concepts. These teachers also participated in interviews about the classes we observed, allowing us to gain insights into instructional decisions being made.

The think aloud interview was mailed to each participant. It included 23 open-ended mathematics tasks focused on proportions. Each teacher used a LiveScribe pen to complete the interview protocol. This allowed us to capture their voice while they were thinking aloud coordinated with the marks they were making to solve each item. The interview protocol included numerous prompts and reminders to the participants to continue thinking out loud as they worked. This protocol took around an hour for teachers to complete. All interviews were transcribed verbatim. Analysis was done using the transcripts combined with the written work.

The clinical interviews were also about one hour each and were videorecorded with two cameras – one focused on participants' hands and what they were writing and one focused on the participant themselves. The interviewer (first author) provided a series of tasks, several capitalizing on dynamic geometry constructions, and asked participants to talk about their thinking as they explored them. In all, there were nine multi-part prompts plus follow-up questions that ranged from asking participants how they define particular terms for their students to follow-up questions related to items in one of the two interviews. As with the think aloud interviews, these were transcribed verbatim and the transcripts were analyzed with the support of the video. In particular, we had to rely on the video for the dynamic geometry items because those involved participants moving around items and talking about the ways in which they did or did not see proportionality as the objects changed.

Classroom observations were done in five classrooms for several days of instruction. As with the larger sample, this was a convenience sample with teachers being selected because of their geographical location and their willingness to allow us to videorecord their teaching. Classroom video was recorded using two cameras–one focused on the whole class and the other zoomed into whatever work the teacher might be looking at (e.g., student's scratch paper). In addition to the classroom videos, we also recorded very short interviews with each teacher at the end of the lesson every few days. That interview focused on the goals of the lesson, what the teacher thought went well, and where the students might still be struggling. This interview was transcribed verbatim.

For the purposes of this paper, we analyzed both interviews for Matt and Tori and we analyzed two classroom videos plus the interviews done on the same day as the classroom video. To remain as consistent as possible in the analysis of teacher practice, we made the decision to only code the actual lesson and not any kind of warm-up tasks given in the classroom or classroom management elements such as passing out papers or listening to morning announcements. This led to Tori having one class day that was only 13 min of instructional time and other that was 31 min of instructional time (total class time was about 55 min). In Matt's classes, we had one session that was 66 min long and one that was 70 min long (total class time was about 90 min). In Tori's class, most of the time not analyzed was dedicated to warm-up activities while in Matt's class most of the uncoded time was dedicated to warm-up activities plus morning announcements.

3.3 Data Analysis

Teacher KiP interviews (the think aloud and the clinical interview) were analyzed by utterance, where an utterance was defined as the reply to a single prompt. For each utterance, we used binary coding to indicate the presence (1) or absence (0) of a given knowledge resource in that utterance. These data were entered into a spreadsheet and uploaded into the ENA tool at http://epistemicnetwork.org. We identified each participant as a unit of analysis, with each task being coded as the conversation. Once we had the ENA model created, we used logical relationships between the knowledge resources as well as the amount of variance accounted for by each axis to arrive at the subset of codes used in this ENA analysis (see Table 1). For the dimensional reduction, we used a singular value decomposition, which produces orthogonal dimensions that maximize the variance explained by each dimension. (See [17] for a more detailed explanation of the mathematics; see [20, 21] for examples of this kind of analysis.)

Networks were visualized using network graphs where nodes correspond to the codes, and edges reflect the frequency of co-occurrence, or connection, between two codes. The result is two coordinated representations for each unit of analysis: (1) a plotted point, which represents the location of that unit's network in the low-dimensional projected space, and (2) a weighted network graph. The positions of the network graph nodes are fixed, and those positions are determined by an optimization routine that minimizes the difference between the plotted points and their corresponding network centroids. Because of this co-registration of network graphs and projected space, the positions of the network graph nodes—and the connections they define—can be used to interpret the dimensions of the projected space and explain the positions of plotted points in the space.

Teacher classroom data, along with the classroom follow-up interviews, were coded using a modified version of the KQ coding set (Table 2). For classroom videos, we coded in three-minute segments. For interviews, we coded by utterance, where an utterance was defined as a teacher's response to one question.

We started from the KQ codes provided by Rowland and Turner (2007), but also watched for emerging trends in the codes that fit the four main categories of KQ, but also were important aspects of the practices we were analyzing. To this end, we ultimately removed one code from the original code set because we were unable to discern it in the participants' videos (Theoretical underpinnings of pedagogy), we added eight codes, and modified one code to broaden it out. We also developed our own definitions for each code because we were unable to find any documents from the KQ team that provided such definitions. The definitions for the categories shown in Table 2 are adapted from Rowland and Turner [9].

Table 1. Robust understandings for proportions codes. (Definitions taken from [19])

Code	Definition
Codes related to solution paths	
Scaling Up or Down	Uses multiplication to scale both quantities to get from one ratio in an equivalence class to another
Equivalence	Describes proportion as a relationship of equality between ratios or fractions
Unit Rate	Uses the relationship between the two quantities to develop sharing-like relationships such as amount-per-one or amount-per-x
Codes related to proportional structures	
Covariation	Recognizes that as one quantity varies in a rational number, the other quantity must covary to maintain a constant relationship
Ratio as Multiplicative Comparison	Shares description of the relationship of the quantities that is multiplicative. The description should have some indication that there is a number that by multiplying one quantity it is possible to get the other quantity (e.g., the amount of lemon juice is always 36/32 as much as the amount of lime juice)
Comparison of Quantities	States ratio is a comparison of two quantities
Between Measure Space	Attends to the adhered nature of the quantities in the ratio. For instance, a participant might say that to triple a batch/jar/mix of two ingredients, we have to triple both ingredients and as a matter of fact we are tripling the "whole thing"/"whole batch"

Working with two other researchers, we coded each of the classroom videos and interviews with the KQ codes. Each data source was coded by at least two researchers. The team met to discuss all codes together and came to full agreement for every segment

Table 2. Knowledge Quartet codes used in this study.

Code	Definition
Foundation Category: what teachers have learned in their own education and in teacher preparation. This includes their knowledge and understandings related to mathematics	
Concentration on procedures	A disposition focused on using procedures to get correct answers
Identifying errors	Evaluative moves, statements, or questions to point out students' errors to them
Overt subject knowledge	Explicit evidence of understanding of content knowledge
Use of terminology	Teacher defines a term in some way
Use of textbook/curriculum map**	Explicit reference to a textbook, curriculum map, or similar
Transformation Category: the capacity a teacher demonstrates to transform content knowledge into powerful pedagogical knowledge (e.g., knowing how to teach mathematics)	
Choice of representation	Teacher or task names a specific visual representation to use or asks students to compare or evaluate a representation
Choice of examples	Indication of the decision to use particular numbers, approaches, or other fundamental elements in a task
*Connect to real life	Making a mathematical connection to real life
Teacher demonstration	Teacher uses mathematical knowledge to show students how to do a procedure
*Driving questions/comments	Use of questions/comments to try to get students to move in their thinking. (Not remediation)
*Classroom Rituals	Teacher engages in particular ritual questions or procedures in the classroom
*Promoting mathematical argument	Making pedagogical moves that promote students' engagement in mathematical argument
Connection Category: choices and decisions that create a coherence across mathematical concepts	
Making connections between concepts	Questions or guidance to compare and evaluate mathematics concepts
Decisions about sequencing	Teacher explains how they decided on order of things (e.g., lessons, students to present, etc.)
Anticipation of complexity	Teacher explicitly notes when something will be difficult

(continued)

Table 2. (*continued*)

Code	Definition
Making connections between procedures	Explicit questions or guidance to compare or evaluate procedures
Recognition of conceptual appropriateness	Evaluative statements regarding conceptual appropriateness of students' approach
Problem solving strategies	Strategies to engage students in process of solving problems
Making connections to context	Explicit questions or guidance to connect math to a context
Contingency Category: the teacher's response to classroom events that were not anticipated, particularly responses to students ideas and preparedness to deviate from the agenda when necessary	
Deviation from agenda	Making changes in the moment in response to students' thinking
Responding to student ideas	Moving students forward from where they are by honoring what they are doing and building from that. (Not redirecting to a preconceived pathway)
Use of opportunities	Capitalizing on opportunities in the room to move learning forward. (Not one-on-one, not remediation)
Reasonableness	Asking students whether they answers make sense

*These are codes that emerged from our analysis of the data.
**This code was originally only use of textbook. We added curriculum map to fit our context

or utterance. We used Dedoose to identify trends in the data related to KQ as well as our conversations about the data. In our conversations, we particularly tried to make sense of the ways in which KQ was helping us to understand the differences in Matt and Tori's classrooms.

4   Findings and Discussion

As noted in the opening section of this paper, our interest in this analysis was to understand how the KiP analysis using ENA could be used with the KQ framework to help make sense of two teachers' practices as they related to their demonstrated knowledge of proportions. In this section, we will provide short descriptions of teachers' classroom, then present data about their KiP analysis and KQ analysis. We will end this section by highlighting our main findings at this point looking across those analyses.

4.1 Matt's Classroom

Matt's classroom was fast-paced and energetic, reflecting Matt's passion for sports. We observed very clear rituals in place. When a task was launched, he quickly took his students through how to approach the problem by asking a series of questions about what they would do. Then, he gave them individual think time, followed by groupwork time, and wrapped up with a whole-class discussion in which students asked each other important mathematical questions. In our observations, Matt never showed the students how to do math. Instead, he asked them questions—questions about whether their answers were reasonable, whether their answers matched other answers in their group, and whether there were other ways the problems could be worked.

Matt generally used one rich math task per lesson. For example, in one class, he wrote a task about how far students would need to run to burn the calories in a 20oz bottle of Gatorade. He told them that it was important to figure this out so he could share the information with the sixth graders because he noticed that all the students at the school drank a lot of Gatorade.

In his interviews about his teaching, Matt was extremely specific and clear about what he was teaching, what the students were struggling with, and where he wanted the students to get in their understanding. In the lessons we observed, a major theme was in developing an understanding that ratio tables have some practical limitations.

4.2 Tori's Classroom

Tori's classroom was calm and serene with ambient lighting and Tori doing her best to be very supportive of her students. As in Matt's class, there were also rituals here. Specifically, she had the students underline and circle key words and phrases when they started a new problem. In her classroom, she did all the question asking, and many of the questions had clear right or wrong answers. However, some were still quite thought-provoking. For example, in one lesson she brought two students' ideas to the board—one using multiplication and the other using repeated addition—and she asked the students why one might be more useful than the other for solving proportional situations.

Tori tended to use a worksheet of questions, some of which had been taken or adapted from the textbook series adopted by the school and others came from other sources. One example of a question that was discussed a lot by Tori as she circulated in her classroom was a question about a whale's growth if it weighed 500 lb at birth and its weight increased by a fixed amount each week.

In her interviews about teaching, Tori was not always very specific about the goals she had for her students or about the issues they had exhibited. In the lessons we observed, a major theme was the need to multiply rather than add when solving a proportion.

4.3 KiP Analysis

In a plotting of all 32 teachers from our larger study, Tori (green point in Fig. 1 with arrow pointing to it) fell in the middle, while Matt showed up as fairly different (purple point in Fig. 1 wit arrow pointing to it). Consistent with his ENA graph, Matt was the

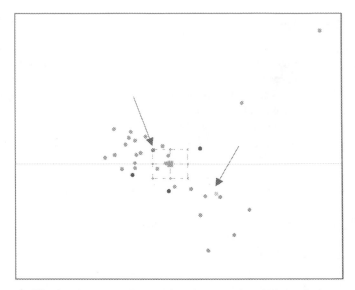

Fig. 1. Placement of 32 teachers in ENA plot of KiP analysis

most unique of the teachers we observed (the other three teachers appear as blue points in Fig. 1).

The ENA model in Fig. 2 shows our analysis of Matt's content knowledge using our Robust Understandings framework (Weiland et al., 2021). As shown in Fig. 2, Matt demonstrated a strong reliance on the knowledge resources that were focused on solving problems, particularly relying on the connection between unit rate and scaling up and down, which was an idea we heard in his classroom, as well. However, he also had connections to structural ideas about proportions and drew upon those in his own mathematical thinking. Specifically, we note that he connected scaling up and down with both covariation and between space (batches) reasoning. This is important because it shows that, for Matt, using scaling procedures was not done in isolation of considering the important relationships between the quantities in the proportional relationship. Similarly, he used unit rate and ratio as a comparison of quantities together, again showing his conceptual connection to the fixed relationship between the quantities in a ratio.

Figure 3 shows the ENA model of our analysis of Tori's content knowledge. In contrast to Matt, we see fewer connections between ideas and the strongest connections are between problem solving approaches. Specifically, like Matt, Tori's main co-occurring codes were scaling up and down and unit rate. Her next most used pairing was scaling up and down with equivalence. Both of these pairings suggest a strong focus on solving problems with less attention to the relationships between the quantities being compared. Tori did have a relatively strong connection between scaling up and down with between space measurement, as well, but it was the weakest of her top three. Also noteworthy, Matt demonstrated a greater ability to use a variety of important knowledge resources than Tori demonstrated. Because we are looking at only two teachers, it is difficult to know whether those differences help explain the differences in their classrooms or whether they are coincidental. However, it suggests a need for further examination of teachers' knowledge as it relates to their teaching.

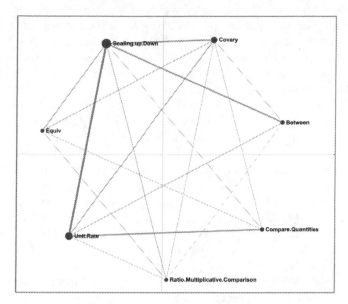

Fig. 2. Matt's KiP interview analysis

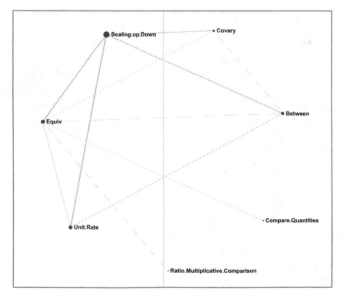

Fig. 3. Tori's KiP interview analysis

4.4 KQ Analysis

Our analysis of Matt and Tori's classroom teaching using KQ showed some important differences in their practice. As a reminder, we coded using a binary approach (present or not present) for every three minutes of video. We then used Dedoose to analyze patterns in the codes we had generated. Across the codes, 17.5% in Matt's class were in the Contingency category—meaning he was making instructional decisions on the fly based on what he heard his students saying. Of the 17%, 10% of the instances were focused on responding to student ideas or making use of opportunities that arose from students' ideas. The rest were in engaging students in opportunities to discern the reasonableness of their work. In contrast, Tori had an average of 2% of her codes as Contingency, all focused on responding to students' ideas and making use of opportunities raised by students.

Interestingly, while Matt and Tori had very similar rates of Foundation knowledge in their practice (Tori's average was 32.5%, while Matt's was 30%), the percent of instances of Transformation was where we saw Tori having considerably more instances (44%) than Matt (35.5%). This speaks to the differences in their teaching style. Tori definitely did more to try to deliver information to the students (consistent with actions in the Transformation category) than Matt, who tried to support students in making sense of the math for themselves (consistent with actions in the Contingency category).

Also interesting, both Matt and Tori had a relatively high number of problem-solving instances, which falls in the Connection category. In all, Tori had 12 of her 89 total codes in this category, while Matt had 11 of his 159 codes. Interestingly, for both teachers, problem solving was a ritual in their classroom that was reviewed at the beginning of each session. For Tori, it was about circling and underlining key words. For Matt, it was about having a plan for what to do if the students were not sure how to solve the problem. To this end, he walked them through their plan in each class by asking them what they would do. So, neither was a using a rich, mathematical problem-solving approach, but both had incorporated some basic structure to support students in trying to solve math problems.

Worth noting were the teachers' interviews. As noted above, Matt's interviews were exceptionally focused on the mathematics the students were working on, the role of the curriculum map, and his plans for continuing to move their understanding forward. We also learned in in interviews that he recognized that he was focusing students on procedural knowledge over conceptual knowledge and that was a deliberate choice he had made. We found the ways Matt talked about his classroom teaching to be very consistent with what we saw in his classroom teaching. In contrast, Tori's discussion about her teaching painted a dramatically different picture of mathematics teaching and learning from what we observed in her classroom. As evidence, in her interview utterances, we found 14% focused on Contingency codes with Tori particularly describing how she brings student work up to the class to support them in making sense of situations. Tori's descriptions of her class were more focused on students' reasoning and engaging students with each other than the segments we analyzed would have suggested. We do not know whether this was an instance of a teacher in the midst of change who was changing her ideas before her practice or who does not understand the ways in which her practice was not aligned to the vision of mathematics she has for her teaching (e.g., [22, 23]).

4.5 Putting KiP and KQ Together

Our work to make sense of the relationship between teachers' knowledge and practice is still developing. In our analysis of Matt and Tori, what we have learned is that we need a third element to make sense of the relationship between their knowledge and their teaching. That element is deep understanding of their classroom teaching. It was because we had observed Matt and coded his teaching then contrasted it to Tori that we were able to see that the Robust Understanding frameworks included knowledge resources that are more focused on finding answers (problem solving) and resources that are more focused on structures. The rich understanding of the two classrooms uncovered aspects of the data that were not apparent at the outset.

We find it interesting that even though KQ was specifically designed to highlight teachers' PCK, which as defined above, includes important ties to CK, that it is insufficient on its own to use to make sense of the data. We found KQ to have specific limitations for teaching that was not didactic, thus the addition of our codes, but also the need for rich understanding.

Consistent with mixed methods approaches, we have found that moving between the rich qualitative data from observing the classrooms and the two quantified data sets (KiP and KQ) has begun to yield a story that makes sense across all the data. That story suggests that Matt has richer access to knowledge of proportions, which positioned him better to support students' novel thinking. That allowed him to teach in ways that relied on less predictability in his classroom. In contrast, Tori clearly knew how to solve proportional problems and she knew important structural aspects of proportions. For example, despite not having connections between understanding proportions as a multiplicative comparison or a comparison of quantities, Tori did have a strong commitment to leading students to understand that a proportional relationship involves multiplication rather than addition. In fact, that was a major focus in her classroom teaching. The shortcoming was that she did not engage her students in thinking about the relationships between quantities, instead focusing on how to scale each individual quantity. By seeing her ENA graph, we can surmise that understandings about the multiplicative names of scaling, while available to Tori, are not well connected to her other ideas about proportions. This is an entirely new way to think about teachers' knowledge that transcends simply looking for its presence or absence and, instead, to look at the teacher's ability to put that knowledge to use in a variety of ways.

5 Conclusion and Implications

This is our first effort to make sense of teachers' knowledge by comparing demonstrated knowledge outside of the classroom to enacted knowledge in the classroom. Because our Robust Understandings framework. Because we are considering the data of only two teachers, our work is raising more questions about teacher knowledge, but it is also leading us to understand how we can use two different frameworks together. In short, the coordination of the two frameworks, which are both quantifications of qualitative data, is made possible through the consideration of rich understanding of the teaching examples. Because we understood the teaching examples deeply, we were able to interrogate particular aspects of the quantified data, which, in turn, helped us better understand the data as a whole.

This work lays the groundwork for thinking about measuring teachers' knowledge using a mixed methods approach in which quantitative ethnography [24] methods are paired with traditional qualitative analysis to uncover rich understandings that can drive further research. This is important because neither qualitative nor quantitative approaches have previously been useful in understanding the connections between teachers' knowledge and practices. Clearly, the work reported here needs to be further refined and expanded, but it is suggesting a promising approach that could lead to actionable work to support teachers in moving toward practices that seem aligned to capitalizing on deep understanding of the content.

Acknowledgement. The work reported here was supported by the National Science Foundation under grant DRL-1054170. The opinions expressed here are those of the authors and may not reflect those of the NSF.

References

1. Hill, H.C., Rowan, B., Ball, D.L.: Effects of teachers' mathematical knowledge for teaching on student achievement. Am. Educ. Res. J. **42**(2), 371–406 (2005)
2. Boston, M.: Assessing instructional quality in mathematics. Elem. Sch. J. **113**(1), 76–104 (2012)
3. Hill, H.C., et al.: Mathematical knowledge for teaching and the mathematical quality of instruction: an exploratory study. Cogn. Instr. **26**, 430–511 (2008)
4. Copur-Gencturk, Y.: The effects of changes in mathematical knowledge on teaching: a longitudinal study of teachers' knowledge and instruction. J. Res. Math. Educ. **46**(3), 280–330 (2015)
5. Kersting, N.B., Givvin, K.B., Thompson, B.J., Santagata, R., Stigler, J.W.: Measuring usable knowledge: teachers' analyses of mathematics classroom videos predict teaching quality and student learning. Am. Educ. Res. J. **49**(3), 568–589 (2012)
6. Ginsberg, H.P.: Entering the Child's Mind: The Clinical Interview in Psychological Research and Practice. University Press, Cambridge, Cambridge (1997)
7. Rowland, T.: The knowledge quartet: the genesis and application of a framework for analysing mathematics teaching and deepening teachers' mathematics knowledge. Sisyphus **1**(3), 15–43 (2011)
8. Rowland, T., Huckstep, P., Thwaites, A.: Elementary teachers' mathematics subject knowledge: the knowledge quartet and the case of Naomi. J. Math. Teacher Educ. **8**, 255–281 (2005)
9. Rowland, T., Turner, F.: Developing and using the 'Knowledge Quarter': a framework for the observation of mathematics teaching. Math. Educ. **10**(1), 107–123 (2007)
10. Turner, F., Rowland, T.: The knowledge quartet as an organising framework for developing and deepening teachers' mathematics knowledge. In: Rowland, T., Ruthven, K. (eds.) Mathematical Knowledge in Teaching, pp. 195–212 (2011). Springer, Dodrecht (2011) https://doi.org/10.1007/978-90-481-9766-8_12
11. Shulman, L.S.: Those who understand: Knowledge growth in teaching. Educ. Res. **15**(2), 4–14 (1986)

12. diSessa, A.A.A.: history of conceptual change research: Threads and fault lines. In: Sawyer, R.K. (edn.) The Cambridge Handbook of the Learning Sciences, pp. 265–282. Cambridge University Press, New York (2006)
13. diSessa, A.A., Sherin, B.L., Levin, M.: Knowledge analysis: an introduction. In: diSessa, A.A., Levin, M., Brown, J.S. (eds.) Knowledge and Interaction: A Synthetic Agenda for the Learning Sciences, pp. 30–71. Routledge, New York (2016)
14. Hon, T.: Expertise. TBV – Tijdschrift voor Bedrijfs- en Verzekeringsgeneeskunde **22**(6), 268 (2014). https://doi.org/10.1007/s12498-014-0115-5
15. Bransford, J.D., Brown, A.L., Cocking, R.R.: How People Learn. National Academy Press, Washington, DC (1999)
16. Shaffer, D.W., et al.: Epistemic network analysis: a prototype for 21st-century assessment of learning. Int. J. Learn. Media **1**(2), 33–53 (2009)
17. Shaffer, D.W., Collier, W., Ruis, A.R.: A tutorial on epistemic network analysis: analyzing the structure of connections in cognitive, social, and interaction data. J. Learn. Anal. **3**(3), 9–45 (2016)
18. Shaffer, D.W., Ruis, A.R.: Epistemic network analysis: a worked example of theory-based learning analytics. In: Lang, C., Siemens, G., Wise, A., Grasevic, D. (eds.), Handbook of Learning Analytics, pp. 175–187. Alberta, Canada, Society for Learning Analytics Research (2017)
19. Weiland, T., Orrill, C.H., Nagar, G.G., Brown, R.E., Burke, J.: Framing a robust understanding of proportional reasoning for teachers. J. Math. Teacher Educ. **24**(2), 179–202 (2020). https://doi.org/10.1007/s10857-019-09453-0
20. Arastoopour, G., Swiecki, Z., Chesler, N.C., Shaffer, D.W.: Epistemic network analysis as a tool for engineering design assessment. Presented at the American Society for Engineering Education, Seattle, WA (2015)
21. Sullivan, S.A., et al.: Using epistemic network analysis to identify targets for educational interventions in trauma team communication. Surgery **163**(4), 938–943 (2017)
22. Ball, D.L.: Reflections and deflections of policy: the case of Carol Turner. Educ. Eval. Policy Anal. **12**(3), 247–259 (1990)
23. Cohen, D.K.: A revolution in one classroom: the case of Mrs Oublier. Educ. Eval. Policy Anal. **12**(3), 311–329 (1990)
24. Shaffer, D.W.: Quantitative ethnography. Cathcart Press, Madison, WI (2017)

Self-regulation in Foreign Language Students' Collaborative Discourse for Academic Writing: An Explorative Study on Epistemic Network Analysis

Ward Peeters[1,2]([envelope]) [ORCID], Olga Viberg[3] [ORCID], and Daniel Spikol[4] [ORCID]

[1] Monash University, Wellington Road, Clayton, VIC 3800, Australia
`ward.peeters@monash.edu`
[2] Kanda University of International Studies, 1 Chome-4-1 Wakaba, Chiba 261-0014, Japan
[3] KTH Royal Institute of Technology, Lindstedsvägen 3, 100 44 Stockholm, Sweden
[4] University of Copenhagen, Universitetsparken 1, 2100 Copenhagen, Denmark

Abstract. Computer-supported collaborative learning (CSCL) settings for academic writing have become a staple in foreign language classrooms in higher education. These settings allow learners to discuss their output, assist others and dialogically assess their learning progress. To successfully do so, however, learners need to be able to effectively self-regulate their learning process. The multiple contingencies of self-regulated learning (SRL) in online collaborative writing settings have hitherto received limited attention in research. Recent advances in learning analytics and quantitative ethnography, nevertheless, offer new opportunities to analyse learner discourse and reveal previously underexplored aspects of SRL. Through the use of epistemic network analysis (ENA), this study examines structural patterns in students' use of SRL strategies and meta-strategies, and models their co-occurrence. Data were collected from a Facebook group integrated into an academic writing course for first-year foreign language majors of English ($N = 123$). The results illustrate how students engage in cognitive and meta-cognitive discourse, and show that other strategies and meta-strategies in the network mainly occur in isolation. The use of ENA, in addition, reveals the different contingencies in the SRL process over time. This study contributes to the fields of quantitative ethnography, learning analytics and SRL by: 1. Showing how ENA can add to our understanding of the SRL process, and 2. by discussing which self-regulatory strategies and meta-strategies are predominantly used in CSCL settings for academic writing, which ones deserve additional attention when integrating CSCL settings in this context, and what educational interventions can be designed as support.

Keywords: Self-regulated learning · Epistemic Network Analysis · Learning Analytics · CSCL · Academic writing · Foreign language learning

1 Introduction

Learners' ability to write in an academic context is an integral part of disciplinary learning, and one of the key aspects of their academic success [1]. To succeed in complex academic writing tasks, students in higher education can benefit from the use of transferable self-regulated learning (SRL) strategies to plan, monitor and effectively govern their writing process [2]. While the awareness and command of SRL strategies have been proven to positively affect writing and learning outcomes [3], studies have shown that a majority of learners are not always capable of adequately and accurately calibrating their own learning and writing activities [4]. This lack of self-monitoring and self-assessment regarding the ways they learn, how they put their knowledge and skills to use, and how they plan their study, in turn, poses challenges for learning designers, instructors and teachers when developing relevant SRL support for academic writing.

Studying the intricate process of SRL is challenging since self-regulation is multifaceted, with many complex cognitive, affective and social dimensions that need to be accounted for [5]. While SRL has been extensively studied on a theoretical or conceptual basis, there has been "little progress in developing methods to make the primary invisible mental regulation processes [...] visible and thus measurable and ultimately interpretable" [6, p.2]. Activities and processes part of SRL continuously interact with one another, making it a dialectic course of action that lies at the very core of learning itself, and thus also at the core of learning how to write in an academic context [7]. To shed more light on this course of action, this study approaches the analysis of self-regulation as describing and illustrating the interconnectivity between different aspects of the writing process as learners plan, monitor and evaluate their learning [8].

The present study focuses on students' use of SRL strategies and meta-strategies in the setting of computer-supported collaborative writing. SRL strategies refer to students' dynamic actions or activities (e.g., reasoning or making deductions) as they engage with writing tasks, learning materials and peers to regulate multiple aspects of their learning trajectory [9]. Meta-strategies are the ways learners control or manage these processes (e.g., by paying attention, monitoring or evaluating their strategy use).

Learning analytics (LA) methods have recently made it possible to visualise the dialectic course of action described above, enabling researchers to connect trace data from online learning contexts and several learning constructs, including SRL [10]. This study builds on recent developments in the field of LA and quantitative ethnography (QE) to reveal foreign language (L2) learners' SRL process in computer-supported collaborative learning (CSCL) settings for academic writing, focusing on the interplay between and co-occurrence of SRL strategies and meta-strategies.

Previous research has shown that the application of LA methods offers valuable insights into different aspects of SRL [11]. Consequently, to understand students' use of SRL strategies and to create better support mechanisms for the development of their academic writing skills, the ways these strategies tend to be applied need to be analysed. This study aims to answer the following research questions:

1. Which self-regulated learning strategies and meta-strategies are applied by foreign language students in a computer-supported collaborative writing setting in higher education?
2. What can co-occurrence between self-regulated learning strategies and meta-strategies in a computer-supported collaborative writing setting reveal about foreign language students' self-regulated learning process for academic writing?

In applying QE methods, this paper aims to contribute to the ways co-occurrences between SRL strategies and meta-strategies in a computer-supported collaborative writing environment can be scrutinised and visualised.

2 Background

2.1 Self-regulation in Academic Writing

In academic writing tasks, learners are often expected to develop their ideas about a given topic and write a cohesive and self-sustained text. Self-regulation in writing refers to the "self-initiated thoughts, feelings and actions that writers use to attain various literary goals, including their writing skills as well as enhancing the quality of the text they create" [2, p.76]. In line with previous research [12], a recent study has shown that there is a significant positive correlation between students' academic performance and their use of SRL tactics such as formulating learning goals, monitoring and assessing the writing process [4]. Scholars have also found that the use of SRL strategies and associated positive motivation results in decreased levels of writing anxiety [13]. Further, students' self-efficacy beliefs about academic achievement and self-regulation of writing can be good predictors of their course grade [12].

Studies that target academic writing in L2 education found that curricula that emphasise strategy-based writing interventions result in students having higher levels of cognitive engagement, positive self-efficacy beliefs about regulating their writing process, and confidence about their written products [14].

2.2 Self-regulation in Online Social Networking Contexts

In CSCL research, considerable attention has been paid to the use of social networking sites to foster academic writing development in L2 learning contexts (e.g., [15, 16]). Next to providing opportunities for formal and informal learning online [17], these spaces have allowed educators and researchers to access new types of (log) data to analyse learners' online activity as well as group dynamics. Examining SRL in these contexts is particularly interesting since "self-regulation extends beyond individualised forms of learning to include self-coordinated collective forms of learning in which personal outcomes are achieved through the actions of others" [18, p.13855].

2.3 LA for Self-regulated (Language) Learning

Using LA, educators and learning designers can better address language learners' needs, predict their behaviour and assist them in creating flexible personalised learning paths [19]. One of the increasingly emerging LA areas is SRL [11]. LA for SRL consists of two interdependent parts. First, it enables us to describe students' SRL actions and activities, based on traces and logs of the actions and activities they perform (i.e., measurement). Second, it allows us to provide recommendations (i.e., support), addressing what should be changed about the ways students engage with learning activities, about the design of the curriculum and the learning spaces, and about how these recommendations can be made applicable and sustainable [20].

2.4   Methods to Measure and Interpret the SRL Process

Recently, LA researchers have started to pay more attention to the ways different aspects of the SRL process interrelate and how they might develop over time [21, 22]. In addition, the field of QE has made considerable progress developing quantitative and qualitative methods to assess learning processes and human meaning-making [23]. One of the methods that has gained ground is ENA, which has been used to analyse SRL in different learning settings [24]. In recent studies, ENA has been applied in combination with LA methods such as process mining and clustering (e.g., [25]) to delve deeper into the dynamic process of SRL. In order to add to this exploration of the use of ENA, this study applies its principles to study the co-occurrence of different strategies and meta-strategies of the SRL process for academic writing, as well as to gain insights into the network of activities and processes learners apply.

3   Theoretical Lens: Strategic Self-regulation in Collaborative Learning Settings

Academic writing is a challenging learning activity that requires learners to be strategic, and self-regulate their learning process. The term 'strategic' is understood in relation to how self-regulated learners approach tasks by selecting strategies they believe to be best suited to the situation, and employing them adequately [26]. Oxford [9] describes the quintessential features of language learning strategies, part of, what she calls, a *Strategic Self-Regulation Model* (S2R) for language education, based on Zimmerman's [8] cyclical SRL model, as follows:

"L2 learning strategies are complex, dynamic thoughts and actions, selected and used by learners with some degree of consciousness in specific contexts in order to regulate multiple aspects of themselves (such as cognitive, emotional, and social) for the purpose of (a) accomplishing language tasks; (b) improving language performance or use; and/or (c) enhancing long-term proficiency. [...] Learners often use strategies flexibly and creatively; combine them in various ways, such as strategy clusters or strategy chains; and orchestrate them to meet learning needs" [9, p.48].

Learners can use strategies before, during and after completing a task, which Zimmerman [8] refers to as *forethought, performance* and *self-reflection* in his SRL model. This is a key feature since guiding learners on how to use learning strategies also requires them to make choices on timeliness, appropriateness and need [27], and thus also requires educators to let learners discover and try out strategies, explicitly or implicitly introduce new strategies to them, and provide scaffolded support along the way [28]. The S2R model covers three key constituting dimensions of self-regulated language learning: *cognitive, affective,* and *sociocultural-interactive.* Cognitive strategies and meta-strategies help learners to construct, transform and apply L2 knowledge. Affective strategies and meta-strategies help them create positive emotions and attitudes and stay motivated. Sociocultural-interactive strategies and meta-strategies aid the learner with communication, navigating sociocultural context, and identity. This study uses the SR2 model as a theoretical lens to examine the phases of the SRL process (*forethought, performance* and *self-reflection* [8]) and the SRL strategies and meta-strategies employed by students in a CSCL academic writing context.

4 Methods

4.1 Context and Data Collection

This study examines the use of SRL strategies and meta-strategies by first-year L2 majors of English ($N = 123$) at a Belgian University who used Facebook as a collaborative space for peer review in an academic writing course. Students used the online space to share their course tasks, discuss and assess their progress, share experiences and review each other's work. The course consisted of 12 face-to-face contact hours, blended with an online self-access module on academic literacy, and a peer review space on Facebook. There were no tutors present in the Facebook group. Students had to hand in three 300-word essays over the course of three months. After an initial brainstorm in class, they finished their essays at home, and were reminded that they could consult with their peers on Facebook at any given time. The tutor was available in class or via email. Tutors provided feedback on the first version of the essay, after which students could hand in a final version two weeks later.

Students generated 2,550 posts and comments on the online group. Log data, including posts, comments, time stamps and participant IDs were collected using an application programming interface available to Facebook developers. In data processing, it was recorded who talked to whom, and when they did so. Informed consent was obtained from all participants and all data were anonymised.

4.2 Data Annotation

In the deductive coding process, the S2R Model for language learning [9] was adopted to annotate students' posts and comments. A team of two coders annotated the corpus in three phases, including iterations of thematic coding, descriptive coding, and refining codes and descriptors [29]. The content of posts and comments was scanned for examples of 'strategies and meta-strategies in context' such as 'planning', 'reasoning' or 'paying attention', part of an extensive list by [9]. All strategies and meta-strategies then received descriptors, based on how they were applied by students. Posts and comments could receive multiple labels as students could address or apply different strategies or meta-strategies in one single post or comment. Posts such as 'Can someone please explain me the difference in use between 'fault' and 'failure'?' was labelled 'Discussing how to approach academic writing tasks, including textual features and structure' or 'activating knowledge' for short. After having annotated the entire data set, a team of four coders independently coded 20% of the transcripts for comparison. The team discussed disputed or ambiguous codes until a consensus was reached. In the end, this social moderation method [30] ensured full inter-rater agreement and accurate descriptions of the different 'strategies and meta-strategies in context'. The list of SRL strategies and meta-strategies was finalised, and final coding approved by all members of the coding team. Table 1 presents the codes of the S2R model, as well as descriptions of how they were annotated in this study.

Table 1. Overview of SRL strategies and meta-strategies [9], keywords and descriptors, as coded in the data set.

SRL Dimension	Strategies & meta-strategies	Descriptors	Key words
Cognitive	Planning	Discussing and implementing learning or writing plans	Planning
	Activating knowledge	Discussing how to approach academic writing tasks, including textual features and structure	Activating knowledge
	Reasoning	Discussing topics and argumentation for academic writing tasks	Reasoning
	Orchestrating strategy use	Discussing goals, objectives and requirements of tasks; discussing practical challenges and strategies to overcome them	Orchestrating strategies
	Obtaining and using resources	Sharing, discussing and evaluating resources and user-generated content	Using resources
	Paying attention	Discussing the purpose of the course and course organisation	Paying attention
	Evaluating	Discussing and applying feedback from peers and tutors about academic performance and collaboration	Evaluating
Affective	Activating supportive emotions, beliefs and attitudes	Talking about hobbies, spare time and leisure; sharing likes and dislikes about shared content	Socialising
	Generating and maintaining motivation	Expressing positive reinforcement and gratitude; strengthening social ties	Motivation
Sociocultural- interactive	Dealing with sociocultural interactive contexts and identities	Sharing and discussing personal stories, expectations and experiences about academic trajectory	Constructing identity

(*continued*)

Table 1. (*continued*)

SRL Dimension	Strategies & meta-strategies	Descriptors	Key words
	Monitoring	Signalling understanding; interacting to learn and communicate	Monitoring

4.3 Data Analysis

First, descriptive statistics were used to examine which SRL strategies and meta-strategies were most frequently applied by students. Later, we applied ENA [23, 31] to our data using the ENA Web Tool (version 1.7.0) [32] to investigate co-occurrence and linkage. To generate the adjacency matrix for the model, we constructed a Python script to transpose the textual codes to binary codes needed for ENA.

We defined the units of analysis as all lines of data associated with a single value of Type (different strategies and meta-strategies) subset by the three assignments they link to (Assignment_level) and the student's unique ID (SourceD). For example, one unit consists of all the lines associated with Assignment 1 and student 87.

The ENA algorithm uses a moving window to construct a network model for each line in the data, showing how codes in the current line are connected to codes that occur within the recent temporal context [33], defined as 4 lines (each line plus the 3 previous lines) within a given conversation. The resulting networks are aggregated for all lines for each unit of analysis in the model. In this model, we aggregated networks using a binary summation in which the networks for a given line reflect the presence or absence of the co-occurrence of each pair of codes.

The ENA model normalised the networks for all units of analysis before they were subjected to a dimensional reduction, which accounts for the fact that different units of analysis may have different amounts of coded lines in the data. For the dimensional reduction, we used a singular value decomposition, which produces orthogonal dimensions that maximise the variance explained by each dimension.

5 Results

5.1 SRL Strategies in the CSCL Context of Academic Writing

The results show that the cognitive strategies *activating knowledge* ($N = 520$) and *reasoning* ($N = 505$) were the most frequently used strategies followed by the sociocultural-interactive strategy of *constructing identity* ($N = 308$) (Table 2). Cognitive meta-strategies such as *orchestrating strategies*, and affective strategies such as *motivation* also appear in the top five. These numbers stress the dominance of cognitive, task-oriented strategies in the CSCL setting for academic writing. That is, L2 learners seem to put considerable emphasis on negotiating content, in addition to negotiating their roles in the CSCL environment.

Table 2. The frequency of strategies and meta-strategies, where one status update or comment can receive more than one label.

Strategies and meta-strategies	Frequency	Ratio
Activating knowledge	520	0.20
Reasoning	505	0.20
Constructing identity	308	0.12
Orchestrating strategies	292	0.11
Motivation	273	0.11
Monitoring	255	0.10
Evaluation	170	0.07
Socialising	104	0.04
Paying attention	75	0.03
Planning	55	0.02
Using resources	12	0.00
Total	**2569**	**1.00**

5.2 ENA Perspective

We generated ENA networks for the different types of strategies and meta-strategies applied by students throughout the entire period of the course (Fig. 1), where we, in addition, made separate networks for status updates and comments.

To analyse our data, we made distinctions between 'Status updates' and 'Comments', the time they were performed (i.e., during one of the three assignments), and the anonymised student IDs. We used the moving stanza window with a size of 6 to account for connected actions between the discussions. To help balance the visualisation, we used unit circle equally spaced nodes. Along the X axis (SVD1), a Mann-Whitney test showed that 'Status update' ($M = -0.39$, $N = 307$) was statistically significantly different at the alpha $= 0.05$ level from 'Comment' ($M = -0.09$, $N = 302$ $U = 68516.00$, $p = 0.00$, $r = -0.48$). Additionally, along the Y axis (SVD2), a Mann-Whitney test showed that 'Status update' ($M = 0.18$, $N = 307$) was statistically significantly different at the alpha $= 0.05$ level from 'Comment' ($M = -0.19$, $N = 302$ $U = 71538.00$, $p = 0.00$, $r = -0.54$).

For 'Status update', it can be observed that meta-cognitive and cognitive strategies tend to co-occur more frequently than any other strategies or meta-strategies in the data set. Weak connections can be observed between both cognitive strategies/meta-strategies and sociocultural-interactive strategies. No other notable connections can be observed in this section, indicating the low level of strategy/meta-strategy co-occurrence in 'Status updates' in the data set. For the 'Comment' section, the network shows more variation and, therefore, more co-occurrences of interrelated strategies and meta-strategies. The link between cognitive strategies and meta-strategies remains strong. Cognitive strategies tend to co-occur with affective strategies and meta-strategies, as well as with

Fig. 1. Types of strategies and meta-strategies applied during the course, equally distributed for 'Status updates' and 'Comments' (top), for 'Status updates' (bottom left) and for 'Comments' (bottom right).

sociocultural-interactive strategies. All observed strategies and meta-strategies co-occur to some degree in the 'Comment' section.

Adding intervals, taking into account that students worked on three different writing assignments over the course of three months, we can examine the evolution of strategy/meta-strategy use in status updates over time (Fig. 2). Here, we could observe that the co-occurrence between cognitive strategies and meta-strategies became more pronounced over time, indicating that they appeared more frequently together in status updates as time went by. Other connections remained weak.

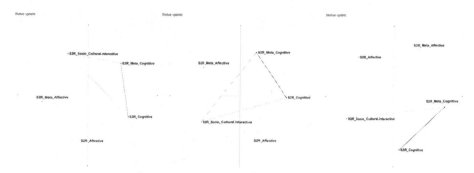

Fig. 2. Types of strategies and meta-strategies applied during the first, second and third assignment in status updates, equally spaced.

Adding intervals to the networks on the 'Comment' section, the evolution of strategy/meta-strategy use can also be examined (Fig. 3). Here, we can observe that cognitive strategies and meta-strategies were used very frequently together, and that their co-occurrence slightly faded over time. This observation contrasts the observations made in Fig. 2, where the link between cognition strategies and meta-strategies only grew over time. Noteworthy increases in co-occurrence can be observed in cognitive and affective meta-strategies, where, over time, the link between both grew. Noteworthy decreases occurred between cognitive strategies and sociocultural-interactive ones, indicating they tended to co-occur less and less in the data set as time went by.

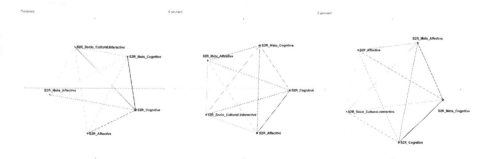

Fig. 3. Types of strategies and meta-strategies applied during the first, second and third assignment in the comment section, equally spaced.

In order to investigate the co-occurrence between SRL strategies and meta-strategies, we visualised both the 'Codes' from the S2R framework with the SRL phases (*forethought, performance, self-reflection*) to gain insights into their relationship (Fig. 4). The ENA graph highlights the centrality of *forethought* and the connection to the cognitive SRL dimension, especially in the 'Status updates'. Comments show a broader connection to the different dimensions with medium and weak ties to cognitive and affective meta-strategies.

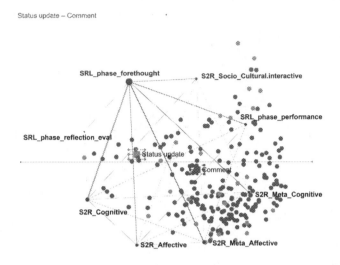

Fig. 4. Types of strategies and meta-strategies applied, connected to the different SRL phases, equally distributed.

When we examine strategies and meta-strategies in connection to the SRL phases, on the X axis (SVD1), the results of a Mann-Whitney test show that 'Status update' (M = 1.02, N = 307) was statistically significantly different at the alpha = 0.05 level from 'Comment' (M = −0.64, N = 302 U = 25118.50, p = 0.00, r = 0.46). Along the Y axis (SVD2), a Mann-Whitney test showed that 'Status update' (M = −0.05, N = 307) was statistically significantly different at the alpha = 0.05 level from 'Comment' (M = 0.11, N = 302 U = 57909.50, p = 0.00, r = −0.25).

As shown in Fig. 4 for 'Status update', the overall connection between all three phases (i.e., *forethought, performance* and *self-reflection*) of the SRL process that ground the S2R model [9] is somewhat weak. Regarding the use of strategies and meta-strategies, the plot shows that the L2 learners' use of cognitive strategies is well-connected to the first phase, i.e., *forethought*, and the use of cognitive meta-strategies has been, to some extent, enabled during the *performance* phase. During the *self-reflection* phase, learners seem to use some cognitive strategies. Other types of meta-strategies and strategies are also employed, but are not closely connected to the SRL phases.

For the 'Comment' section, the link between the *forethought* and the *performance* phase is more pronounced, compared to 'Status update', and there is a weak connection between the *forethought* and the *self-reflection* phase (Fig. 5). Overall, we can see clearer links between these phases. Also, students used a variety of strategies and meta-strategies. These are better connected when compared to the status updates. In particular, they used cognitive strategies during all the phases, as well as cognitive and affective meta-strategies to regulate their writing process during the *forethought* phase when providing comments. Reflection and evaluation, in both cases, seems to lag behind and remained isolated.

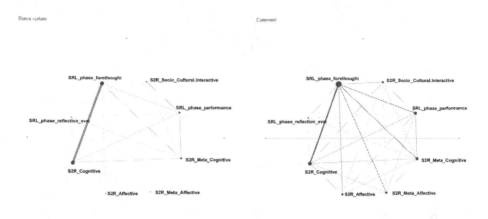

Fig. 5. SRL phases and types of strategies and meta-strategies used, equally distributed for 'Status update' and 'Comment'.

6   Discussion

This study examined how L2 learners used SRL strategies and meta-strategies to master their academic writing process. In line with the first research question, students used a range of cognitive, affective and sociocultural-interactive strategies and meta-strategies throughout the writing course, putting major emphasis on the cognitive strategies *activating knowledge* and *reasoning* in their online written discussions. A previous study [14] reported similar findings as student groups engaged in a range of cognitive processing strategies during SRL-based writing instruction. Similar strategies in the current study took up considerable space in conversation threads (with a combined number of about 40%) and could therefore be considered the main 'actors' or 'facilitators' in the language learning process. Nevertheless, since the SRL process is a dialectic course of action [8], it is important to establish how these strategies are embedded within conversation threads, and how they might relate to one another.

In line with the second research question, ENA showed to what degree certain strategies and meta-strategies co-occurred. The results showed that cognitive strategies and meta-strategies are commonly used together in status updates and comments, indicating that students seem aware of the strategies that can be used to complete tasks at hand, and, to a certain degree, seem aware of the reasons why they used them. 'Status updates' feature very little other strategies or meta-strategies, and strategies and meta-strategies do not tend to co-occur often. In the 'Comment' section, more variation in the use of strategies and meta-strategies has been observed. Also here, cognitive strategies and meta-strategies are prominently co-occurring, albeit to a lesser degree as time went by. The time factor (i.e., by means of the different assignments students had to hand in) demonstrated that the strength of the links between a number of strategies and meta-strategies tends to fluctuate, indicating that the SRL process is a dynamic one. That is, different times and tasks, to a certain extent, require students to apply different strategies and meta-strategies.

Our analysis visualised the dimensions of the SRL process and showed how students can give rise to activating, sustaining and adapting cognition, affect and interaction for academic writing. It has been argued that an adequate interplay between affect and sociocultural-interactive interaction can serve as a basis for a transitional process to improve learning [34]. Harnessing both while supporting learners' cognitive development, therefore, could be an intervention our analysis puts forward.

The findings of this study can be used as a ground to develop adequate and in-time SRL support in the CSCL context of academic writing. For example, selected prompts, adjusted to learners' cognitive abilities, may activate or facilitate students' *identity construction* [35]. Prompting them to, first, reflect on their personal learning goals and expectations, and second, to interact with peers about the learning goals and expectations of others, might give them an understanding of their place within the learning setting. In CSCL contexts, studies have [36] emphasised that providing opportunities for synthesis and reflection is one of the main responsibilities for instructors to maintain a positive, productive learning environment online. Introducing peer feedback or peer collaboration opportunities in the curriculum has proven to be a facilitating factor in language education in this regard, and has allowed learners to explore different aspects of SRL as they can learn from and with others [16]. It is possible to design strategy workshops that focus on students' researching and planning processes in academic proficiency courses or integrate and train peer mentors in writing courses, so students can perform peer review and can get acquainted with the SRL strategies used by peers [37].

7 Conclusion and Future Research

In line with the current discussion in learning analytics and quantitative ethnography for SRL, this study has provided novel insights into L2 learners' use of SRL strategies and meta-strategies in a CSCL setting for academic writing, and the interplay between them. This knowledge is important to different stakeholders, including students, teachers and researchers. However, the generalisation of the results should be carefully considered. In future research, scholars need to complement such findings with qualitative data analysis to understand better why students choose specific strategies or meta-strategies over others at different time points of the learning process. Also, it is critical to consider contextual factors such as language proficiency, which may affect the students' use of SRL strategies. Finally, since there are individual differences between students found in other educational contexts (e.g., [38]), scholars are recommended to delve into the examination of students' individual characteristics in the setting of collaborative computer-supported academic writing to be able to offer more personalised writing support in the future.

One direction for future research is to utilise nCoder to investigate automated coding schemes for comparison since we have a basis for coding with the current data set. This comparison will provide us with an opportunity to examine how tools like nCoder can be used to gain additional insights, and how we apply augmented coding to more data sets from similar ongoing courses.

This study has exhibited how co-occurrences between SRL strategies and meta-strategies in a computer-supported collaborative writing environment can be examined and visualised using quantitative ethnographic methods. Most importantly, it has shown how ENA can help us better understand the SRL process for academic writing as it provides evidence on the roles of cognition, identity construction and motivation.

References

1. Fang, Z.: Demystifying academic writing: Genres, moves, skills, and strategies. Routledge (2021)
2. Zimmerman, B., Risemberg, R.: Becoming a self-regulated writer: a social cognitive perspective. Contemp. Educ. Psychol. **22**(1), 73–101 (1997)
3. Golombek, C., Klingsieck, K., Scharlau, I.: Assessing self-efficacy for self-regulation of academic writing. Euro. J. Psychol. Assess. **35**(5), 751–761 (2019)
4. Peeters, W., Saqr, M., Viberg, O.: Applying learning analytics to map students' self-regulated learning tactics in an academic writing course. In: So, H.-J., Rodrigo, M.M., Mason, J., Mitrovic, A. (Eds.) Proceedings of the 28th International Conference on Computers in Education. vol.1, pp.245–254. Asia-Pacific Society for Computers in Education (2020)
5. Hadwin, A.F., Järvelä, S., Miller, M.: Self-regulation, co-regulation and shared regulation in collaborative learning environments. In: Schunk, D., Greene, J. (eds.) Handbook of Self-Regulation of Learning and Performance, pp. 83–106. Routledge (2018)
6. Noroozi, O., Alikhani, I., Järvelä, S., Kirschner, P., Seppänen, T., Juuso, I.: Multimodal data to design visual learning analytics for understanding regulation of learning. Comput. Hum. Behav. **100**, 298–304 (2019)
7. Li, S., Du, H., Zheng, J., Chen, G., Xie, C.: Examining temporal dynamics of self-regulated learning behaviours in STEM learning: a network approach. Comput. Educ. **158**, 103987 (2020)
8. Zimmerman, B.J.: Attaining self-regulation: a social cognitive perspective. In: Handbook of Self-Regulation, pp. 13–39. Academic Press (2000)
9. Oxford, R.: Teaching and researching language learning strategies: Self- regulation in context (2nd edn). Routledge, Milton Park (2017)
10. Wise, A.F., Knight, S., Shum, S.B.: Collaborative learning analytics. In: International Handbook of computer-supported collaborative learning, pp. 425–443. Springer (2021). https://doi.org/10.1007/978-3-030-65291-3_23
11. Viberg, O., Khalil, M., Baars, M.: Self-regulated learning and learning analytics in online learning environments: a review of empirical research. In: Rensing, C., Drachsler, H. (Eds.) Proceedings of the Tenth Conference on Learning Analytics and Knowledge, pp. 524–533. Association for Computing Machinery (2020)
12. Zimmerman, B., Bandura, A.: Impact of self-regulatory influences on writing course attainment. Am. Educ. Res. J. **31**(4), 845–862 (1994)
13. Csizér, K., Tankó, G.: English majors' self-regulatory control strategy use in academic writing and its relation to L2 Motivation. Appl. Linguis. **38**(3), 386–404 (2017)
14. Teng, L., Zhang, L.: Empowering learners in the second/foreign language classroom: can self-regulated learning strategies-based writing instruction make a difference? J. Second. Lang. Writ. **48**, 100701 (2020)

15. Manegre, M., Gutiérrez-Colón, M.: Foreign language learning through collaborative wiring in knowledge building forums. Interact. Learn. Environ. **28**(7), 1–13 (2020)
16. Peeters, W.: Applying the networking power of Web 2.0 to the foreign language classroom: a taxonomy of the online peer interaction process. Comput. Assist. Lang. Learn. **31**(8), 905–931 (2018)
17. Dressman, M., Sadler, R.: The Handbook of Informal Language Learning. Wiley (2020)
18. Zimmerman, B.: Self-regulated learning. In: Smelser, N.J., Baltes, P.B. (eds.) International Encyclopedia of Social and Behavioral Sciences, pp. 13855–13859. Elsevier (2001)
19. Viberg, O., Wasson, B., Kukulska-Hulme, A.: Mobile-assisted language learning through learning analytics for self-regulated learning (MALLAS): A conceptual framework. Australas. J. Educ. Technol. **36**(6), 34–52 (2020)
20. Winne, P.: Modeling self-regulated learning as learners doing learning science: How trace data and learning analytics help develop skills for self-regulated learning. Metacognition Learn. **17**(3), 773–791 (2022). https://doi.org/10.1007/s11409-022-09305-y
21. Engelmann, K., Bannert, M.: Analyzing temporal data for understanding the learning process induced by metacognitive prompts. Learn. Instr. **72**, 101205 (2021)
22. Saint, J., Fan, Y., Gašević, D., Pardo, A.: Temporally-focused analytics of self-regulated learning: A systematic review of literature. Comput. Educ. Artif. Intell. **3**, 100060 (2022)
23. Shaffer, D.W.: Quantitative Ethnography. Cathcart Press, London (2017)
24. Paquette, L., Grant, T., Zhang, Y., Biswas, G., Baker, R.: Using epistemic networks to analyze self-regulated learning in an open-ended problem-solving environment. In: Ruis, A.R., Lee, S.B. (eds.) International Conference on Quantitative Ethnography, pp. 185–201. Springer (2021)
25. Saint, J., Gasevic, D., Matcha, W., Uzir, N., Pardo, A.: Combining analytics methods to unlock sequential and temporal patterns of self-regulated learning. In: Rensing, C., Drachsler, H. (Eds.) Proceedings of the Tenth Conference on Learning Analytics and Knowledge, pp. 402–411. Association for Computing Machinery (2020)
26. Winne, P., Perry, N.: Measuring self-regulating learning. In: Boekaerts, M., Pintrich, P., Zeidner, M. (eds.) Handbook of self-regulation, pp. 531–556. Academic Press (2000)
27. Peeters, W.: Peer interaction and scaffolded support on social media: Exercising learner autonomy In: Mynard, J., Tamala, M., Peeters, W. (Eds.) Supporting Learners and Educators in Developing Language Learner Autonomy, pp. 118–152. Candlin & Mynard (2020)
28. Kato, S., Mynard, J.: Reflective Dialogue: Advising in Language Learning. Routledge, Milton Park (2015)
29. Jensen, E., Laurie, C.: Doing Real Research: A Practical Guide to Social Research. Sage, Thousand Oaks (2016)
30. Belur, J., Tompson, L., Thornton, A., Simon, M.: Interrater reliability in systematic review methodology: Exploring variation in coder decision-making. Sociol. Methods Res. **50**(2), 837–865 (2021)
31. Shaffer, D.W., Ruis, A.R.: Epistemic network analysis: a worked example of theory-based learning analytics. In: Lang, C., Siemens, G., Wise, A.F., Gasevic, D. (eds.) Handbook of learning analytics, pp. 175–187. Society for Learning Analytics Research (2017)
32. Marquart, C.L., Hinojosa, C., Swiecki, Z., Shaffer, D.W.: Epistemic Network Analysis (Version 1.7.0) (2018). http://app.epistemicnetwork.org
33. Siebert-Evenstone, A., Arastoopour Irgens, G., Collier, W., Swiecki, Z., Ruis, A.R., Williamson Shaffer, D.: In search of conversational grain size: modelling semantic structure using moving stanza windows. J. Learn. Anal. **4**(3), 123–139 (2017)
34. Lajoie, S.P., et al.: The role of regulation in medical student learning in small groups: regulating oneself and others' learning and emotions. Comput. Hum. Behav. **52**, 601–616 (2015)

35. Wong, J., Baars, M., Davis, D.V., der Zee, T., Houben, G.-J., Paas, F.: Supporting self-regulated learning in online learning environments and MOOCs: a systematic review. Int. J. Hum.-Comput. Interact. **35**(4–5), 356–373 (2018)

36. Barett, N., Hsu, W.-C., Liu, G.-Z., Wang, H.-C., Yin, C.: Computer supported collaboration and written communication: tools, methods, and approaches for second language learners in higher education. Hum. Behav. Emerg. Technol. **3**, 261–270 (2020)

37. Xie, Q., Lei, Y.: Diagnostic assessment of L2 academic writing product, process and self-regulatory strategy use with a comparative dimension. Lang. Assess. Q. **19**(3), 1–33 (2021)

38. Akhuseyinoglu, K., Brusilovsky, P.: Data-driven modeling of learners' individual differences for predicting engagement and success in online learning. In: Proceedings of the 29th ACM Conference on User Modeling, Adaptation and Personalization, pp. 201–212 (2021)

Community at a Distance: Understanding Student Interactions in Course-Based Online Discussion Forums

Jennifer Scianna[1](✉) ⓘ, Monique Woodard[2] ⓘ, Beatriz Galarza[3], Seiyon Lee[4] ⓘ,
Rogers Kaliisa[5] ⓘ, and Hazel Vega Quesada[6] ⓘ

[1] University of Wisconsin - Madison, Madison, WI, USA
jscianna@wisc.edu
[2] Drexel University, Philadelphia, PA, USA
[3] University of Texas at San Antonio, San Antonio, TX, USA
[4] University of Pennsylvania, Philadelphia, PA, USA
[5] University of Oslo, Oslo, Norway
[6] Clemson University, Clemson, SC, USA

Abstract. Online discussion forums are often used as a point of contact between students and their instructors for college courses. While asynchronous discourse has proven to be effective for learning, it remains unclear whether the student interactions manifest in socially constructive ways in addition to the cognitive benefits. In this paper, we consider the social dimension of student interactions within a Canvas course discussion forum. In particular, we examine the influence of instructional contexts to shape the mapping of different indicators that constitute social presence within the Community of Inquiry framework. For the analysis, data was collected from two instances of the same course: one taught in a hybrid format and the other in a remote format. The results of epistemic network analysis reveal that elements of social presence manifest differently in hybrid and fully remote modalities. The remote modality yielded more interconnected, balanced networks than their hybrid counterparts. The findings suggest that discourse from online discussions is conducive to collaborative inquiry through the mediation of social presence when pedagogical decisions work with the different instruction modalities to support student-to-student interaction.

Keywords: Discussion Forum · Community of Inquiry · Online Learning · Social Presence

1 Introduction

Online discussion forums have emerged as a popular element of instruction for courses in higher education to engage students in both asynchronous and synchronous classes in rich discussions [1]. Studies have revealed that students in online classes experienced an increased need to collaborate with their classmates, and their interactions and engagement with online discussion boards relate to improved performance [2]. These findings

C. Damşa and A. Barany (Eds.): ICQE 2022, CCIS 1785, pp. 270–284, 2023.
https://doi.org/10.1007/978-3-031-31726-2_19

have been examined prior to the COVID-19 pandemic which caused universities to shift all classed to remote contexts. Educators and learners had to quickly adapt to this sudden transition to online learning [3, 4]. However, concerns arise around whether students may feel isolated from their peers in asynchronous online courses [5]. To mitigate the sense of isolation, discussion boards have been used as a space for classes to engage in interactive conversations with their professors and peers [6].

This paper presents an exploratory study attempting to understand how elements of social presence manifest in a remote learning context within Canvas discussion forums. Earlier research has proposed that social presence progresses from initially identifying with the community, engaging in purposeful communication, and subsequently developing social relationships [7]. In this study, we investigate the implications of this progression and question how students may enact elements of social presence. The findings contribute to the growing body of literature that explores the impact of remote learning while also addressing the importance of social presence and the nuances of understanding the social workings of online discussion. The weeks examined in this paper occurred in 2019 and 2021, prior to and during the COVID-19 pandemic shutdowns. Students in 2019 had options to participate in both face-to-face and online-based classes. On the contrary, students who participated in the class in 2021 only participated in online classes and were isolated from their peers since the start of the pandemic.

2 Background

2.1 Impacts of Remote Learning on Students

Prior to the Covid-19 pandemic, the majority of the literature on remote learning centered on students who had opted-in to participate in online courses. One exception to this was an investigation into the feasibility of online education as a means to provide continuity for students in war zones [8]. Educational researchers have been responsive in their attempts to consider the radically shifting circumstances of the pandemic and potential impact on students and classroom interactions. Myriad concerns regarding student success in a fully remote learning context have been raised by instructors and researchers in the literature citing communication challenges [4], privacy [9], mental health [10], etc. At the center of many of these concerns is a social element either because students have lost access to their peer support group [10] or because there may be accessibility barriers to full participation in the remote environment [11].

The emergency transition to online learning in the wake of COVID-19 resulted in a negative impact in the engagement of students in the classroom [12]. While faculty support during the pandemic was significantly correlated with student social concerns, many instructors were ill-prepared to make the transition to fully-remote teaching [4, 11]. Furthermore, in order to find success in the new context, students needed to self-regulate and self-direct during online discussion settings, but those strategies needed to be taught and practiced over time in order for students to be successful [13]. Students who had previously experienced the opportunity to learn in an online environment were more prepared for the realities of remote learning having a better command of the associated platforms, tools, and expectations that such a context involves [14]. Still, many educators and researchers rely on the ubiquity of technology, embracing it as an efficient tool to promote deeper learning and collaboration between students despite inequities that exist for many [14].

2.2 Online Discussions, Student Engagement, and Social Impact

One of the primary tools used in online and remote learning environments is the online discussion forum. These easily accessible tools can be used to bring students together in collaborative learning tasks and facilitate communication around knowledge construction [15]. Through their participation in peer discussion, students engage in a creative-cognitive process in which ideas are criticized, expanded and developed; when students reflect on peers' contributions, they engage in critical thinking [16], construct personal meaning [17], and provide opportunities for increased engagement and social construction of knowledge [18].

Increased student engagement in online discussion forum environments may stem, in part, from feeling less intimidated and more able to express agency compared to face-to-face settings [19]. Some skepticism remains regarding whether online discussion forums can provide adequate opportunities for active learning strategies that are known to increase engagement due to their asynchronous nature [20]. Pedagogical strategies can help to ensure increased efficacy in the use of discussion forums as a learning tool in the curriculum including setting expectations and continuing to facilitate throughout the discussion [16]. For example, structured teams with well-defined roles were successful in increasing engagement, developing social presence, and fostering a Community of Inquiry through discussion forum collaborative problem solving in an online chemistry course [21]. It seems that for discussion forums to be effective, they need to fit into a greater educational ecosystem where learners understand the role that their social interactions have on the learning process.

2.3 Theoretical Framework: Community of Inquiry

Theoretical and empirical evidence in the learning sciences recognizes that social interactions and collaboration between two or more people are an important source of knowledge construction and can form a basis for mastery of valuable strategies, skills, concepts and knowledge [22]. Vygotsky argued that all cognitive functions originate in social interactions and that learning is the process by which learners are integrated into a knowledge community [22]. This implies that interactions produced during asynchronous online discussions can be used as indicators to understand students' learning processes. One of the common theoretical approaches used in the analysis of online discussions is the community of inquiry framework (CoI) [23].

The CoI framework has three interdependent elements, commonly known as presences, which together characterize students' online learning experience: cognitive presence, social presence, and teaching presence. While all three elements are needed in an effective inquiry process, in this study, we focus on the social presence element since our focus is to explore how students' social engagement in online discussions is influenced by the modality of instruction.

Social presence explores the social environment and interpersonal relationships within online discussion [24] and is defined as the ability of participants to identify with the group or course of study, communicate purposefully in a trusting environment, and develop personal and affective relationships progressively by way of projecting their individual personalities socially and emotionally as real people during the collaborative inquiry process [23]. The role of social presence is to facilitate cognitive and affective objectives of learning by sustaining and supporting critical thinking, and making group interactions appealing, engaging and rewarding [24]. The social presence element is operationalized through three sub-dimensions that capture different elements of social interaction. The affective element captures the students' expression of emotions, moods and feelings through the use of emoticons, self-disclosure, and humor within the online discussion community. The interactive dimension captures the open and interactive nature of student communication which expresses a desire to maintain contact, encouragement and acceptance of a group member (e.g. citing other students' posts). The group cohesion dimension captures activities that build a sense of union and group commitment among students in the learning community (e.g. salutations, addressing other students by name, and addressing the group as we, our, or us) [24]. In this paper, we use the three categories of social presence and their indicators (See Table 1) to identify their presence in asynchronous online discussion posts and how they differ across two different instructional modalities.

Our research seeks to address the contested role of social presence in the CoI framework by investigating how its elements manifest over time. Also, while online discussion forums have been largely integrated as a hybrid element as students engage in a discourse not only synchronously during class but also asynchronously, increasing potential of fully remote modality of instruction raises the need to paint a more comprehensive picture of how the change in modality shapes the discourse within CoI groups.

Prior studies have taken a more comprehensive approach by scoping across all three constructs, or presences. Whereas previous studies have explored the social presence category in online discussions [25], their focus has mainly been on aspects such as the analysis of scripted roles, other than mapping the influence of instructional activities on student engagement. In the field of quantitative ethnography, scholars have looked at associations between the indicators of cognitive and social presences and the characteristics of the participants leading to different patterns in the models [25, 26]. While they have illuminated how different constructs interact with each other, how specific categories of social presence play a transformative role throughout the duration of a course remains relatively unexplored [27]. While the CoI framework has garnered much attention as a theory, empirical evidence pointed out that it was inadequate for describing online learning in practice as students did not engage in deep and meaningful learning, benefiting little from the social interaction in the online space [28]. Instead, students often engage in surface level learning for the purpose of completing the assigned tasks [22]. In acknowledgment, some agreed that the role of social presence for online learning experience has been an overstatement [17]. It is critically important to test the contested literature that the CoI framework fosters deep learning as a model for online learning. In this study, we examine social presence from two angles: through different modalities and over time. In doing so, we address the following questions:

- RQ 1: Does the shift in teaching modality from hybrid to remote learning impact the ways in which social presence manifests across different weeks of a Canvas discussion forum?
- RQ 2: Provided there is a difference in social presence based on modality, how do pedagogical decisions influence the ways elements of social presence manifest in Canvas discussion forum?

3 Methods

3.1 Participants and Context

The data used in this study was collected from a learning management system (LMS) where bachelor's students participated in an online discussion on a weekly basis as a part of their coursework. The course was open to undergraduate students who were interested in the theories and practice at the intersection of learning, design and technology, and was taught multiple times with different students, in different modalities due to the Covid-19 pandemic. Prior to the Covid-19 pandemic, the course was taught as a hybrid where students and instructor met in person for part of the course and participated via the LMS for other aspects. During the Covid-19 closures, the course was taught in a fully remote modality where students participated synchronously for class portions while still using the LMS for others. Both courses used the LMS discussion forum interactions in an asynchronous manner where participants were expected to make a minimum of two contributions every week, although they could do so on their own time. In both cases, the course ran for 7 weeks with the instructor posing a new discussion prompt at the beginning of each week. The prompts from the instructor focused on asking students to make meaning of readings, activities and life experiences in connection to the weekly topic, e.g. "Why do we need to learn about human-machine interaction and interaction design in a course on learning with technology? What is the connection?" Students could choose to respond directly to the main prompt, or they could respond to another peer in the discussion.

3.2 Data Collection

Data was collected from the Canvas discussion forum as a single download at the end of each semester. Data from the 2019 forum included 331 posts from 35 participants while the 2021 forum included 233 posts from 26 participants. The entries were translated from Norwegian into English and checked by two researchers for accuracy. Metadata was added to provide contexts for the specific segment of the discourse such as accounting for when students were responding to the initial thread and when they were responding to another student. Post replies were counted to delineate the conversation; each post and its replies were assigned a number to maintain order of comments and facilitate an understanding of who was responding to whom. For example, if post 3 of the third week had 3 replies, they would be numbered with 3.0, 3.1, 3.2, and 3.3.

3.3 Data Analysis

A team of 6 researchers reviewed the dataset to identify themes of student interactions. A grounded CITE approach was initially taken to best understand the ways individuals were interacting with one another in the discussions. Upon reviewing the data, an alignment was uncovered with the CoI framework [23]. According to this theory, the educational experience involves the elements of teaching presence, cognitive presence, and social presence. In this study, we focused on social presence and used the categories from the coding template provided by Garrison and colleagues [23]. Our unit of analysis were the student posts that signaled social presence. For example, we coded posts that indicated open, purposeful, and collaborative communication [23]. For the categories of open communication and group cohesion, we inductively developed low-level codes through iterative reads of the data and discussions among all the researchers. As a result of this process, we decided on the six codes shown in Table 1 comprising our coding scheme. We coded all the data manually, two raters per code. To calculate inter-rater reliability (IRR), we used Cohen's kappa; scores for each code are shown in Table 1.

One element not captured in the initial codes was the Affective Expression aspect of the CoI framework. To account for this element, we incorporated sentiment analysis as a proxy for affective communication. Sentiment analysis was completed using the VADER (Valence Aware Dictionary and sEntiment Reasoner) component of the Natural Language Toolkit in Python [29]. VADER works by accounting for the valence of each word in a "document," a single post in this dataset, before aggregating the individual word scores to determine an overall score. These scores are passed through a threshold to assign a label to the sentiment outcome. Our thresholds for positive and negative sentiment were set to .25 and $-.25$ respectively, e.g., a post with an aggregate score of .4 would be coded as positive. Prior studies indicate sentiment analysis of translated texts is competitive with analysis of the original language [30].

Table 1. Codebook and Code Validation

Category	Code	Definition, Example, & Validation
Open Communication	Personal	The post shares a personal experience, or the author relates to the prompt or other's posts at a personal level *"[…] I do not feel that technology has influenced my school life to any great extent, but something has been it. When I went to primary school, I remember that the school introduced something they called "super users." […]"* **(rho: 0.00, kappa: 0.76)**
	Risk Taking	The post includes statements denoting honesty, openness to disclose opinions/thoughts/feelings or trust that one's own comments will be valued/respected *"Hello. Hope we will be the course a bit in use of SmartBoard here at the house, had been absolutely top. Want to learn about this. Just honestly admit that I've never tried SmartBoard before."* **(rho: < .01, kappa: 1.0)**

(continued)

Table 1. (*continued*)

Category	Code	Definition, Example, & Validation
Group Cohesion	Agreeing/Disagreeing	The post includes expressions of agreement or disagreement with what is being discussed *"Agree in the answer to S23 over. Feel that technology management is necessary for a good structure for proper use of the technology in the classroom. [...]"* **(rho: 0.01, kappa: 0.74)**
	Asking Questions	The post includes one or more questions, probes, requests to elaborate points discussed previously to keep the conversation going and/or explore new directions *"What learning theories do you think your English teachers used when using the SmartBoard in the classroom?"* **(rho: 0.01, kappa:0.74)**
	Acknowledging	The post considers points mentioned and discussed by others by repeating ideas, relating to it, mentioning the person's name, including a comment showing the value of previous posts *"Now you made me understand why Wertsch wrote in subchapter 3 that mediated actions that serve several purposes tend to end up in conflict. Well reflected that the interest in digital technology can overshadow the primary activity that is learning the subject[...]"* **(rho: 0.00, kappa: 0.84)**
	Expanding	The post expands/elaborates on a point previously discussed by bringing a new related idea or perspective. *"Agree with you S5. I also think that if we look at how school and teaching are today, then this happens mostly digitally. We use various digital platforms and students sit at home while they work [...]"* **(rho: 0.00, kappa: 0.81)**
Affective Expression	Positive, Negative	VADER sentiment analysis was used as a proxy for affective expression

3.4 Epistemic Network Analysis

We conducted Epistemic Network Analysis [31], using the ENA Web Tool [32] to model the coded discourse. As an analysis tool, ENA visualizes patterns of coded data as weighted network plots that display co-occurrences of the codes [31]. To prepare the data for ENA, we followed three levels of segmentation, line, stanza, and conversation to determine temporal context [33]. Individual student discussion posts constituted our lowest level of segmentation (line), the weeks in the course were the middle level (stanza), and the broader level (conversation) were the two years in which data were collected. As suggested by Shaffer and Ruis [34], segmentation should correspond with the delimitations or pauses occurring in the activity studied. In our data, posts, weeks, and years were breaks already embedded in the structure of the course and its online discussions.

To explore the impact of context on manifestation of social presence, we began by generating a model that allowed for the broadest comparisons. Model 1 defined the units of analysis as all lines of data associated with each Student for each week based on the Condition (remote or hybrid). For example, one unit consisted of all the lines associated with Student S1 in the Remote context. The model used a moving window to construct a network model for each line in the data, showing how codes in the current line are connected to codes that occur within the recent temporal context [35], defined as 5 lines (each line plus the 4 previous lines) within a given conversation. According to our qualitative analysis, this sliding window captured relevant connections for a given line. The conversation consisted of all lines associated with a Post within a given Week from a Condition. For example, if a Post in Week 2 of the Remote condition contained 9 replies, the moving window would iterate over the 10 lines creating 10 sets of connections.

To address RQ 2, the team felt a need to further segment the data to see the ways social presence shifted weekly throughout each course discussion. Model 2 utilized the same rotation matrix as Model 1. However, the units were updated to group students by a combined variable of their condition by week. This yielded 14 groups, one for each week (N = 7) in each condition (N = 2). Codes and conversation structure remained consistent between models. This alternate view allowed for comparison between weeks to better understand the overlap between contexts and what was drawing them apart.

4   Results

RQ1 sought to address general differences between learning contexts. To address this, Model 1 used a mean rotation that compared student behavior between the two conditions (Fig. 1A). This plot yielded Pearson correlation values of .88 (x-axis) and .98 (y-axis) and explained 22% of the variance on each axis. Along the X axis, a two sample t test assuming unequal variance showed that Remote (mean = 0.66, SD = 0.58, N = 26) was statistically significantly different at the alpha = 0.05 level from Hybrid (mean = −0.49, SD = 0.41, N = 35; t(42.49) = −8.59, p = 0.00, Cohen's d = 2.34). Due to the means-rotation, there was no significant difference between conditions on the y-axis.

Students in the hybrid environment were more likely to make connections between the triad of *Positive, Expanding*, and *Personal*. Student 20 from the hybrid course responds to several peers who had been discussing the value of Smartboards as they had experienced them in the classroom adding the following comment:

"Agree in the answer to S23 over. Feel that technology management is necessary for a good structure for proper use of the technology in the classroom. Awaken the curiosity and motivation of the students with a solid learning set backed by specialists!"

Student 20 is directly demonstrating that they have read another student's post and are adding what they would like to see done with expanded funding while also showing overall excitement about the topic.

Conversely, the Remote condition of instruction generated more connections between *Agree/Disagree, Acknowledging*, and *Risk Taking*. This is often seen by students demonstrating vulnerability by admitting unsureness about their interpretation of the course textbook or whether their contribution was relevant to the discussion. For example, Student 1 in the remote context closes their very first post by saying, "But

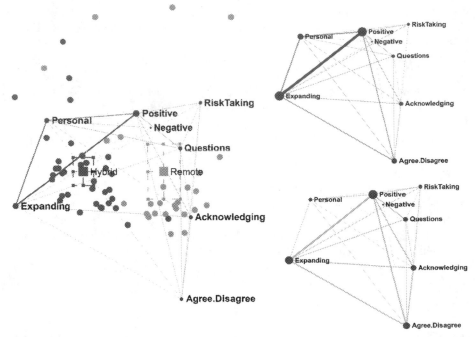

Fig. 1. The comparison plot between Remote (red) and Hybrid (blue) instances of the course highlight that students made more *Personal* connections during the hybrid course while they made more connections between *Acknowledging, Positive,* and *Expanding* in the remote course. Visualization of the networks for each context on its own indicates similar connections in both contexts. (Color figure online)

maybe I'm wrong?:)" This continues into following weeks sprinkled throughout posts as Student 14 in Week 3 of the remote context includes, "But again - maybe I have misunderstood, [...] I have not read the entire text." These elements provide a stark contrast to the strong collaborative effect that connections between *Agree/Disagree* and *Acknowledging* have on the discourse. For example, again in the remote modality in Week 1, Student 7 addresses two peers while both elaborating on their prior posts in the thread and adding their own perspectives:

"Here I would agree with both S14 and S15. Technology is a very large part of the everyday life of the young people in today's society and it will therefore also be both wise and necessary to make this a part of everyday school life. At the same time, it is important to keep in mind that it is not certain that everyone learns best using technology. [...] I think it is important to find a good balance between the use of new technology and other learning methods."

Still, when we consider each of the remote and hybrid plots on their own (Figs. 1B & 1C), the plots themselves are very similar. It appears that both contexts are eliciting all social presence factors.

Model 2 provides greater insight into the way instructors can have influence on their students. This model explains 18% and 14% of the variance across the x and y-axes respectively. This reduction can be attributed to the inclusion of Week into the units, thus asking the same model to incorporate additional data points. When comparing weeks using parametric tests, three of seven remote learning weeks (4, 5, and 7) were significantly different from all hybrid weeks along the x-axis. Two of seven hybrid weeks (2 and 6) were significantly different from all remote weeks along the x-axis. Several week pairs (e.g. Week 2 Remote and Week 2 Hybrid) demonstrated statistically significant differences. Weeks 2, 4 and 7 were each significant across both axes at the alpha $= .05$ level, and Weeks 5 and 6 were each significant on the x-axis at the alpha $= .05$ level (Fig. 1).

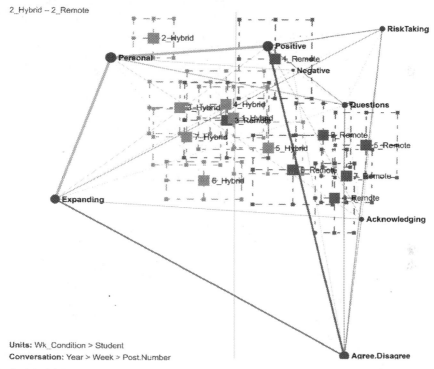

Fig. 2. Model 2's comparison plot of Week 2 hybrid and remote contexts. The hybrid context highlights connections between *Personal* and *Positive* and *Expanding*.

During Week 2, the prompt for the hybrid context included an explicit call to connect the question to personal experience by asking the students, "How has technology changed over time during your time as a learner or student? Do you have any particularly memorable experiences with certain technologies in school?" The students answer keenly, making many connections to their own educational experiences. Student 17 begins one of the more robust conversations with their own experiences about Smartboards:

"I went to primary school in a municipality where little money was allocated to school. We therefore had a relatively tired school with very little resources. There were chalk and blackboard for the teacher and notebooks for us. We never had a smartboard."

Their post is followed by 17 additional posts mentioning the tool including Student 15 noting how the technology fits into their experience, "I remember the week when smart boards were installed in all classrooms, around when I was fifth. There was great fuss around them, and the teachers generally seemed to be uncomfortable with them. They were never used." A similar phenomenon occurs during Week 3 of the remote context. Student 10 begins by discussing their experience with e-learning during job training, "I also have experience with e-learning as training, but then in connection with retail," and it leads to 11 more instances of students citing their own experiences with technological training at work. The instructor's prompt during Week 3 does not directly request that students draw on their personal experiences.

One final consideration for how instructor prompts may be contributing to student engagement with social elements in the discourse is whether the prompt introduces reminders for participation. In both contexts, the instructor does remind students that they should be responding to others, e.g. "Everyone must contribute at least two posts, but all posts will be approved. It is also allowed to formulate questions," (Week 1 - Remote) and "You can form your own thread or respond to others. One answer is OK, but it should be of some length, alternatively you make two posts/answers," (Week 4 - Hybrid). These reminders come early in the course, ending on Week 4 in both contexts. Yet, the weeks that included reminders to participate were not similar in the ways students employed social presence.

5   Discussion

Early research in the effect of remote learning indicated that students have the highest levels of connectedness when they partake in a hybrid learning environment [36]. While technology has reached new levels of ubiquity over the past 20 years, our classrooms continue to conduct business in a status quo model, especially at the undergraduate level. The present study provides support for student capability to adapt to making social connections during remote learning more than previously acknowledged. The students in the remote learning context demonstrated connections between many of the Group Cohesion markers of Social Presence as defined by the CoI framework.

Model 1 demonstrates that there are differences in how students respond to hybrid and remote contexts. In the hybrid context, students were more likely to focus on *Personal* connections and *Expanding* on others' posts, but in the remote context, students were more likely to have balanced connections between many social presence elements such as *Questions, Acknowledging, Risk Taking*, and *Agree/Disagree*. This indicates that the remote context forum supported more diverse social interactions including not only Open Communication but also Group Cohesion elements from the CoI framework [23]. This calls into question whether classroom interactions were fulfilling this role in the hybrid course negating a need for such discussions in the forum. Prior research indicates that instructors noticed the lack of classroom interaction as an area needing support for students during remote learning [4]. Whereas students may have previously taken the opportunity to chat during breaks and before or after class during in-person learning, those opportunities are not available in the remote context. With this in mind, we consider the online discussion forum as a support for students to engage in interactions that lead to Group Cohesion in a modality where otherwise unavailable.

Furthermore, Model 2 demonstrates that instructors can aid in facilitating students to engage in social presence through direct prompting and intentional design of the curriculum. Although the perceived differences were fairly universal across all of the weeks in each context, there were several weeks which stood as outliers. Week 2 in the hybrid context was an outlier in the number of connections students made to Personal experiences. This is likely due to the direct prompt from the instructor to draw on their own experiences. Similarly, by choosing a relatable topic of workplace training, students in Week 3 of the remote context were also able to integrate personal experiences. This aligns with prior work regarding engagement of graduate and professional students in discussions within a CoI framework; drawing on student expertise allows for increased engagement within the community and leads to greater overall student learning and engagement [37]. Extending that to the undergraduate population that is the focus of this study requires modification due to the presumed lack of professional experience. Thus, the employment of more personal questions may allow all students to engage. Model 2 highlights the interconnectedness of social presence with other elements of the CoI framework, Teaching and Cognitive presence [7]; teachers are essential to the community in how they design, organize, and facilitate educational experiences.

Many students during the Covid-19 pandemic did not choose to enter the remote learning context, but in order to maintain continuity in their educational goals, they did so anyway. This shared experience may have also provided an element of shared experience that was enough to overcome the "warm-up period" that has been previously documented in CoI literature [7]. While the literature cites numerous concerns for the social well-being of students throughout the pandemic [4, 10, 11], it is possible that their experiences have allowed them to participate in these less-than-ideal circumstances more fully than they would have otherwise. It would be beneficial to seek student perspectives in the future to understand why they were more willing to engage in Group Cohesion and Open Communication behaviors early in the semester before speculating on their motivations.

6 Limitations

This study was designed in response to the natural experiment that occurred as a result of the course needing to shift to a fully remote context. While this design has the affordance of maintaining consistent instructors and curriculum, the student population changed because of it being the same course. It is possible that the group dynamic of the remote cohort of students was categorically different from that of the hybrid cohort. While acknowledging these potential differences in course dynamics, we note that the ability to engage in productive discourse was an intended learning outcome articulated by the instructor. This may also have influenced the prevalence of students engaging in

Group Cohesion activities during the discussion forums as the instructors grow in their ability to support such discourse. Finally, the course itself was centered on technology. Prior research indicates that when students do not have expertise in the platform used for online discussions, there is a barrier to participation regardless of their sense of belonging [38]. Given that these students chose to take a course on education and technology, the likelihood of them being intimidated by the requisite learning is unlikely.

7 Conclusion

Since the possibility of compulsory distance and remote learning contexts were introduced during the Covid-19 pandemic, educators and researchers alike have been concerned about the possible ramifications of moving all coursework to the new context. While researchers have long focused on the benefits of discussion forums to other distance learning platforms such as Massive Open Online Classes (MOOCs), there has been very little consideration for how to best structure discussions for students who expected a course to be taught in a hybrid or fully in-person context. This is the contribution that this study brings to the literature. First, we demonstrate that students in a remote context do engage in a variety of both Open Communication and Group Cohesion elements of Social Presence from the CoI framework. In some ways their participation is similar to peers in a hybrid course, but in many ways, they draw more connections between Group Cohesion elements.

Given that this experience has provided a proof of concept for long-term remote learning contexts, it is likely that institutions will continue to expand their remote offerings. Based on the exploration of this data, with careful consideration for how instructors structure their prompts within the discussion forum, we would advocate for the use of LMS supported discussion forums to engage students in social elements of learning in order to support their learning.

References

1. Dunn, T.J., Kennedy, M.: Technology Enhanced Learning in higher education; motivations, engagement and academic achievement. Comput. Educ. **137**, 104–113 (2019)
2. Dumford, A.D., Miller, A.L.: Online learning in higher education: exploring advantages and disadvantages for engagement. J. Comput. High. Educ. **30**(3), 452–465 (2018). https://doi.org/10.1007/s12528-018-9179-z
3. Ghazi-Saidi, L., Criffield, A., Kracl, C.L., McKelvey, M., Obasi, S.N., Vu, P.: Moving from face-to-face to remote instruction in a higher education institution during a pandemic: multiple case studies. IJTES **4**, 370–383 (2020). https://doi.org/10.46328/ijtes.v4i4.169
4. Brooks, A., Hardin, C., Scianna, J., Berland, M., Legault, L.H.: Approaches to transitioning computer science classes from offline to online. In: Proceedings of the 26th ACM Conference on Innovation and Technology in Computer Science Education, vol. 1, pp. 81–87. Association for Computing Machinery, New York (2021)
5. Gillett-Swan, J.: The challenges of online learning: supporting and engaging the isolated learner. J. Learn. Des. **10**, 20–30 (2017)
6. Crawford, J., et al.: COVID-19: 20 countries' higher education intra-period digital pedagogy responses. J. Appl. Learn. Teach. **3**, 1–20 (2020)

7. Akyol, Z., Garrison, D.R.: The development of a community of inquiry over time in an online course: understanding the progression and integration of social, cognitive teaching presence. J. Asynch. Learn. Netw. **12**, 3–22 (2008)

8. Rajab, K.D.: The effectiveness and potential of E-learning in war zones: an empirical comparison of face-to-face and online education in Saudi Arabia. IEEE Access **6**, 6783–6794 (2018). https://doi.org/10.1109/ACCESS.2018.2800164

9. Emami-Naeini, P., Francisco, T., Kohno, T., Roesner, F.: Understanding privacy attitudes and concerns towards remote communications during the COVID-19 Pandemic (2021)

10. Zhai, Y., Du, X.: Addressing collegiate mental health amid COVID-19 pandemic. Psychiatry Res. **288**, 113003 (2020). https://doi.org/10.1016/j.psychres.2020.113003

11. Ali, W.: Online and remote learning in higher education institutes: a necessity in light of COVID-19 pandemic. HES. **10**, 16 (2020). https://doi.org/10.5539/hes.v10n3p16

12. Perets, E.A., et al.: Impact of the emergency transition to remote teaching on student engagement in a non-STEM undergraduate chemistry course in the time of COVID-19. J. Chem. Educ. **97**, 2439–2447 (2020). https://doi.org/10.1021/acs.jchemed.0c00879

13. Edyburn, D.: Transforming student engagement in COVID-19 remote instruction: a research perspective. Educ. Tech. Res. Dev. **69**(1), 113–116 (2021). https://doi.org/10.1007/s11423-020-09919-6

14. Katz, V.S., Jordan, A.B., Ognyanova, K.: Digital inequality, faculty communication, and remote learning experiences during the COVID-19 pandemic: a survey of U.S. undergraduates. PLoS ONE **16**, e0246641 (2021). https://doi.org/10.1371/journal.pone.0246641

15. Sun, Z., Lin, C.-H., Wu, M., Zhou, J., Luo, L.: A tale of two communication tools: discussion-forum and mobile instant-messaging apps in collaborative learning. Br. J. Edu. Technol. **49**, 248–261 (2018). https://doi.org/10.1111/bjet.12571

16. Aloni, M., Harrington, C.: Research based practices for improving the effectiveness of asynchronous online discussion boards. Scholarsh. Teach. Learn. Psychol. **4**, 271–289 (2018). https://doi.org/10.1037/stl0000121

17. Annand, D.: Social presence within the community of inquiry framework. Int. Rev. Res. Open Distrib. Learn. **12**, 40–56 (2011)

18. Thomas, M.J.W.: Learning within incoherent structures: the space of online discussion forums. J. Comput. Assist. Learn. **18**, 351–366 (2002). https://doi.org/10.1046/j.0266-4909.2002.038 00.x

19. Wozniak, H., Silveira, S.: Online discussions: Promoting effective student to student interaction (2005)

20. Venton, B.J., Pompano, R.R.: Strategies for enhancing remote student engagement through active learning. Anal. Bioanal. Chem. **413**(6), 1507–1512 (2021). https://doi.org/10.1007/s00 216-021-03159-0

21. Flener-Lovitt, C., Bailey, K., Han, R.: Using structured teams to develop social presence in asynchronous chemistry courses. J. Chem. Educ. **97**, 2519–2525 (2020). https://doi.org/10. 1021/acs.jchemed.0c00765

22. John-Steiner, V., Mahn, H.: Sociocultural approaches to learning and development: a vygotskian framework. Educ. Psychol. **31**, 191–206 (1996)

23. Garrison, D.R., Anderson, T., Archer, W.: Critical inquiry in a text-based environment: computer conferencing in higher education. Internet High. Educ. **2**, 87–105 (1999)

24. Rourke, L., Anderson, T., Garrison, D.R., Archer, W.: Assessing social presence in asynchronous text-based computer conferencing. J. Dist. Educ./Revue de l'ducation Distance **14**, 50–71 (1999)

25. Ferreira, M.A.D., Ferreira Mello, R., Kovanovic, V., Nascimento, A., Lins, R., Gasevic, D.: NASC: Network analytics to uncover socio-cognitive discourse of student roles. In: LAK22: 12th International Learning Analytics and Knowledge Conference, pp. 415–425 (2022)

26. Rolim, V., Ferreira, R., Kovanovic, V., Gasevic, D.: Analysing social presence in online discussions through network and text analytics. In: 19th International Conference on Advanced Learning Technologies, pp. 163–167. Institute of Electrical and Electronics Engineers (2019)

27. Garrison, D.R., Cleveland-Innes, M., Fung, T.S.: Exploring causal relationships among teaching, cognitive and social presence: student perceptions of the community of inquiry framework. Internet High. Educ. **13**, 31–36 (2010)

28. Rourke, L., Kanuka, H.: Learning in communities of inquiry: a review of the literature (Winner 2009 Best Research Article Award). Int. J. E-Learn. Dist. Educ./Revue internationale du e-learning et la formation à distance **23**, 19–48 (2009)

29. Hutto, C., Gilbert, E.: Vader: a parsimonious rule-based model for sentiment analysis of social media text. In: Proceedings of the International AAAI Conference on Web and Social Media (2014)

30. Mohammad, S., Salameh, M., Kiritchenko, S.: How translation alters sentiment. J. Artif. Intell. **55**, 95–130 (2016)

31. Shaffer, D.W., Collier, W., Ruis, A.R.: A tutorial on epistemic network analysis: analyzing the structure of connections in cognitive, social, and interaction data. Learn. Anal. **3**, 9–45 (2016). https://doi.org/10.18608/jla.2016.33.3

32. Marquart, C., Hinojosa, C., Swiecki, Z., Eagan, B., Shaffer, D.W.: Epistemic network analysis [Online software]. Epistemic Analytics (2019)

33. Shaffer, D.W.: Quantitative Ethnography. CathCart, Madison (2017)

34. Shaffer, D.W., Ruis, A.R.: How we code. In: Ruis, A.R., Lee, S.B. (eds.) ICQE 2021. CCIS, vol. 1312, pp. 62–77. Springer, Cham (2021). https://doi.org/10.1007/978-3-030-67788-6_5

35. Siebert-Evenstone, A.L., Arastoopour, G., Collier, W., Swiecki, Z., Ruis, A., Shaffer, D.W.: In search of conversational grain size: modelling semantic structure using moving stanza windows. J. Learn. Anal. **4**, 123–139 (2017)

36. Rovai, A.P., Jordan, H.: Blended learning and sense of community: a comparative analysis with traditional and fully online graduate courses. IRRODL **5**, (2004). https://doi.org/10.19173/irrodl.v5i2.192

37. Waters, J., Gasson, S.: Social engagement in an online community of inquiry. (2006)

38. Aderibigbe, S., Dias, J., Abraham, M.: Understanding issues affecting students' commitment to online discussion forums in undergraduate courses (2021)

Modeling Students' Performances in Physics Assessment Tasks Using Epistemic Network Analysis

Hamideh Talafian[1]([✉]) [iD] and Hosun Kang[2] [iD]

[1] University of Illinois at Urbana-Champaign, Urbana, IL 61801, USA
Talafian@illinois.edu
[2] University of California, Irvine 92617, USA
hosunk@uci.edu

Abstract. The education community continues to struggle to support students to make meaningful connections between disciplinary learning at schools with their everyday life experiences. Even when the students engage in meaningful science learning experiences, recognizing the connections and relations that students make through their engagement is methodologically challenging, especially through the analysis of qualitative data. The purpose of this study was to explore the patterns of connections that students generated through their participation in a co-designed physics unit. We analyzed 76 high school students written and pictorial responses to performance assessment tasks designed to engage students in physics learning. We used quantitative ethnographic techniques and a tool named Epistemic Network Analysis (ENA), to visualize the structure of connections between physics concepts and real-life experiences in students' assessment tasks. The ENA results revealed patterns of connections that students generated between physics concepts they learned at school and their everyday experiences. Notably, the analyses showed differences in patterns of connections between male and female participants and between written and pictorial preferences in momentum and impulse unit assessment tasks. The implications for curriculum design and performance assessment in science are discussed.

Keywords: Learning Science · Epistemic Network Analysis · high school physics · performance assessment in science

1 Introduction

Despite decades of reform efforts, many students struggle to see how the learning of sciences at schools is related to their own life experiences now and in the future [12, 30]. The National Survey of Science and Mathematics Education [2] showed that only 29% of secondary science instruction focus on real-life applications of science and engineering at US schools. Understanding whether and how students make connections between the concepts that they learn at school and everyday experiences are important in that it enables researchers and teachers to gain insights into curriculum design and assessment. Nevertheless, the mode of science teaching that mainly focuses on content delivery continues despite the emphasis made by the National Research Council (NRC) framework and Next Generation Science Standards (NGSS) on bringing students' cultural backgrounds, needs, and concerns into science classes over the past decades [31, 32]. In science classes and specifically in physics, which is the focus of this work, students' sex and racial/ethnic backgrounds further complicate this trend. Female students and students from racially and socioeconomically disadvantaged communities continue to struggle to see meaningful connections between physics concepts that they learn at school and their lives either now or in the future [22, 48, 50].

Even when the students are engaged in science learning activities meaningfully while producing rich learning artifacts, it is challenging to recognize the type and strength of connections that students make between school sciences and everyday life experiences. Currently, there are limited methodological approaches that statistically and visually depict student generated connection making using rich qualitative data. In this study, we explore the affordances of a new methodological approach focusing on connections that students generated through their participation in intentionally designed performance assessment tasks (i.e., written essays and pictorial assessment). To do this, we collaborated with high school science teachers in a research-practice partnership to co-design curriculum and performance assessment tasks to support students' meaningful physics learning. Along with scholars endorsing research practice partnership -where researchers and practitioners engage in co-designing curriculum and assessment- we believe this mode of research has the potential to disrupt the traditional mode of teaching and learning at schools [e.g., 1, 10, 16].

In our co-designed physics unit, the students produced rich written and pictorial responses to performance assessment tasks while making sense of how the safety features of car design might protect their loved ones. We tried to reveal the patterns of students' connection-making structures reflected in the designed physics assessment tasks and gain insights into students' physics understanding. The tasks prompted students to use scientific ideas to explain the safety features in a car collision in real-life situations. Specifically, students were tasked to a) explain the safety features of the car in accidents that they designed for their loved ones, b) give personalized explanations for the reasons why certain features are useful in collisions, and c) sketch and label the car safety features.

We used quantitative ethnographic techniques and a tool named Epistemic Network Analysis (ENA) to quantify and visualize students' physics performances. Although ENA has been incorporated in various fields to represent meaningful connections of coded elements in quantitative data as dynamic network models [46], using this tool to analyze rich qualitative data helped us to better incorporate it in the context of physics learning at the high school level. Unlike traditional coding and counting methods [8] which focus on the frequency of the occurrence of a code, this new approach supported our data analysis in two ways. First, revealing the interdependence between learning actions through connections allowed us to trace any difference in group performances (e.g., male vs. female) in a meaningful way. Second, visualizing the dynamics of learning by focusing on student-generated connections enabled us to better understand student performances reflected in both quantitative and qualitative data [8]. This tool reveals the strengths of connections between different elements of a discourse. The following research questions helped guide this study:

1. What are the type and strengths of the student-generated connections while engaging in deliberately designed physics tasks?
2. Is there any difference in the patterns of student-generated connection depending on their sex?
3. Is there any difference in students' patterns of connection depending on the modes of tasks (written vs. pictorial)?

2 Theoretical Framework

2.1 Situative Theory and Connection-Making Processes in Science Learning

We draw upon sociocultural theories to explore students' learning in a co-designed physics unit. Sociocultural theorists posit that learning is a fundamentally social and relational process that involves one's cultural meaning-making across spaces and time [13, 24, 36–38]. Meaning-making involves generating new relations and connections between learner and environment through embodied experiences situated in contexts [21]. From this perspective, exploring the newly formed connections or relations that students generate while engaging in activities is critical in understanding one's learning.

One implication of the situative perspective is its emphasis on the relational processes between agent and the surrounding world, which constitute activity, cognition, learning, and knowing [23]. In other words, situative theorists attend to interactions among members of the community in a socially and culturally constructed world in order to understand one's learning. Accordingly, the situative approach draws researchers' attention to the interactions between elements of the activity system in context, beyond changes in one's mental structure [14, 15]. Research shows that even cognitive processes, such as problem-solving abilities, are inherently context bound [7, 35, 40]. In short, learning and knowledge are situated in context and are constantly shaping and reshaping as learners participate in communities of practices; hence, learning cannot be reduced into separate processes [21, 28].

This view of learning has many implications for students from non-dominant communities. Scholars in this research tradition believe that participation in scientific practices is more meaningful when students in the community bring their own life experiences and make a deep personal connection [4, 6]. Research shows that these students are more likely to engage in disciplinary practices when the activities are relevant to them [e.g., 41]. Therefore, attending to students' connection-making by bringing their everyday experiences into the class is essential in creating equitable activities and increasing the participation of students who have been historically marginalized [5, 41, 49], such as female students in the context of physics education.

3 Methods

3.1 Epistemic Network Analysis (ENA): A Quantitative Ethnographic Tool for Visualizing Students' Science Learning in Activities

Epistemic Network Analysis (ENA) is a quantitative ethnographic tool (which is different from the ethnographic lens) that allows us to examine the students' connection-making patterns in science discourses both quantitatively and qualitatively [to learn more about ENA see 26, 45, 46, 43]. It measures the structure of connections between the coded elements to identify meaningful and quantifiable patterns in discourse (i.e., which will be students' assessment tasks) and represents them in dynamic network models [25, 43]. ENA is an alternative to the traditional frequency-based assessments or "code and count" approach in data analysis.

ENA is a useful methodological tool to study students' science learning, focusing on connection making (between school sciences and everyday experiences) for at least three reasons. First, ENA allows researchers to visualize the connections that students make among multiple elements of the systems across contexts (i.e., science classroom, home, and/or communities). For example, designing a car for a loved one not only enabled students to think of the safety features of a car in a more personalized way but also allowed them to see how physics concepts introduced in school science classrooms are related to their everyday life. Second, seeing through the strengths and weaknesses of students' connection-making in ENA networks reveal where the students made more connections in discourse. ENA allows us to recognize students' connection-making processes in a systematic way. Lastly, it allows us to compare different groups in a given context, both visually and statistically, by comparing students' networks and centroids. For example, we are interested in exploring how females make connections between physics concepts and everyday life experiences in this co-designed unit and whether these patterns are statistically significantly different from male students.

3.2 Participants and Data Sources

A total number of 76 students from 11th or 12th grades from two classes completed the focal performance assessment of this unit. Hereafter, we named it as letter assessment since it prompted students to explain the safety feature of the car designed for their loved ones. Female students comprised 46.1% (N = 35), male students 42.1% (N = 32) of the population and the other 11.8% (N = 9) did not want to divulge their sex at birth. The students in this school were mainly from Latinx populations (78%) and eligible for free/reduced lunch (66.5%). Hence, the difference in their performances based on the two variables (i.e., race, eligibility for free/reduced lunch program) was not investigated.

Two data sources were used in this study to capture the structure of connections that students made in connecting their school science to everyday science experiences. We used what we called students' letter assessments which consisted of two forms of written and pictorial data. The students designed a car by drawing it for their loved ones and labeling it with design and safety features. Then, they wrote a letter (written component) and explained those features to their loved ones. We used letter assessment with its both written and pictorial components as conversations in that all ideas within the letter are connected to one another. So, the ideas in the letter were interconnected, while ideas across letters that were written by different students were different. Figure 1 below shows an example of letter assessment data with both written and pictorial data.

3.3 Curriculum Storyline

In response to the call for curricular reforms to engage students in three-dimensional learning [33], we designed a phenomenon-driven curriculum [11] and performance assessment tasks using an essential question: "How are modern cars designed to keep you and your family safe in a collision?" (see the details of the unit storyline, embedded assessment tasks, and student performances in Kang et al., [20]). In phenomenon-driven curriculum and assessment tasks, students address a phenomenon or design challenge [39, 42]. In our co-designed unit, the students were tasked to design a dream car for their loved ones considering safety features to protect them in a collision. By assuming the role of an engineer who is designing a car, the students were supposed to make a list of the requirements for building a safe car (DCI aspect) through a series of inquiry labs and revisions. First, the teachers exposed students to fatality data graphs of the Ford Model-T which was a popular car 100 years ago in 1919 and its equivalent rated Toyota Camry in 2018. While learning about the fatality rates in graphs, the students were tasked to hypothesize the reasons under which these two cars showed different fatality rates in collisions as related to car safety features. Real-life collision experiences provided a unique opportunity for the students to get involved in connection-making processes between physics concepts and car safety features. Through various learning activities, such as collaborative chat stations, online collision simulations, egg drop experiment, and invited speakers, the students were able to compare elastic vs. inelastic collisions and the conservation of momentum in collisions. Throughout the course, the students revised their models in groups, including momentum and concepts related to the type of collision and materials. During the research phase, the students were supposed to conduct online research on car safety features (e.g., seatbelts, helmets, crumple zones, and airbags) to learn about impulse, force, and time for collisions using mathematical representations. They learned how these features help reduce the force in the collision by extending the time of the collision.

3.4 Data Collection and Analysis

Written and pictorial data was collected from students' performance assessment tasks at the end of the physics unit. The students' written assessments were digitized by the researchers and their drawings were scanned and attached to the written assessment for further analysis. The data analysis was conducted in four steps. In the first step, the letters were thematically coded to identify descriptive features which led to generating inductive codes. We identified ten codes with two main categories. The categories that encompassed all codes were: 1) science-related and 2) family-related categories. Three coders reached an agreement of 90% on IRR in an iterative process of coding the written assessments. In the second step, the quantitative ethnographic techniques [44] were used to segment and recode data for the existence or non-existence of each inductive code. In the third step, the pictorial data were analyzed based on the inductive codes using

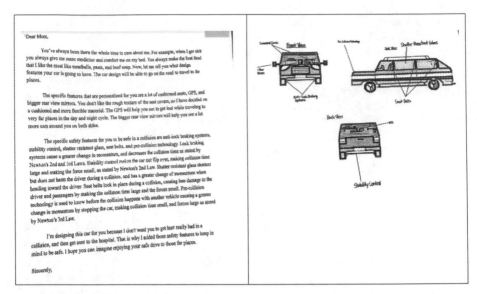

Fig. 1. Mateo's (pseudonym) letter assessment including written and pictorial data.

the same process used for written data. Finally, ENA as a quantitative ethnographic tool was used to visualize the structure of connections between coded segments in the students' performance assessment tasks including both written and pictorial data. Our ENA model included the following codes: physics concepts, safety features, relationship, family dynamics, gratitude (i.e., desire to give back), affection/intimacy, memories/stories, needs, interests and hobbies and preferences/likes and dislikes of loved ones. We defined conversations as all lines of data associated with a single value of sex subsetted by the weight of that code. In coding, we defined two levels for weights (1 = baseline requested information, 2 = baseline plus additional supporting information). For example, one conversation consisted of all the lines associated with the sex of female and weighted coding of 2 in safety code when a female student had explained why lighter materials in designing a car decrease collision fatality rate.

4   Findings

4.1   Research Question #1: What are the Types and Strengths of Student-Generated Connections while Engaging in Deliberately Designed Assessment Tasks?

The results of ENA analysis revealed that male and female students both made connections between physics concepts (i.e., car safety features) and the needs and interests of their loved ones. For instance, Michael's mom needed a safe car which could protect her from probable crashes since she spent a considerable amount of time on the road driving her kids to different places. Michael was able to identify this need and connect it back to car safety features by designing a car with a large crumple zone, fast-locking seatbelts, and light material. Michael not only explained these features in the letter to his mom but also depicted them in his car design and explained how safety features reduce force and how light material (i.e., less mass) reduces momentum change and could be safer in the event of a car collision. Letter and drawing were two forms of data that were coded both as written and pictorial performance assessments. The results were represented as one of the blue dots in the diagram (see Fig. 2).

In technical terms, Fig. 2 shows all students' performances in this assessment along the x and y axis. Please note that the x and y axis in the coordinate is not representing any science-related concepts. The graph simply shows students' performances in a three-dimensional space. In this figure, the blue dots represent male, and the red dots represent female students' performances. The blue and red squares are mean centroid. The boxes around those squares indicate the confidence intervals. Specifically, the width of the box shows the confidence interval on x axis and the height of the box represents confidence interval on the Y axis. There are two ways that we can interpret the findings in this visual: 1) by looking at the plot and comparison models, and 2) by statistically running parametric comparisons between different variables. Just by looking at the red and blue dots, we can see male students (blue dots) have made connections all over the diagram but usually on the right side versus female students made more connections on the left side (red dots). Inherently, there is no negative or positive connection making depending on whether they made connections on the left or right side of the diagram. However, the distance between the mean centroids shows that male and female students made different connections.

Another important finding here is the distance between male means (blue square) and the female means (red square) along the x-axis. This distance means that male and female students made different types of connections, which resulted in locating their performances in different parts of the diagram. As a reminder, from connection making we mean how often and to what extent the students could connect conceptual physics knowledge to their everyday life experiences. In the next section, we explain more about the difference between these connections.

4.2 Research Question #2: Is There Any Difference in Students' Patterns of Connection-Making Depending on Their Sex?

We looked at the primary and secondary plots, coming from the main graph (Fig. 2) to visually examine whether the differences between male and female students were significant. We also looked at the comparison models to better understand where these differences lay. The statistical analysis of paired sample t-tests between male and female students in letter assessment, which was done by ENA tool, showed that male and female students made statistically significantly different connections along the x axis (mean $_{female}$ = 0.12, SD $_{female}$ = 0.59, mean $_{male}$ = −0.10, SD $_{male}$ = 0.48; p < .05, d = .41). If we look closely into Fig. 2, we can see both centroids rest on the x axis but in the distance from each other; hence, the significant difference was detected on the x axis and not the y axis. In order to see where the significant areas were laid down, we ran a difference model (Fig. 3) which showed the connection-making lines between "loved one's interest" and "relationship" among females. This means that female students could better connect two family-related categories (i.e., loved one's interest and relationship) compared to male students who could connect physics concepts to one of those. Even though this type of connection-making does not necessarily imply more learning for

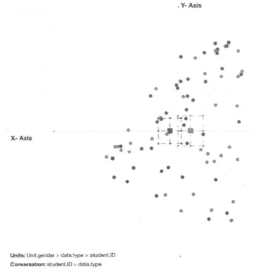

Fig. 2. Physics students' performance in letter assessment. Red = female, blue = male (Color figure online)

female or male students, it implies the ability of females to make more connections among family-related codes and physics concepts in physics discourse.

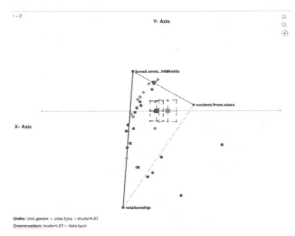

Fig. 3. Male and female comparison model. The model represents three main codes, and the red lines show the areas where female students made more connections compared to male students.

4.3   Research Question #3: Is There Any Difference in Students' Patterns of Connection-Making in Written and Pictorial Assessments?

Comparing written and pictorial assessments in performance assessment tasks (Fig. 4) showed that students made different patterns along the x-axis. Similar to the differences between male and female connection making processes, there is a difference between written and pictorial assessment representations along the x axis. Therefore, we ran a difference model to see 1) if this difference was significant, and 2) where the differences lied down.

The statistical analysis of paired sample t-tests between written and pictorial assessment in letter assessment showed that students' connection making processes were statistically significantly different in written and pictorial letter assessment along the x axis (mean $_{written}$ = 0.56, SD $_{written}$ = 0.79, mean $_{pictorial}$ = -0.60, SD $_{pictorial}$ = 0.67; p < .05, d = 1.58). Specifically, the difference model (Fig. 4) showed that the difference laid on the connection between "loved one's interest" and "relationship" as well as "loved one's interest" and "content from class". These connections were more evident in the letter (the pink lines and dots) than pictorial assessment. A closer look at the secondary models (Fig. 5) also showed the difference in written and pictorial assessment in favor of written assessment. Since the letter was written directly to the loved ones, it created more opportunities for expressing and connecting "loved ones' interest" and "content from class" to "relationship" node in the model. Pictorial assessment, on the other hand, showed to be equally practical in connecting "loved one's interest" to "content from class" indicating that designing a car for a loved one by incorporating their visual skills has the potential of connecting physics concepts to their real-life needs and interests.

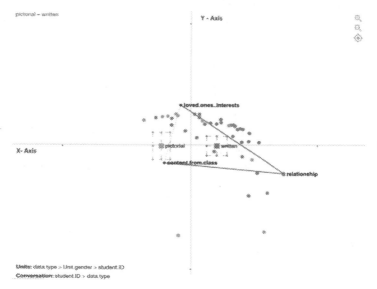

Fig. 4. Difference model between written and pictorial performance assessment physics tasks

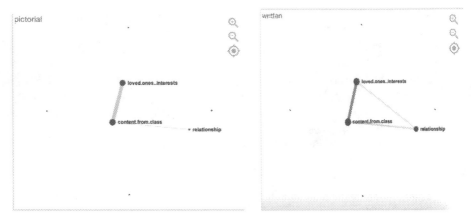

Fig. 5. Students' pictorial (left green) versus written (right red) physics performance assessment depicted by ENA.

5 Discussion

This study aimed to get insights into the students' connection-making processes in physics performance assessment tasks. We intended to identify the patterns of students' connection-making depending on students' biological sex and type of assessment. We used ENA as a tool to visualize students' performance in physics assessment tasks. Specifically, we documented the type and nature of student-generated connections between school sciences and their everyday experiences by analyzing rich qualitative data.

The result of this study revealed statistically significant different patterns made by students depending on their sex and type of assessment. Specifically, female students made more connections among family dynamics codes and male students made more connections between physics concepts codes. In other words, female students showed to make stronger connections between physics concepts when they found them relevant to the needs and interests of their loved ones. However, male students' connection making was not as dependent as females on the needs and interests of their loved ones.

In addition to comparing students' sex, we explored whether different forms of tasks, such as written and pictorial ones, make a difference in the patterns of connection-making among the students. The results of both written and pictorial data analysis using ENA visuals and statistical analyses revealed that some connection-making processes such as showing affection/gratitude toward family members, can be better articulated in written forms of assessments. In contrast, car safety features and their connection to the interests of loved ones could be better supported in pictorial assessment tasks. The differences between these two forms of assessments were shown to be statistically significantly different in favor of letter assessment, indicating that the letter created more opportunities for students to make connections between physics concepts and everyday personal experiences. There was no evidence in favor of any of the sex preferences in written or pictorial forms of assessments.

5.1 Taking a New Methodological Approach to Understand Students' Physics Learning Experiences

In this work, we addressed the challenge of understanding students' science learning experiences by taking a new methodological approach to learning about students' connection-making processes in physics. Through designing a deliberately non-traditional set of curriculum and assessment tasks, we tried to connect physics concepts to students' live experiences [see 20]. Consistent with other researchers' argument on the benefits of making physics more relevant to the students' lives [3, 27, 34], the findings of this study confirmed that connecting physics concepts to personal experiences have positive implications for students' physics learning. Our findings further clarified the type and nature of students' connection-makings to personal experiences through quantitative ethnographic techniques and ENA tool. In education research, there are very few studies that incorporate quantitative ethnographic tools and techniques. In a different context, for instance, Talafian et al. [47] mapped out high school students' identity exploration activities in urban planning while working in a play-based course. In the context of game-based learning other studies have also used QE techniques and specifically ENA to model patterns of participation [46], and patterns of association between theoretical constructs [47]. The similarities of these studies with ours lie in the significance of recognizing patterns and connections in small datasets. Unlike some other network analysis tools that require a big dataset to ensure accuracy, QE allowed us to ensure the richness of the dataset, and ENA helped in depicting accurate visuals of students' connection-making processes in the physics performance assessment tasks. However, any type of analysis or interpretation of the results should be done with caution.

5.2 Expanding Minoritized Students' Ways of Knowing

Previous works have mostly focused on curriculum design features, its impact on females and minoritized students' sense of belonging [18] and career development in STEM fields [17, 19, 47]. In this study, while we took a similar approach in designing a set of curriculum and assessment tasks for minoritized students [20], we tried to untangle the complexities of assessing the effectiveness of those by taking a new methodological approach. We believe understanding the effectiveness of different forms of assessment for students with diverse backgrounds could contribute to expanding minoritized students' ways of knowing. For instance, previous studies have shown that providing tasks with multiple modalities can ensure equity and is effective in including students' cultural and linguistic backgrounds [9] to advance students' success. However, we argue that validating and sustaining multiple ways of knowing through expanding assessing strategies [9, 29] is effective but not enough for expanding minoritized students' opportunities for science learning. Our co-designed unit and assessment tasks [20] are one example of such effort but using QE techniques and ENA tool solidified our understanding of students' connection making in physics.

Aligning ourselves with critical scholars and grounded in sociocultural perspectives, we interpret that the gendered patterns of connection-makings observed in our dataset are one reflection of inequitable opportunities to socialize into sciences, in particular physics, in and out of school setting and over time. These differential patterns of socialization might have been even more complicated along the line of race, ethnicity, language, and socioeconomic status that affect the broader discourses of what it means to do science and who can do science, in particular physics. The focal physics unit was intentionally designed to expand opportunities for minoritized students in high school physics classrooms, such as Latinx female students from low-income families, by facilitating those students to connect themselves to physics.

6 Conclusions and Implications

Prior research in learning sciences and science education has revealed 1) students' connection-making between science concepts and real-life experiences is of utmost importance, 2) new approaches are required to capture the type and strength of these connections. This study offers new insights by addressing these two areas of research by using quantitative ethnographic tools and techniques to reveal the type and strength of students' connection-making processes between physics concepts and real-life experiences. Based on the results of this study and the literature review, three areas of investigation need attention for future research: First, comparing different forms of performance assessment tasks for students with different sex and ethnicity backgrounds help researchers to understand which forms are favorable for students from marginalized backgrounds. Second, recording students' performances over time at different points would be of great value since it allows for comparing students' connection-making trajectories over time. Third, similar to this study that used both written and pictorial forms of data in performance tasks, future studies can use multiple sources of data to better support similar claims and enrich the datasets. Additionally, case studies can help bring a new cycle in informing the type of connections that students make.

References

1. Bang, M., Vossoughi, S.: Participatory design research and educational justice: studying learning and relations within social change making, vol. 34, pp. 173–193. Taylor & Francis (2016)
2. Banilower, E.R., Smith, P.S., Malzahn, K.A., Plumley, C.L., Gordon, E.M., Hayes, M.L.: Report of the 2018 NSSME+. Horizon Research Inc., Chapel Hill, (2018)
3. Bennett, D., Roberts, L., Creagh, C.: Exploring possible selves in a first-year physics foundation class: engaging students by establishing relevance. Phys. Rev. Phys. Educ. Res. 12(1), 010120 (2016)
4. Birmingham, D., Calabrese Barton, A., McDaniel, A., Jones, J., Turner, C., Rogers, A.: "But the science we do here matters": youth-authored cases of consequential learning. Sci. Educ. 101(5), 818–844 (2017)
5. Calabrese-Barton, A., Tan, E.: Funds of knowledge and discourses and hybrid space. J. Res. Sci. Teach. Off. J. Natl. Assoc. Res. Sci. Teach. 46(1), 50–73 (2009)
6. Calabrese-Barton, A.C., Tan, E.: We be burnin'! agency, identity, and science learning. J. Learn. Sci. 19(2), 187–229 (2010)
7. Ceci, S.J., Roazzi, A.: The effects of context on cognition: Postcards from Brazil (1994)
8. Csanadi, A., Eagan, B., Kollar, I., Shaffer, D.W., Fischer, F.: When coding-and-counting is not enough: using epistemic network analysis (ENA) to analyze verbal data in CSCL research. Int. J. Comput.-Support. Collab. Learn. 13(4), 419–438 (2018). https://doi.org/10.1007/s11 412-018-9292-z

9. Fine, C.G.M., Furtak, E.M.: A framework for science classroom assessment task design for emergent bilingual learners. Sci. Educ. **104**(3), 393–420 (2020)
10. Fishman, B., Penuel, W.: Design-based implementation research. In: International Handbook of the Learning Sciences, pp. 393–400. Routledge (2018)
11. Fulmer, G.W., Tanas, J., Weiss, K.A.: The challenges of alignment for the next generation science standards. J. Res. Sci. Teach. **55**(7), 1076–1100 (2018)
12. Fusco, D.: Creating relevant science through urban planning and gardening. J. Res. Sci. Teach. Off. J. Natl. Assoc. Res. Sci. Teach. **38**(8), 860–877 (2001)
13. Greeno, J.G.: On claims that answer the wrong questions. Educ. Res. **26**(1), 5–17 (1997)
14. Greeno, J.G.: The situativity of knowing, learning, and research. Am. Psychol. **53**(1), 5 (1998)
15. Greeno, J.G., Gresalfi, M.S.: Opportunities to learn in practice and identity (2008)
16. Gutiérrez, K.D., Jurow, A.S.: Social design experiments: toward equity by design. J. Learn. Sci. **25**(4), 565–598 (2016)
17. Hazari, Z., Sonnert, G., Sadler, P.M., Shanahan, M.C.: Connecting high school physics experiences, outcome expectations, physics identity, and physics career choice: a gender study. J. Res. Sci. Teach. **47**(8), 978–1003 (2010)
18. Johnson, D.R., et al.: Examining sense of belonging among first-year undergraduates from different racial/ethnic groups. J. Coll. Stud. Dev. **48**(5), 525–542 (2007)
19. Kang, H., Barton, A.C., Tan, E., Simpkins, S.D., Rhee, H.Y., Turner, C.: How do middle school girls of color develop STEM identities? middle school girls' participation in science activities and identification with STEM careers. Sci. Educ. **103**(2), 418–439 (2019)
20. Kang, H., Talafian, H., Tschida, P.: Expanding opportunities to learn in secondary science classrooms using multiple forms of classroom assessments [Structured Symposium Session]. In: Annual Meeting of the American Educational Research Association (AERA), San Diego, CA (2022)
21. Kirshner, D., Whitson, J.A., Whitson, J.A.: Situated Cognition: Social, Semiotic, and Psychological Perspectives. Psychology Press, London (1997)
22. Krakehl, R., Kelly, A.M.: Intersectional analysis of advanced placement physics participation and performance by gender and ethnicity. Phys. Rev. Phys. Educ. Res. **17**(2), 020105 (2021)
23. Lave, J.: Situating learning in communities of practice (1991)
24. Lave, J., Wenger, E.: Situated Learning: Legitimate Peripheral Participation. Cambridge University Press, Cambridge (1991)
25. Lund, K., Burgess, C.: Producing high-dimensional semantic spaces from lexical co-occurrence. Behav. Res. Methods Instrum. Comput. **28**(2), 203–208 (1996)
26. Marquart, C., Hinojosa, C., Swiecki, Z., Eagan, B., Shaffer, D.: Epistemic network analysis (version 1.5. 2)[software] (2018)
27. Nair, A., Sawtelle, V.: Operationalizing relevance in physics education: using a systems view to expand our conception of making physics relevant. Phys. Rev. Phys. Educ. Res. **15**(2), 020121 (2019)
28. Nasir, N.I.S., Hand, V.M.: Exploring sociocultural perspectives on race, culture, and learning. Rev. Educ. Res. **76**(4), 449–475 (2006)
29. Nasir, N.I.S., Lee, C.D., Pea, R., de Royston, M.M.: Rethinking learning: what the interdisciplinary science tells us. Educ. Research. **50**(8), 557–565 (2021)
30. National Academies of Sciences, Engineering and Medicine. How people learn II: Learners, contexts, and cultures. National Academies Press (2018)
31. National Research Council. How people learn: Brain, mind, experience, and school: Expanded edition. National Academies Press (2000)
32. National Research Council. Next generation science standards: For states, by states (2013)
33. NGSS Lead States: Next Generation Science Standards: For States, By States. The National Academies Press, Washington DC (2013)

34. Newton, D.P.: Relevance and science education. Educ. Philos. Theory **20**(2), 7–12 (1988)
35. Nunes, T., Carraher, T.N., Schliemann, A.D., Carraher, D.W.: Street Mathematics and School Mathematics. Cambridge University Press, Cambridge (1993)
36. Packer, M.J., Goicoechea, J.: Sociocultural and constructivist theories of learning: Ontology, not just epistemology. Educ. Psychol. **35**(4), 227–241 (2000)
37. Polly, D., Allman, B., Casto, A., Norwood, J.: Sociocultural perspectives of learning. In: Foundations of Learning and Instructional Design Technology (2017)
38. Rajala, A., Hilppö, J., Lipponen, L., Kumpulainen, K.: Expanding the chronotopes of schooling for the promotion of students' agency. In: Identity, Community, and Learning Lives in the Digital Age, pp. 107–125 (2013)
39. Reiser, B.J.: Designing coherent storylines aligned with NGSS for the K-12 classroom. In: Paper Presented at the National Science Education Leadership Association Meeting, Boston, MA (2014)
40. Rogoff, B.E., Lave, J.E.: Everyday Cognition: Its Development in Social Context. Harvard University Press, Boston (1984)
41. Rosebery, A.S., Ogonowski, M., DiSchino, M., Warren, B.: "The coat traps all your body heat": heterogeneity as fundamental to learning. J. Learn. Sci. **19**(3), 322–357 (2010)
42. Roseman, J.E., Herrmann-Abell, C.F., Koppal, M.: Designing for the next generation science standards: educative curriculum materials and measures of teacher knowledge. J. Sci. Teacher Educ. **28**(1), 111–141 (2017)
43. Shaffer, D.W.: How Computer Games Help Children Learn. Macmillan, New York (2006)
44. Shaffer, D.W.: Quantitative ethnography (2017). https://lulu.com/
45. Shaffer, D.W., Ruis, A.R.: Epistemic network analysis: a worked example of theory-based learning analytics. In: Lang, C., Siemens, G., Wise, A.F., Gasevic, D. (eds.) Handbook of Learning Analytics, pp. 175–187. Society for Learning Analytics Research (2017)
46. Shaffer, D.W., Collier, W., Ruis, A.R.: A tutorial on epistemic network analysis: analyzing the structure of connections in cognitive, social, and interaction data. J. Learn. Anal. **3**(3), 9–45 (2016)
47. Talafian, H., Shah, M., Barany, A., Foster, A.: Promoting and tracing high school students' identity change in an augmented virtual learning environment. In: Paper published in the A Wide Lens: Combining Embodied, Enactive, Extended, and Embedded Learning in Collaborative Settings, 13th International Conference on Computer Supported Collaborative Learning (CSCL), Lyon, France, 17–21 June 2019 (2019)
48. Tan, E., Calabrese Barton, A., Kang, H., O'Neill, T.: Desiring a career in STEM-related fields: how middle school girls articulate and negotiate identities-in-practice in science. J. Res. Sci. Teach. **50**(10), 1143–1179 (2013)
49. Tzou, C., Bell, P.: Micros and Me: Leveraging home and community practices in formal science instruction (2010)
50. White, S., Tesfaye, C.L.: Female students in high school physics: results from the 2008–09 nationwide survey of high school physics teachers. In: Focus on Statistical Research Center of the American Institute of Physics (2011)

Computational Thinking in Educational Policy –The Relationship Between Goals and Practices

Andreas Lindenskov Tamborg[(⊠)], Liv Nøhr, Emil Bøgh Løkkegaard, and Morten Misfeldt

University of Copenhagen, Rådmandsgade 64, 2200 Copenhagen N., Denmark
andreas_tamborg@ind.ku.dk

Abstract. In this paper, we study the relationship between the content and goals of curriculum revisions toward the integration of computational thinking (CT) in compulsory schools in Denmark, Sweden, and England. Our analyses build on data consisting of a combination of official documents such as new curricula, white papers, and implementation strategies and interviews of experts who are either highly knowledgeable about or were involved in developing the curriculum revisions in these three countries. Our study found that there are strong connections between the CT content data practices and goal competitiveness in England. In Sweden, we found that the relationship between data practices and the goal of competitiveness is strongest. In Denmark, we found that the CT content codes related to data practices, modeling and simulation practices, and computational problem solving practices were all strongly represented, but all were weakly related to policy goals.

Keywords: Computational thinking · Curriculum policy · Comparative educational research

1 Introduction

For nearly a decade, the term computational thinking (CT) has played an increasing role in discussions about and revisions of compulsory school curricula across Europe and beyond. A survey conducted by the European SchoolNet in 2022 documented that 25 countries in Europe have implemented curriculum revisions that concern CT [1]. CT, however, remains an ambiguous term with a myriad of definitions, each foregrounding different content areas originating from disciplines such as computer science (e.g., [2]), design processes (e.g., [3]), and the social impact of computation [4–7]. This ambiguity of CT is also reflected in different countries' curriculum revisions. Despite the apparent international consensus that CT is needed, there are notable differences across countries in terms of what CT content is included. Moreover, there are differences in the goals that such CT-related curriculum revisions target.

In this explorative paper, we investigate the relationship between choices of content and declared political goals using an epistemic network approach to analysis. Denmark, Sweden, and England are three countries that make an interesting comparison, as they

C. Damşa and A. Barany (Eds.): ICQE 2022, CCIS 1785, pp. 299–313, 2023.
https://doi.org/10.1007/978-3-031-31726-2_21

have sought to implement different variants of CT for different reasons. This has been documented in [8], in which the rationales and content of curriculum in these three countries were compared based on policy documents and expert interviews of experts on the implementation of CT in the three contexts. This study identified the main goals to be a more democratic education (Denmark), decreased socioeconomic inequality (Sweden), and increased economic competitive power (England) [8].

In this article, we applied an epistemic network analysis (ENA) on the same data as [8]. While [8] used open thematic coding and a classical qualitative approach to analysis, we studied these data sources with ENA. Moreover, [8] primarily focused on the goals of CT-related curriculum revisions and the process of developing its content in Sweden, England, and Denmark. Using ENA, this paper explored and visualized relations between CT content and goals of CT-related curriculum documents as described in policy and research documents and expert interviews.

Our definition of CT builds on the framework of Weintrop and colleagues [9], which described CT as consisting of four different CT practices: systems thinking practices, data practices, modeling and simulation practices, and computational problem solving practices. The research question guiding this paper was "How are Denmark's, Sweden's, and England's goals of implementing CT in the curriculum related to CT practices as depicted in policy documents and expert interviews?" To situate the study, we provide a brief account of the term CT and our rationale for choosing the definition developed by [9] in the following section.

2   Computational Thinking in Education

Although CT is a recent term in educational policy [10], it has existed in mathematics education research since the 1970s. Seymor Papert [11] is often referred to as one of the first to coin the term in his seminal book *Mindstorms* in 1980. Papert and colleagues developed the LOGO programming environment, in which children, by means of simple text programming commands, could navigate a turtle to, among other things, explore and articulate mathematical ideas related to geometry. During the 1980s, Papert's ideas spread to the UK in particular, in which researchers conducted studies on the potential of LOGO for children's learning of several mathematical areas, such as arithmetic, proportion and ratio, geometry, and numbers [e.g. 12, 13]. While this work gained sufficient traction to become mainstream in research, it did not lead to a sustainable impact on educational policy.

In 2006, Jeanette Wing, a professor of computer science at Columbia University, authored a short viewpoint paper in *Association of Computer Machinery*, arguing for the wide relevance of CT as a skill for students of all ages. Wing defined CT as involving solving problems, designing systems, and understanding human behavior by drawing on the concepts fundamental to computer science and to include "a range of mental tools that reflect the breadth of the field of computer science" [14, p. 33]. This paper received significant attention and laid the stepping stones for embedding CT in compulsory school curricula [1]. It also brought with it a number of new definitions of CT as a subject in its own right and as part of existing subjects, most often science and mathematics.

Two of the most widely used definitions came from [15] and [6]. In a line of thinking similar to ENA, [15] described CT as an epistemic frame and primarily focused on how this frame is different from the epistemic frame of mathematics. This study argued that the epistemic frame of CT is outwards-oriented in the sense that tools and concepts typically are used and taught in relation to concrete, real-world problems. Conversely, [15] described the epistemic of mathematics as being inwards-oriented in the sense that mathematics education is often abstract and stays within the realm of mathematics with infrequent use of real-world examples.

In this paper, we have chosen to draw on the definition developed by [6]. Their definition of CT consists of a taxonomy of four distinct practices: data practices, modeling and simulation practices, computational problem solving practices, and systems thinking practices. Each of these practices is composed of five to seven taxonomic levels. This particular framework is relevant for this study because it clearly distinguishes between different components of CT (the four practices), which are described at a relatively granular level in the taxonomic levels compared to other available definitions of CT. Moreover, the framework is empirically built based on diverse data sources, including educational resources (standards and curriculum material) and interviews of people who work with CT as part of their jobs. In the methods section, we describe in detail how we developed codes based on Weintrop et al.'s [6] CT framework. Below, we describe how CT has become part of compulsory school curriculum policy in Denmark, Sweden, and England.

3 Computational Thinking in Denmark, Sweden, and England

3.1 Technology Comprehension in Denmark

As of the time of this writing, Denmark has not yet made a final decision to revise its curriculum to include CT-related topics [9]. However, in 2018, the Ministry of Education launched a pilot project in which 46 schools implemented a new subject called "technology comprehension" (TC) [16]. The purpose of this project was to gain and systematically collect experiences relating to the implementation of this subject to inform a future curriculum revision on a national scale. A central aspect of the intention of the Danish initiative was the proclaimed need to educate K-9 students to be able to critically relate to and shape technology [17–19].

Policy documents stressed that a national curriculum revision was, in fact, needed to ensure that Danish K-9 schooling would continue to live up to the legal purpose of its declaration [18, 20]. Sections 2 and 3 in paragraph 1 of this legislative document specify that Danish schools "*must prepare students for participation, co-responsibility, rights and duties in a society with freedom and democracy*" and that they should create opportunities for students to build "confidence in one's own possibilities and background for taking a stand and acting" [20]. Due to the rapid digitization of society, the reasoning was that living up to the purpose declaration would require a focus on teaching students the mechanisms of digital technology [18, 19].

The curriculum for TC consisted of four competence areas: digital empowerment, digital design and design processes, computational thinking, and technological agency. Further, each competence area was defined by three to five subject matter areas presented as pairs of skill sets and knowledge. In the case of computational thinking, the subordinated subject matter areas were data, algorithms, structures, and modeling.

3.2 Digital Competency in Swedish Schools

In 2017, the Swedish K-9 curriculum underwent a major revision with the goal of strengthening students' digital competence (DC) [22], described as an overarching competence area with no fixed content [23]. DC has been viewed from four different perspectives: 1) understanding the impact of digitalization on society, 2) being able to solve problems and put ideas into action, 3) using and understanding digital tools and media, and 4) having a critical and responsible approach. Together, all four of these perspectives were expected to form an adequate digital competence. The integration of DC led to revisions of all major subjects. This involved different aspects of DC being fitted into different subjects' curricula. Thus, responsible use of digital media and its social, ethical, and legal aspects was embedded in social science and technology, and programming became part of the mathematics curriculum [24, 25]. In mathematics, programming was added to the algebra content and applied to all grade levels in compulsory schooling.

The Swedish mathematics curriculum is organized into six core content areas: understanding and use of numbers, algebra, geometry, probability and statistics, relationship and change, and problem solving. Programming was added to algebra at all grade levels and described in the following way [25, pp. 56–59]:

- Grades 1–3: How unambiguous, step-by-step instructions can be constructed, described, and followed as a basis for programming. The use of symbols in step-by-step instructions.
- Grades 4–6: How algorithms can be created and used in programming. Programming in visual programming environments
- Grades 7–9: How algorithms can be created and used in programming. Programming in a visual and text-based programming environment.

- For grades 7–9, algorithms are also mentioned in relation to problem solving, and computer simulations are mentioned in relation to statistics:
- How algorithms can be created, tested, and improved in programming for mathematical problem solving.
- Assessment of risk and chance based on computer simulations and statistical material.

3.3 Computing in England

In 2014, England was among the first countries to initiate CT-related curriculum revision by introducing a new computing curriculum [26] as a replacement for a previous ICT curriculum. The ICT curriculum had been mandatory in Key Stages 1 and 2 (students aged 5–7 and 7–11) and primarily covered basic usage of ICT tools and information search, including assessing the plausibility and quality of information [27]. However, beginning in 2007, representatives from industry presented concerns that the content of the ICT curriculum was likely to fall short in preparing students to contribute to the IT industry, thereby risking England's future industrial competitiveness. On top of this, the Council of Professors and Heads of Computing (CPHC) documented a continuous decrease in applicants for higher education computing courses, for which they held the unappealing content of the ICT curriculum as partly to blame [28].

The computing curriculum is mandatory throughout Key Stages 1–4 and has four main aims: for students to 1) understand and apply fundamental principles of computer science, 2) have the ability to analyze problems in computational terms, 3) evaluate new and familiar technologies, and 4) become responsible, competent, confident, and creative users of technology [29]. The curriculum content consists of algorithms and programming, logical or computational thinking, digital content and potential uses for digital technology, safety and citizenship, and systems, search, and software. Examples of aims of the subjects are that students should learn "what algorithms are, how they are implemented as programs on digital devices, and that programs execute by following precise and unambiguous instructions" [29, p. 2].

4 Methods

4.1 Choice and Collection of Data

This paper drew on documents that describe the situation and policy process in the three countries and on expert interviews. The documents included policy documents (such as white papers) that described the background for integrating CT-related subjects and the CT content included in the curriculum in the three countries, reports from industry and non-profit organizations, official curricula, policy documents describing the approaches and strategies used to implement the new curriculum, and research papers on CT in the three countries' curricula. We identified these documents by screening relevant resources on educational ministries' websites in the three countries under study. When relevant, we followed a snowball sampling approach [30], which consisted of looking at references of already found documents and their references. Documents were deemed relevant to the extent that they contained information on the content or motivation for curriculum revisions in the three countries. The expert interviews were conducted with ten expert respondents (three from England, three from Sweden, and four from Denmark), which were held subsequent to the collection of documents. The interviews were semi-structured and were conducted as online interviews in English, with the exception of the Danish respondents, as Danish was the mother tongue of both respondent and interviewer. Each interview lasted between 45 and 60 min, and all were conducted in May or June 2021. The interviews primarily sought to gain insights into the motivation and content of CT-related policy revisions in the three countries [8].

4.2 Coding

We coded our material in nCoder [31] to achieve transparent coding across the material. Before doing so, we needed to transform interviews and articles to have common materiality and language, which enabled the coding in nCoder. This had consequences for the types of information that were processed. We briefly highlight this in the following section, and, later, we describe in-depth our deductive coding strategy and coding in nCoder. Our data materials included both articles and interview transcripts. As we were interested in how computational thinking is understood and related to the three goals for implementation in data types, we needed a comparable unit.

The interviews were split into utterances for the coding process. We decided to also include the interviewer's utterances, as this person might have connected goals and components of computational thinking as well. The articles were split into sentences in chapters, only included sentences with more than 30 characters, and excluded tables and pictures. Due to the size of the dataset, we chose to use the semi-automated coding tool, nCoder [31]. As nCoder is expression-based, we needed the materials to be in the same written language. To achieve this, we used Google Translate on both the Danish and the Swedish materials. Using Google Translate can be challenging when dealing with figures of speech (e.g., the Danish saying, "they build upon" was translated into "they build upstairs"). Although this type of mistranslation is confusing, it is manageable in nCoder, in which one can add specific words or phrases that identify a specific code, which the program then applies as rules to the whole dataset. Thus, if we could recognize mistranslation, we could provide a meaningful expression into nCoder.

nCoder helps to improve the set of rules by drawing a random subset of data to be hand-coded and then displaying discrepancies between the hand-coding and the set of rules. We repeated this process to obtain a consistent set of rules for our codes, which is conceptualized in nCoder through a kappa and a rho value. Kappa measures the precision of the machine coding compared to the human coding, and rho provides an estimate of the share of codes that would differ between a full human and a full machine coding of the given rules [31]. To ensure consistent coding across the whole dataset, we aimed for rho values less than .30 and kappa values higher than .80 for a subset of min. 80 units.

The coding strategy used for the study was deductive, as we aimed to explore how the three prior identified goals of enforcing computational thinking related to the conceptualization of computational thinking. To identify content aspects of computational thinking, we used the framework [6]. Although the coding strategy was deductive, we could not derive the relevant terms directly from [6], as the words used to describe CT might not have been exactly the same as when applied or discussed. We thus started the coding process with the terms from [6] but situated them in the data through the circular process embedded in nCoder.

As stated in the research question, our aim was to study the relationship between CT content in curriculum revisions of the proclaimed goals of these revisions in Denmark, Sweden, and England. To develop the codes for the curriculum policy goals, we drew on the recent work of [8]. This study found clear tendencies that the CT curriculum revisions in Denmark primarily were oriented toward a primary goal of democratic education. England was oriented toward competitiveness, while Sweden primarily was oriented toward addressing socioeconomic inequality. Informed by these results, and similar to the development of codes for CT content, we developed the codes for these three goals through the circular process embedded in nCoder. While [8] study primarily investigated the declared aims of CT-related curriculum revisions and the subsequent process of converting these goals to concrete content to embed in the curricula, the analysis in the present paper took a much more focused approach to study the relationship between goals and content in the three countries under review.

4.3   Approach to Analysis

To analyze the data, we performed an Epistemic Network Analysis (ENA) [31–33]. This is a quantitative ethnographic approach to data analysis, that theoretically prioritizes understanding phenomena through their networked constitution rather than understanding them as consisting of isolated sub-elements. As such, it is an approach well suited for the scope of this article, in which the relationships between different parts of CT are central.

We used ENA to visualize and interpret the structure of connections between the different codes we developed through network models. Analytically, ENA thus implies both quantitative and qualitative processes. First, the network models can only be constructed by quantifying the text data, a process not unlike working with nCoder. Our coding and analytical strategy thus complemented each other well. Furthermore, the network models gave us quantitative insights into the structure of connections between the codes in the materials; that is, what codes were most prevalent and what were the "strengths" of the connections between them. Second, by drawing on the epistemic network models, a return to the level of the texts was possible, which effectively closed the so-called "interpretive loop" by allowing us to unfold the qualitative contents of the quantitative connections between the codes within the three countries. As such, the quantitative and qualitative differences between them, in terms of the relationships between their motivations for implementing CT and practices of CT, were key to our analysis.

We applied ENA to our data using the ENA Web Tool (Version 1.7.0) [33]. We defined the units of analysis as all lines of data associated with Denmark, Sweden, or England subsetted by the texts on a "chapter" level. Thus, one unit consisted of all lines associated with, i.e., one of the English texts and one of its respective chapters (0–19). We defined conversations in the same way as the units of analysis; that is, all lines of data associated with any of the three countries subsetted by texts on a chapter level. This implies that the analysis was centered on the interpretation of three distinct network models consisting of the connections between the codes based on each of the different texts related to Denmark, Sweden, or England, respectively. As multiple arguments and practices could be mentioned within the same chapter without building on each other, we chose to employ a moving stanza with seven lines. This allows us to investigate the close context of the arguments and practices employed [33].

Given the diversity of text materials, a question concerning the differences between the interviews on the one hand and documents on the other arose in the process. Therefore, we made a network model to examine the difference between these two types of text materials. As expected, we found that these models reflected the experts' knowledge of elements within CT and the policy-documents interest in the relationship between CT and society overall.

5   Results

The main differences in the data were visualized in two axes. Most of the difference (23.2%) appears on the x-axis, which at one end (x low) relates to the competitiveness, while, at the other end (x high), it relates to an individual's competencies and problem solving. We interpreted this axis as capturing a movement from societal benefits from technology education to more individual aspects.

The y-axis explains 13.8% of the difference between the codes. At the one end of this axis, we find concerns about equality (y low), and at the other end data practices (y high). We interpreted this axis as having concerns related to people on the lower end and data and numbers on the high end. With these interpretations, the first quadrant deals with a very narrow conception of CT as having to do with numbers as well as individual competencies and skills.

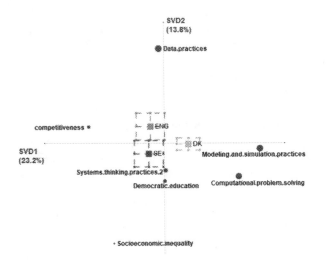

Fig. 1. Comparing the means of different countries. We see that Sweden (SE) and England (ENG) differ from Denmark (DK; but not from one another) in relation to the x-axis, whereas England and Sweden differ on the y axis, where Denmark is placed in the middle.

Figure 1 shows the comparison of the means of the networks for the three different countries. Denmark is significantly different from the two others on the horizontal axis, and Sweden and England differ on the vertical axis. This interpretation shows that the Danish focus on programming and computational thinking is less related to societal concerns (in relation to the corpus). England and Sweden share the societal concern in relation to CT, but where Sweden aims for equity through democratic citizenship, England focus more on technical aspects of computer science, which is connected to aims of increasing competitiveness.

Figure 2 shows the network of the English data. Here, the most pronounced code is the CT policy goal competitiveness, which shares the strongest connections to the other codes. The strongest connection is between competitiveness and the CT content code data practices. Smaller connections can also be observed between competitiveness and the policy goal of socio-economic equality and the content code computational problem solving. It is not surprising and in line with the results in [8] that competitiveness is pronounced in the English data. The connection between this node and that of data practices reveals how the policy goal of CT in England is reflected in a focus on data practice more so than any of the other CT contents (with exception of 'computational

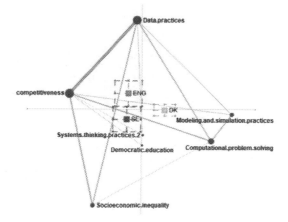

Fig. 2. Network relationship between goals and content in curriculum content in England.

problem solving'). The focus on data practices should be understood in the context of data and digital technologies' impact on the job market especially. In the English materials, data and digital technologies are perceived as promising *"[…] revolutionary transformational changes across the full range of industry sectors and computing"*, and the general conception is that several jobs now either depend on the use or are directly involved the production and maintenance of such technologies. The increasing importance of digital and data technologies from *"industry demands"*, which in the English data is described as requiring a digital literacy: *"Every child should be expected to be digitally literate by the end of compulsory education, in the same way that every child is expected to be able to read and write. Every child should have the opportunity to learn concepts and principles from computing (…) and by age 14 should be able to choose to study towards a recognised qualification in these areas"*.

The quote above emphasizes that education in computational problem solving in England should encourage students to "study towards recognized qualification". This is in line with results found in [8], which found that reports argued that a declining workforce in computing was partly caused by children not being exposed to such subjects in their early schooling and thereby not pursuing formal training in the subject later on.

Figure 3 shows the network between the codes in the Swedish materials. Here, we observe strong relationships between the policy goals competitiveness and socio-economic inequality. We also see a strong relationship between competitiveness and data practices and between data practices and computational problem solving.

The prominence of the policy goal socio-economic inequality is consistent with the findings of [8], but the strong connection it shares with competitiveness is surprising. Closer examination of this relationship reveals that there is a distinct focus on leveling gender differences: *"It has been difficult both for the academy and the industry to attract women to IT-related educations and professions."* a likely explanation for the prominence of the policy goal competitiveness is however that gender equality is not described as a goal in its own right, but as a necessity relative to economic competitiveness: *"The*

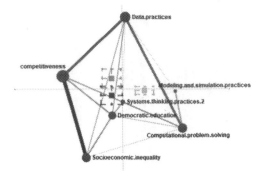

Fig. 3. Network relationship between goals and content in curriculum content in Sweden.

lack of women in the IT industry is not only serious for companies, but also for society as a whole. (…).Women's competence and experience are important parameters for the development of digital tools and services, which contributes to higher competitiveness". In this case, the goal of addressing socio-economic inequality therefore appears to be subordinated, rather than juxtaposed, to the goal of competitiveness. this result is an important nuance of the results found in [8], which we return to in the discussion (Fig. 4).

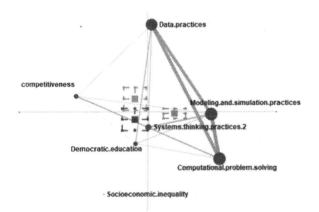

Fig. 4. Network relationship between goals and content in curriculum content in Denmark.

The strongest relation in the Danish model is between the CT content nodes. The most frequently coded node is computational problem solving, followed by data practices. The strongest connection in the Danish network is found between modeling and simulation practices and data practices. These connections often cover close descriptions of what students are expected to do in class, and how TC will affect their work, such as: *"The reasoning and thinking competence as well as the symbol processing competence gain new relevance in combination with technology understanding and especially in the work with the knowledge area programming and data, algorithms and structuring"*. Contrary to England and Sweden, there is no clear relation between the content and a specific goal. There is however some connection between the CT content nodes and policy goals, namely between data practices and democratic education and between computational problem solving and competitiveness. Instances in the data of the relation between the two latter resemble those in England in the sense that industry needs are emphasized: *"Business leaders expect new business models and significant changes in core performance in the coming years due to digitization"*. A difference, compared to the English setting, is however that the Danish material explicitly mentions the pedagogical values through which TC competencies should be cultivated, where it emphasized that the teaching should be *"based on experimentation, ingenuity and testing of ideas"*. In instances in the data where democratic education and CT content is related, it is described how the content areas of TC (here among problem solving, data practices and modelling and simulation) are necessary for students' *"understanding the implications of digital technologies for the individual, community and society"*. The particular way of phrasing CT components as subordinated to a larger goal of building democratic citizens, which is conveyed in this quote, corresponds to the results in [8]. It is however important to stress that although both competitiveness and democratic education are present in the Danish data, the majority of the connections concern content areas and do not include policy goals.

6 Discussion and Conclusion

On a general level, there are several interesting points to discuss in relationship to the analyses of the three countries. As stated in the analysis, the ENA model for Denmark shows that data practices, computational problem solving practices, and simulation and modeling practices were more equally represented in the data than in either Sweden or England. This is consistent with the results found by [9], which described the Danish TC curriculum as being broad compared to other countries. However, while [9] found a relatively clear orientation in Denmark toward democratic education (which also is described by [3]), the ENA model of Denmark indicates that goals of policy as such are somewhat weakly represented in the data. Moreover, the ENA model of Denmark shows a weak relationship between CT content and policy goals. This could indicate that the alignment between content and aims, which in other studies is claimed to be strong in Denmark [3, 9], was less clear in the Danish data than found in other studies.

In England, it was somewhat surprising that socioeconomic inequality was present in the analysis. Previous research, including [8, 34], unanimously found a clear orientation in English policy toward building a strong competitive workforce. In her analysis, Larke [34] found that, in particular, stakeholders from the industry successfully had managed to put significant pressure on the government to give data science and CT-related content a prominent role in the compulsory school curriculum. Moreover, Larke [34] documented that, despite the wide range of stakeholders, including teachers and education researchers, who took part in the initial development of the curriculum, changes were made at the last minute due to lobbying from representatives from industry, which resulted in a more technically oriented curriculum than otherwise planned. While this account of the curriculum development process still holds true, the ENA model of England developed in this paper indicates that goals toward addressing socioeconomic inequality were present.

As depicted in Fig. 3, the ENA model of Sweden shows that the two most prominent goals in Swedish curriculum policy were competitiveness and socioeconomic inequality. In the Swedish data, competitiveness seems to be slightly more strongly represented than socioeconomic inequality. This result, too, deviated from what is found in other studies [9, 24]. Compared to both England and Denmark, Sweden is, however, significantly more oriented to the lower part of the vertical axis (see Fig. 1), which indicates that the Swedish data generally is more strongly oriented toward socioeconomic inequality compared to the two other countries.

The connection between competitiveness and socio-economic differences in both the model for England and for Sweden highlights the strength of ENA to tell a more nuanced and ambiguous story compared to previous studies [9, 36]. Thus, it shows that despite different main goals, there is a similarity in goals for introducing CT in Sweden and England, and a somewhat similar structure in what practices they have included, in particular in terms of data- and computational problem solving practices. ENA's strength of connecting particular singularities, might however also be what makes it difficult to see the connections in Denmark, which Tamborg found to have a more broad conception ofCTcompared to England and Sweden [8]. As the coding is aimed at finding differences between the use of practices in CT and the aims of introducing it, it will be less fitted to see general differences. As the Danish CT understanding is much broader, it might connect the aim of implementing CT more to a general idea, than to the subparts of the whole, than what is the case in England and Sweden. This change in levels is more easily caught in qualitative approaches to coding and analysis, where the analysis is more holistically connected to the coding.

Thus, in qualitative approaches, analysis of relatively large data sets (such as those deployed by both [9] and [35] can, in some cases, be difficult to capture and can represent more subtle nuances of the data. As analysis in general—and qualitative analysis in particular—involves reduction of complexity, it is often the most dominant discourses that end up being represented in the results communicated in a research paper. A central advantage of ENA is that it embraces such complexity and represents the results, however ambiguous they might be. This allows for identifying more nuanced information within data sets, regardless of whether it seems consistent. Moreover, while relationships between goals and content might seem present in data when processed manually by a human being, ENA only represents such relationships to the extent that they appear within the same chapter. In particular, in Denmark, this feature of ENA showed that the goals of CT curriculum revisions were weakly represented and that the relationship between CT goals and CT content was weak. In turn, the opposite can happen, when ENA models show more information than what easily can be reported in results of manual analysis. This was the case in Sweden, in which competitiveness appeared as a policy goal in contrast to previous work [8]. Interestingly, we saw addressing social inequalities in some cases was seen described as a necessity to ensure competitiveness. Also here, ENA confronts the researcher with all the nuances of the dataset and prompts more transparency in the choices and analyses of the data.

In this paper, we set out to investigate how Denmark's, Sweden's, and England's goals of implementing CT in educational curriculum are related to the CT practices as depicted in policy documents and expert interviews. Our results showed strong connections between the CT content data practices and the goal of competitiveness in England. Our results thus indicated a focus on core computer science topics, which is related to a goal of competitiveness. In Sweden, our analysis found the relationship between data practices and the goal of competitiveness to be strongest. While addressing socioeconomic inequality appeared as a strong code in the data, this goal was weakly related to CT content codes. In Denmark, we saw that the CT content codes for data practices, modeling and simulation practices, and computational problem solving practices were all strongly represented, but all were weakly related to policy goals.

As described above, these findings both confirm and add information to what is known through previous research. This indicates that ENA holds the potential for generating valid but also nuanced accounts of relationships between goals and content in curriculum policy. It is, however, important to note that the data on which we have drawn only included accounts for aims and content as declared in policy as expressed by individual experts knowledgeable about or involved in policy decisions in the three countries. Although this data defined the legislative guidelines for teaching within the three countries, the results of our analysis did not necessarily generate insights into the characteristics of practices in schools within the three countries. An obvious next step could thus be to consider collecting data on actual teaching practices and studies by means of ENA.

References

1. Bocconi, S., et al. (eds.): Reviewing Computational Thinking in Compulsory: Education State of Play and Practices from Computing Education. Publications Office of the European Union, Luxembourg (2022). ISBN 978-92-76-47208-7, https://doi.org/10.2760/126955
2. Wing, J.M.: Computational thinking. Commun. ACM **49**(3), 33–35 (2016)
3. Dindler, C., Smith, R., Iversen, O.S.: Computational empowerment: participatory design in education. CoDesign **16**(1), 66–80 (2020)
4. Georgios, F., Stavroula, P.: Computer science teachers' perceptions, beliefs and attitudes on computational thinking in Greece. Inf. Educ. **18**(2), 227–258 (2019). https://doi.org/10.15388/infedu.2019.11
5. Román-González, M., Moreno-León, J., Robles, G.: Complementary tools for computational thinking assessment. In: Kong, S.C., Sheldon, J., Li, K.Y. (eds.) Proceedings of International Conference on Computational Thinking Education - CTE 2017, pp. 154–159. The Education University of Hong Kong (2017). https://www.researchgate.net/publication/318469859_Com plementary_Tools_for_Computational_Thinking_Assessment
6. Sáez-López, J.-M., Román-González, M., Vázquez-Cano, E.: Visual programming languages integrated across the curriculum in elementary school: a two-year case study using "Scratch" in five schools. Comput. Educ. **97**, 129–141 (2016). https://doi.org/10.1016/j.compedu.2016.03.003
7. Upadhyaya, B., McGill, M.M., Decker, A.: A longitudinal analysis of K-12 computing education research in the United States: implications and recommendations for change. In: Proceedings of the 51st ACM Technical Symposium on Computer Science Education, pp. 605–611. Association for Computing Machinery (2020). https://doi.org/10.1145/3328778.3366809

8. Tamborg, A.L.: A solution to what? Aims and means of implementing informatics-related subjects in Sweden, Denmark, and England. Acta Didactica Norden **16**(4) (2022). https://doi.org/10.5617/adno.9184

9. Weintrop, D., et al.: Defining computational thinking for mathematics and science classrooms. J. Sci. Educ. Technol. **25**(1), 127–147 (2015). https://doi.org/10.1007/s10956-015-9581-5

10. Bocconi, S., Chioccariello, A., Dettori, G., Ferrari, A., Engelhardt, K.: Developing computational thinking in compulsory education - implications for policy and practice (No. JRC104188). Joint Research Centre (Seville site) (2016)

11. Papert, S.: Mindstorm. Harvester Press, United Kingdom (1980)

12. Noss, R.: How do children do mathematics with LOGO? J. Comput. Assist. Learn. **3**(1), 2–12 (1987). https://doi.org/10.1111/j.1365-2729.1987.tb00303.x

13. Noss, R., Hoyles, C. Windows on mathematical meanings: Learning cultures and computers. Kluwer (1996)

14. Wing, J.: Computational thinking. Commun. ACM **49**(3), 33–35 (2006). https://doi.org/10.1145/1118178.1118215

15. Pérez, A.: A framework for computational thinking dispositions in mathematics education. J. Res. Math. Educ. **49**(4), 424–461 (2018). https://doi.org/10.5951/jresematheduc.49.4.0424

16. Regeringen. Teknologiforståelse skal være obligatorisk i folkeskolen (2018). https://www.regeringen.dk/nyheder/2018/teknologiforstaaelse-fag-i-folkeskolen/

17. Børne and Undervisningsministeriet. Handlingsplan for teknologi i undervisningen (2018). https://www.uvm.dk/publikationer/folkeskolen/2018-handlingsplan-for-teknologi-i-undervisningen

18. Børne and Undervisningsministeriet. Kontraktbilag 1: Kravspecifikation. Forsøg med teknologiforståelse i folkeskolens obligatoriske undervisning. DocPlayer (2018). http://docplayer.dk/149137888-Kontraktbilag-1-kravspecifikation-forsoeg-med-teknologiforstaaelse-i-folkeskolens-obligatoriske-undervisning.html

19. Børne and Undervisningsministeriet. Handlingsplan for teknologi i undervisningen (2018). https://www.uvm.dk/publikationer/folkeskolen/2018-handlingsplan-for-teknologi-i-undervisningen. Accessed 9 Nov 2021

20. Børne and Undervisningsministeriet. Folkeskolens Formål (2021). https://www.uvm.dk/folkeskolen/folkeskolens-maal-love-og-regler/om-folkeskolen-og-folkeskolens-formaal/folkeskolens-formaal

21. Digitaliseringskommissionen. Gör Sverige i framtiden - digtial kompetans. Regeringen (2015). https://www.regeringen.se/rattsliga-dokument/statens-offentliga-utredningar/2015/03/sou-201528/

22. Olofsson, A.D., et al.: Digital competence across boundaries - beyond a common Nordic model of the digitalisation of K-12 schools? Educ. Inq., 1–12 (2021)

23. Heintz, F., Mannila, L., Nordén, L.-Å., Parnes, P., Regnell, B.: Introducing programming and digital competence in Swedish K-9 education. In: Dagiene, V., Hellas, A. (eds.) ISSEP 2017. LNCS, vol. 10696, pp. 117–128. Springer, Cham (2017). https://doi.org/10.1007/978-3-319-71483-7_10

24. Swedish National Agency of Education: Curriculum for the compulsory school, preschool class and school-age educare 2011. Elanders Sverige AB (2018)

25. Department of Education. National curriculum and assessment from September 2014: Information for schools. Assets Publishing Service (2018). https://assets.publishing.service.gov.uk/government/uploads/system/uploads/attachment_data/file/358070/NC_assessment_quals_factsheet_Sept_update.pdf

26. Department of Education and Employment. Information and communication technology: The national curriculum for England. Teachers TV (1999). http://archive.teachfind.com/qcda/curriculum.qcda.gov.uk/uploads/ICT%201999%20programme%20of%20study_tcm8-12058.pdf

27. Council of Professors and Heads of Computing. *A* Response to the Interim "Digital Britain Report" from the Council of Professors and Heads of Computing UK (2009). https://cphcuk.files.wordpress.com/2014/01/cphc-db-response.pdf
28. Department for Education. Computing programmes of study: Key stages 1 and 2 National curriculum in England. Assets Publishing Service (2013). https://assets.publishing.service.gov.uk/government/uploads/system/uploads/attachment_data/file/239033/PRIMARY_national_curriculum_-_Computing.pdf
29. Given, L.M. (Ed.). The Sage Encyclopedia of Qualitative Research Methods. Sage Publications, Thousand oaks (2008)
30. Shaffer, D.W.: Quantitative Ethnography. Cathcart Press, Madison (2017)
31. Shaffer, D.W., Collier, W., Ruis, A.R.: A tutorial on epistemic network analysis: analyzing the structure of connections in cognitive, social, and interaction data. J. Learn. Anal. **3**(3), 9–45 (2016)
32. Csanadi, A., Eagan, B., Kollar, I., Shaffer, D.W., Fischer, F.: When coding-and-counting is not enough: using epistemic network analysis (ENA) to analyze verbal data in CSCL research. Int. J. Comput.-Support. Collab. Learn. **13**(4), 419–438 (2018). https://doi.org/10.1007/s11412-018-9292-z
33. Siebert-Evenstone, A.L., Irgens, G.A., Collier, W., Swiecki, Z., Ruis, A.R., Shaffer, D.W.: In search of conversational grain size: modeling semantic structure using moving stanza windows. J. Learn. Anal. **4**(3), 123–139 (2017)
34. Larke, L.: Does not compute: Social dissonance in England's computing education policy. Doctoral dissertation, University of Oxford (2018)

Understanding Detectors for SMART Model Cognitive Operation in Mathematical Problem-Solving Process: An Epistemic Network Analysis

Mengqian Wu[1]([✉]), Jiayi Zhang[1], and Amanda Barany[2]

[1] University of Pennsylvania, Philadelphia, PA 19104, USA
wme@upenn.edu
[2] University of Drexel, Philadelphia, PA 19104, USA

Abstract. Understanding indicators in self-regulated learning (SRL) that affect mathematical success using quantitative techniques such as epistemic networks hold potential for providing effective scaffolds that draw directly from the learner's perspective. Tied to learning success, SRL provides a range of frameworks for identifying students' affective, cognitive, and metacognitive performance in a computer-based learning environment. This research can investigate how ENA can contribute as a visualization device to understanding of the metacognitive aspect of math learning. With the aim, we collected text responses from an online math problem-solving environment that encouraged reflections on self-regulated learning patterns that differ by the rate of correctness and familiarity with the educational tool. Student responses consisted of their explanations of strategies and solutions after the scaffolding instructions. Our team deductively designed detectors reflecting on *assembling* and *translating* operations (Winne's SMART model) to examine differences in the learner's self-regulated learning behaviors. We then leveraged Epistemic Network Analysis (ENA) using these detected indicators as codes to compare the results within two categories: performance on correctness and familiarity developed over time. Models show stronger co-occurrence between numerical representation and contextual representation and highlight the critical impact of outcome orientation on learner success. When the final answer is correct, or learners are more familiar with the educational tool, there is a strong outcome orientation connected to contextual representation within SRL operations.

Keywords: self-regulated learning · mathematics education · problem solving · epistemic network analysis

1 Introduction

A growing research interest in understanding cognitive and metacognitive actions using learner data from online learning environments has encouraged the proliferation of self-regulated learning (SRL) theoretical models. Several studies have pointed out the importance of self-regulation in learning science, as it is closely associated with positive

© The Author(s), under exclusive license to Springer Nature Switzerland AG 2023
C. Damşa and A. Barany (Eds.): ICQE 2022, CCIS 1785, pp. 314–327, 2023.
https://doi.org/10.1007/978-3-031-31726-2_22

learning outcomes [1–3]. Learners who regulate their learning are aware of the learning process as they acquire knowledge or skills and actively participate in and control the necessary steps toward mastery [3]. A growing community of scholars proposes a dynamic trajectory model with phases and processes of SRL: that learning behavior is developed over time and composed of preparation, performance, and reflection [4–6]. Despite this landscape, fewer studies have evaluated how these strategies function simultaneously.

Responses to inventories and think aloud are regarded as two categories of self-report data that are commonly collected in computer-based learning environments (CBLEs) to measure SRL constructs [7], and prior research has leveraged quantitative ethnographic approaches for SRL data mining such as Epistemic Network Analysis (ENA) [8–11]. These developments benefit learning analytics by making previously unobservable patterns of the process of thinking visible in online learner data while avoiding issues with the accuracy of memory retrieval. Real-time self-report is complementary to online trace measures, which offers a more direct way to examine learners' thought processes and explain more variance in learners' performance by revealing unobservable problem-solving steps and strategies [12]. Shaffer [13] explained the idea of thick description by noting that language is not just a reflection of how the mind works but also a tiered 'hierarchy of meanings.'

Using learning analytics and quantitative ethnography, we can shed light on the implications of students' self-reported answers during their interactions with computer-based learning environments. The research question seeks to unpack the contextual SRL strategies in math problem-solving and understand how they are associated with successful performance. The following research questions were scrutinized in the paper: (1) What are the differences in connections made between four SRL indicators across learner responses with correct and incorrect answers to math problems? And (2) How do learner patterns of SRL indicators differ as they get familiar with the CueThink and generate more Thinklets (a series of problem-solving tasks)? We develop automatic detectors as codes within an approach of epistemic network analysis (ENA) for SRL process analysis. The current study is concerned with building detectors that detect SRL components of operations based on Winne and Hadwin's SMART model, which consists of five operations: (1) *searching,* (2) *monitoring,* (3) *assembling,* (4) *rehearsing,* and (5) *translating.* Based on data collected from the CueThink, we deductively define four SRL indicators and detect each of them in discourse. These indicators include (1) numerical representation, (2) contextual representation, (3) outcome orientation, and (4) data transformation. Additionally, we defined an indicator called strategy orientation, but there are not enough examples in the dataset to include it in the analysis. We develop a set of epistemic network models to evaluate differences in individual performance on correctness and general development of familiarity. In our study, a method of learning analytics in conjunction with a practice of quantitative ethnography is expected to provide insights about the dynamic associations of SRL indicators detected in math problem solving.

2   Literature Review

Self-regulated learning has gained popularity in education research, and be expanded in use and conceptualization across disparate goals and measurements including: (1) types of measures in data reflecting SRL behaviors, (2) constructed processes or models of SRL processes, and (3) analytical methods to evaluate SRL. Detecting cognitive and metacognitive learning activities in log data that differentiate less efficient learner performance from more efficient learner behaviors could inform the design of more fundamentally conductive prompts and scaffoldings for long-term independent learning. Deeply rooted in established SRL constructs, recent studies explore the idea of developing detectors to investigate SRL patterns [14–17]. These detectors focus on fine-grained micro-level SRL processes to find help-seeking, self-monitoring, self-assessment, goal-setting, and information assembly. According to Zimmerman's cyclical phase model, students with mastery of SRL analyze the learning task and motivate themselves in a forethought phase, control and be aware of the learning progress in the performance phase, and assess and react to their performances in the self-reflection phase [18]. Most approaches for detecting self-regulated learning strategies have not fully explored Winne's [19] theories. Winne and colleagues [19, 24, 35] suggest that higher-level cognitive strategies are integrated into every phase and process of SRL, including both the top-to-bottom processing and their independence and associations with different cognitive abilities in the context of a learning situation. Our broader research aims to develop new operationalized indicators to understand learners' SRL behaviors on an online mathematics problem-solving platform. Winne and Hadwin [20] investigated the process of SRL as four states in sequence, including recognization of the learning task, building goals and plans, implementing them, and reviewing the output of prior steps based on feedback and adaptations. Further developing an integrated theory, Winne's SMART model of SRL [19] identified five operations of cognitive and behavioral actions in task performance: *searching, monitoring, assembling, rehearsing,* and *translating*. It attempts to place diverse constructs into one framework that functions in all of the four SRL sequential tasks [20].

Literature in quantitative ethnography explored SRL in collected log data based on textual inputs and categorized learning events [8, 9, 11, 21]. Paquette and colleagues [8] examined SRL with trace data collected from 98 students in an open-ended online learning environment that allowed students to build models of scientific concepts and phenomena causally. ENA was used to illustrate the problem-solving actions in relation to 'information seeking, solution construction, and solution assessment' (p. 4). Uzir and colleagues [21] studied blended learning environments and investigated time management and learning tactics associated with positive learning outcomes. They used ENA models to illustrate different patterns in different strategy groups. Gamage and colleagues [9] compared MOOC participants based on familiarity (i.e., first-time user/multiple classes completer) and used ENA to compare reflections on video-watching and communication in log data and interviews. Wu et al. [11] developed ENA models to evaluate the metacognitive behaviors of learners in collaborative learning contexts based on self-report reflection. By drawing upon this knowledge, this paper combines a method of labeling log files via text replay with a study of the occurrence of self-regulated learning operations in math problem-solving.

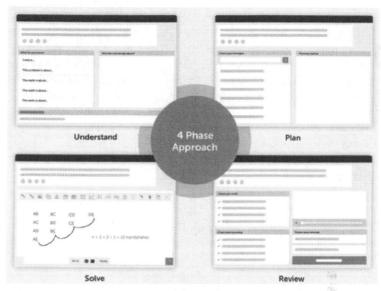

Fig. 1. CueThink's interface. Screenshots of CueThink's Four Phases. Adapted from Jiayi et al. (2022).

3 Method

3.1 CueThink

CueThink is an online learning application that allows middle school students to tackle math word problem practice, aiming at developing their math knowledge, self-regulated learning skills, critical thinking, and independent problem-solving strategies. Students independently complete assignments using CueThink, and teachers review and grades them later. Peer and supervisor feedback can be given asynchronously in CueThink's online classroom community combining with the school setting. Except for students working on randomly assigned math problems, the overall online setting is the same for all students. During the problem-solving procedure, students use CueThink to solve a math problem by manipulating multimedia tools (e.g., create a screencast video, generate a table, make a draft, etc.). CueThink developed four phases (see Fig. 1) aligning with the temporal and sequential nature of self-regulated learning (i.e., Understand, Plan, Solve, and Review) consolidated together as a Thinklet. Learners can move back and forth across the four phases in CueThink, and select any Thinklet to continue with a status of 'Create Thinklet.' At the same time, the tool captures how learners solve the math problem in each phase by recording their performance during learning events, including their textual inputs, answers to multiple-choice questions, a screencast video, and the time spent on each activity. As a means of labeling log files, we use a method known as text replays. It allows us to retrieve a segment of learner behavior that contains a sequence of actions for a selected period, and organize pieces of information in a textual format.

Students create a Thinklet and start with the Understand phase, where students are invited to engage with a math word problem and respond to three question prompts: (1) "What do you notice?" (2) "What do you wonder?" and (3) "What is your estimation about the answer?" In this phase, students look for information from given resources, understand the story, and are encouraged to gather meaningful pieces of information for completing a learning task. The second phase is the Plan phase, in which students will read a multiple-choice question about math problem-solving strategies and will have the option to draw a picture, model an equation, work backwards from the solution, etc. The Plan phase encourages students to write a plan on math problem-solving steps, and discuss solutions from a story. Students develop their thoughts and strategies based on prior understanding and explain their plans through descriptive written responses. In the Solve phase, students explore multimedia scaffolding tools (e.g., ruler, calculator, colorful pen, etc.) and work on a whiteboard space. Students then make a screencast video to describe and demonstrate their use of tools. In the Review phase, students provide final answers to the given math problem and reflect on the quality of their answers, video, and performance in prior phases. CueThink fosters this activity by asking students to fill in a checklist. To evaluate students' performance, the current study will focus on students' textual responses generated in the Understanding phase and Planning phase (phases 1–2), and their final answers provided in the Review phase (phase 4). The structure of phases and events is summarized in Table 1.

Table 1. Learning Events in Three Phases with Textual Inputs.

Phase	Event
Understand	What do you notice? What do you wonder? Estimate your answer?
Plan	Write down (your planning journal)?
Review	Review your estimation? Final answer?

3.2 Participants and Procedures

CueThink has been used by 79 students from six classes in a suburban middle school in California in grades 6th and 7th (approximately 11–12 years old). In 2020, this school's ethnic diversity index is near 50%, and about half of the students are English learners. White students and Hispanic/Latino students both makeup 40% of the student population, while African American students and Asian students each make up 5%.

Data about student usage events and system operations are recorded in log files within the CueThink system. Users' log files, for example, record when they log in, what pages they view, and what text they type or select as their answer to multiple choice questions. Each student spent an average of 5.2 h using CueThink and 1.8 h on each Thinklet [22]. We coded and analyzed 349 Thinklets based on activities and textual responses. We consider a learner high-performing if the learner has more correct final answers than incorrect final answers, which means more than 50% of the solved problems are correct. Otherwise, we regard them as a relatively low-performing group. For the first comparison, we split 349 Thinklets into two categories based on the rate of the correctness of individuals: low performing group (NL = 104) and high performing group (NH = 245). In the second category, we identified four levels of familiarity (i.e., first time/second time/third time generating a Thinklet, and more than three times) in 349 Thinklets. When we talk about learner behaviors, we focus on automatedly detected indicators of SRL processes designed for aligning with Winne and Hadwin's SMART model [20], which we will further discuss in the next section.

3.3 Detectors and Code Book

As a learning analytics team effort, the process of building automated detectors of self-regulated behaviors is challenging, recursive, and iterative. The first step was to convert the log data into human-readable text replays and then operationalize qualitative elements concerning Winne and Hadwin's SMART constructs [22]. Each indicator was classified as one of the strategies relevant to the SMART model, existing in every phase. The log data is usually restructured to reflect the constructs that researchers would like to measure. To define the final codebook, the research team and system developers communicated several times, including seven stages: 1) define concepts of codes and operationalization, 2) refine conceptualization in small groups, 3) build the first codebook, 4) refine it again, 5) implement the codebook, 6) revise the description of codebook based on implementation [22].

In this study, we mainly focus on *assembling* and *translating* operations considering the design of the learning environment and data availability, while other operations not detected in discourse were excluded from our analyses. According to Winne [24], by *tra* you are attempting to identify a relationship, and by *translating* you are changing the way in which a given piece of information is presented. Two coders developed four SRL indicators and coded them manually (See Table 2), including (1) numerical representation, (2) contextual representation, (3) outcome orientation, and (4) data transformation. Numerical and contextual representations, usually defined as strategies used at the beginning of the problem-solving process, contribute to a learner's representation of a problem story and recognition of a learning task [20]. Both indicators reflect *assembling* in the SMART model in that learners actively use, control, and manipulate information provided in the learning environment to make a general representative picture. The other indicator (outcome orientation) reflects *assembling* by explaining a learner's goal-setting and planning behaviors and stressing an outcome-focus. Data transformation is representative of the *translating* operation, in that learners adjust and make a change to the way information is presented in the problem to find a solution. Two raters examine inter-rater reliability in their coding process (see Table 3). Based on clear definition of classification and fully communication, all the Cohen's kappa results are above 0.6 verifying the relatively high agreement between two raters.

Table 2. SRL Code Book with Examples

SMART Category	Codes	Description	Examples
Assembling	Numerical Representation (NR)	The learner's representation of the problems includes numerical components and demonstrates a level of understanding of how the numerical values are used in the math problem	"I will add the total amount of withdrawals. Next, I will add the two deposits (25 + 50)."
Assembling	Contextual Representation (CR)	The learner's representation of the problem includes contextual details relating to the setting/characters/situations within the given math problem	"Jen has $ 20 for walking his neighbor's dog."
Assembling	Outcome Orientation (OO)	The learner provides only a numerical estimate of the final answer for the given math problem, suggesting that learners are focused on the output instead of the process itself	"Last, I will add the −83 and −30 to get −112, then do 113 − 76 = 37."
Translating	Data Transformation (DT)	The learner manipulates the ways information is represented to them in the problem to find a solution. This suggests active problem solving	"I have to make the problem easier and then solve it. I think we have to find the mean of each pen."

Table 3. SRL Code Book Kappa Results

SMART	Codes	Kappa
Assembling	Numerical Representation (NR)	0.832
Assembling	Contextual Representation (CR)	0.628
Assembling	Outcome Orientation (OO)	0.736
Translating	Data Transformation (DT)	0.742

3.4 Epistemic Network Analysis

Using the webtool (version 1.7.0) [27], we generated two sets of epistemic networks to visualize differences in patterns of connections across the generated codes (numerical representation, contextual representation, outcome orientation, and data transformation). The first set of networks compare low-performing and high-performing student groups based on the number of correct final answers. Correctness of final answers is an essential metric in evaluating a student's abilities in math problem solving. CueThink participants were divided into a low-performing student group (0% - 50% of final answers correct) and high-performing student group (51% - 100% of final answers correct). In general, if a learner has more correct answers than incorrect answers, we conceptualize them as high performing. Unit variables consisted of the binary low/high performance groups, subset by user ID. Conversations were segmented by the variable *Thinklet* ID so that associations were only calculated across data within each *Thinklet*. A whole conversation stanza window was used to aggregate co-occurrences across all lines of data in each *Thinklet*. Since the initial unit compares two groups, a mean rotation was used to maximize differences across the x-axis.

The second set of networks track patterns of change across participants as they repeatedly work through *Thinklets*. Learners could begin a new *Thinklet* at any time, and tended to generate more *Thinklets* as they were assigned more math problems. Students' first *Thinklet* serves as a record of their initial experience using and exploring CueThink. As students begin and complete subsequent *Thinklets*, they gain familiarity with the specific online learning environment, and learners are more likely to develop expertise in adapting functions, prompts, and external resources in the tool. Most students generated two to four *Thinklets*, with a few participants creating five or more. To track changes in participants' connection-making between codes across *Thinklets*, models were generated using the unit variable "Order," which groups data into first, second, third, and fourth or more *Thinklet* participation. This unit was also subset by participants' *Thinklet* ID. Conversations were again segmented by *Thinklet* ID, and a whole conversation stanza window was applied. For both sets of networks, goodness of fit was assessed, and Mann-Whitney tests were calculated to assess statistically significant differences between groups. Figures and interpretive descriptions are provided in the following section to examine how learners using CueThink engaged in self-regulated learning practices, which offers insight into SRL behavioral patterns in relation to math problem-solving performance.

4   Results and Discussion

4.1 Group by Low and High Performing

As we evaluate the networks based on correctness, we found that four nodes are connected loosely generally, and data transformation and contextual representation are always closely associated in both networks. To detect the difference between groups as low performing and high performing based on the overall rate of correctness, we compare two networks along the X-axis. Along the X axis, a two sample t-test assuming unequal

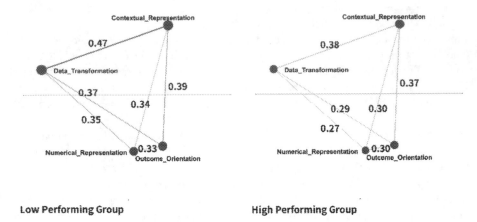

Low Performing Group   **High Performing Group**

Fig. 2. Networks of Low Performers and High Performers

variance showed low performing group (mean $= 0.11$, SD $= 0.26$, N $= 29$) was statistically significantly different from high performing group (mean $= -0.06$, SD $=$
0.44, N $= 51$) at the 0.05 alpha level ($t_{77.96} = -2.24$, p $= 0.03^*$, Cohen's d $= 0.45$).
Observing Fig. 2, there is no extraordinary difference between the two networks if we
conduct Mann Whitney test. However, we find a co-occurrence of data transformation
and contextual representation appears often in both groups, which is more evident in
low-performing group network. Within the network of low performing group, most co-
occurrences of codes are between 0.33 and 0.40, where no specific connection stands out.
When we compare it with high performing group, it shows that lines connected to data
transformation are slightly thicker. We notice that within the network of high performers,
the co-occurrence of contextual representation and outcome orientation (0.37) is stronger
than numerical representation and data transformation (0.27), data transformation and
outcome orientation (0.29), outcome orientation and numerical representation (0.30),
and numerical representation and contextual representation (0.30). The co-occurrence
of contextual representation and outcome orientation stands out more in the high performing group than the low performing group. An example of this would be a student
who goes beyond simply providing the numerical answer to the math problem (outcome orientation) by providing a clarifying contextual representation of a background,
a situation, a character, or a setting. Julia (pseudonym), a student in the high performing group, connected these two codes in the following example: 'I will take the total
from my withdrawals from the bank and add it to the total from my deposits, and my
leftover amount will be my answer (25 + 50).' These results indicate that CueThink
distinguished learners based on their rate of correctness and SRL performance during
the problem-solving process. This can be shown as learners who have a high rate of
correctness focusing heavily on obtaining a numerical answer (outcome orientation), as
well as using contextual details to aid in understanding and solving the problem (contextual representation) within a given situation. Most learners pay attention to contextual

details (contextual representation) and manipulate and transform the given data information within the math problem (data transformation). But when they have the intention or habit of seeing the numerical outcome in the understanding and planning phase, learners tend to improve the correctness of their final answers.

4.2 Group by Familiarity

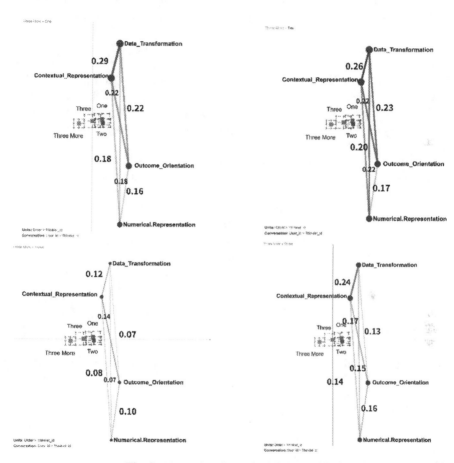

Fig. 3. Networks of Four Levels in Familiarity

To build epistemic networks of familiarity, we grouped Thinklets based on the order they have been generated for each individual. We use *One*, *Two* and *Three* to refer to the Thinklets generated by a learner for the first time, second time, and third time. We use *Four* to refer to the group of 'after-third-Thinklet' conditions, which involves all *Thinklets* generated after the third time. In total, there are 108 items in the *Four* category, 77 in the *One*, 76 in the *Two*, and 65 in the *Three*. Co-occurrences of data transformation and contextual representation show a less and less stable connection from Time 1 to Time

4. As we can observe, the importance of the four codes has been distributed much more evenly in the latter network. However, the diminishing numbers of co-occurrence rates do not simply reflect a failure of self-regulated learning operations to connect in the text. These numbers are impacted by sample format (unit and conversation variables). Every learner at least generates one *Thinklet*, but there are fewer and fewer learners having more than three and four *Thinklets*. The differences in numbers within each network provide more information. The largest number in the first, second, and third networks always represents a strong co-occurrence of contextual representation and data transformation, but there is a decrease in importance compared to other numbers within each network. In contrast, the importance of the association of outcome orientation and contextual representation is stronger from the first to fourth network. Comparing every two-pair of four models, we received results showing significant differences between *One* vs. *Four* (Mdn $= -0.41$, U $= 2525$, p $= 0.00^*$, r $= 0.39$), *Two* vs. *Four* (Mdn $= -0.41$, U $= 2483$, p $= 0.00^*$, r $= 0.40$), and *Three* vs. *Four* (Mdn $= -0.41$, U $= 2701$, p $= 0.01$, r $= 0.23$). In situations where multiple hypotheses get tested, the alpha level will be corrected by Bonferroni approach, that the significant alpha level will be 0.008. In this case, two comparing groups still show significantly differences (Fig. 3).

In summary, network *Four* is mostly different from other three conditions. If we combine datasets of One, Two, and Three together and compared it to Four, along the X-axis a Mann-Whitney test we detected that Thinklets generated after the third time (Mdn $= 0.32$, N $= 45$) were statistically significantly different at the alpha $= 0.05$ level from other conditions (Mdn $= 0.56$, N $= 78$, U $= 926$, p < 0.001, r $= 0.47$). We concluded that as the students get more familiar with the scaffoldings and prompt in the system, they start to use more strategies about outcome orientation. They also consider outcome orientation and contextual representation together much more often in explaining their understandings and problem-solving strategies about the math problem.

5   Conclusion

The findings of this study suggest that researchers can label and measure the connections between various cognitive behaviors with roots in Winne's SMART model. This paper examines how *assembling* and *translating* operations by connecting contextual representation and data transformation could impact the performance of learners as they become more familiar with the learning environment. Additionally, we understand how different aspects or focuses of content can related within the *assembling* operation by connecting contextual representation and outcome orientations. It sheds light on the possibility of deconstructing the unit category in the SMART model to see different patterns.

The innovative approach applied in this paper connects automated detectors of SRL constructs to ENA models based on the textual responses in the learning environment. Epistemic networks can illustrate the co-occurrences of SRL indicators to show a dynamic pattern of SRL behaviors and stress the importance of connections among micro-level SRL operations. Findings offer insights into how math problem-solving languages can reveal and support the intentional SRL process. A range of analyses conducted in this study demonstrated that contextual representation and data transformation are associated with math problem-solving and have been heavily relied on by learners.

Otherwise, students focus more on outcome orientation as they become proficient users of the CueThink platform. When they get familiar with functions and tools embedded in the system and generate more correct answers, we detect more outcome orientation in the text.

It is pertinent to note that there are a limited number of students participating in this study. The future potential of this work is investigating more students and their performances on math problem solving. The current study has limitations in exploring other operations within Winne's [25] SMART model. In the future, we will work on developing more constructs connecting SRL theories and the context of the learning environment. Another challenging problem is how to interpret the connections of our measuring constructs of self-regulated learning within a discourse of teaching and curriculum design. One possible implication is that, in the math problem solving system, we provide suggestions for students about making full use of numbers (numerical representation), building relationships between values and equations (data transformation), and having expectation and estimation about the final answer (outcome orientation). The difference between the two performing groups is not cogent enough to persuade future learners to learn from high-performing group, but it could be a method used for future research. Also, it is a promising direction to consider learner behavioral events and textual responses together in understanding the continuing development of self-regulated learning. It facilitates learning scientists to design more think-aloud activities and foster students to verbalize and visualize their cognitive processes. However, we still have the challenge of making sense of the trajectory nature of log data associated with discourse data when the language is generated based on given prompts and questions. Additionally, instead of only developing codes deductively, we might consider generating codes inductively to better understand special learning environment and learners' personality. It is crucial to frame what is occurring in the internal world of the learner instead of fitting learner words into a pre-structured framework [26]. It argues for the importance of interpreting cultures in discourse rather than straying from textual contexts and relying only on abstract concepts. Overall, this study is an exploratory learning journey, and we will continue to appreciate the power of language in explaining learner behaviors and thoughts.

Acknowledgements. Researchers gratefully acknowledge and appreciate CueThink for the access of data and support. The opinions and conclusions do not reflect the views of the platform or other individuals.

References

1. Cleary, T.J., Chen, P.P.: Self-regulation, motivation, and math achievement in middle school: variations across grade level and math context. J. Sch. Psychol. **47**(5), 291–341 (2009)
2. Nota, L., Soresi, S., Zimmerman, B.J.: Self-regulation and academic achievement and resilience: a longitudinal study. Int. J. Educ. Res. **41**(3), 198–215 (2004)
3. Zimmerman, B.J.: Self-regulated learning and academic achievement: an overview. Educ. Psychol. **25**(1), 3–17 (1990)

4. Molenaar, I., Chiu, M.M.: Dissecting sequences of regulation and cognition: statistical discourse analysis of primary school children's collaborative learning. Metacogn. Learn. **9**(2), 137–160 (2013). https://doi.org/10.1007/s11409-013-9105-8
5. Winne, P.H., Baker, R.S.: The potentials of educational data mining for researching metacognition, motivation and self-regulated learning. J. Educ. Data Min. **5**(1), 1–8 (2013)
6. Azevedo, R., Moos, D.C., Johnson, A.M., Chauncey, A.D.: Measuring cognitive and metacognitive regulatory processes during hypermedia learning: Issues and challenges. Educ. Psychol. **45**(4), 210–223 (2010)
7. Winne, P.H.: Improving measurements of self-regulated learning. Educ. Psychol. **45**(4), 267–276 (2010)
8. Paquette, L., Grant, T., Zhang, Y., Biswas, G., Baker, R.: Using epistemic networks to analyze self-regulated learning in an open-ended problem-solving environment. In: Ruis, A.R., Lee, S.B. (eds.) ICQE 2021. CCIS, vol. 1312, pp. 185–201. Springer, Cham (2021). https://doi.org/10.1007/978-3-030-67788-6_13
9. Gamage, D., Perera, I., Fernando, S.: Exploring MOOC user behaviors beyond platforms. Int. J. Emerg. Technol. Learn. **15**(8), 161–179 (2020)
10. Saint, J., Gasevic, D., Matcha, W., Uzir, N.A.A., Pardo, A.: Combining analytic methods to unlock sequential and temporal patterns of self-regulated learning. In: Proceedings of the Tenth International Conference on Learning Analytics & Knowledge, pp. 402–411 (2020)
11. Wu, L., Liu, Q., Mao, G., Zhang, S.: Using epistemic network analysis and self-reported reflections to explore students' metacognition differences in collaborative learning. Learn. Individ. Differ. **82**, 101913 (2020)
12. van Halema, N., Van Klaveren, C., Drachsler, H., Schmitz, M., Cornelisz, I.: Tracking patterns in self-regulated learning using students' self-reports and online trace data. Frontline Learn. Res. **8**(3), 140–163 (2020)
13. Shaffer, D.W.: Quantitative Ethnography. Cathcart Press, Madison (2017)
14. Aleven, V., Roll, I., McLaren, B.M., Koedinger, K.R.: Help helps, but only so much: research on help seeking with intelligent tutoring systems. Int. J. Artif. Intell. Educ. **26**, 205–223 (2016)
15. Biswas, G., Jeong, H., Kinnebrew, J.S., Sulcer, B., Roscoe, R.O.D.: Measuring self-regulated learning skills through social interactions in a teachable agent environment. Res. Pract. Technol. Enhanc. Learn. **5**(2), 123–152 (2010)
16. Segedy, J.R., Kinnebrew, J.S., Biswas, G.: Using coherence analysis to characterize self-regulated learning behaviors in open-ended learning environments. J. Learn. Anal. **2**(1), 13–48 (2015)
17. Ridgley, L.M., DaVia Rubenstein, L., Callan, G.L.: Gifted underachievement within a self-regulated learning framework: proposing a task-dependent model to guide early identification and intervention. Psychol. Sch. **57**(9), 1365–1384 (2020)
18. Zimmerman, B. J., Campillo, M.: Motivating self-regulated problem solvers. In: The Psychology of Problem Solving, pp. 233–262 (2003)
19. Winne, P. H.: Learning analytics for self-regulated learning. In: Handbook of Learning Analytics, pp. 241–249 (2017)
20. Winne, P.H., Hadwin, A.F.: Studying as self-regulated learning. In: Hacker, D.J., Dunlosky, J., Graesser, A.C. (eds.) Metacognition in Educational Theory and Practice, p. 277–304. Erlbaum, Hillsdale (1998)
21. Ahmad Uzir, N.A., Gašević, D., Matcha, W., Jovanović, J., Pardo, A.: Analytics of time management strategies in a flipped classroom. J. Comput. Assist. Learn. **36**(1), 70–88 (2020)
22. Zhang, J., et al.: In: 15th International Conference on Educational Data Mining. Detecting SMART Model Cognitive Operations in Mathematical Problem-Solving Process (2022)
23. Weston, C., Gandell, T., Beauchamp, J., McAlpine, L., Wiseman, C., Beauchamp, C.: Analyzing interview data: the development and evolution of a coding system. Qual. Sociol. **24**(3), 381–400 (2001)

24. Winne, P. H.: Cognition and metacognition within self-regulated learning. In: Handbook of Self-Regulation of Learning Performance, pp. 36–48 (2018)
25. Winne, P.H.: Experimenting to bootstrap self-regulated learning. J. Educ. Psychol. **89**(3), 397 (1997)
26. Hammer, D., Elby, A., Scherr, R.E., Redish, E.F.: Resources, framing, and transfer. In: Transfer of Learning From a Modern Multidisciplinary Perspective, vol. 89 (2005)
27. Shaffer, D.W., Collier, W., Ruis, A.R.: A tutorial on epistemic network analysis: analyzing the structure of connections in cognitive, social, and interaction data. J. Learn. Anal. **3**(3), 9–24 (2016)

Applications in Interdisciplinary Contexts

Change the Museum: Examining Social Media Posts on Museum Workplace Experiences to Support Justice, Equity, Diversity and Inclusion (JEDI) Efforts

Danielle P. Espino[1]([✉]) [iD], Bryan C. Keene[2], and Payten Werbowsky[3]

[1] Pepperdine University, Malibu, CA 90263, USA
danielle.espino@pepperdine.edu
[2] Riverside City College, Riverside, CA 92507, USA
bryan.keene@rcc.edu
[3] University of Wisconsin-Madison, Madison, WI 53706, USA

Abstract. This study examines experiences in the museum workplace shared by the Change the Museum Instagram account from June–December 2020. These posts were recorded and subsequently hand coded, then put into an Epistemic Network Analysis (ENA) model. Networks were analyzed by month and by construct, in this case looking specifically at BIPOC. Results showed a statistically significant difference between the months of June and December. Main constructs for June were Microaggression, Ignorance, and Senior (Leadership), compared to December with Employment and Wages. For BIPOC networks, the strongest connections throughout all months were linked to White, including Employment and Wages, Senior (Leadership), Microaggression, and Peers/Colleagues. Using these results can help inform meaningful change within museum culture.

Keywords: Museums · Workplace · Diversity · Racism · Microaggressions · Policy Change · Social Media

1 Introduction

The 2020 summer of racial reckoning was a wakeup call for museums and the cultural sector. As a response to the May 25th murder of George Floyd and numerous additional murders of individuals who are Black, Indigenous, or People of Color (BIPOC) earlier in the year, many institutions issued statements of outrage and a commitment to the values of inclusion, diversity, equity, and accessibility (IDEA, also abbreviated as JEDI by substituting justice for accessibility) [1, 24]. It is in this context that the Instagram account Change the Museum (@changethemuseum) emerged on June 16 with the goal of "pressuring US museums to move beyond lip service proclamations of anti-racist missions by amplifying anonymously-shared, crowdsourced tales of unchecked racism" [19]. Stories are generated by anonymous submissions through a Google Form. Anonymity is necessary for highlighting the concerns in a safe space, as retaliation is a real consequence noted by many of the submissions. As of May 2022, Change the Museum boasts over 51K followers, 844 posts, and has tagged over 100 institutions. This dataset includes first-person testimonies and observed accounts of experiences happening in the moment, in the past (sometimes triggered by present posts), or as ongoing issues. An analysis of the account's first six months provides actionable steps museums can take to bridge or repair equity gaps. To date, studies on museums and the plans that these institutions issue are often limited to bar graphs or pie charts about demographics [5]. They effectively miss the human-centered components necessary for understanding the impact of existing structural inequities and neglect to see that the solutions are most often in the anecdotal-experiential data in free response fields [7]. Change the Museum is the *Dear White People* (Netflix, 2017–2021) of the museum industry: a field-wide call for long-overdue JEDI actions.

Throughout the first year of sharing stories of collective professional trauma, the world contended with high mortality related to COVID-19, as well as the related furloughs, loss of work, layoffs, and continued unionizing efforts. People of color have long been most affected by structural inequities, which were only exacerbated during the period of closures [7, 10]. Despite the fact that many organizations issued statements about the death of George Floyd and gradually proposed plans for IDEA/JEDI efforts, few have been transparent about the amount of funds dedicated to this work [22]. To add further pressure on these matters, Change the Museum frequently shares stories from several other accounts, including @artandmuseumtransparency (for salaries), @changetheboard, @changethemuseumaunz (for content specific to Australia and New Zealand); @museumworkersspeak, @salarytransparency, @show_the_boardroom and museum unionizing efforts (in Philadelphia, San Francisco, and Chicago, for example).

The call for changing museums is not new. The historical and fundamental hierarchies in museums and their collections typically privilege and cater to white audiences, respectively, and the institutions enshrine titles and advancement opportunities, especially in senior leadership positions, for white, heterosexual, cisgender men [16, 17]. In 1992, the American Alliance of Museums (AAM) published the report Excellence and Equity: Education and the Public Dimension of Museums, which was built upon the 1984 Commission on Museums for a New Century. These documents outlined the need to involve the entire museum in community engagement with the conviction that, "By making a commitment to equity in public service, museums can be an integral part of the human experience, thus helping to create the sense of inclusive community so often missing in our society" [2]. Twenty years later in 2012, Aletheia Wittman founded the Incluseum as a space, resource, platform, and project for in-person and online dialogue about enacting inclusion in museums [18]. The three years leading up to 2020 alone witnessed several important milestones in redirecting art museums toward this nearly forty-year mission of equity and inclusion, seen in Table 1.

In May 2020 the International Council of Museums (ICOM) issued a communication packet for institutions interested in actionable IDEA initiatives [15]. By summer 2020, LaTanya Autry shared the social justice and museums resource list in Google Docs; the source began as early as 2015 and crowdsourced additional references on social media in the intervening years to the present [9]. This brief timeline reveals that the arts sector has long been aware of the concerns faced by and aspirations of communities and colleagues of color. The references throughout this paper include books, journal articles,

Table 1. Milestones in redirecting art museums towards equity and inclusion.

Year	Milestones
2017	• LaTanya Autry and Mike Murawski began the social media and fundraising campaign #MuseumsAreNotNeutral to signal the vital role museums play in creating social change
	• The Minneapolis Institute of Art became the first museum to create a Center for Empathy and the Visual Arts (CEVA) with an Andrew W. Mellon grant, an initiative that complemented their already-established IDEA efforts
	• AAM hired Nicole Ivy as the director of inclusion, a theme she spoke about during the organization's 2018 annual convening
2018	• Kaywin Feldman was hired as the first female director of the National Gallery of Art in Washington, D.C. and proclaimed a commitment to community engagement
	• The Association of Art Museum Curators (AAMC) annual conference featured the session, "Start Where You Are: Acknowledge Implicit Bias as a First Step Toward More Diverse and Inclusive Museum Initiatives" with Tuliza Fleming and Bryant Marks (Gatherings in the intervening years continued to foreground IDEA discussions)
2019	• Lonnie G. Bunch III became the first Black secretary of the Smithsonian and outlined a plan to tell stories that reflect America's diversity in the various museums under his purview
	• The Arts + All Museums Salary Transparency Google Spreadsheet launched with the goal of exposing inequities in pay based on gender and race
	• A watershed moment was the publication of the AAM report *Facing Change: Insights from the American Alliance of Museums' Diversity, Equity, Accessibility, and Inclusion Working Group*

dissertations, blog posts, and social media campaigns, demonstrating that museum equity work is a continually expanding field of research and is one of the urgent matters of the present.

This study builds upon a previous analysis of Change the Museum posts from June–July 2020 by further examining the power of collective narratives for future policy change decisions [13]. In addition to audiences in the fields of quantitative ethnography and museums, the authors kept students, visitors, and staff from historically marginalized groups in mind. This research affirms that qualitative data of personal testimony is actionable data. Analyzing the posts from June to December 2020 required an intersectional approach. Kimberlé Crenshaw first defined intersectionality in a study about the ways women of color are doubly dealt injustices under the law [11, 12]. The term has expanded as a lens through which we can see where power comes from and where it collides, to see the ways in which oppressive institutions such as racism, sexism, homo- and transphobia, etc. are interconnected and cannot be examined separately from one another. In the museum context, the assessment herein considers the ways people of color (POC) experience racism primarily from white staff through tokenism, microaggressions, discrimination, and harassment. A goal of the study is to examine overall patterns across the stories. Strong connections emerged between POC and white donors and board members, senior leadership, and department heads, and networks were found to exist between these people and issues at times with the themes of inaction and defensiveness. Taken together, institutions and the field of museums are well overdue for meaningful change.

2   Methods

The data examined in this study consisted of posts on the Change the Museum Instagram account from its inception in June 2020–December 2020. A total of 467 posts comprised the dataset, with a breakdown by month seen below in Table 2. Anonymous submissions by museum staff are sent to the Change the Museum Instagram account, whose owners are also anonymous. After July 6, 2020, only first-hand accounts were permitted. While the posts have no formal attribution, the content would often identify certain institutions, locations or members of leadership. For the purposes of this study, the only classifier used on the data was the date posted, as a way to organize a reporting of the data. The text of each entry was extracted and then coded, using constructs developed from a grounded analysis of the data seen in Table 3. Given the rich nature of the data, the process of codebook development was carefully iterated and is outlined in the following section.

Table 2. Number of posts by month.

Month	Number of posts	Month	Number of posts
June 2020	30	October 2020	50
July 2020	171	November 2020	42
August 2020	86	December 2020	27
September 2020	61	Total	467

2.1   Codebook Development

The coding process for this study was foundational to the results and iterative in four phases. Codes are the way meaning is assigned to the constructs and themes to study within a dataset. Generally, codes are theoretical and created in context of the work they are being used in. For example, the definition of collection can just mean a group of items, but within the context of this study, the code for collection means anything involving exhibitions, bilingual labeling, acquisitions, provenance, permanent collections, and funding for collections. Establishing clear and concise definitions for codes is necessary for obtaining meaningful results as well as reliability. The clearer the definition, the less uncertainty is involved when coding the data set [21].

The initial analysis of Change the Museum posts from June-July 2020 compared first-person utterances versus observed occurrences, and it included the following 8 codes:

Race, Gender, Employment, Ignorance, Microaggressions, Positional Influence, Retaliation, and Tokenism [13]. Additional codes were considered but were ultimately masked in order to focus the analysis. These included Invisible, White Fragility, Departure, Institutional Culture, Inaction, and Sexual Orientation. The results of the Epistemic Network Analysis (ENA) models found that stories of personal experiences communicated intimate issues such as retaliation and employment matters (including hiring, advancement, and departure), whereas observed situations commented on ignorance and positional influence of those in leadership [13].

For the additional iterations of the codebook, the researchers applied a hierarchical approach with major themes in the data and multiple sub-theme codes. For example, the theme of parties involved was broken down into positions of power, as well as peers, tour guides/docents, exhibitions, and community. Each of these became individual codes for the second iteration, with the exception of positions of power, which were further divided into donors and board members, paid senior leadership positions, and department heads/supervisors. The team also surveyed the posts for the full first year in order to determine whether concerns for accessibility were expressed, but this potential code did not appear frequently. Using the hierarchical approach helped to identify the themes necessary for examination within the dataset, and then solidified each into specific and concrete codes within each theme. This second iteration included 35 working codes.

After the second codebook was defined, the researchers performed a sample coding of two months. Alterations were made by expanding codes through disaggregation in order to capture the richness and diversity of the posts, while at the same time consolidating others to present the big-picture issues in the posts. The code for Race, for example, now includes a fuller range of utterances: Latinx, Black, White, AAPI, and BIPOC. The code BIPOC was added to capture data that was missing when only coding for specific groups, such as Black or Latinx, since many of the posts did not identify their race specifically. Similarly, it was necessary to take a fuller look at gender – with Male, Female, and Non-Binary – and to also consider the full LGBTQIA2 + spectrum. Based on the responses, more individualized analysis of one aspect of the acronym, such as lesbian or transgender, was not possible for this study (although some utterances included "Latina lesbian" or "Black femmes"). By contrast, the codes for Muslim and Jewish were combined as Religion in order to cover any mention of religion. This decision was necessary because the utterances for each individual code were relatively few, thus the combination had a more significant impact. Other changes were made to add specificity to the definitions. It was also important to add Hurt and Call for Change to the codebook in order to present a snapshot of the harm felt by staff and their hopes for meaningful change. When coding, it is important that a code is decisive; it should be clear by the definition that a code is either present or not. Ambiguity can lead to subjective coding, which can create unreliable coding.

Additional iterations involved further refinement. During the third iteration of the codebook, some categories were found to be ambiguous or underused after coding seven months worth of posts. For example, Bi-Racial was an uncommon code during this time period and was therefore absorbed into the code for BIPOC. Similarly the code for Discrimination had a vague definition and fit better with either Microaggressions or Harassment. This phase also necessitated adding codes for Front-Facing Staff and Hurt.

These additions became the fourth and final iteration, resulting in the current 33 codes (Table 4).

Table 3. Codebook of constructs used in analysis.

Construct	Definition
Male	Directed toward or involves a person/people who are/identified as male
Female	Directed toward or involves a person/people who are/identified as female
LGBTQIA2+	Lesbian, gay, bisexual, transgender, queer, intersex, asexual (sometimes ally), two-spirit, and other gender non-conforming identities or expressions of sexual couplings
Latinx	Directed toward or involves a person/people who are/identified as Latinx
Black	Directed toward or involves a person/people who are/identified as Black
White	Directed toward or involves a person/people who are/identified as White
AAPI	Directed toward or involves a person/people who are/identified as Asian American or Pacific Islander
BIPOC	Directed toward or involves a person/people who are/identified as BIPOC (Black, Indigenous, People of Color), Indigenous/Native American, Brown, non-white, Bi-racial, or unclear intent but historically marginalized group
Religion	Directed toward or involves a person/people who are/identified as a particular religion
Donor, Board Member	Referring to donors, board members, VIPs, stakeholders
Senior (Leadership)	Referring to senior level of leadership, including President, VPs, Directors, "higher-ups," and Chief (C)-suite staff
Department Head, Supervisor	Referring to department heads, supervisors, managers, chief curators
Peers, Colleagues	Referring to peers, colleagues, curators
Tour Guide, Docent	Referring to officially affiliated tour guides, docents, or volunteers
Front Facing	Referring to any front-of-house staff, security, visitor services, custodial, minimum-wage or entry-level position
Collections	Permanent collection, exhibitions, bilingual labeling, acquisitions, provenance, funding or money towards collection
Community	Community, neighborhood, city, region, or visitors

(*continued*)

Table 3. (*continued*)

Construct	Definition
Harassment	Experience of detrimental physical or verbal harassment, includes exploitation, gaslighting, and anything warranting HR intervention
Inaction	No response or action after an incident has been reported or requested
Employment and Wages	Hiring, advancement, recruitment, wage disparity, internships, fellowships, contractors, limited-term staff, career advancement, COVID-19 conditions of employment, unionizing, diversity hires
Tokenism	Referring to instances when an individual is the symbolic representation of diversity; can include instances of fetishization
Microaggression	Commonplace daily verbal, behavioral or environmental slights, whether intentional or unintentional, that communicate hostile, derogatory, or negative attitudes toward stigmatized or culturally marginalized groups; unconscious bias, has some understanding and can include discrimination
Ignorance	Explicit or intentional ignorance on an issue; explicit lack of care/empathy of issue; explicit lack of experience with an issue
Departure	Leaving an organization/institution/field, usually because of the experience at the institution; constructive discharge, leaving when issues were unresolved, or being laid-off
Invisible	Sentiment of not feeling seen or heard, being left out, ignored
Retaliation	Punishing someone for engaging in legally protected activity and/or a fear of retaliation
Defensive	Includes "White fragility"; defensive instincts or reactions (e.g. justifying actions) that a White person experiences when questioned about race or made to consider their own race
Hurt	Sadness, disappointment, hopelessness, despair, exhaustion, pain, regret
Resilience	Appreciation for art and field despite challenges
Call for Change	Explicit suggestion/recommendation on what needs to be addressed
Existing Issues	Acknowledgement of a history within the institution of specific, ongoing issues; calling out institutional culture
Intent for Plan	Intent for IDEA plan/committee etc., but not necessarily follow through; also, the conducting of related IDEA training

Table 4. Example posts with coding.

Codes	Example post
Department Head/Supervisor, Peers/Colleagues, Invisible, Retaliation, Hurt, Intent for Plan	Our museum has recently determined that diversity and inclusion are a priority. My colleagues have been drafting "inclusion statements", many of which are uninformed. When I've pointed out problems with wording and use of language, I have been silenced and reprimanded. Then I was asked if I would discuss my concerns with management. I became upset in the meeting. I was told that I should go to counselling
Female, LGBTQIA2+, BIPOC, Department Head/Supervisor, Senior, Inaction, Employment and Wages	The former AVP of Education and Access terrorized staff the entire six-ish years he was on staff—his anger and work thievery was especially palpable for women, LGBT+, and POC staff, who he constantly belittled, often publicly. When brought to HR and the CEO's attention, he consistently received slaps on the wrist and excuses as to why he couldn't be reprimanded more harshly. When he was finally fired due to messing up a relationship with a significant donor and content partner, we had already lost significant great staff members who couldn't take it anymore. The saddest part is that none of us received any kind of remorse or apology from the CEO, who never took responsibility nor accountability for hiring and protecting a terrible hire over long term and high performing staff
Latinx, BIPOC, Department Head/Supervisor, Front Facing, Collections, Inaction, Ignorance	After years of being asked by floor staff to provide more multilingual signage, the Museum debuted a new, hyper-interactive exhibit which included a single section both in English and Spanish. This section also used the Museum's teen outreach program (which is made of primarily of BIPOC kids) as a way to portray the Museum as being racially "woke." Out of the entire exhibit, it was the only bilingual section. It was also a section simulating a bus stop. Latinx floor staff members came to their supervisors to express their anger at the optics of the only section in Spanish featuring BIPOC kids. They were told that the exhibit designer "didn't see why that would be a problem." and "more multilingual signage isn't a priority"
BIPOC, Harassment, Employment and Wages, Call for Change	The fellowship model is a complete scam–it's a way for museums to boost their diversity numbers while exploiting and underpaying BIPOC without providing any pathways for permanent positions. During my time as a fellow, I was underpaid, overworked, and made to feel as though I barely deserved to be there. I had years more experience than some of the new staff who made thousands of dollars more than I did and I was never paid overtime nor given credit for many of the things I spearheaded. Personally, I don't think I'll ever work in museums again. End the exploitative fellowship system once and for all
AAPI, Department Head/Supervisor, Harassment, Microaggression, Ignorance, Departure	I once overheard a security supervisor making fun of Filipino food, calling it "all dog and disgusting goops". I told him my family is Filipino and attempted to tell him about some of my favorite dishes. He laughed over me and said I must be used to eating dog. I reported it to his director—he also laughed and said I needed to "develop a thicker skin" if I wanted to work there. I quit

While there were many constructs to account for with each post, it was important to the researchers to be as thorough as possible. Once the codebook was developed, each entry was independently coded by two researchers, who then met to review agreement on the final coding through a process of social moderation [14].

Analysis of the data involved the use of epistemic network analysis (ENA) to model the connections between the constructs in the data [20]. Each post served as the unit of analysis and the conversations in which connections were limited. A minimum edge weight of .02 and .03, and scaling to 2.3 were applied to enhance the visibility of the most salient connections. First, a model depicting all posts in the dataset (June 2020– December 2020) was generated. Second, models by month were created to examine the data into organized sections, and consider any key events that may have coincided with posts. Lastly, an initial look at models of certain constructs, given constructs in this context could also serve as metadata, was undertaken. The rich data involved does not allow the complete analysis of the third approach to be included in this paper, so only one model is included to illustrate this level of analysis.

3 Results

The resulting ENA network models are seen below. Constructs are depicted by the dots (nodes) and connections by the lines (edges). Thicker edges indicate stronger connections between the constructs, and opposite for thinner edges. All codes were included in the models, with a minimum edge weight applied and unconnected codes not shown, in order to better identify the strongest and most salient connections and constructs within that model. Figure 1 depicts the overall model of all posts in the dataset, from June 2020– December 2020. The x axis is defined by Microaggressions on the left and Employment and Wages on the right. The y axis is defined by Department Heads and Supervisors at the top, and Ignorance and Senior (Leadership) at the bottom.

For the model on the left in Fig. 1, a minimum edge weight of .03 was applied, in order to narrow the model to the strongest connections. The strongest connection involves White and Ignorance (.06), followed by White and Microaggressions, BIPOC and also Ignorance and Senior (Leadership) (.05). However, it is worth noting that the remaining connections are also quite strong (.04). The overall model on the right in Fig. 1 has a minimum edge weight of .02, and the next strongest connected constructs appear. Additional constructs included in the model with a minimum edge weight of .02 include Male, Latinx, AAPI, Black, and Front Facing.

The means and confidence intervals by month are seen in Fig. 2. For June to August, there is a trend to stay towards the left (Microaggressions) and then progressively down (towards Ignorance and Senior (Leadership)). For September to December, the pattern somewhat repeats, but is situated more towards the right (Employment and Wages). Along the X axis, a two sample t test assuming unequal variance showed June (mean = 0.05, SD = 0.23, N = 31 was statistically significantly different at the alpha = 0.05 level from December (mean = -0.12, SD = 0.21, N = 27; t(55.83) = 2.93, p = 0.00, Cohen's d = 0.77).

The networks for each month can be seen in Fig. 3. Strong connections between codes shift over time and each will be briefly outlined here. For June, the strongest connections

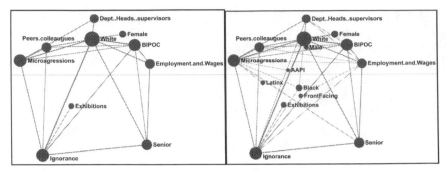

Fig. 1. Overall ENA network models for all posts from June - December 2020, using a minimum edge weight of .03 (left) and .02 (right).

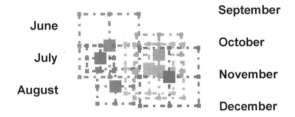

Fig. 2. Confidence intervals and means by month for posts from June–December 2020.

were between Microaggressions and Peers/Colleagues and White and BIPOC, closely followed by Department Heads/supervisors and Microaggressions. In July, Microaggressions and Peers/Colleagues were prominently linked, closely followed by Microaggressions and Ignorance, White and Ignorance, and White and Microaggressions. In August, White and Ignorance, was closely followed by Ignorance and Senior (Leadership). For September, a strong triangle formed between White and BIPOC, Employment and Wages and BIPOC, and White and Employment and Wages. October presented prominent connections between White and Ignorance, while November featured a correspondence between Employment and Wages and Senior (Leadership). In December, a strong network emerged between Peers/Colleagues and Employment and Wages, White and Senior (Leadership), and Employment and Wages and Senior (Leadership).

The network model for BIPOC-related posts from June–December 2020 appears in Fig. 4. The strongest connections (.06) in this network were all linked with White, including White and Employment, Senior (Leadership), Microaggressions, Peers, and Ignorance. The next strongest connections (.05) also involved connections with White, including Department Head, Female, as well as Employment and Wages and Senior (Leadership).

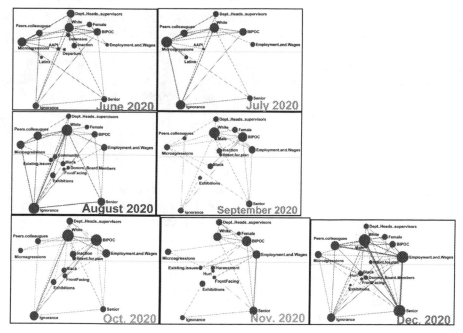

Fig. 3. ENA network models by month for all posts from June–December 2020.

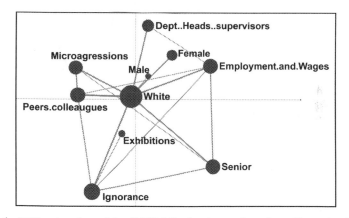

Fig. 4. ENA network models all BIPOC related posts from June–December 2020.

4   Discussion

The network models above help provide a tangible way to examine the rich experiences expressed in these posts. There are several trends to highlight from the models. In looking at the overall model, the strongest connections involve the construct White, notably with Ignorance and Microaggressions. In the breakdown by month, additional strong connections for White are tied to Senior (Leadership) and Employment and Wages. In the network model for the BIPOC construct, the strongest edges all involved connections with White, including White and Employment/Wages, Senior (Leadership), Microaggressions, Peers, and Ignorance. These strong, frequent connections seem to indicate how much the perception of White plays a role in all the constructs it is connected with. For example, with posts raising issues related to employment and salaries, especially in December 2020, the connection with white, senior leadership often arose, and also white department heads/supervisors (though not as mathematically strong as a connection as the Senior (Leadership) construct).

> *I am a woman of color and when I first started my position some of my colleagues and the director of my department were POC. By the time I left, everyone was white. My white manager and white director made the deliberate decision not to renew my contract because they were supposedly looking for someone with more experience (for the job I already had, ha). They actually didn't renew it so they could give it to the administrative assistant, who was essentially the office receptionist (a white woman). She had a personal friendship with the manager and a rumored donor connection.*

> *I'm an immigrant and a writer with 2 degrees. At my interview, after I spoke about my background, the white communications director exclaimed, as if to compliment me, "your English is so good!" I didn't get the job.*

Connections to Female were varied throughout the different models, most often connected to White (as seen in the overall, June, August, September, November, December, and BIPOC models), but also at times to BIPOC (June, September, and inherently BIPOC models). This association is more likely due to the more complicated, nuanced ways females would be involved in the described situation.

> *I have interned at some of the most prestigious museums in Los Angeles, Washington D.C. and San Francisco. All of my supervisors/mentors have been white women. What does that tell you? As a woman of color, I hope to change that experience for the future generation of museum professionals.*

> *We had an excellent pool of applicants for a rare paid fellowship opportunity. Two of three finalists were POC who effectively articulated how the fellowship would be a transformative experience for them. Instead of acting in accordance with our DEI plan, the hiring manager chose the white granddaughter of a wealthy trustee.*

In contrast, strongest connections to Male were much more consistently associated with Senior (Leadership), Inaction, and White, as respectively seen in the September, December, and BIPOC models. The researchers were surprised that more strong connections with Male did not meet the minimum edge weights placed, but note that frequent co-occurrences were observed in the coding process. The node placement of White next to Male also indicates that these constructs tend to have similar patterns of connections other constructs.

Another notably strong connection was between Microaggressions and Ignorance, as seen in the July, August, and September models. Often, the microaggression would occur but with an apparent lack of realization by the white party (or parties) that it was an issue or bothered anyone. This point draws attention to the need for better awareness of microaggressions, perhaps through training and dialogue. While not shown in the models, the researchers often coded Defensive with either Microaggressions or Harassment, associating a need to reason or justify behavior rather than listening to colleagues who are BIPOC, accepting their viewpoints and feedback, and being willing to learn from it. More training and awareness is also needed in how to respond to situations, both for the individuals involved and those observing from the sidelines.

In examining the confidence intervals in Fig. 2, there is a noticeable trend with the posts being more oriented right, towards connecting to Employment and Wages from September - December 2020 which are at many points statistically significant from June, July, and August 2020. Two thoughts could be contributing to this trend. First, perhaps the September - December 2020 posts were somewhat informed by previous posts, while also bringing up additional issues that had not been previously raised. Second, the timing of events happening in the museum industry related to employment may have contributed to a greater sensitivity around the topic, and in turn, raising posts related to it.

Several factors impacted museum staff in the second half of 2020, including loss of work, furloughing, layoffs, and a return to work in uncertain times during the continued pandemic. An AAM survey of the national impact of COVID-19 on US museums revealed that 71% of the 850 respondents had reopened by November 2020 and 26% envisioned reopening in the first quarter of 2021 (95% confidence at ±3%). Additionally 53% of the responding institutions had furloughed or laid off staff, especially those in limited-term or contract positions and more specifically 68% of layoffs/furloughs were in front-line positions, 40% in education departments, and 29% in security/facilities/maintenance [5]. Countless media outlets reported on the discriminatory effects of layoffs on staff of color. For example, on 20 March 2020 the Twitter account Art + Museum Transparency began a thread and Google Spreadsheet to document layoffs and furloughing across the sector – threaded replies amounted to ninety-nine by the final post on 5 August [8].

There were several strong connections the researchers anticipated to see in the network models, and while co-occurrences were frequently coded, likely were not as strong as the other connections dominated by Ignorance, White, Senior (Leadership), Microaggressions, Department Heads/Supervisors and Employment and Wages. One such instance was the co-occurrence of Inaction and Intent for Plan, which usually indicated an institution's intent for a step towards IDEA/JEDI related progress, but ultimately did not act on it. There were many instances in which the posters were given a false hope when the institution says they support IDEA/JEDI work, but staff become disappointed when the efforts do not come to fruition.

I work at a museum in Alaska that recently posted a statement on their social media regarding their plan of action related to the BLM movement. While I am delighted they took the time to craft a statement, I have seen little to no action in the actual museum. Recently, we were in collections storage and many shelving units were labeled with racial slurs ("Es*im*") to identify Alaska Native collections. It's time museums not only look to their staff but every aspect of the institution that perpetuates systemic racism.

As mentioned briefly in the introduction, the museum and arts and culture sector responded to the death of George Floyd by issuing statements and some initial plans for IDEA/JEDI efforts. Regarding such institutional statements, feminist and anti-harassment scholar Sara Ahmed writes, "Such speech acts do not do what they say: they do not, as it were, commit a person, organization, or state to an action. Instead, they are nonperformatives" [1, pg. 104]. She further expands that, "...By putting commitments in writing–as commitments that are not followed by other actions– such documents can be used as supportive devices, by exposing gaps between words and deeds" [1, pg.125]. Change the Museum posts for summer 2020 often commented on institutional inaction or the ineffectiveness of such statements.

These observations and interpretations only start to scratch the surface of the data to extract takeaways that can inform actionable steps for institutions. ENA allows the ability to examine rich qualitative data, such as these posts, in many different ways, but only if institutions and the field are genuinely open to ways to improve and make steps towards becoming more inclusive settings.

4.1 Future Study and Opportunities for Refinement

The dataset is extremely rich, leaving the possibility for various future studies. One approach would be to look at specific groups individually. Whereas this study primarily examined BIPOC as a category, future iterations could examine any of the other code groups, including Black, Latinx, or AAPI, or alternatively Senior (Leadership), Donors/Board Members, and Microaggressions. Analyzing the connected networks between constructs is another promising possibility. For example, assessing how the network of Employment looks when factoring in BIPOC, White, or Women and BIPOC together. Additionally, there is potential to examine the data by institution or region. On June 21, 2021, Change the Museum shared the number of posts by institution, with the most frequently appearing including: Getty (55), MFA Houston (28), Met Museum (24), the Whitney Museum (18). Studying posts about these museums in relation to the IDEA plans or goals that each has issued would have a strong impact on the industry and field of museum studies. Coding the individual plans provides another important angle for addressing the needs of this cultural sector.

The present study can be refined in various future studies. The division of time into months, for example, is subjective since many posts describe experiences that occurred outside of the month in which they were posted. An individual who submitted their story about a past memory or a museum's problematic history did not necessarily align with the month in which the post appeared, unless perhaps as a result of being triggered by previous posts on the account. Additionally, the owner(s) of the Instagram account is (are) anonymous and their posting process is unclear. There could potentially be a post selection or filtration process. Also due to this anonymity, it is unclear why there has been an apparent decline in posts in later months. Possible explanations are that the account owner(s) became worn out and participated in the account less, people shared less submissions, or that a more stringent review process was implemented or institutions may have asked the owner(s) to refrain from posting. It is unclear which explanation or combination of explanations led to the reduction in posts. Each of these areas can be investigated in further research.

In sum, there are several key takeaways for those in the fields of QE and museums. First, qualitative data is actionable data. ENA provides a model for examining datasets that might otherwise be overlooked or dismissed as anecdotal. Collectively, this data reveals connections between shared concerns of a community, such as staff who are BIPOC. Second, as a platform, Change the Museums offers a safe space for sharing experiences of racism, harassment, and discrimination that is not available on an institutional level. The harsh reality is that those who speak up will be targeted, or as Sara Ahmed notes, those who pose a problem often become a problem for institutions unwilling to change [1]. Third, museums have a responsibility to their communities onsite and online, including paying attention to discourses about justice and equity in these venues. Fourth, by considering the strong networks of connections between BIPOC staff experiences of microaggressions from and ignorance of white senior leadership, donors, and board members, this study asserts the following: Those in positions of influence are responsible for and key to bringing about change by creating safe spaces for staff of color that may require a combination of listening carefully without defensiveness to experiences of hurt, trauma, ambition, and joy; acknowledging and apologizing for the historic structural inequities in museums as an ongoing process of healing; together with charting clear, time-based action steps that ensure implicit bias trainings and cultural competency surveys or seminars are more than performative gestures. Listening to and empowering voices, instead of responding in defensiveness or fear to experiences of microaggression and discrimination such as those shared in Change the Museum, can provide a more informed, authentic roadmap for the very change needed in museums.

Acknowledgements. As part of the ongoing process of this work, Danielle and Bryan presented the initial dataset and ideas for future research at an ICQE webinar in April 2022. There, several individuals offered insights that have helped shape this study: We especially thank Mariah Knowles for reminding us to consider Eve Tuck's call to move beyond damage narratives to consider hurt alongside aspirations, joy, and calls for change. We also thank meixi for reminding us of the power of disaggregated data, so that the diversity of stories remains rich and unflattened, and that this approach can also better demonstrate the intersectional connections between utterances. Andrew Ruis encouraged us to share the richness of the personal experiences as part of the interpretation, and David Shaffer suggested the potential for thinking about emancipatory QE as a way to present the data in a way that motivates policy change. In Brendan Eagan's words, this data can speak webs to power (using a heartfelt Spider-Man reference about great data requiring great responsibility). Jaeyoon Choi also posed the important question, "Can QE help question power dynamics between racism/bias and the research methods themselves?" We are still reflecting upon that query as we move forward.

References

1. Ahmed, S.: The Nonperformativity of Antiracism. Meridians Feminism Race Transnationalism (7/1), 104–126 (2006)
2. American Alliance of Museums: Excellence and Equity: Education and the Public Dimension of Museums (2008). http://ww2.aam-us.org/docs/default-source/resource-library/excellence-and-equity.pdf
3. American Alliance of Museums: Facing Change: Insights from the American Alliance of Museums' Diversity, Equity, Accessibility, and Inclusion Working Group (2018). https://www.aam-us.org/wp-content/uploads/2018/04/AAM-DEAI-Working-Group-Full-Report-2018.pdf

4. American Alliance of Museums: Racial Equity and Inclusion Plan Primer (2020). https://www.aam-us.org/2020/06/11/equity-and-inclusion-plan-primer/
5. American Alliance of Museums: National Snapshot of COVID-19 Impact on United States Museums, November 2020. https://www.aam-us.org/wp-content/uploads/2020/11/AAMCOVID-19SnapshotSurvey-1.pdf
6. The Andrew W. Mellon Foundation: Art Museum Staff Demographic Survey (2015). https://mellon.org/media/filer_public/ba/99/ba99e53a-48d5-4038-80e1-66f9ba1c020e/awmf_museum_diversity_report_aamd_7-28-15.pdf
7. The Andrew W. Mellon Foundation: Case Studies in Museum Diversity (2018). https://mellon.org/news-blog/articles/case-studies-museum-diversity/
8. Art + Museum Transparency. (2020). Museum Staff Impact of COVID19 (Google Spreadsheet). https://docs.google.com/spreadsheets/d/1acEaRssONaAlFjThEFybfhBBIb3OIuOne-NHsghOMxg/edit
9. Autry, L.T.: Social Justice & Museums Resource List (2020). https://docs.google.com/document/d/1PyqPVslEPiq0Twnn4YYVXopk3q426J95nISRxvkQI_Q/edit
10. Cohen, A.: Emerging from Crisis. American Alliance of Museums (2020). https://www.aam-us.org/2020/11/01/emerging-from-crisis/
11. Crenshaw, C.: Demarginalizing the intersection of race and gender: a black feminist critique of antidiscrimination doctrine, feminist theory and antiracist politics. University of Chicago (1989)
12. Crenshaw, K.: Intersectionality, identity politics, and violence against women of color. Stanford Law Rev. **43**(6), 1241–1299 (1991)
13. Espino, D.P., Keene, B.C.: Change the Museum: Initial Analysis of Social Media Posts Reflecting on Museum Workplace Experiences. In: ICQE21 Supplement, pp. 88–91 (2021)
14. Herrenkohl, L.R., Cornelius, L.: Investigating elementary students' scientific and historical argumentation. J. Learn. Sci. **22**(3), 413–461 (2013)
15. International Council of Museums: Museums for Equality: Diversity and Inclusion – International Museum Day (Communication Kit) (2020). https://imd.icom.museum/wp-content/uploads/sites/54/2020/01/IMD-2020-kit-EN.pdf
16. Murawski, M.: Museums as Agents of Change: A Guide to Becoming a Changemaker. Rowman and Littlefield, Lanham (2021)
17. Olivares,A., Piatak, J.: Exhibiting inclusion: an examination of race, ethnicity, and museum participation. VOLUNTAS (33), 121–133 (2022)
18. Paquet, R.: Cultivating Inclusion in U.S. museums: insights from the incluseum. Ph.D. dissertation, University of Washington (2021)
19. Rami, T.: The Instagram account 'Change the Museum' is doing just that. The Vulture (2020). https://www.vulture.com/2020/07/change-the-museum-instagram.html
20. Shaffer, D.W.: Quantitative Ethnography. Cathart Press, Madison (2017)
21. Shaffer, D.W., Ruis, A.R.: How we code. In: Advances in Quantitative Ethnography, pp. 62–77 (2020)
22. Small, Z.: After a Year of Reckoning, US Museums Promised to Implement Diversity Policies. Workers Are Still Waiting to See What That Means. Artnet news (2021). https://news.artnet.com/art-world/dei-initiatives-museums-1941407

Ukraine War Diaries: Examining Lived Experiences in Kyiv During the 2022 Russian Invasion

Danielle P. Espino[✉] ⓘ, Kristina Lux, Heather Orrantia, Samuel Green, Haille Trimboli, and Seung B. Lee ⓘ

Pepperdine University, Malibu, CA 90263, USA
danielle.espino@pepperdine.edu

Abstract. This study analyzes early episodes of the Ukraine War Diaries podcast to examine the initial lived experiences of those who stayed in Ukraine after Russia's invasion on February 24, 2022. Aspects of Mezirow's transformational learning theory provided a lens to code the data, as it posits various stages of psychological adaptation after a catalyzing crisis. ENA was used to model the discourse patterns of two residents in the city of Kyiv to identify the most relevant connected constructs that emerged. The most prominent connections were between Self-Examination and Relating Discontent to Others, and Relating Discontent to Others with Disorienting Dilemma. Other strong connections were mostly tied to Self-Examination. These thoughts are consistent with realizations that have not shifted towards change and action, which is expected given the invasion is still ongoing at the time of the episodes, with no resolution in sight. This analysis seeks to document initial experiences of those living in Ukraine through the Russian invasion.

Keywords: Ukraine · war in Ukraine · Russian invasion · reflections · Ukrainian war diaries · podcast · crisis · lived experiences

1 Introduction

In times of crisis, individuals' perceptions and realities can be profoundly affected [2]. Affected individuals often subsume, process, and act on feelings differently than during a non-crisis time. For example, individuals may adjust their communication responses by holding on to current belief systems in an attempt to navigate within new systems and new ways of life [11]. This study seeks to examine how individuals reflect on crisis situations, specifically times of war conflict, through the lens of transformational learning theory, which provides a framework for life adaptation after experiencing crisis.

1.1 Transformational Learning Theory

Mezirow (1997) argues that an individual generally subscribes to a particular view of the world grounded on a set of paradigmatic assumptions derived from the individual's life

C. Damşa and A. Barany (Eds.): ICQE 2022, CCIS 1785, pp. 347–358, 2023.
https://doi.org/10.1007/978-3-031-31726-2_24

experience, upbringing, education, and culture. Mezirow claimed that many individuals often have difficulty shifting or changing their worldviews because their habits are often constructed by unconscious frames of reference and argues that an individual's world-view can become so ingrained, it generally takes crisis, a life altering event, or prevailing human catalyst to disrupt their way of thinking. Underpinned by psychoanalytic theory [1] and critical social theory [7], Mezirow's transformational learning theory is defined as a complex and comprehensive description of how an individual validates, construes, and reformulates an experience. While an individual navigates and reformulates their thinking, new and meaningful cognitive schemes begin to develop through this process of transformative learning.

Transformational learning is generally initiated by either a slow and progressive issue or a sudden and massive crisis. During this catalyst, an individual often realizes a transformation is necessary, requiring deep examination and personal reflection in hopes of creating a new improved experience. Finally, an individual seeks to try out their new behaviors and perspectives while integrating them into a new worldview, dictating future behaviors.

The transformational learning process is further elucidated over ten phases. Building upon each other, the first phase of disorienting dilemma can occur gradually over time or all at once when an individual experiences times of crisis. A disorienting dilemma is seen as a disconnect between an individual's meaning structure and their environment. While engaged in a disorienting dilemma, individuals often challenge preexisting emotional reactions, beliefs, and attitudes requiring them to enter into phase two, otherwise known as self-examination. Self-examination is defined as critical assessment of an individual's current sociocultural or epistemic assumptions. Times of self-examination and self-testing bring about questions to the individual mapping back onto the disorienting dilemma. In phase three, critical assessment requires evaluation or validation of past assumptions, necessitating the individual to remove any biased perspectives.

During this time of assessment and examination, an individual often recognizes that discontent is a shared experience proposing a certain commonality and relatability among individuals. This phase of shared discontent recognizes that many struggle through similar periods of change. Subsequently, the next phase of transformational learning explores new options of behaviors and ideas as they are tested and compared with the compatibility of new relationships, actions, and roles. The next two phases, planning a course of action and acquisition of knowledge, allow for an individual to plot a forward course based on new perspectives and worldviews while acquiring the skills and knowledge necessary for this transformation. Once implemented, the next phase of trying new roles allows an individual to provisionally act on their newly developed skills through experiential or hands-on active learning. As these new roles are tested and new experiences are gained, an individual experiences the phase of confidence building in decision making, leading to the final phase of reintegration and emergence back to a new way of life.

Transformational learning has been frequently used to examine reflections made after life crisis events, such as times of war and refugee experiences [10]. In one study by Magro & Polyzoi examining refugees in Canada and Greece impacted by war, used the theory to discover that earlier stages of transformation were much more long lasting [5].

Mälkki [4] used this theory to analyze the reflections of four women who experienced involuntary childlessness. Participants had a period of time pass from the life crisis so they could expound in more detail. One major finding of the study showed the connection between reflection and sense making: the use of reflection helped the participants draw connections and discuss patterns within their own lives. Also, the more time that passes to come to terms with the trauma of the event, the more critical the reflection will be.

1.2 Examining Reflections During the War in Ukraine

The 2022 war in Ukraine posed yet another major shock to the world, merely two years after the COVID-19 outbreak was declared as a global pandemic. On February 24, 2022, a full-scale invasion of Ukraine was launched by President Vladimir Putin of Russia. Russian forces advanced into parts of Ukraine occupying the north from Belarus advancing towards Kyiv. In response, Ukrainian President Volodymyr Zelensky declared martial law, allowing the military authority to take control over civilian rule. Failing to seize Kyiv, Russian engaged with a more straightforward approach by directly invading Kyiv and Mariupol. With a population of over 40 million, nearly 10 million Ukrainian citizens have fled their homes while four million of these refugees have crossed over to neighboring countries. Often displaced inside Ukraine, another 6.5 million citizens remained behind as they sought to find new ways of life and new norms during this time of crisis.

The study explores the impact of this crisis on two Ukrainians who chose to stay in or near their hometown of Kyiv. Sourced from Sky News podcasts as part of a series titled "Ukraine War Diaries", audio recordings of these Ukrainians were published starting in late March 2022 and continue as of this writing (September 2022). Interviews from two Ukrainians reflecting on their personal experiences were analyzed to examine thought patterns during this crisis. This study exemplifies how Mezirow's transformational learning theory can assist in sense making and decision making process during a disorienting dilemma or times of crisis, such as war, while challenging the validity of an individual's values, assumptions, and worldviews that underpin them.

2 Methods

The data utilized in this study consists of audio diaries recorded by Ukrainian citizens identified by Sky News podcast as part of a series titled "Ukraine War Diaries." The audio diary series started in March 2022, with new episodes being published approximately every 3–5 days as of this writing. For this analysis, episodes from March 2022 to May 2022 were examined. Multiple Ukrainian citizens contribute to the audio diary series and span various life roles such as a daughter, a husband and father, and a CEO. While there are a total of four Ukrainian citizens contributing to the audio diaries, two were selected to be included in this analysis based on their consistency of episodes at approximately 1–2 per week. The other two contributors were excluded due to lack of consistency in uploading new episodes, which took away from providing continuous experiences provided by the two more regular contributors. This ensured a more consistent and equivalent analysis of the war experience through the lens of two Ukrainian citizens.

Furthermore, since the war in Ukraine is still ongoing, any additional episodes published after the researchers extracted data for the analysis were excluded in this study. The final result produced the examination of 16 audio diary episodes from two Ukrainian citizens as represented in Table 1.

Table 1. Podcast diary episodes used in analysis.

Month	Episodes by Ilyas	Episodes by Oksana
March 2022	1 (March 25)	1 (March 30)
April 2022	4 (April 4, 13, 20, 27)	6 (April 1, 6, 11, 15, 22, 29)
May 2022	2 (May 2, 9)	2 (May 6, 11)
Total	7	9

The audio diaries reveal the day-to-day experiences of Ukrainian citizens during the first three months of the war between Ukraine and Russia, and appeared to be recorded in a free-form reflection lasting 3–6 min per episode. Metadata on the participants was limited to what was revealed during the recordings. The Ukrainian citizens provided their first name as part of the diary episodes and spoke to limited personal details throughout their entries. The first Ukrainian citizen analyzed in this study is Ilyas who self-identifies as a husband, father to two children, and an employee of the Information Technology sector. The second Ukrainian citizen analyzed in this study is Oksana who self-identifies as a wife and daughter. In addition to these details, the date of each episode was provided in the title and can be viewed via subscription links on the Sky News Ukraine War Diaries website (https://news.sky.com/story/ukraine-war-diaries-12574741), which will have more episodes beyond those included in this analysis.

Each audio diary was transcribed using an online transcription tool and then reviewed separately by two researchers to verify for accuracy. Researchers made minor adjustments to ensure the final written transcript exactly matched the audio recording and created sentence breaks based on natural pauses in the speakers' utterances. The transcribed utterances were then deductively operationalized based on Mezirow's Transformative Learning Theory (6). Constructs from this theory included Disorienting Dilemma, Self-Examination, Sense of Alienation, Relating Discontent to Others, Explaining Options of New Behavior, Building Confidence in New Ways, Planning a Course of Action, Knowledge to Implement Plans, Experimenting with New Roles, and Reintegration. An additional construct of Reminiscing was added to the codebook to capture a recurring theme in the data of longing for times in the past. The final codebook is represented in Table 2. Each audio diary was coded independently by two raters using the codebook who then came together for a process of social moderation to reach final agreement on the coded data [3].

After the coding process was complete, analysis of the data utilized epistemic network analysis (ENA), an approach in qualitative ethnography to visualize data through

Table 2. Codebook of constructs used in analysis.

Construct	Definition	Examples
Disorienting Dilemma	Being unsure or undecided about thoughts, feelings, or actions; internal conflict. (Current rather than in the past.)	*And I'm not sure whether I'll be able to experience fireworks the same ever again*
Self-Examination	Instance of self-reflection specifically with regard to emotions or feelings	*I'm afraid to become to become full of hate, you know, and and and revenge maybe, but looks like it's not possible to forgive for what they do to us*
Reminiscing	Sense of longing for the past	*They the beautiful spaces that you used to see and you used to enjoy that are no longer there*
Sense of Alienation	Mention of being apart or separated, either physically or mentally/emotionally from others	*He stayed at the house and she told me that he showed the pictures of his family, and he was crying and missing his family*
Relating Discontent to Others	Acknowledgment of conflict, restrictions, negative perceptions. (Current rather than in the past.)	*I'm not sure whether you can hear it, but there is some very loud shooting in the background*
Explaining Options of New Behavior	Describing options for new norms and behavior	*Actually a friend of mine who has lived in Amsterdam for a very long time now, she also reported that she removed all of the Russian music from her playlist*
Building Confidence in New Ways	Expression of hope or faith for future	*I still believe I still have this faith in our forces and I'm pretty sure that we will find our lands back*
Planning a Course of Action	Mention of a logistical plan	*My plan is to see my whole family at some point, maybe in June and maybe a bit later*

(*continued*)

Table 2. (*continued*)

Construct	Definition	Examples
Knowledge to Implement Plans	Process of gaining knowledge for new role, norm, or behavior	*I don't know whether they go to hot cities like Kharkiv or anywhere else like this, but it's quite easy to get a ticket, and there are at least seven different routes from Lviv to Kyiv*
Experimenting with New Roles	Adoption and experimentation of role or responsibility different from norms	*And, you know, like the war basically showed that he is one of the bravest and one of the most sensitive people I have known, actually, like his sensitive side*
Reintegration	Instance of life returning to normal (can be personal or societal reference)	*Kyiv is all right is getting better, and over a million have returned*

statistical methods, to examine the pattern of connections between the codebook constructs. ENA creates a network model of connections among associated constructs by quantifying the frequency that they co-occur within conversations in the data [8]. For this study, a single sentence was defined as the unit of analysis and the separate podcast episodes were defined as the conversations in which the connections were limited. The moving stanza window was set to four (each line plus 3 previous lines) to model the connections among constructs that occurred in recent temporal context [9]. A minimum edge weight of 1.8 was applied in the model to highlight the most salient connections in the data. Researchers initially examined the data across a week-to-week time period, however no clear trend emerged in the ENA model. The researchers hypothesize that this is because the war in Ukraine is ongoing, and therefore, the data suggests that the subjects are still in a constant crisis state. Therefore, the final ENA model examines the data as an aggregate across the entire time period of the included episodes.

3   Results

The resulting ENA network models depict the discourse patterns of the diary entries for Ilyas and Oksana from March–May 2022. For the models below, the nodes indicate the coded constructs coded with the lines representing edges, which show the strength of connections between the constructs within a window size of 4. The thicker the edges, the stronger the connections, in contrast to thinner edges which indicate less connection. Edges were scaled to 2.0. The X axis of the model is defined by Relating Discontent to Others on the left, and Building Confidence in New Ways on the right. The Y axis of the model is defined by Self-Examination at the top and Disorienting Dilemma at the bottom.

The overall discourse pattern of both Ilyas and Oksana are seen in Fig. 1. The strongest connection is between Self-Examination and Relating Discontent to Others, followed by connections between Self-Examination and Disorienting Dilemma, Explaining Options of New Behavior, and Building Confidence in New Ways, and Relating Discontent to Others with Disorienting Dilemma.

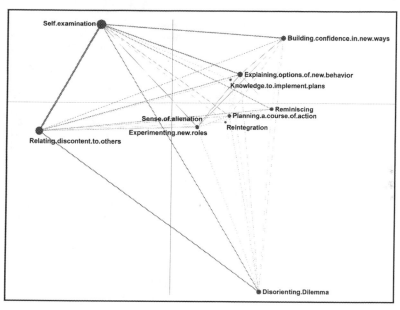

Fig. 1. Overall ENA network model for both Ilyas' and Oksana's entries for the Ukraine War Diaries podcast from March 2022 to early May 2022.

The individual models for Ilyas and Oksana are in Fig. 2. For Ilyas, the strongest connection is between Self-Examination and Relating Discontent to Others, followed by Self-Examination and Planning a Course of Action. For the model for Oksana, the strongest connection is also between Self-Examination and Relating Discontent to Others, but additionally, Self-Examination with Explaining Options of New Behavior and Building Confidence in New Ways, and Relating Discontent to Others and Disorienting Dilemma. It is worth noting that in comparing the two individual network models, both share the strongest connection between Self-Examination and Relating Discontent to Others.

The subtracted network seen in Fig. 3 depicts the differences of the two models. While a two sample t test calculation indicated there was no statistical significance in this difference, the subtracted network shows Oksana having more connected constructs, especially with Self-Examination and Explaining Options of New Behavior, and Relating Discontent to Others and Disorienting Dilemma. In contrast, Ilyas had more of a connection between Self-Examination and Planning a Course of Action.

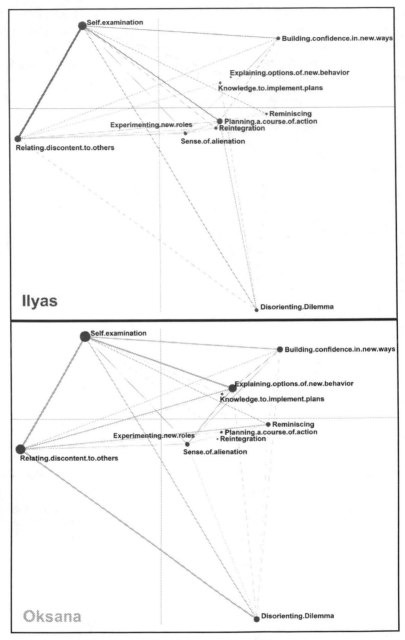

Fig. 2. Individual ENA network models for Ilyas (top) and Oksana (bottom) for their respective episodes for the Ukraine War Diaries podcast from March 2022 to early May 2022.

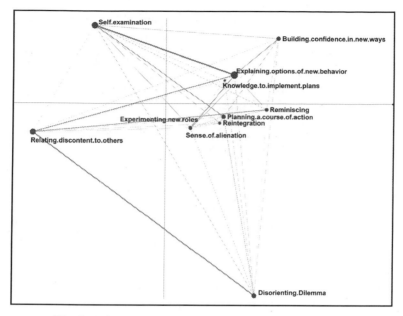

Fig. 3. Subtracted ENA network model for Ilyas and Oksana.

4   Discussion

This examination of almost seven weeks of podcast episodes of the Ukraine War Diaries from late March to early May 2022 gives insight into the lived experiences of two Ukrainians living in the country during the time of the invasion by Russia that began on February 24, 2022, and as of this writing, still continues. The theoretical framework of Transformative Learning by Mezirow provides a lens for the analysis as individuals respond and adapt in times of crisis. This involves a reflection of oneself, shifts in beliefs, which results in behavior changes [6].

In the overall ENA model for entries of the two participants, Ilyas and Oksana, we see the strongest connection between Self-Examination and Relating Discontent to Others. This indicates that a major aspect of the episodes involves the participants reflecting on their emotions related to acknowledging conflict, restrictions, and negative perceptions that surround the situation. The other prominent connections also relate to Self-Examination (notably with Disorienting Dilemma, Explaining Options of New Behavior, and Building Confidence in New Ways), which seems to indicate that for the most part, the participants continue to be focused on the aspect of reflection of themselves during this time of the war. This is not surprising and reinforces the fact that the conflict still continues, so there is limited progression into other thoughts related to Reintegration.

The disaggregation of Ilyas' and Oksana's network models from the overall model seems to indicate that the discourse patterns are similar (there is no statistically significant difference between the two). But examining each model from Fig. 2 closely and the subtracted network in Fig. 3 gives insights on the subtle differences of their reflective thoughts.

4.1 Ilyas

When analyzing the audio diaries created by Ilyas, a strong connection appears between Relating Discontent to Others and Self-Examination. This can be explained by the fact that Ilyas was still in Ukraine during the episode recordings and continued to provide updates on instances of conflict or restrictions in combination with his feelings on these matters as evidenced by the following example:

> We still have horrible deaths of Ukrainian civilians in different cities. And to realize that somewhere in the deaths, a three month old child is dying because of a rocket. How is that to be explained and how is that to be forgiven? I'm afraid to become to become full of hate, you know, and revenge maybe, but looks like it's not possible to forgive for what they do to us.

Throughout the timeframe of his episodes, Ilyas was navigating the difficult decision of how to move forward and create a plan in the midst of this crisis. His wife and children sought refuge in Poland, his mother and grandmother were in a different city in Ukraine, and Ilyas was staying with a friend when the episodes began. With their previous life no longer intact, Ilyas was searching for what the future would hold and how he and his family could move forward together. Throughout his audio diaries, Ilyas discussed many options for both immediate and long-term logistical plans as well as his internal feelings about these options. This correlated theme is demonstrated by the connection between Planning a Course of Action and Self-Examination within the model and evidenced by his discourse:

> I'm staying with my friend and his mother and it's my third place and it's been tiring. I know, of course I know that I'm in a better situation, that many people from other hot cities like Mariupol or Kharkiv, or Chernihiv and I'm in much better conditions. My other thought is about going back to Kiev. We have a really nice apartment in the central part of Kiev. The feelings are mixed.

Constructs that indicate the growth pattern of Transformative Learning Theory, such as Explaining Options of New Behavior, Knowledge to Implement Plans, and Building Confidence in New Ways were not as prominent in Ilyas' utterances, demonstrating that he is still actively in the midst of this crisis experience and may not be able to fully enter a transformative learning state until the crisis is further resolved.

4.2 Oksana

In analyzing the podcast episodes by Oksana, the dominating connection was between self-examination and relating discontent to others. There were several reflections on how the war impacted perspectives to everyday life, motivations, familial and friendship relationships, and awareness of how uniquely different life has become. During Oksana's episodes, there is an arch that occurs throughout her narratives that shows the navigation of life during the early days of the war to a new emerging reality. Oksana's attempts to make meaning of what has occurred in her beloved country and connections to how much her life has changed is reflected in this connection. As a wife and daughter, it appears that she is also interested in how the war has affected them as well.

The emotional stress and trauma caused by the war from Oksana's perspective has forced her to re-examine life prior to the war that has since been destroyed. The next strongest connection, Self-Examination with Explaining Options of New Behavior and Building Confidence in New Ways, highlights Oksana's awareness of how her attitudes, beliefs, and values have changed. During one of the podcast episodes she reveals an inner dilemma on trying to return to normal activities while others affected by the war are not able to. Additionally, she describes how celebrations and other communal behaviors will no longer feel the same for Ukrainians. The struggle to regain the courage to return to social life with her friends and a lifestyle that she was once closely connected to has also been altered. The new behaviors that she notices internally to her mood is opposite of her normal state:

I don't know, I mean, I understand that life goes on for those who have the opportunity to live on, but it just I don't know, it feels weird.

My friends know me as a very optimistic person, and recently I haven't felt this way, and I know, it doesn't feel like me.

Throughout Oksana's episodes, there is evidence of attempting to make meaning from the life-altering events that are happening in real time. She is aware of her life and the lives of others in her worldview that are impacted by the crisis. Her reflections provide a window into how war has the potential to shift dynamics in one's life in a short period of time. Her episodes are an example of how quickly emotional and social constructs can change when facing a life crisis.

4.3 Future Study

Since this study examines published episodes within the late March 2022 - early May 2022 timeline, there are limitations. The crisis situation is still ongoing during the time of the episodes and this writing, so the current analysis can only give a snapshot of the experience. However, the intent of the study was to give insights to and highlight the experience in progress of people in Ukraine, in hopes that a future study might be able to provide a greater longitudinal examination that takes place once the crisis situation has reached somewhat of a resolution. Episodes were likely edited by the publisher, however since the participants continue to record episodes, the study assumes that the participants are satisfied that the episodes adequately portray their thoughts as intended. The study only highlights two participants due to the limitation of the dataset, but because of the shared insights of being in Ukraine and the lack of significant differences between their discourse patterns, the study assumes the episodes conveys a generalized sense of such lived experiences.

The study can also provide insights for how organizations and institutions can integrate trauma-informed practices to their work. The use of social media platforms like podcasts contributes data that can be examined in real time and lead to more immediate responses from transformative leaders. There is also potential for applying transformational learning through critical reflection from less-examined life crises events. This could include examination the impact of previous events, experience of marginalized groups, and other life situations to show similar themes of sense making.

In this study, the use of ENA in this study helped to visualize the progression of thought through the lens of Transformative Learning Theory for Illyas and Oksana in the middle of their experience living in Ukraine during the time of the Russian invasion. On the left side of the model, constructs are oriented towards realization, while the right is more oriented towards action and behavioral adaptation. Since the war in Ukraine is in progress at the time of the last entry examined for this analysis, most of the discourse patterns are consistent with the initial stages of "transformation" and focused on self-examination. Without any resolution in sight, the participants are not able to move from this early stage towards action and reintegration of new beliefs generated from the time of crisis. Only when the war starts to reach its end might start to see shifts towards the right side of the model, reflecting behavioral adaptations and being able to move on.

References

1. Boyd, R.D., Myers, J.G.: Transformative education. Int. J. Lifelong Educ. **7**(4), 261–284 (1988)
2. Capasso, A., et al.: Lessons from the field: Recommendations for gender-based violence prevention and treatment for displaced women in conflict-affected Ukraine. Lancet Reg. Health Eur. (2022)
3. Herrenkohl, L.R., Cornelius, L.: Investigating elementary students' scientific and historical argumentation. J. Learn. Sci. **22**(3), 413–461 (2013)
4. Mälkki, K.: Rethinking disorienting dilemmas within real-life crises: the role of reflection in negotiating emotionally chaotic experiences. Adult Educ. Q. **62**(3), 207–229 (2012). https://doi.org/10.1177/0741713611402047
5. Magro, K., Polyzoi, E.: Geographical and psychological terrains of adults from war-affected backgrounds. J. Transform. Educ. **7**(1), 85–106 (2009)
6. Mezirow, J.: Transformative learning: Theory to practice. New Dir. Adult Continuing Educ. **1997**(74), 5–12 (1997)
7. Scott, S.M.: The grieving soul in the transformation process. New Dir. Adult Continuing Educ. **74**, 41–50 (1997)
8. Shaffer, D.W.: Quantitative Ethnography. Cathcart Press (2017)
9. Siebert-Evenstone, A., Arastoopour Irgens, G., Collier, W., Swiecki, Z., Ruis, A.R., Williamson Shaffer, D.: In search of conversational grain size: modeling semantic structure using moving stanza windows. J. Learn. Anal. **4**(3), 123–139 (2017)
10. Taylor, E.W., Snyder, M.J.: A critical review of research on transformative learning theory, 2006–2010. In: The Handbook of Transformative Learning: Theory, Research, and Practice, pp. 37–55 (2012)
11. Veil, S., Reynolds, B., Sellnow, T.L., Seeger, M.W.: CERC as a theoretical framework for research and practice. Health Promot. Pract. **9**(4_suppl), 26S–34S (2008)

Political Discourse Modeling with Epistemic Network Analysis and Quantitative Ethnography: Rationale and Examples

Eric Hamilton[(✉)] [iD] and Andrew Hurford[iD]

Pepperdine University, Malibu, CA 90263, USA
eric.hamilton@pepperdine.edu, andrewchurford@icloud.com

Abstract. This paper extends an analytic framework for political discourse that takes place over digital social media. First proposed in 2020, the framework applies principles of epistemic frame theory and quantitative ethnography to classify and investigate relationships in political discourse patterns, to situate and visualize broad discourse patterns, and to facilitate ethnographic analysis that incorporates emotion as paramount to explaining these patterns. The paper also reviews the constructs of discursive transactions and emotional grammars to scaffold the framework's explanatory value. This research is meant to use quantitative ethnography and its tools to contribute to a broader dialog on the nature and cost of dysfunctional political discourse patterns, to help researchers articulate both the spiraling nature of dysfunctional political discourse, and the profound damage it inflicts on social goals of fairness, well-being, and prosperity. Commentary threads following political articles from the Washington Post and the Wall Street Journal are modeled with the Epistemic Network Analysis (ENA) software tool to illustrate the viability of a political discourse coding system for the proposed framework.

Keywords: Quantitative ethnography · epistemic network analysis · epistemic frames · political discourse

1 Introduction and Purpose

This paper extends an analytic framework for social media political discourse first proposed [1] at ICQE20. The framework applied principles of epistemic frame theory and quantitative ethnography to investigate and classify political discourse patterns in social media; it incorporated emotion as paramount to explaining dysfunctional patterns and situated appraisal theory [3] and emotion generation as foundational to examining how individuals contribute to increasingly polarized political discourse, especially including acrimonious or hostile discourse. The framework incorporated four major components (Fig. 1), beginning with Epistemic Frame Theory and the use of Epistemic Network Analysis (ENA) [6] to model emotionally charged and distorted conversational threads in political social media. Figure 1 depicts the four components of this analytic framework, which also defined and incorporated two new constructs of discursive transactions and emotional grammars.

© The Author(s), under exclusive license to Springer Nature Switzerland AG 2023
C. Damşa and A. Barany (Eds.): ICQE 2022, CCIS 1785, pp. 359–373, 2023.
https://doi.org/10.1007/978-3-031-31726-2_25

This extension refines the original coding scheme, illustrates its application in two cases, and further develops the underlying rationale for this line of research.

A central thesis of the original framework paper is that, in general terms, individuals actively engaged in social media are evolutionarily unprepared to process the volume and diversity of anger-inciting and anger-escalating messages or signals they process, often responding "in kind" and in ways that foster mistrust and hardened, polarized viewpoints.

Additionally, monetized algorithms purposefully incite new anger and resentment in order to increase viewership [7], and political scholarship has begun to document how public figures use social media to activate anger [8] consistent with popular contemporary assessments of digital social media sites as a "collective outrage factory" [9]. That misinformation bots introduced by hostile interests have such high viewership on Twitter, and historically rank among the most retweeted comments, is another indicator of our national discourse pathology [17–19].

The structure and nature of that pathology arguably should be viewed dispassionately and, this paper argues, scientifically - at a microgenetic level that models how and why contemporary political discourse seems to worsen at every turn. Therapeutically, such reflection can be likened to cognitive-behavioral therapy (CBT) in clinical psychology [10]. CBT is a method of stepping back to recognize, dispassionately examine, and make sense of emotionally charged conflict. Building a science of dysfunctional political discourse analytics may buttress the small but growing number of initiatives (e.g., [11]) seeking more productive and trust-inspiring political discourse. Our framework and this paper seek to contribute to stepping back and helping to clarify dysfunctional discourse dynamics in part by focusing on their emotional dimensions.

Consistent with increased attention in political discourse research, scholarship on political reconciliation in war-torn societies (e.g., Rwanda, South America, or the Middle East) increasingly recognizes that ending conflict involves removing threats to emotional and psychological needs. Nadler and Schnabel ([12, 13], for example, have defined intergroup reconciliation as the process of removing conflict-related emotional barriers that block the way to ending conflict. While widely recognized in political science research, the nature or mechanics of provocation in discourse have not yet been subjected to the type of finely grained analytics possible with ENA. The framework of this paper seeks to employ, investigate, and extend the meaning of the term "emotional grammars".

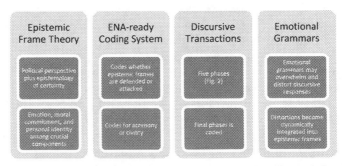

Fig. 1. Four components of proposed model for political discourse analysis [1]

This paper refers to forms of dysfunctional discourse that are self-escalating in hostility. In this context, dysfunctional discourse refers to openly or tacitly hostile conversational threads on social media whose hostility is mainly traceable to the discordance already present in the thread or in the broader discourse it represents. Once a conversation is inflamed with hostility, the underlying issues recede, accounting for a diminishing fraction of the overall conflict. The emotional grammar construct noted in Table 1 delves into and suggests sequences of self-propagating hostility.

The social damage by which such dysfunctionality shapes and distorts the nature of conversation may be far more significant than imagined. It is readily arguable that such dysfunctionality distorts or changes the individuals who engage in it. A difficult to test but likely reasonable conjecture: prolonged engagement in dysfunctional discourse leads many individuals, especially political figures, to morph or gravitate into unappealing versions of their personae, giving added empirical validation and moral certainty to derision and conviction of derision to their adversaries.

2 Epistemic Frame Theory Applied to Political Discourse

Epistemic frame theory [14, 15] has traditionally treated the aggregate structure of an individual's knowledge, skills, and experience, coupled with that person's beliefs and epistemologies, as a unit of analysis (an epistemic frame) [16]. While traditionally treated as personal, i.e., pertaining to individuals, the theory of epistemic frames has been adapted to social groups [17]. An individual's personal epistemic frame is an internal construct that can be modeled by treating discourse patterns as reasonably reliable indicators of that individual's beliefs and epistemologies. Epistemic frames were initially applied to articulate conceptual and belief systems of individuals as they acculturate to learning communities or communities of practice (e.g., [18]).

In practice, epistemic frames are identified relative to specific topics or domains. For example, this paper considers the epistemic frame of an individual's political viewpoints. It is a complex, dynamic, and multifaceted construct. Epistemic frame theory provides language and a means to integrate important considerations underlying political discourse, including how and why individuals build certainty and commitments to political perspectives, justify moral distancing from others, eschew intellectual humility, and treat counterfactuals to political viewpoints as threats to their personal identity [19]. As an object of analysis, an "epistemic commitment" is a subconstruct that refers to guiding beliefs about positions or viewpoints that can spur or hinder academic or professional growth.

Our study applies the epistemic frame construct as a proxy representing individual's political perspective, including their political beliefs, understandings, and epistemic commitments. Under this interpretation, political commentary is considered to express the epistemic commitments of the writer. Such commentary usually seeks to reinforce or defend similar commitments held by others or to convince others of the legitimacy of those commitments. Political discourse in social media can be viewed as a dynamic ecosystem in which individuals express or articulate their epistemic frames, and respond to those of other individuals or groups.

Adapting the epistemic frame construct as a proxy for political perspective enables applying the analytic power of epistemic frame theory to political discourse. Epistemic frame theory naturally leads to epistemic network analysis, or ENA [20–22], to model discourse patterns, the second of two components in Fig. 1. ENA, like any systematic approach to classifying discourse, requires a coding system (Table 2) for classifying discourse patterns. An ENA-ready coding system developed for political discourse also contributes to the QE literature by adding to the growing list of domains that employ the construct.

The word "epistemology," loosely defined as an interpretation or understanding of knowledge, has traditionally been treated as a *cognitive* functionality in ways devoid of reference to affect or emotion. The epistemic frame construct can more holistically treat individual or group dynamics by including affective dimensions. This is consistent with efforts in multiple research communities, especially beginning in the late 20th century, to integrate emotion and cognition. The 1987 founding of the journal *Cognition and Emotion* is a partial metaphor for increasing recognition that these parallel domains serve academic economy but are inseparable in practice.

3   ENA Coding

ENA provides a mathematized means of representing an individual's epistemic frame as a holistic network of beliefs and epistemologies, and particularly, the relationships between them. Relationships between epistemic frames become evident by constructing epistemic network models. The ENA software tool [6, 23] uses discourse transcripts that investigators code according to constructs of interest. Each code represents a node on a network graph; connections between the nodes represent co-occurrences of constructs in discourse segments. A limitation of any effort to apply ENA to political discourse is common to all political discourse analytics: emotion considerations are essential to political discourse analysis, yet emotions are ambiguous to code, especially when converted to the written word or expressed in short social media postings.

3.1   Emotional Grammars

The phenomenon of emotion overwhelming reason is a common part of life. Emotion research in political discourse includes focus on how emotions can overwhelm reason in political discourse (Yu and Lin, 2015), resulting in a combination of what is referred to as emotion exaggeration and cognitive reduction.

The emotional grammar construct serves an emotion-centric analytic framework for political discourse as a sequence of cognitive appraisal of an incoming communication event (e.g., information or commentary) and emotion generation to the message that underpins a response. Emotion science, including Affective Intelligence Theory [24], increasingly treats cognition and emotion either as integrated or different parts of the same mechanism that activate particular neural resources for adapting to external conditions, such as threats [25]. However the relationship is defined, cognition and emotion are no longer treated as meaningfully separate. Appraisal theory originally bridged cognition and emotion [3, 26]. For this framework, emotion can be regarded as a self-regulatory tool that stimulates an adaptive response that cognition modulates [27]. The emotional grammar construct is meant to operationalize this relationship.

Table 1. Six sample emotional grammars (Adapted from [1])

Predicate (the cognitive appraisal of incoming commentary)	→ Emotion generation and preliminary formulation of response
1. *My position (my community's position) on issue A is xyz. These are the reasons it is so. When you do not agree with me, you are disregarding the logic, factual basis, and moral appeal of my position. That is reprehensible*	→ *You are reprehensible*
2. *You have attacked or insulted me; you are hostile to me*	→ *I will be hostile to you.* [2]
3. *You have claimed something about me that is unfair and untrue*	→ *I am going to attack you in return.* [4, 5]
4. *You have claimed something about me or my beliefs that may or may not be true but that puts me in a bad light*	→ *I am going to attack you or divert the discussion to an area where you are vulnerable; I am going to build even more defenses to my position to make me feel better about my position, because if my position is more broadly correct, yours cannot be*
5. *You are intentionally stating that which you know to be false*	→ *You deserve scorn and to be attacked*
6. *You are right or mostly right, but admitting that is too costly*	→ *Divert attention to an area more favorable to defending my point of view*

Table 1, adapted from the original framework paper, proposes a slate of candidate emotional grammars that might be clarified or studied as political discourse components. Some of these are intuitive; each has standing as an "emotion overload" dynamic in interpersonal and emotion research, and can contribute to self-propagating emotional "pile-ups" that take a life of their own in the epistemic frames of the participating individuals. The issue is no longer just the issue, but rather is confounded or eclipsed by the emotional pile up. Efforts by policymakers to resolve issues on merits – the points of public policy consideration – are bound for failure because the causes for disagreement have less to do with underlying political differences than with distortions in the epistemic frames of the policy-makers. Not realizing or fully appreciating this dynamic may leave one doubling down on persuasion to no avail, while concluding that the intransigence of others is empirical validation of their moral deficiency. Once epistemic frames incorporate empirical data that validate or support suspicion or mistrust of others, they become even more challenging to shift, and polarization deepens. But the polarization and moral distancing are not caused by differences on underlying issues as much as by emotionally exaggerated and cognitively reduced discourse patterns [28]. It turns out that efforts to clarify or repair misunderstand can have the opposite effect and deepen polarization.

Table 2. Coded Constructs

Code	Definition
Acrimony	Hostility, anger, nastiness, contempt, scorn, vitriol
Moral Distancing	Distancing oneself from other persons or groups. Creating an "us and them" dichotomy
Cancel	Canceling, shunning, and delegitimizing other persons, groups, or political views. Ostracizing
Sarcasm	Acidic, harsh or bitter derision, ironic
Civic	Focused on community involvement and participation in a democratic society
Civil	Polite, considerate, constructive. Lacking acrimony, derision, or hostility
EF-Held	Promotion of aspects of an epistemic frame; simple assertions with no supporting arguments
EF-Opposed	Assertion against epistemic frames of other persons or groups (e.g., political parties) with no supporting arguments
EF-Held-Justified	EF-Held, with at least one supporting argument
EF-Opposed-Justified	EF-Opposed, with at least one supporting argument

Understanding how discourse deteriorates or cascades downward may help build understanding of the degree to which self-reinforcing conflict surrounding political issues sabotages policymakers personally, our broader polity's capacity to solve problems, and overcome historical wrongs in compassionate, humane, and judicious ways.

4   Research Approach and Methodology

To summarize, this study seeks to apply QE and ENA to building a framework for understanding and eventually contributing to the repair of dysfunctional political discourse. It rests on recent research that has sought to emphasize and define the relationship between emotion and cognition in political discourse, treating appraisal and emotion generation as crucial precursor phases of a discursive transaction (Fig. 2).

Epistemic Network Analysis treats discourse as a proxy or indicator that enables tracing the nature of a political viewpoint, operationalized here as an epistemic frame. The long-term trajectory involves developing more sophisticated and encompassing coding schemes that reflect socioemotional dynamics underlying political discord. Such a trajectory suggests that a significant fraction of the variance in political epistemic frames may be accounted for by factors unrelated to the intellectual merits of held positions or the moral character of the individuals holding those positions.

The vision sought is less related to fostering compromise, but rather more toward fostering clarity concerning the nature of dysfunctional communication patterns, and eventually to greater understanding of how such patterns change the participants of communication.

For this reason, the conceptual tools of quantitative ethnography and ENA may be uniquely well timed for contemporary society. They may help lead to understanding that a large fraction of discord is perceived in parallax manner – that what is perceived is a reflection of an underlying reality situated quite differently from what is perceived. Greater clarity in understanding this parallax is a precursor to relief, reconciliation, and dramatically expanded capacity to address the tremendous challenges that face national and global society.

The ambition to contribute to a science of political discourse analytics that incorporates emotion and integrates it with rationality requires precursor steps of building a coding system and testing it in relatively self-contained discourse settings. An initial coding system in [1] has been revised significantly. This study codes for constructs often seen in political comment threads. Remarks in such threads are typically brief and pointed, but usually include reference to political viewpoints, or what we refer to as epistemic frames. Comments are sometimes acrimonious or angry, sometimes civil, and on rare occasion both. The coding system recognizes the phenomenon of moral distancing, along with a more intense response of individuals asserting not only illegitimacy of others with a differing view but an imperative to curtail their opportunities for income or speech – or canceling.

Coding complexity in discourse is challenging, of course. A realistic coding scheme has only a limited number of slots available. We devoted four slots for references to political viewpoints – whether the individual voiced support for a point of view with no further elaboration (e.g., "We need term limits."); voiced opposition to a political view or antagonism (e.g., "Tax cuts have caused great damage."); voiced support for a point of view with some kind of justification (e.g., "Term limits will enable fresh ideas and prevent long-term corruption"); or opposition to a position with justification (e.g., "Tax cuts prevented greater investment in infrastructure and required borrowing more money).

We included in the coding scheme opportunities not only for recognizing a civil tone in messages, but other conciliatory markers. These might include expressions of gratitude for efforts by a political opponent, expressions of intellectual humility or the possibility of being wrong. Unsurprisingly, while comments were coded for civility, none was coded for gratitude or intellectual humility, two dispositions that dramatically accelerate conflict resolution and reconciliation [29, 30]. Yet these and other attributes are essential tools in micro (e.g., family therapy) and macro (e.g., national reconciliation initiatives) for building trust and the capacity to collaborate in solving problems.

The study used two data sources. One was the comment thread from a Washington Post article on the future of third parties in government. The second was a comment thread from the Wall Street Journal related to the late 2021 maneuverings by both major political parties around the administration's "Build Back Better" plans. A total of 87 comments in convenience samples were coded using social moderation. The intent of the data collection and coding was only peripherally related to making inferences about the particular comment threads. The more significant intent was to test the capacity to build an improved coding system that might help clarify or refine the framework and contribute to a long-term agenda around repairing discourse patterns.

4.1 ENA Codebook and Discourse Selection

Thus, in this study, data takes the form of comment threads in politically oriented social media. ENA assumes that it is possible to systematically identify a set of meaningful features in the data, typically understood as codable constructs; that the data has local structure (conversations); and that an important feature of the data is the way those features connect [31–33]. ENA models the connections between constructs by quantifying when constructs co-occur within conversations. This enables producing a weighted network of co-occurrences and associated visualizations for each unit of analysis in the data. Critically, ENA analyzes all the networks simultaneously, resulting in a set of networks that can be compared visually and statistically.

A fundamental assumption in using ENA is that the structure of connections in the data is central to the data analysis. In other words, ENA is an appropriate technique for any context in which the structure of connections is meaningful. It is thus uniquely useful for modeling political discourse because it can model the relationships between constructs of interest in understanding its deterioration.

4.2 ENA Method

In this study, we applied Epistemic Network Analysis [31–33] to our data using the ENA 1.7.0) [34] Web Tool (version 1.7.0) [34]. We defined the units of analysis as all lines of data associated with a single value of Media (Washington Post or Wall Street Journal) subsetted by Utterance. For example, one unit consisted of all the lines associated with Utterance WSJ1.

The ENA algorithm uses a moving window to construct a network model for each line in the data, showing how codes in the current line are connected to codes that occur within the recent temporal context [35] defined as 4 lines (each line plus the 3 previous lines) within a given conversation. The resulting networks are aggregated for all lines for each unit of analysis in the model. In this model, we aggregated networks using a binary summation in which the networks for a given line reflect the presence or absence of the co-occurrence of each pair of codes.

Our ENA model included the codes appearing in Table 2. We defined conversations as all lines of data associated with a single value of Utterance. For example, one conversation consisted of all the lines associated with Utterance and WSJ1.

The ENA model normalized the networks for all units of analysis before they were subjected to a dimensional reduction, which accounts for the fact that different units of analysis may have different amounts of coded lines in the data. For the dimensional reduction, we used a singular value decomposition, which produces orthogonal dimensions that maximize the variance explained by each dimension. (See [32] for a more detailed explanation of the mathematics; see [36, 37] for examples of this kind of analysis.)

Networks were visualized using network graphs where nodes correspond to the codes, and edges reflect the relative frequency of co-occurrence, or connection, between two codes. The result is two coordinated representations for each unit of analysis: (1) a plotted point, which represents the location of that unit's network in the low-dimensional projected space, and (2) a weighted network graph. The positions of the network graph nodes are fixed, and those positions are determined by an optimization routine that minimizes the difference between the plotted points and their corresponding network centroids. Because of this co-registration of network graphs and projected space, the positions of the network graph nodes—and the connections they define—can be used to interpret the dimensions of the projected space and explain the positions of plotted points in the space. Our model had co-registration correlations of 0.9 (Pearson) and 0.87 (Spearman) for the first dimension and co-registration correlations of 0.92 (Pearson) and 0.9 (Spearman) for the second.

ENA can be used to compare units of analysis in terms of their plotted point positions, individual networks, mean plotted point positions, and mean networks, which average the connection weights across individual networks. Networks may also be compared using network difference graphs. These graphs are calculated by subtracting the weight of each connection in one network from the corresponding connections in another.

5 Results

With the intent to illustrate the development and application of a coding scheme that can eventually accommodate complex constructs such as emotional grammars, the two models and their subtraction model do not enable inferences beyond the 87 comments they represent.

5.1 Data Set 1 (Washington Post)

The first of two coded articles appeared in the Washington Post framed the potential role of third-party voting as a process that might neutralize political partisanship. The network model appears in Fig. 2. The premise and framing of the article neither defended nor attacked left or right positions. Its overall tenor was measured and the commentary thread was, in turn, measured and civil. Interestingly, though, the strongest connections between the comments in civil tone still addressed opposing epistemic frames, either by direct assertion (1) or an assertion with an offered justification (2). Opposition to epistemic frames (with (3) and without (4) justification) also yielded the strongest connections to acrimonious tone. Virtually every sarcastic comment merely identified an opposing political viewpoint, but did not elaborate. The psychology of sarcasm is complex, but we know that the practice of sarcasm often serves to stop further comment and it is not surprising that sarcastic comments never included further discussion. No comments were coded with both acrimonious and civil tones, a semantically possible but realistically unlikely combination for a single utterance or stanza.

Thus, the article about third party voting and non-partisanship heavily elicited individuals making negative comments viewpoints of others, whether those comments were made in civil or acrimonious terms. The article elicited lighter connections from commenters who plainly stated their viewpoints (6) with some justifying notes, but virtually no comments from individuals simply asserting their viewpoint with no further justification were encountered.

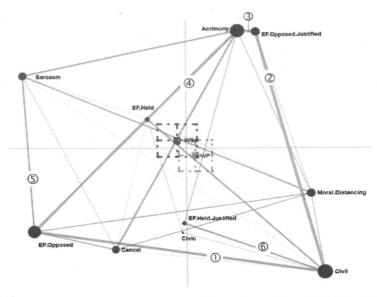

Fig. 2. Comment Thread (n = 44) from Washington Post article on Third-Party Voting

5.2   Data Set 2 (Wall Street Journal)

The second article elicited a much heavier concentration of emotional response. The network model appears in Fig. 3. The Washington Post readership might be considered left or center-left; the Wall Street Journal readers might be considered center-right, and an article that focused on a Democratic administration's signature proposal as it faced intense opposition unsurprisingly elicited significant sarcasm and negative comments about political viewpoints supporting the proposal (1).

Unlike the Post article, there was also significant frequency of instances of sarcastic comments that then provided some added justification for the negativity (2) and expressions of moral distancing. Acrimony, as in the case of the Post article, was the most frequently visible construct. And, like the Post article, this article only lightly elicited comments by which the writer expressed a viewpoint; in each of those cases, the writer provided at least one justification for the viewpoint. There were no comments in the thread by which the writer simply identified their political position. A hypothetical comment supportive of the proposal without further justification might take the form of "This is a Keynesian approach we should adopt." While commenters frequently expressed negative sentiments towards identifiable political viewpoints without further justification in each article, there were no such comments supporting a political viewpoint, unless it was accompanied by at least one justifying statement.

5.3   Subtraction Model

The Post article centered on a less-charged topic (third party voting) than the Wall Street Journal article. The subtraction graph in Fig. 4 is consistent with potential expectations arising from that difference. Comments opposing other political viewpoints were more

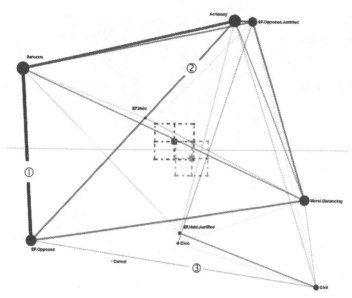

Fig. 3. Comment Thread (n = 43) from Wall Street Journal article on "Build Back Better"

civil. Sarcastic and acrimonious comments addressing opposing political viewpoints (1–2) more commonly occurred in response to the Journal article, as did expressions that could be identified as moral distancing (3). Although the Journal article elicited more outward expressions of acrimony and sarcasm, it did not yield support for delegitimizing or canceling the voice of those holding opposing views, unlike the Post article (4). The two network models though result from a blend of the topic and the readership. Those suggesting "cancellation" in the Post article, for example, primarily suggested that individuals who cast third party ballots in protest of the two-party candidates, or worse, those who refused to vote, should not be entitled to a vote at all. This clarification departs from common discussion around so-called cancel culture, though the construct does apply.

The comparison was not intended to test for statistically significant differences, and indeed, along neither the X (SVD1) nor along the Y (SVD2) axes were differences found. With only 87 utterances between the two publications, this proof of concept is underpowered for a different purpose of claims about statistical significance. Along the X axis, a two sample t test assuming unequal variance showed WSJ (mean = −0.04, SD = 0.28, N = 43 *was not* statistically significantly different at the alpha = 0.05 level from WP (mean = 0.04, SD = 0.24, N = 44; $t(82.21) = -1.41$, p = 0.16, Cohen's d = 0.30). Along the Y-axis, a two sample t test assuming unequal variance showed WSJ (mean = 0.04, SD = 0.24, N = 43 was not statistically significantly different at the alpha = 0.05 level from WP (mean = −0.03, SD = 0.24, N = 44; $t(84.83) = -1.36$, p = 0.18, Cohen's d = 0.29).

However, application of a means rotation that aligns the means along the SVD1 (X) axis alters the values t-test comparisons. That t-test relies on different values originating in the means rotation, producing a different result, this time with a statistically significant difference (p < 0.05) between WP and WSJ. This phenomenon illustrates that a means rotation can partially compensate for underpowering with a new set of comparisons and can make differences not attributable to random variation more visible. Because the comparison in this study was not intended to make conclusions based on tests of statistical significance, however, this point of interest is not central to the study.

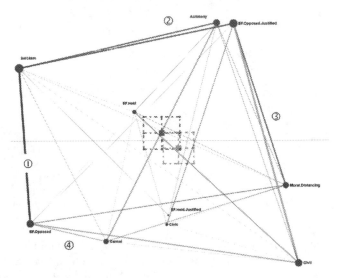

Fig. 4. Subtraction Model

6   Future Directions

This work aims to use QE and ENA to contribute to reshaping and repairing national political discourse. Its prospects for doing so depend in part on whether the ethnography entails descriptions that are explanatory, testable, and may ultimately suggest alternative discourse patterns that are more salubrious than current dominant patterns. Such an ethnography should be able to help explain and visually document how or why polarization is self-intensifying and suggest tractable pathways or norms that restore equilibrium.

That ethnography should be able to articulate the emotional ricochets and escalations that characterize dysfunctional discourse and that can paralyze or reverse our progress as a society. It may help us to understand that convictions that we have of one another, especially those we hold in disdain, may be materially inaccurate. One of the most legendary after-game rants in professional football history came in 2006, after the Phoenix Cardinals lost a game through an epic fourth-quarter collapse to a team – the Chicago Bears – that the Phoenix coach did not believe merited all the esteem with which they were held at the time. The iconic and endlessly replayed scream delivered in that rant – *"They are what we thought they were!"* channeled absolute frustration about correctly sizing up an opposing team's weaknesses but still losing. It may be that in our political discourse, though, we have the opposite problem. It may be that persons or groups we oppose in political discourse are *not* who we think they are, but polarization has so degraded our political personae and has buried us in so much self-reinforcing misperception that efforts to persuade or to progress often result in angry failure – and another round of seemingly but not actually justified polarization and political mistrust.

Tracing these dynamics through discourse coding and an ethnography that relies on constructs such as emotional grammars is meant in part to contribute explanatory power for why our political discourse ecosystem is, in the views of so many, so fundamentally broken and in downward spiral. In that quest for explanations, this effort seeks to justify rethinking discourse patterns and eventually to systematically promote the kinds of repair and healing associated with reconciliation in war-torn societies – without having to experience war first. The goal of building an explanatory ethnography, while seeking equilibrium, is thus not necessarily simply a) to encourage compromise in political discourse, nor b) to diminish full-throated advocacy nor c) to diminish disagreement. Each of these three has crucial roles to play in building a productive, forward-moving, fair, and prosperous civil society. The purpose is *partly* to create better conditions for discourse that enables advocacy, disagreement, and compromise to unfold productively. More fully, it is to create conditions for the deeper and less highly charged inquiry that promotes creativity, exposes and builds on shared aspirations, and fosters more deeply shared connections within the national polity.

Acknowledgements. The authors gratefully acknowledge template language provided by the Wisconsin Center for Education Research for describing statistical results from the study.

References

1. Hamilton, E., Hobbs, W.: Epistemic frames and political discourse modeling. In: Ruis, A.R., Lee, S.B. (eds.) ICQE 2021. CCIS, vol. 1312, pp. 32–46. Springer, Cham (2021). https://doi.org/10.1007/978-3-030-67788-6_3
2. Karadenizova, Z., Dahle, K.-P.: Analyze this! Thematic analysis: hostility, attribution of intent, and interpersonal perception bias. J. Interpersonal Violence, 0886260517739890 (2017)
3. TenHouten, W.D.: Anger, social power, and cognitive appraisal: application of octonionic sociocognitive emotion theory. J. Polit. Power **12**(1), 40–65 (2019)
4. Sanfey, A.G., et al.: The neural basis of economic decision-making in the ultimatum game. Science **300**(5626), 1755–1758 (2003)
5. Dawes, C.T., et al.: Neural basis of egalitarian behavior. Proc. Natl. Acad. Sci. **109**(17), 6479–6483 (2012)
6. Shaffer, D.W., Ruis, A.R.: Epistemic network analysis: a worked example of theory-based learning analytics. In: Handbook of Learning Analytics (2017)
7. Rice, J.: Algorithmic outrage. Comput. Compos. **57**, 102582 (2020)
8. Jacobs, K., Sandberg, L., Spierings, N.: Twitter and Facebook: populists' double-barreled gun? New Media Soc. **22**(4), 611–633 (2020)
9. Hamblin, J.: My Outrage is Better than Your Outrage. Atlantic, vol. 31 (2015)
10. Zettle, R.D., Hayes, S.C.: Rule-governed behavior: a potential theoretical framework for cognitive-behavioral therapy (2016)
11. Jemal, A., Bussey, S., Young, B.: Steps to racial reconciliation: a movement to bridge the racial divide and restore humanity. Soc. Work Christianity **47**(1) (2020)

12. Shnabel, N., et al.: Promoting reconciliation through the satisfaction of the emotional needs of victimized and perpetrating group members: the needs-based model of reconciliation. Pers. Soc. Psychol. Bull. **35**(8), 1021–1030 (2009)

13. Nadler, A., Shnabel, N.: Instrumental and socioemotional paths to intergroup reconciliation and the needs-based model of socioemotional reconciliation. In: The Social Psychology of Intergroup Reconciliation (2008)

14. Shaffer, D.: Epistemic frames for epistemic games. Comput. Educ. **46**(3), 223–234 (2006)

15. Murphy, P.K., et al.: Examining epistemic frames in conceptual change research: implications for learning and instruction. Asia Pac. Educ. Rev. **13**(3), 475–486 (2012)

16. Nash, P., Shaffer, D.W.: Epistemic youth development: Educational games as youth development activities, Vancouver, BC, Canada (2012)

17. Mullen, C.A., et al.: An epistemic frame analysis of neoliberal culture and politics in the US, UK, and the UAE. Interchange **43**(3), 187–228 (2013)

18. Shaffer, D.W.: Epistemic games to improve professional skills and values. Organisation for Economic Cooperation & Development, Paris (2007)

19. Hart, W., et al.: Feeling validated versus being correct: a meta-analysis of selective exposure to information. Psych. Bull. **135**(4), 555 (2009)

20. Shaffer, D.W., et al.: Epistemic network analysis: a prototype for 21st century assessment of learning. Int. J. Learn. Media **1**(1), 1–21 (2009)

21. Wooldridge, A.R., et al.: Quantifying the qualitative with epistemic network analysis: a human factors case study of task-allocation communication in a primary care team. IISE Trans. Healthc. Syst. Eng. **8**(1), 72–82 (2018)

22. Wisconsin Center for Education Research: Epistemic Analytics Website (2022). Software download at http://epistemicnetwork.org

23. Orrill, C.H., Shaffer, D.W.: Exploring connectedness: applying ENA to teacher knowledge. In: International Conference of the Learning Sciences (2012)

24. Brader, T.: The political relevance of emotions: "reassessing" revisited. Polit. Psychol. **32**(2), 337–346 (2011)

25. Gross, J.J., Feldman Barrett, L.: Emotion generation and emotion regulation: one or two depends on your point of view. Emot. Rev. **3**(1), 8–16 (2011)

26. Gratch, J., Marsella, S.: A domain-independent framework for modeling emotion. Cogn. Syst. Res. **5**(4), 269–306 (2004)

27. Zinchenko, A., et al.: Moving towards dynamics: emotional modulation of cognitive and emotional control. Int. J. Psychophysiol. **147**, 193–201 (2020)

28. Luo, J., Yu, R.: Follow the heart or the head? The interactive influence model of emotion and cognition. Front. Psychol. **6**(573) (2015)

29. Zmigrod, L., et al.: The psychological roots of intellectual humility: the role of intelligence and cognitive flexibility. Pers. Individ. Differ. **141**, 200–208 (2019)

30. Xia, L., Kukar-Kinney, M.: Examining the penalty resolution process: building loyalty through gratitude and fairness. J. Serv. Res. **16**(4), 518–532 (2013)

31. Shaffer, D.W.: Quantitative Ethnography. Cathcart Press, Madison (2017)

32. Shaffer, D.W., Collier, W., Ruis, A.R.: A tutorial on epistemic network analysis: analyzing the structure of connections in cognitive, social, and interaction data. J. Learn. Anal. **3**(3), 9–45 (2016)

33. Shaffer, D.W., Ruis, A.R.: Epistemic network analysis: A worked example of theory-based learning analytics. In: Handbook of Learning Analytics (2017)

34. Marquart, C.L., Hinojosa, C., Swiecki, Z., Eagan, B., Shaffer, D.W.: Epistemic Network Analysis (Version 1.7.0) [Software] (2018). http://app.epistemicnetwork.org

35. Siebert-Evenstone, A.L., et al.: In search of conversational grain size: modeling semantic structure using moving stanza windows. J. Learn. Anal. **4**(3), 123–139 (2017)

36. Arastoopour, G., et al.: Epistemic Network Analysis as a tool for engineering design assessment. In: American Society for Engineering Education (2015)
37. Sullivan, S., et al.: Using epistemic network analysis to identify targets for educational interventions in trauma team communication. Surgery **163**(4), 938–943 (2018)

What Makes a Good Answer? Analyzing the Content Structure of Answers to Stack Overflow's Most Popular Question

Luis Morales-Navarro[1][✉][iD] and Amanda Barany[2][✉][iD]

[1] University of Pennsylvania, Philadelphia, PA 19104, USA
luismn@upenn.edu
[2] Drexel University, Philadelphia, PA 19104, USA
amb595@drexel.edu

Abstract. Stack Overflow provides a popular and practical community for software developers to ask and answer questions related to coding. These answers are ranked by users to evaluate their quality. For newcomers, participating in answering questions can be challenging, as they must learn what the expectations for answers in this online community are. In this paper, using epistemic networks, we analyze the content structure of the answers posted to Stack Overflow's most highly ranked question with the goal of understanding characteristics of answers valued by the Stack Overflow community. Network models show that answer content is qualitatively different between high and low ranked answers, with high ranked answers including general explanations and code examples to contextualize question-specific code and explanations. We discuss how these findings could be used to better support and scaffold new participants in crafting their answers.

Keywords: Epistemic Network Analysis · Stack Overflow · Content Structure

1 Introduction

With the increasing need for software development, communities of programmers have organized online to support each other by crowd-sourcing answers to questions and solving problems. These spaces provide new participants with direct access to expert knowledge. Stack Overflow is the most popular technical question-and-answer site on programming available to date, where millions of people seek and provide assistance to each other [15]. It operates as an informal online learning community with software developers sharing and solving programming problems together [9]. On Stack Overflow questions are answered by community members, members comment on the answers to discuss them, and up or down vote them. Answers to a question become part of the repository of discourse for each question, which others use as a resource to solve the problems they encounter when coding. Answers are ranked through a voting system designed to make good content more visible and accessible by displaying high ranked answers first [15]. While studies have looked at how questions are asked [1, 7, 8], the efficiency of

© The Author(s), under exclusive license to Springer Nature Switzerland AG 2023
C. Damşa and A. Barany (Eds.): ICQE 2022, CCIS 1785, pp. 374–387, 2023.
https://doi.org/10.1007/978-3-031-31726-2_26

code shared [23], or the social dynamics of the community [22], less attention has been paid to the structure of answers and how it influences their popularity. Answers are worthy of further study not only because thousands of users consult them, but also because they are one of the most rewarded forms of participation in the community.

Whereas anyone with access to a browser and the internet could join Stack Overflow, research has shown that participating in the community is difficult for newcomers and particularly for women [5, 9, 10]. This is not uncommon in online communities such as this one that operate as affinity spaces—loosely organized socio-cultural spaces where people share practices and a common interest for solving certain kinds of problems [13]. In these spaces, much of the knowledge is tacit, stored in procedures and discursive practices [12]. As such, new participants must learn how to interact with other people and what are the expectations for participating in the space. It is important to make the practices and expectations for participation on Stack Overflow more transparent so that it can be more accessible to newcomers. As part of this effort, research on the content structure of answers to questions on Stack Overflow can be useful to imagine and design scaffoldings that can make the hidden expectations of the community visible in order to support new participants.

This paper reports on the analysis of the content structure of the answers posted to Stack Overflow's most popular question ("Why is processing a sorted array faster than processing an unsorted array?") with the goal of understanding and making transparent the characteristics of high ranked answers. We used epistemic network analysis to compare the structure of high and low ranked answers. The findings address the following research question: What are the similarities and differences in content structure between high and low ranked answers to the most popular question on Stack Overflow? In the discussion section, we offer insights on how these findings could be used to better support and scaffold new participants in crafting their answers.

2 Background

Sites such as Stack Overflow operate as affinity spaces where participants share a common endeavor [11], in this case answering questions and solving problems related to software development. These serve as knowledge repositories that distribute knowledge across participants. From lurkers that observe and upvote answers to experts that edit questions, here new members and experts share a common space. While tacit knowledge is encouraged and honored through participation and interaction in nurturing affinity spaces [13], the structural design and social norms in online affinity spaces often fail to make this explicit to newcomers. For instance, in Stack Overflow, knowledge about how to provide a good answer to a question is not formalized or documented on the site. This kind of implicit knowledge includes what Gee [12] calls "content organization"—that is, how content is designed and organized. In the case of Stack Overflow, since participants themselves generate both questions and answers, there are tacit expectations for what makes an appropriate post. Accessing this tacit knowledge distributed across contributions and in the experiences of experts may not be easily available to newcomers.

On Stack Overflow, it is common for women and new members to report having negative experiences interacting with other members of the community. Ford and colleagues

[10] identified that discursive practices of Stack Overflow, such as how the community welcomes newcomers and provides feedback, create obstacles for new female programmers to participate. Participants in an interview study [10] described fear of contributing to clutter, fear of negative feedback, and onboarding hoops as obstacles for participation. These three obstacles relate to the discursive practices of how the community welcomes newcomers, how it provides feedback and how it deals with duplicate questions or questions already asked. In relation to answers and their ranking, Brooke [5] found that gender determined how answers were scored with contributions of feminine users being undervalued. As Gee and Hayes write [13] affinity spaces can become nurturing by fostering a view where expertise is rooted in the space and not individual participants. This requires making tacit knowledge explicit to make participation more transparent and to support newcomers in learning the expectations and customs of the community.

Most research on Stack Overflow has primarily focused on efficiency, analyzing successful response probabilities, and topics, without considering the discursive practices of formulating answers and the content structure of answers. Novielli and colleagues [17], studied the emotional style of technical questions and its influence on the probability of obtaining a satisfactory answer. Topic modeling has also been used for thematic analysis of the type of questions asked [3] as well as the distribution of questions and answers [24]. Some research on answers has explored how the code shared in answers can be used. Treude and Robillard [23] investigated the reuse of code fragments shared in answers, finding that about half of the code analyzed was not self-explanatory and not necessarily understandable by readers. Nasehi and colleagues [16] also found that explanations accompanying code examples are equally important as the code.

A few studies have investigated what makes a good answer on Stack Overflow. Calefato and colleagues, for instance, [6] argue that several factors contribute to the perception of an answer being "good": the social capital of the author, the timing of the answer and the emotional style of the answer. They found that good answers comply with community standards about length and use code snippets. Early answers tend to be better answers because expert users are the fastest at contributing [2]. At the same time, users with higher site reputation also tend to write high ranked answers [4]. From reader and rater perspective, a study found that readers prefer longer answers because they provide more information, and that good presentation of both code and prose is essential in a good answer [14].

Understanding a process such as answering questions on Stack Overflow requires that users become familiar with affinity space concepts, skills and habits that are related to each other systematically [21]. As such, highly rated answers may display content structures that are valued by the Stack Overflow community and that reflect a desired epistemic frame [19]: the habits, knowledge and skills shared by the community for answering questions. Fewer studies have explored how answers are formulated, what is the structure of the content answers and how the distinct components of answers relate to each other and create meaning. Better understanding how participants communicate and interact with each other could be helpful to comprehend what are the normative practices of the community and what is upvoted as a good contribution.

Epistemic Network Analysis (ENA) can be a particularly helpful method to investigate the content structure of answers on Stack Overflow as it allows for modeling the structure of connections between bits of knowledge and other factors [20]. For instance, Zörgő and colleagues [25] used QE and ENA to analyze the content structure of diabetes support group activity on Facebook coding for both discursive activities (i.e., asking for help, sharing advice) and content shared (i.e., recipes, test results). Building on this analysis, we use ENA to investigate the content structure of Stack Overflow answers. Given that ENA supports the comparison of differences in structure among groups, this method is useful for examining how the content structure of answers varies depending on answer ratings. Consequently, the thick descriptions that can be generated by analyzing quantitative data qualitatively can provide insights into what is the content structure of a good answer according to the community.

3   Methods

3.1   Context and Data Collection

Data was collected from the most popular question on Stack Overflow: "Why is processing a sorted array faster than processing an unsorted array?" This question was first posted on June 27, 2012 and since then has been viewed more than 1.7 million times with a record of 26289 votes. In the question, LHumanRay (all usernames in this paper are pseudonyms) presented two pieces of code in C++, one that processes a sorted array, an indexed collection of values, and an unsorted array. The author then asked why one of the pieces of code is processed faster than the other. Like in any question on Stack Overflow, participants can provide answers, add comments to answers and vote on the answers. The question received 27 answers ranging in popularity from 33864 to 9 votes; these 27 answers had a total of 88 comments as of the time the data was collected. These answers and their respective comments were authored by 69 different participants. In this exploratory study, we focus on this question because it has been recognized by Stack Overflow users as important through user participation and highly rated answers.

Prior to collecting data, the Stack Overflow question was archived using archive.org's Wayback Machine to create a reliable copy of the answers to the question. Following, answers and their comments were sorted by popularity from highest to lowest votes and collected on a spreadsheet. On the spreadsheet, answers, their date posted, number of votes, author, and answer ID were also recorded.

Data was segmented by paragraph to ensure all lines of analysis were of a comparable length. This was important because while some answers were 100 words long, others reached up to 1000 words and included figures and long pieces of code. After segmenting the 28 answers to the question, we had 197 lines. Answer ranks were used to create a variable to divide the data into two categories: high and low ranked answers with 50% of data in one category and 50% of the data in the other. While the difference between answers at the boundary between the groups may not be significant, in this exploratory study the intention is to obtain a general understanding of the differences between the two groups. Future research should look at differences with greater granularity.

3.2   Coding Scheme

We developed a coding scheme after an exploratory chronological reading of the three most popular questions on Stack Overflow and a round of inductive descriptive coding

[18]. From the inductive descriptive coding, several components of answers emerged: general conceptual explanations, Question-specific Explanations, General Code Snippets, Question-specific Code snippets, Advice Based on Previous Experience, Value Judgments, Figures, Authoritative Advice, External Materials, Follow-up Questions and Doubt. Doubt, Follow-up Questions, and Advice Based on Previous Experience were infrequent, and we decided to take them out of the coding scheme. Table 1 displays the final coding scheme and a description for every code.

Table 1. Coding Scheme.

Code	Description	Kappa
General Explanation	Line includes some general explanation of concepts beyond the scope of the question	0.94
Question-specific Explanation	Line includes some conceptual explanation that is related to the question and aims to answer it	0.84
General Code	Line includes some code snippet related to the question that is not a solution or answer including screenshots	0.84
Question-specific Code	Line includes example code that solve/address the question including screenshots	0.79
External Material	Line includes references to external materials that may provide an answer to the question	0.90
Value Judgment	Line includes value judgments (both positive and negative) of the question or other answers	0.85
Figures	Line uses figures including pictures, tables, diagrams to illustrate concepts	1.00
Authoritative Advice	Provides advice without explanation	0.85

3.3 Coding

To begin coding deductively, two graduate-level researchers met, discussed the coding scheme, and applied it together using social moderation to 20 lines of data, coding for presence or absence of the code in each line to develop a common understanding of each inductive code and how it can be applied to the data. Following, each researcher coded 70 lines (35%) of the data independently to check for inter-rater reliability. Finally, the first author coded the remaining data individually. Cohen's kappa was calculated for each code: General Explanation (0.94), Question-specific Explanation (0.84), General Code (0.84), Question-specific Code (0.79), External Material (0.90), Value Judgment (0.85), Figs. (1.00), and Authoritative Advice (0.85). Agreement was strong for all codes except for Question-specific Code, which had moderate agreement.

3.4 Epistemic Network Analysis

After coding, data was uploaded to the Epistemic Network Analysis web tool to model the connections between codes. We chose Answer Id as the conversation variable; all lines of a single answer share an Answer Id assigned by Stack Overflow. While some answers may respond to other answers, usually answers provide new or novel ways of solving the problem posed in the question independently of the content of other answers. As such, Answer Id serves as a useful delimiter for conversations. For this model, we defined the units of analysis as all lines of data associated with a single value of Rank Group (High and Low rated) subset by Answer ID. The ENA algorithm used a moving window to construct a network model for each line in the data, showing how codes in line are connected to codes that occur within the previous 5 lines context [21], within a given answer. The outcome networks were aggregated for all lines for each unit of analysis in the model. Networks were aggregated using a binary summation in which the networks for a given line reflect the presence or absence of the co-occurrence of each pair of codes. Table 2 provides an overview of the parameters used to generate ENA models.

The model normalized the networks for all units of analysis before a dimensional reduction, which accounts for the fact that different units of analysis may have different numbers of coded lines in the data. For the dimensional reduction, it used singular value decomposition, which produces orthogonal dimensions that maximize the variance explained by each dimension (See [20] for a more detailed explanation). A means rotation maximized variance between High and Low rated groups across the x-axis for visual and statistical comparison across the two groups. To assess the goodness of fit of the model, we report Pearson and Spearman correlations. After reviewing the resulting ENA models we returned to the data to close the interpretive loop by writing vignettes that contextualize the findings of the models.

Table 2. Parameters used for generating epistemic network models.

Unit	Rank Group > Answer ID
Conversation	Answer ID
Stanza window size	Moving Stanza, Window Size 5
Codes	General Explanation, Question-specific Explanation, General Code, Question-specific Code, External Material, Value Judgment, Figures, Authoritative Advice
Projection	MR1: 11.0%, SVD2 21.0%

4 Findings

In terms of goodness of fit, the model had co-registration correlations of 0.93 (Pearson) and 0.93 (Spearman) for the first dimension and co-registration correlations of 0.96

(Pearson) and 0.96 (Spearman) for the second. These indicate that there is a strong goodness of fit between the visualizations and the model. Along the X axis (MR1), a Mann-Whitney test showed that high ranked answers (Mdn $= -0.49$, N $= 13$) were statistically significantly different at the alpha $= 0.05$ level from low ranked answers (Mdn $= 0.27$, N $= 14$ U $= 32.50$, p $= 0.00$, r $= 0.64$), which suggests that the patterns of association for high ranked and low ranked answers are different to a degree of statistical significance. In the following paragraphs, we explore how these two groups of answers were qualitatively similar and different by looking at the associations between codes as representative of four key findings to close the interpretative loop.

4.1 General Explanations Matter

The most prominent and central code in the mean networks for both high and low ranked answers was General Explanations, which was strongly connected to at least 7 other codes in each network (see Fig. 1 and 2, we present independent plots instead of a substraction plot to better illustrate the differences in structure), as compared to other code connections. In their answers, users shared General Explanations of concepts beyond the scope of the question to provide context to be able to answer the question. Most answers, 22 out of 28, included General Explanations. For instance, Darkling's answer, the answer with the most votes (33864), provided a detailed explanation of how branch prediction works using a metaphor of a train approaching a railroad junction to illustrate how the processor of a computer works. They wrote:

> I admit it's not the best analogy since the train could just signal the direction with a flag. But in computers, the processor doesn't know which direction a branch will go until the last moment.

Though described as imperfect, the use of the analogy in this case helped to explain a complex process with examples that may be familiar to the reader. This explanation does not directly answer the question "Why is processing a sorted array faster than processing an unsorted array?" but provides the context and information that Darkling uses to address the question later in his answer.

Low ranked answers also included General Explanations demonstrating that General Explanation is a key feature of answers regardless of their ranking. For example, Brain46, whose answer received 18 votes, also provided a General Explanation that situated the answer to the question within the topic of branch prediction. He writes that understanding branch prediction "is important because during the code execution, the machine prefetches several code statements and stores them in the pipeline." These two examples illustrate how General Explanations were used in answering the question.

4.2 Answers Provide Links to Resources Outside of Stack Overflow

For both high ranked and low ranked answers, some of the strongest connections are between General Explanations and External Materials (see Figs. 1 and 2). This highlights how, in answering questions, the Stack Overflow community values explanations that go beyond the scope of the question, provide background knowledge and direct readers to

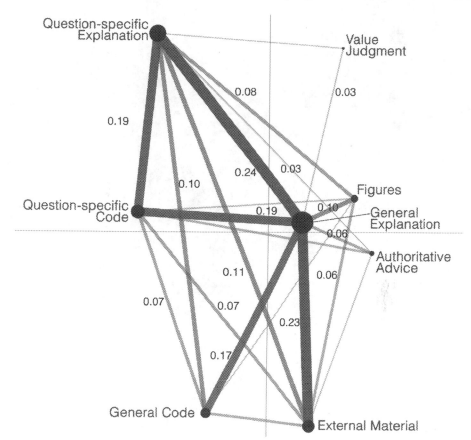

Fig. 1. Mean epistemic network for high ranked answers showing the weighted structure of connections between codes. The thickness of the edges (violet lines connecting dots) indicates the frequency of co-occurrence of each pair of codes, the size of the nodes (gray circles) displays the frequency of the code. (Color figure online)

external materials or resources where they can find more information about the General Explanations. Given that this is prevalent across both groups, providing resources and general explanations are important features of answers that do not determine their raking. For example, Ernest, whose answer received 363 votes, explained how in general branch prediction reduces the amount of time it takes to execute a set of instructions, they also provided a link to for readers to download a "live demo source" that visualizes how branch prediction works by comparing the execution of code with and without branch prediction. Other users such as Mahfuz provided references to their explanations directing readers to academic papers or lecture videos that further explain the issue of branch prediction. Among high ranked answers, the second strongest connection in the means network was between General Explanations and External Materials. Here users like CarlWi explained that pipelining depends on the hardware characteristics of the processor, in the same line

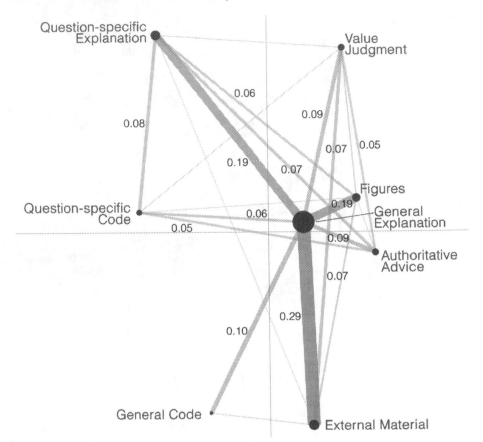

Fig. 2. Mean epistemic network for low ranked answers showing the weighted structure of connections between codes. The thickness of the edges (orange lines connecting dots) indicates the frequency of co-occurrence of each pair of codes, the size of the nodes (gray circles) displays the frequency of the code. (Color figure online)

they added a link to a Wikipedia article on pipelining. Two lines later they also included a link to a book with specific reference to chapters that "explain this in detail."

In the case of high ranked answers external materials were also connected to Question-specific Code, Question-specific Explanations and the use of Figures. At the same time, among low ranked answers external materials were connected to Value Judgments. While these connections were not the strongest, they illustrate how answer authors provide links to external resources and materials to support their question-specific explanations, the code they provide to answer the question and even their value judgments.

4.3   Strong Connections Between General Explanations, General Code, Question-Specific Explanations and Question-Specific Code Characterize High Ranked Answers

The main difference between low ranked answers and high ranked answers is in the connection between General and Question-specific Explanations and their use of code. Each of the four codes (General Explanation, Question-specific Explanation, General Code, and Question-specific Code) are connected to each other in the means network for high ranked answers (see Fig. 1). Indeed, some of the strongest connections in this network are between General Explanation, Question-specific Explanation and Question-specific Code. In contrast, in the low ranked answers network there are no connections between General Code and Question-specific Code and no connections between Question-specific Explanation and General Code. Good answers not only provide General Explanations and links to External Materials. Explanations in high rated answers are highly connected to Question-specific Explanation, use of General Code and Question-specific Code.

When we look at the strength of the connections between the four codes discussed above in both networks, the qualitative differences between high ranked and low ranked questions become more evident. The relationship between Question-specific Code and General Explanation is more than three times stronger in the high ranked network (0.19) than in the low ranked network (0.06). CarlWi, for example, provided a General Explanation of branch prediction linked to Question-specific Code:

> if we look at the code if (data[c] >= 128) sum += data[c]; we can find the meaning of this particular if... Else... Branch is to add something when a condition is satisfied. This type of branch can be easily transformed into a conditional move statement, which would be compiled into a conditional move instruction.

Connecting General Explanations to Question-specific code makes the explanations explicitly relevant to the issue of the question.

The means network for high ranked answers shows a strong connection (0.19) between Question-specific Explanation and Question-specific Code that is more than twice as strong than the same connection (0.08) in the means network for low ranked answers. To illustrate, Hephaestus, in their high-ranked answer, takes individual lines of Question-specific Code and provides Question-specific Explanation of what they do: "then, you can see that the if conditional is constant throughout the execution of the i loop." Here we see the close connection between code use and explanation in how Hephaestus tries to make sure that readers can understand how code works and not just provide a quick answer or a code snippet without explanation.

Similarly, the relationship between General Explanation and General Code is 1.7 times stronger in the high ranked network (0.17) than in the low ranked network (0.10). Mikołaj, for instance, provided a General Explanation:

> Frequently used Boolean operations in C++ produce many branches in the compiled program. If these branches are inside loops and are hard to predict they can slow down execution significantly.

This was followed by General Code snippets that demonstrated how Boolean operations are implemented.

Question-specific Explanation had a slightly stronger (1.2 times stronger) connection to General Explanation among high ranked answers in comparison to low ranked answers. These relationships make explicit how General Explanations address Question-specific issues. Darkling, for instance, after discussing branch prediction in general asked "What can be done?" and provided a brief explanation of how branch prediction can be addressed within the example given in the question. These strong connections between explanations and code among high-ranked answers show that the community values knowledge that provides context when it is well and explicitly connected to the question, its code, and the issues it addresses.

4.4   Strong Connections with Value Judgements and Authoritative Advice Characterize Low Ranked Answers

Value judgements and authoritative advice plays a key role in the low ranked posts network. For instance, while in the high ranked network there is no relationship between Value Judgments and Authoritative Advice, in the lower ranked network these two are connected. User909098's answer provides a good example of how Value Judgments such as "the assumption by other answers that one needs to sort the data is not correct" followed by Authoritative Advice with no explanation "the following code does not sort the entire array, but only 200-element segments of it, and thereby runs the fastest" relate to each other in a low ranked answer. Here there's no justification for the advice given and no explanation behind the value judgment. In the low ranked answers network, Value Judgments has a connection to General Explanation (0.09) that is three times stronger than in high ranked answers (0.03). Inleefyb's answer, which received only 190 votes, includes the following value judgment "the answer to your question is very simple" before a general explanation. We see similar patterns in the relationships between other codes, the connection between General Explanation and Authoritative Advice in low ranked posts (0.9) is 1.5 times stronger than the same relationship in the high ranked posts (0.06) and the connection between Authoritative Advice and Question-specific Explanation is more than two times stronger in the low ranked answers network (0.07) than in the high ranked answers network (0.03).

5   Discussion

From this analysis, we see that high ranked answers to Stack Overflow's most popular question included general explanations that contextualized the issue under discussion and provided access to external resources that readers can consult to learn more. The main determining factors of high ranked answers, however, included making connections between explanations and code—that is, making connections between General Explanations and Question-specific Explanations, General Code and Question-specific Code. Here, authors made the connection between their General Code and Explanations and Question-specific Code and Explanations explicit and made sure to explain how the code shared worked and addressed the question at hand. We also learned that the use of Value Judgments and Authoritative Advice is not appreciated in the community, as these were the main differentiating factors of low ranked answers.

These findings align with earlier research on Stack Overflow answers. For instance, while Nasehi and colleagues [16] found that explanations accompanying code examples are equally important as the code and Treude and Robillard [23] found that code is not self-explanatory and not necessarily understandable by readers, our findings provide a more nuanced understanding on the role that explanation plays as the main connection between answers components. A good answer does not only provide working code but explains why and how the code works with Question-specific Explanations and General Explanations that address the underlying topics of the question.

It is important to note that these findings are only based on the analysis of answers to one question on Stack Overflow and as such may not apply to answers to other or all questions. Further research should sample questions across the rank spectrum to better understand the nature of answers. However, the findings presented in this paper may help make explicit what the affinity space values as a good answer and contribute to make Stack Overflow a more nurturing affinity space for newcomers [13] where expertise is rooted in the space and its scaffoldings and not only individual participants. For instance, when users draft answers, they could receive prompts that encourage them to add General Explanations that provide context to their answers. When users add code to an answer, they could be reminded to add question-specific explanations of how the code works. If a user does not include any links to external materials in their answers, Stack Overflow could ask them if they would like to add any references to external materials before posting their answer. These are some strategies that could help make tacit knowledge explicit, keep participation more transparent, and support newcomers in learning the expectations and customs of the community.

6 Conclusions

In this exploratory study we analyzed the content structure of answers to Stack Overflow's most popular question, revealing some of the characteristics that make up answers that are valued by the community. Moving forward, it is important to analyze the content structure of answers to other questions and online programming affinity spaces to investigate if there are differences between high and low ranked questions. Comments that users add to answers may also be an interesting source of data to better understand what makes a good answer. ENA and automated coding offer valuable possibilities to replicate the work of this paper at scale. Furthermore, this kind of analysis could be valuable to understand the content structure of answers in question and answer sites that are not related to computer programming. We hope that this first effort can contribute to making explicit the implicit knowledge of the affinity space, providing evidence that can help us move towards lowering the barriers to participation that newcomers encounter in Stack Overflow.

Acknowledgements. Special thanks to Nidhi Nasiar for support with data coding.

References

1. Allamanis, M., Sutton, C.: Why, when, and what: analyzing stack overflow questions by topic, type, and code. In: 2013 10th Working Conference on Mining Software Repositories (MSR), pp. 53–56. IEEE (2013)
2. Anderson, A., Huttenlocher, D., Kleinberg, J., Leskovec, J.: Discovering value from community activity on focused question answering sites: a case study of stack overflow. In: Proceedings of the 18th ACM SIGKDD International Conference on Knowledge Discovery and Data Mining, pp. 850–858 (2012)
3. Barua, A., Thomas, S.W., Hassan, A.E.: What are developers talking about? An analysis of topics and trends in stack overflow. Empir. Softw. Eng. **19**(3), 619–654 (2014)
4. Bazelli, B., Hindle, A., Stroulia, E.: On the personality traits of stackOverflow users. In: 2013 IEEE International Conference on Software Maintenance, pp. 460– 463. IEEE (2013)
5. Brooke, S.: Trouble in programmer's paradise: gender-biases in sharing and recognising technical knowledge on stack overflow. Inf. Commun. Soc. **24**(14), 2091–2112 (2021)
6. Calefato, F., Lanubile, F., Marasciulo, M.C., Novielli, N.: Mining successful answers in stack overflow. In: 2015 IEEE/ACM 12th Working Conference on Mining Software Repositories, pp. 430–433. IEEE (2015)
7. Calefato, F., Lanubile, F., Novielli, N.: How to ask for technical help? Evidence based guidelines for writing questions on stack overflow. Inf. Softw. Technol. **94**, 186–207 (2018)
8. Correa, D., Sureka, A.: Fit or unfit: analysis and prediction of 'closed questions' on stack overflow. In: Proceedings of the First ACM Conference on Online Social Networks, pp. 201–212 (2013)
9. Ford, D., Harkins, A., Parnin, C.: Someone like me: how does peer parity influence participation of women on stack overflow? In: 2017 IEEE Symposium on Visual Languages and Human-Centric Computing (VL/HCC), pp. 239–243. IEEE (2017)
10. Ford, D., Smith, J., Guo, P.J., Parnin, C.: Paradise unplugged: Identifying barriers for female participation on stack overflow. In: Proceedings of the 2016 24th ACM SIGSOFT International Symposium on Foundations of Software Engineering, pp. 846–857 (2016)
11. Gee, J.P.: Semiotic social spaces and affinity spaces. In: Beyond Communities of Practice Language Power and Social Context, p. 214232 (2005)
12. Gee, J.P.: Situated Language and Learning: A Critique of Traditional Schooling. Routledge (2012)
13. Gee, J.P., Hayes, E.: Nurturing affinity spaces and game-based learning. In: Games, Learning, and Society: Learning and Meaning in the Digital Age, vol. 123, pp. 1–40 (2012)
14. Hart, K., Sarma, A.: Perceptions of answer quality in an online technical question and answer forum. In: Proceedings of the 7th International Workshop on Cooperative and Human Aspects of Software Engineering, pp. 103–106 (2014)
15. Moutidis, I., Williams, H.T.: Community evolution on stack overflow. PLoS ONE **16**(6), e0253010 (2021)
16. Nasehi, S.M., Sillito, J., Maurer, F., Burns, C.: What makes a good code example?: A study of programming Q&A in stackoverflow. In: 2012 28th IEEE International Conference on Software Maintenance (ICSM), pp. 25–34. IEEE (2012)
17. Novielli, N., Calefato, F., Lanubile, F.: Towards discovering the role of emotions in stack overflow. In: Proceedings of the 6th International Workshop on Social Software Engineering, pp. 33–36 (2014)
18. Saldaña, J.: The Coding Manual for Qualitative Researchers. Sage (2021)
19. Shaffer, D.W.: Models of situated action: computer games and the problem of transfer. In: Games Learning, And Society: Learning and Meaning in the Digital Age, pp. 403–431 (2012)

20. Shaffer, D.W., Collier, W., Ruis, A.R.: A tutorial on epistemic network analysis: analyzing the structure of connections in cognitive, social, and interaction data. J. Learn. Anal. **3**(3), 9–45 (2016)
21. Siebert-Evenstone, A.L., Irgens, G.A., Collier, W., Swiecki, Z., Ruis, A.R., Shaffer, D.W.: In search of conversational grain size: modeling semantic structure using moving stanza windows. J. Learn. Anal. **4**(3), 123–139 (2017)
22. Stephany, F., Braesemann, F., Graham, M.: Coding together–coding alone: the role of trust in collaborative programming. Inf. Commun. Soc. **24**(13), 1944–1961 (2021)
23. Treude, C., Robillard, M.P.: Understanding stack overflow code fragments. In: 2017 IEEE International Conference on Software Maintenance and Evolution (ICSME), pp. 509–513. IEEE (2017)
24. Wang, S., Lo, D., Jiang, L.: An empirical study on developer interactions in stackoverflow. In: Proceedings of the 28th Annual ACM Symposium on Applied Computing, pp. 1019–1024 (2013)
25. Zörgő, S., Jeney, A., Csajbók-Veres, K., Mkhitaryan, S., Susánszky, A.: Mapping the content structure of online diabetes support group activity on Facebook. In: Wasson, B., Zörgő, S. (eds.) International Conference on Quantitative Ethnography, pp. 221–236. Springer, Cham (2021). https://doi.org/10.1007/978-3-030-93859-8_15

Analyzing the Co-design Process by Engineers and Product Designers from Perspectives of Knowledge Building

Ayano Ohsaki[1,2(✉)] [iD] and Jun Oshima[2] [iD]

[1] Musashino University, 1-1-20, Shinmach Nishitokyo-Shi, Tokyo 2028585, Japan
ohsaki.lab@gmail.com
[2] RECLS, Shizuoka University, 836 Ohya, Suruga-Ku, Shizuoka-Shi, Shizuoka 4228529, Japan
joshima@inf.shizuoka.ac.jp

Abstract. This study examines the design activities of engineers and product designers from the perspective of knowledge building. The practice of knowledge building has been studied for more than 30 years. However, in recent years, analytical methods have been developed to analyze it from two directions—idea improvement and epistemic frames—and these methods are currently being enhanced. Nevertheless, studies that have analyzed idea improvement and epistemic frames have focused on practices in the classroom rather than discussing the activities of engineers and designers, who are also knowledge building models. Therefore, this study analyzed the co-design process of a product design team and an engineering team that engaged in creative activities for their work from the perspectives of idea improvement using socio-semantic network analysis (SSNA) and the epistemic frame by epistemic network analysis (ENA). Moreover, this study discussed defining meaning segments using SSNA as a computational approach for quantitative ethnography (QE). As a result, both teams showed good knowledge building characteristics in that they continuously improved their ideas. Furthermore, the engineering team worked under various epistemic actions, while the product designers worked under a limited epistemic frame. We also confirmed that the analysis method of this study was able to extract the characteristic discourse of each team. These results support future knowledge building practices, as they illustrate that designers and engineers engage in the same continuous idea improvement under different epistemic actions. Furthermore, this study contributes to future QE research because the results show the qualitative differences between designers and engineers using determining meaning segments as a computational approach.

Keywords: Knowledge Building · Knowledge Creation · Epistemic Network Analysis · Socio-Semantic Network Analysis · Prototyping · Discourse Analysis

1 Background and Research Purpose

This study discusses the differences in engagement in knowledge building practices between product designers and engineers. Knowledge creation is gaining attention in

C. Damşa and A. Barany (Eds.): ICQE 2022, CCIS 1785, pp. 388–401, 2023.
https://doi.org/10.1007/978-3-031-31726-2_27

this volatile, uncertain, and complex era. The learning theory of knowledge building, a knowledge creation metaphor, has been used to design learning environments to model activities for engineers, designers, and scientists [1–3]. Furthermore, the knowledge building practices in classrooms have been studied for more than 30 years, but the studies have mainly analyzed the differences between high- and low-performance classroom groups and changes in learners over time [4–6]. Hence, little is known about how designers and engineers engage in collective idea improvement from the perspective of knowledge building analytics. By addressing this issue, this study contributes to supporting activities for knowledge creation in industry and the design of the future learning environment. Consequently, this study utilizes a double-layered analytical method, which was used in recent studies to analyze data in classrooms from the perspectives of idea improvement and epistemic agency [7].

The double-layered analytical method uses two analysis tools. First, socio-semantic network analysis (SSNA) is used to analyze idea improvement. The SSNA shows a network of key phases in the discourse, as shown in Fig. 1. Moreover, the total degree centrality (TDC) can be used to measure idea improvement when using SSNA [8]. The score of degree centrality indicates the cohesion of a key phrase based on normalized scores of links. For example, in Fig. 1a, the network has only three nodes, so node A (a black node) has links for all nodes, and the degree centrality of node A is 1. Since knowledge building practices have many networks, as in Fig. 1b, we need to capture the condition of all key phrases. Thus, the TDC sums the degree centrality of all key phrases. The details of the TDC calculation formula can be found in previous studies [8]. SSNA uses the TDC to visualize how ideas and topics change. Moreover, previous studies on knowledge building practice in classrooms using SSNA have suggested that the students in high-performance groups engage in sustainable idea improvement [6, 9–11].

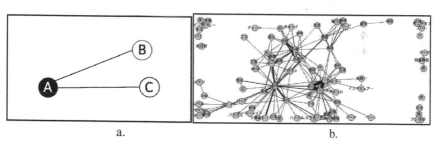

a.   b.

Fig. 1. Example of key phrase network (a. simple network with three nodes; b. case of engineers' network in this study).

The second layer is the epistemic frame of knowledge building. Oshima et al. [7, 9] proposed the use of epistemic network analysis (ENA) [12] and the framework of shared epistemic agency [13]. ENA is used to analyze epistemic frames. Based on a quantitative ethnography (QE) approach, ENA can visualize the differences between more than two sociocultural practices. In the latest research, Ohsaki et al. [14] analyzed knowledge building discourse using directed epistemic network analysis (dENA) [15], an advanced analysis tool of ENA. A previous study on the epistemic frame of knowledge building discourse reported that high-performance groups engaged in generative collaboration more than low-performance groups [7, 9, 14].

Previous research on knowledge building practice for idea improvement and epistemic frames has compared the characteristics of high-performance groups to those of low-performance groups. However, these studies have focused on knowledge building practices in the classroom. As such, it is necessary to clarify how engineers and designers, who are knowledge building models, improve their ideas from the perspective of knowledge building. Consequently, the following research questions were raised: (1) How do engineers and designers improve their ideas in knowledge building discourse? (2) What differences are there in the epistemic frames leading idea improvement between engineers and product designers?

To answer these research questions, this study examined the co-design process of engineers and product designers to elucidate design and engineering processes from the perspectives of idea improvement and epistemic frames. Moreover, for analyzing epistemic frames, we used not only the framework of shared epistemic agency [13], but also the framework of design activities. This is because, in recent years, the quality of design process has become an essential element of innovation, and human-centered design [16, 17] and innovation of meaning [18] processes have attracted considerable attention. Specifically, this study analyzed knowledge building discourse using categories based on design thinking [16, 19] (a famous approach to human-centered design) and innovation of meaning.

2 Methods

2.1 Dataset

The dataset was collected from two cases of knowledge building practice. Both cases involved the same tasks, but the team types differed. The main challenge was to create a new wallet for the user. This workshop consisted of two sessions lasting 90 min in total. In the first 60 min, the participants planned a 3-day project in a planning session. Subsequently, the participants spent 30 min creating a prototype as the first step of their plan in a prototyping session. They understood that their work could be used as models for university classes. The final products were a prototype and presentation video.

The participants in the first case were three engineers studying software engineering at a professional graduate school. All participants had experience working as engineers. The second case involved three students in their final year of an undergraduate product design program. A product designer is a type of design worker with the knowledge and skills required to design and create real products. These three participants had been recommended by a professor, as they had basic design knowledge and skills.

The participants' activities were videorecorded and transcribed. The transcribed discourse data comprised 416 lines for the product designers' team and 309 lines for the engineers' team.

2.2 Coding

Two coding tables were used in this study. The first coding table (Table 1) primarily concerns the design activities perspective based on design thinking [16, 19] and innovation of meaning [18], which have been the focus of much attention in recent years.

Design thinking is an approach to human-centered design [16] that starts with investigating the user's situation and then solves the user's problem. The Stanford model of this approach suggests five steps in the design process: (1) empathize: investigating users and understanding their situation; (2) define: describing the users' critical problems revealed from the investigation of users; (3) ideate: imagining solutions; (4) prototype: creating a model based on the ideas about solutions; and (5) test: evaluating and revising the prototype [19].

In contrast, innovation of meaning is an approach in which one begins with the designer [18]. Thus, the innovation of meaning process involves the following five steps: (1) envisioning: thinking about meaning to create a vision (done individually); (2) meaning factory1: debating similar hypotheses (done in pairs); (3) meaning factory2: clashing and fusing to find new directions (done in a small group); (4) interpreters' lab: questioning each other (done in a big group); and (5) action: testing the vision (done with the wider population).

This study created five coding categories for activities based on participants' focus points, design thinking, innovation of meaning, and the concept of artifact-mediated idea improvement in knowledge creation metaphors [20]. The five categories are as follows: (1) FUNCTION DESIGN involves the final product/service function; (2) APPEARANCE DESIGN concerns visual design (size, color, and tactile impression); (3) USER involves users and interviews; (4) ONE'S OPINION concerns one's opinions or the evaluation of shared ideas; and (5) PROTOTYPE involves PROTOTYPE creation. The first two categories showed the participants' focus points on their activities. The third category focused on design thinking, and the fourth category focused on the innovation of meaning. Moreover, the last category focused on the combination of design thinking, innovation of meaning, and the concept of artifact-mediated idea improvement in knowledge creation metaphors [20].

Table 1. Coding categories for design activities.

Category	Example
FUNCTION DESIGN	This wallet can be used overseas, so it has skimming protection
APPEARANCE DESIGN	Uh, leather. White, black
USER	Is there anything you think is missing from your current wallet?
ONE'S OPINION	But I feel like I don't see much navy blue. Do you?
PROTOTYPE	We can create pockets by pasting on these [materials]

The second coding table (Table 2) shows the codes for shared epistemic agency [13]. This frame is for knowledge building actions constructed from seven categories [13]:

(1) CREATING AWARENESS (CA) –pointing out what is missing; (2) ALLEVIATING LACK OF KNOWLEDGE (ALOK) – trying to acquire missing knowledge and criticizing the information source; (3) CREATING SHARED UNDERSTANDING (CSU) – bringing up their knowledge and checking another person's understanding to create a knowledge object; (4) GENERATIVE COLLECTIVE ACTIONS (GCA) – improving the created knowledge object; (5) PROJECTIVE– planning activities for a goal; (6) REGULATIVE – monitoring the object created by the participants; and (7) RELATIONAL – giving other members space for contribution.

Table 2. Coding categories for shared epistemic agency.

Category [13]	Example
CREATING AWARENESS (CA)	Is there a difference between wallets used in Japan and those used overseas?
ALLEVIATINF LACK OF KNOWLEDGE (ALOK)	By the way, why did you choose the current wallet?
CREATING SHARED UNDERSTANDING (CSU)	Thin is also good, right? Minimalist-like…
GENERATIVE COLLECTIVE ACTIONS (GCA)	Additionally, we can extend the functionality of this wallet by…
PROJECTIVE	We have about 10 min left
REGULATIVE	This [PROTOTYPE] is fine [for us]
RELATIONAL	Oh, that's nice. Let me see your wallet

2.3   Analysis Approach

This study combined SSNA and ENA. For analysis of knowledge building discourse, which is a combination used for double-layered analysis from the perspectives of idea improvement and shared epistemic agency [7, 9]. In other words, SSNA is used for analyzing idea improvement, and ENA is used for analyzing shared epistemic agency and design activities. The Knowledge Building Discourse Explorer (KBDeX) [8] was used as the SSNA analysis tool, and Web ENA [21] was used as the ENA analysis tool. In addition, this study used SSNA to determine the meaning segments for ENA, following Barany et al. [22].

As Barany et al. [22] reported, capturing the meaning segments of discourse is an important consideration in the field of QE. According to Gee [23], one line of discourse may not be sufficient to represent meaning, so it is necessary to consider stanzas a segment of meaning. To handle stanzas computationally, Siebert-Evenstone et al. [24] proposed the moving stanza window method, which moves a window to examine a defined number of lines of discourse data. In addition to the method of moving and incrementally increasing the stanza window at regular intervals, Barany et al. [22] set the point where the TDC, which is the result of SSNA calculation, decays twice in a row as the point at which one stanza ends. These results suggest that SSNA may be effective at setting semantic units. Hence, we applied defined stanza segments using SSNA in this study.

The settings for the analysis tools in this study were as follows. The network lifetime (the duration of the network computing the degree centrality) of the SSNA was set to 4. Moreover, 163 key phrases used in the SSNA were determined by extracting phrases related to ideas from the cases of engineers and product designers. Examples of key phrases include "wallets," "cell phones," "pockets," and "leather." For ENA, we set the unit of analysis as cases (data for engineers and product designers) and subsets by speakers (speakers on a stanza segment detected by SSNA). Conversations were set by case (data for engineers and product designers) and stanza segments (segments detected by SSNA) to prevent associations from being calculated across the different cases and stanza segments. Epistemic networks were visualized as the relationship between the coding categories in Tables 1 and 2. Moreover, this study used an infinite stanza instead of the moving stanza window method.

3 Results

3.1 Analysis of Idea Improvement

Figure 2 shows the TDC transitions of engineers and product designers. In the figure, engineers are indicated by solid red lines, and product designers are indicated by black dotted lines. The x-axis shows the order of the discourse, and the y-axis shows the TDC score.

The analysis results show that the TDC scores of both engineers and product designers changed until the end, indicating that both teams changed their ideas until the end. The common feature of both cases is that the TDC scores are high in the first half. This graph indicates that in the first half, the number of key phrases used was small, and the key phrases that appeared were connected to each other. In comparison, while the number of key phrases used increased in the second half, the focus of consideration narrowed as the degree of completion of outcomes increased. Although changes in ideas were observed, the scores did not increase significantly.

As for the difference between engineers and product designers, the comparison of TDC scores shows that engineers used more key phrases to change their ideas. The members of both teams knew each other before participating in this work, but the engineers' team members were of different ages and had diverse working experiences; therefore, they used a greater variety of words to improve their ideas.

Furthermore, this study calculated the attenuation of the TDC computed using SSNA to determine the stanza segments. Two consecutive decay points were identified for the engineering team at 35 points and for the product engineering team at 29 points. Therefore, we added the last segment and defined the stanza segments as 36 for the engineers and 30 for the product designers.

3.2 Analysis of Epistemic Frame of Knowledge Building

Figures 3, 4, 5, and 6 show epistemic network graphs for the coding categories summarized in Tables 1 and 2. In all graphs, engineers are shown in red and product designers are shown in blue.

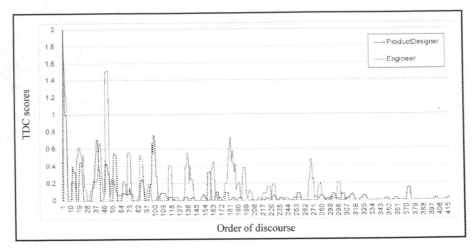

Fig. 2. TDC transitions of engineers and product designers.

Figures 3 and 4 use the coding categories of the design activities listed in Table 1. A graph comparing engineers and product designers is shown in Fig. 3. Figure 4 shows separate graphs for the engineers' and product designers' teams. Along the x-axis (MR1), a Mann–Whitney test showed that product designers (Mdn = 1.42, N = 5) were statistically significantly different from engineers (Mdn = −1.02, N = 8 U = 40.00, p = 0.00, r = −1.00) at the alpha level of 0.05. Along the y-axis (SVD2), a Mann–Whitney test showed that product designers (Mdn = −0.93, N = 5) were not statistically significantly different from engineers (Mdn = −0.08, N = 8 U = 24.00, p = 0.62, r = −0.20) at the alpha level of 0.05.

In the subtracted graph (Fig. 3), the engineers' line shows stronger ties than the product designers' line between FUNCTION DESIGN and the nodes of PROTOTYPE, APPEARANCE DESIGN, ONE'S OPINION, and USER, confirming that functional design played an important role in engineers' idea change. In contrast, the product designers' line shows stronger ties between ONE'S OPINION, APPEARANCE DESIGN, and USER than the engineers' line, indicating that their ideas played an important role in the product designers' activity.

In the respective graphs (Fig. 4), the engineers' graph shows strong connections among the nodes, with the exception of a weak connection between PROTOTYPE and the USER. This indicates that the engineering team engaged in various epistemic actions that were coordinated from the perspective of design activities. Additionally, in the graph of the engineering team, the strongest connection was between USER and FUNCTION DESIGN. This connection may have been due to the emphasis on user-centered design among engineers in recent years and their consideration of this in design ACTIVITES.

In contrast, the graph of product designers (right side in Fig. 4) shows that their epistemic actions were mainly connected between ONE'S OPINION, USER, and APPEARANCE DESIGN. The fact that fewer nodes were connected during the activities of product designers than those of engineers indicates the range of their perspectives. This result may also indicate the characteristics of the product designers. In the product design field,

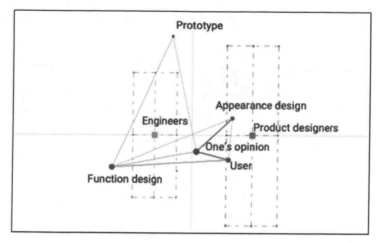

Fig. 3. Subtracted graph of epistemic network for design activities.

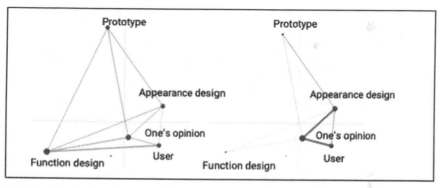

Fig. 4. Graphs of epistemic network for design activities (left: engineers, right: product designers).

designers consider the interface between the user and product, such as the innovation of meaning through the product. Therefore, the team of product designers in this study may have focused on the users, their opinions, and APPEARANCE DESIGN.

Figures 5 and 6 show epistemic networks created by coding the categories of shared epistemic agency in Table 2. Figure 5 shows a comparison between the engineers and product designers. Figure 6 shows separate graphs for the engineers' and product designers' teams. Along the x-axis (MR1), a Mann–Whitney test showed that engineers (Mdn = 0, N = 8) were statistically significantly different from product designers at the alpha level of 0.05 (Mdn = 0.98, N = 5 U = 3.00, p = 0.01, r = 0.85). Along the y-axis (SVD2), a Mann–Whitney test showed that engineers (Mdn = 0, N = 8) were not statistically significantly different from product designers at the alpha level of 0.05 (Mdn = 0, N = 5 U = 19.00, p = 0.94, r = 0.05).

The subtracted graph in Fig. 5 shows that engineers had strong ties between GCA and REGULATIVE, CSU, and RELATIONAL actions and between REGULATIVE and RELATIONAL actions. Product designers had strong ties between ALoK and CSU actions and between RELATIONAL and CSU actions.

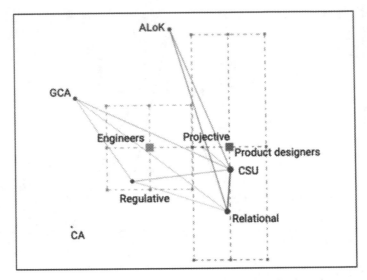

Fig. 5. Subtracted graph of epistemic network for shared epistemic agency.

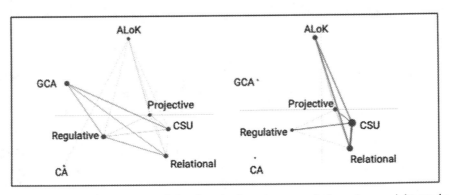

Fig. 6. Graphs of epistemic network for shared epistemic agency (left: engineers, right: product designers).

Because the subtracted graph alone does not sufficiently capture the characteristics of each team, we checked the separate graphs and confirmed that, from the perspective of shared epistemic agency, the characteristics shown by the subtracted graph and those shown by the separate graphs were almost identical. In other words, the engineering team reviewed and revised the prototype while giving others a chance to contribute. In contrast, the product design team was mainly engaged in acquiring information and creating a shared understanding while giving each other space and the opportunity to contribute.

4 Discussion

This study examined the differences between product designers and engineers regarding changes in their perspectives of knowledge building and epistemic frameworks. To answer the first research question (How do engineers and designers improve their ideas in knowledge building discourse?), we conducted SSNA. The SSNA results confirmed that both engineers and product designers continuously improved their ideas until the end. This is similar to the results for high-performance groups in previous classroom studies [6, 9–11]. This confirms the characteristics of good knowledge building practice in this study. In addition, the tendency of the number of key phrases to increase gradually was observed in both the engineer and product designer teams, suggesting that rather than repeatedly discussing the same ideas, the teams produced evolving ideas.

For the second research question (What differences are there in the epistemic frames leading idea improvement between engineers and product designers?), an ENA was conducted to identify the differences in the epistemic frames of the two teams. The design activities showed that engineers were working under various epistemic actions, with a connection between functional design and other epistemic actions. In contrast, product designers engaged in activities based on the limited epistemic actions of ONE'S OPINION, APPEARANCE DESIGN, and USER. This may have been due to the product designers' expertise in the interface with the user and the participants' different work experiences. For example, the engineers worked on the function design based on the user's answers after confirming whether functionality or appearance was more important to the user in the initial user interview.

Furthermore, from the perspective of shared epistemic agency, we confirmed that the engineering team created collaborative ideas and worked to improve them while providing space for the other team members to make their contributions. In contrast, the product designers' team obtained information and created collaborative ideas while providing space for other team members to contribute.

In addition to the visualization by SSNA and ENA, we reviewed the characteristic discourse from both the teams in order to capture the more specific nature of the activities. Table 3 shows the engineering team's discourse, which was identified as the characteristics of the engineering team based on the two ENAs: GCA and FUNCTION DESIGN. The extracted discourse was a situation in which a prototype of a wallet that had already been created was shown, and the members discussed improvements that could be made. The discourse shows participants talking about improvements to create a concrete three-dimensional prototype while praising the activities of other members.

Then, the extracted discourse of the product design confirmed the three product designer characteristics identified in the two ENAs: CSU, APPEARANCE DESIGN, and ONE'S OPINION (Table 4). The discourse showed that the three team members discussed the wallet based on their own opinions on what constitutes good movement for women. In the discourse data, participant PA repeatedly said, "I don't know" and "I'm not sure" while expressing an opinion. In the team culture, this attitude shows that respect for others' opinions. The reason product designers often create shared understandings rather than the most advanced GCA may be that they take the time to confirm others' opinions.

The qualitative examples extracted represent the characteristics of both engineers and product designers; this suggests that our approach is useful for not only capturing

Table 3. Qualitative example of engineers' discourse.

ID	Speaker	Utterance
217	EC	This is meant to be a **card**holder, but what should I do with it? Should I make it exactly like this one? Or should I do something **creative with** it? Or make it a little thicker?
218	EA	Thickness, oh, that's good
219	EC	Add a **gusset**…
220	EA	Add… EC, you're good with your hands
221	EC	EA, you're so good at **flattery**. Complimenting. I guess it's like this
222	EC	Better to use double-sided **tape**
223	EC	Use double-sided **tape**…
224	EA	Sure, it's nice because it gives it a little more of a **3D** effect
225	EB	Sure

Table 4. Qualitative example of product designers' discourse.

ID	Speaker	Utterance
286	PA	Well, I'm not sure. If she's [the user's] the type of a person who wants to appear very neat and tidy, I thought that since it is something the user uses on the outside, it would be better to have something with beautiful **movement**. I don't know about **design** and form
287	PC	If a **woman** uses that the [wallet], it might be not good be opened with one hand, right? It can be opened by one hand… It's certainly convenient, but…
288	PA	Right, [but] I thought it would be better for us to open it like this with both hands and take the **money** out in a beautiful action. I don't know. I thought it would be better for us, but I wonder what **shape** it should take
289	PB	Regarding **movement**, it looks better when there is a lot of **movement**, right?
290	PA	Well… I'm not sure

features through visualized networks but also referring to qualitative data to determine actual phenomena.

5 Conclusion

This study analyzed the engagement in co-design activities of engineers and designers, who are models of knowledge building, from a knowledge building perspective. Co-design, an approach to problem-solving and innovation, is becoming increasingly important in society, and there is growing discussion on how to support collaborative activities outside of the educational context as well. In contrast, knowledge building, which models the knowledge advancement of scientists, designers, and engineers, has been practiced and studied mainly in the classroom for more than 30 years. Therefore, this study focused on the work of engineers and designers, which has not been previously discussed. Specifically, we analyzed the activity processes of engineers and product designers from the perspectives of idea improvement and the epistemic framework of knowledge building.

The results confirmed that the idea improvement of engineers and product designers is continuous and has the same characteristics as the activities of the high-performance groups discussed in previous knowledge building studies [6, 9–11]. From the perspective of the epistemic frame regarding design activities, it was confirmed that engineers engage in idea improvement under various epistemic actions, whereas product designers do not. This is thought to reflect the characteristics of engineers, who prototype functions based on user requests, and the characteristics of product designers, who design the interface between users and products. It was also confirmed that the participants in this study improved their ideas from both perspectives of the user and their own opinions. These results are meaningful for the discussion of the outside-in user-driven design process and the inside-out design-driven innovation process [16, 18]. Furthermore, in the shared epistemic agency framework, which is one aspect of knowledge building discourse analysis, engineers reached the most advanced actions, the GCA, while product designers worked on CSU.

Additionally, this study examined the computational method for defining the meaning segment using the result of SSNA calculation instead of the moving stanza window method. As a result, based on the characteristic epistemic actions identified by the ENA graphs, qualitative examples were extracted from the discourse data, and significant characteristic scenes for each team were identified. Consequently, we confirmed that the engineering team used GCA through functional design scenes in which engineers further improved their prototypes while praising members. For product designers, this study extracted scenes with CSU, APPEARANCE DESIGN, and ONE'S OPINION and confirmed that product designers expressed their own opinions while also respecting their partners' opinions. This is a meaningful result that supports qualitative and quantitative analyses in an age in which the size of data is increasing rapidly and it is becoming important to analyze meaning in data [25].

Of course, this study is limited by the fact that it did not analyze a large amount of data. However, it illustrated that participants took different epistemic actions even if they engaged in similar idea improvement activities and suggested the importance of analysis of the epistemic frame to support knowledge creation activities. Moreover, our computational approach to determining meaning segments helped indicate a pivotal qualitative point. Hence, this study contributes to future knowledge building research and QE analysis.

Acknowledgment. I would like to thank Amanda Barany for her support. The present research was supported by JSPS KAKENHI Grant Numbers JP16H01817, JP18K13238, JP19H01715, and JP20KK0046. This work was funded in part by the National Science Foundation (DRL-1661036, DRL-1713110, DRL-2100320), the Wisconsin Alumni Research Foundation, and the

Office of the Vice Chancellor for Research and Graduate Education at the University of Wisconsin-Madison. The opinions, findings, and conclusions do not reflect the views of the funding agencies, cooperating institutions, or other individuals.

References

1. Paavola, S., Hakkarainen, K.: The knowledge creation metaphor–an emergent epis- temological approach to learning. Sci. Educ. **14**(6), 535–557 (2005)
2. Scardamalia, M., Bereiter, C.: Knowledge building and knowledge creation: theory, pedagogy, and technology. Cambridge Handbook Learn. Sci. **2**, 397–417 (2014)
3. Scardamalia, M., Bereiter, C.: Two models of thinking in knowledge building. Re- vista Catalana de Pedagogia, pp. 61–83 (2017)
4. Chen, B., Hong, H.-Y.: Schools as knowledge-building organizations: thirty years of design research. Educ. Psychol. **51**(2), 266–288 (2016)
5. Zhang, J., Tao, D., Chen, M.H., Sun, Y., Judson, D., Naqvi, S.: Co-organizing the collective journey of inquiry with idea thread mapper. J. Learn. Sci. **27**(3), 390–430 (2018)
6. Oshima, J., Oshima, R., Fujita, W.: A mixed-methods approach to analyze shared epistemic agency in jigsaw instruction at multiple scales of temporality. J. Learn. Anal. **5**(1), 10–24 (2018)
7. Oshima, J., Oshima, R., Saruwatari, S.: Analysis of students' ideas and conceptual artifacts in knowledge-building discourse. British J. Educ. Technol. **51**(4), 1308–1321 (2020)
8. Oshima, J., Oshima, R., Matsuzawa, Y.: Knowledge building discourse explorer: a social network analysis application for knowledge building discourse. Educ. Tech. Res. Dev. **60**(5), 903–921 (2012)
9. Oshima, J., Oshima, R., Ohsaki, A., Splichal, J.M.: Collective knowledge advancement through shared epistemic agency: Socio-semantic network analyses. In: K. Lund, G. Niccolai, E. Lavoué, C. Hmelo- Silver, G. Gweon, M. Baker (Eds.), A wide lens: Combining embod- ied, enactive, extended, and embedded learning in collaborative settings. In: 13th international conference on computer supported collaborative learning (CSCL) 2019, vol. 1, pp. 57–64. Lyon: International Society of the Learning Sciences (2019)
10. Ohsaki, A., Oshima, J.: A Socio-Semantic Network Analysis of Discourse Using the Network Lifetime and the Moving Stanza Window Method. In: Eagan, B., Misfeldt, M., Siebert-Evenstone, A. (eds.) ICQE 2019. CCIS, vol. 1112, pp. 326–333. Springer, Cham (2019). https://doi.org/10.1007/978-3-030-33232-7_29
11. Ohsaki, A., Oshima, J.: Socio-semantic Network Analysis of Knowledge-Creation Discourse on a Real-Time Scale. In: Ruis, A.R., Lee, S.B. (eds.) ICQE 2021. CCIS, vol. 1312, pp. 170–184. Springer, Cham (2021). https://doi.org/10.1007/978-3-030-67788-6_12
12. Shaffer, D.W.: Quantitative Ethnography. Cathcart, Madison (2017)
13. Damşa, C., Kirschner, P.A., Andriessen, J.E., Erkens, G., Sins, P.H.: Shared epistemic agency: An empirical study of an emergent construct. J. Learn. Sci. **19**(2), 143–186 (2010)
14. Ohsaki, A., Tan, Y., Eagan, B., Oshima, J., Shaffer, D.W.: Directed epistemic network analysis of knowledge-creation discourse. In: International Conference on Quantitative Ethnography 2021 (ICQE21) Conference Proceedings Supplement, pp. 34–37 (2021)
15. Fogel, A., et al.: Directed Epistemic Network Analysis. In: Ruis, A.R., Lee, S.B. (eds.) ICQE 2021. CCIS, vol. 1312, pp. 122–136. Springer, Cham (2021). https://doi.org/10.1007/978-3-030-67788-6_9
16. Brown, T.: Design thinking. Harv. Bus. Rev. **86**(6), 84 (2008)

17. Visualization, usability group, The National Institute of Standards usability group, and Technology (NIST).: Human Centered Design (HCD). https://www.nist.gov/itl/iad/visualization-and-usability-group/human-factors-human-centered-design. Aaccessed 29 May 2022.
18. Verganti, R.: Overcrowded. Gildan Media (2017)
19. Stanford d.school.: Get Started with Design Thinking. https://dschool.stanford.edu/resources/getting-started-with-design-thinking. Accessed 29 May 2022
20. Seitamaa-Hakkarainen, P., Viilo, M., Hakkarainen, K.: Learning by collaborative designing: technology-enhanced knowledge practices. Int. J. Technol. Des. Educ. 20(2), 109–136 (2010)
21. Epistemic Network Analysis (ENA), https://www.epistemicnetwork.org/, Accessed 29 May 2022
22. Barany, A., Philips, M., Kawakubo, A.J., Oshima, J.: Choosing units of analysis in temporal discourse. In: Wasson, B., Zörgő, S. (eds) Advances in Quantitative Ethnography. ICQE 2021. Communications in Computer and Information Science, vol 1522. Springer, Cham. (2021). https://doi.org/10.1007/978-3-030-93859-8_6
23. Gee, J.P.: An introduction to discourse analysis: Theory and method, 3rd edn. Routledge, London (2010)
24. Siebert-Evenstone, A.L., Arastoopour, G., Collier, W., Swiecki, Z., Ruis, A.R., Shaffer, D.W.: In search of conversational grain size: Modeling semantic structure using moving stanza windows. J. Learn. Anal. 4(3), 123–139 (2017). https://doi.org/10.18608/jla.2017.43.7
25. Shaffer, D.W.: Big data for thick description of deep learning.: In Millis, K., Long, D. L., Magliano, J. P., Wiemer, K. (eds.) Deep Comprehension. Routledge, New York (2018)

Leveraging Epistemic Network Analysis to Discern the Development of Shared Understanding Between Physicians and Nurses

Vitaliy Popov[✉], Raeleen Sobetski, Taylor Jones, Luke Granberg, Kiara Turvey, and Milisa Manojlovich

University of Michigan, Ann Arbor, USA
vipopov@med.umich.edu

Abstract. In healthcare settings, poor communication between physicians and nurses is one of the most common causes of adverse events. This study used Epistemic Network Analysis to help identify communication patterns in physician-nurse dyad interactions. We used existing video data where physicians made patient care rounds on two oncology patient units at a large academic medical center, and video recordings captured conversations physicians had with nurses on the plan of care. All data was transcribed, segmented and annotated using the Verbal Response Mode (VRM) taxonomy. The results showed that the relationship between Edification and Disclosure was strongest for the dyads that reached a shared understanding, suggesting the importance of these two modes to reaching shared understanding during patient care rounds. Reflection and Interpretation were the least used VRM codes, and this might be one possible area for intervention development. This pilot study provided new insight into how to improve communication between physicians and nurses using ENA coupled with VRM taxonomy.

Keywords: Healthcare · communication · nurse · physician · epistemic network analysis

1 Introduction

In healthcare settings, poor communication between physicians and nurses is one of the most common causes of adverse events (i.e., preventable, or unanticipated events that cause harm to a patient) (Leape and Berwick 2005; Sutcliffe et al. 2004). Although communication, defined as the development of shared understanding, is essential for coordinating care and ensuring that everyone is on the same page, physicians and nurses do not convey their messages in the same way. This leads to communication breaks down, which in turn can lead to errors and mistakes. Quantitative and qualitative methods that have been used to study communication between physicians and nurses have significant drawbacks. For example, quantitative methods often overly rely on self-report measures and fail to capture the contextual nuances and complexities of human communication. Qualitative methods for their part are time-consuming (which adds to their expense) and depend on small sample sizes, which limits generalizability and makes them prone to researchers' interpretation bias. As a result, there is a need for new methodologies that can more effectively study communication between physicians and nurses. Video-based methods are a promising alternative, and involves recording and then analyzing interactions between physicians and nurses. Video-based methods have several advantages over other methodologies. First, they can capture the nonverbal and verbal behaviors of both physicians and nurses to reveal the full range of communication practices. Second, they can be used to study a wide variety of interactions, including those that are informal and brief, yet important to understanding communication. Finally, because video-based methods create a visual and auditory record of communication as it actually occurred, the resulting database of interactions can be further analyzed for future research.

A method in which qualitative data is quantified without reducing the contextual richness of the data, could overcome some of the limitations of both quantitative and qualitative methods. Despite being a relatively new methodology, Epistemic Network Analysis (Shaffer, 2018) is becoming more prevalent in the fields of medicine and health sciences education. Epistemic network analysis (ENA) is a graph-based analytic technique that models the structure of connections in discourse data. ENA produces network models that show the relative frequencies of codes and co-occurrence patterns, as well as allowing aggregations and comparisons both within and between groups.

The use of epistemic network analysis proved to be an effective analytic approach to examine theme relationships in verbal and nonverbal datasets of individual healthcare professionals or teams (Popov et al. 2022; Larson et al. 2021). For example, Wooldridge and her colleagues (2022) developed ENA models to compare networks of medical professionals participating in handoffs between intra-professional (OR to PICU) and interprofessional (OR to ICU) settings. The ENA showed that interprofessional handoffs increased information flow with less precise communication as a tradeoff, whereas intra-professional handoffs resulted in a smaller team and less variety in roles, which may have made communication easier but increased knowledge loss. In a similar vein, Sullivan (2018) studied care transitions of adult and pediatric trauma patients from the operating room to the intensive care unit. ENA has been used in the setting of a 5-trainee trauma team along with the use of Verbal Response Modes (VRM). The team was scored on performance of a simulated resuscitation. Using ENA, communication amongst the trauma teams was able to be analyzed, specifically in that higher scoring teams used questions differently than their lower-scoring counterparts. This enables team members to focus improvement through the use of questions, which benefits the team as a whole. In another study, ENA has been used to analyze interactions within a primary care setting, with a team consisting of a physician, nurse, medical assistant, and unit clerk (Wooldridge et al. 2018). The data suggested that the physician and unit clerk were better at allocating tasks.

This study builds on existing video recordings collected for another study (Manojlovich et al. 2019). In the parent study, the research team followed physicians as they made patient care rounds on multiple patient units at a large academic medical center, and video recorded conversations physicians had with nurses on the plan of care. We were able to observe the natural progression of a conversation from beginning to end and examine if a shared understanding of the day's plan of care was achieved between physician and nurse. The purpose of this pilot study was to test if ENA could help identify improvement targets and design interventions to improve communication by comparing both visually and statistically created communication networks of physician-nurse dyad interactions.

2   Methods

2.1   Context

Video recording occurred at two oncology units in Michigan Medicine hospital. On each oncology unit, two sets of patient care rounds were video recorded, producing four sets of video-recorded rounds. In these video recordings, a GoPro camera device was held by a cameraperson who followed physicians around as they went on their regular rounds across the hospital. There were 4 physicians who were followed in the recordings, and over 200 min of footage were recorded. The footage of interactions between an individual physician and nurse ranged in length from 12 s to over 17 min.

2.2   Data Transcription, Segmentation, and Annotation

As an initial step of data preparation for ENA, we transcribed and segmented the videos to identify portions of the conversations where both the physician and nurse were interacting and present in the scene. Parts of the footage that showed physician-patient interaction, physician-resident interaction, or nurse-patient interaction were excluded from our segmentation process, because the study primary focus was on physician-nurse interaction. These segments were done at the sentence level as the meaningful unit of analysis with the use of ELAN software (version 6.3; see Fig. 1).

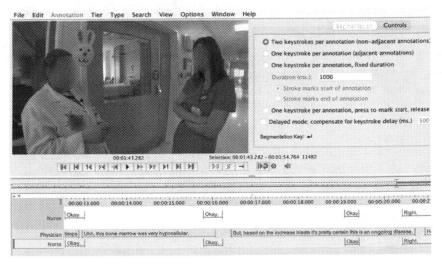

Fig. 1. A screenshot of the ELAN software with one segment depicting physician and nurse with blurred face to protect data privacy.

Physician: "Uhh, this bone marrow was very hypocellular" [Edification/VRM_code]

Nurse: "Okay" [Acknowledgment/VRM_code].

Physician: "But, based on the increase blasts it's pretty certain this is an ongoing disease" [Disclosure/VRM_code]

The segmented data were then annotated using the Verbal Response Mode (VRM) taxonomy. The VRM is a taxonomy of speech acts, used for classifying utterances according to their function in a conversation. VRM taxonomy (Stiles, 1992) has eight classes: disclosure, edification, advisement, confirmation, question, acknowledgement, interpretation, and reflection (see Table 1). The taxonomy categorizes speech acts on two dimensions: literal meaning and pragmatic meaning. The literal meaning of an utterance is the content or message that is conveyed explicitly, without taking into account any implicit or inferred meaning. The pragmatic meaning of an utterance is the meaning that is conveyed implicitly or inferred, beyond the literal meaning of the utterance. For example, the literal meaning of the utterance "I'm hungry" is that the speaker is experiencing the feeling of hunger. The pragmatic meaning of the same utterance could be interpreted as a request for food. In this paper, we focus on pragmatic meaning using the VRM classification. The VRM approach enables differentiation between what is being said and the intent of the speech act. The literal/pragmatic distinction can be important when describing communication because physicians often have difficulty in understanding what nurses are trying to say to them, and literal meanings alone are not enough to bridge the gap in understanding.

Two researchers coded 4 randomly selected data files. The researchers discussed findings and resolved discrepancies between coders through the process of social moderation. The final Cohen's kappa interrater reliability test was at .76. The two researchers then independently annotated the remaining dataset.

2.3 Analysis

In this study, we applied ENA to our annotated data using the ENA web tool version 1.7.0 (Marquart, Hinojosa, Swiecki, Eagan, & Shaffer, 2018). We were interested in two types of analyses: first, an overall comparison of associations across all physician-nurse interaction data, and second, a pairwise comparison between more and less successful physician-nurse dyads at reaching shared understanding. This dyad classification was defined through prior qualitative analysis of this data set (Manojlovich et al. 2019). We defined the units of analysis as all lines of data associated with VRM annotated sentences subsetted by the physician-nurse dyad ids. For example, one unit consisted of all the lines associated with Video Episode 5–1. The ENA algorithm uses a moving window to construct a network model for each line in the data, showing how codes in the current line are connected to codes that occur within the recent temporal context (Siebert-Evenstone et al. 2017), defined as 12 lines (each line plus the 11 previous lines) within a given conversation. The naturally occurring interaction between physicians and nurses are done as exchange of short phrases and sentences. The resulting networks are aggregated for all lines for each unit of analysis in the model. In this model, we aggregated networks using a binary summation in which the networks for a given line reflect the presence or absence of the co-occurrence of each pair of codes. Our ENA model included the following codes: Disclosure, Advisement, Edification, Confirmation, Question, Interpretation, Reflection and Acknowledgment. ENA models depict the relative frequencies of co-occurrences of each unique pair of codes in the segmented data. Co-occurrence of each pair of codes may help identify improvement targets to foster communication.

Table 1. Adapted Verbal Response Mode Taxonomy based on Stiles (1992)

VRM code	Intention	Example from the study
Disclosure	Reveals thoughts, feelings, perceptions, intentions	"But, based on the increase blast, it's pretty certain this is an ongoing disease." (Physician; Video 6–11)
Advisement	Attempts to guide behavior, suggestions, commands	"And if he tolerates well, let us know" (Physician; Video 5–4)
Edification	States objective information	"He walked in the hall….He has not had any fevers Today" (Nurse; Video 5–4)
Confirmation	Agreement, disagreement, shared experience or belief	"I just gave her some Oxy, she hadn't tried that before. She was complaining of pain, so I just did that." (Nurse) "Oh yeah, I saw it." (Physician; Video 9–3)
Question	Requests information or guidance	"This is his first dose, test dose, right?" (Physician; Video 5–4)
Interpretation	Explains or labels the other, judgments or evaluations of behavior	"Yeah, he's doing really good, he asks a lot of good questions" (Nurse; Video 11–4)
Reflection	Repetition, restatements, puts other's experience into words—paraphrasing	"Umm, so I think they're just kind of trying to.. They're looking to each other saying, both of them are saying, well yanno, I want to do what he wants me to do, and he's saying, no we should do what you want to do" (Physician) "Neither of them can decide" (Nurse; Video 6–11)
Acknowledgment	Conveys receipt of communication	"Okay, alright, well thank you for filling me in" (Nurse; Video 6–11, 02:01)

Networks were visualized using network graphs where nodes correspond to the codes, and lines connecting the nodes reflect the relative frequency of co-occurrence, or connection, between 2 codes. Node size indicates frequency of occurrence of the code and thickness of edges shows the strength of the relationship. The ENA model normalized the networks for all units of analysis before they were subjected to a dimensional reduction, which accounts for the fact that different units of analysis may have different amounts of coded lines in the data. For the dimensional reduction, we used a singular value decomposition, which produces orthogonal dimensions that maximize the variance explained by each dimension.

3 Results

Data from all 33 physician-nurse unique interactions were compiled into a single network analysis for an overall comparison of associations (Fig. 2), which demonstrated the strongest associations between Disclosure, Edification, Question and Acknowledgement. Modest associations were most commonly seen involving Interpretation and Reflection across all coded interactions. Confirmation was also associated with only modest associations for groups that both did and did not reach shared understanding.

Figures 3 shows the mean plotted point position for ENA networks for more vs. less successful physician-nurse dyads at reaching shared understanding. A two sample t test assuming unequal variance showed dyads that reached a shared understanding (mean = -0.82, SD = 0.53, N = 6) was statistically significantly different at the alpha = 0.05 level from dyads that did not reach shared understanding (mean = 0.20, SD = 0.59, N = 25; $t(8.21) = 4.13$, p = 0.00, Cohen's d = 1.76). Those dyads that reached a shared understanding engaged in more disclosure and edification behaviors (see Fig. 4). Below are two examples to illustrate this code co-occurrence:

Disclosure and Edification

Nurse: "Oh, and his left arm looks a little more swollen. He doesn't think it does, but I...like bent in. Okay." [Disclosure]

Physician: "It was puffy, it was puffy yesterday." [Edification].

Nurse: "He keeps it strapped to his body all the time." [Edification] "And he's only taking it out when he's showering, so I wasn't sure if we needed some sort of plan, like, to make sure he gets out of that thing every eight hours, or something." [Disclosure]

Physician: "So he is doing some exercises in his room, just with like moving the arm. I don't know how frequently he's doing them, but he did tell me that he was doing them, um... but yeah, I noticed that it was puffy yesterday, and he was noticing that his right hand had some wasting, which it does." [Edification]

Fig. 2. Epistemic network analysis for an overall comparison of associations between Disclosure, Advisement, Edification, Confirmation, Question, Interpretation, Reflection and Acknowledgment across all codes 33 physician-nurse unique interactions.

Questioning was also a part of reaching shared understanding, albeit to a lesser extent. The strongest associations were also seen between Edification and Advisement as well as Edification and Question for dyads who reached a shared understanding. To exemplify these connections:

Edification and Advisement.

Nurse: "His platelets are 13."[Edification].

Physician: "So I would just keep and eye, make sure it's not really bloody, there's no clots…" [Advisement]

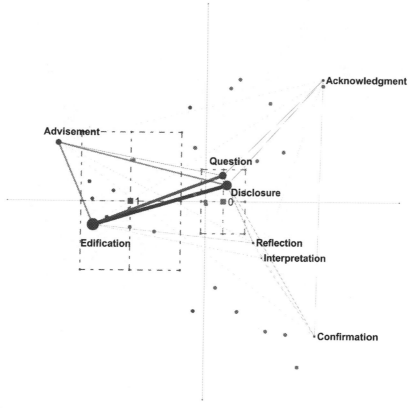

Fig. 3. Comparison epistemic network analysis models showing the mean network locations (colored squares) and 95% confidence intervals (dashed boxes) for the physician-nurse dyads who reached a shared understanding (blue, left) and the dyads who did not reach shared understanding (red, right) along with their respective mean network graphs. (Color figure online)

Edification and Question

Physician: "Do you have his labs? Is his bili [bilirubin] okay?"

[Question]

Nurse: "Um bili... let's see which one it is... 3.6." [Edification].

In the physician-nurse dyads who did not reach shared understanding Disclosure and Confirmation was one of the prevalent code co-occurrences. Confirmation was typically initiated by the physician. For example:

Disclosure and Confirmation

Nurse: "That would be different, but I told her we could work on that." [Disclosure]

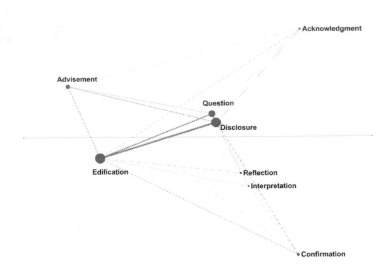

Fig. 4. Mean epistemic network for the physician-nurse dyads who reached a shared understanding.

Physician: "Yeah, so I'll reconcile that with her. It should be... Anything she needs, she should be able to get locally." [Confirmation]

There was more acknowledgment in those dyads that did not reach shared understanding (see Fig. 5). For example:

Disclosure and Acknowledgment

Nurse: "So, I told him not to eat or drink…" [Disclosure].

Physician: "Okay." [Acknowledgment].

Nurse: "Until then." [Disclosure].

Physician: "Sounds good." [Acknowledgment].

4   Discussion

We developed new insight into how to improve communication between physicians and nurses using ENA coupled with VRM taxonomy. ENA provided network graphs of

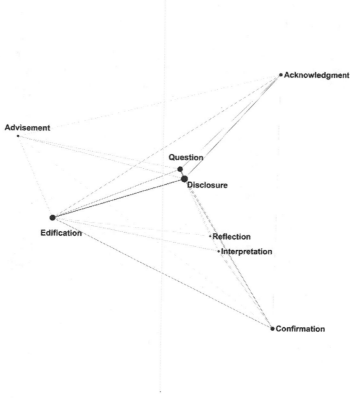

Fig. 5. Mean epistemic network for the physician-nurse dyads who did not reach shared understanding.

communication between physicians and nurses overall, and also how communication differed for those physician/nurse dyads that did and did not reach shared understanding. VRM codes demonstrated where shared understanding could be strengthened. Both groups engaged in more edification and disclosure, which makes sense given that during rounds nurses provide physicians with updated information on patient progress (edification), while physicians then reveal their perceptions of that information (disclosure). The relationship between edification and disclosure was strongest for the dyads that reached a shared understanding, suggesting the importance of these two modes to reaching shared understanding during patient care rounds (Manojlovich et al. 2020). Question and acknowledgement were also frequently used as would be expected, and this finding is consistent with other literature (Gausvik et al. 2015). During patient care rounds, physicians typically ask questions to learn about patient progress and nurses acknowledge receipt of information. Overall, Reflection and Interpretation were the least used VRM codes, and this might be one possible area for intervention development. Reflection and Interpretation involve verbalizing one's thinking as well as paraphrasing another's words and paraphrasing can be a powerful strategy to overcome the differences in how physicians and nurses convey their messages to one another. An interesting finding was that there was more acknowledgement in those dyads that did not reach shared understanding. Acknowledgement simply conveys receipt of information and is consistent with the literature on closed loop communication (Jacobsson et al. 2012) and communication checklists (Justice et al. 2016). Acknowledgement does not consider the perspective or viewpoint of the receiver of the information, and thus may limit the development of shared understanding (where all perspectives are taken into account), as we found in our study.

This study sheds light on the ways nurses and physicians can be more effective in communicating with each other. Nurses play a vital role in communicating with physicians. They act as a liaison between the physician and the patient, and they are often the first point of contact for patients. By communicating effectively with physicians, nurses can ensure that patients receive the best possible care. Achieving shared understanding may require both physicians and nurses to be direct and avoid using indirect communication. Indirect communication may hinder reaching shared understanding, which when one or both interlocuters provide subtle clues (e.g., about their diagnoses or treatment plans), but withhold explicit instructions. By doing this, nurses and physicians rely that their intended message is getting across and another person, or even the patient, will figure out the appropriate course of action on his or her own. However, this tactic can backfire if the receiver of the message does not understand the clue or does not follow the instructions. Nurses and physicians should always be clear and concise when communicating with each other. This study point out the exact communication patterns that should be improved upon, reinforced, or avoided at best.

References

ELAN (Version 6.3) [Computer software]. (2022). Nijmegen: Max Planck Institute for Psycholinguistics, The Language Archive. Retrieved from https://archive.mpi.nl/tla/elan

Gausvik, C., Lautar, A., Miller, L., Pallerla, H., Schlaudecker, J.: Structured nursing communication on interdisciplinary acute care teams improves perceptions of safety, efficiency, understanding of care plan and teamwork as well as job satisfaction. J. Multidiscip. Healthc. **8**, 33 (2015)

Jacobsson, M., Hargestam, M., Hultin, M., Brulin, C.: Flexible knowledge repertoires: communication by leaders in trauma teams. Scandinavian J. Trauma, Resuscitation Emerg. Med. **20**(1), 1–9 (2012)

Justice, L.B., et al.: Improving communication during cardiac ICU multidisciplinary rounds through visual display of patient daily goals. Pediatr. Crit. Care Med. **17**(7), 677–683 (2016)

Larson, S., Popov, V., Ali, A.M., Ramanathan, P., Jung, S.: Healthcare Professionals' Perceptions of Telehealth: Analysis of Tweets from Pre- and During the COVID-19 Pandemic. In: Ruis, A.R., Lee, S.B. (eds.) Advances in Quantitative Ethnography: Second International Conference, ICQE 2020, Malibu, CA, USA, February 1-3, 2021, Proceedings, pp. 390–405. Springer International Publishing, Cham (2021). https://doi.org/10.1007/978-3-030-67788-6_27

Leape, L.L., Berwick, D.M.: Five years after To Err Is Human: what have we learned? JAMA **293**(19), 2384–2390 (2005)

Manojlovich, M., et al.: Formative evaluation of the video reflexive ethnography method, as applied to the physician–nurse dyad. BMJ Qual. Saf. **28**(2), 160–166 (2019)

Manojlovich, M., Harrod, M., Hofer, T.P., Lafferty, M., McBratnie, M., Krein, S.L.: Using qualitative methods to explore communication practices in the context of patient care rounds on general care units. J. Gen. Intern. Med. **35**(3), 839–845 (2020)

Popov, V., Ruis, A.R., Cooke, J.M.: Taking stock and looking ahead: evolution of accreditation feedback for simulation centers over 8 years using epistemic network analysis. Simul. Healthcare : J. Society Simul. Healthcare (2022). https://doi.org/10.1097/SIH.000000000000 0638

Shaffer, D.W.: Epistemic network analysis: Understanding learning by using big data for thick description. In: International Handbook of the Learning Sciences, (pp. 520–531). Routledge (2018)

Siebert-Evenstone, A.L., Irgens, G.A., Collier, W., Swiecki, Z., Ruis, A.R., Shaffer, D.W.: In search of conversational grain size: Modeling semantic structure using moving stanza windows. J. Learn. Anal. **4**(3), 123–139 (2017)

Stiles, W.B.: Describing talk: A taxonomy of verbal response modes. Sage Publications, Newbury Park, CA (1992)

Sullivan, S., et al.: Using epistemic network analysis to identify targets for educational interventions in trauma team communication. Surgery **163**(4), 938–943 (2018)

Sutcliffe, K.M., Lewton, E., Rosenthal, M.M.: Communication failures: an insidious contributor to medical mishaps. Acad. Med. **79**(2), 186–194 (2004)

Wooldridge, A.R.: Team Cognition in Handoffs: Relating System Factors, Team Cognition Functions and Outcomes in Two Handoff Processes. Human Factors (2022). https://doi.org/10.1177/00187208221086342

Wooldridge, A.R., Carayon, P., Shaffer, D.W., Eagan, B.: Quantifying the qualitative with epistemic network analysis: a human factors case study of task-allocation communication in a primary care team. IISE Trans. Healthcare Syst. Eng. **8**(1), 72–82 (2018)

Quantitative Ethnography of Policy Ecosystems: A Case Study on Climate Change Adaptation Planning

Andrew R. Ruis(✉) iD

University of Wisconsin–Madison, Madison, WI 53706, USA
`arruis@wisc.edu`

Abstract. Analysis of policy ecosystems can be challenging due to the volume of documentary and ethnographic data and the complexity of the interactions that define the ecology of such a system. This paper uses climate change adaptation policy as a case study with which to explore the potential for QE methods to model policy ecosystems. Specifically, it analyzes policies and draft policies constructed by three different categories of governmental entity—nations, state and local governments, and tribal governments or Indigenous communities—as well as guidance for policy makers produced by the United Nations Intergovernmental Panel on Climate Change and other international agencies, as a first step toward mapping the ecology of climate change adaptation policy. This case study is then used to reflect on the strengths of QE methods for analyzing policy ecosystems and areas of opportunity for further theoretical and methodological development.

Keywords: Quantitative ethnography · policy ecosystems · policy analysis · climate change policy · health policy

1 Introduction

A key affordance of quantitative ethnography (QE) is the extent to which it can facilitate analyses of complex systems embedded across cultural contexts. For example, *policy ecosystems* [1] are characterized by interactions of actors (institutions, interest groups, bureaucrats, citizens), activities (campaigns, town hall meetings, research, governance), and artifacts (policy briefs, social surveys, budgets) around some agenda. Policies themselves are emergent properties of these interactions in at least four ways:

1. Policies are situated in *narratives*, including what Deborah Stone terms *causal stories* [2]: accounts that convert complex social situations into simpler problems amenable to structural intervention. In this sense, a policy exists as the answer to a question of social importance.
2. Policies are codified as *warrants*, official or semi-official documents that carry institutional or other authority to promote particular behaviors, allocate funds, set priorities, or otherwise guide decision-making and action.

3. Policies are eventuated through *enactments* justified by narratives and warrants. These enactments are often mediated by those Michael Lipsky labels *street-level bureaucrats* [3], functionaries who typically are not involved in the development or codification of policies but are their primary interpreters, implementers, gate-keepers, and enforcers.
4. Policies are manifest in the *experiences* of people and communities (or interpretations of the experiences of non-humans, such as animals or ecosystems) affected by enacted warrants. Experiences often reveal fault lines in policies, which may arise from misalignments of narratives, warrants, and enactments or from mischaracterization of the social situation itself. Ideally, experiences inform the policy development and implementation process, leading to iterative refinement and improvement.

This suggests that multi-level ethnographic and hermeneutic analysis both *of* and *for* public policy is not only useful but likely necessary to improve the processes and outcomes of policy development, implementation, evaluation, and refinement and to broaden participation in policy making [4].

However, policy ecosystems generate massive amounts of data, such as policy drafts and briefs, research reports, training manuals, applications, plans for and records of implementations, and evaluations, in addition to stakeholder data such as records of participatory design sessions or town hall meetings, survey responses, position statements, and online discussions, and there is considerable opportunity to conduct interviews, make observations, and apply other ethnographic methods [5]. The volume of data available (or collectable) can provide a more dynamic and ultimately more accurate view of how policies are made, implemented, and evaluated, and also demystify the process of policy-making to facilitate broader participation, but the scale renders traditional ethnographic or hermeneutic methods less useful if not impossible to implement.

In this pilot study, I explore how techniques and methods from quantitative ethnography can provide expansive but grounded views of policy ecosystems. Specifically, I use *epistemic network analysis* (ENA) [6, 7] to model the policy ecosystem of *climate change adaptation plans*—sometimes called climate change action, preparedness, or resilience plans. Climate change adaptation plans are produced by nations, localities, government agencies, institutions, or other bodies to recommend adjustments that address current and expected effects of climate change. Unlike mitigation efforts, which address the causes of climate change, adaptation aims to reduce harms (to humans, other forms of life, and ecosystems) and exploit opportunities resulting from changes in regional or local climate. As such, adaptations may include action in any sector of human activity or influence, including the built and natural environments and social, institutional, economic, or legal interventions.

In this pilot study, I model four types of policy document: climate change adaptation plans developed by (1) national governments, (2) state and local governments, and (3) tribal nations or other Indigenous communities, as well as (4) climate change adaptation guidelines for policy makers produced by the United Nations' Intergovernmental Panel on Climate Change (IPCC) and other international organizations. In other words, I look at policies and draft policies constructed by three different categories of governmental entity and guidance for policy makers produced by international agencies as a first step toward mapping the ecology of climate change adaptation policy.

2 Data and Methods

2.1 Data

The dataset used in this analysis includes 107 documents: 39 national adaptation plans, 44 state and local adaptation plans, 19 tribal adaptation plans, and 5 reports by international agencies.

The adaptation plans ($n = 102$) were published between 2006 and 2022 and are written in English ($n = 79$), Spanish ($n = 15$), and French ($n = 8$). Nearly all parts of the globe are represented in the dataset, though North America accounts for nearly half of the documents ($n = 47$). The remaining plans come from Africa ($n = 9$), Europe ($n = 10$), Asia ($n = 9$), Oceania ($n = 5$), the Caribbean ($n = 9$), Central America ($n = 2$), and South America ($n = 6$). Plans were identified based on Internet searches and were included in the dataset if they were (a) prepared under the auspices of a national, state, local, or tribal government; (b) written or translated into English, Spanish, or French; and (c) published in a single-column text format. (The final criterion was included because it is very difficult to extract text from PDF files with multi-column formats in a way that preserves the correct order of lines.) Thus, the dataset contains a broad but haphazard sample of climate change adaptation plans.

The reports ($n = 5$) included are those published by an intergovernmental or nongovernmental agency with global scope. These include the third (2001), fifth (2014), and sixth (2022) climate change assessment reports prepared by the IPCC, which cover the approximate range of the adaptation plans in the dataset; the fourth report (2007) was omitted because it was published in a double-column format. Two additional reports are included: the World Bank's *Action Plan on Climate Change Adaptation and Resilience* (2019) and the World Health Organization's *WHO Guidance to Protect Health from Climate Change through Health Adaptation Planning* (2014).

Text was automatically extracted from PDF documents, segmented based on punctuation and line breaks, and placed into a data table with metadata, including the source, year of publication, type of document, region, and language. This resulted in a dataset with more than 82,000 ordered entries, most of which are paragraphs or other discreet pieces of text (e.g., lists, captions, bibliographic entries, &c.).

2.2 Coding

Because there are hundreds of specific adaptations proposed, many of which interact or intersect in complex ways, this analysis focused on the broad domains in which such adaptations occur. In other words, this pilot analysis is an attempt to map the major features of the policy ecosystem's landscape rather than its microterrain. To do this, the study includes seven Codes: HAZARDS, the local and regional consequences of climate change that adaptations are intended to address; four domains that are key targets of adaptation activities (FOOD SECURITY, WATER SECURITY, HUMAN HEALTH, and ENVIRONMENTAL HEALTH); and two governing perspectives proposed to guide adaptation design or implementation: the perspective from justice, equity, diversity, and inclusivity (JEDI) and the perspective from local knowledge and diverse epistemologies (LOCAL KNOWLEDGE). These Codes are described in Table 1.

Table 1. Codes and inter-rater reliability statistics.

Code	Description	Examples	Human vs Computer	
			κ *	$\rho(0.90)$
Hazards	Hazards to human well-being (either direct or indirect) related to climate change, including heat waves, drought, and other forms of extreme weather; sea-level rise and flooding; wildfire; invasive species and algal blooms; and erosion	"Many of the state's programs for home elevations or property buyouts prioritize owner-occupied homes, which leaves renters more exposed to flooding." "Asimismo, ha ocasionado la formación de grandes lagunas glaciares formadas por materiales erosionables que las convierte en una amenaza latente para la ocurrencia de desastres por aluviones."	0.96	0.01
Food Security	Food supply, availability, scarcity, price, or other issues related to maintaining an adequate amount of affordable food for a population, including issues that may affect food security such as plant and livestock disease or management of food supplies, as well as the results of food insecurity, such as malnutrition, hunger, or famine	"Many of the 11 distinct cultures in rural Alaska prioritize their connection to place and subsistence way of life over the conventional Western amenities. This connection is deeply rooted in access to birds, fish, greens, berries and animals for food security." "La Pesca y la Acuicultura desempeñan funciones fundamentales en el suministro de alimentos, en la seguridad alimentaria y en la generación de ingresos."	0.96	0.01
Water Security	Water supply, availability, scarcity, storage, or other issues related to maintaining sufficient water for agriculture, human consumption, and other needs, including issues that may affect water security such as runoff or water quality, as well as approaches to improving water security such as desalinization	"The critical issues emphasized included water resources which are mainly used for agriculture, energy generation in the form of hydro-electricity and human consumption." "Alta vulnerabilidad al desabastecimiento hídrico: la cantidad de agua usada es casi tanta como la oferta disponible promedio, mientras que el sistema hídrico tiene una baja capacidad intrínseca para regular esa oferta."	0.96	0.01

(*continued*)

Table 1. (*continued*)

Code	Description	Examples	Human vs Computer	
			κ^*	$\rho(0.90)$
Human Health	Issues of human physical, mental, and emotional health, including climate-related disease and other health impacts of climate change	"Research shows that carsharing can reduce overall household costs, and of course, walking and biking are important for overall physical health and well-being." "Fortalecimiento del sistema de vigilancia epidemiológica y sanitaria que incorpora los escenarios climáticos para la gestión del riesgo en un contexto de cambio climático en la salud pública."	0.96	0.01
Environmental Health	The health of the natural environment and the functioning, vulnerability, or resilience of ecosystems, including indicators of environmental health such as biodiversity, species extinction/extirpation, habitat destruction, or land degradation	"This adaptation option will strive to enhance natural resilience to the adverse impacts of climate change by enhancing healthy and well-functioning ecosystems." "Los bosques proveen servicios ecosistémicos en favor de la diversidad biológica."	0.92	0.04
JEDI (Justice, Equity, Diversity, and Inclusion)	Issues related to vulnerable, marginalized, or minoritized populations, sovereignty or ownership, and social disparities or discrimination; promotion of planning or decision-making based on rights or what will be just and equitable for, and inclusive of, diverse stakeholders	"The framework highlighted the following values as being important to the NAP process: 1) Participation and inclusivity of all stakeholders and interests. 2) Promotion of 'ecosystem-based' and 'gender and human rights-based' approaches to adaptation." "Los impactos del cambio climático afectan principalmente a los más pobres."	0.92	0.04

(*continued*)

Table 1. (*continued*)

Code	Description	Examples	Human vs Computer	
			κ *	$\rho(0.90)$
Local Knowledge	Local, traditional, or Indigenous knowledge or practices; cultural resources and knowledge transmitted via oral tradition, stories, or intergenerational education; diverse epistemologies or those distinct from Western science	"Identify opportunities for citizen science and community observations to add value to research used by the state. For example, analyze ways for risk assessment to include qualitative methods and local knowledge." "Recupera, valoriza y utiliza los conocimientos tradicionales de los pueblos indígenas u originarios y su visión de desarrollo armónico con la naturaleza."	1.00	< 0.01

* *All kappa values are statistically significant for $\rho(0.90) < 0.05$.*

Automated classifiers for binary coding (indicating only the presence or absence of Codes) were developed and validated using the ncodeR package (version 0.2.0.1) for the R statistical computing platform [8]. Inter-rater agreement was assessed using Cohen's kappa and Shaffer's rho. Agreement between the author and the classifier for all Codes was high, with acceptable Type I error rates: $\kappa > 0.90$ and $\rho(0.90) < 0.05$ (see Table 1). The whole dataset was then coded for these seven constructs.

2.3 Analysis

The dataset was analyzed using the rENA package (version 0.2.3) for the R statistical computing platform [9]. The units of analysis are the individual documents ($N = 107$).

Connections were accumulated for each document using a moving window of 2 lines. The window length of 2 was chosen based on the structure of the data. In formal writing where the lines in the data table correspond roughly to paragraphs, a window of length 1 might be more appropriate, under the assumption that information within paragraphs is more closely related than information in adjacent paragraphs (which is in turn more closely related than information in distal paragraphs). However, the documents in this dataset also contain numerous figures (with captions), tables, lists, and other forms of text data, which are independent lines in the data, and these are typically associated with at least one adjacent paragraph. Moreover, because the data were scraped from PDF documents, single paragraphs often break across two lines in the dataset due to page breaks. Thus, a window length of 2 was chosen to account for these issues.

Dimensional reduction was performed via singular value decomposition (SVD), and networks were visualized in the space formed by the first two SVD dimensions.

3   Model 0 of the Climate Change Adaptation Policy Ecosystem

This pilot study produced a "model zero" [10] of the climate change adaptation policy ecosystem, a model designed less to be analyzed for insights on the topic itself than to guide exploration and further model development. The model was developed using ENA as described above, and the network graphs are shown in Fig. 1.

The first dimension (SVD1) explains 29% of the variance in the structure of connections among documents, and the second dimension (SVD2) explains 17%. The HAZARDS code appears near the origin in the ENA space, as adaptation plans are generally organized around responses to the current and anticipated consequences of climate change. The first dimension (x-axis) differentiates networks with strong connections to WATER SECURITY (high x values) from networks with strong connections to JEDI issues and perspectives, FOOD SECURITY, and ENVIRONMENTAL HEALTH (low x values). The second dimension differentiates networks with strong connections to HUMAN HEALTH (high y values) from networks with strong connections to ENVIRONMENTAL HEALTH and WATER SECURITY (low y values).

As Fig. 1 (top) shows, there are marked differences among the types of document, with only the state and local and tribal adaptation plans showing similar characteristics.

The national adaptation plans differ from both the state and local and the tribal plans in the extent to which they emphasize JEDI issues and perspectives and ENVIRONMENTAL HEALTH, and to a lesser extent, FOOD SECURITY. Both the state and local plans and the tribal plans have stronger connections to WATER SECURITY and HUMAN HEALTH. In comparison with all three types of climate change adaptation plans, the reports intended to inform policy decisions exhibit more and stronger connections to JEDI issues and perspectives, HUMAN HEALTH, and ENVIRONMENTAL HEALTH. Moreover, where the mean networks of the adaptation plans themselves have largely "hub and spoke" structures, dominated by connections between HAZARDS and the other codes, the mean network of the reports has a somewhat more distributed structure.

These differences are largely consistent with expectations. For example, food systems are highly globalized and food policy is typically a national issue, so it makes sense that national adaptation plans would have a stronger emphasis on FOOD SECURITY. Water, in contrast, is often locally managed and consumed. With the exception of bottled drinking water and the *virtual water trade*—the portion of a population's water needs that comes in the form of food or other water-containing commodities that may be globally sourced—water is not commonly distributed more than a few hundred miles from its source. Thus, it makes sense that connections to WATER SECURITY would be stronger in state and local adaptation plans and tribal plans. In addition, coastal tribes are overrepresented in the dataset, in part because the threats of climate change to coastal communities are more immanent, and thus the need for climate change adaptation plans may be greater. Similarly, environmental regulation is typically a national-level issue, while public health has a stronger local component, especially in the United States, which is also overrepresented in the dataset.

The stronger connections to LOCAL KNOWLEDGE in tribal adaptation plans are also not surprising given the emphasis in most tribal plans on traditional knowledge and practices not only as effective means of current and future mitigation and adaptation, but also as past targets of suppression by colonizers through genocide and epistemicide [11].

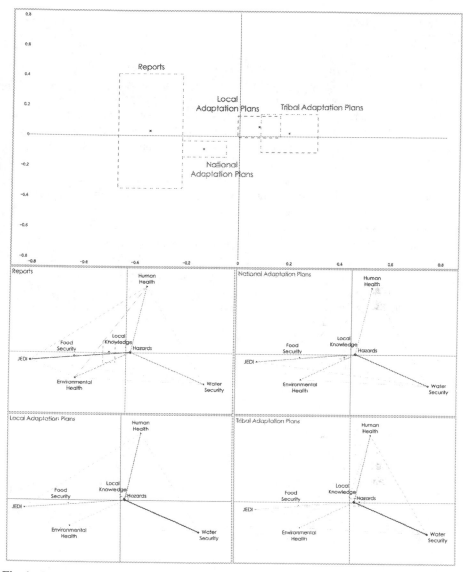

Fig. 1. ENA means and mean network graphs. **Top:** Mean ENA scores (squares) with 95% confidence intervals (dashed boxes) of the reports (purple) and the national (red), state and local (blue), and tribal (green) adaptation plans. **Middle:** Mean ENA networks of the reports (purple; left) and of the national (red; right) adaptation plans. **Bottom:** Mean ENA networks of the state and local (blue; left) and tribal (green; right) adaptation plans. (Color figure online)

For example, the *Karuk Climate Adaptation Plan* (2019) discusses the ways in which USian wildfire management approaches have suppressed traditional Karuk food and fire stewardship and led to the "erasure of cultural landscape, of particular artifacts, and of the future ability to learn from the ancestors and the land" (p. 135). This "exclusion of indigenous management" (p. 135) led to ultimately harmful shifts in the ecological balance of the region (in this case, reduction of sugar pines and expansion of Douglas firs and brush such as ceanothus, poison oak, tanoak, and madrone), reduced germination rates, and increased plant disease, and thus the renewal of traditional practices is a restorative act, not only for addressing climate change but also for Karuk culture.

The weak connections to JEDI issues and perspectives in tribal plans is thus not reflective of a reduced focus on justice, equity, diversity, or inclusion but rather the extent to which those issues are implicit in many tribal approaches to climate change. The explicit reference to JEDI issues and perspectives in national and state and local plans reflects a belated attempt on the part of dominant cultures to reengage subjugated cultures, or perhaps more cynically, the need for dominant cultures to *appear* to address structural and historical inequities despite continuing to uphold systems of oppression.

What is most striking in this analysis, however, is the extent to which reports providing guidance for policy making emphasize JEDI issues and perspectives, HUMAN HEALTH, and ENVIRONMENTAL HEALTH more than the plans produced by national, state and local, and tribal governments. This could suggest that climate change adaptation policies are falling somewhat short of policy goals, or it could reflect differences in the structure of the documents. But as Fig. 2 shows, even policy guidance produced by the same organization can shift markedly over time.

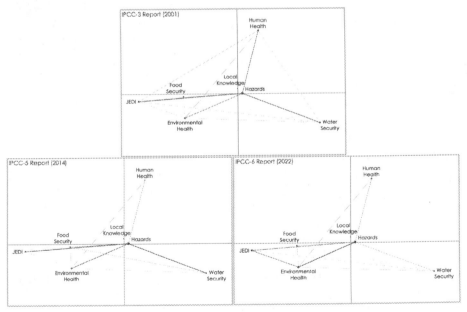

Fig. 2. Mean ENA networks of the three IPCC summaries for policy makers.

The networks of all three IPCC summaries for policy makers three load strongly to the left in the ENA space (see Fig. 2), but the three networks are quite different. Only IPCC-5 (2014) contains a significant connection to LOCAL KNOWLEDGE, while the most recent summary (IPCC-6, 2022) contains far weaker connections to WATER SECURITY yet stronger ones to ENVIRONMENTAL HEALTH. Moreover, the network of the most recent summary (IPCC-6, 2022), which was published in draft form after nearly all of the adaptation plans included in this study, is markedly different from the mean network of the national adaptation plans. Although all the summaries feature fairly rich networks of connections, this suggests that policy makers must navigate a volatile landscape of climate change information, and that frequent updates to adaptation planning may be required.

4   Reflections on Modeling Policy Ecosystems

This pilot study produced a model zero that captures salient features of the climate change adaptation policy ecosystem. The ENA space reflects meaningful characteristics of adaptation planning, the model shows visual and mathematical differences among adaptation plans produced by different types of governmental entity, and comparisons between policies and resources produced for policy makers can be made. Future models could be constructed to explore more fine-grained issues either within or across the Codes included here, different types of adaptation, and a number of other questions that could guide policy development or identify areas for civic engagement.

Yet this study also revealed opportunities and challenges for further development of QE methods as they may be applied to policy ecosystems, and I examine some of these in what follows. My goal is not to detail the limitations of the present study, though there are many, but to use this pilot analysis to explore in a more grounded way some of the theoretical and practical challenges of constructing ecologically sound models of policy ecosystems.

4.1   Time and Space

The development of QE techniques has largely taken as its modal case the modeling of conversations, in the broadest sense of that term: interactions among two or more people that are in person or online; synchronous or asynchronous; structured, semi-structured, or unstructured. This includes collaborative work, idle chit chat, formal debate, mentoring, interviewing, and other forms of human interaction. For example, the concept of a *moving window* [12, 13] in ENA is an operationalization of relational context based on the theory that people in conversations generally respond to prior contributions based on recency (with what counts as recent being, of course, context dependent). In other words, conversations are linear and progressive, much like our experience of time.

When the focus of analysis is documents rather than conversations, *temporality* is less meaningful than *spatiality*. Documents are often multimodal, containing graphs, maps, photographs, and other images in addition to text, but also different types of text: paragraphs, lists, tables, bibliographic entries, and so on. Some text information, such as that contained in tables, is explicitly multidimensional, which poses particular challenges for constructing linearly organized qualitative data tables of the kind needed for most analytic methods, including ENA. Yet it also raises questions about segmentation [14] and relational context [13]. For example, including bibliographic references in an anlysis of policy may be useful, as it reflects the kind of information policy makers draw on to warrant policy decisions, but there is no reason to think that one entry has any relation to those that proceed or follow it in a reference list, which may simply be organized alphabetically by author or in the order of appearance in the text. The relational context for each bibliographic entry is in some other part (or parts) of the document, separated by dozens or even hundreds of pages. Figure captions, in contrast, are almost always proximate to some related discussion in the text, and thus nearly always have a relational context that is the previous or following paragraph. The latter can thus be reasonably modeled with a standard moving window analysis where the former cannot.

This issue is further complicated if we consider not just the structure of documents but the ways in which they are used. For example, a text document is at least mostly linear (excepting things like tables and bibliographies) because words, sentences, and paragraphs are meaningfully ordered. Yet people don't necessarily read documents linearly, particularly professionals who engage documents more like resources to be interrogated than like an authorial monologue [15]. But even setting aside any attempt to model the reading process, simply modeling the content structure of a document is more complex than modeling the content structure of a conversation simply because the former typically *has* a more complex structure—and one that is difficult to preserve when extracting text from machine unfriendly formats like PDFs, the standard file format of digitally disseminated documents.

4.2 Savoir Fair Coding

Another challenge QE researchers face in attempting to model policy ecosystems is linguistic. This small pilot study required developing automated classifiers in three different languages—which essentially meant developing three different codes for each Code. This presents challenges on both pragmatic and theoretical levels.

Pragmatically, it is more challenging to develop coding algorithms using regular expressions because a problem developing effective expressions in any one language reduces the accuracy of coding as a whole *and* introduces the potential for *subgroup unfairness* [16]: systematic inaccuracies in the coding applied to one or more subpopulations. This, in turn, undermines the validity of any model developed based on unfair coding. For example, I intended to develop an AGRICULTURE domain Code, but while this was fairly straightforward in English and Spanish, French posed significant challenges. The French word for "farm" is *ferme*, but *ferme* also means "firm", "solid", "hard", and "definite"; it is part of one term for "land", *terre ferme*; and it is also a conjugation of *fermer*, "to close." It is relatively easy to exclude *terre ferme* using a regular expression, but other disambiguations are far more challenging. Even worse, a common French term for "farming" is *culture*, e.g., "méthodes de culture plus respectueuses de l'environnement."

For the purposes of this pilot study, I simply abandoned my attempt to construct a code for AGRICULTURE. But that is not a viable solution more generally, and with the addition of documents (or other data) in still other languages, this problem only grows more likely. In the current pilot study, there is likely still some bias in the coding. For example, the frequencies of HUMAN HEALTH in English, French, and Spanish are 5%, 3%, and 1%, respectively. It is certainly possible that those differences reflect real variation across contexts—or that they are artifacts of a haphazard sample—but it is also possible that the classifier for HUMAN HEALTH is more accurate for English than for

French and Spanish, and is thus biased. The classifier for ENVIRONMENTAL HEALTH, in contrast, produced frequencies of 3%, 3%, and 4%, respectively, but it is equally unclear whether that indicates the *absence* of bias, as we have already seen that there are meaningful differences in how different cultures think about climate change adaptation.

Another challenge is the ability to involve a second human rater as part of the effort to warrant that the coding is fair and valid, which is predicated on the availability of someone with expertise in both the *content* and the *languages and cultures* involved. In this pilot study, I forewent validation of the coding process using a second human rater in part because my modeling goal was to create a tool for thought and not a tool for action and in part because finding another person with sufficient knowledge of climate change adaptation planning and reading comprehension in English, Spanish, and French is non-trivial.

From a more theoretical perspective, multilingual and multicultural corpora raise questions about the extent to which Codes are similarly meaningful (or not) across different languages and cultures. For example, this analysis included a number of adaptation plans from North American tribes and Indigenous communities, whose epistemologies often differ significantly from those of Western science and governance. The *Confederated Salish and Kootenai Tribes Climate Change Strategic Plan* (2013) argues that.

> Western science has allowed societies to segregate the roles and different functions of each part of nature. Native people to this land understand that these functions cannot be separated from each other. They understand that there is a direct relationship among everything in the natural environment. As such, Traditional Ecological Knowledge is not only incorporating Tribal traditions and culture, but it is applying Salish, Pend d'Oreille, and Kootenai world views into decision-making (p. 28).

The LOCAL KNOWLEDGE Code captured some aspects of this epistemological and ontological perspective, but as discussed above, the JEDI Code was perhaps less successful in this regard. In another sense, the JEDI Code functioned exactly how it was supposed to function, as the very concept is inextricable from systems of oppression, but the ENA model made me reconsider whether that is the best way to understand what is happening in these documents. And that is, after all, what QE is all about, and why the *unification* of methods is so much more important than simply using different tools to solve different problems [10].

This raises another, related theoretical question. Although this pilot study involves only documents, I regard the interpretive process as one that is both hermeneutic and ethnographic, and so the inclusion of documents from such a broad range of cultural and linguistic contexts raises questions about power, and in particular about power imbalance. In the 1970s, Laura Nader challenged ethnographers to "study up," noting that far more ethnographic effort had been expended studying the cultures of oppressed minorities than studying the cultures of the minorities who oppress them [17]. Building on Nader's challenge as well as the field of *critical policy ethnography* [4], this pilot study explicitly included documents from as broad a range of cultures and languages as possible, documents that form a coherent corpus only by virtue of their stated goal of producing plans for dealing with the effects of climate change.

Yet coding (and modeling more generally) is an explicit application of power [16], and the goal of modeling a policy ecosystem in the way I have conceptualized it requires some ability to represent that ecosystem with one, consistent set of Codes. I certainly cannot pretend to expertise on every culture represented in even this small dataset, nor, likely, could anyone else. While there are clear advantages to including as many policy perspectives as possible in a model that purports to represent a policy ecosystem, it is difficult to determine whether my attempt to code and model this dataset is truly fair to all the represented cultures, languages, and perspectives. And given my positionality as a White, male, academic in a position of considerable privilege, it is an important question because the potential for epistemic violence cannot be ignored. Yet in some respects, this is a policy ecosystem in which epistemic violence may also be embedded, in the sense that presumably not all cultures would regard a written document, composed in English or another colonial language, as the most appropriate method of formalizing or communicating policy; yet those cultures that do not engage with the substance as well as the form of climate change adaptation planning may also be unable to obtain the funding and other resources necessary to survive the coming climate crises.

4.3 Seeing What Isn't There

In this pilot study, the only data included in my initial attempt to model a climate change adaptation policy ecosystem were adaptation plans and guidance for policy makers; that is, data on implementation or evaluation of plans were not incorporated. This makes, of course, for a limited theory of ecology, though one that is not without its uses. Yet even when we consider only one part of this ecosystem, the plans themselves, there are intriguing questions raised. For example, the most recent IPCC summary for policy makers (2022) notes that "most observed adaptation is fragmented, small in scale, incremental, sector-specific, designed to respond to current impacts or near-term risks, and focused more on planning rather than implementation" (p. SPM-21). All the more reason to include data on the implementations that *do* exist, an extension of "follow the policy" ethnography [18] in which policies are traced through the four stages I characterize above.

But this also suggests a challenge in modeling policy ecosystems, for what is *not* present in such systems is often as important as what *is*. Absence is not merely lack of presence, for it could come about due to deliberate *exclusion*—the intentional omission of something from the system based, for example, on the choice of narrative that frames the development of policy or decisions about who qualifies as a stakeholder; due to *extinction*—the disappearance of something once part of the system, whether intentional or not; or due to *occlusion*—the inability to see something that is or should be part of the system. For example, when the latest IPCC report (2022) notes that "less attention has been paid to low-regret [adaptation] options, especially at the national and local levels" (p. 4–130), how do we account for that?

Most if not all of the tools of quantitative ethnography are, in one sense, positivist ones: coding is a process of asserting whether *or not* something is present in data, but the "or not" is predicated on there being at least some instances where the Code is positively invoked. Similarly, network analyses are fantastic tools for modeling connections, but they are less useful for showing connections *not made*. And yet as the examples above indicate, scholars routinely attend to what is not present in addition to what is, and this is a particularly powerful approach when we take seriously the task of giving voice to those who may lack full participation in some process. In policy contexts, it is as important to ask who is not sitting at the table as who is, and what is not being discussed as what is.

5   Inconclusion

If it seems that this paper has raised more questions than it answered—or perhaps has answered questions only with more questions—then this pilot study has served its purpose. Modeling something as complex as a policy ecosystem is not something one achieves at first attempt, and it is almost certainly not something that *one* achieves at all. While this pilot study has, I hope, demonstrated the considerable potential of QE methods for modeling policy ecosystems—building on the work of Siebert-Evenstone and Shaffer [19] on the construction of measurement spaces for evaluating alignment of curricula with policy and the work of Schnaider and colleagues [20] on comparative national health policy—my primary goal is to advance the conversation around the theoretical and methodological challenges QE researchers face in attempting to model multinational, multilingual, and multicultural systems.

Acknowledgements. This work was funded in part by the National Science Foundation (DRL-1713110, DRL-2100320), the Wisconsin Alumni Research Foundation, and the Office of the Vice Chancellor for Research and Graduate Education at the University of Wisconsin–Madison. The opinions, findings, and conclusions do not reflect the views of the funding agencies, cooperating institutions, or other individuals.

References

1. Kirby, P., Shepherd, L.J.: Women, peace, and security: mapping the (Re)production of a policy ecosystem. J. Global Secur. Stud. **6**(3), ogaa045 (2021)
2. Stone, D.A.: Causal stories and the formation of policy agendas. Political Sci. Quart. **104**, 281–300 (1989)
3. Lipsky, M.: Street-Level Bureaucracy: Dilemmas of the Individual in Public Service. Russell Sage Foundation (1980)
4. Dubois, V.: Critical Policy Ethnography. In: Fischer, F., Torgerson, D., Durnová, A., Orsini, M. (eds.) Handbook of Critical Policy Studies. pp. 462–480. Edward Elgar Publishing (2015)
5. Eagan, B.R., Siebert-Evenstone, A.L., Hamilton, E., Faul, M., Ashton, L., Wong, N.: Engaging Policy with a QE Lens. In: Wasson, B. and Zörgő, S. (eds.). In: Third International Conference on Quantitative Ethnography: Conference Proceedings Supplement, pp. 139–147. International Society for Quantitative Ethnography (2021)
6. Shaffer, D.W., Collier, W., Ruis, A.R.: A tutorial on epistemic network analysis: analyzing the structure of connections in cognitive, social, and interaction data. J. Learn. Anal. **3**, 9–45 (2016)
7. Bowman, D., et al.: The Mathematical Foundations of Epistemic Network Analysis. In: Ruis, A.R., Lee, S.B. (eds.) ICQE 2021. CCIS, vol. 1312, pp. 91–105. Springer, Cham (2021). https://doi.org/10.1007/978-3-030-67788-6_7

8. Marquart, C.L., Swiecki, Z., Eagan, B.R., Shaffer, D.W.: ncodeR: Techniques for Automated Classifiers. (2018)
9. Marquart, C.L., Swiecki, Z., Collier, W., Eagan, B.R., Woodward, R., Shaffer, D.W.: rENA: Epistemic Network Analysis. (2019)
10. Shaffer, D.W.: Quantitative Ethnography. Cathcart Press (2017)
11. de Sousa Santos, B.: Epistemologies of the South: Justice against Epistemicide. Routledge (2015)
12. Siebert-Evenstone, A.L., Irgens, G.A., Collier, W., Swiecki, Z., Ruis, A.R., Shaffer, D.W.: In search of conversational grain size: modelling semantic structure using moving stanza windows. J. Learn. Anal. **4**, 123–139 (2017)
13. Ruis, A.R., Siebert-Evenstone, A.L., Pozen, R., Eagan, B.R., Shaffer, D.W.: Finding Common Ground: A Method for Measuring Recent Temporal Context in Analyses of Complex, Collaborative Thinking. In: Lund, K., Niccolai, G., Lavoué, E., Hmelo-Silver, C., Gweon, G., and Baker, M. (eds.) A Wide Lens: Combining Embodied, Enactive, Extended, and Embedded Learning in Collaborative Settings: 13th International Conference on Computer-Supported Collaborative Learning (CSCL) 2019, pp. 136–143. In: International Society for the Learning Sciences (2019)
14. Zörgő, S., Swiecki, Z., Ruis, A.R.: Exploring the Effects of Segmentation on Semi-structured Interview Data with Epistemic Network Analysis. In: Ruis, A.R., Lee, S.B. (eds.) ICQE 2021. CCIS, vol. 1312, pp. 78–90. Springer, Cham (2021). https://doi.org/10.1007/978-3-030-677 88-6_6
15. Wineburg, S.S.: Historical problem solving: a study of the cognitive processes used in the evaluation of documentary and pictorial evidence. J. Educ. Psychol. **83**, 73–87 (1991)
16. Shaffer, D.W., Ruis, A.R.: How We Code. In: Ruis, A.R., Lee, S.B. (eds.) ICQE 2021. CCIS, vol. 1312, pp. 62–77. Springer, Cham (2021). https://doi.org/10.1007/978-3-030-67788-6_5
17. Nader, L.: Up the Anthropologist—Perspectives Gained From Studying Up. In: Hymes, D. (ed.) Reinventing Anthropology, pp. 284–311. Vintage Books (1974)
18. Peck, J., Theodore, N.: Follow the policy: a distended case approach. Environ. Plann. a: Econ. Space. **44**, 21–30 (2012)
19. Siebert-Evenstone, A., Shaffer, D.W.: Cause and Because: Using Epistemic Network Analysis to Model Causality in the Next Generation Science Standards. In: Eagan, B., Misfeldt, M., Siebert-Evenstone, A. (eds.) ICQE 2019. CCIS, vol. 1112, pp. 223–233. Springer, Cham (2019). https://doi.org/10.1007/978-3-030-33232-7_19
20. Schnaider, K., Schiavetto, S., Meier, F., Wasson, B., Allsopp, B.B., Spikol, D.: Governmental Response to the COVID-19 Pandemic - A Quantitative Ethnographic Comparison of Public Health Authorities' Communication in Denmark, Norway, and Sweden. In: Ruis, A.R., Lee, S.B. (eds.) ICQE 2021. CCIS, vol. 1312, pp. 406–421. Springer, Cham (2021). https://doi.org/10.1007/978-3-030-67788-6_28

Correction to: Reducing Networks of Ethnographic Codes Co-occurrence in Anthropology

Alberto Cottica, Veronica Davidov, Magdalena Góralska, Jan Kubik,
Guy Melançon, Richard Mole, Bruno Pinaud,
and Wojciech Szymański

Correction to:
Chapter "Reducing Networks of Ethnographic Codes Co-occurrence in Anthropology" in: C. Damşa and A. Barany (Eds.): *Advances in Quantitative Ethnography*, CCIS 1785,
https://doi.org/10.1007/978-3-031-31726-2_4

In the originally published version of chapter 4 the names of the two last co-authors were erroneously merged. The authors' names have been corrected.

The updated original version of this chapter can be found at
https://doi.org/10.1007/978-3-031-31726-2_4

Author Index

A

Arastoopour Irgens, Golnaz   3

B

Barany, Amanda   58, 185, 201, 314, 374
Bright, Dara   185
Brohinsky, Jais   163
Brown, Rachael Eriksen   239

C

Cai, Zhiqiang   17, 30, 58, 101
Choi, Jaeyoon   30
Condon, Lara   201
Cottica, Alberto   43

D

Davidov, Veronica   43

E

Eagan, Brendan   3, 17, 30, 87
Ebby, Caroline   201
Espino, Danielle P.   331, 347

F

Folkestad, James   227

G

Galarza, Beatriz   270
Ghaffari, Sadaf   227
Goldsmith-Markey, Lindsay   201
Góralska, Magdalena   43
Granberg, Luke   402
Green, Samuel   347

H

Hamilton, Eric   359
Hurford, Andrew   359

J

Jones, Taylor   402

K

Kaliisa, Rogers   270
Kang, Hosun   285
Keene, Bryan C.   331
Kim, Yoon Jeon   214
Knowles, Mariah A.   58, 101, 214
Kubik, Jan   43

L

Lee, Seiyon   270
Lee, Seung B.   347
Løkkegaard, Emil Bøgh   299
Luther, Yanye   227
Lux, Kristina   347

M

Manojlovich, Milisa   402
Marquart, Cody   17, 101
Melançon, Guy   43
Misfeldt, Morten   299
Mole, Richard   43
Moraes, Marcia   227
Morales-Navarro, Luis   374

N

Nøhr, Liv   299

O

Ohsaki, Ayano   388
Orrantia, Heather   347
Orrill, Chandra Hawley   239
Oshima, Jun   388

P

Peeters, Ward   254
Pinaud, Bruno   43
Popov, Vitaliy   402

Q

Quesada, Hazel Vega   270

© The Editor(s) (if applicable) and The Author(s), under exclusive license
to Springer Nature Switzerland AG 2023
C. Damşa and A. Barany (Eds.): ICQE 2022, CCIS 1785, pp. 429–430, 2023.
https://doi.org/10.1007/978-3-031-31726-2

R
Remillard, Janine   201
Ruis, Andrew R.   30, 71, 101, 132, 414

S
Saravani, Sina Mahdipour   227
Scianna, Jennifer   214, 270
Shaffer, David Williamson   17, 30, 58, 71,
      101, 132
Sobetski, Raeleen   402
Spikol, Daniel   254
Swiecki, Zachari   87
Szymański, Wojciech   43

T
Talafian, Hamideh   285
Tamborg, Andreas Lindenskov   299

Tan, Yuanru   101
Trimboli, Haille   347
Turvey, Kiara   402

V
Vega, Hazel   117
Viberg, Olga   254

W
Wang, Yeyu   132
Werbowsky, Payten   331
Woodard, Monique   270
Wu, Mengqian   314

Z
Zhang, Jiayi   314
Zörgő, Szilvia   146, 163

Printed in the United States
by Baker & Taylor Publisher Services